ANALECTA BIBLICA
INVESTIGATIONES SCIENTIFICAE IN RES BIBLICAS
72

The Divine Sonship of Christians in the Johannine Writings

ROMAE
E PONTIFICIO INSTITUTO BIBLICO
1977

MATTHEW VELLANICKAL

The Divine Sonship of Christians in the Johannine Writings

ROME
BIBLICAL INSTITUTE PRESS
1977

233
V545

7902133

© Iura editionis et versionis reservantur
PRINTED IN ITALY

TYPIS PONTIFICIAE UNIVERSITATIS GREGORIANAE — ROMAE

Preface

The fact that the theme of the 'Divine Sonship of Christians' is central to the message of the 'Beloved Disciple' is universally acknowledged. But little effort has been made so far on the part of the Exegetes to give an adequate treatment to this Johannine theme. Hence the present attempt to investigate the Johannine doctrine of Christian Sonship.

This book is a thesis defended at the Pontifical Biblical Institute, Rome, on the 14th of February 1970, corrected and updated for publication. We avail ourselves of this opportunity to express our deep gratitude to Rev. Fr. Ignatius de la Potterie who has directed this work with his extremely valuable suggestions and constructive criticism. We would like to recall with gratitude also Fr. L. Sabourin who has helped us with his careful observations for preparing this work for publication. It is our great pleasure to acknowledge the assistance and encouragement of Prof. R. Schnackenburg of the University of Würzburg, whose suggestions have been of great help in preparing this work.

With sentiments of deep gratitude, we would like to recall the painstaking care with which Dom. Bernard Orchard O. S. B., the Editor of the Catholic Commentary of the Bible, went through this work brushing up its language. Finally, we would like to thank in a special way the authorities of the Pontifical Biblical Institute, who have accepted this work to be published in the 'Analecta Biblica' series of the Institute.

MATTHEW VELLANICKAL

St. Thomas' Apostolic Seminary
Vadavathoor, Kottayam
Kerala, India
October 1976

Table of Contents

Preface V
Table of Contents VII
List of Abbreviations XIX
Bibliography XXIII
Introduction 1

PART ONE: THE DIVINE SONSHIP OF MAN OUTSIDE THE JOHANNINE WRITINGS 7

CHAPTER I. THE DIVINE SONSHIP OF MAN IN THE OLD TESTAMENT 9
  I. The Divine Sonship of Israel through the Saving act of Yahweh (Ex 4:22-23) 10
    A. The Divine Sonship of Israel and Exodus 10
    B. Yahweh, the *Gō'ēl* 10
    C. The Substitutional Character of the Liberation of Israel . . 11
    D. Israel the Firstborn of Yahweh 12
  II. Israel's Sonship through the establishment of the Covenant (Ex 4:23) 13
    A. Israel's Sonship and the Covenant 13
    B. Yahweh gives Israel existence as a Nation 14
    C. Restoration of the Covenant - Restoration of the Father-son relationship 14
  III. Israel's Sonship: Adoptive but real 15
    A. The Family character of the Sinai Covenant 15
    B. Relation of Love between Yahweh and Israel 16
      1. The Fatherly Love of Yahweh for Israel 16
      2. Filial love of Israel for Yahweh 16
  IV. Israel's Sonship - A Dynamic Sonship 17
  V. The Divine sonship of the Davidic King and Israel's Sonship . 18
    A. The Davidic King: a Son of Yahweh 18
    B. The King and Israel sharing the same sonship 20
  VI. The Divine Sonship and the Individual Israelite 20
    A. A Homogeneous development of the traditional concept . . 20
    B. The Divine sonship and Personal Justice 21

		1. Wisd 2:13,16,18	21
		2. Eccl 23:1,4, and 51:10	22
	C.	The Universal Fatherhood of God (Wisd 14:3)	23
VII.	The Divine Sonship of Israel in terms of a begetting by God		23
	A.	The Old Covenant as a begetting by God	23
	B.	The New Covenant - A New Creation	24
VIII.	The Eschatological Character of Israel's Sonship		25
	CONCLUSION		26

CHAPTER II. THE DIVINE SONSHIP OF MAN IN LATER JUDAISM — 29

I.	The Divine Sonship of the Community through Election and Covenant		29
	A.	Prayer of Intercession (4 Q Dibrê ham - Me'orôt) 3:4-10	30
		1. Context	30
		2. Structure of the Section 3:4-10	31
		3. Analysis of words	31
	B.	I QH 9:35	32
		1. The Context in the section I QH 9:30-36	32
		2. Structure of I QH 9:35-36	32
		3. Analysis of words	33
	C.	In the Apocrypha	35
II.	The Sons of God and the Just		35
	A.	In the Qumran Literature	35
	B.	In the Apocrypha and the Rabbinic Writings	36
III.	Sons of Light (God) and Sons of darkness (devil)		36
	A.	Sons of Light - Sons of God	36
	B.	Sons of Light-Believers	37
IV.	Birth of the Community through the Teacher (I QH 3:1-18)		38
	A.	The Structure of the Section	38
	B.	Vocabulary	40
	C.	The Community born of the Power (Spirit) of God	41
V.	Community born through the Truth (revelation)		42
	CONCLUSION		42

CHAPTER III. THE DIVINE SONSHIP OF MAN IN HELLENISM AND PHILO — 45

I.	In Hellenism		45
	A.	Men - Sons of God	45
	B.	Individual Sonship	46
	C.	Rebirth in the Mystery Religions	47
		1. Adoption Rites in the Mystery cults	47
		2. Regeneration in Corpus Hermeticum XIII	47
		a. Description of the Regeneration	48
		b. Characteristics of this Regeneration	49
	Conclusion		49

TABLE OF CONTENTS

II. In Philo 50
    A. Men - Sons of God 50
        1. Sons of God : Those who serve God 50
        2. Sons of God : Those who have the knowledge of God 50
        3. Sons of God : Those who worship and love God . . . 51
    B. Logos - Mediator of the Divine sonship 51
    C. Divine sonship and Spiritual birth 51
Conclusion 52

CHAPTER IV. THE DIVINE SONSHIP OF CHRISTIANS IN THE SYNOPTIC GOSPELS 53

I. Sons of God : Peacemakers (Mt 5:9) 53
    A. Matthean Redaction 53
    B. Analysis of the Text 54
        1. Εἰρηνοποιοί : ' Peacemakers ' 54
            a. Messianic peace 54
            b. Peacemakers : the merciful 55
        2. 'They shall be called sons of God' 55
II. Sons of God - Those who love their enemies (Mt 5:43-48 ; Lk 6:27-28,32-36) 56
    A. " Love your enemies ... " (Mt 5:44) 56
    B. God the model and exemplar of this love (Mt 5:45b) . . . 57
        1. Love of the Father 57
        2. Perfection of the Father (Mt 5:48) 57
            a. Structure of Mt 5:44-48 57
            b. Comparison with Lk 6:36 58
    C. " That you may become sons of your Father in Heaven " (Mt 5:45a) 58
        1. Argument from the Structure 58
        2. Τέλειος in Mt 59
        3. Ὡς ὁ πατὴρ ὑμῶν (Mt 5:48) 59
    D Ὅπως γένησθε (Mt 5:45) 59
        1. Γίνεσθαι in Mt 18:1-4 60
        2. Dynamism of γένησθε in Mt 5:43-48. 61
III. Lk 20:36 Sons of God - Sons of the Resurrection 61
    A. Lukan Redaction 62
    B. Literary Structure 62
    C. Analysis of the Text 63
    D. Other eschatological references on sonship 64
IV. God the Father of the Disciples 64
    A. Texts speaking of God as Father 64
    B. Contexts of texts speaking of sonship in Mt 65
    C. Other Indications 65
V. Christ and the Divine sonship of man (Mt 17:25-27 ; 12:48-50 ; 11:25-27) 66
    A. Mt 17:25-27 66

	B. Mt 12:48-50	67
	C. Mt 11:25-27	67
	CONCLUSION	67

CHAPTER V. THE PAULINE DOCTRINE OF CHRISTIAN SONSHIP   69

I.	Use of the term υἱοθεσία in Paul	69
	A. Israel's sonship as background	69
	B. Adoption of the Sons of God - The Blessing of Abraham	70
	C. Origin of the term υἱοθεσία	71
II.	Adoption through liberation	71
III.	Adoption by God the Father	72
IV.	Sons of God in Christ (Gal 3:26-28)	74
	A. The Structure of the Text	74
	B. Grammatical and Philological Analysis	74
	1. Εἷς ... ἐν Χριστῷ Ἰησοῦ (v. 28)	74
	2. Χριστὸν ἐνεδύσασθε (v. 27)	75
	3. Υἱοὶ Θεοῦ ... διὰ τῆς πίστεως (v. 26)	76
V.	Birth through the Gospel (I Cor 4:15)	77
VI.	The Divine Sonship of Christians and the Holy Spirit (Gal 4: 4-7; Rom 8:14-17)	78
	A. The Holy Spirit - Witness of adoption (Gal 4:6)	78
	1. The Structure of Gal 4:4-7	78
	2. " Πνεῦμα κρᾶζον "	79
	B. The Holy Spirit - Cause of our adoption	79
	C. The Holy Spirit - Active Principle of our life as sons of God (Rom 8)	80
	1. The Use of the verb ἄγειν in Rom 8:14	80
	2. 'The Spirit of the Son dwells in us' (Rom 8:11)	81
	3. The Structure of Rom 8	81
	D. The Corresponding life of the sons of God	82
	1. Life of Faith	82
	2. The Condition of Suffering	83
VII.	Eschatological Adoption (Rom 8:23)	83
	A. The 'Already' and 'not yet' of adoption	83
	B. Waiting for the adoption as sons	84
	1. The Structure of Rom 8	84
	2. The Vocabulary of Rom 8	85
	C. The Spirit and the Eschatological adoption	86
	CONCLUSION	87

PART TWO: THE JOHANNINE DOCTRINE OF CHRISTIAN SONSHIP   89

Introduction	89
The Johannine Terminology	90
A. The use of τέκνα Θεοῦ	90

1. The usage of τέκνον in general 90
2. The Johannine use of τέκνα Θεοῦ 91
   a. Τέκνα Θεοῦ and υἱὸς Θεοῦ 92
   b. Τέκνα τοῦ Θεοῦ and τέκνα τοῦ διαβόλου 93
   c. Τέκνα τοῦ Θεοῦ and εἶναι ἐκ τοῦ Θεοῦ 94
   d. Εἶναι ἐκ τοῦ Θεοῦ and γεγέννηται ἐκ τοῦ Θεοῦ . . 95
B. Usage of γεννηθῆναι ἐκ Θεοῦ. 98
   1. The use of γεννηθῆναι in general 98
   2. The Johannine usage of γεννηθῆναι 99
   3. The distinctive character of the begetting by God . . 101
Conclusion 103

Chapter VI. THE POWER OF BECOMING CHILDREN OF GOD (Jn 1:12-13) 105

I. History of the Exegesis of Jn 1:12-13 105
   A. Dynamic Sonship 105
      1. In the Patristic Period 106
      2. In the Middle Ages 106
      3. In the Reformation and Post-Reformation period . . 108
      4. In Modern Times 109
   B. Static Sonship 110
      1. In the Patristic Period 110
      2. In the Middle Ages 110
      3. In the Reformation and Post-Reformation Period . . 111
      4. In Modern Times 111
II. Textual Criticism : 112
   A. External Criticism 113
      1. Witness of the plural reading 113
      2. Witnesses of the reading in the singular 114
      3. Evaluation of the data of the External Criticism . . . 115
   B. Internal Criticism 116
      1. Reasons in favour of the reading in the singular . . . 117
         a. The Threefold Negation 117
         b. The Context 117
         c. Grammatical reasons 117
         d. Reasons from Johannine doctrine and vocabulary . 118
            i. The Fundamental scheme 118
            ii. The Divine origin of Christ 118
            iii. 'Those who believe in his name' 119
            iv. The Johannine vocabulary of the Supernatural begetting 121
         e. Reasons from the Structure 124
      2. Objections against the Singular 126
      3. Answer to the objections 126
         a. The singular reading of v. 13 - more explanatory . 126
         b. Generation of Christ : both eternal and temporal . 127

				i.	The Divine Sonship of Christ	127
				ii.	The revelatory nature of Christ's divine sonship	128
				iii.	Pre-existent and temporal sonship.	128
				iv.	Jesus: the μονογενής	129
				v.	The Phrase in v. 13	130
				vi.	Comparison with the Synoptics	130
				vii.	The temporal generation: Sign of the eternal generation.	131

        4. The change from singular to the plural 132
  III. Exegetical Analysis 132
      A. Context in the Prologue 132
          1. The Structure of Jn 1:1-18 132
          2. The Scheme of the Structure 134
      B. Analysis of the Text. 136
          1. Grammatical Considerations 137
              a. The different elements of the verses 137
              b. Evaluation of the tenses 138
          2. Study of the Vocabulary 139
              a. ' to become children of God ...' (v. 12b) 139
              b. '... who believe in His name ...' (v. 12c) 141
                  i. The different constructions of Πιστεύειν . . . 141
                  ii. Πιστεύειν with dative. 142
                  iii. Πιστεύειν followed by ὅτι 143
                  iv. Πιστεύειν εἰς τινα 143
                  v. Πιστεύειν εἰς τὸ ὄνομά τινος 145
              c. '... who received Him ...' (v. 12a) 146
              d. '... He gave them power ...' (v. 12b) 149
  IV. Analysis of related Texts. 152
      A. " From his fulness we have all received ..." (Jn 1:16). . . 152
          1. The Only begotten Son full of Grace and Truth . . . 153
          2. Grace of Truth (Revelation) in Jesus Christ 153
          3. Grace of Truth (Revelation): Grace of Sonship . . . 154
          4. Sharing from the fulness of Grace - Sonship - in Christ 154
      B. Becoming sons of Light through faith in the Light . . . 157
          1. Christ as Light 157
          2. "... believe in the Light that you may become sons of Light ..." 158
          3. The Structure of Jn 12:35-36 159
  Conclusion 160

Chapter VII. THE BIRTH INTO THE LIFE OF THE CHILDREN OF GOD (Jn 3:3-10) 163

  I. The Context of Jn 3:3-10 163
  II. Exegetical Analysis of Jn 3:3-10 165
      A. The Structure of Jn 3:2-10 165
      B. The Absolute Necessity of the Supernatural begetting (Jn 3:3-5). 167

- C. The Nature of the Supernatural begetting 169
  - 1. Begetting from above (from the Spirit) 169
    - a. Ἐὰν ... γεννηθῇ 169
    - b. Critical problem of v. 5 170
    - c. The meaning of ἄνωθεν 172
    - d. Begetting from the Spirit 174
      - i. The OT concept of a begetting from the Spirit 174
      - ii. In Later Judaism 175
      - iii. The Synoptic Teaching on the matter 176
      - iv. The Johannine vocabulary 177
  - 2. Begetting from Water and Spirit 179
    - a. History of the Exegesis 179
      - i. The Signification of water. 179
      - ii. The relation between water and Spirit 181
        - (a) Water as instrumental cause 181
        - (b) Water and Spirit as distinct and complementary causes 183
    - b. Interpretation of the text 186
      - i. The Pre-Johannine doctrine on the matter . . 186
      - ii. The relation between faith and Baptism in Jn 187
      - iii. Begetting brought about by Baptism and Spirit working through faith 190
  - 3. Begetting from the Spirit : A Continued life of faith . . 191
    - a. The Holy Spirit : the principle of birth 191
      - i. " Holy Spirit that is given to us " (I Jn 4:12-13 ; 3:23-24) 192
      - ii. The Structure of I Jn 3:23-24 193
      - iii. Love infused in us through the Holy Spirit . 193
    - b. Continuous influx of the parent source in the life of sonship 194
    - c. Permanent communion of life between the Father, the Son and the Children 195
    - d. The dynamism of the divine begetting 197
- D. The Nature of the one who is born of the Spirit (Jn 3:6-8) 197
  - 1. Born of the Spirit versus Born of the flesh (Jn 3:6) . 197
  - 2. Born of the Spirit is Spirit (Jn 3:8) 199
    - a. Use of πνεῦμα in the context 199
    - b. Other expressions in the context 200
    - c. The unfathomable character of the divine begetting 202
- E. The Kingdom of God and the Divine Sonship of men (Jn 3:3,5,15) 203
  - 1. See (enter) the Kingdom of God (Jn 3:3,5) 203
    - a. Different explanations 204
    - b. The Kingdom of God and the person of Christ . . 205
    - c. Seeing and entering 207
  - 2. Have eternal Life in Him (Jn 3:15) 208
    - a. The Structure of the section Jn 3:11-21 208
    - b. The Kingdom of God and Eternal Life 209

		c.	Eternal Life - Life of the children of God	210
		d.	Member of the Kingdom - a child of God	211
			i. The Synoptic teaching on the matter	211
			ii. Development of the doctrine	212
			iii. The Johannine teaching.	213
	III.	The Divine Sonship of the Believers through the Death of Christ (Jn 11:52)		214
		A. History of the Exegesis		214
		B. A Prophecy after the event		215
		C. Imparting the Divine Sonship and gathering into one		216
			1. The Structure of Jn 11:47-53	217
			2. Vocabulary	218
			a. Λαός and Ἔθνος in the LXX	219
			b. Λαός and Ἔθνος in the NT	220
			c. Johannine use of ἔθνος and λαός	221
			3. Dying for the People and gathering the scattered Children of God	223
	Conclusion			224

Chapter VIII. RIGHTEOUSNESS: CRITERION OF THE LIFE OF THE CHILDREN OF GOD (I Jn 2:29-3:10; Jn 8:31-47) 227

	I.	The Divine Sonship in Two Stages	228
		A. Witness of the Ecclesiastical Writers	228
		B. The Synoptic Teaching on the matter	228
		C. In the Specific Johannine Context	229
		1. Presentation of the Epistle	229
		2. The use of εἶναι ἐκ τοῦ Θεοῦ.	230
	II.	The Twofold Johannine scheme in the manifestation of the Sonship	231
	III.	The Literary Criticism of I Jn 2:29-3:10.	232
		A. Different attempts on the History of Redaction	232
		B. The Baptismal Tradition in I Jn.	234
		C. The Baptismal Liturgy underlying the Section.	235
		D. Eschatological and Dualistic Context	237
		E. Locating the Section in the frame of the Baptismal Parenesis	238
	IV.	The Structural and Grammatical Considerations	240
		A. The Structure of I Jn 2:29 - 3:10a	240
		B. The Scheme of the Structure	242
		C. Evaluation of the tenses of the verbs in 2:29	243
	V.	Vocabulary	245
		A. Εἰδῆτε and γινώσκετε	245
		B. δίκαιος: God or Christ?	246
		1. Comparison with I Jn 3:7	246
		2. The use of δίκαιος in Jn	247
		3. Transition from Christ to God	247

        C. Christ as Righteous 248
            1. Christ's Righteousness in Jn 16:8-10 248
            2. Christ the Righteous in I Jn 2:1-2 249
            3. Christ the Righteous in filial relationship with God . . 250
                a. The Pre-Johannine teaching on the matter 250
                b. In the Johannine texts 251
        D. 'Everyone who does righteousness' 252
            1. Comparison between 1 Jn 2:29 - 3:10 and Jn 8:31-47 . 252
            2. The Structure of Jn 8:31-47 253
            3. Sonship manifested in Conduct 256
            4. Diabolic Sonship manifested in committing sin 256
                a. The concept of sin in concrete 257
                b. The Specific character of sin in the context . . . 258
    VI. Divine Sonship manifested in doing righteousness 261
        A. Sonship of Christ and Sonship of Christians 261
        B. Likeness of Conduct in the Children of God 261
    CONCLUSION 262

CHAPTER IX. IMPECCABILITY: FRUIT OF THE LIFE OF DIVINE
    SONSHIP (I Jn 3:9; 5:18-20; Jn 8:31-36) 265

    I. The Notion of impeccability in I Jn 3:9 265
        A. Different Interpretations 265
        B. Impeccability in the Johannine context 266
    II. Impeccability of the one who is born of God (I Jn 3:9) . . . 268
        A. The Structure of I Jn 3:9 268
        B. Different Interpretations of σπέρμα 268
        C. Source of Impeccability in the Jewish and Primitive Christian Tradition 269
        D. Source of Impeccability in Jn 271
            1. Dwelling of the Word and Victory over the evil one
               (I Jn 2:12-14) 271
            2. Faith: Victory over the World (I Jn 5:4) 272
            3. Sinlessness: Effect of a Mutual Dwelling (I Jn 3:6,9) 272
                a. The Johannine usage of μένειν 274
                b. The Χρῖσμα in Jn 274
    III. Impeccability of the Children of God through the Son of God
         (I Jn 5:18-20) 276
        A. Textual criticism of I Jn 5:18 276
            1. External Criticism 276
            2. Internal Criticism 277
        B. Analysis of the Expressions 278
            1. "... He who was Begotten of God keeps him ..." . . . 278
                a. The Context 279
                b. The Vocabulary 280
                    (1) Ὁ γεννηθεὶς ἐκ τοῦ Θεοῦ 280
                    (2) Τηρεῖ 280

        c. The Structure of I Jn 5:18-20 281
           (1) The Literary unity of the Section 281
           (2) Comparison between 5:18-20 and 3:5-10 ... 281
           (3) The Structure 282
     2. " ... has given us understanding ..." 284
IV. Freedom proper to the Divine Sonship (Jn 8:31-36) 286
  A. The Structure of Jn 8:31-36 286
  B. Vocabulary 287
     1. ' Son ' and ' Slaves ' 287
     2. " If the Son makes you free, you will be free indeed "
        (v. 36) 288
        a. Freedom from sin 289
        b. Freedom inherent to the nature of Sonship. ... 289
        c. True freedom : True self-determination 290
     3. " You are truly my disciples and ... the Truth will make
        you free " (vv. 31-32). 290
        a. Freedom of the Children of God and discipleship . 291
        b. Freedom of the Children of God through the Truth 292
           (1) Jesus - the Truth in his sonship 292
           (2) Knowledge of the Truth - Communion with the
              Truth (Son) 292
     4. " ... If you remain in my word ..." 293
Conclusion 294

Chapter X. LOVE : THE EXPRESSION OF THE LIFE OF DIVINE
SONSHIP (I Jn 3:10-12 ; 4:7-8) 295

I. Brotherly Love : Manifestation of the life of Divine Sonship
  (I Jn 3:10-12) 295
  A. Tradition and Redaction 295
  B. Brotherly Love and Righteousness 295
     1. Brotherly Love and Righteousness as Parallels 295
        a. In the construction of v. 10 295
        b. In the whole context of the Epistle 296
     2. The Specific relation of brotherly love to divine sonship 296
        a. Grammatical Consideration 297
        b. Analysis of expressions 297
           (1) " For this is the message ..." (v. 11) 297
           (2) " ... love his brother ..." (v. 10) 299
  C. Lack of Brotherly love : Manifestation of the Diabolic Son-
     ship 300
     1. The Structure of I Jn 3:10-12 300
     2. Cain and Abel : Prototypes of sonship 301
     3. The Diabolic Sonship : source of hatred 302
II. Ὁ ἀγαπῶν : The Existential Definition of a Child of God (I Jn
  4:7-8). 302
  A. The Literary Unity and Structure of the Section 4:7-21 .. 303
  B. The Structure of I Jn 4:7-8 304

	C.	Evaluation of the Tenses.	306
	D.	Analysis of the Expressions.	306
		1. ' Love is of God '	306
		2. ' God is love '.	307
	E.	Love : Means of Growing in the Life of Divine Sonship	309
		1. ' to know God ' and ' to be born of God '	309
		2. An experiential Knowledge of faith and love	310
		3. Γινώσκει	311
III.	Analysis of Related Texts		312
	A.	" ... His love is perfected in us ..." (I Jn 4:12-13)	312
	B.	" See what love the Father has given us that ... children of God (I Jn 3:1)	313
		1. Ἀγάπη	313
		2. Δέδωκεν ἡμῖν	314
		3. " ... that we should be called children of God ".	314
	Conclusion		315

CHAPTER XI.   LIFE OF DIVINE SONSHIP : A LIFE OF FAITH

	(I Jn 5:1-4)	317
I.	The Literary Criticism.	317
	A. The Context of I Jn 5:1-4.	317
	B. The Literary Unity and Structure of the Section	318
II.	Experience of Sonship : A Faith Experience.	319
	A. Faith : The Concrete form of the Life of Sonship	320
	B. Faith in Jesus as Christ and Son of God	321
	C. Faith as a Baptismal Experience.	322
	1. The Baptismal formula	322
	2. The Baptismal Tradition	323
	D. Victory of the Divinely Born over the world through Faith	324
III.	Faith : The root of love in the Children of God (v. 1)	325
	A. Love Flowing from the Life of the Children of God (v. 1)	326
	1. The ' Begetter ' and the ' begotten '	326
	2. Difference between I Jn 4:7 and I Jn 5:1	327
	B. Love for God - Proof of genuine love for the Children of God (v. 2)	328
	1. " Ἐν τούτῳ ... ὅτι ... ὅταν " (v. 2)	328
	2. " Τὰ τέκνα τοῦ Θεοῦ "	329
	Conclusion	330

CHAPTER XII. THE ESCHATOLOGICAL DEVELOPMENT OF THE DIVINE SONSHIP OF CHRISTIANS (I Jn 3:1-2)   331

I.	Present Life of sonship - Foretaste of the Future Life (I Jn 3:1-2a)	331
	A. Community of Life and similarity of nature with God	331
	1. The Use of the term τέκνα Θεοῦ	332
	2. The use of the term ὁ πατήρ	333

XVIII TABLE OF CONTENTS

        a. In the baptismal contexts parallel to I Jn 3:1-2 . 333
        b. The Johannine usage 334
    B. Community of Life and Knowledge of God (Christ) 335
       1. Incapability of the world to know the children of God 335
       2. Children of God and the knowledge of God 337
II. The Future state of sonship - Unfolding of the present state
   (I Jn 3:2b) 337
    A. The Vocabulary 338
       1. Τί ἐσόμεθα 338
       2. Οὔπω ἐφανερώθη 339
    B. Comparison with parallel texts 339
III. Nature of the Future State of Sonship (I Jn 3:2cd) 340
    A. A State of perfect likeness to and vision of Christ (God) . 340
       1. Ἐὰν φανερωθῇ 340
       2. Ὅμοιοι αὐτῷ ἐσόμεθα 341
       3. Ὅτι ὀψόμεθα αὐτὸν καθώς ἐστιν 342
         a. History of Interpretation 342
         b. Vision of Christ (God) - Fulfilment of the Knowledge
           of Communion 343
         c. Christ the direct object of vision 343
    B. Assimilation through vision 344
       1. The meaning of ὅτι 344
       2. The Johannine text in the light of the parallel NT
         Texts 345
       3. Faith unfolded in vision 346
IV. Filial Hope and Confidence of the Children of God (I Jn 4:17-18;
   3:3) 347
    A. The Eschatological Confidence of the Children of God (I Jn
      4:17-18) 347
       1. Condition of the Children of God - basis of Confidence 347
       2. Similarity with Christ gives confidence 348
    B. Filial Hope - Incentive for a Dynamic Life of sonship . . 349
   Conclusion 350

GENERAL CONCLUSION 353

  I. The Theological Synthesis 353
 II. The Originality of the Johannine Concept of Sonship 358
    A. Against the OT and Jewish background 358
    B. Against the Background of Hellenism and Philo 360
    C. Against the Background of other NT Writings 362
       1. The Synoptic Gospels 362
       2. The Pauline Epistles 363

INDICES 365

List of Abbreviations

Abh. z. Theol. ANT :	Abhandlungen zur Theologie des Alten und Neuen Testaments, Basel-Zürich.
AJT	American Journal of Theology, Chicago.
Anal. Bibl.	Analecta Biblica, Rome.
Angelicum	Angelicum, Roma.
ATR	Anglican Theological Review, Evanston.
BBB	Bonner Biblische Beiträge, Bonn.
BibKi	Bibel und Kirche, Stuttgart.
BibLeb	Bibel und Leben, Düsseldorf.
Biblebhashyam	Biblebhashyam, An Indian Biblical Quarterly, Kottayam.
BibOr	Bibbia e Oriente, Genova.
BiTod	Bible Today, Collegeville, Minn.
BiViChr	Bible et Vie Chrétienne, Maredsous.
BJ	Bible de Jerusalem, Paris.
BNTW	Beihefte zur Zeitschrift für die Neutestamentliche Wissenschaft (Giessen), Berlin.
BS	Bibliotheca Sacra, Dallas, Texas.
BThW	Bibel-Theologisches Wörterbuch.
Bull. Lit. Eccl.	Bulletin de Littérature Ecclésiastique, Toulouse.
BZ	Biblische Zeitschrift, Paderborn.
BzFCTh	Beiträge zur Förderung Christlicher Theologie, Gütersloh.
CBQ	Catholic Biblical Quarterly, Washington, D. C.
C. H.	Corpus Hermeticum
ChQ	Church Quarterly Review, London.
Coll. BG	Collationes Brugenses et Gandavenses, Brugge.
Conc.	Concilium, An International Review of Theology, London.
CSCO	Corpus Scriptorum Christianorum Orientalium, ed. by I. B. Chabot and others, Louvain-Paris-Rome 1903.
CSEL	Corpus Scriptorum Ecclesiasticorum Latinorum, ed. by Academia Scientiarum Austriaca, Vindobonae 1866 onwards.
CuBib	Cultura Biblica, Segovia.
DBS	Dictionaire de la Bible, Supplément, ed. L. Pirot, Paris.
DomS	Dominican Studies, Oxford.
DTC	Dictionnaire de Théologie Catholique, Paris.
DTh	Divus Thomas, Piacenza.
EspVie	Esprit et Vie, Langres.
EstBib	Estudios Biblicos, Madrid.
ET	Expository Times, Edinburgh.

ETL	Ephemerides Theologicae Lovanienses, Louvain.
EvQ	The Evangelical Quarterly, London.
EvTh	Evangelische Theologie, München.
Exp.	The Expositor, London.
Foi et Vie	Foi et Vie, Paris.
GCS	Die Griechischen Christlichen Schriftsteller der Ersten Drei Jahrhunderte, ed. by Corpus Berolonese, Leipzig-Berlin 1897 onwards.
HeythJ	The Heythrop Journal, Oxford.
HNT	Herders Theologischer Kommentar zum Neuen Testament, Freiburg.
ICC	International Critical Commentary.
IDB	Interpreters' Dictionary of the Bible.
IEJ	Israel Exploration Journal, Jerusalem.
Interpretation	Interpretation, Richmond, Va.
JBL	Journal of Biblical Literature, Philadelphia.
JBR	Journal of Bible and Religion, Brattleboro, Vt.
JHS	Journal of Hellenistic Studies, London.
JNES	Journal of Near Eastern Studies, Chicago.
JSS	Journal of Semitic Studies, Manchester.
JTS	Journal of Theological Studies, Oxford-London.
LavThéolPhil	Laval Théologique et Philosophique. Québec.
LThK	Lexicon für Theologie und Kirche, Freiburg.
Lum et Vie	Lumière et Vie, Lyon.
Mél. ScRel.	Mélanges de Science Religieuse, Lille.
MelT	Melita Theologica, Valletta, Malta.
MKNT	H. A. W. Meyer, Kritisch-Exegetischer Kommentar über das Neue Testament, Göttingen.
MünchTheolZeit.	Münchener Theologische Zeitschrift, München.
NeotPatr.	Neotestamentica et Patristica. Eine Freundesgabe Herrn Prof. Dr. O. Cullmann zu seinem 60. Geburtstag überreicht. Leiden 1962. (Supplements to Novum Testamentum VI).
NKZ	Neue Kirchliche Zeitschrift, Leipzig.
NRT	Nouvelle Revue Théologique, Louvain.
NovTest.	Novum Testamentum, Leiden.
NtAbh	Neutestamentliche Abhandlungen, Münster.
NThSt	Nieuwe Theologische Studien, Groningen-Wageningen.
NTS	New Testament Studies, Cambridge.
OTS	Oudtestamentische Studien, Leiden.
ParVi	Parole di Vita, Torino-Leumann.
PG	Patrologiae Cursus completus, series Graeca, ed. Migne (1857-1866).
PL	Patrologiae Cursus completus, series Latina, ed. Migne (1878-1890).
PrincTR	Princeton Theological Review, Princeton, N. J.
RB	Revue Biblique, Paris.
RDiocNamur	Revue Diocésaine de Namur, Namur.

RechBibl	Recherches Bibliques. (Journées Bibliques de Louvain), Bruges.
RefTR	Reformed Theological Review, Hawthorn, Australia.
RExp	Review and Expositor, Louisville, Ky.
RGG	Die Religion in Geschichte und Gegenwart, Tübingen.
RHPR	Revue d'Histoire et de Philosophie Religieuses, Strasbourg.
RHR	Revue del'Histoire des Religions, Paris.
RivBib	Rivista Biblica, Rome.
RNT	Regensburger Neues Testament, Regensburg.
RQ	Revue de Qumran, Paris.
RScPhTh	Revue des Sciences Philosophiques et Théologiques, Le Saulchoir.
RScRel	Revue des Sciences Religieuses, Strasbourg.
RSR	Recherches de Science Religieuse, Paris.
RTh	Revue Thomiste, Toulouse-Bruxelles.
SacPag	Sacra Pagina. Miscellanea Biblica Congressus Internationalis Catholici de re Biblica, Bruxelles-Louvain 1958. 2 vols. Ed. by J. Coppens, A. Descamps, E. Massaux, Gembloux (Duculot) 1959.
ScotJT	Scottish Journal of Theology, Edinburgh.
Scripture	Scripture, London.
SOr	Studia Orientalia, Helsinki.
ST	Studia Theologica, Lund-Kobenhavn.
StANT	Studien zum Alten und Neuen Testament, München.
StCath.	Studia Catholica, Nijmegen.
St.d.ThFr.	Studien der deutschen Theologie und Frömmigkeit, Weimar.
StEv	Studia Evangelica. Papers presented to the International Congress on 'the Four Gospels in 1957' held at Christ Church, Oxford 1957 = TU 73, 1959.
TBLNT	Theologisches Begriffslexikon zum Neuen Testament, Wüppertal.
TDNT	Theological Dictionary of the New Testament, the Translation of Kittel's " Theologisches Wörterbuch zum Neuen Testament ", Michigan.
ThBl	Theologische Blätter, Leipzig.
THK	Theologisches Handkommentar zum Neuen Testament, Leipzig.
ThSt	Theologische Studien, Zürich.
ThStKr	Theologische Studien und Kritiken, Hamburg.
ThZ	Theologische Zeitschrift, Basel.
TLZ	Theologische Literaturzeitung, Berlin.
TS	Theological Studies, Woodstock, Md.
TsTNijm.	Tijdschrift voor Theologie. Redactie: Nijmegen.
TU	Texte und Untersuchungen zur Geschichte der altchristlichen Literatur, Leipzig-Berlin.

TWNT	Theologisches Wörterbuch zum Neuen Testament, Stuttgart.
VD	Verbum Domini, Roma.
VieSpir	Vie Spirituelle, Paris.
VT	Vetus Testamentum, Leiden.
Way	The Way, London.
WUNT	Wissenschaftliche Untersuchungen zum Neuen Testament, Tübingen.
ZAW	Zeitschrift für die Alttestamentliche Wissenschaft, (Giessen) Berlin.
ZDMG	Zeitschrift der Deutschen Morgenländischen Gesellschaft, (Leipzig) Wiesbaden.
ZKT	Zeitschrift für Katholische Theologie, Innsbruck.
ZNW	Zeitschrift für die Neutestamentliche Wissenschaft und die Kunde des alten Christentums, Berlin.
ZRG	Zeitschrift für Religions - und Geistesgeschichte, Köln.
ZTK	Zeitschrift für Theologie und Kirche, Tübingen.

Bibliography

I. Commentaries

ALEXANDER, N., *The Epistles of St. John*, London 1962.
BARRETT, C. K., *The Gospel according to St. John*, London 1962, (reimpression).
BAUER, W., *Das Johannesevangelium* (HNT 6), 3rd ed., Tübingen 1933.
BELZER, J. E., *Die Briefe des hl. Johannes*, Freiburg in Br. 1906.
BERNARD, J. H., *A Critical and Exegetical Commentary on the Gospel according to St. John* (ICC), 2 vols., Edinburgh 1962, (6th impression).
BLASS, F., *Philology of the Gospels*, London 1898.
— — *Evangelium Secundum Johannem cum Variae Lectionis Delectu*, Lipsiae 1902.
BONSIRVEN, J., *Épîtres de s. Jean* (Verbum Salutis IX), 2nd ed., Paris 1954.
BOUYER, L., *Le quatrième évangile*, 3rd. ed., Paris 1956.
BROOKE, A. E., *The Johannine Epistles* (ICC), Edinburgh 1957, (reimpression).
BROWN, R. E., *The Gospel according to John I-XII* (The Anchor Bible 29), New York 1966.
— — *The Gospel according to John XIII-XXI*, New York 1970.
BÜCHSEL, F., *Das Evangelium nach Johannes* (Das Neue Testament Deutsch), Göttingen 1934.
— — *Die Johannesbriefe* (THK XVII), Leipzig 1933.
BULTMANN, R., *Das Evangelium des Johannes* (Kritisch-Exegetischer Kommentar über das Neue Testament II), 10th ed., Göttingen 1964 (18th impression).
— — *Die drei Johannesbriefe*, Göttingen 1967.
CALMES, Th., *L'Evangile selon S. Jean*, Paris 1904.
CALMET, A., *Commentarius Literalis in Omnes Libros Novi Testamenti*, vol. II, Würzburg 1787.
CHAINE, J., *Les épîtres catholiques* (Etudes Bibliques), 2nd ed., Paris 1939.
CHARUE, A., *Les épîtres catholiques* (La Sainte Bible XII), Paris 1938.
DODD, C. H., *The Johannine Epistles* (The Moffat New Testament Commentary), 2nd ed., London 1947.
FEUILLET, A., *Les épîtres johanniques*, in *Introduction à la Bible*, II, Tournai 1959, pp. 685-708.
GAUGLER, E., *Die Johannesbriefe*, Zürich 1964.
HOLTZMANN, H. J., *Evangelium, Briefe und Offenbarung des Johannes*, (Handkommentar zum N. T. IV), 3rd ed., Tübingen 1908.
HOSKYNS, E. C., *The Fourth Gospel* (ed. by F. N. DAVEY), 2nd ed., London 1947.
HOULDON, J. L., *The Johannine Epistles*, London 1973.
HUNTER, A. M., *The Gospel according to John*, Cambridge 1965.

HUTHER, J. E., *Critical and Exegetical Handbook to the General Epistles of James and John*, Edinburgh 1882.
KOHLER, M., *Le cœur et les mains*, Neuchâtel 1962.
KUSS, O., and MICHL, J., *Der Brief an die Hebräer und die katholischen Briefe* (RNT 8), Regensburg 1953.
LAGRANGE, M. J., *Le quatrième évangile* (Études Bibliques), 3rd ed., Paris 1925.
LAPIDE, CORNELIUS A, *Commentaria in Quatuor Evangelia*, vol. IV, Turin 1906.
LIGHTFOOT, R. H., *St. John's Gospel, A Commentary* (ed. by C. F. EVANS), Oxford 1956.
LOISY, A., *Le quatrième évangile*, Paris 1903.
LUTHER, M., *De. Martin Luthers Evangelien Auslegung* (hrsg. E. MÜHLHAUPT), 2nd ed., vol. IV, Göttingen 1961.
MACGREGOR, G. H. C., *The Gospel of John* (Moffat Commentary), London 1928.
MALDONATUS, J., *Commentarii in Quattuor Evangelistas* (ed. by CONRAD MARTIN), vol. II, Moguntiae 1863.
MELANCHTON, P., *Enarratio in Evangelium Johannis*, (ed. C. J. BRETSCHNEIDER), vol. XV, Halle 1848.
MEYER, H. A. W., *Kritisch-Exegetisches Handbuch über das Evangelium des Johannes*, Göttingen 1862.
MILLIGAN, W. M., and MOULTON, W. M. F., *Commentary on the Gospel of St. John*, Edinburgh 1898.
MORRIS, L., *The Gospel according to John*, Eerdmans 1971.
NATALIS, A., *Expositio Literalis et Moralis S. Evangelii Jesu Christi Secundum Lucam, Marcum et Johannem*, Paris 1743.
ODEBERG, H., *The Fourth Gospel, Interpreted in Relation to Contemporaneous Religious Currents in Palestine and the Hellenistic Oriental World*, Uppsala 1929.
O'NEILL, J. C., *The Puzzle of Ist John. A New Examination of Origins*, London 1966.
REVILLE, J., *Le quatrième évangile, son origine et sa valeur historique*, 2nd ed.' Paris 1902.
RIBERA, F., *In Sanctum Jesu Christi Evangelium secundum Johannem Commentarii*, Lyon 1623.
RICHARDSON, A., *The Gospel according to St. John*, (Torch Bible), London 1964.
ROTHE, R., *Der Erste Brief Johannes*, Wittenberg 1878.
SCHANZ, P., *Kommentar über das Evangelium des Hl. Johannes*, Tübingen 1885.
SCHLATTER, A., *Der Evangelist Johannes, wie er spricht, denkt und glaubt. Ein Kommentar zum Vierten Evangelium*, 3rd ed., Stuttgart 1960.
SCHNACKENBURG, R., *The Gospel according to St. John*, vol. I, trans. from the German " Das Johannesevangelium, I Teil " (HNT IV, 1), by K. SMYTH, New York – London 1968.
—— *Das Johannesevangelium* II Teil, Herder 1971.
—— *Die Johannesbriefe* (HNT XIII), 2nd ed., Freiburg 1963.
SCHULTZ, S., *Das Evangelium nach Johannes*, Göttingen 1972^{12}.
THOMAS, St., *Super Evangelium S. Joannis Lectura*, ed. R. CAI, 5th ed., Taurini-Romae 1955.

TILLMANN, F., *Das Johannesevangelium*, 4th ed., Bonn 1931.
TOLETUS, F., *In Sacrosanctum Johannis Evangelium Commentarii*, Romae 1588.
VAN DEN BUSSCHE, H., *Jean. Commentaire de l'Évangile spirituel*, Bruges 1967.
VREDE, W., *Der Erste Brief des Hl. Johannes*, Bonn 1916.
WEISS, B., *Das Johannesevangelium* (Krit. Exegetischer Kommentar über das Neue Testament II), 9th ed., Göttingen 1902.
— — *Die drei Briefe des Apostels Johannes* (Krit. Exegetischer Kommentar über das Neue Testament XIV), 6th ed., Göttingen 1899.
WELLHAUSEN, J., *Das Evangelium Johannis*, Berlin 1908.
WENDT, H. H., *Die Johannesbriefe und das Johanneische Christentum*, Halle 1925.
WESTCOTT, B. F., *The Gospel according to St. John*, 2nd ed., London 1958.
— — *The Epistles of St. John*, 4th ed., London 1966.
WINDISCH, H., *Die katholischen Briefe* (HNT 15), 3rd ed. by H. PREISKER, Tübingen 1951.
ZAHN, Th., *Das Evangelium des Johannes* (Kommentar zum N. T. IV), 5th ed., Leipzig 1921.
ZAHN, Th., *Das Evangelium des Johannes* (Kommentar zum N. T. IV), 5th ed., Leipzig 1921.

II. Special Literature on Sonship

BAUER, G., " Geburt ", *TBLNT* I, 444-454.
BAUERNFEIND, O., " Gotteskindschaft ", *RGG*, 3rd ed., vol. III, col. 1798-1800.
BAUR, P., " Gott als Vater im Alten Testament ", *ThStKr* 72 (1899), 483-507.
BENOIT, P., " Nous gemissons, attendant la délivrance de notre corps, (Rom VIII, 23) ", in *Mél. J. Lebreton I* (Paris 1951), 267-280.
BLINZLER, J., " Sohnschaft, Sohn Gottes, Söhne Gottes, Kinder Gottes ", *BThW* II, 1050-1060.
BÖHLIG, A., " Vom ' Knecht ' zum ' Sohn ' ", in *Myst. Wahr.* Leiden, 1967, 58-66.
BOISMARD, M. E., " Dieu notre Père ", in *Grandes thèmes bibliques*, Paris 1958, 67-75.
BORNKAMM, G., " Sohnschaft und Leiden, Judentum, Urchristentum und Kirche ", *Fs. für J. Jeremias*, (*BNTW*), Berlin 1960, 188-198.
BRAUN, F. M., " Qui ex Deo Natus Est ", in *Aux Sources de la Tradition Chrétienne* (Mél. M. Goguel), Neuchâtel 1950, 11-31.
BRAUN, F. M., " La vie d'un haut (Jo 3,1-15) ", *RScPhTh* 40 (1956), 3-24.
CALDER, W. M., " Adoption and Inheritance in Galatia ", *JTS* 31 (1930), 372-374.
CALLE, F. De La, " La ' huiothesian ' de Rom 8,23 ", *EstBib* 30 (1971), 77-98.
CANDISCH, J. S., " Children of God ", in *Hasting's Dictionary of the Bible*, Edinburgh 1909, 124-126.
CASTELLINI, G., " De Jo 1,13 in Quibusdam Citationibus Patristicis ", *VD* 32 (1954), 155-157.

CIPRIANI, S., " Il potere di diventare figli di dio ", Il battesimo : *Catechesi*, 167-188.
COOKE, G., " The Israelite King as Son of God ", *ZAW* 73 (1961), 202-225.
DE BOER, P., *De Zoon van God in het O. T.*, Leiden 1958.
DEY, J., ΠΑΛΙΓΓΕΝΕΣΙΑ. *Ein Beitrag zur Klärung der religionsgeschichtlichen Bedeutung von Tit 3,5*, (NtAbh. XVII, 5), Münster 1937.
—— " Wiedergeburt ", *BThW* II, 1228-1235.
DODD, C. H., " The Prophecy of Caiaphas, John XI, 47-53 ", in *Neot. Patr.*, (Supplement to NT VI), Leiden 1962, 134-143.
DONATUS, Ab HAMRUN., Τέκνα Θεοῦ ἐκ Θεοῦ ἐγεννήθησαν. *A Biblical-Theological Approach to Jo 1:12-13 and to Its Parallel Johannine Passages* (Diss. Pont. Univ. Greg.), Roma 1953-1954.
DONATUS, A Marsa., " An Outline of St. John's Doctrine on the Divine Sonship of the Christian ", *MelT* 8 (1955), 1-26 ; 53-71 ; 9 (1956), 14-38.
GALOT, J., *Être né de Dieu, Jo 1,13*, (Anal. Bibl. 34), Rome 1969.
GOPPELT, L., " Wiedergeburt ", *RGG* (3rd ed., 1962), vol. VI, cols. 1697-1699.
GRUNDMANN, W., *Die Gotteskindschaft in der Geschichte Jesu und ihre seligionsgeschichtlichen Voraussetzungen*, (St.d.Th.Fr. 1), Weimar 1938.
——, " Zur Rede Jesu vom Vater im Johannes Evangelium ", *ZNW* 52 (1961), 213-230
GRUNDMANN, W., " Der Geist der Sohnschaft ", *Disciplina Domini* 1 (1963), 180ff.
GYLLENBERG, R., " Gott der Vater im A. T. und in der Predigt Jesu ", *SOr* 1 (1926), 51-60.
HALLER, A. H., " Der Begriff der Wiedergeburt nach der Schrift ", *NKZ* 11 (1900), 614ff.
HARNACK, A. v., " Die Terminologie der Wiedergeburt und verwandter Erlebnisse in der ältesten Kirche ", *TU* 42-3 (1918) 97-143.
HAVET, J., " Dieu notre Père ", *RDiocNamur* 12 (1958), 19-40 ; 155-169.
HEUSCHEN, J., " Wiedergeburt ", *Bibel Lexikon* (2nd ed., 1968), cols. 1888-1891.
HOUSSIAU, M. A., " Le milieu théologique de la leçon ' ἐγεννήθη ' (Jo 1,13) ", *SacPag* II (Paris 1959), 169-188.
HUNTRESS, E., " Son of God' in the Jewish Writings prior to the Christian Era ", *JBL* 54 (1935), 117-123.
JANKOWSKI, A., " The Grace of Filiation in Johannine Theology " (In Polish), *AtKap* 55 (1957), 26-42.
JEREMIAS, J., " Abba ", *TLZ* 79 (1954), cols. 213ff.
—— *Abba. Studien zur neutest. Theologie und Zeitgeschichte*, G, Vandenhoeck 1966.
KÜRZINGER, J., " Συμμόρφους τῆς εἰκόνος τοῦ υἱοῦ αὐτοῦ (Rom 8,29) ", *BZ* (NF) 2 (1958), 294-299.
LAGRANGE, J. M., " La paternité de Dieu dans l'Ancien Testament ", *RB* 17 (1908), 481-499.
—— " La régénération et la filiation divine dans les mystères d'Éleusis ", *RB* 38 (1929), 68-81 ; 201-214.
LEANEY, A. R. C., " Conformed to the Image of His Son ", *NTS* 10 (1963-1964), 470-479.

LOFTHOUSE, W. F., " Fatherhood and Sonship in the Fourth Gospel ", *ET* 43 (1931), 442-448.
LYONNET, S., " La libertà dei figli di Dio ", *Humanitas* (Nuova Serie) 1 (1969), 76-94.
McCARTHY, D. J., " Israel, My Firstborn Son ", *The Way* 5 (1965), 183-191.
—— " Notes on the Love of God in Deut. and the Father-Son Relationship between Yahweh and Israel ", *CBQ* 27 (1965), 144-147.
McKENZIE, J. L., " Divine Sonship and Individual Religion ", *CBQ* 7 (1945), 32-47.
—— " The Divine Sonship of Men in the Old Testament " *CBQ* 7 (1945), 326-339.
—— " The Divine Sonship of Israel and the Covenant " *CBQ* 8 (1946), 320-331.
MARCHEL, W., *Abba Père! La prière du Christ et des chrétiens*, (Anal. Bibl. 19) Romae 1963.
MENSCHING, G., " Vatername Gottes ", *RGG* (3rd ed., 1962), vol. VI, cols. 1232-1233.
MERSCH, E., " Filii in Filio ", *NRT* 65 (1938), 551-582 ; 651-702 ; 809-830.
MICHEL, O., and BETZ, O., " Von Gott gezeugt' in Judentum, Urchristentum und Kirche ", *Fs. J. Jeremias (BNTW)*, Berlin 1960, 3-23.
MONTEFIORE, H. W., " God as Father in the Synoptic Gospels ", *NTS* 3 (1956), 31-46.
MORALDI, L., " La paternità di Dio nell'Antico Testamento ", *RivBib* 7 (1959), 44-56.
OKE, C. C., " A Suggestion with regard to Romans 8,23 ", *Interpretation* 11 (1957), 455-460.
PAX, E., " Gotteskindschaft ", *LThK* (2nd ed., 1960), IV, cols. 1114-1116.
—— " Wiedergeburt ", *LThK* (2nd ed., 1960), X, cols. 1099-1102.
PESCH, H., " Ihr müsst von oben geboren werden (Jo, 3,1-12) ", *BibLeb* 7 (1966), 208-219.
RENARD, H., and GRELOT, P., " Fils ", in *Vocabulaire de Théologie Biblique* Paris 1964, cols. 381-384.
ROMANIUK, K., " Spiritus Clamans (Gal 4,6 ; Rom 8,15) ", *VD* 40 (1962), 190-198.
ROOSEN, A., " Testimonium Spiritus (Rom 8,16) ", *VD* 28 (1950), 214-226.
ROSSELL, W. H., " New Testament Adoption - Graeco-Roman or Semitic ? ", *JBL* 71 (1952), 233-234.
SAILLARD, M., " C'est moi qui, par l'Évangile vous ai enfantés dans le Christ, (I Cor 4,15) ", *RSR* 56 (1968), 5-42.
SCHLAFER, F. G., *The Johannine Doctrine of Christian Sonship*, Diss. Southern Baptist Theological Seminary, Louisville 1948-1949.
SCHMID, J., " Jn 1,13 ", *BZ* (NF) 1 (1957), 118-125.
SCHOENBERG, M. W., " Huiothesia. The Word and the Institution ", *Scripture* 15 (1963), 115-123.
SCHOENBERG, M. W., " St. Paul's Notion on the Adoptive Sonship of Christians (Gal 4,5) ", *Thomist* 28 (1964), 51-75.
SCHRUERS, P., " La paternité divine dans Mt 5,45 et 6,26-32 ", *ETL* 36 (1960), 593-624.

SCHWEITZER, E., " υἱός ", *TWNT* VIII, 392-395.
SCHWEITZER, W., *Gotteskindschaft, Wiedergeburt und Erneuerung im NT und seiner Umwelt*, Diss. Masch. T 1944.
SISTI, A., " La carità dei figli di Dio (I Giov 3,10-18) ", *BibOr* 9 (1967), 77-97.
SJÖBERG, E., " Wiedergeburt und Neuschöpfung im Palästinischen Judentum ", *ST* 4 (1951), 44-85.
SPARKS, H. F. D., " The Doctrine of the Divine Fatherhood in the Gospels ", *Studies in the Gospels* (1955), 241-262.
SUMMERS, R., " Born of Water and Spirit ", *Studies in Memory of H. Trantham*, Texas 1964, pp. 117-128.
SWETNAM, J., " On Romans 8,23 and the Expectation of Sonship ", *Bib* 48 (1967), 102-108.
THERON, D. J., " Adoption in the Pauline Corpus ", *EvQ* 28 (1956), 6-14.
TWISSELMANN, W., *Die Gotteskindschaft der Christen nach dem Neuen Testament* (Beitr.z.Förd.Christl.Theologie 41-1), Gütersloh 1939.
VIARD, A., " Singulier ou pluriel dans S. Jean 1,13, ' Qui ex Deo natus est ' ou ... ' nati sunt ' ? ", *AmiCl* 68 (1958), 516-520.
VILLAPADIERNA, C. De., " Dedit Potestatem Filios Dei Fieri (Jn 1,12f) ", *NatGrac* 11 (1964), 97-104.
VOSTÉ, J. M., " De Spirituali Regeneratione ex Aqua et Spiritu ", in *Studia Joannea* (Rome 1930), 101-138.
WHALING, T., " Adoption ", *PrincTR* 21 (1923), 223-235.
WILLIAMS, A. L., " My Father' in Jewish Thought of the First Century ", *JTS* 31 (1929-30), 42-47.
WINDISCH, H., " Friedensbringer-Gottessöhne ", *ZNW* 24 (1925), 240-60.
WINTER, P., " Der Begriff ' Söhne Gottes ' im Moseslied, Dt 32:1-43 ", *ZAW* 75 (1955), 40-48.
WITTICHEN, C., *Die Idee Gottes als des Vaters*, Göttingen 1865.
ZEDDA, S., *L'adozione a figli di Dio e lo Spirito Santo. Storia dell'interpretazione e teologia mistica di Gal 4,6.* (Anal. Bibl. 1), Roma 1952.
— — " L'adozione a figli di Dio ", *ParVi* 13 (1968), 43-45.

III. *Other Select Literature*

AALEN, S., " Reign' and ' House ' in the Kingdom of God in the Gospels ", *NTS* 8 (1961-1962), 215-240.
ABBOTT, E. A., *Johannine Vocabulary*, London 1905.
— — *Johannine Grammar*, London 1906.
AHERN, B. M., " The Fellowship of His Sufferings ", *CBQ* 22 (1960), 1-32.
ALAND, K., *Die Säuglingstaufe im Neuen Testament und in der Alten Kirche* (Theologische Existenz Heute 86), München 1961.
ALFARO, J., " Cognitio Dei et Christi in I Jo ", *VD* 39 (1961), 82-91.
— — " Christo Glorioso, Revelador del Padre ", *Greg.* 39 (1958), 222-230.
ARGYLE, A. W., " I Jo 3,4 ", *ET* 65 (1935), 62-63.
AUGUSTINOVIC, A., *Critica ' Determinismi ' Joannei*, Jerusalem 1947.
AUZOU, G., *De la servitude au service*, Paris 1961.

BAERT, E., " Het Thema van de Zalige Godsaanschouwing in de Griekse Patristiek tot Origines ", *NsTNijm* 1 (1961), 289-308.
BAILLET, M., " Un recueil liturgique de Qumran, Grotte 4 : ' Les paroles des luminaires ' ", *RB* 68 (1961), 195-250.
BALTZER, C., *Das Bundesformular*, Neukirchen 1964.
BARBERIS, A., " Sangue e acqua od acqua e sangue ? (Giov 19:34) ", *Sindon* 10 (1967), 31-33.
BARRETT, C. K., *The Prologue of St. John's Gospel*, London 1971.
BARTH, M., *Die Taufe – Ein Sakrament ? Ein exegetischer Beitrag zum Gespräch über die kirchliche Taufe*, Zollikon-Zürich 1951.
BARTHELEMY, D., " La sainteté selon la communauté de Qumran et selon l'Evangile " : Rech. Bibl. IV, *La Secte de Qumran et les origines du Christianisme* (1959), 203-216.
BATES, H. W., " Born of Water (Jn 3,5) ", *BS* 85 (1928), 230-236.
BAUERNFEIND, O., " νικάω ", *TDNT* IV, 942-945.
BAUMGARTNER, J. and MANSOOR, M., " Studies in the New Hodayot (Thanksgiving Hymns) – II ", *JBL* 74 (1955), 188-195.
BEILNER, W., " Vollmacht ", *BThW*, II, 1171-1176.
—— " Aufbau und Aussage des Johannes Prologs (Jo 1:18) ", *BibKi* 20 (1965), 98-105.
BERTRAM, G., " πατέω and Compounds in the LXX ", *TDNT* V, 941-943.
—— " ἔθνος ", *TDNT* II, 364-369.
BETZ, O., " Die Geburt der Gemeinde durch den Lehrer ", *NTS* 3 (1956-57), 314-326.
—— " Das Volk seiner Kraft, Zur Auslegung der Qumran-Hodayoth III, 1-18 ", *NTS* 5 (1958-59), 67-75.
BEUTLER, J., Μαρτυρία. *Traditionsgeschichtliche Untersuchungen zum Zeugnisthema bei Johannes*, Frankfurter Theologische Studien 10 (Frankfurt a. M. 1972).
BIELER, L., ΘΕΙΟΣ ΑΝΗΡ, *Das Bild des göttlichen Menschen in Spätantike und Frühchristentum*, 2 vols., Wien 1935-1936.
BIENECK, J., *Sohn Gottes als Christusbezeichnung der Synoptiker* (Abhandlungen zur Theologie des Alten und Neuen Testaments, 21), Zürich 1951.
BLACK, M., *The Scrolls and Christian Origins*, New York 1961.
BLANK, J., " Das Johannesevangelium, Der Prolog, II Teil ", *BibLeb* 7 (1966), 112-127.
BLIGH, J., " Four Studies in St. John, II : Nicodemus ", *HeythJ* 8 (1967), 40-51.
BOISMARD, M. E., " La Connaissance de l'Alliance nouvelle d'après I Jean ", *RB* 56 (1949), 365-391.
—— " Critique textuelle et citations patristiques ", *RB* 57 (1950), 388-408.
—— " Je ferai avec vous une Alliance nouvelle. Introduction à la lecture de I Jean ", *Lum et Vie* 8 (1953), 94-110.
—— *Le prologue de saint Jean* (Lect. Div., 11), Paris 1953.
—— " Une Liturgie Baptismale dans la Prima Petri ", *RB* 63 (1956), 182-208 ; 64 (1957), 161-183.
—— " Le Papyrus Bodmer II ", *RB* 64 (1957), 363-398.
—— " L'évolution du thème eschatologique dans les Traditions johanniques", *RB* 68 (1961), 507-524.

— — *Quatre hymnes baptismales dans la première épître de Pierre*, (Lect. Div., 30), Paris 1961.
BONHÖFFER, A., *Epiktet und das Neue Testament*, Giessen 1911.
BONNARD, P., *L'évangile selon saint Matthieu*, Neuchâtel 1963.
— — " Connaître Dieu selon le Quatrième Evangile et la Gnose Hellenistique : La connaissance de Dieu selon le NT et son milieu ", *Foi et Vie* 64 (1965), 483-492.
BONSIRVEN, J., *Le judaisme palestinien au temps de Jesus Christ*, 2nd ed., 2 vols., Paris 1934-1935.
BORIG, R., *Der wahre Weinstock* " (Studien zum Alten und Neuen Testament, 16), München 1967.
BORNKAMM, G. ; BARTH, G. ; Held, H. J., *Überlieferung und Auslegung im Matthäus-Evangelium*, Neukirchen 1960.
BOTTERWECK, G., *Gott erkennen im Sprachgebrauch des Alten Testaments*, Bonn 1951.
BOUSSET, W., *Kyrios Christos* (FRLANT, 21), 4th ed., Göttingen 1935.
BOVER, J. M., " Χάριν ἀντὶ Χάριτος (Jn 1,16) ", *Bib* 6 (1925), 454-460.
BRAUN, F. M., *La mère des fidèles*, Tournai 1953.
— — " Hermetisme et Johannisme ", *RTh* 55 (1955), 22-42 ; 259-299.
— — *Jean le théologien, sa théologie. Le mystère de Jésus Christ* (Études Bibliques), Paris 1966.
BRAUN, H., " Literaranalyse und theologische Schichtung im Ersten Johannesbrief ", *ZTK* 48 (1951), 261-272.
— — " ποιέω ", *TWNT* VI, 456-483.
BRINKMANN, B., " Prolog und Johannesevangelium ", *BibKi* 20 (1965), 106-113.
BROWN, R. E., " The Eucharist and Baptism in John ", in *New Testament Essays*, Milwaukee 1965, 77-95.
— —, " The Qumran Scrolls and the Johannine Gospels and Epistles ", *CBQ* 17 (1955), 560-567.
BUCH, F., *Die Liebe Gottes beim Propheten Osee*, Rome 1953.
BÜCHSEL, F., " ἄνωθεν ", *TDNT* I, 378.
— — " γεννάω ", *TDNT* I, 665-666 ; 668-672.
— — " δίδωμι ", *TDNT* II, 166.
— — " Μονογενής ", *TDNT* IV, 737-741.
— — *Johannes und der hellenistische Synkretismus* (BFChTh, II, 16), Gütersloh 1928.
BÜCHSEL, F., " Zu den Johannesbriefen ", *ZNW* 28 (1929), 235-241.
BULTMANN, R., " Analyse des Ersten Johannesbriefes ", in *Festgabe für A. Jülicher*, Tübingen 1927, 138-158.
— — " ζάω ", *TDNT* II, 832-872.
— — " γινώσκω ", *TDNT* I, 689-714.
— — " Die kirchliche Redaktion des I Johannesbriefes ", in *Memoriam Lohmeyer*, Stuttgart 1951, 189-201.
— — " Die Eschatologie des Johannes-Evangeliums ", in *Glauben und Verstehen*, Tübingen 1954, vol. I, 134-152.
— — *Theologie des Neuen Testaments*, Tübingen 1958.
BURNEY, F. C., *The Aramaic Origin of the Fourth Gospel*, Oxford 1922.

CADBURY, H. J., " The Ancient Physiological Notions Underlying Jn. 1:13a ; Hebr. 11:11 ", *Exp* 9 (1924), 430-439.
CAEVEL, J. de, " La connaissance religieuse dans les hymnes d'action de grâces de Qumran ", *ETL* 38 (1962), 435-460.
CALHOUN, G. M., " Zeus the Father in Homer ", *TPAPhA* 66 (1936), 1-17.
CAMELOT, Th., " Credere Deo, Credere Deum, Credere in Deum ", *RScPhTh* 30 (1941-42), 149-155.
CARPENTER, J. W., " Water Baptism in Jn 3,3-5 ; Acts 2,38 ; 22,15-16 ", *RExp* 54 (1957), 59-66.
CASALIS, M., " Le thème de la connaissance dans les milieux literaires essenien, paulinien et johannique : La connaissance de Dieu selon le NT et son milieu ", *Foi et Vie* 64 (1965), 493-522.
CERFAUX, L., " La Charité fraternelle et le retour du Christ (Jn XIII, 33-38)," *Recueil Lucien Cerfaux* vol. I, Gembloux 1954, 27-40.
—— " Les sources scripturaires de Mt 11,25-30 ", *ETL* 30 (1954), 740-746 ; 31 (1955), 331-342.
CERFAUX, L., *Le chrétien dans la théologie paulinienne* (Lect. Div., 33), Paris 1962.
CHARLIER, C., " L'Amour en Esprit (I Jn 4:7-13) ", *BiViChr* 10 (1955), 57-72.
CLIFFORD, M. F., " Aspects of Freedom in the Writings of John and Paul ", *BibTod* 29 (1967), 2035-2039.
CLIMBLIN, J., *Théologie de la paix*, Paris 1960.
CONCHAS, D. A., " Redemptio Acquisitionis ", *VD* 30 (1952), 14-29 ; 81-91 ; 154-169.
COOK, W. R., " Hamartiological Problems in First John ", *BS* 123 (1966), 249-260.
COOPER, E. J., " The Consciousness of Sin in I Jn ", *LavThéolPhil* 28 (1972), 237-248.
COUTURE, P., *The Teaching Function in the Church of Ist John*, Rome 1968.
CREED, J. M., *The Gospel according to St. Luke*, London 1957.
CULLMANN, O., " Der johanneische Gebrauch doppeldeutiger Ausdrücke als Schlüssel zum Verständnis des Vierten Evangeliums ", *ThZ* 4 (1948), 360-372.
—— *Die Tauflehre des Neuen Testaments* (Abh.z.Th.d.Alt.u.Neu.Test., 12), Zürich 1948.
—— *Die ersten christlichen Glaubensbekenntnisse*, (Theologische Studien, 15), Zürich 1949.
D'ARAGON, J. L., " La notion johannique de l'unité ", *ScE* 11 (1959), 111-119.
DAVIES, W. D., *The Setting of the Sermon on the Mount*, Cambridge 1964.
DECOURTRAY, A., " La conception johannique de la foi ", *NRT* 81 (1959), 561-576.
DELCOR, M., " Le vocabulaire juridique cultuel et mystique de l'initiation dans la secte de Qumran ", in *Qumran Probleme*, by H. BARDTKE, Berlin 1963, 109-134.
DELLING, L. G., " λαμβάνω ", *TDNT* IV, 5-7.
DEMKE, C., " Der sogenannte Logos-Hymnus im johanneischen Prolog ", *ZNW* 58 (1967), 45-68.

DESCAMPS, A., *Les justes et la justice dans les évangiles et le christianisme primitif, hormis la doctrine proprement paulinienne*, Louvain 1950.
DES PLACES, E., " Hymnes grecs au seuil de l'ère chrétienne ", *Bib* 38 (1957), 113-129.
—— *Syngeneia. La parenté de l'homme avec Dieu d'Homère à la patristique* (Études et Commentaires LI), Paris 1964.
DINECHIN, O. De, " ΚΑΘΩΣ : La similitude dans l'évangile selon saint Jean ", *RSR* 58 (1970), 195-236.
DODD, C. H., *Historical Tradition in the Fourth Gospel*, Cambridge 1963.
—— *The Interpretation of the Fourth Gospel*, Cambridge 1965.
DUPONT, J., *Essais sur la christologie de S. Jean*, Bruges 1951.
—— *Les beatitudes*, 2nd ed., Louvain 1958.
—— " Soyez parfaits – Mt 5:48 ; soyez misericordieux – Lk 6:36 ", *SacPag* II, (1959), 150-160.
—— " Matthieu 18,3 ", *Neotestamentica et Semitica*, Edinburgh 1969, 50f.
DUPONT-SOMMER, A., " La mère du messie et la mère de l'Aspic dans un hymne de Qumran ", *RHR* 147 (1955), 174-188.
FELICE, F. Di, " La Nascita dall'acqua e dallo Spirito (Giov. 3,5) ", *Asprenas* 17 (1970), 301-307.
FENTON, J. C., *St. Matthew* (Pelican Gospel Commentaries), London 1963.
FESTUGIÈRE, A. J., *La révélation d'Hermès Trismégiste*, 4 vols., Paris 1944-1954.
—— *Observations stylistiques sur l'évangile de s. Jean*, Paris, 1974.
FEUILLET, A., " L'Heure de la femme (Jn 16,21) et l'heure de la mère de Jésus (Jo 19,25-27) ", *Bib* 47 (1966), 169-184 ; 361-380 ; 557-573.
—— *Le mystère de l'amour divin dans la théologie johannique*, Paris 1972.
—— " Dieu est Amour ", *EspVie* 81 (1971), 537-548.
FLUSSER, D., " Two Notes on the Midrash on 2 Sam VII ", *IEJ* 9 (1959), 104-109.
FOERSTER, L. W., " ἐξουσία ", *TDNT* II, 560-574.
FORESTELL, J. T., *The Word of the Cross. Salvation as Revelation in the Fourth Gospel* (Anal. Bibl. 57), Rome 1974.
GAECHTER, P., *Das Matthäus-Evangelium*, Innsbruck-Wien 1962.
GAETA, G., *Il dialogo con Nicodemo*, Brescia 1974.
GÄRTNER, B., *The Temple and the Community in Qumran and the New Testament*, Cambridge 1965.
GAFFNEY, J., " Believing and Knowing in the Fourth Gospel ", *TS* 26 (1965), 215-241.
GALBIATI, E., *La struttura letteraria dell'Esodo*, Roma 1956.
GALTIER, P., " Le chrétien impeccable (I Jean 3,6 et 9) ", in *Mél. de Sc.Rel.*, 4 (1947), 137-154.
GELDENHUYS, N., *Commentary on the Gospel of Luke*, London 1954.
GIBLET, J., " Jésus et le Père dans le IVe Évangile ", in *L'Évangile de Jean*, Bruges 1958, 111-130.
GRÄSSER, E., " Die Juden als Teufelssöhne nach Joh. 8,37-47 ", in *Abh.z. Christl.Jud. Dialog* 2 (Münster 1967), 157-170.
GRAY, G. B., *Studies in Hebrew Proper Names*, London 1896.
GROSS, J., *La divinisation du chrétien d'après les Pères grecs*, Paris 1938.

GROSSOUW, W., "The Dead Sea Scrolls and the New Testament", *StCath* 26 (1951), 289-299.
GRUNDMANN, W., " δέχομαι ", *TDNT* II, 50-54.
—— " δύναμαι-δύναμις ", *TDNT* II, 284-317.
—— " Die ' Nepioi ' in der urchristlichen Parenese ", *NTS* 5 (1958-59), 188-205.
—— *Das Evangelium nach Lukas*, (THK III), 2nd ed., Berlin 1961.
—— *Das Evangelium nach Matthäus*, (THK I), Berlin 1968.
GUNDRY, R. H., " In My Father's House Are Many μοναί ", *ZNW* 58 (1967), 68-72.
GUTIERREZ, P., " Conceptus Lucis apud Johannem Evangelistam in relatione ad Conceptum ' Veritatis ' ", *VD* 29 (1951) 3-19.
HAMILTON, N. Q., *The Holy Spirit and Eschatology in Paul*, SJT Occasional Papers 6 (1957).
HANSE, H., " ἔχω ", *TDNT* II, 816-827.
HÄRING, T., " Gedankengang und Grundgedanke des Ersten Johannesbriefes ", in *Theologische Abhandlungen für C. von Weizsäcker*, Freiburg in Br., 1892, 171-200.
HARNACK, A. v., " Zur Textkritik und Christologie der Schriften des Johannes ", in *Sitzungsberichte der Königlich Preussischen Akademie der Wissenschaften*, Berlin 1915, 534-573.
HAWTHORNE, G. F., " The Concept of Faith in the Fourth Gospel ", *BS* 116 (1959), 117-126.
HEHN, J., " Zum Problem des Geistes im Alten Orient und im Alten Testament ", *ZAW* 43 (1925), 210-225.
HEILER, F., *Das Gebet. Eine religionsgeschichtliche und religionspsychologische Untersuchung*, 2nd ed., München 1920.
HERING, J., " Y a-t-il des aramaïsmes dans la première epître johannique ? ", Prolégomènes à une nouvelle traduction de cet écrit, *RHPR* 36 (1956), 113-121.
HEISE, J., *Bleiben.* μένειν *in den Johanneischen Schriften*, Tübingen, 1967.
HESTER, J. D., *Paul's Concept of Inheritance*, (SJT Occasional Papers, 14), 1968.
HOLTZMANN, H. J., *Lehrbuch der Neutestamentlichen Theologie*, 2nd ed., 2 vols., Tübingen 1911.
HORT, J. A., *Two Dissertations, I : On Monogenes Theos in Scripture and Tradition*, Cambridge 1876.
HOWARD, F. W., *The Fourth Gospel in recent Criticism and Interpretation*, 3rd ed., London 1945.
—— *Christianity according to St. John*, London 1943.
HUBY, J., " De la connaissance de foi dans s. Jean ", *RSR* 21 (1931), 385-421.
IRIGOIN, J., " La composition rhythmique du prologue de Jean ", *RB* 78 (1971) 501-14.
JACOB, E., *Théologie de l'Ancien Testament*, Neuchâtel 1955.
JAUBERT, A., *La notion d'Alliance dans le judaïsme aux abords de l'ere chrétienne*, (Patristica Sorbonensia, 6), Paris 1963.
—— " ' Croire ' dans l'évangile de Jean ", *VieSpir* 119 (1968), 137-148.

JEREMIAS, J., *Infant Baptism in the First Four Centuries*, trans. from German, " Die Kindertaufe in den Ersten Vier Jahrhunderten ", 2nd. ed., London 1964.
JERVELL, J., " Er kam in sein Eigentum, zum Joh. 1,11 ", *StTh* 10 (1956), 14-27.
JONGE, M. DE, " Jewish Expectations about ' Messiah ' according to the Fourth Gospel ", *NTS* 19 (1973), 246-270.
JOÜON, P., " Jean 1-16 : καὶ χάριν ἀντὶ χάριτος ", *RSR* 22 (1932), 206.
KENNEDY, H. A. A., " The Covenant Conception in the First Epistle of John ", *ET* 28 (1916), 23-26.
KERN, W., " Der symmetrische Gesamtaufbau von Joh. 8,12-58 ", *ZKT* 78 (1956), 451-454.
KLEIN, F. N., *Die Lichtterminologie bei Philon von Alexandrien und in den Hermetischen Schriften*, Leiden 1962.
KÖNIG, E., *Theologie des Alten Testament*, 4th ed., Stuttgart 1923.
KRUIJF, Th. DE., *Der Sohn des lebendigen Gottes* (Anal. Bibl. 16), Roma 1962.
KUSS, O., *Der Brief an die Römer*, Regensburg, 1940.
KUYPER, L. J., " Grace and Truth ", *Interpretation* 18 (1964), 3-19.
LACOCQUE, A., " L'idée directrice de l'Exode I à IV ", *VT* 15 (1965), 345-353.
LAGRANGE, M. J., *Évangile selon saint Matthieu*, Paris 1923.
— — " L'hermetisme ", *RB* 35 (1926), 240-264.
LAMARCHE, P., " Le Prologue de Jean ", *RSR* 52 (1964), 502-512.
LAMBERT, G., " Le maître de justice et la communauté de l'alliance ", *NRT* 74 (1952), 259-297.
LAW, R., *The Tests of Life. A Study of the First Epistle of St. John*, Edinburgh 1909.
LAZURE, N., *Les valeurs morales de la théologie johannique* (Évangile et épîtres), (Etudes Bibliques), Paris 1965.
LÉGASSE, S., *L'Appel du riche*, Paris 1966.
— — *Jésus et l'enfant*, Paris 1969.
LEIPOLDT, J., *Die urchristliche Taufe im Lichte der Religionsgeschichte*, Leipzig 1928.
LEWIS, E., " A Christian Theodicy : An Exposition of Romans 8:18-39 ", *Interpretation* 11 (1957), 405-420.
LINDBLOM, J., *Das Ewige Leben, Eine Studie über die Entstehung der religiösen Lebensidee im Neuen Testament*, Uppsala-Leipzig 1914.
LOHMEYER, E., *Das Evangelium des Matthäus* (MKNT I), Göttingen 1956.
— — *Das Vater-Unser erklärt*, 3rd ed., Zürich 1952.
LOHMEYER, H., " Über Aufbau und Gliederung des Ersten Johannesbriefes ", *ZNW* 27 (1928), 225-267.
LOHSE, E., " Wort und Sakrament im Johannesevangelium ", *NTS* 7 (1960-1961), 110-125.
LOUW, J., " De Vraag naar de Beteekenis van ἄνωθεν, Johannes 3:3 ", *NThSt* 23 (1940), 53-56.
LÜHRMANN, D., " Liebet eure Feinde (Lk 6:27-36 – Mt 5:39-48) ", *ZTK* 69 (1972), 412-438.

LYMAN, M. E., " Hermetic Religion and the Religion of the Fourth Gospel ", *JBL* 49 (1930), 265-276.
LYONNET, S., *Les épîtres de saint Paul aux Galates et aux Romains* (BJ), 2nd ed., Paris 1959.
—— *Exegesis Epistulae ad Romanos. Cap. V ad VIII* (except. Rom 5,12-21), Roma 1966.
MCCARTHY, D. J., " II Samuel and the Structure of the Deuteronomic History," *JBL* 84 (1965), 131-138.
MCCOOL, F. J., " Living Water in John ", in *Bible in Current Catholic Thought*, New York 1962, 226-235.
MCHUGH, J., *The Mother of Jesus in the New Testament*, London 1975.
MCPOLIN, J., *The " Name " of the Father and of the Son in the Johannine Writings*, (Excerpt.Diss.P.B.I.), Rome 1972.
MALATESTA, E., *Interiority and Covenant* (Excerpt. Diss. P.B.I.) Rome 1974.
MANSON, T. W., *The Teaching of Jesus*, Cambridge 1931.
—— " Entry into Membership of the Early Church ", *JTS* 48 (1947), 25-33.
MARSILI, S., " Pasqua centro della storia e atto di nascita del popolo di Dio ", in *Il Popolo di Dio*, Corso Biblico di Padova (1964-1965), 51-62.
MENDNER, S., " Nikodemus ", *JBL* 77 (1958), 293-323.
MERLIER, O., " ' ONOMA ' et ' EN ONOMATI ' dans le IVe Évangile ", *RÉG* 47 (1934), 180-204.
MICHAELIS, W., " Der Beitrag der LXX zur Bedeutungsgeschichte von πρωτότοκος ", in *Sprachgeschichte und Wortbedeutung*, Fs. A. Debrunner, 1954, 313-320.
MICHEL, O., " ὁμολογέω ", *TDNT* V, 199-220.
—— *Der Brief an die Römer* (MKNT), Göttingen 1955.
MICHL, J., " Der Geist als Garant des rechten Glaubens ", in *Vom Wort des Lebens* : Fs. für Max. Meinertz, (Münster 1951), 142-151.
MIRANDA, J. P., *Der Vater, der mich gesandt hat*, Frankfurt 1972.
MOLLAT, D., " La divinité du Christ d'après Saint Jean ", *Lum et Vie* 9 (1953), 101-134.
—— " La foi dans le quatrième evangile ", *Lum et Vie* 22 (1955), 91-107.
—— " La fede nel quarto vangelo ", in *Catechesi con San Giovanni*, (Brescia 1965), 35-43.
MOORE, G. F., *Judaism in the First Centuries of Christian Era*, 3 vols. Cambridge 1927-1930.
MORAN, L. W., " The Ancient Near Eastern Background of the Love of God in Deuteronomy ", *CBQ* 25 (1963), 77-87.
MOUROUX, J., " L'Expérience chrétienne dans la première épître de s. Jean ", *VieSpir* 78 (1948), 381-412.
NAGL, E., " Die Gliederung des Ersten Johannesbriefes ", *BZ* 16 (1924), 77-92.
NAUCK, W., *Die Tradition und der Charakter des Ersten Johannesbriefes* (WUNT 3), Tübingen 1957.
NEUGEBAUER, F., " Das paulinische ' In Christo ' ", *NTS* 4 (1957-58), 124-138.
NIEDERWIMMER, K., *Der Begriff der Freiheit im neuen Testament*, Berlin 1966.
NILSSEN, M. P., *Geschichte der griechischen Religion*, 2nd ed., 2 vols., München 1961.
NOACK, B., *Zur johanneischen Tradition*, Kobenhavn 1954.

NÖTSCHER, F., *Vom Alten zum Neuen Testament* (BBB 17), Bonn 1962.
—— *Zur theologischen Terminologie der Qumran Texte* (BBB 10), Bonn 1956.
NORDEN, E., *Die Geburt des Kindes. Geschichte einer religiösen Idee*, Leipzig-Berlin 1924.
NOTH, M., " David und Israel in II Sam 7 ", in *Mél. Bibliques redigés en l'honneur de André Gobert* (1957), pp. 122-130.
NYGREN, A., *Eros et Agapè. La notion chrétienne de l'amour et ses transformations* (trans. from German), Aubier 1944.
O'CONNELL, M., " The Concept of Commandment in the Old Testament ", *TS* 21 (1960), 351-403.
OEPKE, A., " ἐν ", *TDNT* II, 537-543.
—— " παῖς ", *TDNT* V, 636-654.
—— *Der Brief des Paulus an die Galater* (THK IX), Berlin 1960.
OKE, C. C., " The Plan of the First Epistle of John ", *ET* 51 (1939-40), 347-350.
OLIVIERA, C. J. P. de, " Le verbe ' ΔΙΔΟΝΑΙ ' comme expression des rapports du Père et du Fils dans le IVe evangile ", *RScPhTh* 49 (1965), 81-104.
PANCARO, S., " People of God in St. John's Gospel ", *NTS* 16 (1969), 114-129.
PANIMOLLE, S. A., *Il dono della legge e la grazia della verità* (Gv 1,17), Roma 1973.
PERCY, E., *Untersuchungen über den Ursprung der johanneischen Theologie*, Lund 1939.
PHILIPS, G. L., " Faith and Vision in the Fourth Gospel ", in *Studies in Fourth Gospel*, ed. by F. L. CROSS, London 1957, 83-96.
PLUMMER, A., *An Exegetical Commentary on the Gospel according to St. Matthew*, London 1909.
—— *The Gospel according to St. Luke*, (ICC), 5th ed., Edinburgh 1922.
POTTERIE, I. de la, " οἶδα et γινώσκω – Les deux modes de la connaissance dans le quatrième évangile ", *Bib* 40 (1957), 709-725.
—— " La notion de témoignage dans s. Jean ", *SacPag* II, 193-208.
——, " L'emploi dynamique de εἰς dans s. Jean et ses incidences théologiques ", *Bib* 43 (1962), 366-387.
—— " L'impeccabilité du chrétien d'après I Jn 3,6-9 ", in *La vie selon l'esprit, condition du chrétien*, (Paris 1965), 197-216.
—— " Naître de l'eau et naître de l'esprit, le texte baptismal de Jn 3,5 ", in *La vie selon l'esprit*, 31-63.
—— " L'onction du chrétien par la foi ", in *La vie selon l'esprit*, 107-167.
—— " Le paraclet ", in *La vie selon l'esprit*, 85-105.
—— " Le péché, c'est l'iniquité (I Jn 3,4) ", in *La vie selon l'esprit*, 65-83.
——, " Le rapport de la foi et du baptême dans la mission après le Nouveau Testament ", in *Repenser la mission*, (Louvain 1965), 161.
—— " Jesus et Nicodemus : de necessitate generationis ex Spiritu : Jo 3,1-10 ", *VD* 4 (1969), 193-214.
—— " Χάρις paulinienne et Χάρις johannique ", in *Jesus und Paulus* (Fs. W. G. Kümmel), Göttingen 1975, 256-282.

PRÜMM, K., *Religionsgeschichtliches Handbuch für den Raum der Altchristlichen Umwelt*, Rome 1954.
PRUNET, O., *La morale chrétienne d'après les écrits johanniques* (Évangile et épîtres), Paris 1957.
QUELL, G., " πατήρ ", *TDNT* V, 959-974.
RANDALL, J. F., " The Theme of Unity in John 17,20-23 ", *ETL* 41 (1965), 373-394.
RATZINGER, J., *Die christliche Brüderlichkeit*, München 1960.
REITZENSTEIN, R., *Poimandres*, Leipzig 1904.
— — *Die hellenistischen Mysterienreligionen nach ihren Grundlagen und Wirkungen*, Berlin 1927.
RESCH, A., *Ausserkanonische Paralleltexte zu den Evangelien*, 4 Teil, (TU 10,3), Leipzig 1896.
RESCH, G., " Was versteht Paulus unter der Versiegelung mit dem Hl. Geist ", *NKZ* 6 (1895), 991-1003.
REUSS, J., " Die Erklärung des Johannesevangeliums durch den Patriarchen Photius von Konstantinopel ", *BZ* (NF) 6 (1962), 279-282.
RICCA, P., *Die Eschatologie des Vierten Evangeliums*, Zürich 1966.
RICHTER, G., " Die Fleischwerdung des Logos im Johannesevangelium ", *NovTest* 13 (1971), 81-126 ; 14 (1972), 257-276.
RIDDERBOS, H., " The Structure and Scope of the Prologue to the Gospel of St. John ", *NT* 8 (1966), 180-201.
RIEDL, J., " Strukturen christologischer Glaubensentfaltung im Neuen Testament (Lk 1,35 ; Rom 1,3f ; Jn 1,14) ", *ZKT* 87 (1965), 443-452.
RIESENFELD, H., " Zu den joh. ' hina' Sätzen ", *ST* 19 (1965), 213-220.
ROBINSON, J. A. T., " The Destination and Purpose of the Johannine Epistles ", *NTS* 7 (1960-61), 56-65.
ROBINSON, P. W. B., " Born of Water and Spirit : Does John 3,5 Refer to Baptism ? ", *RefTR* 25 (1966), 15-23.
ROLLA, A., " Il dialogo con Nicodemo ", in *Cento problemi biblici*, (Assisi 1961), 364-368.
ROMANIUK, K., " Die vollkommene Liebe treibt die Furcht aus. Eine Auslegung von I Joh 4,17-18 ", *BibLeb* 5 (1964), 80-84.
ROUSTANG, F., " L'entretien avec Nicodème ", *NRT* 78 (1956), 337-358.
RYLE, J. C., *Expository Thoughts on the Gospels*, vol. I, London 1896.
SANDERS, J. T., *The New Testament Christological Hymns*, Cambridge, 1971
SASSE, H., " αἰώνιος ", *TDNT* I, 208-209.
SCHÄDEL, K., *Das Johannes Evangelium und die Kinder des Lichtes*, Diss. Wien 1953.
SCHAEFER, O., " ' Gott ist Licht ', I Jo 1,5 ", *ThStKr* 105 (1933), 467-476.
SCHLIER, H., *Lettera ai Galati*, trans. from the German : " Der Brief an die Galater ", by M. BELLINCIONI, Brescia 1966.
SCHLIER, H., " Le révélateur et son oeuvre dans l'évangile de saint Jean ", in *Essais sur le Nouveau Testament* (Paris 1968), 295-305.
— — " Zum Begriff des Geistes nach dem Johannesevangelium ", in *Besinnung auf das Neue Testament*, (Freiburg 1964), 264-271.
SCHMID, J., *Das Evangelium nach Matthäus* (RNT), 3rd ed., Ratisbonne 1956.

SCHMID, R., *Das Bundesopfer in Israel* (Studien z. Alt. u. Neu. Testament), München 1964.
SCHMIDT, K. L., " ἔθνος ", *TDNT* II, 369-372.
SCHNACKENBURG, R., *Das Heilsgeschehen bei der Taufe nach dem Apostel Paulus*, München 1950.
—— " Logos-Hymnus und Johanneischer Prolog ", *BZ* (NF) 1 (1957), 66-109.
—— *The Moral Teaching of the New Testament*, trans. from the German " Die sittliche Botschaft des Neuen Testaments ", by J. H. SMITH and W. J. O'HARA, London 1967 (4th impression).
SCHNIEWIND, J., " ἀγγελία ", *TDNT* I, 58-60.
——, *Das Evangelium nach Matthäus*, Göttingen 1954.
SCHRENK, G., " πατήρ ", *TDNT* V, 945-959 ; 974-1022.
SCHÜTZ, R., *Die Vorgeschichte der johanneischen Formel* ὁ Θεὸς ἀγάπη ἐστίν, Göttingen 1917.
SCHWEIZER, E., " πνεῦμα ", *TWNT* VI, 436-449.
SCHWERTSCHLAGER, R., *Der I Joh. in seinem Grundgedanken und Aufbau*, Coburg 1935.
SCOTT, C. A. A., *Christianity according to St. Paul*, Cambridge 1961.
SEEBASS, H., " Gerechtigkeit ", *TBLNT* I, 502-509.
SEESEMANN, H., " Der Begriff ΚΟΙΝΩΝΙΑ im Neuen Testament ", *BNTW* 14 (1933).
SEGALLA, G., *Volontà di Dio e dell'uomo in Giovanni*, Brescia 1974.
SEGOND, A., " Ire épître de Jean, chap. 5,18-20 ", *RHPR* 45 (1965), 349-351.
SELWYN, E. G., *The First Epistle of St. Peter*, London 1947.
SIDEBOTTOM, E. M., " Reward in Mt 5,46etc. ", *ET* 67 (1956), 219-220.
SILBERMANN, L. H., " Language and Structure in the Hodayot (I QH 3) ", *JBL* 75 (1956), 96-106.
SJÖBERG, E., " Neuschöpfung in den Toten-Meer-Rollen ", *ST* 9 (1955), 131-136.
SKRINJAR, A., " Errores in Epistola I Jo impugnati ", *VD* 41 (1963), 60-72.
—— " Theologia Primae Epistolae Joannis ", *VD* 42 (1964), 3-16 ; 49-60.
SLIPYJ, J., *Die Auffassung des Lebens nach dem Evangelium und I. Briefe des hl. Johannes*, Rom 1965.
SMITH, M., " God's Begetting the Messiah in I QSa ", *NTS* 5 (1958-59), 218-224.
SPICQ, C., *Agapè dans le Nouveau Testament. Analyse des Textes*, 3 vols., Paris 1958-1959.
—— *Dieu et l'homme selon le Nouveau Testament* (Lect. Div. 29), Paris 1961.
STÄHLIN, G., " Zum Problem der johanneischen Eschatologie ", *ZNW* 33 (1934) 225-254.
STAUFFER, E., " ἀγαπάω ", *TDNT* I, 35-55.
STEVENS, G. B., *The Johannine Theology*, London 1894.
STRATHMANN, H., " λαός ", *TDNT* IV, 50-57.
SUITBERTUS, A S. JOANNE A. Cruce, " Die Vollkommenheitslehre des ersten Johannesbriefes ", *Bib* 39 (1958), 319-333 ; 449-470.
SURJANSKY, A. J., *De Mysterio Verbi Incarnati ad Mentem Beati Johannis Apostoli*, Rome 1941.
SYNGE, F. C., " I Jo 3,2 ", *JTS* 3 (1952), 79.

TAYLOR, T. M., " ' Abba Father ' and Baptism ", *ScotJT* 11 (1958), 62-71.
THOMAS, St., *Super Evangelium S. Mathaei Lectura*, ed. by R. CAI, 5th ed., Torino 1951.
THÜSING, W., *Die Erhöhung und Verherrlichung Jesu im Johannes-Evangelium* (NAbh. 21), Münster 1960.
—— *Herrlichkeit und Einheit*, Düsseldorf 1962.
TÖPEL, L. J., " A Note on Methodology of Structural analysis in Jn 2:23 - 3:21 ", *CBQ* 33 (1971), 211-220.
TRAETS, C., *Voir Jésus et le Père en Lui selon l'évangile de saint Jean*, Rome 1967.
TURNER, W., " Believing and Everlasting Life, A Johannine Inquiry ", *ET* 64 (1952-53), 50-52.
VANCELLS, J. O. T., *La Verdad os hará libres (Jn 8,32)*, Barcelona 1973.
VANHOYE, A., " Notre foi, oeuvre divine d'après le quatrième evangile ", *NRT* 86 (1964), 337-354.
VAN IERSEL, B. M. F., ' *Der Sohn* ' *in den Synoptischen Jesusworten*, Leiden 1961.
VAN IMSCHOOT, P., " L'esprit de Yahvé, source de vie dans l'A. T.", *RB* 44 (1935), 481-501.
—— " L'esprit de Yahvé, principe de vie morale dans l'A. T.", *ETL* 15 (1939), 457-467.
——, " L'esprit de Yahvé, source de la pieté dans l'A. T. ", *BiViChr* 6 (1954), 17-30.
VENARD, L., " Jean (Saint) ", in *DTC* VIII, 1, cols., 537-593.
VERGOTE, A., " L'exaltation du Christ en croix selon le quatrième évangile ", *ETL* 28 (1952), 5-23.
VIAU, E., " ' Connaître Dieu ', une expression johannique ", *VieSpir* 77 (1947), 324-333.
VILLETTE, L., *Foi et sacrament, du Nouveau Testament à saint Augustine*, I, Paris 1959.
VINCENT, M. R., *Word Studies in the New Testament*, vol. II, London 1887.
WALVOORD, J. F., " The Kingdom of Heaven ", *BS* 124 (1967), 195-205.
WARNACH, V., *Agape. Die Liebe als Grundmotiv der neutestamentlichen Theologie*, Düsseldorf 1951.
WEINEL, H., *Biblische Theologie des Neuen Testaments*, Tübingen 1928.
WEISENGOFF, J. P., " Light and its Relation to Life in St. John ", *CBQ* 8 (1946), 448-451.
WHITE, R. E. O., *The Biblical Doctrine of Initiation*, London 1960.
WIDENGREN, G., " King and Covenant ", *JSS* 2 (1957), 1-32.
WINDISCH, H., *Der Sinn der Bergpredigt*, Tübingen 1937.
WINTER, P., " Monogenès para Patros (Jo 1) ", *ZRG* 5 (1953), 335-365.
WOHLENBERG, G., " Glossen zu I Jo ", *NKZ* 13 (1902), 233-240 ; 632-645.
WRIGHT, G. E., " The Terminology of the O. T. Religion and its Significance ", *JNES* 1 (1942), 404-414.
WUEST, K. S., " Deity of Jesus in the Greek Texts of John and Paul ", *BS* 119 (1962), 216-226.
WURZINGER, A., " Glauben nach Johannes ", *BibLit* 39 (1966), 203-208.

YSEBAERT, J., *Greek Baptismal Terminology. Its Origins and Early Development* (Graecitas Christianorum Primaeva, I), Nijmegen 1962.
ZAHN, Th., *Das Evangelium des Matthäus*, 4th ed., Leipzig-Erlangen 1922.
ZIMMERMANN, H., " Christushymnus und Johanneischer Prolog ", in *Neues Testament und Kirche* (Fs. R. Schnackenburg), Herder 1974, 249-265.

Introduction

Taking as the determinative concept Jesus' favorite name for God, Father, John interprets the ideal relationship of men to God as that of spiritual children, having the Life — eternal — from the Father. According to Jn this life of sonship to God, having a definite beginning other than the physical birth, and being manifested in very definite moral and spiritual qualities, defines the very being of a Christian. It is in the measure that one understands clearly, experiences personally and expounds persuasively this truth of Christian Sonship, that one lays hold upon the very heart of Christian faith and life. Hence this investigation of ours to find the formulas, the content and the meaning of the Johannine doctrine of the divine sonship of Christians.

When we start investigating the Johannine doctrine of the divine sonship of Christians, we are confronted with certain questions regarding its nature and origin: Is the Johannine concept of sonship something purely juridical or moral, or does it suppose an ontological reality? If it supposes such a reality, in what does it consist? How do men obtain this reality so as to become children of God? What are the practical consequences of this divine sonship in the life of men? What is the origin of the vocabulary employed by Jn to express his concept of sonship? Only an attentive study of all the relevant texts in the Johannine Writings can provide satisfactory answers to all these questions.

Jn expresses his doctrine of Christian sonship mainly by two expressions: τέκνα θεοῦ (Jn 1:12; 11:52; I Jn 3:1,2,10; 5:2) and γεννηθῆναι ἐκ τοῦ θεοῦ (Jn 1:13 [in plural]; 3:3-8 [πνεύματος]; I Jn 2:29; 3:9; 4:7; 5:1,4,18). For a right understanding of the Johannine concept of sonship it is of utmost importance to see whether and how these two expressions are mutually related. If they are identical in meaning, τέκνα θεοῦ is not a mere title of honour, and supposes a reality, and γεννηθῆναι ἐκ τοῦ θεοῦ receives a valuable interpretation. There are, in fact, numerous attempts to study the origin of the Johannine concept and vocabulary regarding the new birth[1]. But

---
[1] Cf. the special bibliography, giving the studies on the Johannine concept of divine sonship of men.

little effort has been made to investigate the Johannine concept of the divine sonship of men as expressed in the above mentioned Johannine terms.

The treatment given to Christian sonship in works on biblical theology is generally sketchy, partial and inadequate. Here and there will be found paragraphs or sections dealing with one or another phase of the doctrine. The commentaries, of necessity, carry only a patch-work, a scanty and scattered presentation of ideas related to the subject in the course of a running discussion of chapters and verses in the Johannine Writings. The articles on one or another Johannine text giving one or another phase of the doctrine of sonship, are naturally inadequate to give a complete notion of sonship. In short, there has been found no thorough-going and adequate treatment on this important theme in the Johannine Writings.

To our knowledge, there are only two dissertations that make a real attempt to give the Johannine notion of sonship, namely, that of F. G. Schlafer at the Southern Baptist Theological Seminary, Louisville [2], and that of Donatus Ab Hamrun at the Gregorian University, Rome [3]. While we acknowledge the valuable contribution made by these authors to the understanding of the Johannine doctrine on sonship, we should, nevertheless, say that these works do not sufficiently explain all the relevant texts in the Johannine Writings, and hence are inadequate to give a complete notion of the Johannine doctrine on sonship. We could mention in this regard also the dissertation of W. Twisselmann [4], which gives in 14 pages just an outline of the Johannine doctrine on this point. So the lack of an adequate treatment of this Johannine theme, based on an exegetical study of the relevant texts, leaves room for this present work.

We do not claim that the present dissertation is an exhaustive treatment of the doctrine set forth. Yet an honest attempt has been made to make an exegetical study of all the relevant Johannine texts and thus to formulate from them ' the Johannine doctrine of the divine sonship of Christians '.

---

[2] Cf. F. G. Schlafer, *The Johannine Doctrine of Christian Sonship*, Diss. Southern Baptist Theological Seminary, Louisville, 1948-1949.

[3] Cf. Donatus ab Hamrun, τέκνα Θεοῦ ἐκ Θεοῦ ἐγεννήθησαν. *A Biblical Theological Approach to Jn* 1,12-13 *and to its parallel Johannine Passages*, Diss. Pont. Univ. Gregoriana, Roma, 1953-1954. This is later resumed and published in three issues of Melita Theologica. Cf. Donatus a Marsa, " An Outline of St. John's Doctrine on the Divine Sonship of the Christian ", *MelT* 8 (1955), 1-26 ; 53-71 ; 9 (1956), 14-38.

[4] Cf. W. Twisselmann, *Die Gotteskindschaft der Christen nach dem Neuen Testament*, (BzFCTh 41-1), Gütersloh, 1939, 77-91.

Definition of Terms

In the following discussion, all the ideas occurring in the title will be employed or assumed in the development of the main body of thought. It is well, therefore, at the outset to state precisely what is meant by each of the terms in the title.

Divine

The adjective 'divine' corresponds to the Greek θεῖος. Jn actually does not make use of the term θεῖος [5]. Speaking of the sonship of men, he uses the terms τέκνα θεοῦ and γεννηθῆναι ἐκ τοῦ θεοῦ. So when we make use of the adjective 'divine', we mean by that the ideas expressed in these terms θεοῦ and ἐκ τοῦ θεοῦ. The term 'divine' therefore, refers to the relation of men to the One, Personal God, to whom they stand in a filial relation.

Sonship

The term 'sonship' actually does not correspond exactly to the Johannine idea of the relation of the believers to God as their Father, because Jn makes use of the term τέκνον exclusively to express this relation, and 'son' is both an inexact and inadequate translation of the word τέκνον in the context of Johannine Theology. In fact, υἱός the corresponding word for 'son' is reserved by Jn exclusively and deliberately for references to Jesus Christ as 'Son of God' or 'Son of Man', while τέκνον is never used to refer to the sonship of Christ. Besides, τέκνα θεοῦ is used in Jn alike for men, women and children, namely, for all those who by their faith and life are actually spiritual children of God. Consequently, the masculine form 'sonship' does not fully express the broader relationship, unless it is made clear that the term is used in the generic sense. Certainly, the term 'childship'[6] would be more consistent with the context and expression of the Johannine ideas in this regard. Yet 'sonship' has a more common usage and clearer theological connotation than 'childship' and is the more euphonious of the two titles. Besides, it is specified by the subject 'Christians'. Given this, the term 'sonship' could convey the exact meaning of the Apostle John on this vital point, without being misunderstood. Hence our title 'divine sonship of Christians'.

---

[5] In the NT θεῖος occurs only in Acts 17: 29 and II Pet 1:3-4.

[6] G. B. STEVENS, *The Johannine Theology*, London, 1894, p. 253ff. where he makes use of this term to express the Johannine idea.

Christians

Although the term 'Christian' is foreign to the vocabulary of the Johannine Writings [7], the term 'Christians' is used in the title to designate a distinction, which underlies and determines the content of the entire investigation. The point under discussion is the sonship of *believers*, rather than the sonship of men in general, because it is only those who accept the 'Logos', that receive the power to become children of God (Jn 1:12). Moreover, it focusses our attention on the sonship of the believers in Christ [8], rather than on the sonship of Christ Himself, although the latter remains the type and source of the former [9].

Johannine Writings

Anyone with a limited knowledge of NT studies and NT Theology is aware of the fact that the authorship of the so-called Johannine Writings is a crucial problem. It is self-evident that a work of the nature and scope of this thesis cannot possibly review and pronounce upon the multiform views, which have been expounded in the voluminous body of literature concerned. As far as our own purpose is concerned, it would avail little to go into these details. An investigation of this sort must concern itself primarily with the content and teachings of the books, regardless of who the author is.

The striking similarity of style, of theme, of spirit, of thought and of expression would stamp the Epistles as teaching essentially the same truth as the Gospel and in the same general manner [10]. Therefore they would need to be considered together in any doctrinal presentation. The term 'Johannine Writings', therefore, will be used to designate the Fourth Gospel and the three Johannine Epistles. The Apocalypse falls into a category by itself because of style, intent and content [11] aside from any consideration of authorship, and accordingly it will not be involved in the discussion which follows.

---

[7] In the NT the term 'Christian' occurs only in Acts 11:26; 26:28 and I Pet 4:16.

[8] Note that the very adjective Χριστιανός derives from Χριστός and the adjectival ending designates belonging. Cf. G. BOUWMAN, art. "Christ", in Bibellexikon, 2nd ed., (Benziger Verlag 1968), col. 293.

[9] Cf. W. N. CLARKE, *An Outline of Christian Theology*, N. Y., 1902, p. 268; W. GROSSOUW, *Revelation and Redemption*, London, 1965, pp. 35-41.

[10] For a common authorship for the Gospel and the First Epistle of John, cf. A. ROBERT and A. FEUILLET, *Introduction à la Bible*, II, Tournai, 1959, pp. 694-697; W. G. KÜMMEL, *Introduction to the New Testament*, London, 1966, pp. 310-312.

[11] Cf. W. G. KÜMMEL, op. cit., pp. 329-331. Here it is worth noting that

Plan of Procedure

In developing the doctrine of the divine sonship of Christians in Jn, it has been thought best to approach the subject historically by investigating briefly the background and setting of the Johannine teaching regarding the believers as children of God. Part One, therefore, will present the historical and literary setting of the doctrine by pointing out contrasting, similar and related ideas that are found in the OT, Later Judaism, Hellenism, the Synoptic Gospels and the Pauline Epistles [12]. In Part Two, the discussion turns into a detailed exegetical study of the main sonship passages in the Johannine Writings. In pursuing this exegetical study, the student beholds the panorama of the doctrine clearly delineated: the 'who' and the 'how' and the 'what' of the divine sonship of Christians according to the Johannine Writings. At the end, a brief summary of the main points characteristic of the Johannine doctrine and a confrontation of these with the related ideas will mark out the originality of the Johannine doctrine of Christian Sonship.

---

speaking of the sonship of men the Apocalypse does not make use of the usual Johannine term τέκνα but υἱοί (cf. Apoc 21:7).

[12] We do not give a special section treating on texts in the other Books of the NT, since we speak of them in the Second Part in the course of our exegesis of the Johannine texts.

Part One

THE DIVINE SONSHIP OF MAN OUTSIDE THE JOHANNINE WRITINGS

John does not stand isolated in his presentation of the 'Divine Sonship of Christians'. He could not invent a new language in order to present his doctrine. Even to present new realities, he had to make use of the language of the environment in which he lived. Therefore, a study of the vocabulary and thought patterns of the literary environment of John regarding the theme of the divine sonship of man becomes necessary.

If John the Evangelist, according to the Tradition, comes from a Jewish background, constituted by the Old Testament and Later Jewish Literature including that of Qumran, for many years he had to live in a Hellenistic environment. Hence our study of the theme of the divine sonship of man in the Old Testament, Later Jewish and Hellenistic Literature.

On the other hand, it is quite probable that the New Testament language has influenced, more than any other, the Johannine concept and terminology. Therefore we make the study of the Synoptic and Pauline concept of the Divine sonship of Christians in Chs. IV and V respectively.

Such an exposition will also help us to see the possible influence of one current of thought on the other. Thus Part One will give us a better preparation to enter into the world of the Johannine thought.

Chapter I

The Divine Sonship of Man in the Old Testament

In the Old Testament, the term 'Son of God' is applied to angels (Job 1:2), Sethites (Gen 6:2), the people of Israel (Exod 4:22), the King of Israel (2 Sam 7:14) and the just man (Wisd 2:13). The first two categories are excluded from our consideration here, because the aspect in which they are called 'sons of God' is not relevant to our specific problem of the divine sonship of man.

As to the divine sonship of the people of Israel, the majority of scholars interpret it metaphorically, though they use different terminology [1]. Our task here is to clarify further the nature of this sonship. Is it a real sonship? Is it a sonship that is peculiar and exclusive to Israel? [2] If so, what is the relation between God and Israel resulting from this singular position of Israel? [3] Does the position as 'son of Yahweh' belong to the people as such or also to the individuals who make up the people? These are some of the questions we try to answer in the following pages.

---

[1] Cf. C. WITTICHEN, *Die Idee Gottes als des Vaters*, Göttingen, 1865, p. 11; M. J. LAGRANGE, "La paternité de Dieu dans l'A. T.", *RB* 17 (1908), 481; O. PROCKSCH, *Theologie des Alten Testaments*, Gütersloh, 1949-50, p. 509; P. VAN IMSCHOOT, "L'esprit de Yahvé source de la piété dans l'Ancien Testament", *BiViChr* 6 (1954), 18; G. A. F. KNIGHT, *A Christian Theology of the Old Testament*, London, 1951, p. 120; W. MARCHEL, *Abba Père! La prière du Christ et des chrétiens*, Anal. Bibl. 19, Rome, 1963, pp. 5-44.

[2] The majority of Critics admit a divine sonship that is exclusive to Israel Cf. M. J. LAGRANGE, art. cit., p. 483; J. L. MCKENZIE, "The Divine Sonship of men in the Old Testament", CBQ 7 (1945), 326; P. BAUR, "Gott als Vater im Alten Testament", *ThStkr* 72 (1889), p. 484; W. MARCHEL, op. cit., p. 40: " En effet, vu la position tout à fait particulière créée par son élection, il semble qu'il s'agisse plus probablement d'une filiation singulière, exclusive et absolue d'Israel ".

[3] There are some who reduce this relation to a merely juridique one. Cf. P. BATIFFOL, *L'enseignement de Jésus*, Paris, 1905, p. 95: " Cette paternité n'était envisagée que sous son aspect juridique et national : si Dieu était proclamé Père, c'était surtout pourqu'Israel pût se réclamer de ses droits de fils, de fils aîné ".

I. The Divine Sonship of Israel through the Saving Act of Yahweh (Ex 4:22-23)

A. The Divine Sonship of Israel and Exodus: The divine sonship of Israel is affirmed for the first time in Ex 4: 22-23 in the context of the liberation from Egypt and in an essential association with it: " And you shall say ... Israel is my first-born son, I say to you, let my son go ..." The expression ' my first-born son ' seems to have an important explanatory role within this great story of the liberation of Israel. An analysis of the concentric stylistic structure of the section Ex 1:1 – 7:7 reveals the central role of 4:21-23 in the whole section [4]. In this structure the divine sonship of Israel appears to be the central factor in the liberation of Israel.

The literary structure of the oracle of Yahweh (Ex 4:22-23) shows this:

v. 22 A   And Thou ... Israel is MY FIRST-BORN SON
   23 B   And I say to you, LET my son GO
       C   THAT HE MAY SERVE ME
       B'   And if you refuse to LET him GO
       A'   Behold I will slay YOUR FIRST-BORN SON

Note the literary parallels in AA' and BB'. In this concentric structure, Yahweh substituting the first-born of Egypt for his own (AA') redeems them from slavery (BB') so that they may serve him as his own sons (C).

It is worth noting that the affirmation of Israel's divine sonship reappears often in this context. The return from the exile is pictured as a new Exodus described in the classical terms of the original Exodus (cf. Is 56:1 – 66:24) and the father-son relationship is repeated several times in the context of this return. Jeremias sees the return as the restoration of the father-son relationship between Yahweh and Israel (cf. Jer 31:9).

B. Yahweh, the *Gō'ēl*

The use of *Gō'ēl* for Yahweh in the contexts of both the Exodus (Ex 6:6) and the Return (Is 49:7; 59:20) is also an indication of this

---

[4] Cf. E. GALBIATI, *La Struttura letteraria dell'Esodo*, Roma, 1956, pp. 234-249 where he divides the section of Ch. 1:1 to Ch. 7:7 into four groups: 1:1 – 2:22 Introduzione; 2:23 – 3:12 Ciclo iniziale; 3:13 – 6:9 Ciclo centrale and 6:10 – 7:7 Ciclo conclusivo. Then he brings out the concentric structure of 2:23 – 7:7 in the centre of which come 4:21-23.

link between the divine sonship and redemption of Israel, since *gō'ēl* was always connected with the idea of salvation by a member of the family [5] which would in turn impose lasting obligations on those on whose behalf he intervened [6]. The main idea is that of getting back a person into his original place in the family. From Dt. Isaiah onwards, the redeeming '*ge'ulla*' becomes central to the thought about salvation [7]. Is 63:16 shows clearly that it is the redemption that established this father-son relationship between Yahweh and Israel: " ... thou O Lord art our *Father*, our *Redeemer* from of old ...".

C. The Substitutional Character of the Liberation of Israel

The substitutional character of the liberation of Israel from Egypt shows how Israel became the first-born son of Yahweh on the paschal night. In Israel all the first fruits were to be offered to Yahweh (Num 3:12, 41;8:16-17). If they were not offered to God, the whole household remained impure (Lev 19:23). But this supposed the death of the first-born. At the same time human sacrifice was rigorously prohibited in the OT (Dt 12:31 ; Jer 7:31). So in order to keep the right of Yahweh, they had the substitutional sacrifice in which an animal representing the first-born is sacrificed and thus the firstborn were saved from death (Ex 34:19-20 ; Num 18:15-16). Thus the substitutional sacrifice had a representative and redemptive element. It is in the same way that Yahweh accomplished his saving act. By substituting and sacrificing the first-born of Egypt Yahweh redeems his own first-born [8].

This substitutional character is clearly brought out in the very structure of the oracle of Ex 4:22-23. Note the parallel expressions of ' first-born ' in AA'. Thus on the paschal night, Yahweh could

---

[5] Here it is worthwhile to note that '*gō'ēl*' in Hebrew, meaning redeemer was originally a family concept. Originally it meant the member of a family to whom the Mosaic Law gave the right and responsibility to protect and redeem his relatives. Cf. F. ZORELL, *Lexicon Hebraicum et Aramaicum Veteris Testamenti*, Roma, 1964, p. 136.

[6] Cf. D. DAUBE, *The Exodus Pattern in the Bible*, London, 1963, p. 13 where he speaks of the existence of such a social custom at the time of Exodus.

[7] It occurs over 20 times from Is 40 onwards and that in connection with the Return. Prior to that it occurs only once in Is 35:9.

[8] Cf. A. LACOQUE, " L'idée directrice de l'Exode ", *VT* 15 (1965), 345-353 in which he proves the substitutional character of several elements in this section and concludes that the key idea of the section Exod 1-15 is ' substitution '.

really call Israel his first-born, as a result of this substitutional sacrifice[9]. This substitutional character of the slaughter of the first-born of Egypt is referred to in Ex 13:11-16 [10].

A substitutional sacrifice in order to save one's own people was also known to Pharaoh. Hence the command to throw into the River Nile all the sons born to Israel after the reign of a new dynasty in Egypt (Ex 1:22) [11]. The act of Pharaoh is parallel to a similar act on the part of Yahweh. Yahweh simply reverses the same act intended by Pharaoh [12].

All the above considerations show how Israel's sonship was based on the unique experience of the Exodus, the saving act of Yahweh in which God showed himself a loving father to Israel.

D. Israel — the First-born of Yahweh

The Hebrew '$b^ek\bar{o}r$' in itself does not imply having more children [13]. The Bible itself gives the definition of the 'first-born' as 'whatever is the first to open womb' (Ex 13:2; Num 3:12; 8:16; 18:15), without any further consideration of what follows. Parents had to fulfill their duties regarding the first-born, regardless of other children who followed (Mt 1:25; Lk 2:7).

In LXX we have υἱὸς πρωτότοκος, and πρωτότοκος in its primary sense says nothing about other children born afterwards [14]. The expression in Ps 89:27 'I will make him the first-born' points to a sense of adoption. Its parallel expression 'the highest of the kings' also gives the same impression. The words 'he shall cry to me, "Thou art my father"' in v. 26 of the same psalm, show that only this first-born is entitled to call God 'father' and that the other kings do not have God as father in the same way. This means that the Mes-

---

[9] Note the acknowledgement of the Egyptians in Wisd 18:13 "... when their First-born were destroyed, they acknowledged thy people to be God's son".

[10] Note the word '$p\bar{a}d\bar{a}h$' used in this context which has a familiar sense near to that of '$g\bar{a}\bar{a}l$'. '$P\bar{a}d\bar{a}h$' has also a sense of 'redeeming by ransom', hence the substitutional idea contained in it. Cf. G. AUZOU, *De la servitude au service*, Paris, 1961, p. 176; cf. also S. DRIVER, *Exodus*, (ICC), ad v. 4:22, where he says: "the deliverance from Egypt stamped Israel as the First-born of God".

[11] Cf. A. LACOQUE, op. cit., p. 347.

[12] Note the parallel use of 'people' and 'sons' in Hos 1:10.

[13] Cf. G. SCHARBERT, art. 'Erstgeburt'', *LThK*, III, p. 1052.

[14] Cf. F. ZORELL, *Lexicon Graecum Novi Testamenti*, Paris, 1961, cols. 1161-1162.

sianic king is called 'first-born' in his quality of being chosen and beloved of God.

When speaking of the first-born, the idea that is predominant in the OT is that of 'inheritance' (Dt 21:17). This right could even pass to a younger brother (Gen 27 and 49:3,8). But it remains the right of the 'first-born'. The right of Israel as the first-born of Yahweh is shown in giving Palestine, the heritage of Yahweh (Ex 19:5; Dt 10:14), as a possession to her (Ex 6:8). In Eccl 36:11-12 God is asked to restore to Israel its inheritance and the fact that she is his first-born is stressed; on the other hand, Yahweh is called father only of Israel (Jer 31:9). All these show that this divine sonship is something exclusive to Israel.

II. Israel's Sonship through the Establishment of the Covenant (Ex 4:23)

A. Israel's Sonship and the Covenant

Exodus was only the beginning of the event by which Israel was made the son of Yahweh. It was by the establishment of the Covenant that Israel became the son of Yahweh in the full sense of the term. In fact the Exodus and the Covenant are two phases of the same event by which Israel is made a son of Yahweh [15].

The word $W^eya'abdēnî$ of Ex 4:23 expresses this Covenant relation, Yahweh was going to establish with Israel. The 'ābad used with a suffix relating to God, is linked into the idea of cult as indicated in Ex 3:12, 'When you have brought forth the people out of Egypt, you shall serve God upon this mountain.' But when it is used to express the relation of man to God it could mean the very activity of love, expressed in a complete faithfulness and dedication to God [16]. And this refers to the Covenant relationship. So Yahweh liberated Israel in order to establish this Covenant relationship and thus Israel's sonship becomes a Covenantal sonship [17].

---

[15] Cf. W. BEYERLIN, Herkunft und Geschichte der ältesten Sinai-traditionen, Tübingen, 1961, in which he denies Von Rad's hypothesis that the Sinai traditions and the Exodus traditions were originally separate. He maintains that the Exodus is the Historical event, the subject of the narrative, while the happenings at Sinai are acts in which the Covenant between Yahweh and His people was formalized and given external expression.

[16] Cf. G. AUZOU, op. cit., pp. 79-82.

[17] Cf. F. C. FENSHAM, " Father and Son as Terminology for Treaty and Covenant ", in Fs. ALBRIGHT W. F., London, 1971, pp. 121-135.

B. Yahweh gives Israel existence as a nation (Dt 32:6,15,18)

It was their allegiance to Yahweh through the Covenant that gave Israel, a collection of peoples with different backgrounds of clans and cultures, their unity as one people [18]. The initiative in this belongs to Yahweh (Dt 7:8). Thus the Covenantal relationship becomes a father-son relationship.

Dt 32:6,15,18 speak clearly of this father-son relationship based on the creation of Israel as a nation and rebukes them for their grievances against Yahweh, because of the particular malice of their sins as treachery to their father. 'Is not he your father, who created you?' (v. 6). 'He forsook God who made him and scoffed at the rock of his salvation' (v. 15). 'You were unmindful of the rock that begot you and you forgot the God who gave you birth' (v. 18). The verbs used here such as 'yālad' and 'hôlēl' are used respectively for father and mother in giving existence to the child.

Other texts that describe the Covenant relationship as parallel to the father-son relationship are Dt 14:1-2; Mal 2:10; 3:17; Is 43:6-7; 63:8; 64:8 etc. The very name that Israel used for itself as a nation ''am' in contradistinction to other peoples who are 'gōyîm' points to the concept of Israel as a family [19]. The ''am' indicates a group conceived of having somehow a family relationship, while 'gōyîm' refers to a social or political grouping of men [20]. Yahweh calling the faithful Israelites 'my people' and the unfaithful 'this people' [21] also suggests this special relationship implied in the Covenant relationship.

C. Restoration of the Covenant — Restoration of the Father-Son relationship

Jer 31:1-9 speaks of the restoration of Israel in terms of the Exodus from Egypt. This section begins with a formula characteristic of the Covenant: " I will be the God of all the families of Israel and they shall be my people." It ends with a formula that expresses the

---

[18] Cf. M. J. COURTNEY, *The Problem of God*, Yale, 1964, p. 11.

[19] Cf. Ex 34:24; Lev 18:24; 25:44; Num 14:15; Dt 4:27 etc. where 'gōyîm' is used about the nations who are inimical to Israel.

[20] Cf. Th. C. VRIEZEN, *Hoofdlijnen der Theologie van het Oude Testament*, Wageningen, 1954, p. 229 " Het woord volk ('am) is oorspronkelijk de aanduiding voor de gemeenschap van Bloedverwanten ".

[21] Cf. Is 3:12-15; 5:13 etc. where 'my people' is used in a context showing intimate relation, while in Is 6:10; 8:6 etc. 'this people' is used in a context of failure of Israel to realize the ideal, hence showing a distance between God and Israel.

father-son relationship between Yahweh and Israel: "for I am a father to Israel and Ephraim is my first-born son." The fact that Ephraim is called Yahweh's first-born son does not make any difficulty, because Ephraim is part of Israel the first-born. The fundamental reason of this restoration is the everlasting love of Yahweh (v. 3), which reminds us of Hos 11:1 and Dt 7:8-9. Thus the restoration of the people of Israel is presented as the restoration of the Covenant [22] and father-son relationship.

III. Israel's Sonship: Adoptive but Real

By the very fact that it is Covenantal sonship it is clear that it is an adoptive sonship. We are accustomed to make a clear distinction between an adopted child and a natural child. But it was not so with ancient Israel. The result of the Covenant was thought of as a kind of blood-relationship. So the Covenant between Yahweh and Israel did in fact make Israel the family of God in a very real sense.

A. The Family Character of the Sinai Covenant

In the Israelite tradition, the covenant relationship had always something of the family about it [23]. The family character of the Covenant of Sinai could be seen from the rites by which it was ratified. Thus in Ex 24:5-8 we have the description of the ceremony of throwing half of the blood on the altar (representing Yahweh) and sprinkling half of it on the people, as if making both parties members of one family. Moreover the Sinai Covenant is accompanied by some sort of sacrificial rite and a meal of Communion (Ex 24:11) uniting Yahweh and the people in a family relationship [24]. There are also other texts such as Hos 8:1; Jer 12:7 which present Israel as members of family of which God is the head.

---

[22] Cf. v. 2 where it is said "They have found pardon in the wilderness". The wilderness as the scene of conversion (cf. Hos 2:16) reminds us certainly of Exodus and Covenant.

[23] Cf. for instance, II Kg 16:7 in which Ahaz calls himself the son of the brutal Assyrian king, because of a covenant with Assyria.

[24] The most solemn and in their historical effect most far-reaching covenants as the Abrahamite and the NT Covenants as also the Sinaitic Covenant are all connected with a sacrifice and meal.

B. Relation of love between Yahweh and Israel [25]

1. *The Fatherly love of Yahweh and Israel*

There are several texts testifying to the fatherly love of Yahweh for Israel. The very expression ' first-born ' with which Israel is called (Ex 4:22) refers to Israel as beloved of Yahweh. The creation of Israel as a nation is solely an act of pure love on the part of Yahweh (Dt 7:7-8). The care of Yahweh for Israel while in Egypt (Dt 32:10), on their way to the heritage (Dt 32:11-14) etc. is described as the affectionate care of a father for his son; ' The Lord bore you as a man bears his son ...' (Dt 1:31). See also the tender love of Yahweh expressed in Dt 32:6; Is 63:8; 64:7; Ps 103:13 where he is said to be nearer to his children than any earthly father.

Now, the relation of love arising from the father-son relationship between Yahweh and Israel was conceived in terms which correspond to the definition of Covenantal love. The Covenantal love with which Deuteronomy is concerned is a love like that between overlord and vassal [26]. But this is in no way prejudicial to the love described above. It means only that the filial love of Israel for Yahweh is a love that can be commanded and which is expressed in reverential fear, loyalty and obedience [27].

2. *Filial love of Israel for Yahweh*

As it is in the Covenant that the filial love of Israel is realized, we see all relevant texts referring to the Covenant relation. Though all these texts do not call this mutual relation expressly ' love ' nevertheless the underlying force is always ' love '.

Thus we have some texts in which the father-son relationship is brought as a motive to obey a particular command (Dt 14:1) and

---

[25] On this aspect of the father — son relationship of Yahweh and Israel, cf. L. MORALDI, " La paternità di Dio nell'Antico Testamento ", *RivBib* 7 (1959), 44-56; P. BAUR, art. cit., pp. 483-507; M. J. LAGRANGE, art. cit., pp. 481-499; R. GYLLENBERG, Gott der Vater im AT und in der Predigt Jesu, *SOr* I (1926), 51-60; F. E. BARKER, " The Fatherhood of God ", *ChQ* 132 (1941), 174-196.

[26] Cf. Dt 8:5; 14:1. Cf. W. L. MORAN, " The Ancient Eastern Background of the Love of God in Deuteronomy ", *CBQ* 25 (1963), 77-87.

[27] Cf. Dt 14:1; Is 1:2; Mal 1:6. Considering the eastern mentality even to this day concerning the father-son relationship, there is nothing strange about it. Reverence for Parents is an outstanding semitic virtue (cf. Dt 5: 16; 21:18-21), and according to the semitic concept, fatherhood connotes reverence, though not exclusive of love, rather it is a reverence that is inspired by love.

other texts in which the infidelity of Israel in turning away to other gods is shown as a denial of the father-son relationship (Dt 32:17-19; Is 30:1-5; 8:14; Mal 1:6 etc) [28].

In Is 1:2-3 the example of domestic animals is brought to show the unchanging and totally reliable fidelity expected of Israel: "...Sons have I reared ... they have rebelled against me. The ox knows its owner ... but Israel does not know ...". 'To know' in biblical sense often denotes the activity of the whole man in his thinking, willing and feeling implying love and obedience [29]. So here Yahweh complains of the lack of loving fidelity expected of Israel, his people and his sons.

So for Israel the demands of the Covenant are the demands of a loving father and the response to the Covenant is the response of sons to their father.

Mutual love implies the communication of goods too. And the first and foremost good is oneself. This is what we see in the Covenant formula: 'I will be your God and you will be my people' (Ex 6:4-7; Lev 26:12; Dt 26:17-18). It is in this mutual giving of self that the father-son relationship between Yahweh and Israel is realized.

IV. Israel's Sonship — A Dynamic Sonship

Since the Covenant and the father-son relationship implies a union of mutual love, as explained above, the sonship is certainly dynamic. It had to be a conscious sonship expressed in actions according to the wishes of the father's heart. And it is these actions that are actually defined by the Law. Thus Law enters as an integral factor in this father-son relationship [30]. As the Father is Father in terms, not of what he is, but of what he does, so the son is son precisely in the continued action of his life as son. Thus a day-to-day living according to the Father's standards constitutes this divine sonship on the part of man [31].

---

[28] Cf. D. J. McCarthy, "Notes on the love of God in Deuteronomy and the father-son relationship between Yahweh and Israel", *CBQ* 27 (1965), 146.

[29] Even about God it is used as an equivalent for 'love'. Cf. for instance, Amos 3:2: "You only have I known of all the families of earth", and Ps 139:1: "Thou hast searched me out and known me".

[30] Here we have to forget the pejorative connotations often attached to this term 'Law'. These connotations came as a result of the misconceptions regarding the role of the Law in this relation of man to God expressed in the OT.

[31] Cf. M. J. O'Connell, "The Concept of Commandment in the Old Testament", *TS* 21 (1960), pp. 351-403.

The dynamism involved in this sonship is indicated also by the moral likeness to the Father demanded of Israel, his son: "Be ye holy, for I Yahweh, your God am holy" (Lev 19:2 ; 20:7,26). This comes especially as an introduction to the commandments, so that the observance of the commandments becomes, so to say, an imitation of God in his holiness [32]. This command to imitate is given in connection with the Covenant relationship (cf. Lev 11:45 ; 20:26) and hence also the father-son relationship.

Moreover, it is quite normal that sons imitate their father, without an explicit invitation to it on the part of the father. In fact we see such an assumption in the OT. In Dt 32:4-5, having said about God that "there is no corruption in him", about Israel it is said that "His children have the blemish, a generation twisted and perverse". It supposes that Israelites were expected to be like their Father and had failed to be so [33].

V. The Divine Sonship of the Davidic King and Israel's Sonship

A. The Davidic King: a Son of Yahweh

A divine sonship is attributed to the King of Israel in II Sam 7:14 ; Ps 89:27 ; Ps 2:7 ; Ps 110:3 [34]. Though the exact dating of these texts could be discussed, there is no doubt that they represent concepts which were utilized in the Monarchic period [35].

II Sam 7:14 says: "I will be a father to him and he will be a son to me". Here the promise is made to David regarding his son

---

[32] Holiness is one of the essential attributes of the God of Israel (cf. Lev 11:44-45 ; 19:2 ; 20:7 etc). The original idea of separateness and transcendence (Ex 33:20) undergoes a transformation through ritual purity and developes into a spiritual purity under the influence of the moral demands made by God under the title of His holiness.

[33] Cf. D. J. McCarthy, 'Israel, My First-born Son", *The Way* 5 (1965), 189.

[34] Some authors try to exclude Ps 2:7 as not pertaining to this category, because there the king is addressed as the representative of the authority of Yahweh, while in the other texts he is addressed as the Davidic King (cf. J. L. McKenzie, "The Divine sonship of men in the OT", p. 326). But this does not seem to be convincing. The kingship in Israel was always Davidic, and it is on the basis of the Davidic election and covenant that the king becomes the representative of the authority of Yahweh. Besides, there is no evidence that the king as such enjoyed the title 'son of God' either among the Israelites or among other Semites (cf. M. J. Lagrange, art. cit., p. 487). So for our purpose we may put Ps 2:7 in this category.

[35] Cf. G. Cooke, "The Israelite King as Son of God", *ZAW* 73 (1961), 202-206 where he discusses the dating of these texts.

(cf. v. 12). The promise of this sonship is made not to the King as such, but to the descendant of David and the bearer of the Davidic Covenant (cf. vv. 9-10). The expression ' *ehyeh lô l^{e}âb w^{e}hû yih^{e}yeh lî l^{e}bēn* ' using the verb ' to be ' with a ' *lāmĕd* ' in the dative and a ' *lāmĕd* ' in the accusative indicates an adoptive relationship as that between Yahweh and Israel, expressed in Jer 31:9.

In Ps 89:26-27 " He shall cry to me — Thou art my Father ... and I will make him my First-born ..." the word ' *b^{e}kôr* ' (first-born) is the same title applied to Israel in Ex 4:22 and similarly it expresses the privileged position of David resulting from his adoption as the son of Yahweh.

Ps 2:7 says : " I will declare the decree of the Lord : He said to me, ' You are my son ; today I have begotten you ' ". The connection of this verse to Nathan's promise in II Sam 7:14 as a pattern for its modelling is generally admitted [36] and it indicates the distinctive character of the verse. The expressions ' Today I have begotten you ' and ' you are my son ' are ordinary formulas of adoption [37]. The word ' *y^{e}lidtîkā* ' in this context gets from the word ' *hayyōm* ' an emphasis on the immediate occasion on which the King has become God's son, and it meant that from the day of enthronement onwards, the King was favoured by Yahweh as if he was His son. The word ' *hōq* ' (decree), as it is associated in the OT with the Law and is used almost always in connection with the Covenant (cf. Ex 24:5-8 ; Jos 24:1-28 ; I Kg 8:58 ; II Kg 23:3), here seems to indicate the relation between God's act of adoption and renewal of Davidic Covenant on the occasion [38].

The text of Ps 110:3 is uncertain [39]. Anyhow, an idea of the

---

[36] Cf. L. ROST, *Die Überlieferung von der Thronnachfolge Davids*, Stuttgart, 1927, p. 51.

[37] Cf. The text of the Code of Hammurabi, para 170-171 and 190-191 in DRIVER and MILES, *The Babylonian Laws* II, London, 1955, pp. 65f and 75f. In fact Noth argues from these adoption formulas that a change of the royal ideology took place in Israel under the influence of the Syrian Palestinian tradition (cf. M. NOTH, " God, King and People in the Old Testament " : *The Bultmann School of Biblical Interpretation : New Directions*, I, New York, 1965, p. 43). It is beyond our competence to enter here the big question of this God-King ideology of the Myth-Ritual school. Whatever it be, the special divine sonship of the Davidic King as affirmed in this verse and similar passages can be given sufficient explanations in Biblical tradition itself. And that is enough for our purpose.

[38] Cf. G. H. JONES, " The Decree of Yahweh " (Ps 2:7), *VT* 15 (1965), 336-344.

[39] The Heb. says : " Your people is generosity on the day of your strength, in sacred splendours, from the womb of the dawn, to you the dew of your

birth of the King in relation to God is asserted here and hence it could be given an interpretation in the same line as that of Ps 2:7.

B. The King and Israel sharing the same sonship

It is the Election and Covenant, the fundamental titles for the divine sonship of Israel, that provided the form and basic content of the election of David and his seed, and of the Davidic Covenant [40]. This could be seen from the different aspects of solidarity between the King and the people. II Sam 7:14-17 make it clear that the Covenant made by Yahweh with the Davidic dynasty, and the sonship accompanying it in vv. 11-14 is not limited to David himself. The oracle of Nathan begins with a proclamation of David as the ' prince ' ' nāgîd ' over Israel, a Covenanted people (II Sam 7:8). Note the expression ' to be a prince over my people Israel '. Also in the earlier texts of the OT, the ' nāgîd ' is used in relation to ' my people ', and the ' nāgîd ' was always ' the Anointed of Yahweh ' (cf. I Sam 9:16 ; 10:1 ; 13:14 ; 25:30 ; II Sam 5:2 ; 6:21 etc.) [41]. In Dan 9:25 it is used of the future Messiah. So the Davidic Covenant and the resulting sonship is based on his solidarity with the Covenanted people, Israel. The Davidic Covenant continues and specifies the Sinaitic Covenant [42], and therefore the Davidic divine sonship seems to give Israel's divine sonship a new centre of gravity. So we may say that it is the same sonship that is shared by the Davidic King and Israel.

VI. The Divine Sonship and the Individual Israelite

A. A Homogeneous Development of the Traditional Concept

The dynamic character of the sonship, realizing itself in the day-to-day existence of man according to the divine Father's standards

---

youth ". The LXX gives : " With you is the royal dignity ... from the womb before dawn I begot you ".

[40] Cf. G. COOKE, art. cit., p. 217.

[41] For the meaning of ' nāgîd ', cf. A. ALBRECHT, *Die Staatenbildung der Israeliten in Palästina*, Leipzig, 1930, p. 29 ; cf. also W. RICHTER, " Die ' nāgîd ' — Formel in Beitrag zur Erhellung des ' nāgîd ' problems ", *BZ* 9 (1965), 71-84 where an examination of the history of evolution of the word ' nāgîd ' is made, which shows clearly the intimate connection of this term with the salvation of Israel.

[42] Cf. D. J. MCCARTHY, " Covenant in the OT ", *CBQ* 27 (1965), 235-241 where he discusses the problem of integrating the Davidic Covenant with the Mosaic one as the Davidic Covenant becomes actually the backbone of a theological structure which explains the continuity of Israel.

is a proof that the sonship belongs to the individual Israelite. An individual responsibility is implied in the Covenant relation and hence in the father-son relationship as it demands fidelity to the Commandments of God [43]. The Covenant placed Israel in the state of sonship, not automatically making him son as a nation, but imposing the obligation of being the sons, which could be realized only in the individual relation to Yahweh as such [44]. The theophoric names in the OT composed of 'ab perhaps show a personal family relation to Yahweh [45].

However, it is in the later books of the OT that we find the divine sonship passed on explicitly to the individual, inviting on the personal interior quality of the sonship, ' Be like a father to orphans... you will then be like a son of the Most High ' (Eccl 4:10). The passages in which virtuous men are called sons of the personified Wisdom are all witnesses to this change into the individual divine sonship, because the divine wisdom renders them similar to God [46]. As a result of the insistence on the imitation of the heavenly Father, the divine sonship becomes more and more personal so that finally the Sapiential Books identify the ' divine sonship ' with ' personal justice ' (Wisd 2:13,16,18 ; 16:26). This is simply a homogeneous development of the original idea of sonship of which ' holiness ' or ' fidelity to the Law ' was a constituent element. It is the constant failure of the Israelites to realize their divine sonship in the course of ages that brings about a greater emphasis on this personal justice. Thus the individual sonship comes to the fore [47].

B. The Divine Sonship and Personal Justice

1. *Wisd 2:13,16,18* : Wisdom 2 speaks of the opposition between the just and the unjust and the unjust say that this just man is a son

---

[43] For a detailed study of this personal relationship of Israel with God, cf. J. L. McKenzie, " The Divine Sonship and Individual Religion ", *CBQ* 7 (1945), 32-47.

[44] Cf. W. Marchel, op. cit., p. 52 where he, after examining all the texts speaking of the father-son relationship of Yahweh and Israel, concludes : " Ces aspects de l'amour et de la sainteté dans l'idée de la paternité de Dieu et de la filiation d'Israel semblent capitaux ".

[45] Cf. G. B. Gray, *Studies in Hebrew Proper Names*, London, 1896, p. 254 ; cf. also pp. 277-279 where he gives a complete list of names compounded with 'ab.

[46] Cf. Wisd 9:12 and 11:10 where the divine sonship of those with divine wisdom is affirmed.

[47] Cf. W. Marchel, op. cit., pp. 53-82 where he, analysing the texts in which God is invoked as father of the individual, excludes the Hellenistic influences in this respect.

of God [48]. The justice is the same Covenantal justice. The just man is a general term for the faithful Israelite and the enemies are the breakers of the Law (Wisd 2:12) [49]. In v. 13 this sonship of the just is connected with the knowledge of God: " He professes to *have the knowledge of God* and calls himself a *child of Lord.*"

We saw in Is 1:2-4 the knowledge of God as the concrete expression of the father-son relationship between Yahweh and Israel. So the sonship of the just is exactly that which results from the Covenant but realized in the life of the individual [50].

2. *Eccl 23:1,4 and 51:10*

These are texts in which God is invoked in prayer as father by an individual. In 23:1,4 the just calls God father and God (ruler) of his life, and he invokes God for protection against his enemies [51], for assistance against the sins of pride and covetousness, and thanks for the paternal care. This shows a filial confidence in God as Father which the just enjoyed. Thus the Father of the nation becomes the Father of the individual, who being faithful to the will of God invokes him in prayer as his own Father.

Eccl 51:10, according to the Hebrew text, affirms the fatherhood of God in terms identical with that of Ps 89:27 [52]. In this text it is suggested that the divine sonship of the individual results from the salvific act of Yahweh. " ... O Yahweh thou art my father because thou art the hero of my salvation ". Thus the individual just man experiences God as his Father in the quality of being his saviour and redeemer.

---

[48] The παῖς here has the same meaning as υἱός as seen from the use parallel to the υἱός in v. 16 and 18. Besides, allusion is made to the fatherhood of God in v. 16. The same interchange of use is seen also in Wisd 9:4, 7 ; 12:7,19,20,21.

[49] A Christian interpretation here about Christ does not seem admissible, because in the following chapter ' just man ' and ' just men ' are used indiscriminately. A Christian interpolator would not introduce the Passion of Christ without mentioning a word about the Resurrection. Moreover, the persecutors of Christ are not breachers of the Law. Cf. A. T. S. GOODRICK, *The Book of Wisdom*, Oxford Church Bible Commentary, London, 1913, ch. 2.

[50] Cf. Jn 8:54-55 where Jesus speaks of the knowledge of God lacking in His adversaries whose father is not God.

[51] Cf. Wisd 2:18 where the conviction in God's protection for ' the just ' is expressed.

[52] Cf. W. MARCHEL, op. cit., pp. 63-66 where he discusses all the textual problems regarding this text and concludes that it is an affirmation of the fatherhood of God parallel to Ps 89:27.

C. The Universal Fatherhood of God (Wisd 14:3)

Wisd 14:3 forms part of a prayer and in it the author invokes God simply as 'father' in a context speaking of the providence of God [53]. The context shows that the providence mentioned here is the providence of God in the Exodus of Israel: " because thou hast opened a pathway even through the sea, a safe way over the waves " [54]. Nevertheless, since the merciful love and providence of God is extended to all in the OT tradition (cf Ps 47; 50:12; 145:9; Is 60:11; Jer 12:15), it is not impossible that in a Book like that of Wisdom, where the divine sonship becomes more and more a matter of personal choice (justice) and consequently has a possibility of being universal, the author thinks also of a universal fatherhood of God. So we may say that the OT doctrine on divine sonship of man while based on the particular relation between Yahweh and Israel, ends with an opening towards a sonship that exceeds the national boundaries of Israel.

This opening towards a universal sonship may be perhaps traced back to the Covenant. Israel becomes the bearer of the Covenant, which is eventually destined for all men (cf Gen 22:18). Actually the first Covenant of God was with Adam, father of all men (Gen 3:14 f) which is not excluded in the succeeding Covenants [55].

VII. The Divine Sonship of Israel in Terms of a Begetting by God

A. The Old Covenant as a Begetting by God

The constitution of Israel as a people of God through the Covenant is often represented as a 'begetting by God'. Dt 32:15-18, which

---

[53] W. MARCHEL analyses the vocabulary of the text on the basis of the traditional doctrine of the OT, comparing it to that of the Greek world and he concludes that the idea expressed in it is entirely traditional, while it is expressed in a language familiar to the milieu of the writer. Cf. W. MARCHEL, op. cit., p. 80 : " Si donc les Juifs pouvaient entendre ce πατήρ dans le sens traditionel et national, d'autre part, ainsi formulée, cette invocation était susceptible d'atteindre les paiens, et de s'en faire plus facilement accepter, puisqu'elle ne leur était pas étrangère ".

[54] Note the conjunction ὅτι which shows that the basis of the assertion of the providence of God here is the special providence of Yahweh for Israel shown in the Exodus. Note the same expression in Is 43:16 where the prophet speaks of the miracles of the New Exodus, in which he appears to be a father to the Israelites scattered abroad (vv. 6-7), by referring to his providential act in the Exodus from Egypt.

[55] Cf. J. L. McKENZIE, " The Divine Sonship of Israel and the Covenant ", *CBQ* 8 (1946), 320.

makes a literary unit, puts 'God saving Israel' parallel to 'God begetting Israel'.

The unit actually begins in v. 15c because v. 15a-b is a recapitulation of the preceding verses about the parental care of Yahweh for Israel and the consequent well-being as the cause of her sins.

v. 15   A   He forsook GOD WHO made him
           B   And scoffed at THE ROCK of his salvation
v. 16-17   C   They stirred him ... provoked him ... sacrificed
                                                        to demons ...
v. 18   B'   You are unmindful of THE ROCK that
                                                        begot you
           A'   You forgot GOD WHO gave you birth

The parallelism between AB and B'A' is clear. In ABB'A' the sin of Israel is stated in general terms with special reference to their relation to God as the cause of their being, while in C the sin is described in specific terms of idolatry. In this parallel structure the creation of Israel (A) through the saving act of Yahweh (B) (v. 15c) [56] is presented as begetting (B') and a giving birth (A') by God (v. 18) [57].

In the same way, Is 1:2 affirms that Yahweh has brought forth sons speaking of Israel. The Hebrew *gādal* is often used in the sense of *yālad* (cf. Is 23:4 ; 49:21 ; 51:18 ; 2 Kg 10:6 ; Hos 9:12). The LXX uses ἐγέννησα thus explicitly referring to birth.

Also Is 45:9-11 speaks of the creation of Israel by Yahweh comparing it to a father and mother bringing forth a child. Jer 2:26-27 sees in the sin of idolatry of Israel the denial of father-son relationship between Yahweh and Israel, and that in terms of a begetting by Yahweh.

B. The New Covenant—a New Creation

Jer 31:31-34 speaks of the New Covenant in which God engraves the 'Law' in the heart of each one. The Law is said to be 'planted' within each individual (v. 33). Thus the Law becomes an inner source out of which a new life springs forth and grows. The Law

---

[56] Note that God is often termed as 'rock of salvation' in the OT (cf. II Sam 22:47 ; Ps 95:1) (Note how LXX uses Θεός in all the four places in vv. 15ed and 18ab), and in Ps 89:27 God is said to be the 'rock of salvation' parallel to his role as father to the king.

[57] The Judaic Tradition had a concept of New Birth regarding the Covenant relation connected specially with Law. Cf. Midrash on the Cant. of Canticles 8.2 " Why does he call Sinai 'house of my mother'? Because it is there that the Israelites became new born children ".

which was already a constituent element of Israel's sonship, now becomes an inner source of spontaneous activity, and the knowledge of God parallel to sonship (Is 1:2-3) becomes spontaneous arising from the interior of man (cf. v. 34) [58].

In Ez 36:16f the Spirit of Yahweh is shown as the principle of a new life, which implies a moral regeneration of the individual to the life of a more perfect divine sonship (vv. 25-27). Indication of this new sonship through a moral regeneration is seen in Is 1:2-4; 30:1, 9; Jer 3:19-22 etc. where Yahweh calls his disloyal sons back, to restore them to the position of his sons which can be done only through a decisive conversion to Him [59]. This is realised in the New Covenant where the Spirit of Yahweh becomes the origin and source of this decisive conversion — a moral regeneration.

Unlike the Old Covenant, this New Covenant is presented in terms of a New Creation and not a new birth from God, because here it concerns the individual, not the community as such, and to speak of it as a birth from God could easily lead to misunderstanding. Nevertheless the idea of the beginning of a new life having God as the source is already implicit in it [60]. Here we have the basis of the doctrine of rebirth of the proselytes in Later Judaism and of Christians in the NT [61].

VIII. The Eschatological Character of Israel's Sonship

Israel's sonship had also an eschatological dimension. Many factors contributed to this. The fact that Israel is called the 'first-born' of Yahweh made Israel hope for some heredity (cf. 1 Sam 26:19). But the lack of realization of the sonship in the life of Israel on account of their constant infidelity kept the sonship together with the heritage as a salvific good to be hoped for in future, namely, eschatological [62].

---

[58] Cf. v. 34 " No longer shall each man teach his neighbour saying ' know the Lord ', for they shall all know me ...". Cf. also Dt 30:11-14 where though the Law is written in the Book (v. 10), an indication of its interiorization is given.

[59] Cf. O. BAUERNFEIND, " Gotteskindschaft ", *RGG*, III, 1798.

[60] Cf. Is 66:7-14 describing the advent of the New Israel using the metaphor of a mother giving birth and God is pictured as the one who causes this new birth. And this new birth is a source of an incessant joy as it opens the bosom of Jerusalem and brings forth a heap of children.

[61] Cf. E. SJÖBERG, " Wiedergeburt und Neuschöpfung im Palästinischen Judentum ", *ST* 5-6 (1951-52), pp. 44-85.

[62] O. BAUERNFEIND, art. cit., p. 1798.

The Covenantal love of Yahweh that made Israel, Son of Yahweh (cf. Dt 7:8) was a steadfast love, lasting forever (cf. 1 Chr 16:34, 41; 2 Chr 5:13; 7:3,6; Ps 100:5; 103:7 etc)[63]. But again on the part of man faithfulness to the Covenant was necessary for the realization of sonship. Thus the time of the restoration of this sonship was called a time 'when steadfast love and faithfulness meet' (cf. Ps 85:10). This hope of realizing this sonship always existed in Israel. That gave rise again to the eschatological concept of Israel's sonship.

The moral regeneration of the New Covenant as expressed in Jer 31:31f and Ez 36:25-28 also opens the way to this eschatological concept. They speak of a new existence of man which is to take place in the future. All the expressions there show perspectives of a great eschatological renewal[64].

In the Book of Wisdom this sonship becomes more individual and something to be enjoyed in the Messianic time. It becomes more individual, because its realization has to take place in each individual. At the same time in the announcement of the sonship the moral regeneration is mixed up with the material restoration (cf. Ez 36:25-27). Since this material prosperity was not realized in the case of the 'just', this sonship was considered to be enjoyed in the Messianic time, when God will gain victory over all adversaries (cf. Wisd 2:13,16,18)[65].

Conclusion

Israel becomes 'son of God' as a result of their creation as 'people of God' through the saving act of Yahweh in Exodus and through the Covenant. So Israel's sonship is essentially adoptive and as the first-born of Yahweh, Israel enjoys a sonship that is peculiar to it and not common to all the nations.

Though adoptive, it is a real sonship resulting in a loving communion of a love of paternal care and nurture on the part of God and response of filial love on the part of Israel expressed in loyalty and obedience and hence sonship is essentially dynamic in nature.

---

[63] Cf. Ps 136 in which the formula *kî le'Ôlām ḥasdû* accompanies as a litany the recital of the event of Exodus.

[64] Cf. also Is 55:3; 59:21 and 61:8 which all speak of an everlasting Covenant in the same perspective.

[65] Note how in Wisd 5:5 the impious admit their delusion and final victory of the 'sons of God'. Also the background of the Book of Wisdom points to the same. It rose from a situation of the loyal Alexandrian Jews who were derided and persecuted by their pagan allies. Cf. the Jerusalem Bible, p. 1009, note 1.

This implies an individual relation of divine sonship in Israel, which becomes more and more explicit in the later books of the OT, thus opening the way to a universal sonship. The individual sonship is characterised by the knowledge of God and a filial confidence in the Father.

A likeness to the Father is indicated in Israel's filial relation to Yahweh, though not explicitly mentioned, because Israel is asked to imitate God in his holiness.

A divine sonship is attributed to the Davidic King which is based on the Covenant relationship with God and is expressed in terms of Israel's sonship which is an indication that the King and Israel share in the same divine sonship.

The concept of a begetting by God through which Israel becomes a son of God is not entirely absent from the OT, though it refers exclusively to the Community as such. Of the individual, OT speaks in terms of a new creation rather than a new birth, though there we have the concept of a new life with the Law and the Spirit of Yahweh as its interior principle and implying a moral renewal of the individual.

The non-realization of the sonship at present, combined with the steadfast Covenantal love of Yahweh who calls Israel back to the restoration of their sonship, gave rise to the eschatological concept of this divine sonship.

Chapter II

The Divine Sonship of Man in Later Judaism

The problem of the father-son relationship between God and man as conceived in Later Judaism has been the object of detailed discussion among scholars. There are critics who deny absolutely the idea of such a relationship in the Jewish Religion [1], while there are others who see in Judaism an idea equivalent to that in the New Testament [2]. The majority of the authors, however, admit the existence of the idea of the divine sonship of man in Later Judaism, though they differ in details. Some restricted the divine sonship to Community as such [3], while others extended it to the individuals [4].

In the following pages, it is our aim to examine the main texts in the Jewish Literature of Qumran, Apocrypha and Rabbinic Writings which speak of the divine sonship of man. In the main, we follow the Qumran Literature, since we see there especially some of the aspects of the divine sonship of man, which will be relevant to our study of the theme in the Johannine Writings.

I. **The Divine Sonship of the Community through Election and Covenant.**

It is generally accepted that the community of Qumran believed themselves to be the ideal regenerated House of Israel, the small

---

[1] Cf. W. Bousset, *Jesu Predigt in ihrem Gegensatz zum Judentum*, Göttingen, 1892, p. 43.

[2] Cf. C. G. Montefiore, *The Religious Teaching of Jesus*, London, 1910, pp. 90-95.

[3] Cf. A. L. Williams, "'My Father' in Jewish Thought of the First Century", *JTS* 31 (1929-30), pp. 42-47; J. Jeremias, "Abba", *TLZ* 79 (1954), col. 213f. Cf. also W. Marchel who, having considered the different opinions of authors regarding the individual invocations of God as 'Father', concludes: " Dans le Judaisme Palestinien l'invocation à titre individuel à Dieu Père avant la venue de J. C., semble peu probable " (cf. W. Marchel, op. cit., p. 93).

[4] Cf. J. Bonsirven, *Le Judaisme Palestinien au temps du Jesus Christ*, Paris, 1934, I, p. 138; B. M. F. Van Iersel, *Der Sohn in den synoptischen Jesusworten*, Leiden, 1961, p. 106; M. E. Boismard, *Dieu notre Père*: in Grands thèmes bibliques, Paris, 1958, pp. 67-75.

remnant that stayed faithful to the Covenant [5]. This belief is manifested in several books of the Qumran Community [6]. As a result of this conviction, they did not hesitate to attribute to themselves the status of the Old Israel as ' Son of God ' [7].

A. *Prayer of Intercession (4 Q Dibrê ham – Me'orôt) 3:4-10*

The belief of the Community to be in a filial relation to God is best expressed in the ' Prayer of Intercession ' or ' The Words of the Heavenly Lights ' 3:4-10 which makes use of the different texts regarding the sonship of Israel in the Old Testament [8].

1. *Context*

Our particular section comes in the centre of a large section 1:8 – 7:2, in which the preceding part speaks of the Mosaic Covenant and pardon given through it (2:7b-19), while the subsequent part speaks of the Davidic Covenant and the punishment and pardon following it (4:4b – 6:4a) concluding it with a prayer to deliver his people from the present tribulations (6:4b – 7:2) as in the introduction (1:8 – 2:7a). The thematic structure will show the central thought of their consciousness of being the sons of God.

1:8 – 2:7a		I n t r o d u c t i o n : Imploring the mercy of God
2:7b – 12a	A	*Pardon* given through Moses
2:12b – 19	B	Mosaic *Covenant* — The Promulgation of the Law
3:1 – 4:4a	C	The predilection for I s r a e l a n d Q u m r a n C o m m u n i t y w h o e n j o y a f i l i a l r e l a t i o n s h i p w i t h G o d
4:4b – 14	B′	The *Covenant* with David and Solomon
5:1 – 6:4a	A′	Punishment in ' Exile ' and *Pardon* in ' Return '
6:4b – 7:2		C o n c l u s i o n : Imploring the mercy of God

---

[5] Cf. Th. GASTER, *The Dead Sea Scriptures in English Translation*, New York, 1964, pp. 3-6.

[6] Cf. for instance, I QS 5:7-10 ; 8:1-7 ; CD 8:14-17 etc.

[7] Though the theme of the divine sonship of men is not so frequent in the Qumran Writings, it is nevertheless sufficiently attested by a few explicit texts and by many references to the filial trust which the Community of Qumran enjoyed in their relation to God.

[8] Cf. J. CARMIGNAC, *Les textes de Qumran*, Paris, 1963, pp. 302-303 ; M. BAILLET, " Un recueil liturgique de Qumran grotte 4 : Les paroles des luminaires " : *RB* 68 (1961), pp. 202-203.

This shows how the Community of Qumran was conscious of its being the New Israel, having the right to implore the mercy of God on the title of 'sonship' resulting from the Covenant.

2. Structure of the Section 3:4-10

Line 4	A	It is on Thy name alone that w e h a v e b e e n c a l- l e d [9]
	B	It is for Thy glory that THOU HAST C R E A T E D U S
5	C	THOU HAST MADE US THY SONS in the sight ... nations
6	D	For THOU HAST NAMED ISRAEL 'MY FIRST-BORN SON'
7	C'	THOU HAST chastised US as a man chastises his SON
	B'	THOU HAST m a d e U S G R O W throughout ... generations
8-10	A'	Thou hast delivered us ... through faithfulness ... Covenant, For it is we whom y o u h a v e c h o s e n ... to be Thy people

The whole section is phrased in such a way that the ELECTION – COVENANT (AA') CREATION (BB') and SONSHIP (CC') of the Community are centered round the SONSHIP OF ISRAEL (D).

3. Analysis of Words

It is worth noting that this section starts with the word *'ābî* 'my father'. The particle *kî* before the affirmation of the sonship of Israel (D) shows that the divine sonship of the Community is a result or continuation of the sonship of Israel. As in the OT, also in the Qumran Community the Election and Covenant are the basic titles for sonship [10]. The creation, of which mention is made, is the special creation of the Community, as it is used parallel to the special calling of the Community in contrast to other nations [11]. The expression

---

[9] This is a quotation from Is 43:7 and therefore the unr(qn) seems to be restituted as *niqᵉrēnû*. Cf. J. CARMIGNAC, op. cit., II, p. 303 note 3.

[10] While 'D' quotes Exod 4:22, 'C' 'C'' apply Dt 14:1 and 8:5 respectively, which are all keytexts for the divine sonship of Israel resulting from the Covenant. Hence all the references to sonship in this section are applications of the sonship of Israel in the OT.

[11] This is reinforced by the fact that line 4 (AB) is a quotation from Is 43:7 where the creation and calling by God's name of Israel are parallels. This is all the more remarkable, because in Isaiah, as here, the same is said in a context, in which the divine sonship of Israel is mentioned (cf. Is 43:6).

ûbānîm s'amtēnû also indicates this sonship resulting from the special Election and hence an adoptive sonship, because *sîm* with accusative, when used of persons, denotes 'planting' (establishing) someone in a special position which he did not have before. All these show how the Community of Qumran considered themselves to be the sons of God in the traditional way.

B. 1 QH 9:35

The same notion of father-son relationship is expressed in 1 QH 9:35 : " For thou art a Father to all (the sons) [12] of thy truth ". This is a crowning statement regarding the paternal predilection of God for the members of the community, which is a theme running throughout the Thanksgiving Hymns and is certainly the 'Leitmotif' of the whole strophe 1 QH 9:30-36. The members of the Community are here represented by the psalmist, as is usual, in the Thanksgiving Hymns [13].

1. *The Context in the Section, 1 QH 9:30-36*

This section could be divided into three subsections :

i. Lines 30-31 : God is a father in a truer sense than the natural parents are. This is manifested in the Election and predestination.

ii. Lines 32-34 : God's fatherhood is manifested in the Covenantal gifts such as enlightenment (l. 32), knowledge of eternal Truth (l. 32), peace (l. 33), forgiveness of sins (l. 34) etc.

iii. Lines 35-36 : God is the only real Father.

---

[12] The word *b*e*ni* is not clear in the scroll and hence is left out in the edition of E. L. SUKENIK. But the 'sons of thy truth' is a frequent phrase specially in the Thanksgiving Hymns. So here too we may reasonably fill in with *b*e*ni* as done by all the translators and also by some Hebrew editions. Cf. for instance, A. M. HABERMANN, *Megilloth Midbar Yehuda, The Scrolls from the Judean Desert*, Machbaroth, Israel, 1959, p. 125.

[13] It is true that the 'I' in the Hymns is individual as seen clearly from I QH 7:6-25. But this does not in any way affect his representing the experience of the Community. Cf. H. BARDTKE, " Considerations sur les cantiques de Qumran ", *RB* 63 (1956) pp. 232-233 where he says : " A Supposer que le Maître de Justice ait été l'auteur, même alors ce que il rapporte de ses propres éxpériences n'aura, pas trouvé place dans les 'Hodayoth' qu'à condition d'être également applicable à tout membre de la Secte. Dès lors le Maître de Justice n'est plus que le premier dans la série de tous ceux qui ont vécu les mêmes expériences dans la conquête de la vérité ". Note how the Psalmist in the end of this section identifies himself with the sons of God's truth.

So the statement in lines 35-36 comes after the statement of the Election and Covenant.

2. *Structure of IQH 9:35-36*

Line 35   A   For, my FATHER hath not acknowledged me
            B   And my MOTHER hath abandoned me to THEE
            C   For THOU ART A FATHER TO ALL THY FAITHFUL SONS
" 36   B'   And Thou rejoicest [14] ... like a MOTHER over ... babe
          A'   And Thou upholdest ... as a FOSTER-FATHER in the bosom

Note the parallelism in AA' and BB' between actions of their natural parents and of God taking their place [15]. So it makes a concentric structure emphasizing the fact that God is a Father to all his faithful sons.

3. *Analysis of Words*

The '*kî*' at the beginning of the statement makes it the ground for all the previous affirmations. If the '*kî*' in line 35a gives the negative reason for God's paternal love, namely, the disappearance of the natural relationship in the face of the new relationship with God, the '*kî*' in line 35c gives the positive reason for this paternal love, namely, the existence of the only real father-son relationship between God and the faithful [16].

An allusion to the adoptive character of this divine sonship may be seen in the statement ' My mother hath abandoned me to thee ', which could be a reference to the practice of adoption which existed among the Essenes attested by Josephus in Bell. Jud II, 120 : The

---

[14] Some translate it as ' you reveal yourself ' taking the word as *gālāh*. But *gîl*, ' rejoice ' seems better in the context as it suits better the illustration. Cf. S. H. NIELSON, *Hodayoth-Psalms from Qumran*, Aarhus, 1960, p. 164, note 159. Besides, this phrase seems to be inspired by Is 49:13 which chapter, as we have seen, has already influenced the passages in the beginning of this strophe.

[15] The parallelism between A and A' has been denied by some who see in line 36b a relation of God to the creatures in opposition to the ' sons of His truth ' (cf. for instance, J. LICHT, *The Thanksgiving Scroll, A Scroll from the Wilderness of Judea*, Jerusalem, 1957, p. 149). But the affirmation about the foster-father in 36b is exactly like the mother in 36a. So "all thy works' should be the same as ' the sons of thy truth ' (cf. F. NOTSCHER, " Hodayot (Psalmenrolle) ", *BZ* 2 (1958), p. 132 ; cf. also S. H. NIELSON, op. cit., p. 165, note 160.

[16] Cf. S. H. NIELSON, op. cit., p. 164.

abandoning of the child to God by the mother is certainly to consecrate him to the service of God [17].

The expression ' Sons of his truth ' (literally) [18] reveals the nature of this father-son relationship. A definition of this phrase is given in IQP Hab 7:10-12, namely, " those who practise the Law and whose hands do not leave the service of truth ". This definition is quite significant, because it resumes the various connotations implied in the word 'emet. The word 'emet has a revelatory significance in Qumran, designating the divine plan revealed to man [19]. The Law is also nothing but the revealed plan of God. In fact ' Law ' and ' Truth ' are interchangeable in Qumran as seen from the parallel expressions ' the truth of the laws of God ' (1 QS 1:12) and ' the laws of His truth ' (1 QS 1:15). So the expression ' sons of truth ' implied the whole religious relationship between God and the Community based on the revelation by God and fidelity to it. It is such a life that gives the Father-son relationship between God and man.

The fact that this sonship is based on the Election and Covenant is again clear from its parallel expressions such as ' sons of his good will ' (1 QH 4:31-33 ; 11:9-11) and ' sons of his Covenant ' (1 QM 17:8).

---

[17] It is worth noting here that the OT expressions to mean ' abandon to ' are usually '$\bar{a}z\bar{a}b$ with l^e or byd and not 'al. On the other hand '$z\bar{a}b$ '$\bar{a}l$ is used to express the ' committing of oneself to God ' (cf. Ps 10:14). Cf. M. DELCOR, Les hymnes de Qumran, Paris, 1962, p. 222.

[18] It is interesting to note that this expression has something special about it, which is absent from the various expressions composed of ' sons ' as ' sons of light ', ' sons of justice ' etc., namely, that it is always used with a suffix relating to God hence the translation ' thy faithful sons '. This shows that this expression has much more relevance to the father-son relationship between God and the faithful, and is characteristic of the relationship in the Qumran literature. This is all the more true, because, this father-son relationship is explicitly affirmed using this phrase alone. (It is worth noting here that I QpHab 7:10 where the phrase ' men of truth ' is used, also lacks the suffix that usually goes with it, indicating thereby that the suffix has something to do with the ' sons ' unlike the other phrases of the same category). If this is true, it would not be wrong to see an allusion to the father-son relationship in all the places where this phrase is used, such as I QH 6:29 ; 7:29 ; 10:27 ; 11:11 ; and I QM 17:8. (Note that J. Carmignac translates on all these occasions ' thy faithful sons '. Cf. J. CARMIGNAC et P. GUILBERT, Les textes de Qumran, Paris, 1961).

[19] Cf. I. DE LA POTTERIE, "La Verità in San Giovanni", in San Giovanni, Brescia, 1964, pp. 125-127 ; cf. also I QH 11:7 where the ' truth ' is identified with the ' mouth ' (word) of God, which also indicates this revelatory character.

C. *In the Apocrypha*

The traditional OT theme of divine sonship of Israel is found also in the Apocrypha (cf. Jub 2:20; 19:29; 22:11; Ps. Sol 1:8; 8:14; 18:4; 2 Bar 13:9; Asc. Mos 10:3). Ps 18:4 shows that the Jews considered themselves as the true Israel who is the son of God [20]. The designation of God as 'Father' in the forms of both affirmation and invocation in the Rabbinic literature also points to the same (cf. Y. Hag II, 1, 77a) [21].

II. The Sons of God and the Just

A. *In the Qumran Literature*

The Qumran Community is a new Israel created out of the 'Remnant' of the Old Israel, and in this sense, is the bearer of the 'New Covenant' $b^e rît\ hadašā$' (cf. CD 6:19; 20:12), which points unmistakably to the prophetic ideal of Jeremiah and Ezekiel [22]. But it is not entirely new because it is a restoring of the Old Covenant through the Remnant that remained faithful [23]. This shows the gradual stress laid on the human response to the Covenant, which we may call 'Justice'. Note that in 1 QM 17:8 the rejoicing of 'Justice' and of 'the Sons of his truth' are parallels. So the divine sonship of the Community, though based on 'Election' and 'Covenant' is strictly restricted to those who are 'Just'.

According to many texts, an interior change or conversion from iniquity to justice is required to enter the Covenantal community (cf. 1 QS 2:24,26; 3:3) [24]. In 1 QS 3:4-9 and 4:21-23 this change is said to be worked out by the Holy Spirit through the 'Truth' and the 'Law of God' [25]. Thus the notion of the divine sonship, though

---

[20] Cf. G. BORNKAMM, *Sohnschaft und Leiden* : *BNTW*, 2nd ed., München, 1964, pp. 188-198. Cf. also IV Ezra 6:58 where it is said: " We thy people whom thou hast called, Thy First-born, Thy only begotten, Thy beloved ".

[21] Cf. J. BONSIRVEN, *Textes rabbiniques des deux premières siècles chrétiens*, Rome, 1955, p. 280; for more examples of affirmation and invocations of God as 'Father' in the Rabbinic Judaism, cf. W. MARCHEL, op. cit., pp. 83-89.

[22] Cf. M. BLACK, *The Scrolls and Christian Origins*, New York, 1961, p. 92.

[23] This is indicated by the different names of this Covenant as the 'Covenant of repentance' (cf. CD 19:16), and 'Covenant of mercy' (cf. I QS 1:8).

[24] Cf. E. SJÖBERG, " Neuschöpfung im Toten Meer ", *ST* 9 (1953), pp. 135-136; O. BETZ, Die Taufe in der Qumransekte und im Neuen Testament ", *RQ* 1 (1958), 218-221.

[25] Cf. R. E. BROWN, " The Qumran Scrolls and the Johannine Gospels and Epistles ", *CBQ* 17 (1955), 560-567.

in a way outgrows the national boundaries of Israel, becomes much more restricted, because, they identify the ' Just ' with their own Community.

B. *In the Apocrypha and the Rabbinic Writings*

This characteristic of the divine sonship is attested also by the Apocrypha and the Rabbinic Writings. It was now more the faithfulness to the Covenant that made the Jews the true Israel who is the son of God (cf. Ps Sal 17:17,21 ; 10:5). In Jub 1:25 God is described as their father in justice. It is only when they will be faithful to God and his Commandments that they will be God's children (cf. Jub 1:23-25 and 28 ; cf. also other texts as Ps. Sal. 9:11-15 ; Enoch 62:11-12 ; 3 Mach 5:7 ; 6:8 ; 7:6).

In the Rabbinic literature if one is a son of God by belonging to the Covenantal Jewish fold [26] this sonship is conditioned by one's moral conduct [27].

III. Sons of Light (God) and Sons of Darkness (devil)

A. *Sons of Light - Sons of God*

This peculiar concept of divine sonship is expressed in the dualistic terms of Qumran Literature ' sons of light ' and ' sons of darkness '. ' Sons of light ' are those who accomplish the will of God expressed in the Torah, entering the Covenant according to the design of God (1 QS 1:7-8,12-13). Thus they are identified with the true Israel covenanted with God [28] as the ' sons of truth ' [29].

In 1 QS 1:9-10 the ' sons of light ' are those who imitate God loving their fellow members according to their dispositions in the

---

[26] Cf. Aboth 3:14 " R. Aqiba said : Beloved are the Israelites, because they are called sons of God. As a special love it will be announced to them that they are called sons of God, see Dt. 14:1 — You are ...". Cf. Str. Bill., *Das Evangelium nach Matthäus erläutert aus Talmud und Midrash*, München, 1922, p. 219, where he gives other texts belonging to this category.

[27] Cf. Qid 36a Bar : You are the children of Yahweh (Dt 14:1). If you live according to the nature of his children, you are called children ; if not, you are not called children. These are the words of R. Jehuda (cf. Str. Bill., op. cit., I, p. 220).

[28] Note the same expression in Ex 30:33,38 ; Lev 17:9,14 etc. applied to the sons of light in I QS 2:16.

[29] This is reinforced by the fact that ' the prince of the lights ' (According to I QM 9:15,16 ; 13:9,10 ; 17:6,7 etc. this ' prince of lights ' seems to be St. Michael who represents the power of God), who dominates all the sons of justice (IQS 3:20), is identified with the angel of God's truth (IQS 3:24-25).

party of God, and hating the sons of darkness with the vengeance of God [30]. This shows in the 'sons of light' a similarity in nature and attitude to God pointing thereby to the father-son relationship. This is confirmed by 1 QS 4:23 where all the glory of Adam is destined for the 'sons of light' in the final victory, since Adam is created in the image of God [31].

B. *Sons of Light - Believers*

We saw above how the knowledge of truth (revealed plan of God) is preliminary to becoming 'sons of Truth (God)' (cf. 1 QH 10:20,27, 29). The 'knowledge of the Most High' is characteristic of them [32]. This knowledge is revealed to them: "... and thereafter knowledge will be revealed to them, abundant as the waters of the sea" (1 Qp Hab 10:14-11:2). 1 Qp Hab 2:1-6 says: "... this refers to the traitors who have aligned themselves with the man of lies, for they did not believe the words of the Teacher of Righteousness from the mouth of God ... and to the traitors of the New Covenant, for they did not believe ..." [33]. From this it is clear that the 'sons of darkness' (cf. 1 QH 1:1-7) (of the devil - man of lies) are those who refuse to accept the Truth - Revelation [34]. Hence the 'sons of Light' are those who accept the Revelation of God - Truth [35].

---

[30] Cf. E. F. SUTCLIFFE, "Hatred at Qumran", *RQ* 2 (1955-60), 342-355.

[31] The Judaic Tradition attributed to the just as eternal recompense all that Adam was deprived of by sin, cf. B. OTZEN, "Some Textual Problems in I QS", *ST* 11 (1957), 96-98.

[32] Cf. E. SJÖBERG, art. cit., pp. 131-136 in which he emphasizes the great role of the 'knowledge' of the divine mysteries together with the 'giving of the Spirit' in the renewal which takes place at the entrance in the Community of the New Covenant.

[33] About the Teacher of Righteousness, cf. L. MORALDI, *Il Maestro di Giustizia*, Fossano, 1971.

[34] Cf. R. E. BROWN, art. cit., in *CBQ* 17 (1955), pp. 415-416 where he defines the 'sons of light' as 'doers of the Law in the house of Judah whom God will deliver from the house of judgement for the sake of their labour and their faith in the Teacher of Righteousness'. This is actually the definition of the 'just' according to I Qp Hab 8:1, who are the sons of God for Qumran.

[35] Cf. I QpHab 8:2f where 'truth' is taken in the sense of 'loyalty' to the Teacher of Righteousness — the faith in the person sent by God. Cf. F. NÖTSCHER, *Vom Alten zum Neuen Testament*, BBB 17 (1962), p. 115.

IV. Birth of the Community through the Teacher (I QH 3:1-18)

This text speaks of the birth connected with the Messianic age. As to who is being born, some think of the Messiah, others, of the Teacher of Righteousness, and some others, again of the community [36]. The imagery of birth pains certainly indicates the dawn of the eschatological Messianic age [37] and considering the general trend of Qumran texts it seems more likely that here we have the birth of the Messianic Community. Because the centre of gravity for Qumran texts was the Community [38] and there was only a minor interest in a Saviour - Messiah. Hence the collective unit became the bearer of so many Messianic characteristics [39].

A. *The Structure of the Section*

The whole section seems to have been built of three concentric structural divisions: 1. Lines 1-6; 2. 7-12a; 3. 12b-18. We give only the second and third parts, because the first part is almost entirely lost.

Lines 7-12a

Line	7	A	I was in distress as a WOMAN IN TRAVAIL bringing ... first-born
		B	For her BIRTHPANGS COME SUDDENLY
	8	C	And AGONIZING PAINS to her pangs
		D	To GIVE BIRTH TO THE FIRST-BORN of her pregnancy
		E	For CHILDREN have COME to the BREAKERS of death
	9	F	And SHE WHO CONCEIVED a male child ... by her PAINS
		X	FOR IN THE PAINS OF DEATH SHE GIVES LIFE TO A MAN - CHILD.
	10	F'	And in the PAINS of sheol, from...PREGNANT ONE

---

[36] A discussion on this problem could be seen in S. H. NIELSON, op. cit., pp. 61-64.

[37] Cf. for instance, II Ezra 4:42 and I Enoch 62:4-5 where the birth agony is used as a representation of pain and suffering in the eschatological age.

[38] Cf. J. B. GÄRTNER, *The Temple and the Community in Qumran and the New Testament*, Cambridge, 1965, p. 138.

[39] This does not mean that we exclude the Messiah from this, because the Messiah comes naturally from the Messianic Community, that is created by God through the mediation of the Teacher.

BIRTH OF THE COMMUNITY THROUGH THE TEACHER

	E'	There ... BREAK FORTH a wonderful counsellor people...
	D'	There COMES FORTH A MAN CHILD from the BIRTH canal
11	C'	During the breakers and AGONIZING PAINS ... in their birth
	B'	And in his hour of BIRTH all PANGS COME SUDDENLY
12a	A'	In the womb of the PREGNANT ONE

Lines 12b-18.

Line 12b	A	THE WOMAN PREGNANT WITH viper with shooting pain
	B	And the breakers OF THE PIT with all DEEDS of terror
13	C	The foundations ... crumble like a ship ... on WATERS
		and the clouds ROAR with a ROARING VOICE
14	D	THOSE who dwell upon ... like ... who go DOWN TO THE SEA
	E	Terrified BY THE ROARING OF THE waters
	F	And THEIR WISE MEN
	X	ARE LIKE MARINERS IN THE DEPTHS
15	F'	When all THEIR WISDOM is confused
	E'	By THE ROARING OF THE seas
16	D'	When the DEPTHS see the ... THEY shall rage ... of waves
	C'	And the WATER — breakers with their ROARING VOICE
17		and when they rage ... descend into the deep ...
18	B'	And the gates open ... DEEDS of wickedness ... OF THE PIT
	A'	Behind THE WOMAN PREGNANT WITH iniquity ... wickedness

Note the literal, synonymous and thematic parallelisms in both parts. In the first part, as far as we can judge from the remaining lines, the author speaks of the persecution of the Teacher by his enemies using the metaphor of a ship in a troubled sea and of a beseiged city. In the second part he describes these eschatological tribulations using the metaphor of birth, and the outcome of these tribulations is the deliverance of the child — the messianic community — through God's power (X). In the third part he describes the situation of the enemies who also are object of the eschatological tribulations using both the metaphors of the first and second parts and the outcome is their eternal imprisonment in the deep sheol as the mariners in the depths (X). For this reason, the birth imagery in the third part *harāyat 'ap ^{e}'eh* (AB) is transformed to actual inimical figures *harāyat 'āwel* (A' B') going down to the depths (CC' DD') through the calamities of the roaring waters (DD' EE') and finally ending as mariners in the depths (FF'X)[40].

B. *Vocabulary*

The first line 7 gives the key to understand the allegory developed in the following lines. The psalmist describes his condition as that of a woman in travail bringing forth her first-born. The *mab^{e}kîrāh* is to be taken as plural as parallel to 'children' in line 8 and 'their birth' in line 11 [41]. So the Teacher undergoes pains and tribulations to give life to a first-born that is collective. In Column 6 it is quite clear that he suffers on account of his disciples and the imagery is that of the ship in the troubled waters of the sea. The same imagery is used here also in 3:6,13-16 parallel to birth pangs, which shows that the first-born here are his new Community [42].

'The children who came to the breakers of death' reminds us of Is 37:3 combined with 2 Sam 22:5 and points to the twofold pains connected with this Messianic birth, namely, the sufferings of the one who gives birth and the tribulations that are held in store for the Messianic Community.

In *gebber hēṣērâ* of line 9 the *hē* could be causative of the verb 'ṣārar' meaning 'to be in distress' as used in Jer 48:41; 49:22 etc. precisely referring to birth pains. So there is no question of a 'man of suffering' here with allusion to Is 53:3 as some adherents of exclusive Messianic interpretation have held [43].

The expression "for in the pains of death she gives life to a man-child" is a quotation from Is 66:7-8, where the male child is the people of the New Jerusalem (sons of Zion). So here too the male child *zākār* represents the Community [44]. 'The wonderful coun-

---

[40] Cf. S. BROWN, "Deliverance from the Crucible: Some further reflexions on I QH III, 1-18", *NTS* 14 (1968), pp. 247-259 where he maintains the two births, resulting differently.

[41] But even if it is taken as singular, it could be understood as collective when used of Israel as in Ex 4:22, which is quoted in PL 3:6 and applied to the Qumran Community.

[42] This is quite in agreement with the Jewish concept, because in Num 11:12 Moses' work is compared to a giving birth. It is interesting to note here that the same concept was in use in the Primitive Christian Tradition as seen from Jn 16:21-22; Rom 8:22; Gal 4:19 etc.

[43] Cf. A. DUPONT-SOMMER, "La mère du messie et la mère de l'Aspic dans une hymne de Qumran", *RHR* 147 (1955), p. 180.

[44] Cf. O. BETZ, "Die Geburt der Gemeinde durch den Lehrer", *NTS* 3

sellor' in line 10 is also collective. The expression is taken from Is 9:5 where 'Emmanuel' is called 'wonderful Counsellor', 'God Almighty'. The absence of the words 'God Almighty' suggests that it is the Community, while the use of this Messianic formula suggests the salvific role of the Community that is being born [45]. They have to bring in the day of salvation in the distress of the last days [46].

C. The Community Born of the Power (Spirit) of God

The phrase '$\bar{a}m\ g^e b\hat{u}r\bar{a}t\hat{o}$ of v. 10 is liable to three interpretations: 1. 'with his power' [47], 2. 'the wonderful counsellor of the power of God' [48] or 3. 'people of his power' [49]. The third one seems to be the correct one. It is supported by the structure. Note how in E that is parallel to this stanza the plural $b\bar{a}n\hat{i}m$ is used. Moreover, 'power' is characteristic of God in Qumran and they, so to say, identified the power of God with God himself (cf. 1QS 11:4-5). Though the one who gives birth is the Teacher, it is the power of God that brings forth the Community.

The 'power of God' and the 'Holy Spirit' go together (cf. 1QH 7:6f). In I QS 4:4-9 and 21-23 we see that the Holy Spirit is the power of God working in men through 'Truth' and 'Law of God' effecting thereby a purification and a birth into the Community of the Covenant. In I QH 7:6ff the Holy Spirit is said to have come upon the Teacher. So the Community is born through the Teacher by the Power (Spirit) of God.

(1956-57), p. 319 where he refers also to Rev 12:7 where mention is made of the rest of the seed of the woman, which represents the Community of Christ, against whom the fight of the Dragon and his angels is described making use of expressions similar to the fight between the 'sons of light' and 'sons of darkness' in Qumran.

[45] Cf. S. MOWINCKEL, "Some Remarks on Hodayot" 3,5-20, *JBL* 75 (1956), 276; O. BETZ, art. cit., p. 320 where he takes the wonderful counsellor as collective, meaning those who follow the teaching and advice of the Teacher, namely, the real wise men, the members of the Community in opposition to the 'wise of this world' in I QH 3:14ff.

[46] Cf. J. B. GÄRTNER, op. cit., p. 132; M. BLACK, *The Scrolls and Christian Origins*, N. Y., 1961, p. 150.

[47] Cf. S. H. NIELSON, op. cit., p. 56; A. DUPONT-SOMMER, *Les écrits esséniens découverts près de la Mer Morte*, Paris, 1959, p. 223; J. CARMIGNAC, *Les textes de Qumran*, I, p. 194.

[48] Cf. J. LICHT, *The Thanksgiving Scroll*, Jerusalem, 1957, p. 80, where he gives also the possibility of reading the '$\bar{a}m$ as meaning the 'people' and hence as 'the wonderful counsellor of the people of the power of God'.

[49] Cf. O. BETZ, "Das Volk seiner Kraft, zur Auslegung der Qumran-Hodayot III, 1-18", *NTS* 5 (1958-59), 67-75.

V. Community born through the Truth (revelation)

I QH 7:20ff presents the Teacher as 'the father ... before whom the Community opens mouth as a child at its mother's breast ...'. This indicates the manner in which the teacher is a father to them, namely, by giving the milk of doctrine. In doing this he participates in some way in the fatherhood of God himself. This is all the more true, because his parental relation to the Community is completely dependent on his relation to God. He is only the mediator who leads the Community to the Truth (revelation of God) which is transparent in himself [50]. In 1 QH 5:5-6a the Psalmist thanks God for the Light (Revelation) he received [51] and in v. 27 he says that through him the members of the Community were given the Light [52]. So the birth of the Community takes place through the Truth (Revelation).

Conclusion

In Later Judaism the fundamental titles to the divine sonship are the same as in the OT, namely, the salvific Election and Covenant and the realization of this sonship depends entirely on the fidelity to this Covenantal relation. But a reversal of values takes place here. If in the OT, the whole nation of Israel was the son of God and was therefore obliged to realize this sonship through their fidelity, in Later Judaism, only those Israelites, who are faithful to the Covenant relation, are sons of God. Thus the sonship becomes a salvific and eschatological good to be acquired. This reversal of values creates a tension, between the two aspects, namely, possessing it on the title of 'Election' and 'Covenant' and meriting it on the title of 'Justice'.

The sons of God are called 'sons of his Truth' as it is the positive response to the Truth (Revelation) that makes them sons of God. An interior change from iniquity to justice is required to enter this filial relationship to God and it is worked out by the Holy Spirit through the 'Truth' and the 'Law of God'.

This peculiar concept of divine sonship is expressed in the dualistic terms 'sons of light' and 'sons of darkness'. 'Sons of light' are those who accept the revelation of God and live accordingly, while the sons of darkness are the 'unbelievers'.

---

[50] Cf. O. Betz, " Die Geburt der Gemeinde ...", p. 320.

[51] Note the parallelism between 'Thou hast made my face to shine' in v. 5 and 'Thou hast revealed thyself to me' in v. 6.

[52] Note the parallel expressions 'Thou hast made my face to shine' in v. 5 and 'Through me thou hast enlightened the face of many' in v. 27.

This divine sonship is presented also as a birth of the Community through the Teacher who communicates the revealed truth, or birth that is worked out by the Power (Spirit) of God.

CHAPTER III

The Divine Sonship of Man in Hellenism and Philo

I. In Hellenism

The Writers and Poets of the Greeks in every age — from Homer to the time of Christianity — invoke God as 'father'[1]. It is 'creator-motif' that is prominent behind this invocation[2]. It was a projection of the family concept among the Greeks, applied to the Creator. So it did not really mean a real divine sonship of man, rather it meant a total dependence on God[3].

In the Hellenistic philosophical writings there are texts referring to a kinship of man with God. Two texts of the Stoic school may be brought here in this connection. These are v. 4 of the 'Hymn of Zeus' by Cleanth " ἐκ σοῦ γὰρ γένος ἐσμέν " and v. 5 of the 'Phenomena' by Aratos " τοῦ γὰρ καὶ γένος εσμέν [4]. The " γάρ " in both hemistichs shows that here the divine origin of man is shown as the basis of prayer. Some scholars refuse to attach these expressions to a real divine sonship of man[5]. But it may refer to a concept of divine sonship marking the divine origin of man, though based on a pantheistic concept of creation. But we are interested here more in texts speaking of men clearly as 'sons of God' and of a Rebirth.

A. *Men - Sons of God*

Epictetus in particular uses many times the phrase 'son of God' and other similar expressions about men which show an idea of divine sonship. In Dissert. Book I Ch. 3:1-3 he concludes that there should

---

[1] Cf. W. MARCHEL, op. cit., p. 53 where he gives a list of such Greek Writers, and the literature concerning it.

[2] Cf. W. TWISSELMANN, op. cit., p. 10.

[3] E. des PLACES, *Syngeneia*, Paris, 1964, p. 21; G. MENSCHING, " Vatername Gottes ", *RGG* 3rd ed., Tübingen, 1962, col. 1233.

[4] For the text of the hymn cf. J. U. POWELL, in *Collectanea Alexandriana*, Oxford, 1925, pp. 227-229.

[5] Cf. for instance, M. P. NILSSON, *Geschichte der griechischen Religion*, II, 2nd ed., München, 1961, p. 689.

not be any base thought in man as a consequence of his being the son of God. The texts of Dissert. I 13:3 ; 19:9 and II 16:44 speak of a divine sonship of man resulting from the love of God and of the consequent fraternal charity. The sonship shows the " συγγένεια " of men to God (Dissert. I 9:6f) and their divine origin (II 8:11) which grant them the dignity (I 3:1-3) and freedon of children (I 19:8f ; 17:29). Man being " συγγενὴς τῷ θεῷ " (I 9:22,25) stands as " ὁ ἴδιος υἱός " to God (I 19:9). In Dissert. IV 10:14 it is God who begot man " σὺ ἐγέννησάς με ". All these are ideas that recall Jn and I Jn about divine sonship of man though, at least partially, they rest within the framework of Stoic Pantheism. But perhaps we should admit an influence of Christianity on Epictetus [6]. However in these texts there is no idea of a special personal divine sonship that elevated some above other people.

B. *Individual Sonship*

Though the sentiments of an individual and personal relation of man to God as father are expressed in general in theophoric names [7], a real individualization of the divine sonship is seen only in cases of men who distinguished themselves from other people by their wisdom or authority. It is in the case of the kings that we see mostly this individualization of sonship. The prayers of the kings throughout the various ages manifest this [8].

In the Hellenistic period, anyone believed to possess some kind of divine power was also called ' son of God '. The " θεῖος ἀνήρ " is a figure of the period [9]. Thus in popular hellenistic usage the expression υἱὸς θεοῦ reflects a certain confusion of divinity and humanity.

In more philosophico-religious circles, the absolute transcendence of the ultimate divinity was emphasized and consequently the relation of man to God required mediating essences which came to be called ' sons of God.' There the ' cosmos ' and ' Logos ' were ' sons of God '. In more spiritual circles, priests and teachers were called ' sons of

---

[6] Cf. É. DES PLACES, *Syngeneia*, pp. 156-157 where he says that Epictetus comes closer to Christianity and that the doctrine of the Ancient Stoics becomes in him Spirit and Life ; cf. also M. J. LAGRANGE, " La Philosophie Religieuse d'Epictète et la Christianisme ", *RB* 9 (1912), pp. 193-194.

[7] Cf. W. MARCHEL, op. cit., p. 20.

[8] Cf. the various examples given by W. Marchel in his book ' *Abba Père* ', p. 21-22.

[9] Cf. L. BIELER, ΘΕΙΟΣ ΑΝΗΡ, *Das Bild des göttlichen Menschen in Spätantike und Frühchristentum*, Wien, 1935-1936, 2 vols.

God'. Here generally the view was held that a man might become a 'son of God' through the 'gnosis' obtained by the mediation of the priest through a cultic rite [10].

C. Rebirth in the Mystery Religions

1. Adoption Rites in the Mystery Cults

In the Mystery Cults of the Greek the divine sonship comes through a consecration understood as a 'rebirth' or 'adoption'. In the Eleusian Mysteries, Demeter is the earth mother who gives life to all, and who alone can give a second life. They tried to ensure this life through a consecration, a sacramental act by which the initiates become the children of the goddess. From traditions we know that the sacramental act consisted in the 'mystic' touching a model of the maternal womb, a symbolic act of birth [11].

In the cults of a male divinity too, there are indications of a divine sonship, thought of in terms of a man becoming a 'child of God' through a begetting by the divinity. It is in the *Mithraic liturgy* that we find for the first time such a rite of initiation. It contains an initiation rite, which implies a new birth to immortality " ἀθανασία " (2:3) [12], " ἀθανάτῳ γενέσει " (4:7) and divine sonship " ἐγὼ γάρ εἰμι ὁ υἱός " (6:2), " πατρός μου θεοῦ " (6:12). Thus Mithras becomes the father of the initiates, and they are begotten of him, though it is to be noted that we never have an explicit affirmation of a 'birth from or begetting by God'. In the Attis and Isis mystery cults also, there are initiation ceremonies which mark the beginning of a new life through the divinity [13].

2. Regeneration in Corpus Hermeticum XIII

The Corpus Hermeticum XIII speaks of a " παλιγγενεσία " of the mystic. The word is composed of " πάλιν " and " γίνεσθαι " meaning etymologically 'restoration' or a 'new beginning'. Till the Hermetic usage, it had no meaning of 'rebirth'. It had other meanings such as 'world restoration after the cyclic conflagration', 'reincarnation of the soul in the body' etc. In C.H. XIII different terms are used to signify the rebirth such as : " παλιγγενεσία " (7b, 10, 13a, 16, 22b),

---

[10] Cf. C. H. XIII, 2 where Hermes himself is called Θεός Θεοῦ παῖς who mediates the same thing to Tat who also is going to be a παῖς Θεοῦ.

[11] Cf. O. KERN, *Die Religion der Griechen*, Berlin, 1935, II, p. 193.

[12] The references here are according to the pages and lines as given in A. DIETERICH, *Eine Mithrasliturgie*, 2nd ed., Leipzig, 1910.

[13] Cf. W. TWISSELMANN, op. cit., pp. 18-20 where he speaks of these ceremonies as found in the Attis and Isis cults.

"γένεσις ἐν θεῷ" (6a), "γένεσις τῆς θεότητος" (7a), "ἀνεγεννήθην ἐν νῷ" (v. 3)[14], "ὁ γεννώμενος" (v. 2) "τῆς κατὰ θεὸν γενέσεως" (v. 10) etc. All these show that in the C.H. it is a matter of a rebirth effected by God.

a) Description of the Regeneration

C.H. XIII has 3 parts : 1-8a, the teacher describes the rebirth ; 8b-14, the pupil experiences it ; 15-20, they give thanks to God for it.
The doctrine of ' rebirth ' is not to be taught until one is ready to experience it. And the condition of experiencing it is ' alienation from the material world ', and ' alienation of the thoughts of the heart from the world's deceptions '. It is an indispensable condition for salvation. It is not a new creation, but a new begetting to the status of a child of God (cf. the words μήτρα (womb), πατήρ (father) σπόρα (seed) etc)[15]. The minister who mediates it is also a son of God reborn in the same way. ' Teaching ' and ' experiencing ' of the rebirth are not clearly distinguished. It is a wonder that takes place solely by the mercy of God. Human teaching is merely an occasion for it to happen[16]. It is a rebirth in mind (ἐν νῷ) and is mediated through a spiritual vision (ἄπλαστον θέαν). In this new birth man passes to a new self — ' an immortal body ' — composed of divine δυνάμεις, which can be seen only with the eyes of the mind. This regeneration supposes the death of the old man ' I am no longer what I was '. This mystical experience causes an ethical change.

The 12 vices (τιμωρίαι) which trouble man are expelled by the 10 virtues, (δυνάμεις θεοῦ), which constitute the new man, the divine logos in us. He sees things hereafter with the eye of the mind. He finds himself one with all that exists. He feels himself to be omnipresent and eternal. The new self is imperishable.

---

[14] It is much discussed, whether the word ἀναγεννᾶν belongs to the traditional text or not. FESTUGIERE gives ἐγεννήθην. F. BÜCHSEL in his art ἀναγεννάω in *TDNT* I, p. 673 says that ἀναγεννᾶν here is a conjecture made by SCOTT and REITZENSTEIN influenced by the NT. However we cannot deny that it was a current word at that time, though the genuineness of its technical meaning as seen in C. H. XIII is to be doubted.

[15] It is interesting to note here that the divine sonship through this regeneration is expressed only through παῖς and otherwise only once in another context expressed by υἱοί in plural, which in the singular is used only for λόγος. But τέκνον is used only to express the human relationship, which is the technical term for John to express the divine sonship.

[16] Cf. W. SCOTT, *Hermetica*, Oxford, 1925, vol. II, p. 379.

b) Characteristics of this Regeneration

It is *Pantheistic*: In the highest rapture, the initiated calls " Father, I see the whole (all) and myself in the intellect ". The Pantheistic character is clear too from the fact that the ' Logos ' that constitutes the essence of the new man is ' son of God ' because he comes forth from God (C.H. I, 6).

It is *essentially Gnostic*: It takes place through the recalling of the doctrine to the mind. The final result is the self-knowledge and the knowledge of God. The rebirth is an illumination and the light received is knowledge (C.H. XIII, 18) and it is God himself, who dwells in the man and becomes the spiritual eye of the man and transforms the essence of man.

It is *essentially connected with salvation and morality*: The rebirth is effected once for all. He is ' Reason ', ' Logos ' himself and hence cannot sin any more. If he sins it is only in appearance, not real. He is identified with God — παῖς θεοῦ θεός (C.H. XIII 2,14).

Conclusion

Unlike the Biblical notion, in Hellenism it is the initiative of man to infer a father-son relationship between himself and God, transferring the human relationship to the divine.

The title of the divine sonship is a total dependence on God as regards his essence and existence, a dependence connected with creation and providence. Though there are ideas similar to those found in Jn and I Jn, they are found mostly within the framework of Stoic Pantheism.

There is no real personal divine sonship of man as such. Only some intermediaries between God and man as kings, priests, wise men etc. are called ' sons of God ' and that in the sense of a ' divine man '.

In the mystery cults rebirth is stressed, but in terms of a divinization. The birth takes place, so to say, magically through the divine intervention, and the part played by the individual is reduced to a minimum. The renovation that takes place in man is of a mystical order and not properly ethical. The ethics mentioned are within a strongly cosmological speculation.

No mystery religion speaks explicitly of a ' birth from God ' γεννᾶσθαι ἐκ τοῦ θεοῦ which gives him a real sonship of God, but a birth through God which divinizes him.

II. In Philo

The naming of God as 'Father' is frequent in the Writings of Philo. As regards the terms that express the father-son relationship between God and man, Philo proceeds rather in the line of the Greek Writers, except that he makes use of the terminology of a begetting by God, when speaking of creation (cf. Spec. Leg. II, 30ff; III, 189; Op Mund 84). The divine sonship of man in Philo, however, does not rest on this begetting by God or on this common paternity of God.

A. Men - Sons of God

1. Sons of God: Those Who Serve God

That which properly constitutes the divine sonship of man in Philo is a kinship based on a common belief, which is of greater dignity and sanctity than kinship based on bodily descendence (Spec. Leg. I, 58. 317) [17]. It is this kinship that he sees in the title 'sons of God' given by Holy Scriptures to 'those who do what is pleasing to God' (Spec. Leg. I, 318). This means that for Philo divine sonship does not belong to all men without distinction. It is the privilege of those who are willing to serve God, and is constituted by this readiness to serve God (Spec. Leg. I, 317).

But it is not enough to serve God in any way, but in a manner prescribed by the Law of Moses, since Israel was the model of this service of God. Israel became capable of seeing God and becoming 'sons of God' from this habit of serving God (Congr 10,51; Post. Cain. 26,92; De Sacr. 36,120) [18].

2. Sons of God: Those Who Have The Knowledge of God

In Conf. Ling. 145 'the sons of God' are those who have knowledge of the 'One' and are identified with 'Israel' whom Moses calls in Dt. 14:1 and 32:6,18 'sons of God'. This knowledge, however, does not divinize them, as does the vision of God in Hellenism. In De Praem 43-45 this knowledge of God is presented as a vision of God in which man has a mystical awareness of the Absolute Being. Here he brings in Israel with its name 'seer of God' "ὁρῶν θεόν" [19].

---

[17] Cf. H. A. WOLFSON, *Philo*, Cambridge, 1948, vol. II, p. 357.

[18] Cf. H. A. WOLFSON, op. cit., p. 358.

[19] Cf. Conf. Ling. 92 where it is said that 'Israel alone has the right to contemplate God' and Conf. Ling. 144 where Israel is called the 'race that sees' "τὸ ὁρατικὸν γένος".

This sonship is necessarily adoptive, because by this they acquire something natural only to the angels [20].

3. *Sons of God*: *Those Who Worship and Love God*

Worship is also a constitutional element of divine sonship in Philo. In Conf. Ling. 142-145 after speaking of the 'sons of men' who are polytheists, he speaks about the 'sons of God' who do recognise and worship the one true God [21]. 'Love of God' also plays its role in this sonship; it is characteristic of the wise to love God and thus be worthy of this noble birth. God becomes to them as father and they are adopted by God as sons (De Sobr 55-56).

B. *Logos - Mediator of The Divine Sonship*

Since it is the knowledge of God that makes man son of God, it is through the mediation of Logos, the first-born Son of God, that one becomes a son of God. Conf. Ling. 146 says: " If there be any as yet unfit to be called son of God, let him be eager to be ranked on the side of His First-born, the Logos ... If we have not yet become fit to be ... children of God, at least we are children of his eternal image, ... Logos ".

This is so because the Logos, the First-born of God is the same logos who is a transcendent 'heavenly man' above us " λόγος ἐνδιάθετος ", and who is also immanent 'real man' in us " λόγος προφορικός ", and this fact gives man a kinship with the universal Logos. This kinship enables him to rise to the knowledge of God by communion with the Logos, and thus to the condition as son of God [22].

C. *Divine Sonship And Spiritual Birth*

The idea of a spiritual begetting of man by God, symbolized in the mystery of the generation of Isaac is seen in Philo. Speaking of the Covenant of God with Isaac in Qu. in Gen. III, 60 he says: " The birth of Isaac is not a birth that belongs to the actual temporal life, but a birth that belongs to another great, holy, sacred and divine life ". Somn. I, 173 distinguishes the status of Isaac as a 'son begotten by God the Father' from that of Abraham as a 'disciple instructed by God the guide'. Leg. All. III, 219 says: " The Lord

---

[20] Cf. Quest. in Gen I, 66, 92 where the wise are compared to the angels in this respect.

[21] Cf. R. ARNALDEZ, *Les oeuvres de Philon d'Alexandrie*, Paris, 1963, vol. 13, p. 177.

[22] Cf. C. H. DODD, *The Interpretation of the Fourth Gospel*, Cambridge, 1965, pp. 70-71.

has begotten Isaac; for it is he, who is the father of the perfect nature, who sows in the soul and begets joy". In Mut. Nom 131 this joy and divine sonship are identified: "Isaac who will be born... will be joy... the immanent son of God... who gives it to the most pacific souls". Thus Isaac becomes the symbol of the divine sonship (joy) given by God to souls. Elsewhere he speaks of a σπείρειν of God the Father in the soul (Vit. Contem. 68) [23]. This joy (sonship) comes unexpectedly from God and takes man in a rapture that is not foreseen (Migr. Ab. 140, 142). So here we have a kind of mystical generation that is the work of God as Father [24] of which Isaac is the symbol.

Conclusion

The divine sonship of man in Philo is inspired by both Jewish and Hellenistic elements. It is essentially adoptive and is obtained through the knowledge of God, which culminates in a mystical experience of God, which however is accompanied by elements of worship, love and service of the true God.

This sonship is possible for man only through the mediation of Logos, who is the Firs-born Son of God, because it is the communion with the Logos that gives him the knowledge of God.

A spiritual begetting through the power of God, which transforms the soul giving it a perfect nature similar to that of God is attested by him and is personified in the figure of Isaac.

---

[23] Cf. F. BÜCHSEL, art. "γεννάω", *TDNT* I, p. 669, where he sees behind this σπείρειν of God the wisdom of the Mysteries.

[24] Cf. A. BRÉHIER, *Les idées philosophiques de Philon d'Alexandrie*, Paris, 1925, p. 234.

CHAPTER IV

The Divine Sonship of Christians in the Synoptic Gospels

After having analysed the pre-Johannine background of the concept of divine sonship of man in the OT, Later Judaism, Hellenism and Philo, now we come to examine the NT background, specially, in the Synoptics and in St. Paul. First we take the Synoptic Gospels. In the Synoptics, we find two series of texts connected with the doctrine on the divine sonship of man: one, texts speaking of God as the 'Father' in relation to the believers [1], and the other, texts speaking of men as 'sons of God' [2]. There are also other texts where the father-son relationship between God and man is implicitly affirmed. The main object of our study here are the texts speaking explicitly of men as 'sons of God: namely Mt 5:9,45; Lk 6:35 and 20:36.

I. Sons of God: Peacemakers (Mt 5:9)

A. *Matthean Redaction*

Mt 5:9 says "Blessed are the peacemakers, for they shall be called sons of God". There is no parallel for Mt 5:9 in the other gospels and εἰρηνοποιός is hapax in the whole New Testament [3]. On the other hand, the theme of peace, the verb καλέω and the expression 'sons of God' are all characteristic of Lk [4]. And this beatitude composed of words of Lukan preference is not found in Lk. All these indicate that it is a purely redactional work of Matthew [5]. The moral character of three beatitudes concerning the 'merciful',

---

[1] Cf. Mt 5:16,45,48; 6:1,4,6,8,9,14,15,18,26,32; 7:11; 10:20,29; 13:43; 23:9; 28:19; Mk 11:25,26; Lk 6:36; 11:2,13; 12:30,32.
[2] Cf. Mt 5:9,45 (Lk 6:35); Lk 20:36.
[3] The corresponding verb εἰρηνοποιέω is found in Col 1:20.
[4] The noun εἰρήνη occurs in Mt 4 times, in Mk once, in Jn 6 times, in Lk 13 times and in Acts 7 times, while the verb καλέω occurs in Mt 27 times, in Mk 3 times, in Jn 3 times, in Lk 42 times and in Acts 16 times; 'sons of God' occurs apart from here only in Lk 20:36 and 6:35.
[5] Cf. J. Dupont, *Les béatitudes*, Louvain, 1958, pp. 258-259.

'pure of heart' and the 'peacemakers' that are absent in Luke also points to the Matthean redactional character [6].

B. *Analysis of the Text*

1. εἰρηνοποιοί : '*Peacemakers*'

Some understand it as those who are ready for peace and forgiveness [7] while others understand it as those who make peace among others [8]. However, the word is not εἰρηνικός (cf. Jam 3:17 ; Hb 12: 11) which could be translated as 'peaceable', but εἰρηνοποιός which refers to the one who makes peace [9]. In Judaism such peacemaking was highly esteemed and such peacemakers were promised great blessings [10].

a. Messianic Peace

In the Old Testament the Messianic kingdom is a kingdom of peace and the Messiah, a prince of peace [11]. Is 52:7 identifies peace with a salvation and reign of God : "'How beautiful are the feet of ... who publishes peace ... salvation ..., says to Zion 'your God reigns'".

In the New Testament also God is the 'God of Peace' (I Thes 5:23 ; Phil 4:9) and Christ's work is to bring peace (Lk 2:14 ; Jn 14: 27 ; Col 1:20). In Lk 19:42-45 Jesus says of Jerusalem that rejects his work, "she did not know on this day that which is for her peace ... the time of her visitation".

Christ brought peace, establishing peace between God and man and making men a family of God in which peace reigns between the members (cf. Eph 2:14f). It is the making of this peace that is meant here. So those who participate in the work of the Messiah — the peace making, participate in his dignity also — the divine sonship [12].

---

[6] Cf. J. SCHMID, *Das Evangelium nach Matthäus*, Ratisbonne, 1956, (3rd ed.), p. 76.

[7] Cf. J. WELLHAUSEN, *Das Evangelium Matthaei*, Berlin, 1914, p. 14.

[8] Cf. B. WEISS, *Das Matthäus-Evangelium*, Göttingen, 1898, p. 94 ; P. BONNARD, *L'Evangile selon saint Matthieu*, Neuchâtel, 1963, pp. 57-58 ; W. GRUNDMANN, *Das Evangelium nach Matthäus*, Berlin, 1968, p. 131.

[9] Cf. W. BAUER, *A Greek English Lexicon*, Chicago, 1957, p. 227.

[10] Cf. Str. Bill., I, 215-218 ; H. WINDISCH, " Friedensbringer-Göttessöhne, Eine religionsgeschichtliche Interpretation der 7. Seligpreisung " *ZNW* 24 (1925), pp. 241-251.

[11] Cf. Ps 72:3,7 ; Is 9:6,7 ; 26:3,12 ; 32:17 ; 52:7 ; 54:10,13 ; 60:17 ; 66:12 ; Jer 33:6,9 ; Ez 34:25 ; 37:26 ; Mich 4:3 ; 5:5 ; Hag 2:10 ; Zach 6:13 ; 9:10.

[12] Cf. W. GRUNDMANN, *Das Evangelium nach Matthäus*, Berlin, 1968, p. 132:

b. 'Peacemakers': the Merciful

The three beatitudes of Matthean origin (Mt 5:7-9) form a triad in which 'purity of heart' stands in the centre referring back and forth to the two beatitudes of the social character, which are parallels. So the peacemaking is something that is parallel to the activity of showing mercy. In Mt men are called merciful only here in 5:7. That shows that this mercy is not simply a human feeling, but something divine. The ἐλεήμων in the OT is above all God (Ps 86:5 ; 145-8f etc.). God shows his mercy above all by forgiving those who offended him (Ps 78:38 ; 103:8f ; 121:7f). Jesus showed by his life, words and deeds what it meant to be merciful (Mt 9:36 ; 20:28). It means a new type of human existence with concrete acts of merciful love towards all including the sinners and enemies. So the peacemaker is a man who is capable of new attitudes that reverse entirely the ordinary course of the fallen human nature which lets itself be led by desires leading to all sorts of conflicts [13]. It is such an existence that was realized in Christ and that made peace between God and man and among men themselves. This 'peacemaking' and 'being merciful' seem to be again concretely expressed in the 'love of enemies' spoken of in Mt 5:45. The fact that Mt speaks of the divine sonship of man again in that context shows that 'peace-making' and 'loving enemies' are interrelated and mutually explanatory.

2. 'They shall be called sons of God'

What is the specific relation that exists between peacemaking and divine sonship ? Some see the divine sonship simply as a reward in the kingdom of God [14], while others see in it the sign of being the object of God's love (Gottgeliebtheit) [15]. Again some others see in it a similarity to God, a similarity that should exist between the Father and his children [16]. The fact of being a reward, in itself, does not go against the similarity of nature implied. Since God is the God of

---

" Friedenstiftung und Sohnschaft (vgl. 1, 21, 23 ; 2, 15 ; 3, 17) sind Werk des Messias und teilen darum seine Würde ".

[13] Cf. J. COMBLIN, Théologie de la paix, 1960, pp. 196-201.

[14] Cf. J. WELLHAUSEN, Das Evangelium Matthaei, p. 14.

[15] Cf. B. WEISS, Das Matthäus Evangelium, p. 94.

[16] Cf. H. WINDISCH, art. cit., p. 259 : " Als vermittelnder Begriff ist also der Gedanke der Nachahmung Gottes oder der Ähnlichkeit mit Gott in die Interpretation einzulegen " ; W. GRUNDMANN, Das Evangelium nach Matthäus, p. 132 : " Das Wort ' Sohn ' bezeichnet dabei die Analogie mit und die Genealogie aus Gott in Sein und Wirken ".

peace, and his kingdom a kingdom of peace, the idea of similarity seems to lie behind this sonship [17].

The verb καλεῖσθαι stands for εἶναι or γενέσθαι (cf. Dt 14:1 ; Mt 5:19 ; Mk 11:17) [18]. It is a thoroughly Hebraic concept that the name reveals and is identical with one's nature and that sons are those who share in their father's nature (Mt 23:31 ; Jn 8:39, 41f ; Apoc 21:7 etc.).

II. Sons of God — Those who love their enemies (Mt 5:43-48; Lk 6: 27-28, 32-36)

A. " Love your enemies ..." (Mt 5:44)

Out of the 8 occurrences of ἀγαπᾶν in Mt, five come in the Sermon on the Mount, the Charter of the Kingdom. The Law in the New Kingdom is the law of love [19]. In Mt God is mentioned as 'father of men' almost exclusively in the Sermon on the Mount. So Mt sees the morality of the New Kingdom as a filial morality consisting in love.

In the context of Mt, the enemies seem to be the enemies (persecutors) of the Messianic Community formed by the early Christians [20]. In the LXX the word ἐχθρός usually refers to the enemies of the people of God (Ps 31:7 ; 139:21 etc.). The allusion to 'persecutors' in v. 44 also points to the same. The Epistles of the NT also testify to this usage of the word (2 Th 3:15 ; Rom 5:10 ; Col 1:21 ; Jam 4:4). Though it is concretely the enemies of the Community that are intended here in Mt they simply represent all the enemies in general. In fact the parallel text in Lk 6:27-28 has brought out the individual and universal aspect of this love of enemies.

This love does not mean absence of hatred or vengeance but love of living Communion expressed in concrete actions of praying for them (Mt 5:44), saluting them (Mt 5:47) and doing good to them (Lk 6:27). The phrase καὶ προσεύχεσθε does not mean that prayer is the only expression of this love. The καί is not explanatory. It means 'in particular' [21].

---

[17] Cf. H. WINDISCH, art. cit., p. 246 : " Während ... der Gedanke, dass Gott der grosse Friedenstifter in aller Welt ist, vom AT her dem Judentum geläufig geworden und geblieben ist, so dass unsere Seligpreisung, wenn man den Begriff der Gottähnlichkeit hineinschiebt sofort verstanden werden konnte ...".

[18] Cf. E. KLOSTERMANN, Das Matthäus-Evangelium, Tübingen, 1927, p. 38.

[19] Note the imperative mood of ἀγαπᾶτε in 4 of the 5 instances.

[20] Cf. W. FOERSTER, art. " ἐχθρός " TDNT II, pp. 811f.

[21] Cf. P. BONNARD, L'évangile selon saint Matthieu, Neuchâtel, 1963, p. 73.

B. *God the model and exemplar of this Love* (Mt 5:45b)

1. *Love of the Father*

Mt 5:45b 'Who makes his sun rise ... unjust' shows God the Father as the exemplar of a universal and disinterested love. In the Synoptics ἀγαπᾶν is usually used to express the relation of man to man, and not of God to man. God is always spoken of as 'merciful' (Lk 1:50, 54, 58, 78 ; 6:36 etc.). And here we see the new aspect of the new order established by Christ, namely, the order of merciful love. Jesus brings forgiveness of sins, expression of God's merciful love and in those who experience it, a similar love is released. This is expressed in the words of Jesus in Lk 7:47 " He who is forgiven little, loves little ". The episode in Lk 7:36-50 points to a communication of the pardoning love of God to the justified sons of God which should animate their whole life. Note the absolute use of ἀγαπᾶν in this passage, meaning that the person has now a new life — ' love '.

It is this relationship of God to man that lays the foundation for a new relationship of man to man. Constantly needing to ask forgiveness for his sins presupposes in him a constant readiness to forgive (Mt 5:7 ; 18 : 21 ; Lk 11:4). In the Lord's Prayer, after imploring forgiveness of one's sins, the demand for a forgiving charitable heart immediately follows (Mt 6:14-15 ; Mk 11:25). This solidarity between the heavenly Father and his children is manifested in the fact that in Mk this is the only place where we have the phrase ' Your Father who is in heaven '. The parable of the unmerciful servant also teaches the same (Mt 18:23-25) [22].

2. *Perfection of the Father* (*Mt 5:48*)

" You therefore must be perfect as your heavenly Father is perfect ". Here it is the merciful and pardoning love that is presented as the perfection of the Father that is to be imitated by his children. This is clear first of all from the structure of the section Mt 5:44-48.

a. Structure of Mt 5:44-48.

V. 44 A   LOVE your enemies and pray for ... who persecute you ...
45   B   So that YOU BECOME sons of YOUR FATHER IN HEAVEN who makes his ... on the evil and the good ...
46-47 A'   If you LOVE ... what reward ... If you salute ... what more ...

---

[22] Cf. C. SPICQ, *Agape in the New Testament*, (trans. from the French without footnotes), vol. I, London, 1963, p. 54.

48 B'   So YOU BE perfect as YOUR FATHER IN HEAVEN is perfect.

According to this structure, B' (v. 48) develops the same idea of B (v. 45) in different words. The parallelism between ' Your Father ... who makes his ... on the unjust ' in v. 45 and ' Your Father is perfect ' in v. 48 shows that the perfection of God consists in his pardoning and disinterested love.

b. Comparison with Lk 6:36

A comparison with the parallel statement in Lk 6:36 ' Be merciful even as your Father is merciful ' proves the same. Οἰκτιρμός in Lk seems to be more original [23], because τέλειος is nowhere applied to God in the Bible except here. On the contrary, οἰκτιρμός is applied to God 12 times in the OT and only once to man. Being a divine attribute οἰκτιρμός is quite in keeping with the pardoning love of the Father, characteristic of the Synoptics. Lk invites Christians to imitate a quality proper to God, while Mt invites them to have a quality proper to man, but applied to God, starting from the ideal proposed to the disciple. This difference is on account of the immediate context. In Lk it comes immediately after Jesus has spoken of the conduct of God, while in Mt other considerations intervene (vv. 46-47) and v. 48 forms a conclusion to the whole section of the 6 antitheses going back to the introduction [24]. So, though the accent is different, the concept is the same.

C. *" That you may become sons of your Father in Heaven "* (Mt 5:45a)

' So that you may become sons ' of Mt 5:45 orientates the idea towards a real sonship implying a similarity of nature with the Father. He who loves his enemy will conduct himself as a son of God, will be recognised as such and will be that effectively.

1. *Argument from the structure*

As in the structure the τέλειος of v. 48b (B') is parallel to and therefore refers to the merciful love of God the Father in v. 45b (B)

---

[23] Cf. G. BARTH, in *Überlieferung und Auslegung im Matthäus Evangelium*, Neukirchen, 1960, 90; For a comparative study of Mt 5:48 with Lk 6:36 cf. D. LÜHRMANN, " Liebet eure Feinde (Lk 6:27-36 - Mt 5:39-48) ", *ZTK* 69 (1972), pp. 412-438.

[24] Cf. J. DUPONT, " Soyez parfaits " Mt 5:48, " Soyez miséricordieux " Lk 6:36, in *SacPag* II, 1959, pp. 150-160.

so the τέλειοι of v. 48a (B') is parallel to the 'sons of the Father' in v. 45 a (B) and therefore refers to them as having the same merciful love [25]. Some find here really a theology of 'agape' [26] as we present it here, while others see in it the perfection of a specifically legal nature [27]. But both could be reduced to the same, because for Mt the fulfilment of Law is in Love.

2. τέλειος in Mt

This is clear from the use of the word τέλειος in Mt. He uses the word only in two places, namely, here and in Mt 19:21. In both contexts he begins by speaking of the commandments (5:44-45 ; 19:19) and ends with a call to perfection (5:48 ; 19:21). Note the expression 'follow me', which runs parallel to the call of perfection in 19:21 which is an invitation to imitate Christ whose life was a giving himself up for his enemies - sinners. Hence the 'perfection' is the highest form of charity expressed in the 'love of enemies'.

3. ὡς ὁ πατὴρ ὑμῶν (Mt 5:48)

This phrase seems to stand in apposition to the ὡς σεαυτόν of Lev. 19:18 which is understood in Mt 5:43 [28]. The child of God rises above the ordinary human level, namely, loving others as himself, and loves others as God loves them (Mt 5:45) and thus acquires a perfection analogous to God his Father [29]. Hence the divine sonship certainly points to a community of nature and life with God. From love of enemies, the concrete expression of this divine love, which should animate our relations with other men, will emerge a resemblance to the Father, and our divine sonship will be actually in proportion to this resemblance to Him.

D. Ὅπως γένησθε (Mt 5:45)

There is a discussion as to whether the divine sonship of man affirmed here is static [30], namely, only a possessed sonship to be

---

[25] Cf. C. Spicq, *Agapè dans le Nouveau Testament*, I, p. 26 : " La double répétition de τέλειος accentue l'assimilation de l'homme à Dieu, de l'enfant à son Père, par l'amour ".

[26] Cf. C. Spicq, *Agapè dans le Nouveau Testament*, I, pp. 24-34.

[27] Cf. J. Dupont, *Les béatitudes*, p. 152.

[28] Cf. Mt 19:19 ; 22:39 where it is said explicitly.

[29] Cf. A. Plummer, *An Exegetical Commentary on the Gospel according to St. Matthew*, London, 1928, p. 89 : " To return evil for good is devilish ; to return good for good is human ; to return good for evil is divine ".

[30] Cf. St. Thomas, *Super Evangelium S. Matthaei Lectura*, a cura di R. Cai, Torino, 1951, p. 85 ; Th. Zahn, *Das Evangelium des Matthäus*, 4th ed., Leipzig,

demonstrated, or dynamic [31], namely, a sonship that is gradually brought to perfection. The verb γίνεσθαι is frequently used in Mt as in the other Synoptics instead of εἶναι (Mt 6:16; 10:16; 24:44). But this does not mean that it has the same sense everywhere [32]. In this context the sense and the form are different from that in the above mentioned texts.

1. γίνεσθαι *in Mt 18:1-4*

In Mt 18:1-4 the same verb comes in the same tense and mood. A structural division of this text will show the dynamic character of γίνεσθαι.

Vv. 1-2   A   The disciples ... who IS THE GREATEST IN THE KINGDOM OF HEAVEN ? ...

3   B   Unless ... be converted and become LIKE a CHILD

     C   YOU WILL NOT ENTER THE KINGDOM OF HEAVEN

4   B′   Whoever humbles himself LIKE this CHILD

     A′   He IS THE GREATEST IN THE KINGDOM OF HEAVEN

The v. 4 is Matthean creation, as it has no parallel in Mk. It repeats in a positive form what was said negatively in v. 3 and rounds off the paragraph making an 'inclusion'. In this structure 'Entering the Kingdom' is the fundamental issue and the two parallel statements in BB′ express the disposition required. Now both these statements in BB′ contain dynamic elements. The 'be converted' (στραφῆτε) shows a fundamental change from one condition to another that is implied in the verb γένησθε [33]. The term στρέφω in Mt is always used to show a turning towards something or someone (cf. 5:39; 7:6; 9:22; 16:23; 27:3). The parallelism of this text with Jn 3:5 shows also the relevance of this dynamic change to the divine sonship of man.

1922, pp. 253-257; A. PLUMMER, *An Exegetical Commentary on the Gospel according to St. Matthew*, p. 88; J. SCHNIEWIND, *Das Evangelium nach Matthäus*, Göttingen, 1954, pp. 71-72.

[31] Cf. J. CHRYSOSTOM, PG 57, 268ff; M. J. LAGRANGE, *Évangile selon S. Matthieu*, 3rd ed. Paris, 1927, p. 97; P. BONNARD, *Évangile selon S. Matthieu*, pp. 74ff; W. GRUNDMANN, *Das Evangelium nach Matthäus*, p. 177; J. SCHMID, *Das Evangelium nach Matthäus*, p. 112; Th. SOIRON, *Die Bergpredigt Jesu*, Freiburg, 1941, pp. 295-302.

[32] Some authors give the texts using γίνεσθαι for εἶναι as exemplar for a static explanation of γένησθε in Mt 5:45. Cf. A. PLUMMER, op. cit., p. 87.

[33] Cf. P. BONNARD, *Évangile selon S. Matthieu*, p. 268.

The 'ταπεινώσει' of B' which is parallel to 'becoming like a child' of B also shows this dynamism [34]. In the Synoptics ταπεινώσει signifies a concrete service of God and neighbour (cf. Mt 23:12; Lk 18:14) [35] which comes near to the 'love of enemies' proposed by Mt 5:44-45 to become sons of God.

2. Dynamism of γένησθε in Mt 5:43-48

In the section Mt 5:43-48 itself there is a movement from v. 45 to v. 48. He who loves his enemies as God loves them, will be (ἔσεσθε-future) perfect (note the οὖν concluding the section), and thus he arrives at the end indicated in the movement that began in γένησθε of v. 45. If love of enemies is an obligation of sonship, the integrity and plenitude of sonship is acquired only by the exercise of it, so as to resemble perfectly the heavenly Father and thus tending towards the eschatological perfection of the sonship [36].

This dynamic character is expressed also in the idea of reward "μισθός" in Mt 5:46. In Lk 6:35b the μισθός is identified with sonship: "Your reward will be great, you will be sons of the Most High". So the reward is something inevitable in the nature of the case. This connection appears in I Pet 2:21; 3:9 'Do not return evil for evil, but bless ... that you may obtain a blessing' [37]. So the 'reward' is to become sons of God through the love of enemies.

III. Sons of God — Sons of the Resurrection (Lk 20:36)

In Lk 20:36 the sons of God are said to be the 'sons of the resurrection'. Some take the 'sons of God' simply for being in the

---

[34] This parallelism is defended by J. DUPONT, in his article on Mt 18:3 in *Neotestamentica et Semitica*, Studies in honour of Mathew Black, Edinburgh, 1969, p. 59; cf. also S. LEGASSE, *Jésus et L'enfant*, Paris, 1969, pp. 215-231.

[35] Cf. P. BONNARD, *L'Évangile selon S. Matthieu*, p. 337 speaking of Mt. 23:12 "L'idée d'abaissement dans le v. 12 doit être interprétée par celle de service du v. 11"; W. GRUNDMANN, *Das Evangelium nach Matthäus*, p. 487 speaking of humility in 23:12 says: "Nur im bruderschaftlichen Helfen, in dem sich einer dem anderen zum Diener macht, erfüllt der Jünger den willen Gottes und gewinnt die rechte Stellung zu ihm, die Gott — im Passiv verborgen — mit Erhöhung beantwortet".

[36] Cf. W. GRUNDMANN, *Das Evangelium nach Matthäus*, pp. 177-178, where speaking of becoming sons of God in Mt 5:45 he says: "Als Kinder dieses Vaters, die seine reifen Söhne zu werden bestimmt sind, wachsen sie zu dieser eschatologischen Reife, in dem sie in ihrem Handeln den Menschen gegenüber das Handeln Gottes abbilden".

[37] Cf. E. M. SIDEBOTTOM, art. "μισθόν" in Mt 5,46", *ET* 67 (1956), pp. 219ff.

natural condition befitting the angels as sons of God (Ps 89:7; Job 2:1)[38]. Others put emphasis on the υἱοί ' children ' in contradistinction to those grown up, who marry or are married[39]. Again some take the καὶ υἱοί εἰσιν Θεοῦ as an anticipation of thought of the next section, explaining it as ' the sons of the resurrection live unto God as their Father '[40].

A. Lukan Redaction

Here in Lk καὶ υἱοί εἰσιν[41] is redactional and has an important role in the argument. The expressions " οἱ υἱοὶ τοῦ αἰῶνος τούτου " and " ὁ αἰὼν ἐκεῖνος " are found only in Lk in the whole NT. The υἱοὶ τῆς ἀναστάσεως is hapax in the NT. For καταξιόω and τυγχάνω there are no parallels in the NT. So the Lukan character of this section is evident. Perhaps Lk had a special source for the pericope.

B. Literary Structure

We present here a structure of the section Lk 20:34-36 which will help us to see better the intention of Lk in his redactional work.

V. 34 A The sons OF this AGE
   B MARRY AND ARE GIVEN IN MARRIAGE
 35 A'a But those ... OF that AGE
    b AND to THE RESURRECTION from the dead
   B' Neither MARRY NOR ARE GIVEN IN MARRIAGE ...
 36 A²a' Because they are equal to angels
    b' AND are sons of God being sons of THE RESURRECTION

The ἰσάγγελοι (v. 36), hapax in the whole Bible, is the Lukan redaction of ὡς ἄγγελοι. The answer to the Sadducees was over by this phrase as seen from the other Synoptics. By introducing ἰσάγγελοι which is less clear than ὡς ἄγγελοι and adding ' καὶ υἱοί εἰσιν ... ' the accent in Lk is shifted to the divine sonship. In the structural recomposition of Lk A' corresponds to A. In these corresponding

---

[38] Cf. N. GELDENHUYS, *Commentary on the Gospel of Luke*, London, 1954, ad loc.; B. RIGAUX, *Temoignage de l'évangile de Luc*, Louvain, 1970, p. 280.

[39] Cf. J. DILLERSBERGER, *Lukas*, Wien, 1942, vol. VI, p. 71.

[40] Cf. J. M. CREED, *The Gospel according to St. Luke*, London, 1957, ad. loc.

[41] Certain Mss such as D 157 it Syr sin and Marcion do not give the καὶ υἱοί εἰσιν. But this omission could be explained as ' homoeotheleuton '. All the important Mss give it. So the genuineness of the phrase is to be admitted.

texts, again the οἱ δὲ καταξιωθέντες (a) corresponds to the ἰσάγγελοι (a') (the traditional matter) and the καὶ τῆς ἀναστάσεως (b) corresponds to καὶ υἱοί εἰσιν Θεοῦ (b') (the redactional matter). The b seems to be an explanation of a. But the b' seems to be more than a mere explanation of a'. The repetition of εἰσιν is a sign against a merely explanatory interpretation [42]. There seems to be a progress in argument and the ' καὶ υἱοί εἰσιν Θεοῦ ...' seems to contain the final basis of the argument in vv. 35-36.

C. *Analysis of the Text*

The particle ὄντες in v. 36 is very significant. It is in as much as they are 'sons of the resurrection' namely, they belong to God and the resurrection (note the parallelism between b and b'), that they are 'sons of God' and 'equal to the angels' and the consequent 'immortality' and the 'non-marriage'. Thus the resurrection becomes the cause and condition of the 'divine sonship' and the 'equality to the angels' [43]. It is only here that the divine sonship is explicitly connected with the resurrection in the whole NT. In the theology of Lk, resurrection is an eschatological good of great importance promised by God (Lk 7:22; 14:14; Acts 13:30-34; 25:8) and is already a reality in Christ (Lk 24:6,32; Acts 1:22; 2:31; 13:30-34), which is the hope and pledge of our resurrection (Acts 3:15,26; 23:6 " πρῶτος ἐξ ἀναστάσεως ").

In Lk the resurrection is inseparable from the kingdom of God (Lk 14:14) which he calls 'eternal life' (Lk 10:25; 18:18). So it is the culmination of this eternal life that is affirmed in the sons of God at the resurrection. It is by possessing the culmination of this divine life that the sons of God are similar to the angels and immortal, denying thereby the necessity of marriage in the age to come.

Thus we have here an affirmation of the eschatological glorious state of the life of the sons of God. As Christ was installed in power as the Son of God by his resurrection (Acts 13:33; Rom 1:4) those possessing the eternal life, belonging to the kingdom of God (Lk 10:25; 18:18), will also be sons of God in the full sense of the term at the resurrection.

---

[42] Cf. A. PLUMMER, *The Gospel according to St. Luke*, (ICC), 5th ed., Edinburgh, 1964, p. 470.

[43] Cf. W. GRUNDMANN, *Das Evangelium nach Lukas*, Berlin, 1961, p. 375: " ... sie sind Gottes Söhne und haben damit Gottes Art. In diese Art werden sie durch die Auferstehung umgeschaffen ".

D. Other Eschatological references on Sonship

The future κληθήσονται of Mt 5:9 points to this eschatological aspect of sonship. The verb κληθήσονται is virtually ἔσονται (cf. Mt 5:19; 21:13; Lk 1:32,35) [44]. As we saw above, this beatitude is resumed in other terms in Mt 5:44-45, in which ὅπως γένησθε orientates the idea towards a real sonship to be acquired in its fulness by means of realising in oneself gradually the nature of the Father. So the promise contained in κληθήσονται carries with it the idea of a real acquisition of sonship in its eschatological perfection [45].

Mt 5:46 which describes the sonship as a reward also indicates the eschatological character of this sonship. The parallel text of Mt 5:45 in Lk 6:35 makes it explicit. There the ἔσεσθε υἱοὶ ὑψίστου is parallel to ἔσται ὁ μισθὸς ὑμῶν πολύς. So the divine sonship is a reward that is held in store for those who love their enemies [46].

IV. God the Father of the Disciples

A. Texts speaking of God as 'Father'

Since the Synoptics speak of men as 'sons of God', the texts speaking of God as 'Father' have special relevance to this sonship of man. It is interesting to note the use of the name 'Father' for God and its connection with the Kingdom. Mt uses the phrase 'the Kingdom of the Father' when speaking to the disciples and that with eschatological overtones (Mt 6:10; 13:43; 26:29), but, 'the Kingdom of God, when speaking to Jesus' adversaries (Mt 12:28; 21:31,43). In Mt 6:26-32, though Jesus speaks of the paternal love for men in general, it is in the context of the Kingdom, and perspectives of faith, eternal life, judgement etc. are present. The name 'Father' is used of God often in connection with his will (Mt 18:14) and Spirit (Mt 10:20) both of which are intimately connected with the Kingdom. It is worth noting that the title of God as 'Father' of men comes 14 times in the Sermon on the Mount, and 'Father' of Jesus only twice, while outside the Sermon 'Father' of Jesus comes 20 times and 'Father' of men only 5 times. This shows the intimate connection of the Fatherhood of God to the membership in the Kingdom the norms of which are promulgated in the Sermon on the Mount.

---

[44] Cf. A. H. McNEILE, *The Gospel according to St. Matthew*, p. 53.

[45] Cf. W. GRUNDMANN, *Das Evangelium nach Matthäus*, p. 132 : " Es (κληθήσονται) meint im sprechen Gottes, das ein neues Sein hervorruft, weil es ein gültiges sprechen ist ".

[46] Cf. H. SCHÜRMANN, *Das Lukas Evangelium*, HThKNT, III, vol. I, Freiburg, 1969, p. 355; E. SCHWEIZER, art. υἱός, *TWNT* VIII, p. 393.

It is the disciples who find God as Father in Prayer (Mt 6:9, 14-15 ; 7:7-11 ; 18:19-20). In Mt the name 'Father' for God comes entirely on the lips of Jesus and He uses it for God only in relation to himself and others who are of like mind with himself, men with similar relations with God though keeping the distinction between his unique sonship and the sonship of man expressed in his distinctive use of 'my Father' and 'your Father'. From the fact that Mt adds 'my Father' and 'your Father' to his sources [47] it is clear that Mt develops with equal emphasis the thoughts that God is Jesus' Father and that He is the Father of the disciples [48].

B. *Context of texts speaking of Sonship in Mt*

The very context of the Sermon on the Mount in Mt gives indications that it is a sonship of the disciples that is in question. In Mt the Sermon on the Mount comes just after the calling of disciples. Mt 5:1-2 says : "when he sat down his disciples came to him and he opened his mouth and taught them ..." The word in Mt 5:12 "thus they persecuted the prophets" could be said only of the disciples. The observation at the end in Mt 7:28-29 about the crowd belongs to the secondary redaction which shows the tendency to widen the audience in the primitive Church [49].

C. *Other Indications*

In Mt 5:9 the technical signification of 'the sons of God' is already defined as those who belong to the Kingdom of God. Note how Mt, beginning and ending the beatitudes in v. 3 and 10 with the promise of this Kingdom, shows that all other beatitudes are a living description of the Kingdom. The 'reward' and the 'more' of Mt 5:46-47 is a negative affirmation and detailed explanation of v. 45 showing the distinction of the 'sons of God' from the others. Hence the insistence of the conclusion οὖν opposing 'you' to 'publicans' and 'gentiles' [50].

---

[47] For 'my Father' cf. Mt 15:13 ; 16:17 ; 18:10,19,35 ; 25:34 ; 26:53. For 'your Father' cf. Mt 5:16 ; 6:1,4,6,18 ; 18:14 ; 23:9.

[48] Cf. S. E. JOHNSON, "Son of God", in *IDB*, New York, 1962, vol. IV, p. 411.

[49] Note the stereotyped formula of Mt "Jesus having finished the Sermon" at the end of each of the five discourses (Mt 7:28-29 ; 11:1 ; 13:53 ; 19:1 ; 26:1).

[50] For the Christian sonship in this context, cf. W. C. ALLEN, *The Gospel according to Mathew*, (ICC), 3rd ed., Edinburgh, 1962, ad loc. ; G. SCHRENK, art. πατήρ, *TDNT* V, pp. 990-991 ; T. W. MANSON, *The Teaching of Jesus*,

In Mt 13:37-43 the sons of the Kingdom are compared to the 'good seed' and the sons of the evil to the 'weeds'. If in the sowing time (vv. 37-38) the good seeds are the 'sons of the Kingdom', in the reaping time (v. 43) they are the 'just who shine forth in the Kingdom of their Father' showing thereby the divine sonship of the 'sons of the Kingdom'.

V. Christ and the Divine sonship of man (Mt 17:25-27; 12:48-50; 11:25-27)

A. Mt 17:25-27

In Mt 17:25-27 the disciples are said to be 'sons' together with Jesus in contradistinction to the foreigners who are not 'sons'. In v. 27 Jesus applies to himself and Simon the parable in vv. 25-26 about the freedom of the sons of the King from paying tax. The application of the parable is implicit in the fact that they are to give the tax in order not to scandalize others meaning thereby that they are not bound to do it as 'sons' [51]. Note the adversative δέ at the beginning of v. 27 which has an emphatic significance in this application of the parable.

The joining of Jesus with Simon in the divine sonship is also seen from the fact that here it is a question of the temple tax, which is the revenue of the royal family of God, as the temple is the house of God [52]. Peter stands here in his quality of the disciple of Jesus. So this freedom extends also to other disciples who together with Jesus and Peter enjoy this freedom as sons of the heavenly King [53]. Hence the sharing of the sonship of Jesus by his disciples is implicit in this passage.

Cambridge, 1931, 89-115; P. SCHRUERS, "La paternité divine dans Mt 5:45 et 6:26-32", *ETL* 36 (1960), pp. 593ff; R. LOHMEYER, *Das Vater-Unser*, Zürich, 1952, pp. 18-41.

[51] That Mt thinks of the divine sonship of men here is perhaps suggested by the fact too that they are obliged precisely as sons of God to avoid scandal — to love (Mt 5,9,44-45). Cf. W. GRUNDMANN, *Das Evangelium nach Matthäus*, p. 410.

[52] It was the oriental custom to consider the tax as the revenue of the royal family.

[53] Cf. W. G. THOMPSON, *Mathew's Advice to a Divided Community*: Mt 17:22 – 18:35, Rome, 1970, pp. 57-58.

B. Mt 12:48-50

The above conclusion is reinforced by Mt 12:48-50 where Jesus explicitly calls his disciples his brothers [54]. Compared with the parallel text in Mk 3:31-35 we notice significant differences in Mt. In v. 49 Mt changes into 'the will of my Father', 'the will of God' of Mk 3:35. So Jesus proclaims here implicitly the sonship of the disciples because of their filial obedience to the Father, which was characteristic of his own sonship (cf. Mt 26:42; Heb 10:7) [55].

C. Mt 11:25-27

The so-called 'Johannine Logion' of the Synoptics makes it clear that Jesus as the Son possesses 'the knowledge of the Father' (v. 27bc) and the power to communicate this knowledge to those who accept Him (v. 27ad). If in v. 25 it is the Father who reveals the mystery of the Kingdom (the knowledge of the Father) to the children (disciples) [56], in v. 27 it is the Son who, possessing the power to reveal (v. 27a) and the knowledge of the Father to be revealed (v. 27bc), reveals it to the disciples (v. 27d). Note the verb ἀποκαλύπτειν which forms an 'inclusion' to the section. If the knowledge of the Father which Christ enjoys is in his quality of the Son, the communication of this knowledge also carries with it a communication of the same sonship. So Christ becomes the mediator of the divine sonship of man.

Conclusion

Those who participate in the work of the Messiah in establishing peace between God and man and between themselves, through concrete acts of mercy towards all, even enemies, will share also in his dignity as Son of God. Through love of enemies one becomes similar to God the Father, who is the model and exemplar of disinterested and pardoning love and thus becomes a real son of God. The divine

---

[54] Note also that Jesus goes on speaking about brotherly relations that should exist among his disciples, just after the pericope of the temple tax, in which he illustrated the divine sonship of the disciples as that of Himself.

[55] Cf. W. GRUNDMANN, *Das Evangelium nach Matthäus*, p. 336, where speaking of this Matthean change into the 'will of my Father' in v. 50 he says: "Damit aber wird der Grund der Familia Dei in Gott als dem Vater des Sohnes selbst begründet. Sind die Jünger als Täter des Willens Gottes seine Brüder, so sind sie damit des Vaters Kinder; sein Vater ist ihr Vater".

[56] Cf. S. LEGASSE, op. cit., p. 168, where he takes the νήπιοι for the small circle of the disciples who received the Messianic revelation.

sonship of man will be actually in proportion to this resemblance to the Father and hence this sonship is essentially dynamic.

The eschatological character of the divine sonship is clear from the fact that it is as the 'sons of the resurrection' that they will be 'sons of God' in the full sense of the term.

It is the disciples who find God as Father in prayer, and the divine sonship in the Synoptics is parallel to membership in the Kingdom of God.

The disciples are sons of God, because they share in the sonship of Christ and by communicating the knowledge of God which Christ possesses in his quality of the Son of God, he communicates also the divine sonship. Thus Christ becomes also the mediator of the divine sonship of man.

Chapter V

The Pauline Doctrine of Christian Sonship

Paul makes use of different terms to express the father-son relationship between God and man, such as: υἱοὶ τοῦ θεοῦ (Rom 8:14, 19; 9:26; 2 Cor 6:18; Gal 3:26; 4:6f), τέκνα τοῦ θεοῦ (Rom 8:16,17, 21; 9:8; Phil 2:15), τέκνα ἐπαγγελίας (Rom 9:8; Gal 4:28), θυγατέρες (2 Cor 6:18) and υἱοθεσία (Rom 8:15,23; 9:4; Gal 4:5; Eph 1:5). Unlike John, Paul uses both υἱοί and τέκνα to express the divine sonship of man, while Jn reserves the term υἱός for Jesus. This usage, when seen as concomitant to the figure of adoption [1], characteristic of Pauline doctrine, seems to emphasize the dignity and privilege of sonship, rather than the nature of sonship as in John [2].

I. Use of the term υἱοθεσία in Paul [3]

A. *Israel's Sonship as background*

The general practice of adoption in the Greco-Roman world and the absence of the term υἱοθεσία in the LXX and the lack of a corresponding term in the Massoretic Text, led many authors to find the Greco-Roman influence in the Pauline doctrine of adoption [4]. But recently, the scholars are becoming more and more convinced of its background in Israel's sonship [5].

---

[1] It is to be remarked that υἱοθεσία in Paul is best translated as ' adoption ', and not as ' sonship ' which does not convey the total idea behind the word. Cf. J. D. HESTER, *Paul's Concept of Inheritance*, (SJT Occasional Papers, no. 14), 1968, p. 59.

[2] Cf. M. R. VINCENT, Word Studies in the New Testament, New York 1924, II, p. 49.

[3] On ' adoption ' in St. Paul, cf. W. M. CALDER, " Adoption and Inheritance in Galatia ", *JTS* 31 (1930), 372-374; T. WHALING, " Adoption ", *Princ TR* 21 (1923), 223-235; M. W. SCHOENBERG, " Huiothesia : The Word and the Institution ", *Script* 15 (1963), 115-123; E. SCHWEIZER, art. υἱός, *TWNT* VIII, p. 402.

[4] Cf. W. M. RAMSAY, *A Historical Commentary on St. Paul's Epistle to the Galatians*, New York 1900, p. 339, 343; P. FEINE, *Theologie des Alten Testaments*, 8th ed., Berlin, 1951, p. 227, note 1.

[5] Cf. W. H. ROSSELL, " New Testament Adoption - Graeco-Roman or Se-

The adoptive nature of Israel's sonship is clear from its relation to the liberation from slavery and the connection with the Covenant. St. Paul himself attributes the υἱοθεσία to the Israelites (Rom 9:4). He calls the children of God as ' sons of the promise ' (Rom 9:8) and true sons of Abraham (Rom 9:7-8 ; Gal 3:29), thus referring to the sonship of Israel as the antecedent of the Christian sonship [6]. Also the use of the Aramaic ἀββᾶ precisely and only in the contexts speaking of adoption in Paul (Rom 8:15 ; Gal 4:6) is also significative of its semitic background [7].

B. *Adoption of sons of God - The Blessing of Abraham*

In all the texts speaking of υἱοθεσία, Paul appeals to the testimony of the Old in writing the doctrine of the New Testament. Besides, in all these texts, the idea of liberation from the bondage of slavery is predominant. In speaking of this liberation from bondage and adoption to sonship, Paul seems to think of the liberation and adoption of Israel as the background and the basis of Christian liberation and adoption. The parallelism between Gal 3:10-14 and 4:1-5 is enlightening. Both texts follow the same order: situation under the Law (3:10-12 = 4:1-3), the redemption worked out by Christ (3: 13 = 4:4) and the effect of their redemption (3:14 = 4:5). The effect is described in three parallel phrases : " that we might receive ' adoption of sons ' " (4:5), " that ' the blessing of Abraham ' might come " and " that we might receive ' the promise of the Spirit ' " (3:14). The parallelism between the two clauses in 3:14 is clear from the fact that both are equally dependent on the clause " Χριστὸς ..... ἐξηγόρασεν ". This shows a continuation of Israel's sonship in the Christian's sonship.

Originally the adoption to divine sonship was the right of Israel, by Election, Covenant and Promises. But already in the O. T., the realization of it was only in those who were faithful to the Covenant, as seen in the gradual transfer of this title to the ' just '. So, not all the Israelites according to the flesh are the ' sons of God ' but only the true posterity of Abraham who were born under promise

---

mitic ? ", *JBL* 71 (1952), 233-234 ; D. J. THERON, " Adoption in the Pauline Corpus ", *EvQ* 28 (1956), 6-10 ; A.v. HARNACK, *Die Terminologie der Wiedergeburt und verwandter Erlebnisse in der ältesten Kirche*, TU 42-3 (1918), pp. 103-104 ; compare also K. NIEDERWIMMER, *Der Begriff der Freiheit im Neuen Testament*, Berlin 1966, pp. 70-72.

[6] Cf. M. W. SCHOENBERG, " St. Paul's Notion on Adoptive Sonship of Christians (Gal. 4:5) ", *Thomist* 28 (1964), 51-75.

[7] Cf. W. H. ROSSELL, art. cit., p. 234.

namely, symbolized in Isaac understood spiritually (Rom 9:7-8; Gal 4:21-31). So the divine sonship of Israel was in view of the Christian sonship [8].

C. *Origin of the term* υἱοθεσία

Though Paul's concept of Christian adoptive sonship is deeply rooted in Israel's sonship, the term υἱοθεσία seems to be inspired by the Roman system of adoption, as it was quite suitable to express his concept of Christian sonship. Paul could have in mind the Roman ceremony of adoption (adrogation) where a man is bought out from under the ' Patria Potestas ' of one man and placed under the ' Patria Potestas ' of another [9]. In fact Gal 4:3-7 speaks of the redeeming work of Christ, by which men are bought from the power of στοιχεῖα τοῦ κόσμου and placed under the power of God, whom they call ' Abba Father '. Also other elements of the Roman form of adoption seem to be present in Paul's adoption metaphor, namely, the adopter (God) [10], the purchase price (Jesus Christ) (Gal 4:4) and the witness (Holy Spirit) (Gal 4:6; Rom 8:16) [11]. So Paul seems to have taken a term that was most expressive of Christian sonship for his hearers.

II. Adoption through liberation

As Israel was made ' son of God ' through the liberation from the slavery (Exodus) so also Christian sonship presupposes a liberation from various forms of slavery, viz: sin (Rom 6:16-20), law (Gal 4:5), beings that by nature are no gods (Gal 4:8), carnal body (Rom 8:23) and death (Rom 8:21). Only a complete liberation from all these

---

[8] Cf. A. v HARNACK, *Die Terminologie der Wiedergeburt* ..., p. 103 : " Dieser (Adoptionsgedanke) ist letztlich die Anwendung des ATlichen Gedankens vom Bunde Gottes mit seinem Volke (bzw. von der Annahme der Volksgenossen zu seinem Söhnen und Töchtern) auf jeden einzelnen Christen, der als solcher zum wahren Israel gehört ".

[9] Cf. J. D. HESTER, op. cit., p. 59; cf. also W. ELMERT, " Redemptio ab Hostibus ", *TLZ* 71 (1947), cols. 265-270 where he rejects the idea of buying out of slavery, since the redeemed comes again under the power of the buyer, and he sees in Paul's use of adoption only an allusion to the redemption from the enemies. It is interesting in the sense that the ' patria potestas ', out of which one is bought, is described as inimical and as such fits in well in the Pauline concept of adoption. But the fact that under this system the buyer was to be paid back by the redeemed goes against God's free grace and electing love in adoption to sonship.

[10] Cf. W. TWISSELMANN, op. cit., pp. 62-64.

[11] Cf. J. D. HESTER, op. cit., p. 61.

will give the final consummation of 'Adoption' (Rom 8:23). To be adopted is more than to be liberated. But liberation is always a prerequisite for sonship [12].

It is interesting to note how Paul follows always the same order by describing first, the situation of slavery (Gal 3:10-12; 3:22-23; 4: 1-3), then, the liberation from the slavery (Gal 3:13; 3:25; 4:4) and finally the giving of adoption (sonship) (Gal 3:14; 3:26; 4:5). Again in the Epistle to the Romans in Chs. 5-7 he speaks of the slavery to sin, law and death and freedom from it and then in Ch 8 he speaks of the divine sonship. This necessity of liberation from the slavery of sin shows also the unique significance of Christ in mediating this sonship. It is Christ who freed all men, " ἡμᾶς ἐξηγόρασεν " (Gal 3:13; 4:4) [13], from the slavery of sin and law. It is Christ who represented us in this redeeming work (γενόμενος ὑπὲρ ἡμῶν). It is only passing through this redemption by Christ, that we attain this divine sonship.

III. Adoption by God the Father

The term υἱοθεσία (υἱὸν τινα τιθέναι) signifies in the active the act of adopting one as a son and in the passive the condition of the one thus adopted. It is the aspect of election on the part of God that is emphasized by this term, rather than the juridical aspect of the right to heredity [14]. As in the OT, the initiative lies with God in the act of our adoption. It is God who destined us beforehand in love (προορίσας) to the adoption of sons (εἰς υἱοθεσίαν) through

---

[12] Cf. Gal 4:5 where the redemption is explicitly said to be leading to adoption. Cf. H. SCHLIER, *Lettera ai Galati*, trans. from German by M. Bellincioni, Brescia 1966, p. 203 : " Quel totale donarsi del Figlio al cosmo ... aveva lo scopo di liberare ... A questo scopo negativo ne corrisponde un altro, positivo : il dono della υἱοθεσία agli uomini ".

[13] The fact that ἡμᾶς includes all Jews and Non-Jews and not the Jews only (the latter is defended by E. D. BURTON, " Redemption from the Curse of the Law. An exposition of Gal 3:13,14 ", *AJT* 11 (1907), 624-646; also Commentators like Zahn, Lagrange, Lietzmann, Lyonnet etc.) is clear from the fact that it is repeated in the same v. 13 in ὑπὲρ ἡμῶν which is certainly to be referred to all men. Cf. H. SCHLIER, *Lettera ai Galati*, p. 142.

[14] This is perhaps insinuated also from what we said above on the use of the term υἱοθεσία by Paul emphasizing the aspect of drawing men out of the power of the world and bringing under the power of God. Perhaps a further confirmation is seen in the way in which the Syrians called the adopted son even in their juridical books as ' son of goodness ' or ' son of grace '. Cf. S. LYONNET, *Exegesis Epistulae ad Romanos, Capita V ad VIII*, Rome 1966, p. 207.

Christ according to his salvific will (Eph 1:5 ; Rom 8:28f). Thus God sends his own Son (Gal 4:4 ; Rom 8:3) and the Holy Spirit (Gal 4:6) in view of our adoption [15]. Hence the adoption, from its origin to its realization, is due to the initiative of the Father.

Because of this initiative of God the Father, it is He alone, who is our Father and not the Holy Trinity as such [16]. Though all the three persons are active (participate) in the work of our adoption, it is the Father *who sends* the Son and *who gives* the Holy Spirit to realize our adoption (Rom 5:5 ; 2 Cor 1:22 ; 5:5 ; Gal 3:5).

The paternity of the Father is all the more real, because he infuses in man the divine life. It is on this basis that the Christians adopted the invocation " Abba " (Rom 8:15 ; Gal 4:6) which was otherwise used only by Jesus in relation to God [17]. There are authors who limit this invocation to a few charismatics [18]. But there is every indication that it is the invocation of all christians as sons of God[19]. The argument of Paul in the context of Rom 8:15 is to arouse hope in all Christians. So it should be common to all those who are led by the Spirit (v. 14), are in the Spirit (v. 5) or walk according to the Spirit (v. 4). And the testimony of the Spirit in v. 16 is the same as the cry mentioned in v. 15 because v. 16 is an apposition to v. 15. Besides, Gal 4:6 says clearly that it is the Spirit himself, who cries ' Abba, Father '. It could be also an allusion to the ' Lord's prayer ' in as much as it expresses the relation of Christians to God, especially considering the place of this prayer in the baptismal rite [20].

---

[15] The verb ἐξαπέστειλεν is found in Paul only in this context, and it indicates the supernatural mission of this sending, namely, adoption.

[16] Cf. J. HAVET, " Dieu Notre Père ", *RDiocNamur* 12 (1958), 19-40 where he speaks of the authors who affirmed that we are sons of the Trinity.

[17] For this singular use of ' Abba ' for God in the mouth of the Christians, cf. S. LYONNET, *Exegesis Epistulae ad Romanos*, Cap. V-VIII, pp. 207-215.

[18] Cf. for instance, A. ROOSEN, " Testimonium Spiritus ", *VD* 28 (1950), pp. 214-226.

[19] Cf. W. MARCHEL, *Abba, Père*, p. 243 where concluding his elaborate study on ' Abba, Père ' as the prayer of Christ and the Christians, he says : " L'invocation ' Abba ' que Paul mentionne dans Gal 4:6 et Rom 8:15 nous révèle la profondeur de la prière chrétienne au Père. Son fondement est l'adoption divine ". Cf. also H. SCHLIER, *Lettera ai Galati*, p. 206 ; S. C. V. CASLAND, " Abba, Father ", *JBL* 72 (1953), 79-91.

[20] Cf. O. CULLMANN, *The Christology of the New Testament*, (trans. from the German ' Die Christologie des Neuen Testaments '), 2nd ed. London 1963, pp. 208-209 ; A. OEPKE, *Der Brief des Paulus an die Galater*, 2nd ed. Berlin, 1957, ad. loc.

IV. Sons of God in Christ (Gal 3:26-28)

The fact that the Christians invoked God with ' Abba, Father ', the same invocation of Christ (Mk 14:36), shows that it is in Christ that they are sons of God. Our sonship is based on the sonship of Christ. This solidarity and union with Christ as the basis of our sonship is expressed in Gal 3:26-28.

A. *The Structure of the Text*

Vv. 24-25   So ... until Christ came ... now that faith has come,
         A   We are NO LONGER (οὐκέτι) ...
     26   FOR YOU ARE ALL *sons of God* ... IN CHRIST JESUS
     27   B   For as many ... WERE BAPTIZED INTO CHRIST
                                HAVE PUT ON CHRIST
     28   A'   There is NEITHER (οὐκ) ... NOR (οὐδέ) ...
                FOR YOU ARE ALL *one*   IN CHRIST JESUS

Note the literary parallelism in AA'. This parallelism shows that the ἐν Χριστῷ Ἰησοῦ determines the υἱοὶ θεοῦ ἐστε in V. 26 as it does determine ὑμεῖς εἷς ἐστε in v. 28 [21]. The parallelism between υἱοὶ θεοῦ ἐστε and εἷς ἐστε shows that the sonship of man through faith is the result of being one with Christ.

B. *Grammatical and philological analysis*

1. εἷς ... ἐν Χριστῷ Ἰησοῦ (V. 28)

The masculine εἷς (not ἕν) shows that it is Christ the Son of God who stands in our place thus making us sons of God [22]. The phrase ἐν Χριστῷ Ἰησοῦ [23] also points to this union with Christ. In

---

[21] There are authors who connect the ἐν Χριστῷ Ἰησοῦ to διὰ τῆς πίστεως. Cf. M. J. LAGRANGE, *St. Paul, épître aux Galates*, Paris 1918, p. 92 ; W. TWISSELMANN, op. cit., p. 61, note. But in the sense of faith in Jesus Christ, Paul never says πίστις ἐν Χριστῷ Ἰησοῦ, but πίστις Χριστοῦ (Gal 2:16,20 ; 3:22 ; Rom 3:22,26 ; Eph 3:12 ; Phil 1:27 ; 3:9 ; Col 2:12 ; II Thes 2:13) or πίστις πρὸς τὸν κύριον Ἰησοῦν (Philm 5) or πίστις εἰς Χριστόν (Col 2:5). Also in Eph 1:15 and Col 1:4 Χριστός is to be taken not as object, but as the basis of faith (cf. I Tim 1:14 ; 3:13 ; II Tim 1:13 ; 3:15). Cf. H. SCHLIER, *Lettera ai Galati*, pp. 176-177.

[22] Cf. H. SCHLIER, *Lettera ai Galati*, p. 180 : " ... tutti sono in Christo Gesù un solo, ossia Christo stesso ".

[23] On the use of this formula in Paul, cf. A. DEISSMANN, *Die Formel in Christo Jesu*, Marbourg 1892 ; X. M. VALLISOLETO, " In Christo Jesu ", *VD* 13 (1933), 311-319 ; F. BÜCHSEL, " In Christus " bei Paulus, *ZNW* 42 (1942),

itself the preposition ἐν indicates only an undetermined relation to Christ. But Paul gives to this expression in many texts the sense of a communication of life [24]. This communication of life certainly supposes an intimate union between Christ and the Christians [25].

2. Χριστὸν ἐνεδύσασθε (V. 27)

The B (v. 27) in the centre of the structure shows that 'being sons of God' (A) and 'being one in Christ' (A') takes place concretely in 'being baptized into Christ' and 'putting on Christ'. Note the γάρ in v. 27 which explains v. 26 and hence also its parallel v. 28 [26]. In this construction, the 'putting on Christ' is the formal explanation of 'being sons of God through faith', while the relative 'as many ... baptized into Christ' shows that the 'putting on Christ' is materially realized in 'being baptized into Christ'.

The verb ἐνδύω [27] has in the OT always a metaphorical sense of identification with the thing or person that is the object (cf. Is 50:3; 51:9; 52:1; 59:17 etc.). In Paul it occurs 12 times and always in this metaphorical sense. Out of these, 4 have a person as object (cf. Rom 13:14; Gal 3:27; Eph 4:24; Col 3:10), and all of these are in a parenetical context calling for a renewal of life. So 'putting on Christ' refers to the union with Christ and the renewal of life based on this union.

Rom 13:14, which is the only other text speaking of 'putting on Christ', shows a subjective and radical process of life in the Christian which began in Baptism. Rom 6:3-11, in which v. 3 is literally parallel to Gal 3:27a, shows that 'to be baptized in Christ' results in a change of life, a change into a new life in Christ (cf. Rom 6:4 and 10f). Col 2:11-12 which is again parallel to both Rom 6:3-11 and Gal 3:26-27 speaks of baptism in which 'you were buried with Him' and 'you were also raised with Him through faith'. So in Gal 3:27

141-158; F. NEUGEBAUER, " Das Paulinische ' In Christo ' ", *NTS* 4 (1957-58), 124-138.

[24] Cf. L. CERFAUX, *La théologie de l'église suivant S. Paul*, 2nd ed. Paris 1948, pp. 168ff.

[25] For a study of the different uses of ἐν Χριστῷ, cf. W. MARCHEL, op. cit., pp. 227-230.

[26] The motivation in v. 27 (γάρ) seems to be specifically directed to ἐν Χριστῷ Ἰησοῦ (Cf. H. SCHLIER, *Lettera ai Galati*, p. 178), because it is the 'being one in Christ' parallel to 'being sons of God in Christ' that are explained in v. 27, resuming twice the word Χριστόν.

[27] For the usage of this metaphor, cf. W. STRAUB, *Die Bildersprache des Apostels Paulus*, Tübingen, 1937, pp. 24ff; A. OEPKE, art. " ἐνδύω ", *TDNT* II, pp. 319ff; J. LEIPOLDT, *Die urchristliche Taufe im Lichte der Religionsgeschichte*, Leipzig 1928, pp. 60ff.

the 'putting on Christ' shows this union with Christ in rising with Him through faith (v. 27b) to a new life of the sons of God through faith (v. 26), which begins in dying with Him in Baptism (v. 27a) [28]. If 'putting on Christ' happens materially in baptism, it happens formally in an act of faith, which marks the beginning of the life of the sons of God, a life of faith in Christ [29].

This shows also the dynamic character of the divine sonship. It is worth noting that the verb ἐνδύω is used in the active while the verb ἐβαπτίσθητε is in the passive. So the life of sonship is a life of faith in Christ which began in the sacramental happening of Baptism and which remains dynamic throughout.

3. υἱοὶ θεοῦ ... διὰ τῆς πίστεως (v. 26)

From the above considerations we come to understand the fundamental role of faith in the divine sonship. This is in agreement with the Synoptic teaching regarding sonship through membership in the Kingdom, where conversion was an indispensable condition. Actually 'conversion' and 'faith' were inseparable conditions of entering the Kingdom (cf. Mk 1:15 "... μετανοεῖτε καὶ πιστεύετε ..."). In fact conversion was a response to preaching. Hence both conversion and faith indicated the same reality. As the statistics show, the μετάνοια was gradually replaced by πίστις [30]. Hence, if for the Synoptics the condition of sonship was μετάνοια, for St. Paul it is the πίστις.

Faith here does not seem to be used in a mere subjective sense [31]. The contraposition of πίστις to νόμος in the proximate context (3: 19-29) shows that πίστις here stands for the whole happening in Christ.

---

[28] Cf. H. SCHLIER, *Lettera ai Galati*, p. 178: "Χριστὸν ἐνδύεσθαι ... non sta dunque ad indicare l'inizio di un rapporto etico, ma di un rapporto ontologico con Christo. Designa l'inizio della (commune) partecipazione all'essere di Christo stesso, che si realizza, come dice 2:20, nella nascita di un nuovo 'io', di 'Christo in me'...". Th. ZAHN interprets it as a mere moral imitation of Christ, which does not seem to be correct.

[29] Cf. I. DE LA POTTERIE, "Le rapport de la foi et du baptême dans la mission d'après le Nouveau Testament", in *Repenser la Mission*, Louvain 1965, pp. 160-161.

[30] When the μετάνοια and μετανοεῖν is used in Mk. 3 times, in Mt 7 times, in Lk 14 times, in Acts 11 times, in Paul 8 times and in Jn not at all, the word πίστις and πιστεύω is used in Mk 19 times, in Mt 20 times, in Lk 20 times, in Acts 52 times, in Paul 221 times and in John 90 times.

[31] It is the faith that has arrived, of which is said in Gal 3:25. The διὰ τῆς πίστεως of Gal 3:26 resumes the ἐλθούσης τῆς πίστεως of v. 25 (cf. Fr. SIEFFERT, *Der Brief an die Galater*, (Kritisch-Exegetischer Kommentar über das Neue Testament, VII), 9th ed., 1899, ad loc.).

However the distinction is not very clear in Paul. For him both objective and subjective faith contributed to the realization of sonship. It is the coming of Christ that gives deliverance from slavery of sin and law to everyone who accepts him and thus gives him sonship.

V. Birth through the Gospel (I Cor 4:15)

In I Cor 4:15 Paul speaks of a father-son relationship between himself and the faithful, because " he begot them through the Gospel " [32]. This points to the birth to the divine life, through the Word of God. Actually the πίστις in Gal 3:26 through which we become sons of God is not much different from the concept of the ' preached Word of faith ' in Rom 10:8, in as much as it is the expression of faith itself [33].

In Paul the word εὐαγγέλιον is used with διά 5 times in all. In the other 4 texts it is a means of salvation presented as a life in and with Christ in its different aspects : ' Glory of Christ ' (2 Thes 2:14), ' life and immortality ' (2 Tim 1:10-11), ' heritage ', ' incorporation into Christ ' (Eph 3:6), ' salvation ' introducing the theme of resurrection with Christ in the whole chapter (1 Cor 15:1-2). All these indicate that ' to beget through the Gospel ' means ' to introduce to the new divine life in Christ ', namely, to the life of Christian sonship. The formula ἐν Χριστῷ Ἰησοῦ also refers to this birth to the Christian sonship.

The occurrence of the word γεννάω here in the form of aorist has a parallel in Philm 10 where Paul speaks of his son Onesimus, whom he begot in chains. In the light of 1 Cor 4:15 it seems to be interpreted as referring to the conversion of Onesimus by Paul in his captivity [34]. Gal 4:19 also forms a parallel to our text, as it speaks of Paul begetting the faithful in pain until Christ be formed in them, though the word used is ὠδίνω [35]. Hence I Cor 4:15 refers to a birth to the life of Christian sonship, which takes place through the Word of God preached by Paul [36].

---

[32] For a detailed exegetical study on this verse, cf. M. SAILLARD, " C'est moi qui, par l'Évangile, vous ai enfantés dans le Christ Jésus (I Cor 4,15) ", RSR 56 (1968), 5-41.

[33] Cf. H. SCHLIER, Lettera ai Galati, p. 177.

[34] Cf. M. SAILLARD, art. cit., p. 24.

[35] Ὠδίνω is applied usually to the mother, while γεννάω could be applied to both father and mother. Nevertheless here the similarity of the metaphor cannot be denied.

[36] Cf. W. MEYER, Der Erste Korintherbrief, Zürich, 1948, p. 153 where he paraphrases the verse as : " Ich habe euch zur Welt gebracht als Kinder Gottes durch das Evangelium in Jesus Christus ".

VI. The Divine Sonship of Christians and the Holy Spirit (Gal 4:4-7; Rom 8:14-17)

Gal 4:6 speaks of the Spirit of the Son of God and both Gal 4:6 and Rom 8:15 speak of the Spirit of adoption which we received and by virtue of which we cry to God 'Abba Father'. Whatever be the exact nature of the Spirit — the H. Spirit himself or the result of the action of the H. Spirit [37] — the Spirit of adoption is not a purely subjective disposition, but a divine element communicated to man.

A. The Holy Spirit - Witness of adoption (Gal 4:6)

Here we meet with the problem of the relation between the Spirit and adoption : whether the Spirit is the cause of adoption testifying to it or the consequence of it [38]. The whole difficulty comes from the meaning of ὅτι in this text, which can have a causal sense (sonship as cause of sending the spirit) [39] and a completive or demonstrative sense (sonship witnessed by the spirit) [40].

1. The structure of Gal 4:4-7

```
v. 4   A       When ... GOD SENT FORTH
       B                HIS SON born ...
   5   C                    So that we might receive a d o p t i o n
                                                    a s   s o n s
   6   D                AND             YOU ARE SONS
       A'      GOD HAS SENT FORTH
       B'      The Spirit of HIS SON
```

---

[37] Cf. R. CORNELY, *Epistula ad Romanos*, Paris 1896, p. 416 ; M. J. LAGRANGE, *Epître aux Galates*, Paris 1950, p. 104.

[38] For the history of the exegesis on this point, cf. S. ZEDDA, *L'Adozione a Figli di Dio e lo Spirito Santo*, Roma, 1952 ; A. DUPREZ, " Note sur le role de l'Esprit Saint dans la Filiation du Chrétien. A Propos de Gal 4:6 ", RSR 52 (1964), 421-423.

[39] For this causal sense, cf. E. BURTON, *The Epistle to the Galatians*, (ICC), Edinburgh 1921, 221-222 ; H. SCHLIER, *Lettera ai Galati*, 204 ; A. OEPKE, *Der Brief des Paulus an die Galater*, 2nd ed., Berlin 1960, p. 97 ; L. CERFAUX, *Le chrétien selon saint Paul*, Paris 1963, pp. 254, 299.

[40] For this completive sense cf. O. KUSS, *Der Brief an die Römer*, Regensburg 1940, pp. 270-271 ; S. LYONNET, *Épître aux Galates, aux Romains* (BJ), 2nd ed., 1959, p. 34 ; F. AMIOT, *Épîtres aux Galates*, Paris, 1946, pp. 191-192 ; H. W. BEYER, *Der Brief an die Galater* (Das N. T. Deutsch), 6th ed., Göttingen, 1953, pp. 33-34 ; M. ZERWICK, *Der Brief an die Galater*, Düsseldorf, 1964, pp. 77-78.

   C' Into our hearts c r y i n g 'A b b a, F a t h e r'
7 D' So ... YOU ARE ... a SON, and if
      a SON, ... an heir.

As we see from the structure, it is God who sends (AA') the son and the spirit (BB'). The Spirit is the Spirit of the Son. The correspondence of C and C' shows that the activity of the Spirit crying ' Abba, Father' is in direct relation to the ' Adoption '. Hence the mission of the Spirit is ordained towards the mission of the Son and is within the function of adoption.

  2. " Πνεῦμα κρᾶζον "

This phrase, though unique in the Bible, is common in Rabbinic literature and there it is used to add authority to a scriptural text which always follows it [41]. This favours the testimonial value of the cry of the Spirit here [42].

The conclusion " so ... you are ... son ..." (v. 6) (D' in the structure) shows that the whole argument is to prove the sonship, and not the sending of the Spirit through sonship. Hence the ὅτι (D) is to be taken in the demonstrative sense. The parallel text Rom 8:15-16 says clearly " when we cry ' Abba, Father ', it is the Spirit himself bearing witness ... that we are children of God ". So the Spirit is Witness of our adoption as sons.

B. *The Holy Spirit - Cause of our adoption*

The testimony in the form of a prayer, points certainly to the Holy Spirit also as the cause of divine sonship [43]. This is reinforced by the fact that this Spirit is the Spirit of the Son. It is this causality of the Spirit in our sonship that is expressed in Rom 8:14. " All

---

[41] Cf. K. ROMANIUK, " Spiritus Clamans (Gal 4:6 ; Rom 8:15) ", *VD* 40 (1962), pp. 190-198.

[42] Cf. A. ROOSEN, " Testimonium Spiritus ", *VD* 28 (1950), 214-226.

[43] In fact, the Antiochian and Greek Fathers clearly saw in this text the Holy Spirit as the cause of adoption. Cf. for example, ATHANASIUS, PG 25, 473 : " Because the Spirit of the Word that is in us calls His Father as ours (Father) through us (δι' ἡμῶν). That is what the Apostle says : ἐξαπέστειλεν ... 'Αββᾶ ὁ πατήρ " ; cf. also J. CHRYSOSTOM, *Commentarius in Epistola ad Galatas*, PG 61, 657 ; CYRIL OF ALEXANDRIA, *in D. Joannis Evangelium*, PG 74, 260 where commenting Jn 14:16-17 he quotes Gal 4:6 to prove that the Holy Spirit renders us sons of God. It is the same with Latin Fathers, though less clearly. The later interpretation of ' ὅτι causal ' seems to have its source in the translation ' quoniam '. For a detailed study of its history, cf. S. ZEDDA, op. cit. pp. 1-123.

who are led by the Spirit of God are sons of God ". In Rom 8 we find an increased emphasis on our participation of the Spirit and on the casual role of the Spirit in our sonship. In Gal God sends the Spirit while in Rom we receive the Spirit. In Gal the Spirit cries ' Abba, Father ', while in Rom we cry in the Spirit which we received. In Rom the Spirit testifies with our Spirit. So there is an intimate relation between the activity of the Spirit and our activity as sons of God under the influence of the Spirit. So the Holy Spirit stands out as the cause of our sonship.

C. *The Holy Spirit-Active Principle of our Life as Sons of God* (*Rom 8*)

We saw above how in the sonship, our spirit is intimately connected with the Holy Spirit and is penetrated so to say with the Spirit of the Son. Thus the Holy Spirit becomes a new principle of action in the sons of God. This seems to be expressed in Rom 8:14 " All who are led by the Spirit of God are sons of God ".

1. *The use of the verb* ἄγειν *in Rom 8:14*

The verb ἄγειν is used absolutely, and having God as subject in the OT almost exclusively in contexts speaking of the Exodus from Egypt and of the New Exodus from the exile, and that often in texts speaking of the father-son relationship between God and Israel (cf. Dt 8:2-5 ; 32:5-12 ; Is 43:5-6 ; 63:7-64:11 ; Jer 31:8-9).

In the NT outside Paul (except in Jn 10:16) it is used in connection with the sonship of Christ (Lk 4:1 ; Acts 13:23,33) or Christians (Heb. 2:10). In Heb 2:10 Christ leads the ' son of God ' from slavery of sin to the glory. The context of Exodus is clear from the fact that here Jesus is compared to Moses, and from the description of the life of Israel in the desert quoted here.

The very fact that Rom 8 speaks of an adoption that is fully realized in the final liberation from the slavery of corruption (8:21-23) seems to show that Paul had in mind a typological comparison with the liberation of Israel out of Egypt leading them to the adoption as sons of Yahweh [44]. As Israel, the son of God, was led by God through the desert towards their heritage of the promised land, so the Christians becoming sons of God through liberation from slavery of sin, law and death are led towards their heritage-eschatological adop-

---

[44] Generally the Commentators do not observe this fact and sometimes put this sentence precisely against the OT concept of sonship. Cf. O. MICHEL, *Der Brief an die Römer*, p. 167 : " Unser Vers (v. 14) klingt wie eine im Kampf gegen das Judentum gewonnene Bestimmung dieser Sohnschaft ".

tion at the resurrection — by the Spirit of God. Though this leading is orientated towards the eschatological adoption, nevertheless it is a leading that takes place at present. Thus the Holy Spirit remains as the active principle of our present life as sons of God.

2. 'The Spirit of the Son dwells in us' (Rom 8:11)

As we saw when speaking of 'putting on Christ', our life of sonship is realized by a dynamic union with Christ the Unique Son of God. Now this is possible only through His Spirit. This is expressed in Rom 8:11 "If the spirit of him who raised Jesus from the dead dwells in you, he who raised Jesus from the dead will give life to your mortal bodies also through his Spirit which dwells in you". It is the same Spirit that led Jesus through death to the resurrection and thus to the consummation of his sonship (Act 13:23-33), that leads us now through death to the resurrection in union with Christ, namely to the consummation of our divine sonship. So the Holy Spirit becomes the active principle of our life in Christ — our life of sonship. Actually the whole chapter of Rom 8 is a commentary of this principle in Rom 8:11.

3. The Structure of Rom 8

Vv. 1-13	A		Life IN CHRIST JESUS — through the Spirit
			The Redemptive work of CHRIST.
14-18	B	a	For all w h o a r e l e d by THE SPIRIT OF GOD are *sons of God*, for you have received THE SPIRIT OF *sonship*. When w e c r y "A b b a F a t h e r" it is THE SPIRIT himself
		b	bearing witness ... that we are CHILDREN OF GOD and if CHILDREN, then h e i r s ... w i t h C h r i s t provided we s u f f e r ... also be g l o r i f i e d with him
		c	I consider that the s u f f e r i n g of this present time ... comparing with the GLORY ... to be revealed ...
19-25	C	a	*For the* c r e a t i o n WAITS WITH eager longing for the r e v e a l i n g of the Sons of God
		b	for the c r e a t i o n ... who subjected it IN HOPE
		c	because the creation will be FREED from the slavery of corruption
		d	and obtain the *freedom of the glory of the children of God*
			We know that THE whole CREATION ...
			GROANING

```
              d'         Not only THE CREATION, but we ...
                                                      GROAN ...
                         As we wait for adoption as sons
              c'         the redemption of our bodies
              b'         for IN this HOPE we were saved ... HOPE ...
              a'         For who hopes for what he sees ... hope for
                                                 what we do not see
                         we WAIT FOR it WITH patience.
     26-30  B'a'         Likewise THE SPIRIT helps us ... to pray ...
                         but THE SPIRIT HIMSELF intercedes for the saints...
              b'         We know ... who are called ... he also predestined
                         to be c o n f o r m e d  to  the  image  of
                                                             THE SON ...
                         He ... the Firstborn among many
                                                        brethren
              c'         And those whom ... he also GLORIFIED
     31-39   A'         Love of CHRIST — Love of God IN CHRIST JESUS
                         The Redemptive work of CHRIST.
```

In this structure, if AA' (vv. 1-13 and 31-39) speak of Christ and those who are in and with Christ, BB' (vv. 14-18 and 26-30) speak of this union with Christ in terms of sonship [45] and put the Holy Spirit as the one who realizes this sonship with Christ [46]. Finally C (vv. 19-25) speaks of the consummation of this sonship led by the Spirit. Being thus the active principle of our life in Christ, our life as sons of God, the Spirit of the Son dwelling in us, leads us to the eschatological consummation of our divine sonship, in the definite possession of our heritage in the glorious revelation of our sonship at the resurrection.

D. *The Corresponding life of the sons of God*

1. *Life of Faith*

Speaking of Gal 3:26 we saw how faith is a constitutive element of the life of sonship. It is this life of faith that is the corresponding docility to the leading of the Spirit in us. Note how the ' Putting on Christ' which was a reality and the formal explanation of being

---

[45] We are children of God and co-heirs with Christ (vv. 16-17) and conformed to the image of the Son, the First-born among many brothren (v. 29). (Note the parallelism of Bb and B'b').

[46] The Spirit leads us (v. 14) and helps us to pray (v. 26) as sons of God 'Abba, Father' (v. 15). (Note the parallelism of Ba and B'a').

the sons of God in Gal 3:26-27, is still an ethical demand in Rom 13:14. It is the Holy Spirit leading us, and our spirit being docile to it through faith, that together constitute the filial spirit and filial life.

Though in Rom 8 the word πίστις does not occur, for Paul, Holy Spirit and Faith are inseparable. If in Gal 3:23 faith liberated us from law, in Gal 5:18 it is the Spirit that liberated us from the law. If in Gal 3:26 we are sons of God through faith, in Rom 8:14 it is through the Spirit that we are sons. If in Col 2:12 we owe our resurrection to the faith, in Rom 8:11 we owe it to the Spirit. So it is the mutual corresponding activity of the Holy Spirit and our spirit through faith that constitute the filial life.

2. *The condition of suffering*

Rom 8:17 says that one of the present results of being sons and heirs of God is suffering with Christ. If the sons of God are similar to Christ in his sonship, they should be similar to him also in his suffering, as it was an essential condition of his sonship [47]. And as the suffering of the Son brought with it salvation and glorification, so also the suffering of the sons signify salvation [48], and lead to glorification.

VII. Eschatological Adoption (Rom 8:23)

A. *The 'Already' and 'not yet' of adoption*

Adoption in Paul is both present (already) and eschatological (not yet). It is present because it is manifest through the actual experience of redemption by Christ and testified in our crying in the Spirit 'Abba, Father' (Rom 8:14f; Gal 4:6). But the final consummation of it is yet to come. The Christian, though he has the first fruits of the Spirit, groans within himself, waiting for the adoption as sons (Rom 8:23) [49].

---

[47] Note the parallelism between τέκνα — κληρονόμοι — συγκληρονόμοι — συμπάσχομεν in v. 17 and συμμόρφους τῆς εἰκόνος τοῦ υἱοῦ αὐτοῦ ... πρωτότοκον ἐν πολλοῖς ἀδελφοῖς in v. 29 in the structure Bb and B'b' of the section in Rom 8.

[48] This differentiates Paul from the Rabbinic consideration of suffering as due to sin. Cf. G. MONTEFIORE and H. LOEWE, *A Rabbinic Anthology*, New York 1963, xiii.

[49] The word υἱοθεσίαν is contained in the overwhelming majority of witnesses such as X ABCKP Ψ, all the minuscules, it ar, Vg, Syr, p, h, copsa,bo, arm, and also quoted by the Fathers such as Origen, Methodius and Augustine etc., while it is omitted by a few Mss such as p⁴⁶, D G and also by Ambrosiaster, Ephrem, Ambrose, Pelagius etc. It is rejected by P. Benoit on the

The obligations of sonship are present obligations, because they have future ramifications. The present moral and ethical behaviour of the sons of God affects his future inheritance and the suffering in this world has its counterpart in the glorification in the next (Rom 8:14-18).

The consequence of man's position as a 'son of God' is a constant ethical tension. He has the spirit of adoption and knows that he is a son of God, liberated from the power of flesh and death (στοιχεῖα τοῦ κόσμου). But still he continues to be subject to their influences until the end [50]. He cannot escape this eschatological tension. But he has the Spirit of God and hence the power to struggle successfully against the στοιχεῖα, though it causes suffering. And the suffering is an indication of future glorification.

B. *Waiting for the adoption as sons*

1. *The structure of Rom 8*

In the concentric structure of Rom 8 in ABCB'A', the C forms the central point speaking of the eschatological situation of the children of God as the basis of hope. Other sections ABB'A' prepare this central point, speaking of the redemptive work of Christ orientated towards completion in the resurrection (A A') and of the present sonship moving towards its manifestation in glory (BB') (cf. vv. 18 and 30) [51]. In the central part this manifestation of the sons that is expected (Caa') gives hope for the entire creation (Cbb'). It consists in a definite liberation or redemption of bodies from the slavery

---

reason that those who are already sons cannot wait for adoption (cf. P. BENOIT, " Nous Gemissons, attendant la délivrance de notre corps (Rom VIII, 23) ", *Mél. J. Lebreton*, I (Paris 1951), 267-280, where he gives also other reasons). But we do not intend to enter into a discussion on this point, since the reading is accepted by the majority of the Writers and also because it is possible to understand the word υἱοθεσίαν in the context as will be clear from our exposition below. For arguments in favour of the authenticity of υἱοθεσίαν cf. S. LYONNET, *Exegesis Epistulae ad Romanos*, pp. 248-250 and also other recent interpreters such as O. MICHEL, C. K. BARRETT, and F. J. LEENHARDT. J. SWETNAM, " On Romans 8:23 and the Expectation of Sonship ", *Bib* 48 (1967), 102-108 proves the authenticity of υἱοθεσίαν giving the meaning ' infer ' to the verb ἀπεκδεχόμενοι in the context ; cf. also F. DE LA CALLE, " La ' huiothesian ' de Rom 8,23 ", *EstBib* 30 (1971), pp. 77-98.

[50] Note how Paul after having spoken of the liberation from the powers and adoption in Gal 4:1-7 goes on to warn the Christians against falling slaves to the same powers again (Gal 4:8-11).

[51] Note also the idea of heritage that points towards this future manifestation.

of corruption (effect of death and sin) (Ccc') and it is the freedom of the glory of the sons of God and the final consummation of adoption (Cdd'). This naturally refers to the resurrection in glory in which the revelation of the sons of God takes place [52].

2. The Vocabulary of Rom 8

Note the vocabulary in the central part (C) that manifests this looking forward to the future such as: ἀποκαραδοκία, ἀπεκδέχομαι (3 times), ἐλπίς (4 times) ἐλπίζειν (2 times) ὑπομονή. The words συμπάσχομεν and συνδοξασθῶμεν in 8:17 express the idea of being co-heirs with Christ and hence of the need of being glorified with him in the future after having suffered with him at present. The phrases such as συμμόρφους τῆς εἰκόνος τοῦ υἱοῦ αὐτοῦ and πρωτότοκον ἐν πολλοῖς ἀδελφοῖς (Rom 8:29) refers to the community of nature between the Son and the sons which comes to perfection by the obtaining of the δόξα at the resurrection [53]. It is only the resurrection with the glorified body as that of Christ, that gives us the perfection of adoption.

The omission of the article before υἱοθεσίαν seems to emphasize the eschatological nature of adoption in 8:23 and τὴν ἀπολύτρωσιν τοῦ σώματος ἡμῶν seems to be an explicative apposition to υἱοθεσίαν [54]. The word ἀπολύτρωσις in the NT, when used of man, has always an eschatological sense (Lk 21:28; Eph 1:14; 4:30). When used in the present tense, it is because it is viewed as already taken place in Christ (Cf. Col 1:14; Eph 1:7; 1 Cor 1:30) and is also connected with the forgiveness of sins which agrees with the eschatological sense, as the need of liberation from the body is the result of sin. In the other eschatological contexts, it is connected with the possession of the Spirit as here (Eph 1:14; 4:30). In Eph 1:14 Redemption seems to be defined as an acquisition of man by God [55]. So the redemption

---

[52] Note how v. 19 introducing the central section on expectation and hope speaks of the revelation of the sons of God, and how the word ἀπεκδέχεται forming an inclusion to the section (aa') is resumed in v. 23 (d') the central affirmation on waiting for the ' adoption as sons '.

[53] Note the correspondence of the two sections vv. 14-18 and vv. 26-30 (BB' in the structure) speaking of this community of nature with Christ coming to perfection in the obtaining of δόξα.

[54] Cf. E. PERCY, *Die Probleme der Colosser und Epheserbriefe*, Lund 1946, p. 24 where he takes it so, adducing parallels such as Rom 7:14; 12:1; 13:4; I Cor 4:13; II Cor 5:1 etc.

[55] On this argument, cf. D. A. CONCHAS, " Redemptio acquisitionis ", *VD* 30 (1952), 14-29; 81-91; 154-169; S. LYONNET, *De Vocabulario redemptionis*, Roma 1960, pp. 61-66.

of body here should be understood not negatively, as a liberation from the body of sin and death but positively as the glorification of the whole man, soul and body, by which the acquisition of man by God is completed.

C. *The Spirit and the Eschatological Adoption*

The structure of Rom 8 shows also the role of the Spirit in leading the sons of God to the eschatological adoption. In the structure, the parallel sections B and B' speak of the role of the Spirit in the divine sonship of man. Verse 14 introduces the section B saying "Those who are led by the Spirit of God are sons of God", and goes on describing the sonship, moving towards its eschatological stage in the glory to be revealed (v. 18)[56]. So it is the leading of the Spirit, that seems to conduct the sons of God towards the glory to be revealed[57]. Hence the role of the Spirit in the adoption that is present and eschatological[58]. If the present work of the Spirit is to witness to the reality of the divine sonship of man, his future work is to reveal them as 'sons of God'. If his present work is to give man power to live up to his sonship, his future work is to give man power to bring it into completion. If his present work is to guarantee the believer that he is a 'son' and 'heir' of God, his future work is to make good that guarantee by providing entrance into the inheritance[59].

---

[56] Note the same procedure in section B' (vv. 26-30) thus forming a structural parallelism between B-abc and B'-a'b'c'.

[57] Note how the very central affirmation regarding this eschatological adoption in v. 23 speaks of those who 'possessing the first-fruits of the Holy Spirit ... wait for adoption'.

[58] Cf. W. MICHAELIS, *Reich Gottes und Geist Gottes nach dem Neuen Testament*, Basel 1931, 24 : " Der gegenwärtige Geistbesitz, wiewohl das Höchstmass göttlicher Hilfe (Rom 8:26), steht in einer Spannung zur Enderwartung, die sich mit der 'Erlösung des Leibes' (Rom 8:23) erfüllen wird, das heisst, der Auferstehung der Toten die das Reich Gottes einleitet ". We should like to add that Rom 8:14 being parallel to v. 26 (cf. the structure) also stands orientated towards the adoption in v. 23.

[59] Cf. E. LEWIS, " A Christian Theodicy : An Exposition of Romans 8:18-39 ", Interpretation 11 (1957), 416 ; cf. also C. C. OKE, " A Suggestion with regard to Romans 8:23 ", Interpretation 11 (1957), 455-460, where he argues that ἀπαρχή is a technical legal term for the birth certificate of a free person. Then the activity of the Spirit in the context of vv. 16-23 would mean 'the certification of the Spirit'. This interpretation accords quite well with the role of the Spirit as guaranteeing and providing entrance into the inheritance. For further discussion on the work of the Spirit in the resurrection and exal-

Hence the parallel terms such as 'freedom of the glory of the sons of God', 'redemption of our bodies', 'freedom from the slavery of corruption' indicate the eschatological condition of adoption by the Father (C), towards which the Spirit of God leads the children of God (BB′) effecting an intimate union with Christ the Son of God (AA′).

Conclusion

The term υἱοθεσία is characteristic of the Pauline doctrine of sonship and it emphasizes the dignity and privilege rather than the nature of sonship. Christian sonship is a continuation of Israel's sonship, and it presupposes a liberation from slavery of sin, law, beings that by nature are not gods, body, death etc. Hence the unique significance of Christ the redeemer in mediating this sonship.

Adoption to divine sonship is made by God the Father, and the Christian sonship is a sharing in the sonship of Christ. The life of this sonship is concretely expressed in a life of faith in Christ, which remains dynamic throughout, resulting in a renewal of life. It is the Gospel or the Word of God that introduces man to this life of sonship and hence Paul speaks of a begetting through the Gospel.

The Holy Spirit is the Witness and Cause of this adoption and remains the active principle of this life of sonship. It is the same Spirit that leads the sons of God to the eschatological consummation in glory, the glorification of the whole man. Hence the eschatological adoption is the object of our hope.

The condition of man as 'son of God' is of a constant ethical tension, since the 'liberated' son of God is still subject to the influences of inimical powers. But he has power to overcome it, though the struggle causes suffering. But it is a suffering with Christ, which will end up in glory with Christ the Son of God.

---

tation of Christ and the believers, cf. N. Q. HAMILTON, " *The Holy Spirit and Eschatology in Paul* ", SJT Occasional Papers 6, 1957, pp. 17-21.

PART TWO

THE JOHANNINE DOCTRINE OF CHRISTIAN SONSHIP

INTRODUCTION

Having seen the theme of the divine sonship of man in the OT, Jewish, Hellenistic and the Pre-Johannine NT Writings, now we proceed to an exegetical analysis of the Johannine texts on Christian Sonship. Before the study of the texts themselves, we present a preliminary study of the terminology characteristic of the Johannine doctrine of Christian Sonship.

As to the analysis of the texts themselves, we try to have a strictly critical and exegetical approach, so that the texts will be made to speak for themselves. Hence the analysis will be based mainly on the grammatical and structural considerations and the study of the Vocabulary.

After the preliminary study of the Johannine Vocabulary on Christian sonship, we present a study of the Johannine texts which speak explicitly of the divine sonship of the believers. Hence the different chapters are arranged according to the texts indicating the different aspects of Christian Sonship expressed in them. The analysis of the basic text will, in each case, be accompanied by a short study of the other texts or themes connected with it.

Finally, in the general conclusion, we will try to point out the originality of the Johannine concept of Christian Sonship against the Pre-Johannine background studied in Part One.

The Johannine Terminology

To express the divine sonship of men, John makes use of two main phrases: "τέκνα Θεοῦ" (Jn 1:12; 11:52; I Jn 3:1,2,10; 5:2) and "γεννηθῆναι ἐκ τοῦ Θεοῦ" (I Jn 2:29; 3:9; 4:7; 5:1,4,18). First of all we have to see what these phrases mean in themselves, and then their Johannine usage.

A. Usage of "τέκνα Θεοῦ"

1. The usage of 'τέκνον' in general

"τέκνον" comes from the root "τίκτειν" which literally means 'to beget', 'to engender', 'to procreate', 'to give birth to', namely, pointing always towards the origin [1]. Thus literally it points to the offspring, which results from such action on the part of either or both of the parents. The proper translation of the word in English would be 'child', without regard to sex [2].

In the LXX it corresponds predominantly to the Hebrew word 'bēn'. The sex of the child can be made clear only by the context (cf. Mt 21:28; Rev 12:5).

In a more general sense the plural of the word is used for descendants or posterity. In this sense it is used in Mt 2:18; 3:9; 27:25; Acts 2:39; 13:33. The Hebrew usage of denoting peoples and tribes by bᵉnê joined to the name of the progenitor [3] seems to lie behind this usage in the NT.

The metaphorical meanings of 'τέκνον' are quite numerous. In the vocative it generally expresses a familiar address, denoting the reciprocal and intimate relationship formed between men by bonds of love or authority (cf. Mt 9:2; Mk 2:5; Lk 16:25; and Gal 4:19).

---

[1] Cf. A. OEPKE, art. "παῖς", *TDNT* V, p. 638.

[2] In this sense we find the word in Mk 13:12; Lk 1:7; Acts 7:5 and Rev 12:4 in the singular and in Mt 7:11; 10:21; 18:25; 19:29; 22:24; Mk 13:12; Lk 1:17; 14:26 and I Cor 7:14 in the plural. Cf. W. BAUER, *A Greek English Lexicon of the New Testament and Other Early Christian Literature*, Chicago, 1957, p. 815.

[3] Cf. the names such as bᵉnê yisrā'ēl (Gen 42:5; 45:21; 46:5; Exod 1:1 etc.) and bᵉnê yᵉhûdâ (Gen 46:12; 26:19; I Chr 2:3,10; 4:1 etc. for the Israelites).

In a metaphorical sense it is used of the disciples or the spiritual children of a teacher or an apostle (cf. I Cor 4:14,17; I Tim 1:2; Tit 1:4; Philm 10; 3 Jn 4) [4]. Here we have genealogy and analogy to ancient ideas of adoption, which are partly Jewish and partly Greek, but which are reorientated by the Christian eschatological context [5]. In Jn ' τέκνα ' in this sense is applied with special reference to the members of particular Churches (cf. 2 Jn 1:4,13).

The designation of the inhabitants of a city as its ' τέκνα ' (Mt 23:37; Lk 13:34; 19:44; Gal 4:25) and the use of ' τέκνον ' or ' υἱός ' with a genitive of quality or condition as a substitute for an adjective (Eph. 2:3; 5:8; I Pet. 1:14) is certainly of Hebraic derivation [6].

Again ' τέκνον ' is used with a noun in the genitive to show that somebody bears a perfect likeness or a similarity of nature to some other person, to whom for the same reason some relation of paternity is attributed [7]. In this expression is implied the derivation of the person's nature, and following therefrom, his character and belongings, though sometimes the one and sometimes the other element is prominent. In this category the use of ' τέκνα ' with abstract things to signify an intimate relationship of connection, origin or dependence could also be grouped (cf. Rom 9:7,8; Gal 4:28,31) [8].

2. *The Johannine use of* " τέκνα Θεοῦ "

John makes use of ' τέκνα ' 15 times altogether in his writings and every time he makes use of the plural, with the exception of Rev 12:4,5 [9]. In 7 cases the use is metaphorical and the word is

---

[4] In this sense, John uses rather " τεκνία " ' little children ', the diminutive of τέκνον (cf. I Jn 2:12,28; 3:7,18; 4:4; 5:21; Jn 13:33). It is a term of keener affection.

[5] Cf. A. OEPKE, art. παῖς, *TDNT* V, p. 639.

[6] Cf. L. RADERMACHER, *Neutest. Grammatik*, (Handbuch zum Neuen Testament 1), 2nd ed., 1925, p. 28; J. H. MOULTON and W. F. HOWARD, *A Grammar of New Testament Greek*, vol. II, London, 1919-29, 441.

[7] Note the expressions such as τὰ τέκνα τοῦ 'Αβραάμ (Mt 3:9; Lk 3:8; Jn 8:39; Rom 9:7) (τὰ) τέκνα (τοῦ) Θεοῦ (Rom 8:16,21; 9:8; Phil 2:15; Eph 5:1; Jn 1:12; 11:52; I Jn 3:1,2,10; 5:2); τὰ τέκνα τοῦ διαβόλου (I Jn 3:10).

[8] Cf. A. DEISSMANN, *Bible Studies*, Edinburgh, 1901, p. 161f., where he shows that the use is both Oriental and Greek.

[9] In Rev 12:4,5 the word is used of Christ, which also makes an exception to the ordinary use characteristic of the other Johannine writings, where Christ is exclusively called υἱός and τέκνα is used exclusively for men, when speaking of their relation to God. Here it is worth noting that in the Book of Revelation υἱός is also attributed to men in relation to God and there it is in the singular (cf. 2:7), a use that is foreign to the ordinary use in the Johannine Writings.

followed by a genitive of a noun such as "Θεοῦ" (cf. Jn 1:12; 11: 52; I Jn 3:1,2,10), "Ἀβραάμ" (Jn 8:39) and "διαβόλου" (I Jn 3:10)[10]. In all other cases the use of "τέκνα" refers to children who are physically descendants. It is interesting to see that the metaphorical usage is found exclusively in the Gospel and the First Epistle of John, while the other usages are confined to II and III Jn and the Book of Revelation. Needless to say it is the metaphorical usage of "τέκνα Θεοῦ" that comes under our consideration.

a. Τέκνα Θεοῦ and υἱὸς Θεοῦ

First of all we have to exclude from "τέκνα Θεοῦ" a meaning that is equal to "υἱὸς Θεοῦ". The very Johannine usage of the terms favours this exclusion. The Evangelist, who, on the one hand, speaks of the divine sonship both with regard to Christ and with regard to men, on the other hand, carefully makes a clear distinction between them. The exclusive use of "υἱός" for Christ and "τέκνα" for men is expressive of this distinction. It is only of Jesus that the word "μονογενής" is used, which points to the unique relation of divine sonship and generation of the "υἱὸς τοῦ Θεοῦ"[11]. While men have to *become* the children of God, and their divine sonship is a gift due only to the love of God towards men (Jn 1:12; I Jn 3:1), Jesus *was* the Only Begotten Son, who was sent into the world (Jn 3:16-18). If Jesus in his temporal existence is 'the Only Begotten Son of God' (Jn 1:14,18) and his temporal generation (Incarnation) is called a generation from God (Jn 1:13; I Jn 5:18), it is because his temporal sonship and generation is a continuation and manifestation of the eternal sonship and generation. Thus it is again different from the sonship and generation of the faithful, which Jn shows through a different usage in his vocabulary. If Jesus is "ὁ υἱὸς τοῦ Θεοῦ" and "ὁ γεννηθεὶς ἐκ τοῦ Θεοῦ", the faithful are "τέκνα τοῦ Θεοῦ" and "ὁ γεγεννημένος ἐκ τοῦ Θεοῦ"[12].

This distinction between the divine sonship of Christ and Christians is manifested also in the use of "πατήρ" for God by Jn. The fact that in the Johannine Writings, where the name "πατήρ" is used

---

[10] In this connection it is worth noting that John never connects the word τέκνα with an abstract noun. With abstract nouns he uses instead the noun υἱός (cf. 12:36; 17:12).

[11] Cf. F. BÜCHSEL, art μονογενής, TDNT IV, p. 741; R. BULTMANN, *Das Evangelium des Johannes*, Göttingen, 1941, p. 47.

[12] In spite of the differences, the similarity of expressions emphasizes the relation between the υἱὸς τοῦ Θεοῦ and the τέκνα τοῦ Θεοῦ in the divine sonship and generation as we will see in the section speaking of the divine sonship of men as a participation of the divine sonship of Christ.

for God about 136 times, the expression ' Our Father ' never occurs, and ' Your Father ' only once, and that after the resurrection, marks the singular relation of the " υἱὸς τοῦ Θεοῦ " to the Father which is different from the relation of the " τέκνα τοῦ Θεοῦ " to the Father. Hence the " υἱὸς τοῦ Θεοῦ " who was the son of God by virtue of a strictly natural generation, is clearly differentiated by John from the " τέκνα τοῦ Θεοῦ " who are by natural generation men, and become children of God through a supernatural generation.

b. Τέκνα τοῦ Θεοῦ and τέκνα τοῦ διαβόλου

Having seen that " τέκνα τοῦ Θεοῦ " has in Jn a metaphorical meaning, we now proceed further to see what is implied in this metaphorical usage, because as noted above, the metaphorical usage of " τέκνα ", though it always includes some relation of origin, could neverthless imply a relation of origin extending from any kind of dependence, to the derivation of the very nature of the person.

First of all we see in Jn a use of " τέκνα τοῦ Θεοῦ " that is parallel to " τέκνα τοῦ διαβόλου ". In I Jn 3:10 those who do justice are indicated as the " τέκνα τοῦ Θεοῦ " in opposition to those who do not do justice, and are indicated as " τέκνα τοῦ διαβόλου ". The " ἐν τούτῳ " in v. 10 could refer to that which precedes or that which follows. Actually it refers to both. In as much as v. 10 forms an inclusion with 2:29 [13], it refers to what precedes. Thus the children of God are manifested in their ' doing justice ', and the children of the devil in their ' not doing justice ' (committing sin). What follows in v. 10b is a repetition of the same thing negatively. The sentence " πᾶς ὁ μὴ ποιῶν " of v. 10b, which corresponds to 2:29 – 3:9, describes the " ἐν τούτῳ " of v. 10a. Thus John puts here the " τέκνα τοῦ Θεοῦ " in antithetical parallelism to the " τέκνα τοῦ διαβόλου ".

This parallelism to " τέκνα τοῦ διαβόλου " seems to give " τέκνα τοῦ Θεοῦ " a meaning of belonging on the mere ground of likeness of character. It is interesting to note that John speaks of the devil in terms of a father-son relationship only in two contexts, namely, here in I Jn 3:8-10 and in Jn 8:44. In both these contexts the devil is described as the one who sins from the beginning, and a person who sins is said to be in a filial relation to the devil [14]. Hence the whole context of these passages clearly shows that the filial relation is based on the simple fact of likeness of character [15]. So, if the " τέκνα τοῦ διαβόλου " indicates a moral likeness of character, its antithetical

---

[13] Cf. the literary structure of the section I Jn 2:29 – 3:10 on p. 240.
[14] Τέκνα τοῦ διαβόλου (I Jn 3:10) and ἐκ τοῦ πατρὸς τοῦ διαβόλου (Jn 8:44).
[15] It is worth noting here that also in Jn 8:39 the ' children of Abraham ' are said to be those who ' do the works of Abraham '.

parallel " τέκνα τοῦ Θεοῦ " indicates a filial relation to God, based on a moral likeness of character.

c. Τέκνα τοῦ Θεοῦ and εἶναι ἐκ τοῦ Θεοῦ

We go further and try to see if the phrase could be elucidated still more by some other equivalent expression. And here we meet a phrase that is used parallel to the " τέκνα τοῦ Θεοῦ ", namely, the phrase " εἶναι ἐκ τοῦ Θεοῦ."

The parallelism of these two phrases is clear from the fact that we see them precisely in the same contexts, as we saw the " τέκνα τοῦ Θεοῦ " used in antithetical parallelism to " τέκνα τοῦ διαβόλου ", namely, in I Jn 3:10 and Jn 8:47 speaking of the fatherhood of the devil. This parallelism is reinforced by the fact that John speaks of "εἶναι ἐκ τοῦ διαβόλου" only in these two contexts (cf. I Jn 3:8 and Jn 8:44) and that also in antithetical parallelism with " εἶναι ἐκ τοῦ Θεοῦ ".

The preference of Jn for the preposition ἐκ is well known [16]. The phrase " εἶναι ἐκ τοῦ Θεοῦ " is a use characteristic of Jn who has used it 13 times, while outside Jn we find it only in Acts 5:39 [17]. Out of these 13 occurrences in Jn, 8 are used of men (cf. Jn 8:47 bis ; I Jn 3:10 ; 4:4,6 bis ; 5:19 ; III Jn 11) while the others are of doctrine (Jn 7:17), of the spirits (I Jn 4:1,2,3) and of love (I Jn 4:7). Thus it is worth noting that the use of " εἶναι ἐκ τοῦ Θεοῦ " for men is exclusively Johannine.

Another characteristic of the Johannine use of " εἶναι ἐκ τοῦ Θεοῦ " for men is that it occurs precisely in the contexts that speak of the father-son relationship between God and man (cf. Jn 8:41-47 ; I Jn 3:10 ; 4:4-7 ; 5:18-20) [18]. This points to a difference of signification in " εἶναι ἐκ τοῦ Θεοῦ " when used of men, than when used of doctrine, or spirits or love where it means a simple derivation or belonging. It is also worth noting that it is in these contexts that John speaks of those who are " ἐκ τοῦ διαβόλου " (cf. Jn 8:44 ; I Jn 3:8) and " ἐκ τοῦ κόσμου" (cf. I Jn 4:5), hence in antithetical parallelism to those who are of God [19].

Again there is another peculiarity that we find in the use of

---

[16] In the Johannine Writings alone we find ἐκ 336 times, while in Mt 82, Mk 67, Lk 87, Acts 84, Paul 210, Heb 20, and the Catholic Epistles 28 times.

[17] In the other few occurrences of ἐκ τοῦ Θεοῦ it is used without the verb εἶναι (cf. Rom 2:29 ; I Cor 2:12 ; 11:12 ; II Cor 3:8 ; 5:18 and Phil 3:9).

[18] The only exception is in 3 Jn 11, in which he does not treat of the divine sonship of men.

[19] Note that in Jn 15:19 ; 17:14,16 and 8:23 the εἶναι ἐκ τοῦ κόσμου is denied of Christ and the Disciples.

"εἶναι ἐκ τοῦ Θεοῦ", namely, that it is never used of Christ. When speaking of Christ, Jn employs "εἶναι παρὰ τοῦ Θεοῦ" (cf. Jn 6:46; 7:29; 9:16,33) and this is used exclusively of Christ. At the same time, it is to be noted that "ἐκ τοῦ Θεοῦ" is used of Christ when speaking of His coming into the world [20], or His temporal generation [21]. From the above considerations it is clear that "εἶναι ἐκ τοῦ Θεοῦ" used of men in Jn shows a peculiar aspect of the divine sonship of men which is diametrically opposed to the diabolic sonship of men.

The preposition ἐκ when used with εἶναι denotes origin [22]. The use of "εἶναι ἐκ" occurs 52 times in John and is distinctly characteristic of him. Sometimes it denotes place of origin or derivation (cf. Jn 1:46; 4:22; 7:17,22,52; I Jn 4:17) while in other contexts it denotes a belonging to a group or community (cf. Jn 3:1; 6:64,70; 7:50; 10:16,26; 12:20; 18:17,25). Here it is to be noted that sometimes this belonging is considered not merely as something external but as a communion (cf. I Jn 2:19). Finally, it denotes a spiritual belonging to a determined sphere and the influence from it determines the nature of the thing or person. This is the most frequent usage in John and it is mostly in dualistic contexts. Thus we have in Jn 3:31 "ἐκ τῆς γῆς" opposed to "ἐκ τοῦ οὐρανοῦ" in Jn 8:23 "ἐκ τῶν κάτω" opposed to "ἐκ τῶν ἄνω", in I Jn 2:16 "ἐκ τοῦ πατρός" opposed to "ἐκ τοῦ κόσμου" and in I Jn 4:5-6 "ἐκ τοῦ Θεοῦ" opposed to "ἐκ τοῦ κόσμου". As we can see from the examples, this is the usage under which the formula "εἶναι ἐκ του Θεοῦ" comes.

In the light of the other parallel Johannine phrases such as 'to be of the earth' (Jn 3:31; 8:23), 'to be of the world' (Jn 8:23; 15:19; 17:14,16; 18:36; I Jn 2:16; 4:5) the "εἶναι ἐκ τοῦ Θεοῦ" seems to indicate a moral connection of derivation and dependence on God [23]. At the same time, the parallelism with other similar phrases shows that this idea of origin or derivation is far from being a derivation by birth. So a simple identification of "εἶναι ἐκ" and "γεγεννῆσθαι ἐκ" made by scholars is not at all justifiable [24]. So practically,

---

[20] Cf. Jn 8:42 "ἐκ τοῦ Θεοῦ ἐξῆλθον καὶ ἥκω"; 16:28 "ἐξῆλθον ἐκ τοῦ πατρὸς καὶ ἐλήλυθα εἰς τὸν κόσμον".

[21] Cf. Jn 1:13 "ἐκ Θεοῦ ἐγεννήθη" I Jn 5:18 "ὁ γεννηθεὶς ἐκ τοῦ Θεοῦ".

[22] Cf. W. BAUER, *A Greek English Lexicon*, p. 234.

[23] As WESTCOTT says: "It expresses the ideas of derivation and dependence and of a moral correspondence between the issue and the source". Cf. B. F. WESTCOTT, *Epistles of St. John*, 4th ed., London, 1966, p. 123.

[24] Cf. BULTMANN, *Evangelium*, p. 97, note 3 where he sees in Gnosticism the source of the formula εἶναι ἐκ and says that in Jn εἶναι ἐκ is of the same signification as γεγεννῆσθαι ἐκ. Cf. also C. H. DODD, *Interpretation*, p. 259, where he expresses a similar opinion.

" εἶναι ἐκ τοῦ Θεοῦ " comes to the same as " τέκνα τοῦ Θεοῦ "[25]. The parallelism between these two phrases in Jn favours this interpretation.

d. εἶναι ἐκ τοῦ Θεοῦ and γεγέννηται ἐκ τοῦ Θεοῦ

But is there some indication in John that " εἶναι ἐκ τοῦ Θεοῦ " tells something more about " τέκνα Θεοῦ " ? It seems that the answer is to be given in the affirmative. John uses " εἶναι ἐκ τοῦ Θεοῦ " not only in contexts where it is parallel to " τέκνα Θεοῦ " but also in contexts where it is parallel to " γεγέννηται ἐκ τοῦ Θεοῦ " (cf. I Jn 4:4,6 ; 5:19)[26]. This shows that there is some element in " εἶναι ἐκ τοῦ Θεοῦ " that is in the line of " γεγέννηται ἐκ τοῦ Θεοῦ " without, however, expressing the idea of a begetting.

At this point I Jn 5:19 seems to come to our aid. There the " εἶναι ἐκ τοῦ Θεοῦ " of the believers is put antithetically parallel to the fact that ' the world lies in the power of the evil one '[27]. The ' evil one ' is here described as an active influence to which there is a corresponding receptivity in the life of the world[28]. The order " ὁ κόσμος ὅλος " (not " ὅλος ὁ κόσμος " as in I Jn 2:2) suggests that the world is wholly or completely, in all its parts and elements placed in the domain of the evil one[29]. This active influence of the evil one is absolutely excluded in the case of those who are begotten of God. This is affirmed by v. 18c : " and the evil one does not touch him ", which according to the structure of the section corresponds to v. 19b. So if the nature of the world (the sinner) is fully determined by the evil one (v. 19b) the nature of those begotten of God is completely free from the influence of the evil one (v. 18c) and hence is determined by some other principle. This other principle is expressed positively in v. 19a : " we know that we are from God — ἐκ τοῦ Θεοῦ ἐσμεν ". So the εἶναι ἐκ τοῦ Θεοῦ points to the nature of the children of God, a nature that is fully determined by God.

It is the same idea of antithetical parallelism that we see between the children of God who are from God, and the children of the devil who are not from God (I Jn 3:10), but from the devil (I Jn 3:8).

---

[25] We will see later, how far in Jn the εἶναι ἐκ τοῦ Θεοῦ unlike the other formulas with εἶναι ἐκ assumes a special meaning that coincides with the characteristic Johannine use of γεγεννῆσθαι ἐκ τοῦ Θεοῦ.

[26] It is to be noted that this parallelism is found also in I Jn 3:10, which forms an inclusion to I Jn 2:29.

[27] Cf. the literary structure of I Jn 5:18-20 on p. 282.

[28] It is to be remembered that the world is here taken as alien from and opposed to God.

[29] Cf. WESTCOTT, *Epistles*, p. 195.

It is the devil who gave the first impulse to human sinning or who sins from the very beginning (cf. Jn 8:44 ; I Jn 3:8b) and who always gives fresh impulse to it (cf. Jn 13:2). So directly or indirectly all human sins may be described as the work of the devil, to destroy which the Son of God appeared (cf. I Jn 3:5,8cd). Thus the devil becomes the father of those who commit sin, by determining their nature of sinning, expressed in the phrase εἶναι ἐκ τοῦ διαβόλου (cf. I Jn 3:8,12 ; Jn 8:44). In the same way God becomes the father of the believers, by determining their nature, their manner of thinking and acting expressed in the phrase εἶναι ἐκ τοῦ Θεοῦ (cf. Jn 8:47 ; I Jn 3:10 ; 4:4,6 ; 5:19 ; III Jn 11).

So far we have tried to see the meaning of τέκνα τοῦ Θεοῦ and εἶναι ἐκ τοῦ Θεοῦ in the light of their philology and their Johannine use in antithetical parallelism with τέκνα τοῦ διαβόλου and εἶναι ἐκ τοῦ διαβόλου. Thus we saw that they express a relation of vital dependence of man on God, which constitutes the father-son relationship between God and man, and this is parallel to the father-son relationship between the devil and the sinner.

But, though parallel, are they in fact equivalent ? Some authors do not shrink from drawing this inference [30]. But in spite of the apparent similarity of expressions, the phrases " τέκνα τοῦ Θεοῦ " as well as " εἶναι ἐκ τοῦ Θεοῦ " might admit of a deeper significance, which could by no means ever be included in the phrases " τέκνα τοῦ διαβόλου " as well as " εἶναι ἐκ τοῦ διαβόλου ". And actually this difference is implied in Jn, because John also speaks of a begetting from God. There are authors who attribute to the devil an imparting of life to the sinner [31]. But it is quite evident that the devil cannot give life, while God can. An examination of the Johannine phrase regarding the begetting from God will bring to light this difference.

---

[30] Cf. ROTHE, *Der erste Brief Johannes*, Wittenberg, 1878, as quoted by R. LAW, *The Tests of Life. A Study of the First Epistle of St John*, Edinburgh, 1909, p. 143, where he says : " It is an appalling thought that man may enter into the same relation to the devil, in which he originally stands to God "; cf. also, J. E. HUTHER, *Critical and Exegetical Handbook to the General Epistles of James and John*, Edinburgh, 1882, pp. 393-398, where he also expresses himself in similar terms.

[31] Cf. J. E. HUTHER, op. cit., p. 393, where he says that " the life that animates the sinner emanates from the devil ".

B. *Usage of* γεννηθῆναι ἐκ Θεοῦ

1. *The Use of* γεννηθῆναι *in General*

" Γεννάω " from the philological point of view is liable to different interpretations. The general idea is quite simple, namely, that of begetting, generating, giving birth to, producing etc. But this action may be thought of from different points of view, and consequently " γεννάω " can have different implications or shades of meaning.

In the LXX " γεννάω " corresponds almost constantly to the verb *yālad* and its derivatives. *Yālad* translated by " γεννάω " in the LXX usually refers to the mother bearing or bringing forth a child, rather than to the father begetting a child, though the latter is also found[32].

" Γεννάω " is also used of the begetting of the father and the ' bringing forth of the mother ' both in Greek generally[33] and in the NT[34]. When speaking of the mother, it could mean the ' conception ' (cf. Mt 1:20) or the ' bringing forth ' (cf. Lk 1:35). But primarily " γεννάω " is used for the father who generates the children[35], while for the mother the verb " τίκτω " is used (cf. Mt 1:21,23,25 ; Lk 1:31 ; 2:7 ; Rev 12:4,5,13). This difference comes from the fact that " τίκτω " properly designates the bodily act of bringing forth a child, while " γεννάω " includes also the act and the element of conception[36]. When " γεννάω " is used of the father in the active, the role of the mother is expressed with ἐκ and the genitive (cf. Mt 1:3,5). When used in the passive, speaking of the natural begetting from the father, " ἀπό " is used introducing the male principle (cf. Heb 11:12)[37]. But it is to be noted here that the " ἑνός " in Heb 11:12 is considered as the remote principle of those who are begotten and hence the preposition " ἀπό " and not " ἐκ "[38]. When " γεννάω " is used of the mother in the passive, almost invariably " ἐκ " is used introducing

---

[32] It is said of the mother about 208 times, while it is said of the father only about 22 times. Rarely it refers also to both parents (cf. Za 13:3 ; Gen 20:17).

[33] For examples, cf. W. BAUER, *A Greek English Lexicon*, pp. 154-155 ; Th. ZAHN, *Kommentar zum Johannesevangelium*, 5th ed., Leipzig, 1921, p. 74, no. 64. Cf. Lk 1:13,57 ; 23:29 ; Jn 16:21.

[34] Of the father, cf. Mt 1:2-16 ; of the mother, cf. Lk 1:13,57.

[35] Cf. F. ZORELL, *Lexicon Graecum Novi Testamenti*, Paris, 1961, col. 247.

[36] Cf. G. BAUER, art. " Geburt ", *TBLNT*. I, Wuppertal, 1967, p. 444.

[37] There is a variation of the reading ἐγεννήθησαν, namely, ἐγενήθησαν which is actually the reading attested by many important Mss and accepted by the Editors such as Weiss Bern, Von Soden, Vogels, Merk, Nestle, Bauer etc.

[38] Cf. T. E. ROBINSON, *Greek and English Lexicon of the New Testament* New York, 1872, p. 224.

the female principle (cf. Mt 1:16; 19:12; Lk 1:35; Gal 4:23). But as we have seen, speaking of the natural birth, in the NT as also in the LXX, it is not possible to attribute to " γεννάω " a reference exclusive to the father, and hence it can mean both 'begetting' and 'bringing forth' according to the context.

Now as " τέκνον " is taken sometimes in a metaphorical sense, so also " γεννᾶν " may point to a metaphorical begetting. Thus in the sense of begetting " γεννάω " is used to indicate the influence of a person exerted on others so as to mould their lives, thus constituting the beginning of a new life and establishing a filial relation. Thus Paul is said to have begotten the faithful through the Gospel (cf. I Cor 4:15,17; Gal 4:24; Philm 10). In the sense too of 'bringing forth' " γεννάω " is used metaphorically to indicate something that is produced or caused (cf. II Tim 2:23).

Speaking of God as the subject, a metaphorical usage is found in the OT for the begetting of the King-Messiah by God; it refers to his kingly enthronement (cf. Ps 2:7; 110:3) and this usage is taken up by the Christological texts of the NT (cf. Acts 13:33; Heb 1:5; 5:5), though here the idea of a natural begetting cannot be excluded, which only gives perfection to the OT Messianic idea. It is true that the OT is reluctant to express the father-son relationship between God and Israel in terms of a generation, probably because of the surrounding Religions which abounded in generation myths [39]. But it cannot be said that the metaphorical usage of " γεννάω " to express the father-son relationship between Yahweh and Israel is completely absent from the OT. Texts like Dt 32:15-18; Is 1:2; 45:9-11; Jer 2:26-27 etc., certainly speak of the formation of Israel as the people of God through the Exodus and Covenant in terms of a generation, and the father-son relationship between Yahweh and Israel is admittedly a result of the Exodus and Covenant [40]. Also the Johannine expression 'to be begotten by God' speaking of men comes under the metaphorical usage of " γεννάω ", since a divine origin by a strictly natural generation from God cannot be attributed to men.

2. The Johannine Usage of γεννηθῆναι

The verb " γεννάω " is a word of Johannine preference. Out of the 99 occurrences in the whole NT, 28 are in the Johannine Writings [41]. Jn makes use of " γεννάω " almost always in the passive [42],

---

[39] Cf. G. BAUER, art. " Geburt ", *TBLNT* I, p. 445.

[40] Cf. our treatise on the divine sonship of men in the OT pp. 23-24.

[41] Here we have to remember that out of the rest, 45 are in Mt with his genealogy. Apart from that it occurs in Mk once; Lk 6 times; Acts 7 times; Paul 7 times; Heb 4 times; and II Pet once.

and except in ch. 9 treating of the blind man, he always speaks of a supernatural generation [43]. Speaking thus of a supernatural generation in the passive, the verb "γεννᾶσθαι" or "γεννηθῆναι" is always followed by the preposition ἐκ with the name of the begetter in the genitive [44]. And always it is "ἐκ τοῦ Θεοῦ" except in Jn 3, when he replaces the "Θεός" with "πνεῦμα".

In our examination of the general usage of "γεννάω" in the NT, we saw how it is used in the active and in the passive, referring to both the father and mother. So "γεννάω" in itself can refer to the moment of conception or to the moment of birth. But God being the Father of men, the "γεννηθῆναι ἐκ τοῦ Θεοῦ" should naturally refer to the moment of conception. On the other hand, all the examples of "γεννηθῆναι" in the passive referring to the natural generation, when followed by the preposition ἐκ, introduce the role of the mother and hence refer to the moment of 'bringing forth' (cf. Mt 1:16; 19:12; Lk 1:35; Gal 4:23).

Now, to what moment does the 'generation from God' in Jn refer? It seems that Jn does not refer to any specific moment either of conception or of birth. Nor does he distinguish between these two moments, when speaking of the supernatural generation. The distinction between the 'aorist' and 'perfect' does not seem to refer to the two moments of conception (aorist) and birth (perfect). As we will see later, this distinctive use of aorist and perfect has another theological importance for John. Hence when speaking of "γεννηθῆναι ἐκ τοῦ Θεοῦ" what really matters for Jn is the idea of an origin from God through generation. He deliberately does not envisage the different moments of conception and birth.

This is perhaps reinforced by the fact that Jn never makes use of the aorist indicative to express the divine generation of men. In the divine generation of men, what is of interest to him, is the nature of the generation, and not the moment of the generation, while in the divine generation of Christ the historical event of Incarnation was of great importance, and hence was expressed in the aorist indicative (Jn 1:13) and participle (I Jn 5:18) [45].

---

[42] The only two exceptions are Jn 16:21 speaking of the woman bringing forth the man and I Jn 5:1 speaking of God as the begetter of the faithful.

[43] Cf. Jn 1:13; 3:3,4,5,6,7,8; 8:41; I Jn 2:29; 3:9; 4:7; 5:1,4,18. Jn 18:37 speaks of the coming of Christ into the world as being born.

[44] The only exception is Jn 3:3,7 where ἄνωθεν stands for the ἐξ ὕδατος καὶ πνεύματος of Jn 3:5.

[45] Note that also in the divine generation of Christ, the moment of importance for Jn is the historical moment of Incarnation as such, without further specification as to the moment of conception or birth.

Since it is the origin itself that is of importance in the Johannine concept of the divine generation of men, the preposition ἐκ deserves particular consideration. We saw above how ἐκ in itself, when joined to verbs such as " εἶναι " " γεννᾶν " and " γίνεσθαι " indicates origin. In this sense ἐκ points to that from which anything proceeds or is derived, and which is put in the genitive. In as much as the phrase " γεννηθῆναι ἐκ " in Jn refers to origin, it could be made to approach the frequently recurring Johannine phrase " εἶναι ἐκ " (Jn 8:47 ; I Jn 3:10) and " ἐξέρχεσθαι ἐκ " (Jn 8:42 ; 16:28) [46]. We will see below how the " ἐκ Θεοῦ ἐγεννήθη " referring to the divine generation of Christ, expressed in the aorist indicative in Jn, is parallel to the historical coming of Christ expressed as " ἐκ τοῦ Θεοῦ ἐξῆλθον ". If the phrase " ἦλθεν ἐκ τοῦ Θεοῦ " is used as parallel to the " ἐγεννήθη ἐκ τοῦ Θεοῦ " in the aorist indicative referring to Christ, the phrase " εἶναι ἐκ τοῦ Θεοῦ " always used in the present tense, is used as parallel to " γεννᾶσθαι ἐκ τοῦ Θεοῦ " always used in the perfect tense referring to Christians [47].

3. *The Distinctive Character of the Begetting by God*

The fact that the two phrases " εἶναι ἐκ τοῦ Θεοῦ " and " γεγέννηται ἐκ τοῦ Θοεῦ " are parallel in Jn, means that they have something in common. This is, as we have seen when speaking of the phrase " εἶναι ἐκ τοῦ Θεοῦ ", the idea of an origin from God and an essential similarity of nature determined by God as a result of this origin. The parallelism, however, does not mean an absolute identification of the two phrases. The fact that the use is metaphorical also may suggest an identification. It is metaphorical in contradistinction to natural generation. But as we will see soon, it is not a mere metaphor [48]. A close examination of the typically Johannine use of " γεγέννηται ἐκ τοῦ Θεοῦ " will show that the two phrases are not identical.

Actually we have three phrases in Jn that are closely related to the concept of divine sonship, namely, " γεγέννηται ἐκ τοῦ Θεοῦ ", " τέκνα τοῦ Θεοῦ " and " εἶναι ἐκ τοῦ Θεοῦ ". It is really interesting to note that while Jn makes constant use of the other two phrases to denote both the relation of men to God and to the devil alike, he never says that those who do wickedness are ' begotten of the devil '. The concept of a generation of the wicked by the devil, is alien to the mind of John. The verb " γεγέννηται ", wherever it

---

[46] Cf. G. BAUER, art. " Geburt ", *TBLNT*, vol. I, p. 446.

[47] Note the parallel usage of εἶναι ἐκ τοῦ Θεοῦ and γεννᾶσθαι ἐκ τοῦ Θεοῦ in I Jn 2:29 – 3:10 and 5:18-20.

[48] The opinion of G. BAUER in the art. " Geburt " in *TBLNT* I, p. 446 that the two phrases are ' gleichbedeutend ' seems to be an overstatement.

occurs throughout the Johannine Writings to denote the spiritual generation of men, is exclusively employed for the generation from God.

Even in contexts where according to the usual Johannine style we would expect the phrase " γεγέννηται ἐκ τοῦ διαβόλου " as antithetically parallel to " γεγέννηται ἐκ τοῦ Θεοῦ ", John avoids it. Thus in I Jn 3:10b which is parallel to 2:29 forming an inclusion of the section, John changes the expression, and the change seems to be intentional.

a   2:29   Everyone who does justice ... *is begotten of Him*
b   3:1   See what love the Father ... the children of God
b'   3:10a In this is manifested   the children of God
                           and
                                    the children of the devil
a'   3:10b Everyone who does not do justice *is not of God*

As we see from the above structure, the phrase one naturally expects in 3:10b ' begotten of the devil ' as parallel to the ' begotten of Him ' in 2:29, is changed into ' is not of God '. On the one hand Jn wants to express the parallelism, but on the other, he avoids an identity of expression. While the ' children of God ' are ' begotten of God ', ' children of the devil ' are only ' of the devil (not of God) ', and not ' begotten of the devil '. This implies a great distinction. Divine sonship is based on a begetting, namely, on an initial communication of life on the part of God, which remains active throughout and which determines the nature of the children of God, and thus forms the basis of the similarity of nature between God and His children. The diabolic sonship is not based on such an initial communication of life on the part of the devil, and the similarity of nature between the devil and his children is based on his influence which is of a purely moral nature [49].

The fact of this communication of life by God in begetting His children implies in the divine sonship the idea of growth and the development of this life to full maturity. On the contrary, the diabolic sonship, which lacks such a communication of life, is not destined to the same growth and development. Besides, this shows that the divine sonship is more than a merely moral relationship, based on a supernatural ontological endowment, while the diabolic sonship is purely of a moral nature and depends entirely on moral actions.

---

[49] Cf. St. AUGUSTINE, *Commentarius in Ep. Jo.* Tract IV, 10, P 135, 2007 where he says : " Neminem fecit diabolus, neminem genuit, neminem creavit ; sed quicumque fuerit imitatus diabolum, quasi de illo natus, fit filius diaboli imitando, non proprie nascendo ".

This distinctive characteristic of the children of God in being begotten by God is communicated also in the words of John in I Jn 3:9 regarding the seed of God that dwells in him who is begotten of God, while he never speaks of a 'seed of the devil'.

Such an exclusive affirmation of the divine begetting regarding the children of God gives, therefore, to the phrase εἶναι ἐκ τοῦ Θεοῦ and τέκνα Θεοῦ a signification that is more profound and superior to that of the parallel phrases εἶναι ἐκ τοῦ διαβόλου and τέκνα τοῦ διαβόλου. Unlike the children of the devil, the essential connection of similarity of nature existing in those who are ἐκ τοῦ Θεοῦ is in virtue of the initial communication of the divine life in the γεννηθῆναι ἐκ τοῦ Θεοῦ and it is by virtue of this communicated divine life that one grows into a τέκνον Θεοῦ. Hence the expression τέκνα Θεοῦ in Jn is not a matter of a merely metaphorical title, but implies a reality. Christians are really children of God and really, though in a way thoroughly peculiar to this wonderful filiation, begotten of God.

Conclusion

By way of conclusion to this analysis of the Johannine terminology we may make the following remarks. John makes use of the phrases 'τέκνα Θεοῦ' and 'γεννηθῆναι ἐκ τοῦ Θεοῦ' to express his idea of the divine sonship of man, and that in a metaphorical but real sense.

The parallelism of 'τέκνα Θεοῦ' with 'τέκνα τοῦ διαβόλου' indicates a filial relationship to God based on a moral likeness of character. The same idea is expressed also by another parallel phrase 'εἶναι ἐκ τοῦ Θεοῦ', which, however, adds to it a sense of moral connection of derivation from and dependence on God.

The exclusive affirmation of a divine begetting regarding the children of God with the phrase 'γεγέννηται ἐκ τοῦ Θεοῦ' gives to the phrases 'τέκνα Θεοῦ' and 'εἶναι ἐκ τοῦ Θεοῦ' a deeper meaning, namely, the divine sonship of man is based on a begetting or an initial communication of life from the part of God. The tendency of John to use the perfect tense 'γεγέννηται' or 'γεγεννημένος' about the children of God shows that the divine life that is communicated remains active throughout and determines the nature of the children of God. Hence the divine sonship of Christians is more than a mere moral relationship and is based on a supernatural endowment, a communication of the Life of God, and therefore destined to growth and development to full maturity.

Chapter VI

The Power of Becoming Children of God (Jn 1:12-13)

After studying the Johannine terminology regarding the divine sonship of Christians in its philological dimensions, we now come to examine it in the different contexts in which it occurs. The first thing to attract our attention is the fact that the first reference to the believers' sonship occurs in the very Prologue of the Gospel (Jn 1:12-13). This is indeed significant. The Prologue is, as admitted by all, a most solemn introduction to the Gospel, announcing with wonderful clarity the principal themes dealt with therein [50].

I. History of the Exegesis of Jn 1:12-13

In the course of history, we see an explanation of these texts, supposing the reading 'ἐγεννήθησαν' in the plural in v. 13, as it is the 'textus receptus' to the present day. We give below a summary of the different explanations of the texts. We meet with two main currents of explanation regarding them, which could be characterized as 'Dynamic' and 'Static'. This difference of explanation is based on the relation between the " οἳ ἐγεννήθησαν " ' of v. 13 and the " ἔδωκεν ... τέκνα Θεοῦ γενέσθαι " of v. 12.

A. Dynamic Sonship

Those who give a dynamic explanation dissociate the two phrases, and see some kind of growth and development intervening between the 'divine begetting' in v. 13 and the 'becoming children of God' in v. 12. They see in the " ἐκ Θεοῦ ἐγεννήθησαν " the communication

---

[50] Cf. B. F. Westcott, *The Gospel according to St. John*, London, 1958, p. 1; R. Bultmann, *Das Evangelium*, p. 1; F. Tillmann, *Das Johannesevangelium*, 4th ed. Bonn, 1931, 47; J. Reville, *Le quatrième évangile, son origine et sa valeur historique*, 2nd ed., Paris, 1902, pp. 110-129; A. Loisy, *Le quatrième évangile*, Paris, 1903, p. 47f, 153f, 144. B. Brinkmann, *Prolog und Johannes-Evangelium*, Bibki 20 (1965), pp. 106-113; J. A. T. Robinson, " The Relation of the Prologue to the Gospel of John " NTS 9 (1962-63), pp. 120-129.

of the divine life (germinal sonship), and in the " τέκνα Θεοῦ γενέσθαι " the progressive realization of this germinal divine sonship with a dynamic co-operation from the part of man, which comes to its culmination in the celestial condition of glory. Their maxim is " Werde was du bist ". The defenders of this position are the following.

1. *In the Patristic Period*

The Greek Fathers such as Dydymus Alexandrinus [51], J. Chrysostom [52] and Cyril of Alexandria [53] exphasize the fact that in Jn 1:12 it is said that ' He gave them power to become ' (ἔδωκεν αὐτοῖς ἐξουσίαν ... γενέσθαι) and not that ' He made them ' (ἐποίησεν αὐτούς) sons of God, which indicates a progressive evolution, throughout the whole terrestrial life, of the gift of the initial and germinal divine sonship received through Faith in Christ and Baptism [54]. Didymus Alexandrinus, speaking of I Jn 3:1, refers to Jn 1:12 and says : " He who has only this power, is only virtually and not actually son of God. When, however, he makes use of this power well, then he becomes son also actually ". As a proof of this dynamic character, he points to the present tense of " ποιῶν " in I Jn 2:29, and in I Jn 3:2 he sees the fulness of this divine sonship which is to be revealed in future [55]. For Cyril of Alexandria, v. 12 points to a calling to the adoption of sons (διὰ πίστεως ... εἰς υἱοθεσίαν κεκλημένοι) and v. 13 expresses the gratuitous nature of the gift of this sonship on the part of God [56].

2. *In the Middle Ages*

Greek Writers such as Theophylactus [57], Euthymius [58], and also a few Latin Writers such as Bede the Venerable [59], B. Alcuinus [60], J. Scottus Erigena [61], Rupertus Abbatus Tuitiensis [62], and Albert the Great [63].

---

[51] Cf. PG 39, 1785.
[52] Cf. PG 59, 75-78.
[53] Cf. PG 73, 151-162.
[54] Cf. PG 59, 76.
[55] Cf. PG 39, 1785.
[56] Cf. PG 73, 156.
[57] Cf. PG 123, 1151-1155 ; PG 126, 34.
[58] Cf. PG 129, 1119.
[59] Cf. PL 92, 641-642.
[60] Cf. PL 100, 748.
[61] Cf. PL 122, 297.
[62] Cf. PL 169, 219.
[63] Cf. *Opera Omnia*, ed. Aug. Borguet, vol. 24, Paris, 1898, pp. 46-47.

Theophylactus and Euthymius speak in the same line as John Chrysostom, insisting on the aspect of the power that is received to become children of God, which is to be actualized later. For Euthymius it is one thing 'to be adopted by God in baptism' (v. 13), and another thing 'to become son of God through the observance of the Evangelical precepts; the former is the beginning (ἀρχή) the latter, the end (τέλος) '[64]. For Bede the Venerable and B. Alcuinus, Jn 1:12 expresses the dynamism of the divine sonship received in Baptism (Jn 3:5). They emphasize the necessity of a faith that produces good works of charity and justice which vivifies the faith, referring to James 2:17; Rom 1:17; Heb 2:4, which point to the dynamism implied in becoming children of God. V. 13 shows only the supernatural order in which the believers can become children of God [65].

J. Scotus Erigena distinguishes between v. 12a and v. 12c. In v. 12a he sees the simple fact of having believed at a definite point of time. But in v. 12c he sees a progressive knowledge of faith which ends in the life after death [66]. In v. 13 he sees a birth through Baptism, but a birth that is only a beginning [67]. Thus he sees in vv. 12-13 a dynamism in the faith and in the 'becoming children of God'.

For Rupertus Abbatus Tuitiensis, 'to believe' is to 'receive the seed of God — the Word', which remains in him, and by the power of which one is turned into a child of God [68]. V. 13 shows only the universality and individuality of this divine sonship, namely, no human qualification plays a role in this birth and sonship.

Albert the Great too conceives of a dynamic and progressive attainment of a perfect divine sonship by virtue of divine generation in vv. 12-13 [69].

---

[64] Cf. PG 129, 1120.

[65] " Quo autem ordine credentes filii Dei possent fieri ... Evangelista designat " (cf. PL 92, 641; PL 100, 748).

[66] " His qui credunt in nomine ejus i. e., qui credunt notitiam ejus et intelligentiam per fidem in hac vita et per speciem in altera recepturos " (cf. PL 122, 297).

[67] " Sed ex Deo nati sunt, per gratiam videlicet Baptismatis, in quo incipiunt credentes in Christum ex Deo nasci " (cf. Ibid.).

[68] " Credere namque est Semen Dei Verbum cum amore susceptum, impregnata mente portare ... quod tantae virtutis ... ut ... de hominibus deos (Ps. 8) de filiis irae filios gratiae faciat (Ephes II) " (cf. PL 169, 219).

[69] " Hoc enim fieri est generationis divinae, quo primo movemur per consensum. Secundum est acceptum donum gratiae quod dat facultatem. Tertium est, quod movemur ad opus bonum et meritum per quod efficimur opus divinum facientes. Et in hoc completa est filiatio Dei et forma Dei in nobis " Cf. *Opera Omnia*, ed. Aug. Borgnet, vol. 24, Paris, 1898, p. 46.

3. *In the Reformation and Post-Reformation Period*

J. Maldonatus really puts the question how those who are begotten by God are not sons of God ? He answers this question, understanding the power of becoming children of God in v. 12 as the power of becoming heirs of God, and coheirs of Christ, in the sense that Paul speaks of the divine sonship in Rom 8:15,23 [70]. Thus he admits a dynamic and progressive becoming in the divine sonship as conceived here.

The same outlook on dynamic sonship is held by Francis Ribera [71], A. Calmet [72] and A. Natalis [73]. Toletus distinguishes two grades of sonship, namely, sonship as such and the state of sonship, which supposes freedom of action. This state of sonship which supposes freedom of action (as in those who are ' sui juris ') is more perfect than the simple sonship (as in the children). He then applies it to the history of salvation and sees in the Old Covenant the simple divine sonship, and in the New, the state of the divine sonship, implying freedom from the Law. Again this state of sonship is only actuated in baptism giving freedom from sin, which comes to its perfection only at the resurrection when one gets complete freedom from sin and corruption, which is justly called by Paul in Rom 8 the ' adoption of sons '. Thus the ' fieri ' of Jn 1:12 according to him refers to the progress towards this perfect adoption of sons [74]. Cornelius a Lapide sees a dynamic sonship, without referring to the celestial beatitude, actualized in our co-operation with the Grace of God [75].

---

[70] *Commentarii in Quatuor Evangelistas*, ed. Conrad Martin, vol. II, Mognutiae, 1863, p. 413 " ... iis qui jam vere erant filii Dei, quique non ex ..., sed ex Deo nati erant, potestatem, id est, jus dedit, ut haeredes quoque illius fierent, quod est alio sensu filios Dei fieri ".

[71] *In Sanctum Jesu Christi Evangelium secundum Johannem Commentarii*, Lyon, 1623, pp. 40-41 : " ... dedit potestatem, i. e. facultatem, ut filii Dei effici possint filiatione consummata, quae est adoptio beatitudinis ... et ita ponitur hic filiatio inchoata per baptismum et eadem perfecta per beatitudinem ".

[72] *Commentarius Literalis in Omnes Libros Novi Testamenti*, vol. II, Würzburg, 1787, pp. 16-17.

[73] *Expositio Literalis et moralis S. Evangelii Jesu Christi secundum Lucam, Marcum, et Johannem*, Paris, 1743, p. 450.

[74] *In Sacrosanctum Johannis Evangelium Commentarii*, Romae, 1588, cols 73-74.

[75] Cf. *Commentaria in Quatuor Evangelia*, vol. IV, ed. Ant. Padovani, Turin, 1906, p. 28 : " ... in nostra enim potestate est filios Dei fieri ... Deus enim fidem ... reliquasque virtutes ... hominibus non induit invitis ..., sed cogitantibus, volentibus, consentientibus et cooperantibus libere ...".

4. *In Modern Times*

P. Schanz says that Jn 1:12 indicates a temporal evolution by Grace and human co-operation of the divine sonship received through baptism (Jn 1:13) [76]. Calmes too sees in the same way in v. 13 the spiritual birth and in v. 12 the progress towards perfection as the children of God, which is in an initial stage at the moment of baptism [77]. Also Tillmann sees in Jn 1:12-13 a beginning of the divine sonship in baptism through faith and a progress towards the culminating perfection of it at the resurrection [78].

From the Protestant side too, a few hold this dynamic position. According to Westcott, it is only the seed that is given, and not the fruit of the divine sonship. Men are placed in the position of sons, that so they may become children actually. Thus in Jn 1:12-13 the divine and the human sides in the realization of sonship are harmoniously united [79]. According to J. H. Bernard, v. 13 refers to God as the immediate cause of the new spiritual life that begins in the believer, while the present participle of " πιστεύουσιν " in v. 12 points to a continual life of faith, which is the life of sonship [80]. According to Th. Zahn, v. 12 speaks only of a power and a possibility to become the children of God, and not of the realization of it. He emphasises the fact that it is not said ' they became children of God ' [81]. He insists also on the present tense of " τοῖς πιστεύουσιν εἰς τὸ ὄνομα αὐτοῦ " which is incompatible with the aorist " ἐγεννήθησαν " of v. 13, if this latter only explains v. 12 [82]. A. Guillerand says : " On

---

[76] Cf. *Kommentar über das Evangelium des hl. Johannes*, Tübingen, 1885, pp. 89-94.

[77] Cf. *L'évangile selon saint Jean*, Paris, 1904, pp. 114-115 : " ... c'est la filiation divine sans doute, mais à l'état initial et ce premier état peut être appelé une puissance, par rapport a une union plus intime avec la divinité, que l'homme ... doit réaliser par actes libres ".

[78] Cf. *Das Johannesevangelium*, 4th ed., Bonn, 1931, p. 59 : " Der Glaube ... ist also die Wurzel und das Fundament der Gotteskindschaft. Auf dieser Grundlage baut die Taufe, 3:3-12 weiter, bis die Wiederkunft des Herrn einst die volle Einsetzung in die Sohnschaft ... Daran schliesst v. 13 ..., die ... das tiefste Wesen der so gewonnen Gotteskindschaft aus ihrer Entstehung ableitet ".

[79] Cf. *The Gospel according to John*, pp. 8-10.

[80] Cf. *The Gospel according to John*, Edinburgh, 1928, pp. 15-19.

[81] Cf. *Das Evangelium des Johannes*, Leipzig, 1908, p. 71 : " Da nicht gesagt ist : τέκνα Θεοῦ ἐγένοντο oder γεγόνασιν, so dürfen die vorliegenden Worte auch nicht so verstanden werden, als ob jenes dastünde ".

[82] Cf. Ibid., pp. 71-72.

devient enfant de Dieu par la foi ; on dévelope le germe de vie divine en développant la foi " [83].

B. *Static Sonship*

Those who defend the static position do not dissociate the two phrases οἵ ... ἐγεννήθησαν (v. 13) and ἔδωκεν ... τέκνα Θεοῦ γενέσθαι (v. 12) and meet the problem of combining both : namely, how to become what they are already by birth ? And they try to solve this problem by seeing in v. 13 only an explanation of what is said in v. 12. Hence according to them, ' the becoming children of God ' projected in v. 12 is already realized in the fact of ' being begotten by God ' in v. 13. The believers' life that progresses towards the celestial condition of sonship has nothing to contribute to the making of the divine sonship itself. It is only a manifestation or revelation of that sonship, which one actually and fully possesses. Their maxim is : " sei und zeige was du geworden bist ". The defenders of this position are the following.

1. *In the Patristic Period*

St. Augustine [84] explains the divine sonship of Christians here comparing it to the divine sonship of Christ. According to him the " τέκνα Θεοῦ γενέσθαι " of v. 12 expresses the temporal condition of the divine sonship of the faithful, which they received in baptism (v. 13), in contraposition to the eternal divine sonship of Christ. The faithful had to ' become ' the children of God (which took place already in baptism) while Christ ' was ' eternally Son of God. None of the Greek Fathers holds this position of Static Sonship.

2. *In the Middle Ages*

The Latin Writers such as St. Bruno Astensis [85], St. Thomas [86] and St. Bonaventure [87] speak in favour of static sonship identifying the ' becoming children of God ' of v. 12 with the ' birth from God ' of v. 13. St. Thomas sees in vv. 12-13 a procedure towards baptism. Thus the faith in v. 12 prepares one to become a child of God, which actually takes place in the generation through baptism as is described in v. 13 [88].

---

[83] Cf. A. GUILLERAND, *Au seuil de l'abîme de Dieu*, Rome, 1961, p. 44.

[84] Cf. Sermo 121, in PL 38, 678-680.

[85] Cf. PL 165, 454.

[86] Cf. *Super Evangelium S. Johannis Lectura*, ed. R. Cai, Marietti, Roma, 1952, p. 32.

[87] Cf. *Opera Omnia*, Ed. Quaracchi, Florence, 1893, vol. 6, p. 252.

[88] " ... primo requiratur fides, quod fit in Catechumenis, qui debent primo

3. In the Reformation and Post-Reformation Period

In this period the Protestant authors mostly stick to the static character of the sonship denying to the faith in v. 12 any possibility of dynamic and progressive relation to the sonship. Thus Luther [89] and Philip Melanchton [90] explain vv. 12-13 without admitting any subjective dynamic role. Calvin, in identifying the 'becoming children of God' and the 'being begotten by God' in vv. 12-13 expresses clearly his intention of refuting Catholics who see a dynamic element in the power of becoming children of God [91].

Apparently, as a reaction to the contemporary reformation movement, all the Catholic authors of this period insist on the dynamic element of the divine sonship as we saw above.

4. In Modern Times

Among the Modern Authors, we see both Catholics and Protestants who favour the Static sonship. Among the Catholics could be mentioned Lagrange [92]. H. Van den Bussche [93], Schnackenburg [94], and Brown [95]. According to Lagrange, the power to become the children of God in v. 12, shows only the power to be something that was not and could not be through natural power, and which is realized in baptism (v. 13) [96]. According to Van den Bussche, the two affirmations ' recevoir — enfants de Dieu ' and ' croire — être nés de Dieu '

---

instrui de fide, ut scilicet credant in nomine ejus, et deinde regenerentur per baptismum, non quidem ex sanguinibus carnaliter, sed ex Deo spiritualiter " (cf. op. cit., p. 32, no. 164).

[89] " Das Kinder werden haben alle, die an ihn glauben, ohne Verdienst, allein durch den Glauben an seinen Namen ... er (Gott) lässt sein Licht durch die Taufe, durch das Sakrament und die Predigt leuchten. Alsdann macht dich der Glaube zu einem Kind Gottes" (cf. D. Martin, *Luthers Evangelien Auslegung*, ed. E. Mülhaupt, vol. IV, Göttingen, 1961, pp. 49-50).

[90] Cf. *Enarratio in Evangelium Joannis*, ed. C. G. Bretschneider, vol. XV, Halle, 1848, pp. 20-24.

[91] " ' Nomen ' ἐξουσίας mihi dignitatem hoc loco significat : et praestaret ita vertere ad reffellendum papistarum commentum ... nam continuo post subjicit Evangelista, fieri Dei filios ... quum ex Deo nascuntur" (cf. *J. Calvini Opera*, ed. G. Bann, Brumsvigae, 1892, v. 47, 11).

[92] Cf. *Le quatrième évangile*, Paris, 1925, pp. 13-19.

[93] Cf. *Jean*, Bruges, 1967, p. 96.

[94] Cf. *The Gospel according to St. John*, (trans. from German), London, 1968, pp. 258-265.

[95] Cf. *The Gospel according to St John*, New York, 1966, p. 12.

[96] " ... devenir enfant de Dieu, c'est être engendré par lui d'une façon spirituelle ..." (Cf. op. cit., p. 15).

are parallels. There is no anteriority of one to the other [97]. For R. Schnackenburg, vv. 12-13 speak of the supernatural process which takes place in baptism. Thus for him as for R. Brown, the relative clause in v. 13 adds a fuller explanation of how one becomes a child of God [98].

Among the Protestants could be mentioned, R. Bultmann [99], who considers v. 13 as a ' weitere Erläuterung ' of what is said in v. 12. For Hoskyns, faith and rebirth in baptism are not two distinct stages in Christian enlightenment, and those who believe are not potentially children of God. They are already His children, though it is not yet made clear what they will become (I Jn 3:2) [100]. According to Lightfoot, the right or authority granted to those who received the Logos (v. 12) is that of a new, divine birth, whereby they might become sons of light (Jn 12:36) [101].

As we see from the above data, the Greek Fathers in general defended the dynamic position, while the Latin Fathers are more inclined to the static position. Coming to the Reformation period, there seems to be a great barrier of apologetic tendency, that divides the Catholics and Protestants into dynamic and static positions respectively. But in modern times, again both Catholic and Protestant Scholars go together and without any barrier of prejudice hold the dynamic or static position merely on exegetical grounds. After having had thus a panorama of the history of the Exegesis of Jn 1:12-13 up to the present time, now we come to examine the text in itself.

II. Textual Criticism: Jn 1:12-13

Before starting with the analysis of the text, we have to make sure of the text to be analysed. So we proceed to the textual criticism of vv. 12-13. The main critical problem is in v. 13, and it is, whether it should be read in the plural " οἵ ... ἐγεννήθησαν " [102], or in the singular " ὅς ... ἐγεννήθη " [103].

---

[97] Cf. op. cit., p. 96.
[98] Cf. op. cit., p. 262.
[99] Cf. *Das Evangelium des Johannes*, Göttingen, 1964, pp. 36-37.
[100] Cf. *The Fourth Gospel*, London, 1947, p. 146.
[101] Cf. *St John's Gospel, A Commentary*, Oxford, 1956, p. 81.
[102] In favour of the plural, cf. G. CASTELLINI, " De Jo. 1,13 in quibusdam citationibus patristicis ", *VD* 32 (1954), 155-157; A. VIARD, " Singulier ou pluriel dans S. Jean 1,13 " Qui ex Deo natus est " ou " nati sunt " ?, *Ami CL* 68 (1958), 516-520; A. HOUSSIAU, " Le milieu theologique de la leçon ἐγεννήθη (Jn 1,13) ", *Sac Pag* II, paris, 1959, 169-188; P. LAMARCHE, " Le prologue de Jean ", *RSR* 52 (1964), 502-512; J. SCHMID, " Jn 1:13 " *BZ* 1

Those who defend the plural connect the " οἵ ... ἐγεννήθησαν " to " τοῖς πιστεύουσιν " or to " τέκνα " and see in it the divine generation of Christians. Those who defend the singular connect the " ὅς ... ἐγεννήθη " to " αὐτοῦ " and see in it the divine generation of Christ. The controversy is very old going back to Tertullian. For a detailed study of the controversy, and the evaluation of the arguments ' pro and contra ', we refer the reader to the excellent work of J. Galot [104], in which he treats the question elaborately and ' ex professo '. We give below only an outline of the evidences from external and internal criticism, in the light of which, we have to choose the text for our analysis.

A. *External Criticism*

1. *Witnesses of the Plural reading*

All the Greek Mss, Uncials and Cursives give the plural reading with the following variants. D omits " οἵ "; E omits " οὐδὲ ἐκ θελήματος σαρκός " and has " τοῦ Θεοῦ " in the place of " Θεοῦ ". A and B and a few other Mss have " ἐγενήθησαν " instead of " ἐγεννήθησαν ".

(1957), 118-125; G. SEGALLA, *Volontà di Dio e dell'Uomo in Giovanni* (Vangelo e Lettere), Brescia, 1974, pp. 237-244. Also the recent Commentaries on Jn mostly adopt the plural reading. Cf. the Commentaries of C. K. Barrett, A. Wikenhauser, R. Schnackenburg, R. E. Brown, etc.

[103] In favour of the singular, cf. A. RESCH, *Ausserkanonische Paralleltexte zu den Evangelien*, 4 Teil, TU 10, 3, Leipzig, 1896, 57; F. BLASS, *Philology of the Gospels*, London, 1898, 237f; *Evangelium secundum Johannem cum Variae Lectionis Selectu*, Lipsiae, 1902, XII, 2; A. LOISY, *Le Quatrième Évangile*, Paris, 1903, pp. 174-183; A. v. HARNACK, " Zur Textkritik und Christologie der Schriften des Johannes ", in *Sitzungsberichte der Königlich Preussischen Akademie d. Wissenschaften*, Berlin, 1915, pp. 542-552. Th. ZAHN, *Das Evangelium des Johannes*, Leipzig, 1921, 74f, 711-714; R. SEEBERG, *Festgabe A. Harnack dargebracht*, Tübingen, 1921, pp. 267-269; F. C. BURNEY, *The Aramaic Origin of the Fourth Gospel*, Oxford, 1922, p. 34f; F. BÜCHSEL, *Das Evangelium nach Johannes* (NT Deutsch 4), Göttingen, 1934, p. 527f; G. H. C. MACGREGOR, *The Gospel of John*, (Moffat Commentary), London, 1928, p. 15; M. E. BOISMARD, " Critique textuelle et citations patristiques ", *RB* 57 (1950), 388-408 and *Le prologue de S. Jean*, Paris, 1953, p. 62f; F. M. BRAUN, " Qui ex Deo Natus est ", in *Aux sources de la tradition chrétienne* (Mélanges M. Goguel), Neuchâtel, 1950, pp. 11-31 and *La mère des fidèles*, Tournai, 1953, pp. 33-46; C. CHARLIER, *La lecture chrétienne de la Bible*, Maredsous, 1950, p. 57; J. MCHUGH, *The Mother of Jesus in the New Testament*, London, 1975, pp. 255-268.

[104] Cf. J. GALOT, *Être né de Dieu*, Jean 1, 13, Rome, 1969.

Apart from the exceptions, which will be indicated below regarding the Vet. Lat. and Vet. Syr., the Latin, Syriac, Coptic, Arminian and Ethiopian Versions follow the text of the Greek Mss.

The majority of the Ancient Ecclesiastical Writers, mostly posterior to the Third Century such as Clement of Alexandria [105], Origen [106], John Chrysostom [107], Cyril of Alexandria [108], Theodor of Mopsuestia [109], Hilarius [110], Ambrosiaster [111], Ambrose [112] and Augustine [113] give both readings.

2. *Witnesses of the Reading in the singular*

The Latin Version b (Codex Veronensis) which is resumed also in the Liber Comicus [114], and the Syriac Versions Cureton (Syc) and Sinaiticus (Sys) give the singular reading. Besides, the Apocryphal 'Epistula XI Apostolorum' known to us in two versions, Coptic [115], and Ethiopian [116] also give the reading in the singular [117].

The Ancient Ecclesiastical Writers [118] such as Tertullian [119], Ire-

---

[105] Cf. Strom. 2,13 ; 58,2 ; SC 38,81.

[106] Cf. GCS Origenes IV, p. 489, l. 28-31 ; 490, l. 14 ; 565, l. 19.

[107] Cf. PG 59, 76.

[108] Cf. PG 73, 153D.

[109] Cf. PG 66, 732 A and B.

[110] Cf. De Trinit. 1,10 in PL 10, 32A.

[111] Cf. Questio 123,16-17 ; CSEL 50, 380-381.

[112] Cf. Liber de Noe et Arca c. IV (PL 14, 366b) ; De Spiritu Sancto, Liber 2, c. 7 (PL 16, 756A) ; Expl. in Ps. 36,48,61 (CSEL 64, p. 96, l. 15-16 ; p. 364, l. 5-9 ; p. 396, l. 4-6).

[113] Cf. In Johannem (PL 35, 1395, no. 15) ; Sermo 121 in Jo. l. 10-14 (PL 38, 679, no. 4) ; De Consensu Evangelistarum, Lib. 2, c. 3 (CSEL 43, p. 87, l. 1) ; De Peccatorum meritis et remissione, Lib. 2, c. 23 (CSEL 60, p. 110, l. 10-18).

[114] *Liber Comicus sive Lectionarius Missae quo Toletana Ecclesia ante annos mille et ducentos utebatur*, ed. D. G. Morin, Maredsoli, 1893.

[115] Cf. C. SCHMIDT, *Gespräche Jesus mit seinen Jüngern nach der Auferstehung. Ein katholischapostolisches Senschreiben des 2. Jahrhunderts nach einem koptischen Papyrus des Institut de la mission Archéologique française au Caire*, unter Mitarbeit von Herrn Pierre Lacan (TU, Dritte Reihe, 13, Leipzig, 1919).

[116] Cf. L. GUERRIER, *Le testament en Galilée de Notre Seigneur Jésus Christ. Texte éthiopien édité et traduit en français* (PD 9, p. 141-236).

[117] Cf. L. GUERRIER, op. cit., no. 14, p. 190.

[118] For a detailed exposition of the Patristic authority in favour of the singular reading, cf. A. RESCH, op. cit., p. 57f ; Th. ZAHN, op. cit., p. 73f ; A. v. HARNACK, art. cit., p. 543f.

[119] Cf. De Carne Christi 210-212, c. 19 (CSEL 70, p. 236, l: 1-8) and c. 24 (CSEL 70, p. 248, l: 10-13).

neus [120] and Sulpice Severius [121] certainly witness the singular reading. To these could be added the witness of Tychonius [122] and of Pseudo Athanasius [123], whose texts, though actually giving the plural, should be corrected into the singular, to be coherent with their argument [124]. Among the Greek Writers, Hyppolytus [125] and Methodus of Olympe [126], though they do not quote the text literally, seem to have in mind the singular reading [127]. Recently, another witness of Appollinarius of Laodicea has been brought forward in favour of the singular reading by H. de Riedmatten [128].

There are also some traces of witnesses to the singular even before Ireneus, namely in Ignatius of Antioch [129], and in Justin [130]. Although we do not find them quoting literally Jn I:13, nevertheless, the idea and the vocabulary of the relevant passages certainly recall to one's mind Jn I:13 read in the singular [131].

3. *Evaluation of the data of the external Criticism*

It is true that no Greek Mss give John 1:13 in the singular. But the Greek Mss are all relatively late. The testimony of the Sy^c and Sy^s points to a text that goes back to the Second Century translation of the Old Syriac, from which both have sprung or of which both are the legitimate descendants [132]. Moreover the 'Epistula XI Apostolorum' is also dated by scholars between the second half of the Second and the beginning of the Third Century [133]. The fact that

---

[120] Adv. Haer. III, 17,1 ; 20,2 ; 26,1 ; V, 1,3.

[121] Cf. ESCL 1, p. 59, i. 9-10.

[122] Cf. Liber Regularum, ed. Burkitt, p. 7.

[123] Cf. PL 62, 318B.

[124] Cf. C. TISCHENDORF, *Novum Testamentum Graece*, 8ed., I, Lipsiae, 1869, p. 743 ; F. M. BRAUN, art. cit., in Mélanges M. Goguel, p. 18.

[125] Cf. Elenchos VI, 9 (GCS 26, p. 136, l. 5-8).

[126] Cf. De Resurrectione, I, 26 (GCS 27, p. 102, l: 13-14).

[127] Cf. F. M. BRAUN, art. cit., p. 19.

[128] Cf. H. DE RIEDMATTEN, " Some Neglected Aspects of Appollinarist Christology ", *Dom S*, Oxford, 1948, pp. 239 245.

[129] Cf. Smyrn. 2,1 ; Sc. 10.154 ; Cf. P. BRAUN, art. cit., p. 22 ; J. GALOT, op. cit., pp. 11-17.

[130] Apol. 1,32 (Otto, Corpus Apologetarum I,1, p. 100, l. 2-3) ; Dial. C.54 (I, 2, p. 182, l. 18-19) ; Dial. C.76 (I, 2, p. 270, l. 25 to p. 272, l. 1) ; Dial. C.61 (I, 2, p. 214, l. 2) ; Dial. C.63 (I, 2, p. 222, l. 13-14) ; Apol. I, 22 (I, 1, p. 68, l. 16 to p. 70,1).

[131] Cf. J. GALOT, op. cit., pp. 11-27.

[132] Cf. A. S. LEWIS, *Light on the Four Gospels from Sinai Palimpsest*, London, 1913, p. 132.

[133] Cf. C. SCHMIDT, op. cit., p. 402 where he dates it between 160 and 170

the 'Epistula XI Apostolorum' does not depend on the 'Diatessaron of Tatian'[134] seems to suggest that it depends on a version of the Gospel — Old Syriac or Greek — that existed in Syria in the 2nd Century[135].

Speaking of the Patristic witnesses, we saw how the most ancient Witnesses are in favour of the singular, going back to the 2nd century[136], while the witnesses favouring the plural are mostly posterior to the 3rd century. Besides, we see Ireneus and Tertullian accusing the Gnostics of having changed the sense or the words of the text into the plural[137]. Hence, the unanimity of the Greek Mss cannot be considered as a decisive argument, in face of the 2nd century evidence brought forward by the few versions and the Patristic literature, which show evidently the history of the text before it was fixed up in the plural as reproduced by the Greek Mss. The importance of the versions and the Patristic quotations in this respect is illustrated by the Bodmer Papyrus as shown by P. Boismard, who gives a list of 49 readings ignored by the Greek Mss, where the text of P66 agrees with the witness of the Fathers and the versions[138].

B. *Internal Criticism*

Having seen the external evidences of the text, now we come to examine the text in itself and in its context both proximate and remote. As the external criticism does not allow us to decide for one or the other reading, the internal criticism should be decisive in the matter. First of all we give the reasons in favour of the singular reading[139]. Then we will try to solve the apparent difficulties in adopting the singular reading.

A. D. This is followed by B. H. STREETER, *The Four Gospels. A Study of Origins*, treating the Manuscripts tradition, sources, authorship, and dates, London, 1930, p. 70; cf. also, L. GUERRIER, op. cit., p. 161f.

[134] Cf. C. SCHMIDT, op. cit., p. 226.

[135] Cf. F. M. BRAUN, art. cit., in Mélanges Goguel, p. 16.

[136] For a detailed evaluation of the Patristic evidences, we refer the reader to J. Galot, op. cit., pp. 11-86, where he, after a detailed analysis of the evidences decides in favour of the singular reading.

[137] Cf. TERTULLIAN, *De Carne Christi*, in CSEL, 70, p. 236, l. 1-8; IRENEUS, as quoted in Opera S. Isidori Hisp. Proleg., PL 81, 639.

[138] Cf. P. BOISMARD, "Le papyrus Bodmer II," *RB* 64 (1957), 391-393. However here it is to be noted that, in spite of this phenomenon P66 here reads plural.

[139] We give in detail the reasons in favour of the singular reading, because they will be of help also to understand the concept of the divine sonship of Christians affirmed in the context.

1. Reasons in Favour of the Reading in the Singular

a. The Threefold Negation

The exclusion of a birth according to the ordinary laws with such a threefold negative insistence would be very strange, if attributed to the believers, because they are first of all born according to the ordinary laws, and the supernatural birth of men does not suppress or exclude natural birth, but rather presupposes it. In Jn 3:3-6 he does not say that those who are born of the Spirit are not born of the flesh. He only distinguishes the two births. Here he does not distinguish, but denies human birth. On the contrary, if it is applied to Christ, in His temporal generation, this threefold negation is quite understandable, because it excludes a birth according to the ordinary laws of natural birth.

b. The Context

One of the main themes of the Prologue, the temporal generation of the Logos, is better understood by this threefold negation which prepared very well for the culminating affirmation of it in v. 14. Applying it to the Christian, v. 13 becomes a useless and emphatic repetition of v. 12 [140]. How can those who are already born of God, receive the power to become children of God? [141]. The attempts made by the defenders of the plural to do away with this tension through exegetical explanations are not convincing [142]. If applied to Christ, it gives good sense in affirming that the Word has given the believers power to become sons of God, just as He Himself is begotten of God, since our sonship has as source the sonship of Christ.

c. Grammatical reasons

" οἵ ... ἐγεννήθησαν " of v. 13 in the plural should go with the simple appositional clause " τοῖς πιστεύουσιν ". In this case, the present tense of " πιστεύουσιν " would require either an atemporal present or a perfect tense, and not an aorist [143]. This difficulty does not disappear, even if it is applied to " τέκνα Θεοῦ ". It only doubles

---

[140] Cf. LOISY, Le quatrième évangile, p. 101.

[141] Cf. BOISMARD, Le prologue, p. 56.

[142] Cf. J. SCHMID, " Jn 1:13 ", BZ 1 (1957), p. 122; Boismard, art. cit., p. 55f.

[143] Here it is to be noted that the difficulty is more grammatical, because theologically it is possible to explain that the believers (πιστεύοντες) are those who are already begotten of God (aorist).

the difficulty, namely, it goes over an apposition to explain a predicative clause ¹⁴⁴. So the aorist plural here, seems to be out of place¹⁴⁵.

The " αὐτοῦ " of v. 12c requires to be continued with " ὅς " and not with " οἵ ". Much more than a useless repetition of v. 12, one is inclined to expect here a development of the person of the Logos, to determine His situation in relation to those who become children of God through Him, and to prepare the solemn and precise definition of the Incarnation ¹⁴⁶.

The " καί " in the beginning of v. 14 requires that v. 13 also speaks of the Logos. The use of " καί " in the beginning of a phrase in Jn always recalls an idea that preceded. Thus, for example, the " καί " in Jn 9:1 recalls the action of Jesus in Jn 8:59. The " καί ... μαρτυρία " of Jn 1:19 recalls the " μαρτυρεῖ " of Jn 1:15. In the Prologue itself, the καί in v. 5 recalls the idea mentioned in v. 4. Hence, the καί in v. 14 also seems to recall what is said in v. 13. This naturally points to a singular reading in v. 13 ¹⁴⁷.

d. Reasons from the Johannine doctrine and vocabulary

i. The Fundamental scheme

The fundamental scheme found in Jn regarding the relation of Christ to the Father as the principle of our relation to God, and our participation through faith in that which is Christ in Himself, favours the singular reading. The singular reading in v. 13 would be in perfect agreement with this fundamental scheme. Thus as Christ is begotten by God ' par excellence ' (v. 13), He could give to believers the same quality of being the children of God (v. 12) ¹⁴⁸.

ii. The divine origin of Christ

The origin of Christ is a predominant theme in Jn. The basis of the mission of Christ is His being itself expressed in terms of origin, namely, that He does not come from Himself, but from God. This heavenly origin of Christ is mentioned in different ways by Jn. In Jn Ch. 6 Christ identifies Himself with the bread that came down

---

[144] Cf. HARNACK, art. cit., p. 547.

[145] Cf. SCHMID, art. cit., p. 122, where he says: " Sodann erscheint der Aorist ἐγεννήθησαν an dieser Stelle ganz unpassend ".

[146] Cf. LOISY, op. cit., p. 101.

[147] Cf. LAGRANGE, évangile, p. 19, where he says that if we admit the singular the ' καί ' in the beginning of the v. 14 " serait limpide dans ce cas ". For this connection demanded by καί cf. also F. M. BRAUN, art. cit., in Mélanges M. Goguel, p. 22 ; T. ZAHN, Evangelium, p. 75 ; Schmid, art. cit., p. 122.

[148] Cf. BOISMARD, Le prologue de saint Jean, p. 57 ; J. GALOT, op. cit. pp. 107-108.

from heaven. His mysterious origin becomes the object of discussions and interrogations among the people (cf. Jn 7:27,28-29 ; 8:14,23) [149]. In Jn 8:31-47 Jesus speaks of His origin from God (v. 42) parallel to His filial relationship to God (v. 38). The indirect accusation of prostitution brought forward by the Jews regarding the origin of Jesus in this context (v. 41) also points to the mysterious birth of Jesus from God, unknown to the Jews. The quasi identification of His mission and origin expressed in the titles ' Christ ' and ' Son of God ' used equivalently by Jn in different contexts [150], shows that the ' coming of Christ into the world ' is a manifestation of His ' divine sonship '. All these are well explained, if we admit that Jn has already affirmed in 1:13 the temporal generation of Christ as a divine generation, as a generation from God.

iii. ' Those who believe in his name '

Also the phrase ' to those who believe in his name ' confirms the reading in the singular applying v. 13 to Christ. If the " αὐτοῦ " is not specified by the verse 13, to whom does it refer ? In that case it should refer to " Θεοῦ " in v. 12b, for two reasons. First of all, stylistically it is the nearest one [151]. Secondly, according to the context the point at issue is ' becoming children of God ', and hence it refers better to " Θεοῦ ".

But the use of " ὄνομα " in Jn does not allow us to refer this " αὐτοῦ " to " Θεοῦ ". In Jn we see " ὄνομα " applied to God and Christ. When applied to God it is always connected with the name " πατήρ " and never with the name " Θεός " [152]. So in 1:12 the " αὐτοῦ " cannot refer to " Θεοῦ ", because it would be a use quite foreign to Jn. Also it cannot refer to " πατήρ " here, because it is out of context. Hence it should refer to Christ-Logos, if we suppose a reading in the plural. But in Jn " ὄνομα " when applied to Christ, is never used with ' Logos '. Moreover, in Jn, it is always applied to Christ with particular reference to Him as Son of God (cf. 3:18 ; 20:31 ; I Jn 3:23 ; 5:13) [153]. Note too the parallelism of Jn 20:31 to

---

[149] Cf. J. GALOT, op. cit., p. 114, n. 302, where he shows the ignorance of the Jews about the origin of Jesus, hence of his heavenly origin, in Jn 7:28-29, against Dodd (*The Interpretation of the Fourth Gospel*, Cambridge, 1958, p. 260), who excluded this mystery in this context.

[150] Cf. Jn 1:49 ; 11:27 ; 20:31 ; 1 Jn 5:1,5.

[151] Λόγος is farther than Θεοῦ and is already taken up by the αὐτόν in v. 12a.

[152] Cf. Jn 5:43 ; 10:25 ; 12:28 ; 17:6,11,12,26. Jn 12:13 where it is connected with the name κυρίου is a quotation from Ps 117.

[153] Cf. also Jn 14:13,14,26 ; 15:16,21 ; 16:23,24,26 where it is connected with μου speaking of Jesus and 17:6,11,12,26 where it is connected with τοῦ

1:12-13 admitted by all exegetes, which also points to the reference of "αὐτοῦ" to Christ as 'Son of God'.

In fact the entire phrase "πιστεύουσιν εἰς τὸ ὄνομα αὐτοῦ" points to the same conclusion. In Jn the phrase in this form comes only four times, namely, in Jn 1:12; 2:23; 3:18; and I Jn 5:13. In 3:18 and I Jn 5:13 it is expressly connected with the title 'Son of God'[154]. Jn 2:23, as we will see below, is parallel to Jn 3:18. Thus all the cases seem to refer to Christ as 'Son of God'. Hence, also in Jn 1:12 it is quite normal that the "αὐτοῦ" refers to Christ as 'Son of God' — 'Begotten of God' as specified in 1:13[155].

This argument is reinforced by the hypothesis according to which vv. 12c-13 is a Johannine addition to the primitive hymn, and the Johannine redactional character of these verses is admitted by all[156]. If this is a Johannine addition, this shows that vv. 12c-13 form a unity in which the affirmation in v. 13 is complementary to the mention of faith in v. 12c. Thus v. 13 becomes a Johannine precision of the name of the one "αὐτοῦ", in whom one should believe, in order to become a child of God.

The precision in v. 13 of the object of faith is quite coherent in the Johannine context. "πιστεύειν εἰς τό ὄνομά τινος" in John means to believe and adhere to the person, precisely as expressed by the name[157]. In the words of Westcott, 'to believe in His name' is to believe in Him as characterised by the specific title implied[158]. And this formula is seen in its full implication in Jn 3:18: 'to believe in the name of the Only Begotten Son of God'. Hence, the object of the Johannine faith in the formula is Jesus as "μονογενής υἱός". The word "μονογενής" contains the idea of generation in Jn. So it is the divinely Begotten Son of God that is the object of this faith.

---

speaking of God. It is interesting to note that in the chs. 14-17 the same πατήρ occurs 51 times, while the name Θεός only 5 times, which also shows the reference of ὄνομα to the Father and the Son. For a detailed study of it cf. J. McPolin, *The "Name" of the Father and of the Son in the Joh. Writings*, Rome, 1972.

[154] It is worth noting here that the object of faith in the parallel text in Jn 3:18 is μονογενής, and the same is applied to Logos in the Prologue, after the affirmation of the generation from God.

[155] The refutation of this argument by G. Segalla in his book (cf. op. cit., p. 242) seems to miss the point, because the formula in question is not 'to believe in him', but 'to believe in his name'.

[156] Cf. J. Schmid, art. cit., p. 124; A. v. Harnack, art. cit., p. 550; R. Schnackenburg, "Logos-Hymnus und Johanneischer Prolog", *BZ* I (1957), p. 75; cf. also Commentaries of Schnackenburg, Käsemann, Bernard etc.

[157] Cf. I. de la Potterie, "L'emploi dynamique...", art. cit., in *Bib* p. 376.

[158] Cf. Westcott, *The Gospel*, on Jn 8:30.

Note also that in Jn 1:14 and 18, this Incarnate Logos is called " μονογενής ". So it is this specific character of the unique sonship resulting from the begetting by God that is the object of faith as described by Jn in 1:13, and thus gives precision to the name mentioned in 1:12c.

So in the Johannine thought the divine begetting of Christ mentioned here in Jn 1:13 is not only the principle of our sonship, but also the object of our faith, through which we participate in that which the name expresses. The Johannine faith enters into the very mystery of the reality of the sonship of Christ [159], in order to make us capable of participating in the same mystery. Hence, the Johannine redactional character of vv. 12c-13 is just an argument in favour of applying v. 13 to Christ and not in favour of the plural reading as Schmid says in his article [160].

iv. The Johannine Vocabulary of the Supernatural Begetting

Finally, the vocabulary of Jn regarding the supernatural birth also suggests that here Jn speaks of the generation of Christ. John speaks often, both of the children of God (Jn 1:12 ; 11:52 ; I Jn 3:1, 2,10 ; 5:2) and of those who are begotten by God (I Jn 2:29 ; 3:9 ; 4:7 ; 5: 1-4,18). A close study of the use of the terms used in Jn to express these concepts, shows certain peculiarities.

Speaking of the believers, the " τέκνα Θεοῦ " is used by Jn always in the plural, while " γεννηθῆναι ἐκ τοῦ Θεοῦ " is used always in the singular, even when both expressions come closely one after the other (cf. I Jn 2:29 and 3:1 ; 5:1 and 2). I Jn 5:1-2 shows this peculiarity very clearly, because there both are used in connection with the same idea :

> " Everyone who loves the one who begat, loves him who is begotten of Him. By this we know that we love the children of God ".

Also in the Gospel the same peculiarity of usage is seen (cf. Jn 3:3-8 and 11:52). So if Jn 1:13 is said of the believers (in plural), it would be the only exception to the regular Johannine usage with regard to the theme of believers' sonship. This exception seems to be all the more strange, when we see that in Jn 1:12 the usage of " τέκνα Θεοῦ " is as usual in the plural.

---

[159] Cf. D. MOLLAT, " La Fede nel Quarto Vangelo ", in *Catechesi con San Giovanni*, Brescia, 1965, p. 39.

[160] Cf. J. SCHMID, art. cit., pp. 124-125.

Another peculiarity of the Johannine usage in this matter is in the tense of the verb of "γεννάω". When speaking of the believers' birth Jn uses the verb "γεννάω" always in the perfect indicative (I Jn 2:29; 3:9; 4:7; 5:1) and a participle (Jn 3:6-8; I Jn 3:9; 5:1, 4,18) or aorist conjunctive (Jn 3:3,5) and infinitive (Jn 3:4,7), but never in an 'aorist indicative and participle'. And Jn uses an aorist indicative and participle only in two places (Jn 1:13 indicative, and I Jn 5:18 participle), and in these two places it seems to refer to Christ [161]. Already scholars have acknowledged the difficulty in reconciling the aorist in the plural in Jn 1:13 with the context [162], and they all agree that the present tense of "πιστεύουσιν" requires an atemporal present or perfect tense in Jn 1:13. Now this is confirmed also by the very vocabulary of John. Hence the singular seems to be much more fitting in the context of v. 13.

This distinctive use of "γεννάω" is seen also on the level of the sense of Johannine vocabulary. Making use of the perfect tense of "γεννάω" for the believers, Jn considers the divine birth of the believers in its actual influence on the life of the believer. Note how Jn goes so far as to put "γεγέννηται ἐκ τοῦ Θεοῦ" and "ἔστιν ἐκ τοῦ Θεοῦ" as parallels (cf. I Jn 2:29 and 3:10). Note also how the divine birth of the believers in John is always connected with the manifestation of it in a life of doing justice (I Jn 2:29; 3:10), not committing sin (I Jn 3:9; 5:18), loving (I Jn 3:10; 4:7) and of believing (I Jn 5:1,4). Even when the aorist is used, it is the aorist conjunctive or infinitive (cf. Jn 3:3-7) and not indicative, which shows that for John, in the believers' birth, it is not the historical event of the birth that is of interest, but the profound change of life, that is involved in this new beginning. Note the use of the neuter "τὸ γεγεννημένον" in Jn 3:6, used to explain the birth expressed in the aorist conjunctive.

On the contrary, when speaking of the birth of Christ, it is the historical event of birth (Incarnation) that is of the utmost importance for Jn, because it is the basis of the divine birth of men. This could be seen from the way in which Jn speaks of the gift of the divine sonship of men. In I Jn 3:1, he says that the divine sonship of men is the result of the love of the Father, and in Jn 1:12 it is the gift of the Word. Now, how to combine these two affirmations? It means that for Jn the divine sonship of men is the gift of both the Father and the Son. John himself has done this combination, where he speaks of the love of God towards men. In I Jn 4:9 he says of the manifestation of this love of God: "In this the love of

---

[161] About I Jn 5:18 see our textual criticism on pp. 276-278.
[162] Cf. A. v - HARNACK, art. cit., p. 547; J. SCHMID, art. cit., p. 122.

God was manifested among us, that God sent His Only Begotten Son into the world that we might live through Him ". In Jn 3:16, he expresses the same idea and explains that it is through faith, that we obtain this life: " For God so loved the world, that He gave His Only Begotten Son, so that whoever believes in Him ... has eternal life ".

It is worthwhile to note the different tenses used in this connection. In I Jn 3:1 it was perfect tense " δέδωκεν " used of the love of God, which denotes the love of God rather as a reality remaining in us, by virtue of which we are already sons[163]. But in I Jn 4:9 and Jn 3:16 he speaks of the manner in which this love of God becomes a reality in us, namely, through the historical event of the manifestation of this love in the Only Begotten Son of God[164]. Hence the historical coming of Christ into the world is the concretization of the love of God and the divine life is communicated to us through Him. The role of the Father in this communication of life, namely in the divine generation of Christians, is described by John as " τὸν γεννήσαντα " (I Jn 5:1). The role of Christ in this divine generation of Christians, which Jn emphasises in the Prologue, is also His historical coming, and the acceptance of Him by the believers. This is quite compatible with his affirmations in Jn 3:16 and I Jn 4:9. Now it is interesting to note that it is only in these two contexts outside the Prologue, that Christ is qualified as " μονογενής " which as we will see below, points to His origin by generation. Hence, Jn seems to describe the role of Christ in the divine generation of Christians, as the One who is generated by God " ὁ γεννηθεὶς ἐκ τοῦ Θεοῦ " (cf. I Jn 5:18), in the aorist, referring to His temporal generation in the Incarnation. Thus John specifies the roles of the Father and the Son in the generation of Christians: The Father as the One who generates (ὁ γεννήσας) and the Son as the One who is generated (ὁ γεννηθείς).

Now it is quite reasonable that in the Prologue, where Jn emphasises the role of the Son in communicating sonship to Christians, he also mentions expressly the precise characteristic of this role of the Son, namely, the quality of being begotten by God.

But John had to differentiate the generation of Christ, which was unique in quality, and capable of communicating the divine generation to Christians, from that of Christians. This he does in different ways. First of all, unlike the other NT Writers, he reserves the

---

[163] Note the indicative present of τέκνα Θεοῦ ἐσμέν.

[164] Note the use of the aorist tense ἠγάπησεν ὁ Θεός (Jn 3:16), ἐφανερώθη ἡ ἀγάπη (I Jn 4:9) and the conjunctive use of ἵνα ἔχῃ ζωήν (Jn 3:16) and ἵνα ζήσωμεν (I Jn 4:9).

name " υἱός τοῦ Θεοῦ " for Christ, calling the Christians exclusively " τέκνα τοῦ Θεοῦ ". Besides, he applies to Christ his characteristic term " μονογενής " showing thus the unique character of His sonship and begetting [165]. Moreover he employs the aorist indicative of " γεννάω " exclusively for Christ, to refer to the unique moment of history, the moment of Incarnation as the moment of this unique generation of Christ, which becomes the source of the generation of Christians.

Hence, with all probability in Jn 1:13, we should read the singular referring to this unique generation of Christ from God, of the One who is called " μονογενής " in the same Prologue, just after the declaration of this generation and Incarnation (cf. Jn 1:14,18) [166].

e. Reasons from the Structure

The very structure of the Prologue favours the singular reading. The Prologue forms a literary unit in which 5 verbs seem to mark the decisive stages of the development of the argument. These words are : 1) ἦν(ὤν), 2) ἐγένετο, 3) λαμβάνειν, 4) μαρτυρεῖν and 5) ἔρχομαι. If ἦν(ὤν) marks the presentation of the Logos (Jesus) in his relation to God (Father) (vv. 1-2,18), ἐγένετο marks the presentation of his role in the history and economy of salvation (vv. 3,17) [167]. The verb λαμβάνειν marks the response on the part of man to the salvific role of Jesus (vv. 4-5,16 ; also vv. 11 and 12). If μαρτυρεῖν marks the witness of John the Baptist to the salvific role of Jesus (vv. 6-8,15), ἔρχομαι marks the more concrete presentation of the salvific and revelatory presence and activity of Jesus among men and their response to it (vv. 9-10,11 to which vv. 12-13 and 14 form a parallelism as will be explained below).

Note the occurrence of these words in the different verses so as to constitute a concentric structure :

A	ἦν	(vv. 1-2)	(v. 18)		ὤν	A'
B	ἐγένετο	(v. 3)	(v. 17)		ἐγένετο	B'
C	οὐ κατέλαβεν	(vv. 4-5)	(v. 16)		ἐλάβομεν	C'
D	μαρτυρήσῃ	(vv. 6-8)	(v. 15)		μαρτυρεῖ	D'

---

[165] Cf. F. BÜCHSEL, art. μονογενής, *TDNT* IV, p. 740 ; R. BULTMANN, *Evangelium*, p. 47.

[166] Cf. A. v HARNACK, art. cit., p. 548 where he observes that the value of the expression μονογενοῦς παρὰ πατρός in v. 14 will be considerably weakened, if we take the plural in Jn 1:13.

[167] Note the word γίνομαι and not κτίζω or ποιέω used in v. 3 parallel to that of v. 17, which indicates that John speaks here not only about creation, but about the whole economy of salvation (from creation to redemption) realized through the Son (Logos). Cf. P. LAMARCHE, art. cit., p. 524.

E ἐρχόμενον εἰς τὸν   (v. 14)   ... σὰρξ E'
   κόσμον (vv. 9-10)   ἐγένετο
F ἦλθεν εἰς τὰ ἴδια   ὅς ... ἐγεννήθη F'
   οὐ παρέλαβον (v. 11)   (vv. 12-13) ἔλαβον αὐτόν

In this concentric structure the ἐρχόμενον εἰς τὸν κόσμον of v. 9 (E) and εἰς τὰ ἴδια ἦλθεν of v. 11 (F) are parallels to σὰρξ ἐγένετο of v. 14 (E') and ὅς ... ἐγεννήθη of v. 13 (F') respectively. This parallelism is confirmed by the thematic parallelism of the accompanying phrases ' he was in the world ' of v. 10 which is parallel to ' he dwelt among us ' of v. 14b, and ' the world did not know him ' of v. 10c which is antithetically parallel to ' we have seen his glory ' of v. 14c [168]. So the coming of Christ into the world (unto his own) [169] is parallel to his Incarnation and birth from God.

Here it is interesting to examine how Jn speaks of the coming of Christ into the world. Jn speaks of Christ's coming in the aorist or perfect tense with the phrase ' εἰς τὸν κόσμον ' precisely in contexts reminding us of His sonship or generation. In Jn it occurs apart from the Prologue in 3:19 ; 12:46 ; 16:28 and 18:37. In 3:19 it is in the context of speaking of Him as ' μονογενής ' (3:16,18). Jn 12:46 is parallel to 3:19 and 12:35-36 [170], and also 12:35-36 speaks of ' sons of Light ', which is a participation in the sonship of Christ who is ' Light '. In 16:28 it is used parallel to the coming forth from the Father [171]. The same expression ' εἰς τὸν κόσμον ' is used in 16:21 with the verb ' ἐγεννήθη ' in which the birth of the man into the world in this eschatological context seems to refer to the Messianic coming of Christ [172]. Finally, in Jn 18:37 the ' birth of Christ ' is

---

[168] It is worth noting that there is also a literary parallelism of the word ἐγένετο in both vv. 10 and 14. For ἔρχεσθαι referring to Jesus' coming as the revelation of the Father, cf. J. P. MIRANDA, *Der Vater, der mich gesandt hat*, Frankfurt, 1972, p. 40.

[169] Note that in Jn 1:11a τὰ ἴδια and the οἱ ἴδιοι are the same as τὸν κόσμον in v. 9 where the κόσμος stands for the humanity in general. Cf. J. JERVELL, " Er kam in sein Eigentum Zum Joh. 1:11 ", *ST* 10 (1956), pp. 14-27.

[170] Note the occurrence of the same theme of ' Light ' and ' belief '.

[171] It is worth noting that in the Patristic tradition this coming forth from the Father is seen as a generation from God. Quoting Jn 8:42b, Epiph: Haer. LXIX, 53, p. 775C says : ἐγέννεσάς με, φησί, πάτερ, καὶ ἐγὼ ἐκ τοῦ πατρός ἐξῆλθον καὶ ἥκω. Cf. A. RESCH, *Ausserkanonische Paralleltexte zu den Evangelien*, III in *TU* X, 4, 1896, p. 120.

[172] Cf. A. FEUILLET, " L'heure de la femme (Jn 16:21) et l'heure de la mère de Jésus (Jn 19:25-27) ", *Bib* 47 (1966), pp. 366-368.

made synonymous to 'His coming into the world' (γεγέννημαι καὶ ἐλήλυθα εἰς τὸν κόσμον).

The Johannine vocabulary, therefore, favours the parallelism of 'εἰς τὰ ἴδια ἦλθεν' with 'ὃς ἐγεννήθη' of v. 13. Hence with considerable probability we can take the 'ἐγεννήθη' of v. 13 in the singular referring to Christ's generation from God extended and manifested in His coming into the world, namely, in His Incarnation.

2. Objections against the Singular

a. According to Calmes [173] and Schnackenburg [174], v. 13 explains v. 12, and the singular reading would destroy this explanatory character.

b. Another objection to the singular reading arises from the difficulty of applying it to both the eternal and temporal generation of Christ. According to some critics, it cannot be applied to the eternal generation because then it should have been mentioned in vv. 1-2 speaking of the eternal relation of the Word to God; and Jn never presents the eternal relation between the Father and the Son as a generation. Moreover, it would be absurd to exclude with such an emphasis the carnal elements in order to speak of the eternal generation. On the other hand, they find it difficult to apply it to the temporal generation, because in this case it anticipates v. 14 and thus destroys the newness of the declaration in v. 14, which appears to be a new and solemn declaration both as to the form and as to its content [175].

3. Answer to the Objections

a. The Singular reading of v. 13: more explanatory

Our answer to the objection no. 1 is that the singular reading only gives v. 13 a more profound explanatory character, than when it is read in the plural. It explains first of all the sonship, not simply exposing the process of the divine generation of Christians, but presenting the divine generation of Christ as the 'prototype' and 'source' of the sonship of Christians. Moreover, it explains also the specific

---

[173] Cf. *L'évangile*, pp. 119-120.
[174] Cf. *The Gospel according to St. John*, pp. 263-265.
[175] This difficulty is admitted by SCHMID, who favours the plural (cf. art. cit., in *BZ* pp. 118-124) and by HARNACK who favours the singular (cf. art. cit. p. 549), and both of them try to solve the problem, by seeing vv. 12c-13 as a later addition, though characteristically Johannine, thus leaving the difficulty in itself unsolved.

character of the faith that leads to this divine sonship. Namely, it is not enough to have any faith in general, but the faith that reaches Christ as Begotten of God, which is quite in accordance with the idea expressed in John elsewhere (cf. Jn 3:16 ; 20:31 ; I Jn 5:1,5,13).

b. *Generation of Christ: both eternal and temporal*

We answer to the second objection by proving that in Jn there is a combination of the eternal and temporal generation of Christ. Certainly, if we take the eternal and temporal generation of Christ so separately and try to see exclusively one of these generations in v. 13, we meet with the difficulty mentioned above. But does John make such an exclusive consideration about the generation of Christ? To see the real nature of the generation of Christ, we should have a glimpse of the Johannine concept of Christ's divine sonship itself.

i. The divine sonship of Christ

The divine sonship of Christ seems to get an extraordinary emphasis in the Writings of John. Faithful to his purpose (Jn 20:31 ; I Jn 5:13), Jn develops the doctrine of the divine sonship of Christ throughout. The abundant use of the word " πατήρ " for God [176] is in itself a distinctive mark of the importance of this theme in Jn [177]. The fact that the expression ' Our Father ' does not occur in Jn and ' Your Father ' only once and that after the resurrection of Christ, marks the singular relation between the Father and the Son, as developed by Jn.

This use of the term ' Father ' for God in a singular relation to Jesus, shows that the use of the term ' Son of God ' for Jesus also expresses the singular divine sonship of Jesus. Different statements regarding Christ point to the divine nature expressed by the term ' Son of God '. His preexistence [178], His equality with the Father in knowledge (cf. 2:24 ; 5:18 ; 6:65 ; 12:33 ; 16:29 etc.) and power (cf. 5:17,20,36), His community with the Father (cf. 16:15 ; 17:10), the mutual communication of the divine nature and attributes (cf. 10:30 ; 14:10-12 ; 17:22-23), all are important proofs of His divinity that is expressed in the term ' Son of God '. Therefore, though in the mouth

---

[176] It occurs in the Gospel 115 times ; in the Epistle 16 times and in Rev 5 times.

[177] Cf. W. F. LOFTHOUSE, " Fatherhood and Sonship in the Fourth Gospel ", *ET* 43 (1931), pp. 442-448 ; BULTMANN, *Evangelium*, pp. 36ff.

[178] ' He is before Abraham was ' (8:58) ; ' He goes back to heaven where He was and from where He descended ' (6:7,38,62) ; ' He was glorified before the world existed ' (17:5) ; ' God loved Him before the creation of the world ' (17:24) ; ' He was with God before the existence of anything else ' (1:1-2).

of others it could be simply a synonym for the Messiah [179], in the mouth of Jesus [180] and the Evangelist [181], it certainly meant that Christ is the Son of God by nature.

ii. The Revelatory nature of Christ's divine sonship

But it is interesting to note that Jn makes use of the title 'Son of God' almost exclusively in contexts expressing Christ's mission among men, and never in contexts expressing solely the relation existing between God and Christ. This seems to point to the special revelatory nature characterising the divine sonship of Christ in Jn [182].

The special character of Jesus' sonship seems to be implied in the fact that Jn interchanges the titles 'Christ' and 'Son of God' for Jesus (cf. Jn 20:31 and I Jn 5:1,5). The interchanging of these two titles modifies both the concept of divine sonship and that of Messianism in the Johannine Jesus. For Jn Jesus is not the Son of God because He is Christ, but He is Christ because He is Son of God [183]. The Messianic character of Jesus as Christ is singular, because it seems to define His being itself. Christ's Mission seems to be confused with His being itself. He lives not 'for' His mission, as the prophets, but 'of' His mission [184]. His Mission is His coming itself [185].

iii. Pre-existent and temporal sonship

Actually the Johannine formula of self-witness of Jesus is either " ἐγὼ ἦλθον " or " ἐγὼ ἐλήλυθα " (cf. 8:42 ; 16:27,28 ; 17:8 ; 18:37 etc.). The basis of the Messianic claim of Jesus is that He does not come from Himself (cf. Jn 7:28 ; 8:42) but from God the Father (cf. Jn 8: 42 ; 16:27,28). According to John the Baptist, the Messiah is " ὁ ἄνωθεν ἐρχόμενος " (Jn 3:31). Even for the Jews, the Messiah is to be recognised on the basis of His origin (cf. Jn 7:27). Thus the divine origin (sonship) becomes the basis of His Messiahship, and His Messiahship becomes the expression of His sonship. Thus Jn seems

---

[179] By John the Baptist (1:34 ; 3:35,36) ; By Nathanael as parallel to King of Israel (1:49) ; by Peter (6:69) ; by Martha as parallel to Christ (11:27) ; by the Jews (19:7).

[180] Cf. 3:16-18 ; 5:19-23,25,26 ; 6:40 ; 8:36 ; 9:35 ; 10:36 ; 11:4 ; 14:13 ; 17:1.

[181] Cf. 1:18 ; 20:31 and the texts in I and II Jn.

[182] For the revelatory nature of the term 'Father' for God in John. Cf. G. SCHRENK, art. πατήρ, *TDNT* V, pp. 997-999.

[183] For the revelatory nature of Jesus' divine sonship, cf. M. VELLANICKAL, " Jesus of the Fourth Gospel ", *Biblebhashyam* 1 (1975), pp. 60-73.

[184] Cf. BULTMANN, *Evangelium*, p. 143f.

[185] Cf. D. MOLLAT, " La divinité du Christ d'après saint Jean ", *LumVie* 9 (1953), p. 116.

to combine the two sonships in Christ: The preexistent sonship and the Messianic temporal sonship [186].

The preoccupation of the Evangelist is to show Jesus as the Son of God, and to explain this divine sonship through the union between the Word and Humanity. He is not preoccupied with the origin of the humanity of Christ or of the manner of union of this humanity to the Word [187]. The fact that Jn speaks of the divine sonship of Christ as based on the fact that He comes from God the Father in virtue of a generation, seems to confirm this special characteristic of the sonship of Christ in Jn.

iv. Jesus: the 'μονογενής'

The idea of the divine generation of Christ seems to be implied in the title 'μονογενής', which Jn several times attributes to Christ (cf. Jn 1:14,18; 3:16,18; I Jn 4:9). First of all it is to be noted that in Jn "μονογενής" is connected directly with the notion of sonship, from the fact that it is joined to "υἱός" (cf. Jn 3:16,18; I Jn 4:9), or is put in correspondence with "πατήρ" (cf. Jn 1:14,18). This shows that Jn wanted to show by this term the dependence of origin. The divine sonship and divine generation being characteristically Johannine arguments, this idea of origin could hardly be excluded from the full meaning of "μονογενής". John does not exclude the affectionate note of the term (cf. Jn 3:16 and I Jn 4:9). But in him the term connotes much more the fundamental reason for God's fatherly affection towards Christ [188].

Moreover, in Jn 1:18 the Word Incarnate is "μονογενὴς Θεός" [189]. Jesus Christ is not only 'the only Begotten of God', but He is 'the only Begotten God'. He strictly shares with God the Father (note the article with πατρός) the divine essence and being. In virtue of His unique origin or generation from God, He Himself is true God [190].

---

[186] In this connection cf. J. RIEDL, " Strukturen christologischer Glaubensentfaltung im Neuen Testament ", *ZKT* 87 (1965), pp. 445-452 where he tries to show how a process in combining the two sonships of Christ took place in the Primitive Christian Community, traces of which are found in Rom 1:3-4 and Lk 1:35, and how Jn 1:14 marks the final stage of this process, where the Johannine Logos — Son of God — becomes the revealer of God from the beginning to the end.

[187] Cf. L. VENARD, art. cit., in *DTC* VIII, 1, col. 569.

[188] Cf. A. M. DONATUS, art. cit., p. 11; A. J. SÜRJANSKY, op. cit., p. 115.

[189] The reading μονογενὴς Θεός is to be preferred in the light of evidences both external and internal. Cf. J. A. HORT, *Two Dissertations*, (I On Monogenes Theos in Scripture and Tradition), Cambridge, 1876, pp. 1-72; M. J. LAGRANGE, *L'Évangile*, pp. 26ff; WESTCOTT, *Gospel*, pp. 32-33.

[190] The 'only' modifies not the 'Son' but 'begotten' and that in a

The image of the bosom connected with the relation between the Father and the Monogenes also points to the concept of generation implied in " μονογενής "[191].

It is this implicit affirmation of the divine generation of Christ, that seems to be explicitly affirmed by Jn in the two places, namely in Jn 1:13 and I Jn 5:18. The fact that in both these contexts the aorist tense is used shows that the divine begetting of Christ as conceived by Jn refers specially to the moment of Incarnation.

Thus John seems to combine both the eternal and temporal generation. The term " μονογενής " does not speak only of the temporal generation in the sense that Jesus became " μονογενής " by becoming man, because in Jn 3:16 and I Jn 4:9 God sends the One who was already " μονογενής ". It does not either speak only of the eternal generation, because the " μονογενής " is used in Jn only after the affirmation of the Incarnation and in strict connection with it. Note also the phrase that accompanies " μονογενής " in Jn 1:14 'full of Grace and Truth', which could be said only of the Incarnate Christ [192].

v. The Phrase in v. 13

In the phrase " ἐκ Θεοῦ ἐγεννήθη " of v. 13, the aorist ' ἐγεννήθη ' shows an event that took place at a moment in time. This cannot be referred to the eternal generation. At the same time, the compliment " ἐκ Θεοῦ " shows that it is a generation from God. For Christ, this should be eternal. Hence we see a combination of both the eternal and temporal generation of Christ in the very expression of v. 13.

vi. Comparison with the Synoptics

This combination of the historical and eternal generation in v. 13 is seen better, if we compare it with the Synoptic presentation of the Incarnation of Christ. The Synoptic formula of the temporal generation of Christ is " γεννηθῆναι ἐκ πνεύματος ἁγίου" (Mt 1:20 ; Lk 1:35), and not " γεννηθῆναι ἐκ Θεοῦ". While the emphasis in the Synoptic formula is on the manner of Jesus' generation (virginal) [193], the emphasis in the Johannine formula is on the divine sonship itself of

---

qualitative sense. Cf. K. S. WUEST, " Deity of Christ in the Greek Texts of John and Paul ", *BS* 119 (1962), p. 219.

[191] Cf. I. DE LA POTTERIE, art. " L'emploi dynamique de εἰς dans saint Jean et ses incidences théologiques ", *Bib* 43 (1962), p. 385.

[192] Cf. M. J. LAGRANGE, *L'Evangile*, p. 22.

[193] Jn is not ignorant of this aspect, but he refers to it rather in an indirect manner and negatively with the phrases " neither ... nor ... nor ...".

Christ. The paradox of the Johannine formula consists in the fact that while the aorist tense refers to an historical event (temporal - virginal generation) the formula itself refers to the transcendent reality of Jesus' generation from God.

vii. The Temporal Generation: Sign of the Eternal Generation

What Jn wants to express here is the divine generation of Christ, and he wants to explain this divine generation through the temporal generation or Incarnation. The wonderful manner itself of the temporal generation is not of great interest to Jn, though it is included in this affirmation [194]. John speaks of the temporal (virginal) generation in as much as it is the sign and continuation of the eternal generation. This combined generation of Christ in Jn is expressed by the Ecclesiastical Writers of the 2nd Century using different terms for Christ such as ' carnal and spiritual ', ' begotten and not begotten ', ' God made in flesh ' ... ' from Mary and from God ' etc.[195] It is this combined generation of Christ, both eternal (from God) and temporal (from Mary), namely, the eternal generation from God expressed and continued in the temporal generation, that becomes the object of faith for the believers, and the source and prototype, for their sonship and generation.

Combining the eternal and temporal generation, v. 13 forms a good transition to the explicit declaration of the Incarnation in v. 14, which keeps its newness in the fact that it mentions for the first time the temporal generation in contradistinction to the eternal generation of vv. 1-2 resuming the word ' Logos '.

On the other hand, it is to be noted that v. 14 is not totally new, excluding all sorts of anticipation. In fact, we see anticipations of it in vv. 9-10 " ... coming into the world. He was in the world..." (E) forming parallel to v. 14 (E') and also in v. 11 " he came to his own " (F). Hence it is not surprising to see a certain anticipation of it also in v. 13 (F') " ὅς ἐγεννήθη ", it being parallel to v. 11a (F). So the reading in the singular of v. 13 gives only more harmony to the movement of thought in the Prologue.

---

[194] Note how in excluding the elements of the ordinary human birth, John does not exclude the will of the woman, which had an essential role in the Incarnation. Cf. J. GALOT, op. cit., pp. 118-122.

[195] Cf. IGNATIUS OF ANTIOCH, Ad Eph 7,2 in PG 5, 649.

4. *The Change from Singular to Plural* [196]

There is no need to suppose a voluntary change of the text. In a Christian milieu, penetrated by the Gnostics, it was perfectly natural that the change into plural seemed quite conformable to the intention of the text expressing the sonship of v. 12 in a spiritual birth, because the Gnostic doctrine applied the spiritual birth of the Word to the 'Spirituals'. Applied rightly, it was quite acceptable in such a Christian milieu. So there is no wonder, if in the Alexandrian Christian milieu the plural was accepted without difficulty.

This does not imply a conscious abandoning of the doctrine of the virginal birth of Christ included in the profession of faith as claimed by Schnackenburg [197]. In a circumstance where the virginal birth was taken for granted, when the Anti-Ebionite polemics was no more actual, this transformation does not mean an abandoning of the doctrine of the virginal birth of Christ.

The reason why this transformation into the plural had such a success, so that it was introduced into all the Mss of the Greek tradition is simple. The Church of Alexandria, where this change took place, had a decisive influence in the fixing up of the Greek text of the Gospel. So this change took place in a circumstance favourable to its acceptance and expansion in the whole Church of the Greek world. And as the change was quite conformable to the doctrine of the divine sonship of Christians mentioned in the context, it continued to be the accepted text throughout the Centuries to this day.

III. Exegetical Analysis

A. *Context in the Prologue*

First of all, we try to fix up the position of Jn 1:12-13 in the Prologue through a structural analysis of the latter, which will show the importance of the theme of the divine sonship of Christians as presented in these verses. This structural analysis will also help us to see the different parallelisms, occurring in the different verses, which will explain one or another aspect of the same theme of Christian sonship.

1. *The Structure of Jn 1:1-18*

Vv. 1- 2 A   In the beginning WAS the W o r d ... WAS w i t h
                                                            GOD ...
                            WAS GOD ... WAS w i t h GOD

---

[196] On this problem, cf. J. GALOT, op. cit., pp. 86-94.
[197] Cf. *The Gospel according to St. John*, pp. 263-265.

3	B	All things WERE MADE THROUGH him ... WAS ... MADE
4-5	C	What was made in HIM was Life ... Light of men
		The Light shines ... darkness DID NOT RECEIVE IT
6-8	D	There WAS ... JOHN ... HE CAME for WITNESS TO BEAR WITNESS TO the Light ... TO BEAR WITNESS TO ...
9-10	E	The Light ... was coming into the world ...
		And the world did not know HIM.
11	F	HE came to His own and His own RECEIVED HIM not
12-13	F'	Who RECEIVED HIM ... who believe in his name, He gave them power to become children of God ... WHO was born ... of God
14	E'	The Word WAS MADE Flesh and dwelt among us We saw HIS glory ... as of the Only Begotten Son ...
15	D'	JOHN BORE WITNESS TO him and cried ... HE who COMES ... WAS ...
16	C'	From HIS Fulness WE HAVE all RECEIVED Grace for Grace
17	B'	For the Law ... THROUGH ... Grace and Truth WAS MADE THROUGH ...
18	A'	No one ... GOD ... the Only Begotten Son who IS in the bosom of the Father ...

There are several studies made on the structure of the Prologue based on the literary indications [198]. They can be classified into two

---

[198] Cf. M. E. BOISMARD, *Le prologue de saint Jean*, Paris, 1953, pp. 99-108; M. Fr. LACAN, "Le prologue de saint Jean. Ses thèmes, sa structure, son movement", *Lum et Vie* 33 (1957), pp. 91-110; H. RIDDERBOS, "The Structure and Scope of the Prologue of the Gospel of John", *NovTest* 8 (1966), pp. 180-201; A. FEUILLET, *Le prologue de quatrième évangile*, Paris, 1968, pp. 137-177; J. IRIGOIN, "La composition rythmique du prologue de Jean (1,1-18)", *RB* 78 (1971), pp. 501-514; S. A. PANIMOLLE, *Il Dono della Legge e la Grazia della Verità* (Gv 1,17), Roma, 1973, pp. 71-105; A. J. FESTUGIÈRE, *Observations stylistiques sur l'évangile de s. Jean*, Paris, 1974, pp. 124-141.

main categories: one, those who propose a concentric structure (thus Boismard, Feuillet), and the other, those who propose a circular or spiral structure (thus Lacan, Ridderbos, Panimolle), though in details they may differ again one from the other.

As it can be seen from our presentation, the general structure of the Prologue is concentric, moving towards the all important affirmation of John in vv. 11-13. The words ὅσοι δέ (the δέ occurs only here in the whole Prologue) introduce the strong antithesis of the second part (vv. 12-18) to the first part (vv. 1-11). The general theme of the Prologue is nothing else but the theme of the Gospel itself, as expressed in Jn 20:30-31, namely, Jesus Christ, the salvific revealer (Son of God), who gives the gift of Life (a share in his sonship) to those who give a positive response to Him. It is this theme that pervades the whole structural presentation of the Prologue, emphasizing in each part one or other aspect of this general theme. The different aspects may be described as follows: 1) Jesus Christ in his relation to God, which enables Him to be the salvific revealer (vv. 1-2,18 = AA'); 2) His role in the economy of salvation as the salvific revealer (vv. 3,17 = BB'); 3) The participation, negative or positive, on the part of man, in the salvific revelation realized in and through Christ (vv. 4-5,16 = CC'); 4) John the Baptist bearing testimony to the revelatory role of Jesus Christ (vv. 6-8,15 = DD'); 5) The salvific presence of Christ the revealer and the response, negative and positive, on the part of man are expressed more concretely (vv. 9-10,14 = EE'); 6) Finally, the salvific revelatory presence of Christ, negative and positive response on the part of man, and the consequence of the positive response: sharing in the divine sonship of Christ by receiving the gift of becoming children of God (vv. 11-13 = FF').

2. *The Scheme of the Structure*

For a clearer perception of the movement of the argument, we present below a scheme of the structure of the Prologue:

Vv. 1- 2 A   Jesus Christ the Revealer
     3 B   Christ's role in the economy of salvation
    4- 5 C   Salvific revelation realized in and through Christ
                   Response and Participation - Negative
    6- 8 D   The testimony of John the Baptist
    9-10 E   The salvific presence of Christ the Revealer
                   Response of man - Negative
     11 F   The revelatory presence of Christ
                   Response - Negative

12-13	F'	The revelatory presence of Christ
		Response - Positive
		Consequence - Sharing in the sonship
14	E'	The salvific presence of Christ the revealer
		Response of man - Positive
15	D'	The testimony of John the Baptist
16	C'	Salvific revelation realized in and through Christ
		Response and Participation - Positive
17	B'	Christ's role in the economy of salvation
18	A'	Jesus Christ the Revealer

As it can be seen from the scheme, the movement of the argument is towards the centre, where it culminates in the presentation of the central theme, namely, the gift of divine sonship to those who believe in the Incarnate Son of God, in whose filial life the salvific revelation is fully realized (vv. 11-13). This is very well prepared, and to some extent anticipated, in the other parallel statements, emphasising the negative and positive side of it in the first half and the second half respectively. In presenting it thus, the second half of the Prologue (vv. 14-18) uses a vocabulary that is distinct from the first half (vv. 1-10) remaining, however, parallel to it in the basic outline of the structure. The second half makes use of a vocabulary which reflects the concrete Christian experience, with the terms such as 'Jesus Christ', 'the Only Begotten', 'his glory', 'his fulness', 'Grace and Truth', 'the Father' etc. These are certainly more concrete expressions of Christian experience than those found in the first half such as 'the Word', 'God', 'Life', 'Light' etc, but, nevertheless, parallel to them. It is no wonder that the second half is so distinctive, because it is precisely in the second half that the positive response to and participation in the Christ event is expressed. It is worth noting how v. 14 which forms a transition to the second half of the Prologue, after the central statement in vv. 11-13, combines in it the two titles 'the Word' (v. 14a = vv. 1-2) and 'the Only Begotten of the Father' (v. 14c = v. 18), with which Jesus is introduced in the Prologue in the first and second halves respectively. It is quite natural that in a concentric structure, the second half, remaining basically parallel to the first half in its argument and movement, presents a vocabulary which shows more progress and development.

It is this distinctive and progressive vocabulary that has led some authors to find a circular or spiral structure in the Prologue [199]. Though in the stylistic structure of the small units taken in them-

---

[199] Cf. S. A. PANIMOLLE, op. cit., pp. 71-105.

selves such a spiral procedure may be admitted, the overall structure is concentric. The main thrust of the Prologue, as that of the Gospel, is not simply to present Christ as the Son of God in his relation to the Father, and consequently the salvific revelation realized in Christ, as expressed in vv. 17-18, which becomes the culminating point in the theory of the circular or spiral structure of the Prologue. The main thrust of the Gospel and the Prologue goes far beyond that. It is to show the gift of divine sonship or Life shared by those who give a positive response to Christ. It is to be noted that, whether the Prologue originally goes back or not to a hymn about Logos or Jesus Christ [200], at present it is an introduction to the Gospel that contains synthetically the main argument of the Gospel. The fact that the theme of Christian sonship holds the central place in the Prologue shows how integral it is to the message of the Evangelist.

If, therefore, the doctrine of the divine sonship of the believers is a central theme to Jn, we have every reason to think that he meant something more than a mere figure of speech by the words " τέκνα Θεοῦ γενέσθαι " in 1:12. If the other facts related in the Prologue, such as, the relation of the Logos to God, His coming into the world, the testimony of John the Baptist, the negative and positive response given to the Incarnate Logos, are all true and real facts, it would be very strange, if he were to place in the centre of these affirmations something that is only a mere metaphor [201].

B. *Analysis of the Text*

First of all we have to remark that we adopt the singular reading " ἐγεννήθη " in v. 13 on the basis of our arguments exposed in the

---

[200] We do not intend to enter upon the discussion regarding the complex question of the derivation of the Prologue, as it is impossible to do in a limited work as ours, and also because it is of little use for the scope of our work. On the matter, cf. R. SCHNACKENBURG, " Logos-Hymnus und Johanneischer Prolog ", *BZ* 1 (1957), pp. 66-109; J. BLANK, " Das Johannesevangelium. Der Prolog ", II Teil, *BibLeb* 7 (1966), pp. 112-127; C. DEMKE, " Das sogenannte Logos-Hymnus im Johanneischen Prolog ", *ZNW* 58 (1967), pp. 45-68; J. T. SANDERS, *The New Testament Christological Hymns*, Cambridge, 1971, pp. 20-24; G. RICHTER, " Die Fleischwerdung des Logos im Johannesevangelium ", *NovTest* 13 (1971), pp. 81-126; 14 (1972), pp. 257-276; H. ZIMMERMANN, " Christushymnus und Johanneischer Prolog ", in *Neues Testament und Kirche: Festschr.* R. SCHNACKENBURG, Herder, 1974, pp. 249-265.

[201] Cf. A. M. DONATUS, art. cit. in *MelT* 8 (1955), p. 19 where he says that " in this case it would be the only thing not real, attested by him, or, in other words, he would have given a strong testimony to a thing, which does not imply any reality at all ".

textual criticism. By this very fact it is clear that we dissociate the two verses, and thereby we are freed from the task of combining the two phrases " ἔδωκεν ... τέκνα Θεοῦ γενέσθαι " of v. 12 and " ἐκ Θεοῦ ἐγεννήθησαν " of v. 13. So our task will be to analyse the implications of v. 12 in the matter of the divine sonship, and its relation to the relative clause of v. 13 taken in the singular, understanding the latter as referring to Christ, the object of faith, which plays a fundamental role in the divine sonship of men as mentioned in v.12[202].

1. *Grammatical Considerations*

a. **The Different Elements of the Verses**

Verses 12-13 are composed of the following elements:

vv. 12 a. ὅσοι ... ἔλαβον αὐτόν
     b. ἔδωκεν αὐτοῖς ... τέκνα Θεοῦ γενέσθαι
     c. τοῖς πιστεύουσιν ... αὐτοῦ
   13. ὃς οὐκ ... ἀλλ'ἐκ Θεοῦ ἐγεννήθη

Out of these four elements v. 12b forms the principal clause, representing the Logos who gives the power to become children of God. The relative clause in the nominative in v. 12a is an expansion of " αὐτοῖς " the indirect object of " ἔδωκεν " in v. 12b. It is an example of the 'casus pendens' construction, which is characteristically Johannine [203], in which a word or phrase is taken out of its normal place in the sentence and is put first. Thus it represents men, who received the Logos and to whom the power is given to become children of God. The participial clause in v. 12c also explains " αὐτοῖς " the indirect object of ἔδωκεν, and this time it refers to those who believe in the name of the Son of God. Verse 13 is a relative clause referring to the " αὐτοῦ " of v. 12c, explaining thus the specific character of the one, in whose name they believe.

Thus if the two phrases in v. 12a and 12c speaking of the believers are subordinated to v. 12b, explaining the indirect object of " ἔδωκεν ", v. 13 is a compliment of v. 12c explaining the direct object of the faith.

Now, the mutual relation of the verbs in the verses is to be examined more closely. This relation could be drawn schematically as follows:

---

[202] Here it is worth mentioning that in our exegesis of the texts, we do not intend to repeat the arguments exposed in the textual criticism, many of which are of considerable importance for the actual understanding of the texts.

[203] This construction occurs in John 27 times, while it occurs in the Synoptics, only 21 times in all.

ἔλαβον
ἔδωκεν . . . . γενέσθαι
                              πιστεύουσιν
ἐγεννήθη

The use of different tenses brings forward the problem of chronological relation between " ἔλαβον ", " πιστεύουσιν " and " γενέσθαι ".

It seems that there is an interval between " ἔλαβον " and " τέκνα Θεοῦ γενέσθαι " an interval marking a process of becoming children of God, and in this process " πιστεύουσιν " seems to play the role of a dynamic factor. The solution of this problem depends partly on an evaluation of the different tenses used and their mutual relation.

b. Evaluation of the Tenses

The verb " ἔλαβον " marking the reception of the Logos is in the aorist indicative. The ordinary significance of the aorist indicative is a punctiliar action in the past. From the grammatical point of view, nothing could be said about its priority or posteriority in relation to another action. This has to be determined by the context.

On the other hand, " πιστεύουσιν " is a present participle. The ordinary signification of the present participle is a continuous action, without temporal specification [204]. So the act of believing is conceived as something that is going on. As we saw above, both phrases refer to those to whom the power is given to become children of God. This repetition of the same idea with a different word and in a different tense, naturally points to a progress of signification in this element of faith. If v. 12a speaks of men as having received the Logos at a definite time in the past, v. 12c describes them as continuing or persisting in that reception and belief.

The verb " γενέσθαι ", an aorist infinitive, according to the ordinary sense means an action in itself. So the ' becoming children of God' is here considered as something that takes place without any special reference of priority or posteriority to another action. It simply explains " ἐξουσίαν " the object of the principal verb " ἔδωκεν " [205]. The " ἔδωκεν " being an aorist indicative, does not give any specific temporal nuances. But its parallel use with " ἔλαβον " shows that the reception of the Logos and the giving of the power are contemporaneous.

The above evaluation of the tenses seems to show that the punctiliar action of the reception of the Logos in the past (ἔλαβον) is

---

[204] Cf. M. ZERWICK, *Biblical Greek*, Rome, 1963, no. 371.

[205] Note, however, that γενέσθαι in its verbal expression has a meaning that points towards future, by the very fact that it means ' to become '.

vitalized by means of a continual and ever dynamic faith (πιστεύ-ουσιν) which in its turn results in becoming children of God (τέκνα Θεοῦ γενέσθαι).

Now, to bring out the full significance of the different elements of the verses, we pass on to a study of the Vocabulary.

2. Study of the Vocabulary

a. '...to become children of God...' (v. 12b)

First of all, we take the word " γενέσθαι " which being part of the predicate speaking of the divine sonship, is more significant than any other words in the verse for understanding the specific character of the divine sonship affirmed here [206]. " Γίνομαι " in its original and ordinary sense means 'to come into being', 'to become', or 'to originate'[207]. This original meaning is kept specially when it is used of persons and things which change their nature, to indicate their entering a new condition [208]. There are numerous examples of such a use in the NT referring to both natural and supernatural relations [209].

There is no doubt that there are texts in the NT, where " γίνομαι " is used as a substitute for the forms of " εἰμί " (cf. Mt 10:16; 13:22; Mk 4:19 etc.). But this does not mean a complete lack of distinction between " γίνεσθαι " and " εἶναι " in the NT usage. Actually the Johannine usage of " γίνομαι " seems to keep the original meaning, specially when used with a noun or adjective, as complement of the predicate. Out of the 50 occurrences of " γίνομαι " in Jn, 17 are with such complements of nouns or adjectives and all of them signify a change from one condition to another [210]. Mostly it is when speaking of men, that Jn makes use of it in this sense [211].

---

[206] Usually the modern Commentators neglect this verb as being insignificant. Cf. the Commentaries of LAGRANGE, VAN DEN BUSSCHE, LOISY, BERNARD, BULTMANN, SCHNACKENBURG etc.

[207] MOULTON-MILLIGAN, *The Vocabulary of the Greek Testament* ..., p. 126.

[208] Cf. W. BAUER, *A Greek English Lexicon*, p. 158; cf. also J. GUHRT, art. γίνομαι, *TBLNT* I, p. 448 where he describes it as: " zu etwas werden, um eine eintretende Veränderung, einen anderen Zustand zu beziehen ".

[209] Cf. Mt 5:45; Mk 1:17; Lk 6:16; 23:12; Jn 12:36; Acts 26:29; Rom 4:18; I Cor 3:18; 4:9; 13:11; Gal 3:13; Heb 5:5 etc. In front of these numerous examples, it is quite embarrassing to hear BÜCHSEL saying that ' Usually the term has no particular religious or theological interest in the New Testament " cf. art. γίνομαι, *TDNT*, I, p. 681.

[210] Cf. Jn 1:12,14; 2:9; 4:14; 5:4,6,9,14; 9:22,27,39; 10:16; 12:36,42; 15:8; 16:20.

[211] Out of the 14 occurrences, only one speaks of Christ (Jn 1:14) and 3 speak of things (Jn 2:9; 4:14 and 16:20).

Here it is worth noting that, while Jn makes use of the aorist indicative to signify the bodily becoming of Christ (1:14) and also the bodily change that takes place in the paralytic (5:4,9), he never makes use of it to signify the moral or spiritual change that takes place in man [212]. When speaking of a moral and spiritual change in men, Jn makes use of " γίνομαι " in the aorist infinitive or conjunctive, which is a form often similar to future indicative. This seems to show that Jn considers the spiritual change in men, not as something static that takes place once for all at a definite moment in history, but as something that gradually takes place, and remains dynamic moving towards a final perfection.

Another interesting thing to note regarding the Johannine usage of " γίνομαι " to indicate the spiritual change that takes place in men, is that he makes use of a noun as complement of the predicate exclusively to denote the change into the condition of the disciples of Christ, such as " μαθηταί " (9:27 ; 15:8), " τέκνα Θεοῦ " (1:12), " μία ποίμνη " (10:16) and " υἱοὶ φωτός " (12:36). When he speaks of a spiritual change in a pejorative sense, always he makes use of an adjective such as " τυφλοί " (9:39) and " ἀποσυνάγωγος " (9:22 ; 12:42). This phenomenon perhaps points to the radical change that takes place in the spiritual change into the condition of the disciples of Christ.

Jn makes use of the aorist infinitive of " γίνομαι " in the sense of 'becoming' only in 3 instances apart from Jn 1:12. In all these 3 instances, it indicates a sense in contradistinction to " εἶναι " (cf. Jn 5:6 ; 8:58 ; 9:27). In fact, this distinction is explicitly brought out in 8:58 " πρὶν 'Αβραὰμ γενέσθαι ἐγώ εἰμί ". In the other two cases where it indicates properly a change from one condition to another, it is used as the object of " θέλεις " which points to the dynamism involved in the change, on the part of those who undergo the change. This naturally points to a change that takes place in the " τέκνα Θεοῦ γενέσθαι " of Jn 1:12 and the dynamism implied in it.

Besides, " γίνομαι " in the sense of becoming has always a dynamic sense, whenever it is applied to Christians in Jn. In all these cases we see a dynamic process of a continuous heading towards perfection in knowledge and adhesion to Christ. Thus in 12:36 it is a continuous dynamic adhesion to Christ [213] (πιστεύετε εἰς τὸ φῶς) that

---

[212] Note that speaking of men Jn makes use of γίνομαι to indicate the bodily change only in Ch. 5 (cf. vv. 4, 6, 9, 14) speaking of the paralytic. All the other times, it is used to indicate a moral or spiritual change that takes place in man.

[213] Note how in 12:46 which is parallel to v. 36 Christ is said to be the 'Light' that has come into the world and demands faith on the part of men.

makes men ' sons of Light '. Also in 10:16 the sheep become one fold and one pastor by means of an adhesion to Christ, hearing his voice. In the same way in 15:8 they become disciples of Christ by means of a life that brings forth much fruit. The dynamism implied in this bringing forth of fruits and becoming disciples, is seen from vv. 4-5 of the same chapter, where the bringing forth of the fruits is ascribed to an intimate union (μένειν) with Christ. This phenomenon of a dynamic adhesion to and union with Christ that always accompanies the process of becoming disciples, naturally points to the dynamic element of faith in becoming children of God in Jn 1:12 [214].

All the above considerations speak for a dynamism implied in the " τέκνα Θεοῦ γενέσθαι " (becoming children of God) by means of a dynamic adhesion to Christ (τοῖς πιστεύουσιν εἰς τὸ ὄνομα αὐτοῦ).

b. '...who believe in His name...' (v. 12c)

Now we pass on to the dynamic element of faith in the process of becoming children of God. " Πιστεύειν " is characteristically a Johannine word [215]. The Johannine preference for the verb rather than noun could be noticed from the fact that the noun " πίστις " does not occur at all in the Gospel [216]. In addition, the present tense accounts for 60 of the 107 occurrences, which indicates the linear concept of action expressed in the use of " πιστεύειν " in Jn. The participial expression " ὁ πιστεύων " is almost proper to John [217]. The preference of Jn for the verb shows that for Jn faith is not a static disposition, but an active commitment [218], and the Johannine predilection for the participial expression shows that this active commitment is a continual life of commitment [219].

i. The Different constructions of πιστεύειν

The verb ' πιστεύειν ' in Jn is found in different constructions such as " πιστεύειν τινί " with the dative [220]; " πιστεύειν " followed

---

[214] Also Jn 9:27 shows this dynamism, where the γενέσθαι implies a change from the state of enmity into a state of friendship-discipleship of Christ.

[215] Out of the 241 occurrences in the NT, 107 are in the Johannine Writings, while in the Synoptics it occurs only 34 times.

[216] It occurs once in I Jn.

[217] The only exception we find in the NT is in Acts 13:39, while John uses it 23 times.

[218] Cf. R. E. Brown, *The Gospel*, p. 512.

[219] In John the life of faith is so essential to a Christian, so that ὁ πιστεύων becomes a sort of quasi proper name for a Christian. The frequent use of πᾶς in the construction is indicative of this.

[220] Cf. 2:22 ; 4:21,50 ; 5:24,38,46(bis),47(bis) ; 6:30 ; 8:31,45,46 ; 10:37,38(bis) ; 14:11 ; I Jn 3:23 ; 4:1 ; 5:10.

by " ὅτι "[221]; " πιστεύειν εἴς τινα "[222]; " πιστεύειν εἰς τὸ ὄνομα τινός "[223] and " πιστεύειν " used absolutely[224]. The absolute use of " πιστεύειν " could be classified with one of the other constructions because there does not seem to be any clear instance where the verb is completely absolute. The object of faith can be inferred from the context[225]. Some authors think that these different constructions are equivalent in meaning[226]. But a close examination of the texts will show a variety of important shades of meaning for the different constructions.

ii. Πιστεύειν with dative

Πιστεύειν with the dative occurs in Jn 20 times. This is the common classical construction found in Greek literature, which means in Jn ' to believe ', ' to give credence to ', ' to accept as true ' etc. Thus Jn speaks of believing the word (Jn 4:50), the Writings (5:46-47), in the works (10:38) etc. For Jn these dative objects of πιστεύειν are indirect objects of belief, the sense that they lead the action of believing to someone or something beyond what they represent. In other words, they are believed precisely as attesting or signifying. And this is true even where Jesus Himself is presented as the object of πιστεύειν in the dative, because there He is viewed as One who testifies, by his words and deeds, to his own person and mission[227]. Hence, the πιστεύειν with the dative in Jn could be said to mark a faith that leads towards a faith which is of more profound significance, marked by the construction of πιστεύειν with εἰς and the accusative, as will be seen below[228].

---

[221] Jn 6:69; 8:24; 11:27,42; 13:19; 14:10; 16:27,30; 17:8,21; 20:31; I Jn 5:1,5.

[222] Jn 2:11; 3:16,18,36; 4:39; 6:29,35,40; 7:5,31,38,39,48; 8:30; 9:35,36; 10:42; 11:25,26,45,48; 12:11,36,37,42,44(bis),46; 14:1(bis),12; 16:9; 17:20; I Jn 5:10(bis).

[223] Jn 1:12; 2:23; 3:18; I Jn 5:13.

[224] Jn 1:7,50; 3:12(bis),15,18; 4:41,42,48,53; 5:44; 6:36,47,64(bis); 9:38; 10:25,26; 11:15,40; 12:39; 14:11b,29; 16:31; 19:35; 20:8,25,29,31.

[225] Cf. G. F. HAWTHORNE, " The Concept of Faith in the Fourth Gospel ", BS 116 (1959), pp. 125-126.

[226] Cf. F. BLASS and A. DEBRUNNER, *A Greek Grammar of the New Testament and Other Early Christian Literature* (Eng. ed. by R. W. FUNK), Cambridge, 1961, 187, 6; Th. CAMELOT, " Credere Deo, Credere Deum, Credere in Deum ", RScPhTh 30 (1941-1942), pp. 149-155.

[227] Cf. J. GAFFNEY, " Believing and Knowing in the Fourth Gospel ", TS 26 (1965), pp. 230-231.

[228] The Notion of Johannine Faith as proceeding in stages of development is supported by J. HUBY, " De la connaissance de foi dans s. Jean ", RSR 21 (1941), pp. 385-421; D. MOLLAT, " La foi dans le quatrième évangile ", Lum-

iii. Πιστεύειν followed by ὅτι

Πιστεύειν followed by ὅτι introduces a noun clause and reveals the content of the believers' faith. The object of belief in this construction usually concerns the origin and mission of Jesus (cf. Jn 11: 27 ; 14:10 etc.). This marks a step further towards the commitment and allegiance to the Person of Jesus, expressed in the construction of πιστεύειν with εἰς and the accusative.

The construction of πιστεύειν with the dative τῷ ὀνόματι (I Jn 3:23) could be classified with πιστεύειν ὅτι constructions, as it expresses the belief in the doctrine that Jesus is really that which is signified by the name, namely, the Son of God. Perhaps the aorist πιστεύσωμεν points to the definite act of faith, that led the Christians towards the above mentioned allegiance and committal to Christ.

iv. Πιστεύειν εἴς τινα

Πιστεύειν εἰς followed by the accusative is the favourite Johannine construction. This expression which is original with the NT Writers[229], is distinctive of the Fourth Evangelist. Out of the 45 NT examples, John accounts for 35 of them. The very fact that it outnumbers all the other constructions of πιστεύειν in Jn, shows the specifically Johannine character of this construction. Jn seems to be struggling with a new concept or a new dimension of faith.

The very use of the preposition εἰς points to the dynamism implied in this concept of faith [230]. Also the use of the tenses of the verb πιστεύειν in this construction is revealing. Out of the 39 occurrences (including the phrase 'believe in the name of') in the Johannine writings, 24 are used in the present tense, and mostly (18 times) as present participle [231]. On the other hand 9 are used in the aorist indicative, and in 8 of these 9 cases, it indicates an imperfect faith, an imperfect act of adhering to Christ, which took place on account of the miraculous signs, and the subject of this faith is always πολλοί [232]. Only Jn 2:11 makes exception to this, the subject being

---

Vie 22 (1955), pp. 91-107 ; A. DECOURTRAY, " La conception johannique de la foi ", *NRT* 81 (1959), pp. 561-576.

[229] There are no similar examples in the LXX and in the profane Greek Literature. Cf. C. H. DODD, *Interpretation of the Fourth Gospel*, Cambridge, 1965, p. 183 ; R. E. BROWN, *The Gospel*, I, p. 512.

[230] For the dynamic sense of εἰς in Jn, cf. I. DE LA POTTERIE, art. "L'emploi dynamique de εἰς ...", *Bib* 43 (1962), pp. 366-387 ; cf. also E. A. ABBOTT, *Johannine Grammar*, London, 1906, nos. 2305-2323 and 2706-2713.

[231] Cf. Jn 1:12 ; 3:16,18,36 ; 6:29,35,40 ; 7:38,39 ; 9:35 ; 11:25,26 ; 12:36,44, 46 ; 14:1,12 ; 16:9 ; 17:20 ; I Jn 5:10,13.

[232] Cf. 2:23 ; 4:39 ; 7:31,48 ; 8:30 ; 10:42 ; 11:45 ; 12:42. Jn 7:48 where the subject is not πολλοί is an embarrassing question of the pharisees. Note also that these uses of the aorist indicative are all in the Book of Signs.

the μαθηταί. But there the miracle, being the first action of His ministry, is explicitly said to be the manifestation of His glory before His disciples, and hence their faith seems to be different from that given merely an account of miraculous signs [233]. Hence, the present tense and mostly the participle used in this construction, when speaking of the real believers seems to show that the faith involved here is ever present and active.

The concept of πιστεύειν εἰς in Jn seems to be clarified by an analogous phrase ἔρχεσθαι πρός often used in parallel (cf. 3:18-21; 6:35; 7:37-38). In 3:18-21 " He who does not believe in Him (Christ) (μὴ πιστεύων εἰς αὐτόν) is judged and the judgement is that he does not come to the Light (Christ) (οὐκ ἔρχεται πρὸς τὸ φῶς)." In 6:35 is said " He who comes to me (ὁ ἐρχόμενος πρὸς ἐμέ) will never hunger and he who believes in me (ὁ πιστεύειν εἰς ἐμέ) will never thirst". So πιστεύειν εἰς signifies a movement of adhesion or allegiance to the person of Christ, a giving of oneself to Christ in full confidence [234].

The dynamic character of this adhesion to Christ is seen also from the content of the above parallel texts. In 3:18-21 the coming or not coming to the light depends on the works that are good or evil respectively. So the faith that is implied here is a faith that is living and dynamic accompanied by works. This is indicated also in the answer of Jesus to the crowd in 6:29 that the 'work of God' to be done is 'to believe in Him' (ἵνα πιστεύητε εἰς ὅν). So the belief in Him is essentially connected with the work of God. Again the parallelism between Jn 6:47 " The one who believes in me has eternal life " and 6:54 " The one who eats my flesh ... has eternal life " shows that faith is that which appropriates the person of Christ, and assimilates him until he becomes the very life-principle of the believer [235].

There are also other associated terms such as 'to receive' (Jn 1:12), 'to hear' the voice or the words of Jesus in the sense of obeying (Jn 5:24; 6:45; 8:43,47; 12:47; 18:37), 'to see' (6:40; 12:45), 'to know' (14:7-10; 17:8,21-23 etc.), which can stand for the Johannine faith. It is not possible, nor is it necessary to discuss them in detail here [236]. The association of such terms with faith shows that

---

[233] The other few cases, where imperfect, aorist conjunctive, future or perfect are used, are either in the negative (3:18; 7:5; 12:37), or in the interrogative (9:36), or are in the words of the Pharisees (11:48) or refer to the subject πολλοί (12:11).

[234] Cf. I. DE LA POTTERIE, art. " L'emploi dynamique ...", in Bib 43 (1962), p. 376.

[235] Cf. G. F. HAWTHORNE, art. cit., p. 121.

[236] Cf. J. GAFFNEY, art. cit., pp. 219-223 where he gives a complete list of such associated terms and speaks of their relation to Faith.

the Johannine faith is the personal acceptance of the unique Revealer and Saviour, personal union with Him in a growing understanding and an active life according to His commandments and example [237].

It is important to note that the faith followed by εἰς with the accusative has always a person as object (the only exception is I Jn 5:10), and is directed almost exclusively to the person of Jesus [238]. This peculiarity gives to the Johannine faith its special characteristic, namely, the faith for Jn is to accept the self-revelation of Christ and to commit oneself to Him, who is the only Mediator of salvation, in order to possess eternal life.

v. Πιστεύειν εἰς τὸ ὄνομα τινός·

This characteristic is expressed much more clearly in the expression that interests us most, namely, in πιστεύειν εἰς τὸ ὄνομα αὐτοῦ. It does not mean only 'to believe in the person of', taking the 'name' for the 'person' in a semitic way [239], but it means to accept fully what the name expresses, and to adhere to His person, as formally signified by the name. This expression seems to be a synthesis of all the different shades of meaning of Johannine faith as expressed in different constructions.

Thus it expresses the acceptance of the testimony of Christ (πιστεύειν with the dative), leading to the acceptance of the self-revelation of Christ regarding His mission and origin as Christ and Son of God (πιστεύειν followed by ὅτι), which leads inevitably to a self-committal and allegiance to His person (πιστεύειν followed by εἰς with the accusative) as formally signified by the name of Christ and Son of God (πιστεύειν εἰς τὸ ὄνομα αὐτοῦ).

The name that is the object of this faith is expressed in 3:18 and I Jn 5:13 as the 'Only Begotten Son of God'. The divine sonship of Christ, as we saw above, comprises in Jn both the eternal and temporal sonship, or better, is the eternal sonship continued and manifested in the temporal sonship. So the personal commitment to

---

[237] Cf. R. Schnackenburg, *The Gospel according to St. John*, pp. 563-567.

[238] The only exception is Jn 14:1 where the object of faith is God, which should be explained from the context, of the taking leave of Jesus (cf. R. Schnackenburg, *The Gospel*, p. 560). Besides, the juxta-position of the objects of faith εἰς τὸν Θεόν, καὶ εἰς ἐμέ shows that it is the same faith that is directed to God and Christ, precisely because for Jn Christ is the revelation of the Father and faith in John is based upon this relation between the Father and the Son. Note that this verse introduces the successive discourse in Ch. 14 describing the work of the Son, in which God is called exclusively πατήρ (23 times).

[239] Cf. L. Bouyer, *Le quatrième évangile*, 3rd ed., Paris, 1956, p. 61; Van den Bussche, *Jean*, p. 95.

the name of Jesus means a commitment to Jesus as Christ and Son of God, which presupposes a complete acceptance of the self-revelation of Jesus as Christ and Son of God [240]. This is indicated in the fact that in many texts πιστεύειν εἰς is used parallel to πιστεύειν followed by ὅτι [241]. Thus ' to believe in His name' points to an acceptance of the self-revelation of Jesus as Christ and Son of God and a self-commitment to Him as such, which in its turn brings the believer to the attainment of eternal life [242].

In the light of the above considerations, Jn 1:12c seems to speak of this dynamic faith implied in the πιστεύειν εἰς τὸ ὄνομα αὐτοῦ. Verse 13, taken as singular, goes well with such an understanding, because it explains the αὐτοῦ, which should be Christ, the Son of God. Here John contemplates this divine sonship of Christ explicitly as a divine begetting, which is already implied in μονογενής of 3:18. As we have explained above, speaking of the divine begetting of Christ, it comprises both the eternal and temporal generation of Christ, and hence implies both ideas of ' Christ ' and ' Son of God ' [243].

This faith, as we have said, appropriates its object and assimilates it, until it becomes the very life-principle of the believer. Now, the object here is Christ as begotten of God, which implies His life as ' Son of God '. So the believers appropriate the divinely Begotten Son of God, so that the divine begetting and the divine sonship of Christ is shared by them, and thus becomes their very life-principle. In this manner, the believers are given the power to become children of God. Here we see the great dynamism implied in the τοῖς πιστεύουσιν εἰς τὸ ὄνομα αὐτοῦ which leads to the τέκνα Θεοῦ γενέσθαι of Jn 1:12.

c. ' ... W h o r e c e i v e d h i m ...' (v. 12a)

The ὅσοι δὲ ἔλαβον αὐτόν of v. 12a and τοῖς πιστεύουσιν εἰς τὸ ὄνομα αὐτοῦ of v. 12c are mutually related and explain each other.

---

[240] We saw above how the object of πιστεύειν ὅτι in Jn is precisely His mission and origin, namely, the quality as Christ and Son of God, which is explicitly stated in Jn 20:31 ; I Jn 5:1,5.

[241] Compare Jn 4:39 with 42 ; 11:45 with 42 ; 14:12 with 11 ; 17:20 with 8 and 21 etc.

[242] Note how in Jn 3:18 and I Jn 5:13 ' to believe in the name of the Only Begotten Son of God ' and in Jn 20:31 ' to believe that Jesus is Christ the Son of God ' are resulting in the attainment of eternal life.

[243] Many authors have acknowledged that ' believing in His name ' here means ' to believe in Him as Christ and Son of God ', though they do not see well the dynamism implied here (cf. BERNARD, *St. John*, I, p. 17 ; W. BAUER, *Das Johannesevangelium*, p. 21 ; Th. CALMES, *L'évangile*, p. 112 ; WESTCOTT, *Gospel*, p. 9.

But this does not mean that they are completely equivalent [244]. The difference of the words (λαμβάνειν and πιστεύειν) and tenses (aorist and present) points to a difference of signification too.

Λαμβάνω etymologically meaning ' to grasp ', ' to seize ', develops in Greek Literature in two directions, namely, active and passive : — in active, meaning ' to welcome ', and in passive meaning ' to receive ' [245]. Both meanings are found in the NT, and in Jn, specially when spoken of men, we find a consistent use of active and passive meanings, according as the object is Christ or the Holy Spirit [246]. Thus when the verb λαμβάνω has for object Christ (cf. Jn 1:12 ; 5:43 ; 13:20) or His witness (cf. Jn 3:11,32,33) or His words (cf. Jn 12:48 ; 18:8), the emphasis is rather on the active meaning of ' welcoming '. But when the verb has for object the Holy Spirit (cf. Jn 7:39 ; 14: 17 ; 20:22), the emphasis is rather on the passive meaning of ' receiving ' [247]. The active meaning of λαμβάνω that is predominant in Jn, specially in these theologically significant verses is clear from the frequent use of λαμβάνω with object in the accusative, and not with prepositions παρά or ἐκ with genitive [248].

So in Jn 1:12a ἔλαβον seems to imply an active sense and this is favoured by its antithetical parallels οὐ παρέλαβον of v. 11 and οὐ κατέλαβον of v. 5 in the Prologue, which speak of the non-acceptance of the Logos on the part of men [249]. The οὐ παρέλαβον of v. 11 suggests that His own did not recognise and hence did not approve of the Logos, and thus remains more at the intellectual level of ' accepting ' and ' recognising ' [250]. The parallel statement in v. 10 ' the

---

[244] Usually authors speak of both as having the same meaning. Cf. R. E. BROWN, *The Gospel I*, p. 11 where he sees a complete equivalence between v. 12a and v. 12c, and attributes the omission of either of these two verbs in the Mss to this identification.

[245] Cf. G. DELLING, art. λαμβάνω, *TDNT* IV, p. 5.

[246] Cf. I. DE LA POTTERIE, " La Parole de Jesus ' Voici ta Mère ' et l'accueil du disciple (Jn 19,27b) ", *Marianum*, 1974, pp. 34-36.

[247] The passive meaning is indicated by the fact that the Spirit is here ' given ' and the reception of the Spirit follows faith (7:39).

[248] Note that out of the 19 occurrences of λαμβάνω in the theological sense speaking of men, 17 have the object in the accusative.

[249] The equivalence of παρέλαβον (v. 11) and ἔλαβον (v. 12) is generally admitted by all. Cf. for instance, C. K. BARRETT, *The Gospel according to St. John*, 2nd ed. London, 1958, p. 136 ; BULTMANN, *Evangelium*, p. 35, note 4 ; for the omission of the compound preposition, cf. J. H. MOULTON, *A Grammar of New Testament Greek*, Edinburgh, 1908, vol. I, 115.

[250] Cf. W. BAUER, *A Greek English Lexicon*, p. 625 where he says that here emphasis is laid not so much on receiving or taking over, as on the fact that the word implies agreement or approval.

world did not know Him' favours this interpretation. The ἴδιοι in v. 11 is the interpretation of κόσμος in v. 10 [251], and not Israel as supposed by some authors [252], because the context does not make any special reference to Israel, and Israel in relation to God is never spoken of as λαός ἴδιος [253]. The δέ of v. 12a shows that the reception mentioned here is the opposite of the non-welcoming mentioned in v. 11 [254].

The οὐ κατέλαβεν of v. 5 which is also parallel to vv. 10 and 11 seems to favour this interpretation [255]. The parallelism with vv. 10 and 11 urges us to accept the meaning ' to grasp ' or ' to comprehend ' for καταλαμβάνειν [256].

In the light of the above considerations, it seems that the ἔλαβον in v. 12a refers to the faith, but specifically to the definite acceptance of the self-revelation of Jesus, the one coming from God (as Christ and Son of God), which leads men to a self-commitment to Him as expressed in v. 12c. So if v. 12a expresses an active acceptance or welcome of the self-revelation of Jesus as Christ and Son of God, v. 12c expresses an active commitment to Him. If the aorist of ἔλαβον in v. 12a points to the definite step taken by the acceptance of the self-revelation of Jesus in the beginning, the present participle of πιστεύειν of v. 12c points to the ever dynamic self-committal to Him throughout one's life, on the basis of that acceptance, which eventually constitutes men children of God (v. 12b).

---

[251] Cf. BULTMANN, *Evangelium*, pp. 34ff ; A. SCHLATTER, *Der Evangelist Johannes, wie er spricht, denkt und glaubt*, 3rd ed., Stuttgart, 1930, p. 17 ; LOISY, *L'Evangile*, p. 173 ; W. BAUER, *Evangelium*, pp. 20-21.

[252] Cf. the Commentaries of WESTCOTT, SCHANZ, KNABENBAUER, TILLMANN, LAGRANGE, HOSKYNS, and DODD, *Interpretation*, p. 402.

[253] The LXX speaks of Israel as λαὸς περιούσιος (Exod 19:5 ; 23:22 ; Dt 7:6 ; 14:2 ; 26:18).

[254] Cf. BERNARD, *St. John* II, p. 15 where he says that the δε of v. 11 must be given its full adversative force.

[255] Cf. above pp. 124-125 where we spoke of the structure of the Prologue, in which the whole Prologue refers to the Incarnate Logos, and the stanzas speaking of the attitude of men towards this Logos (positive or negative) marked by the verb λαμβάνειν are parallels.

[256] Cf. W. BAUER, *A Greek English Lexicon*, p. 414 where he admits the possibility of this meaning. This is the interpretation given by CYRIL OF ALEXANDRIA, The Latin Fathers, LAGRANGE, MACGREGOR, BRAUN etc. Cf. R. E. BROWN, *The Gospel* I, p. 8, where he gives the different interpretations of the text. He does not accept this interpretation, but admits that this meaning is quite intelligible, if the ' Light ' is a reference to the Incarnate Word.

d. "... He gave them power ..." (v. 12b)

To those who took the definite step of accepting the self-revelation of Christ, He gave the power (ἐξουσίαν) to become children of God. The two aorists ἔλαβον and ἔδωκεν mark the simultaneous character of the ' reception ' of Christ and the ' giving ' of the power. The term ἐξουσία has been translated by interpreters in different ways. As a matter of fact, it admits of various interpretations such as ' freedom or right to do something ' (Jn 10:18 ; Acts 5:4 ; Rom 9:21 ; Rev 13:5), ' power or might ' (Mk 6:7 ; Lk 9:1 ; 10:19 ; Rev 11:6), ' authority ' (Mt 9:8 ; 28:18 ; Mk 11:28 ; Lk. 7:8 ; 12:5 ; Jn 5:27 ; 17: 2 ; 19:10 etc.). Thus the biblical notion of ἐξουσία is a complex one [257].

Ἐξουσία philologically coming from ἔξεστιν implies a freedom to dispose of something and the ability to do it [258]. It implies a meaning in contradistinction to δύναμις, ἰσχύς and κράτος which all indicate an indwelling objective physical or spiritual power [259]. In Jn ἐξουσία is always a power that is given either by the Father (5:27 ; 10:18 ; 17:2 ; 19:10-11) or by Christ (1:12), accompanied by the verb δίδωμι in all these contexts [260].

Another interesting thing to be noted regarding the Johannine use of ἐξουσία is that it is used always in connection with ' life '. Thus in Jn 10:18 Christ has the power to dispose of His life, and in 19:10 it is also the question of power over the life of Christ. In 17: 2 and 5:27 it is the power of Christ over divine life to be given to men. This power over the life is implicit in the power to ' judge ' (to give life or death) in 5:27 [261]. Note how the two verses 26-27 are co-ordinated with καί which points to the fact that the power to ' judge ' is intimately connected with Christ's having life in Himself, of which the divine life of the Christians is a participation.

---

[257] Cf. W. BEILNER, art. " Vollmacht ", *BThW* II, p. 1.

[258] Cf. W. BAUER, *A Greek English Lexicon*, p. 227.

[259] Cf. W. FOERSTER, art. ἐξουσία, *TDNT* II, p. 566. Here it is worth noting that John uses only ἐξουσία and no other words to express the concept of ' power ', while the Synoptics make use of other words too, such as δύναμις (Mt 13 times ; Mk 10 times ; and Lk 15 times), ἰσχύς (Mk 2 times ; Lk once), and κράτος (Lk once).

[260] The only exception is Jn 10:18 where we do not have the verb δίδωμι. But from 5:26 we know that the life over which the Son has power is given by the Father. That He had been given this power is also in accordance with the consistent teaching of the NT Writers, that it is God the Father who was the agent of the resurrection of Christ.

[261] Cf. Jn 5:21-22 where ζωοποιεῖν and κρίνειν are used in antithetical parallelism.

The above characteristics of ἐξουσία in Jn seem to show in Jn 1:12 the power of the believers to dispose of the divine life which makes them children of God. Some authors, limiting ἐξουσία to this meaning see in 1:12 only man's free will as a co-operative agent to the Grace of divine sonship [262]. But the meaning of ἐξουσία should not be limited to this. This meaning of a free co-operation on the part of man is already indicated by the sharp distinction between those who did not receive the Word (v. 11) and those who did (v. 12a). Others have given to ἐξουσία a meaning of ' right ' implying the idea of privilege and dignity [263], thus reducing the ἐξουσία to an equivalent of τέκνα Θεοῦ γενέσθαι, meaning thereby ' the privilege which consists in being the children of God ' [264]. This all but destroys the dynamism implied in the verb γενέσθαι.

It is to be noted that this is the only place in Jn, where he speaks of the power given to men concerning their divine life or sonship, and hence we must be careful in applying to it the notion of ἐξουσία in other contexts. In Jn 1:12 the power is given to ' become ' children of God. So the emphasis seems to lie on the aspect of ability, though received from outside, rather than on that of freedom [265]. The suggestion of Bultmann [266], supported by Boismard [267], Schnackenburg [268] and Brown [269], that the Greek ἐξουσίαν is probably an awkward attempt to render the idea behind the Semitic expression ' *nāthān* ', meaning that ' He gave them to become ' is questionable, because as we have seen, wherever it occurs in Jn it is used in the proper sense of power. Besides in Jn 1:12 it is a question of really becoming (γενέσθαι) the children of God, which presupposes an ability to become [270]. Hence it seems that ἐξουσία here should be taken as a real ability to become children of God, which concretely consists in the life of faith.

---

[262] Cf. SIMON DORADO, *Praelectiones Biblicae, Novum Testamentum*, I, Taurini, 1950, p. 254 ; LAGRANGE, *L'Évangile*, p. 15.

[263] Cf. J. M. VOSTÉ, *De Prologo Joanneo et Logo*, Romae, 1925, p. 25 ; F. ZORELL, *Lexicon Graecum*, col. 458 ; G. B. STEVENS, *The Johannine Theology*, London, 1894, p. 251.

[264] Cf. A. M. DONATUS, art. cit., p. 21.

[265] Cf. W. BAUER, *A Greek English Lexicon*, p. 227 where he puts Jn 1:12 in this category.

[266] Cf. *Das Evangelium*, p. 36.

[267] Cf. *Le prologue de saint Jean*, pp. 42-43.

[268] Cf. *The Gospel according to St. John*, p. 262.

[269] Cf. *The Gospel according to John*, I, p. 11.

[270] Note that in none of the texts with διδόναι and infinitive adduced by them as parallel to the διδόναι of Jn 1:12 (3:27 ; 5:26 ; 6:31,65) occurs the verb γενέσθαι.

Besides the verb ἔδωκεν that always accompanies the ἐξουσία points to the fact that this bestowal of the power to become children of God is a special gift of God through Christ. The relationship of the children of God is an arrangement in the gracious decree of God and not a claim by right, nor an internal ability on the part of man [271], as perhaps the Jews presumed [272]. So ἐξουσία expresses a real ability to become children of God, which is at the same time a special gift of God through the Incarnate Logos [273].

So the definite acceptance of the self-revelation of Christ in the past (aorist) (v. 12a) is the condition for the receiving of the power to become children of God (v. 12b). The 'believing in His name' of v. 12c is not a simple apposition just reminding us once more of the condition expressed in v. 12a [274]. In v. 12c Jn passes on to the present, referring to the Christian Community in the concrete [275], which, having received the power at the historic moment of the definite act of faith, continues to realize that power, by a continuous and dynamic adhesion to Jesus as Christ and Son of God.

From the parallel texts speaking of the ἐξουσία it seems that this giving of the power consists in imparting the divine life, because the ἐξουσία given to the Son is always in view of the believers [276]. This imparting of life which marks the beginning of the life of sonship, is called in Jn a 'begetting by God', as will be seen later, when dealing with the texts concerned [277].

The fact that the power of becoming sons of God is a gift imparted through Grace (ἔδωκεν) shows that this right did not always exist

---

[271] Cf. H. A. W. MEYER, *Kritisch- Exegetisches Handbuch über das Evangelium des Johannes*, Göttingen, 1862, p. 65.

[272] Cf. Jn 8:41 where the Jews on account of their racial birth claim to have God as their Father without accepting the self-revelation of Jesus, the real condition to become children of God.

[273] Cf. Th. ZAHN, *Evangelium*, p. 71; W. BAUER, *Evangelium*, p. 21; LAGRANGE, *L'Évangile*, p. 11.

[274] In that case it would require πιστεύσασιν in the aorist. Cf. Th. ZAHN, *Evangelium*, p. 71.

[275] Cf. the article τοῖς which would have been lacking, if it was a mere expression of a quality of those already mentioned.

[276] Note that in John the scheme is that the Father gives always to the Son and the Son gives always to the believers. Out of 77 occurrences of διδόναι in Jn only 6 speak of God as giving something to men. But in these 6 cases, either God gives the Son (3:16; 6:32) or He brings men to the Son (6:65), or He gives through the Son (16:23; 14:16; 15:16).

[277] It is worth noting that, if we accept the plural reading, the aorist ἐγεννήθησαν would mark this giving of the power consisting in imparting the divine life, which develops into the state of the children of God.

for the one who thus enters the condition of sonship. Jn states quite plainly that, those who received Christ are given the power 'to become' children of God. This means that 'being a child of God' is a relationship that has a definite beginning in the conscious life of the one who enjoys that experience. This beginning is marked by the two aorists ἔλαβον and ἔδωκεν. Thus the Evangelist here speaks of the divine sonship of men with special reference to the beginning (the divine sonship in seed), in concrete, the beginning of the life of faith with an allusion to its progressive development towards the perfect state of divine sonship through a continued life of dynamic adhesion to Christ. Thus Jn 1:12 expresses the twofold dynamism: the dynamism of Christian faith (ἔλαβον πιστεύουσιν) and of sonship (τέκνα Θεοῦ γενέσθαι).

IV. Analysis of related Texts

This concept of receiving the gift of the divine sonship as a result of the faith in the Incarnate Logos, seems to be again developed in the following verses. This is clear from the structure, in which vv. 11-13 form the central part expressing the essential elements, namely, the salvific revelation in the coming of Jesus Christ (ἦλθεν and ἐγεννήθη), the negative and positive response given to Him (οὐ παρέλαβον and ἔλαβον), and the result of it (ἔδωκεν ... τέκνα Θεοῦ γενέσθαι). If the part that precedes takes up these elements, laying emphasis on the negative response given to Him, the part that follows takes up these elements laying emphasis on the positive response given to Him and its result. Thus we have a further development of the positive result of the coming of Jesus Christ, and the response given to Him in the following verses [278].

A. "*From His fulness we have all received...*" (Jn 1:16)

Speaking of 'believing in His name' we saw how the faith causes an appropriation of, or a participation in, the nature of the object towards which the faith is directed. Consequently, in those who believe in Jesus Christ as the 'Begotten of God', the power to become children of God denotes a participation in the divine begetting that belongs to Him. It is the same idea that is further developed in the following verses, and specially referred to in v. 16 " and of His fulness we have all had a share ... " [279].

---

[278] Cf. A. M. DONATUS, art. cit., p. 22.

[279] It is worth noting here that, if the Johannine usage of διδόναι in contexts of 'Father giving to the Son' is an expression of their father-son

1. The Only Begotten Son full of Grace and Truth

The exact connotation of the 'fulness' (πλήρωμα) here depends certainly on what the πλήρης in v. 14 modifies [280]. The πλήρης, as it now stands, could modify the 'Logos' or the 'δόξα' or the 'μονογενής' as this adjective is sometimes treated as indeclinable [281]. Anyway, χάρις and ἀλήθεια are attributed by Jn to Jesus Christ (Jn 1: 17). So it is certainly the Incarnate Logos or His glory that is full of Grace and Truth, and not the Logos before being made flesh. And the Incarnate Logos is here the μονογενής. On the other hand, δόξα as that of the Only Begotten Son needs no further description [282]. So the πλήρης goes better with μονογενοῦς.

This is suggested also by the variant reading for v. 14c with ὡς preceding the δόξαν: "αὐτοῦ ὡς δόξαν μονογενοῦς παρὰ πατρός" attested by very ancient Oriental versions going back to the 3rd Century such as syc, syp etc, and also by Syrian Writers of the early centuries, and which seem to have good reasons to be original [283]. In this reading, the sentence runs as follows: "We saw His glory equal to (as) the glory of the Only Begotten Son of the Father, full of grace and truth". Besides, the structure of the whole sentence suggests that 'full of grace and truth' be taken as the reason of comparison. So the phrase should naturally go with μονογενοῦς with whom (whose glory) comparison is made.

2. Grace of Truth (Revelation) in Jesus Christ

The very meaning of the phrase 'full of Grace and Truth' (vv. 14 and 17) leads us to the same conclusion. The expression 'Grace and Truth', according to some, is the resumption of the Hebrew expression '*hesed we'emet*' which is frequent in the OT and which goes back to the Sinai Covenant (Ex 34:6) [284]. But this Hebrew expression is translated ordinarily in the LXX with "ἔλεος καὶ ἀλήθεια" (cf. Jos 2:14; II Sam 2:6; 15:20; Ps 84(85):11, and not with

---

relationship (cf. C. J. P. DE OLIVEIRA, " Le Verbe ΔΙΔΟΝΑΙ comme Expression des Rapports du Père et du Fils dans le IVe Évangile ", *RScPhTh* 49 (1965), 81-104), it is probable that the usage of διδόναι in Jn 1:12 speaking of the Son giving to the sons is an expression of their mutual relation of communion in sonship.

[280] Cf. R. E. BROWN, *The Gospel* I, p. 15.
[281] Cf. BLASS-DEBRUNNER, *A Greek Grammar*, 137, 1.
[282] Cf. R. SCHNACKENBURG, *The Gospel*, p. 272.
[283] For an evaluation of arguments of external and internal criticism in favour of this reading, cf. P. KACUR, " De Textu Joh. 1,14c ", *VD* 29 (1951), 20-27.
[284] Cf. L. J. KUYPER, " Grace and Truth ", *Interpretation* 18 (1964), 3-19.

" χάρις καὶ ἀλήθεια ". In Ex 34:6 it is translated with ' πολυέλεος καὶ ἀληθινός '. Besides, in the OT both these words signify a subjective disposition rather than an objective reality as is the case in the Prologue. The ' Truth ' in Jn means the Revelation brought by Christ[285]. Therefore the ' Grace ' also seems to indicate something objective such as a ' gift ' in this context. ' Grace ' seems to form a ' hendiadys ' with ' Truth '[286], and thus seems to refer to the ' Grace of Truth (revelation) made in Jesus Christ ' which substitutes the ' Law given through Moses ' (Jn 1:17). This seems to be confirmed by the reference of Jn 1:16 to this as ' grace for grace ', namely, the grace (gift) of Truth in Jesus Christ which substitutes the gift of Law given through Moses. Note the ὅτι at the beginning of v. 17, which indicates that v. 17 is an explanation which goes to clarify the statement in v. 16.

3. *Grace of Truth (Revelation)*: *Grace of Sonship*

Now, in Jn the ' Grace and (of) Truth ' that takes place through Jesus Christ seems to be intimately connected with His divine filial life, because it is in His quality of being the Only Begotten Son of the Father that Jesus becomes the revelation of God (Jn 1:18). Note that the word ἐξηγήσατο (he revealed) in v. 18 has no object and the emphasis on the person of the Only Begotten Son as to the revelation is given by means of the pronoun ἐκεῖνος. Therefore we may translate v. 18 better as the following : " ... the Only Begotten Son, who is in (in constant orientation to) the bosom of the Father, it was he, the revelation "[287]. So it was the fulness of the divine sonship possessed by Jesus that made him possess the fulness of the Grace of Truth (Revelation).

4. *Sharing from the Fulness of Grace — Sonship — in Christ*

It is from this fulness of Grace — sonship — that we have all received (Jn 1:16). Therefore v. 16 presents Jesus as the fulness of

---

[285] Cf. I. DE LA POTTERIE, " Je suis la voie, la vérité, et la vie (Jn 14, 6) ", *NRT* 88 (1966), pp. 907-942.

[286] Cf. R. BULTMANN, *Das Evangelium des Johannes*, Göttingen, 1968, pp. 49f ; S. A. PANIMOLLE, op. cit., pp. 293-390 ; I. DE LA POTTERIE, " Χάρις Paulinienne et Χάρις johannique ", *Festschr.* W. G. KÜMMEL, Göttingen, 1975, pp. 269-282.

[287] Cf. J. M. GARRIGUES, " Theologie et Monarchie, l'entrée dans le mystère du ' sein du Père ' (Jn 1,18) comme ligne directrice de la Théologie apophatique dans la tradition orientale ", *Istina* 25 (1971), pp. 435-465 ; specially p. 437 : " ἐξηγήσατο n'a pas de complément d'objet, car le Fils est en lui-même l'exégèse du Père sans aucun intermédiaire ".

the gift of divine sonship, and the believers (we) as those who share in this divine sonship. This is clearly indicated in the very structure of the Prologue in its second half, in which vv. 12-13 correspond more to v. 16, and v. 14 to vv. 17-18 in the resumption of the themes. This correspondence may be shown as the following:

Vv. 17-18 A   for the Law ... GRACE AND TRUTH
                WAS MADE through Jesus Christ
                No one has ... but THE ONLY BEGOTTEN OF THE FATHER ...
   16 B   for from his fulness WE HAVE ALL RECEIVED
                G r a c e f o r G r a c e
   14 A'   And ... Word WAS MADE Flesh and dwelt ...
                we saw the glory ... THE ONLY BEGOTTEN FROM THE FATHER full of GRACE AND TRUTH
  12-13 B'   Whoever ... RECEIVED HIM
                He gave them p o w e r t o b e c o m e C h i l d r e n o f G o d
                To those w h o b e l i e v e in His name
                Who was born ... of God.

Note the literary parallelisms in AA' and BB'. If AA' presents Jesus Christ the Incarnate Word as the salvific revelation (full of Grace and Truth) in his quality of being the Only Begotten Son of the Father (in his fulness of divine sonship), BB' presents the positive response given by man to this revelation (Truth — revealed sonship) and its result of sharing in the sonship of Christ. If in v. 16 (B) this is expressed in a very condensed and implicit manner, in vv. 12-13 (B') it is expressed in an explicit and descriptive manner. Besides, BB', in a way, partially resume also the argument of AA' though in different terms. Perhaps the following diagram will help us to see better the mutual correspondence of AA'BB'.

AA' = vv. 17-18 and 14	B = v. 16	B' = vv. 12-13
	We have all received	Who received Him He gave power to become
Only Begotten of the Father	from His fulness	Children of God who believe in his name
Full of Grace and Truth	Grace for Grace	who was born ... of God

The salvific revelation in Jesus Christ (fulness of Grace and Truth — His divine sonship in vv. 14 and 17-18 = AA′) is resumed in v. 16 = = B as 'his fulness' and 'grace for grace', which is again resumed in vv. 12-13 = B′ as 'his name' and 'who was born... of God'. Because, as we have seen, the name of Jesus, when referred to as the object of faith, means the Son of God (Jn 20:31) or the Only Begotten of God (Jn 2:23 ; 3:18) and 'He who was born... of God' refers to his historical generation as the extension and expression of his eternal generation (sonship) from God.

The positive response and the resulting participation in this sonship revealed in Christ is expressed in v. 16 (B) by the word λαμβάνειν. In vv. 12-13 (B′), however, while the response is expressed by the words λαμβάνειν (received him) and πιστεύειν (believe in his name), the resulting participation in his sonship is expressed by the words 'he gave them power to become children of God' (v. 12b). Now, the verb λαμβάνειν in Jn, as we have seen, moves in two directions: one, active, when the object is Christ, and the other, passive, when the object is the Spirit or a spiritual gift. The ἐλάβομεν of v. 16, in which the Evangelist places himself together with the believers, seems to oscillate between these two directions. It moves in the active direction, referring to the Grace as the grace of Truth or Revelation in Christ which the believers welcomed or accepted into their life, and in this sense it corresponds to v. 12a and v. 12c. It moves in the passive direction referring to the Grace as the grace of divine sonship of Christ in which the believers were enabled to participate, and in this sense it corresponds to v. 12b. This double movement of ἐλάβομεν seems to be confirmed by the double movement of the phrases 'his fulness' and 'grace for grace' in v. 16, which as we have seen correspond to the grace of 'Truth' and 'Sonship'. Hence 'to receive from his fulness' means 'to welcome the Truth in Christ' and thus 'to share in his sonship'[288]. Hence the divine sonship of Christians is a sharing in the sonship of Christ by means of faith in Him.

---

[288] Cf. CSCO, 116, 26 where Theodore of Mopsuestia gives a similar interpretation to this verse : " De humana ejus natura dicit omnem gratiam ei inesse ; at simul hoc manifestat dignitatem quae in eo est. Per unionem enim cum Deo Verbo, mediante Spiritu, factus est consors *filiationis verae*. Nos ex ejus gratia spirituali partem accipimus atque per eandem participes efficimur una cum eo filiationis adoptivae, quamvis multum ab ea dignitate distemus ". Cf. also the Commentary of Cyril of Alexandria in PG 73, 169.

B. *Becoming Sons of Light through faith in the Light* (Jn 12:36)

Jn 12:36, where Christ is called the 'Light', and those who believe in Him are said to 'become sons of Light' is of particular interest in this respect, because 'Light' is a favourite Johannine term [289] to express the revelatory character of Christ, which, as we saw, is essentially connected with His divine sonship itself.

It is all the more important in this context because vv. 4-5 of the Prologue, which is parallel to v. 16 [290] presents Christ as the Life which is the Light of men. The Life (ζωή) is the Life by which God himself lives and which the Son of God possesses from the Father (Jn 5:26; 6:57). Therefore, it is the Life of divine sonship by virtue of which Jesus becomes the Revelation — the Light of men.

1. *Christ as Light*

There is no doubt that the 'Light' in Jn 12:36 is Christ. Jn 12:35 clearly resumes Jn 7:33 speaking of the departure of Christ [291]. The idea of the death of Christ is diffused all over the section chs. 7 to 12 [292]. Besides, in other contexts in the Gospel, 'Light' always refers to Christ (cf. Jn 1:9; 3:19-21; 8:12; 9:5; 12:46). In the very context of Jn 12:35-36 the words of Jesus are an answer to the question of the crowd regarding the Son of Man. This parallelism between the 'Light' and the 'Son of Man' is seen also in Ch. 9, where Jn began with Jesus as the 'Light of the world' (v. 5) and ended with an indication of Jesus as the 'Son of Man' (vv. 35-37) [293].

The formulation itself of vv. 35-36 shows the 'Light' as Christ, the Revelation of the Father. Faith in the Light in v. 36 is expressed by the formula of " πιστεύειν εἰς " with the accusative of the

---

[289] It occurs in the Gospel of John 23 times and in I Jn 6 times, while in the Synoptics it occurs only 15 times in all, and in Paul 13 times. The Johannine characteristic of the use of φῶς is also clear from the fact that in Jn the metaphorical usage of φῶς is always referring to God or Christ. Cf. J. C. Bott, "De Notione Lucis in Scriptis S. Joannis", *VD* 19 (1939), p. 82.

[290] Cf. the parallelism of C C′ in the structure of the Prologue on p. 133.

[291] Cf. the literal parallelism of expression ἔτι χρόνον μικρὸν μεθ' ὑμῶν (ἐν ὑμῖν) εἰμι (ἐστιν).

[292] Cf. 7:33; 8:21; 9:4; 10:18; 11:9,10,51; 12:32-33,35-36.

[293] It is worth noting here that the Isaian picture of the suffering Servant, which provided the background for the concept of being lifted up in glory (cf. R. E. Brown, *Gospel*, pp. 477-479), also offers background for the image of Christ as Light, because Is 49:5,6 speak of the Servant as the Light to the Nations. For the salvific character of the Revelation, cf. J. T. Forestell, *The Word of the Cross. Salvation as Revelation in the Fourth Gospel*, (Anal. Bibl. 57), Rome, 1974.

object, which, as we saw, denotes acceptance of the self-revelation of Christ and a self-committal to Him.

The fact that Jn demands the "πιστεύετε" and "περιπατεῖτε" while you have the Light [294] and that he says 'the Light is with you a little longer' (v. 35a), shows Christ as the Light in his earthly life. This is quite in agreement with what we said of Christ as the Revealer of the Father in his quality of being the Only Begotten Son of God, because speaking of the Prologue we saw how the coming of Christ into the world — the Incarnation — is for Jn the extension and manifestation of His eternal generation from God. So Christ is the Light in his divine generation and in his life of divine sonship manifested in His earthly life.

2. "... believe in the Light that you may become sons of Light"

Now, the effect of faith in Christ who is the Light is 'to become sons of Light'. The Hebraic construction, υἱός with genitive of the thing [295], usually denotes one who shares in this thing, or who is worthy of it, or who stands in some other close relation to it. It is remarkable that Jn, who makes use of τέκνα to denote the divine sonship of men never makes use of it with an abstract noun. With abstract nouns he uses always υἱός (cf. Jn 12:36 and 17:12). This shows that in these phrases with υἱός, it is not the personal relation that is stressed as in the phrases with τέκνα, but the qualitative relation. So the expression 'sons of Light' emphasises the quality of Christ as Light which is shared by men. As we saw above, this quality of Christ as Light consists mainly and fundamentally in his divine sonship, in which He becomes the revelation of the Father. So to become 'sons of Light' means to share in the life of the sonship of Christ.

That which makes men 'sons of Light' is faith in Christ the Light. Πιστεύετε being the present imperative expresses an action that is to be continued. So the faith required is a 'life of faith', and not a single act of faith. The verb γένησθε in subjunctive aorist together with ἵνα introducing the final clause, points to a 'becoming sons of Light' that is to be realized as a result of the life of faith [296]. At the same time it is not a simple future that is used here, which warns us against postponing the 'becoming sons of Light' to a distant future. So long as men live the life of faith in Christ who is the

---

[294] Cf. the Parallelism of ABB'A' in the structure given below.

[295] Cf. BLASS-DEBRUNNER, *A Greek Grammar*, 162, 6; J. H. MOULTON and W. F. HOWARD, *A Grammar of New Testament Greek*, vol. II, 441; A. DEISSMANN, *Bible Studies*, pp. 161-166.

[296] Cf. M. ZERWICK, *Biblical Greek*, 340-341.

Light, they share more and more in the Light, that is the life of sonship in Christ.

3. *The Structure of Jn 12:35-36*

The dynamism that is involved in this 'becoming sons of light' is indicated also by the parallelism of περιπατεῖτε in v. 35 with πιστεύετε in v. 36. The parallelism could be seen from the following structure:

V. 35   A   For a little while THE LIGHT is with YOU
          B   *Walk*
          C   WHILE YOU HAVE THE LIGHT
          D   That THE DARKNESS may not overtake you
          D'   He who walks in THE DARKNESS does not know ...
36   C'   WHILE YOU HAVE THE LIGHT
          B'   *Believe in the Light*
          A'   That YOU may become sons of THE LIGHT

Περιπατεῖν is a typically semitic expression to indicate man's religious and ethical walk [297], and is often connected with 'Light' in OT and later Jewish literature [298]. In the NT too this ethical usage of περιπατεῖν connected with 'Light' is found [299]. But, unlike the predominantly hortatory use in Paul, in Jn it has a specific sense pointing to the whole stance of the believer or of faith itself [300]. In Jn ethical life is life in conformity with the Revealed Truth [301], and hence a life of union with Christ realized in faith [302]. So the parallelism between περιπατεῖτε in v. 35 (B) and πιστεύετε εἰς τὸ φῶς in v. 36 (B') is quite Johannine and shows the dynamism of the life of faith, that makes men 'sons of Light' [303].

All the above considerations make it clear that a dynamic faith in Christ, who is the revelation of the Father in his filial life, results

---

[297] Cf. A. KUSCHKE, "Die Menschenwege und der Weg Gottes im AT", *ST* 5 (1951), 106-118.

[298] Cf. G. BERTRAM, art. πατέω, *TDNT* V, 943.

[299] Cf. Eph 5:8; Jn 8:12; 11:9; 12:35; I Jn 1:7.

[300] Cf. H. SEESEMANN, "Πατέω and Compounds in the New Testament", *TDNT* V, 945; F. BÜCHSEL, *Die Johannesbriefe (Theol. Hdk. NT*, XVII), Leipzig, 1933, p. 261, note 1.

[301] Note the characteristic Johannine use of 'walking in the Truth' (II Jn 4; III Jn 3,4). which indicates the life in conformity with the Revealed Truth.

[302] Cf. R. SCHNACKENBURG, *The Moral Teaching of the New Testament*, London, 1967, pp. 307ff.

[303] Note this dynamism already indicated by πιστεύειν with εἰς and accusative and the present imperative of περιπατεῖτε and πιστεύετε.

in the sharing of His filial life itself. Since in Jn the source of Light and Life is the same, the conditions for attaining them are the same (cf. 12:36,46 ; 3:16) and their essential signification is the same, we see a quasi-identification of ' Light ' and ' Life ' in Jn [304]. So to become sons of Light through faith in the Light, that is Christ, means that the life of the believers is determined by the life of the Son of God.

This is reinforced by the parallelism between ' becoming sons of Light ' (A') and ' Light being in (with) [305] us ' (A). The presence of the Light, though primarily it refers to the historical presence of Christ, cannot be exclusively an external presence, because this presence gives the possibility of ethical life (περιπατεῖτε) which is a life of faith — communion — (πιστεύειν εἰς) in Christ, and hence implies also an internal presence of communion [306].

Again the correspondence of AD' to DA' [307], shows this life of Christ shared by the believers, because ' to be conquered by the darkness ' means ' to be determined by the force that is opposed to the Light ' that is Christ [308]. Note also how in Jn 8:12 ' to walk in the darkness ' is opposed to ' have the Light of Life '. Hence Jn 12:35-36 shows in a special manner the dynamism involved in the sharing of the sonship of Christ by the believers through faith, as expressed in Jn 1:12 [309].

Conclusion

The analysis of Jn 1:12 shows that the divine sonship of men in St. John is essentially dynamic implying a change from the state of ' not being children ' to that of ' being children of God ', that supposes a dynamic process of a continuous heading towards becoming

---

[304] Cf. J. P. WEISENGOFF, " Light and its Relation to Life in St. John ", *CBQ* 8 (1946), pp. 448-451.

[305] Cf. the variant reading μεθ' ὑμῶν attested by Δ 700 28s 124 1424 pl. mr U al. 245s Λ - 1093 ΑΓr 850s Syspi gg cor.

[306] Note the distinctive Johannine use of ἐν with εἶναι indicating a religious fellowship (cf. Jn 10:38 ; 14:10a,11,20 ; 17:21,23,26 ; I Jn 2:5b ; 5:20 etc). Cf. A. OEPKE, art. " ἐν ", *TDNT* II, p. 543. Regarding its use in the context of Jn 12:35, cf. Th. CALMES, *L'Évangile*, p. 356.

[307] Note the ἵνα that introduces both D and A' in the structure.

[308] Cf. P. GUTIERREZ, " Conceptus Lucis apud Johannem Evangelistam in relatione ad Conceptum ' Veritatis ' ", *VD* 29 (1951), p. 8.

[309] Note that Jn 12:35-36 and 44-50, being parallel to the Prologue, form, so to say, an inclusion to the first part of the Gospel. (Cf. H. VAN DEN BUSSCHE, *Jean*, pp. 53-59). It is worth noting that a comparison between the two parts shows a strict parallelism between Jn 1:10-13 and 12:35-36.

(γενέσθαι) children of God. The main element in this dynamic process is 'faith' in the characteristically Johannine form (to believe in the name of him) as given in v. 12, which means a life of adhesion and commitment to the person of Christ as Son of God, in which the believer appropriates its object, namely, the divine sonship and begetting of Christ, until it becomes the very principle of his life.

The starting point of this dynamic process is the definite step taken by the acceptance of the self-revelation of Christ in the beginning of Christian life (ἔλαβον), which shows that the 'becoming child of God' has a definite beginning in the conscious life of the one who enjoys that experience.

The fact that the divine sonship of Christians is a participation in the Sonship of Christ, is expressed in v. 16 of the Prologue: " and of His fulness we have all had a share ...". It was the fulness of the divine sonship that made Jesus possess the fulness of the Grace of Truth (Revelation). Hence 'to receive from His fulness' means to accept the Revelation in Christ and consequently to share in his sonship.

Also Jn 12:36 speaking of Christ as the 'Light', and those who believe in Him as 'becoming sons of Light', refers to this participation of the believer in the sonship of Christ, since the 'Light' is here Christ as the Revealer of the Father in his sonship.

CHAPTER VII

The Birth into the Life of the Children of God (Jn 3:3-10)

From the consideration of Jn 1:12 we saw how 'the power to become children of God' is concretely realized in the life of faith (adhesion to Christ), so that 'the life of the children of God' becomes practically synonymous with the 'life of faith'. In Jn 1:12 the beginning of this life is marked by a definite acceptance of the Incarnate Logos. This beginning of the life of the children of God is called by John in his so-called 'biological conception of salvation'[1], most appropriately a 'begetting by God'[2].

Now in Jn 3, in the Nicodemus discourse, this life of the children of God (life of faith) is considered with special reference to the beginning of it, namely to the birth which introduces one to the life of sonship. That Jn 3 speaks of this life of faith is clear from the fact that the same expression 'πιστεύειν εἰς τὸ ὄνομα' occurs apart from Jn 1:12 exclusively in the section Jn 2:23-3:21, and that it forms practically an 'inclusion' of the section, occurring in the beginning (2:23) and in the end (3:18) of the passage[3]. This is reinforced by the fact that the objects of faith in 1:12-13 (ὅς ... ἐκ Θεοῦ ἐγεννήθη) and 3:18 (μονογενής υἱὸς τοῦ Θεοῦ) express the same concept of Christ as the Begotten by the Father, in whose life the believers participate.

I. The Context of Jn 3: 3-10

The structure of the Nicodemus' dialogue will make clear the role of the verses speaking of the spiritual birth in relation to the life of faith (life of the children of God). Scholars are not unanimous in the

---

[1] Cf. WALTER F. ADENEY, *The Theology of the New Testament*, London, 1894, p. 244.

[2] Cf. Jn 1:12-13 in which if v. 13 is read in the plural, the ἐκ Θεοῦ ἐγεννήθησαν in the aorist marks this beginning of the life of the children of God, being contemporaneous to the other two aorists ἔλαβον and ἔδωκεν ... ἐξουσίαν.

[3] Cf. I. DE LA POTTERIE, " Naître de l'eau et naître del'Esprit " Le texte baptismal de Jn 3,5, in *La vie selon l'Esprit*, Paris, 1965, 48-50.

way they present the structure of the section. If some divide the section according to the form, namely, distinguishing the proper dialogue from the commentary of the Evangelist [4], others divide it according to the themes [5]. But all these norms have their drawbacks, as being liable to arbitrary divisions, for which the very diversity of the divisions even following the same norm is a clear proof.

Hence, it seems best to follow the structure based on literary criteria such as vocabulary, chaining of words, the usual literary procedure of the dialogue in Jn, inclusions etc.[6] Thus we divide the section into three parts: An Introduction, speaking of the imperfect faith of the Jews (2:23 – 3:2); a first part, speaking of the necessity of birth from the Spirit to see or to enter the kingdom of God (3:3-10); and a second part, speaking of the authentic faith of the believers (3:11-21).

Jesus tries to bring Nicodemus from an imperfect faith (2:23 – 3:2) to an authentic faith, of which the first part (3:3-10) gives the conditions, and the second part (3:11-21) gives the content [7].

So from the structure we see that the verses speaking of the spiritual birth come exclusively in the first part of the section (vv. 3-10), which gives the conditions of the life of faith as described in the second part, and hence form a passage from the imperfect faith of

---

[4] Westcott, Bernard, Lagrange and Van den Bussche divide thus in a) vv. 1-15 and b) vv. 16-21, while Belser, Tillmann, Calmes and Schnackenburg divide following the same norm in a) vv. 1-12 and b) vv. 13-21.

[5] For example cf. E.C. HOSKYNS, *The Fourth Gospel*, pp. 201-209; BULTMANN, *Evangelium*, pp. 91-93; BROWN, *The Gospel*, vol. I, pp. 136-137; F. ROUSTANG, " L'entretien avec Nicodème ", *NRT* 78 (1956), 338; M. BALAGUE, " Diálogo con Nicodemo ", *CuBib* 16 (1959), 193; U. HOLZMEISTER, " Grundgedanke und Gedankengang im Gespräche des Herrn mit Nikodemus (Jn 3,3-21) ", *ZKT* 45 (1921), 528. All these authors, though they follow the same norm, do not give the same division.

[6] Cf. I. DE LA POTTERIE, art. Naître, pp. 41-48, where he gives the structure of the section following these literary criteria. As he gives the literary indications of this structure very well, we do not intend to repeat the same here. We do not enter upon a discussion on the original position and form of the Nicodemus dialogue (On this point cf. S. MENDNER, " Nikodemus ", *JBL* 77 (1958), 293-323) as it is of little use for our purpose. Whatever be the original position of the dialogue, our present task is to analyse the section in its present context and form.

[7] Cf. C. TRAETS, *Voir Jésus et le Père en Lui selon l'évangile de saint Jean*, Rome, 1967, p. 128; cf. also J. BLIGH, " Four Studies in St. John, II : Nicodemus ", *HeythJ* 8 (1967), 40-51, where he also gives the same division of the section, and that in three concentric structures. But he follows other norms for the division, and the concentric structure that he gives is not based on literary evidences.

the Jews in vv. 2:23-3:2 to the authentic faith of the believers in vv. 3: 11-21 [8].

II. Exegetical Analysis of Jn 3:3-10

The first part of the section, speaking of the condition for the life of faith (vv. 3-10) interests us most, as it gives this condition in terms of a spiritual birth. First of all we give a structure of the section, as it will often be revealing in the following exposition of the texts. In giving the structure of vv. 3-10, we begin with v. 2, because it forms a transition to the section vv. 3-10, and also because the answer of Jesus in v. 3 is intimately connected with the question of Nicodemus in v. 2 [9]. This connection will be clear from the very structure given below, in which v. 2 forms an ' inclusion ' with vv. 9-10. Besides, it is to be noted that the formula introducing v. 3 ' Ἀμὴν ἀμὴν λέγω σοι ' never introduces a new argument but always has reference to something that has been said already, which is expanded or set in a new light [10].

A. The Structure of Jn 3:2-10

v.			
2	A		Nicodemus said ... WE KNOW ... YOU ARE A TEACHER come ...
	B		No one CAN do THESE signs ... unless ...
3		C	Jesus said ... UNLESS ONE IS BEGOTTEN FROM ABOVE
		D	HE CANNOT (οὐ) SEE (ἰδεῖν) THE KINGDOM OF GOD
4	B'		Nicodemus said ... HOW CAN
		C'	A MAN BE BEGOTTEN when he is old
		D'	CAN HE ENTER (εἰσελθεῖν) INTO the womb ...
5		C²	Jesus ... I say ... UNLESS ONE IS BEGOTTEN FROM WATER AND SPIRIT

---

[8] Note how the verb γεννᾶν occurs exclusively in the first part (vv. 3-10) 8 times, while the verb πιστεύειν occurs exclusively in the other two sections of introduction (twice) and the second part (7 times).

[9] It is worth noting here that the Ancient Fathers such as CYRIL OF ALEXANDRIA (PG 73, 241-244) and THEOPHYLACTUS (PG 123, 1203-1204) show this connection existing between the question of Nicodemus and the answer of Jesus, namely, Jesus brings Nicodemus to a fuller concept corresponding to that which is expressed in his question.

[10] Cf. BERNARD, St. John, vol. I, pp. 368 and 66-67.

	D²		HE CANNOT ENTER (εἰσελθεῖν) INTO THE KINGDOM OF GOD
6		E	That which IS BORN OF THE flesh IS flesh
			That which IS BORN OF THE SPIRIT IS SPIRIT
7		C³	Do not ... I said ... YOU must BE BEGOTTEN FROM ABOVE
8		D³	The Wind (Spirit) blows ... You do not know (οὐκ οἶδας) whence it comes (ἔρχεται)..
		E'	So is everyone who IS BORN OF THE SPIRIT
9	B²		Nicodemus replied ... HOW CAN THESE THINGS BE
10	A'		Jesus replied ... YOU ARE A TEACHER ... YOU DO NOT KNOW ...

As we can see from the above presentation, the structure of this section is mainly circular or spiral with the repetitive and progressive presentation of the same elements BCD (vv. 2b-3), B'C'D' (v. 4), C²D²E (vv. 5-6) and C³D³E' (vv. 7-8), with the inclusion AB (v. 2) and B²A' (vv. 9-10), which marks off the passage from the other units. The main theme of the passage is the 'rebirth' marked by the verb 'γεννᾶν' which occurs in all the central verses 3 to 8. The different elements occurring in this passage move around this verb 'γεννᾶν' and go to specify it. The specification regards the subject, the nature and the consequence of the rebirth, and finally, the very nature of the 'reborn'.

The subject of the rebirth is 'one' in C, 'a man' in C', 'one' in C² and 'you' in C³. If the general reference to the subject with the terms 'one' or 'a man' gives the subject a universal tone addressed to each and every member of the humanity, the term 'you' (C³) makes the subject more concrete, namely, men whom Nicodemus concretely represents, and who are called to a life of perfect faith — of divine sonship.

The nature of the 'rebirth' is specified as 'again' (from above) in C and C³ and as 'from Water and Spirit' in C² in contrast to physical birth (C'). The 'ἄνωθεν' sets out the temporal (again) and spatial (from above) dimensions of this birth, which arouses the misunderstanding of Nicodemus about the physical birth and the further specification of Jesus about the birth from Water (the temporal dimension) and from the Spirit (the spatial dimension). If

'Water' marks the point of transition between the before and after of the new Life, 'Spirit' marks the environment (space) where this new Life is realized, or the transcendental nature of this new birth.

If the consequence of the rebirth is specified in D and D^2 as 'seeing and entering into the Kingdom of God' namely, the life of faith and communion with Jesus Christ, or the life of sonship [11], D' and D^3 contrast the two spheres: the sphere of the physically born (entering into the womb of the mother and being born) (v. 4) and of the Spirit (the Kingdom of God — Christ) (v. 8), with the two imageries of the 'womb' (D') and the 'wind' (D^3) [12].

The nature of the 'reborn' is specified in E and E'. If in E it is specified with a contrast to 'that which is born of the flesh' and with a reference to its necessary connection with its origin, in E' it is specified more positively with a reference to the nature and working of the Spirit itself which is the source of the life of the 'reborn'.

The structural consideration of the passage shows the general movement of the theme with the different aspects and their inter-relationship. The author begins by stating the absolute necessity of the new birth as an indispensable condition for the life of the children of God. Then he tries to specify the nature of this new birth and then the nature of the 'reborn'. Then in vv. 11-21 he will proceed to specify further the content of the life of faith — of the children of God, which is announced here as 'seeing and entering into the Kingdom of God'.

In our exposition too, we follow the same procedure. First, we try to see the relation between the condition and its effect, namely, the absolute necessity of the supernatural begetting. Then we will see the nature of this supernatural begetting itself, followed by the treatise on the nature of the 'reborn'. Finally we will examine how far the 'seeing and entering the Kingdom of God' corresponds to the life of the children of God, which should be the natural consequence of the supernatural begetting.

B. *The Absolute Necessity of the Supernatural Begetting (Jn 3:3-5)*

In the two parallel affirmations of vv. 3 and 5 a supernatural begetting is put as the condition 'sine qua non' for 'seeing and entering the Kingdom of God'.

---

[11] For a Christological interpretation of the 'Kingdom of God' see our explanation below on pp. 205f.

[12] For further explanation of the correspondence between v. 4 and v. 8 cf. G. GAETA, *Il Dialogo con Nicodemo*, Brescia, 1974, pp. 53-64.

Grammatically both texts have the same construction:

v. 3 ἐὰν μή τις γεννηθῇ ... οὐ δύναται ἰδεῖν ...
v. 5 ἐὰν μή τις γεννηθῇ ... οὐ δύναται εἰσελθεῖν ...

' Ἐὰν μή ' with the subjunctive in the protasis and the present indicative in the apodosis points to a general or universal condition implied in both statements [13]. The γεννηθῇ in the aorist subjunctive simply refers to the fact of being begotten as a condition without any specific reference to time. However, as John more than many Greek authors, utilized the shades of difference between the aorist and the present subjunctive [14], the aorist subjunctive here shows that the supernatural begetting is not conceived as present and progressive, but as something that takes place at a definite moment of time.

The ' οὐ ' with the indicative ' δύναται ' points to a categorical denial of the possibility of seeing or entering the Kingdom of God, unless the condition is verified. The aorist infinitive of ' ἰδεῖν ' and ' εἰσελθεῖν ' which follow the verb ' δύναται ' is also of some importance. John usually makes use of the present infinitive after δύναμαι, when the infinitive represents something that one can habitually ' do ' or ' not do ' in accordance with the law of one's nature, while the aorist infinitive following δύναμαι does not have this character of permanence or habit [15]. So the aorist of ἰδεῖν and εἰσελθεῖν in the passage denotes the definite act of seeing and entering into the Kingdom of God [16].

Hence from the above considerations, we see that here Jesus announces a general and universal condition that is relevant to all men without exception. This condition of supernatural begetting is con-

---

[13] Cf. M. ZERWICK, *Biblical Greek*, Rome, 1963, no. 325.

[14] Cf. for example Jn 10:38 where he uses both aorist and present subjunctive immediately following one another, thus contrasting the present and progressive recognition (γινώσκητε) with the past when the believer first recognised (γνῶτε). Cf. E. A. ABBOTT, *Johannine Grammar*, London, 1906, no. 2511.

[15] Cf. Jn 5:19-30; 9:16-33 etc. The only exception seems to be Jn 11:37 where the aorist is used, because the reference is not to a course of action, but to a particular act in the case of Lazar. Cf. E. A. ABBOTT, *Johannine Grammar*, no. 2496; F. ZORELL, *Lexicon Graecum Novi Testamenti*, 3rd ed.. Paris, 1961, col. 339.

[16] Note that in our section this construction occurs six times (3:2,3,4(bis), 5,9) and out of these six occurrences, only once it is used with the present infinitive, namely, in 3:2 where it represents the ability of Christ to work miracles, which is a habitual ability. All the other instances give the aorist infinitive referring to spiritual begetting or the consequent vision of the Kingdom.

ceived as a fact that takes place at a definite moment in the life of men. The categorical denial οὐ δύναται followed by the aorist infinitive suggests the absolute necessity of this spiritual begetting, even to enter the condition of seeing and entering the Kingdom of God.

C. *The Nature of the Supernatural Begetting (Jn 3:3-5)*

1. *Begetting from Above (from the Spirit)*

The condition is expressed in two ways, namely, as a begetting ' from above ' and as a begetting ' from water and Spirit '. As we have already seen, speaking of the Johannine phraseology, ' begetting ' implies an initial communication of life. The repeated use of the verb ' γεννᾶν ' in the inceptive aorist form (cf. vv. 3,4(bis), 5, 7) points to the intention of the author to show that the new life of the children of God always has a definite beginning at a specific, chronological point of conscious experience. That is to say, birth from above is actually a new birth, that brings one forth as God's child, and begins thereby a new relationship, one not previously experienced.

a. ἐὰν ... γεννηθῇ

It cannot be by chance that in the Gospel, when speaking of the supernatural ' begetting ' of the believers, the Evangelist makes use of the inceptive aorist form. It is remarkable that out of the 10 instances, only 3 are in the perfect tense, and that in perfect participles (not indicative), in which either an abstract principle is being stated (v. 6) [17], or a general personal application is being made (v. 8). So the purpose at hand in the Gospel and specifically in Jn ch. 3 speaking of the spiritual begetting, is to state a ' fact ' or to refer to a definite ' act '.

On the contrary, in the Epistle, when the spiritual begetting of the children of God is spoken of, we find only the perfect tense (both indicative and participle) [18]. This is in perfect agreement with the avowed purpose of the Epistle, which is to bring encouragement, assurance and renewed faith and joy to those who already believe and who are children of God (cf. I Jn 1:4 and 5:13) [19].

---

[17] For the perfect participle in the neuter stating the principle in abstract, cf. M. R. VINCENT, *Word Studies in the New Testament*, vol. II, London, 1887, p. 93.

[18] The only exception is the ὁ γεννηθείς in I Jn 5:18, which as we will see, refers to Christ.

[19] Note the difference between the purpose expressed in Jn 20:31 and I Jn 5:13. If in Jn 20:31 the purpose is to believe, and thus to have life, in I Jn 5:13 the purpose is to know that they already have life (ἵνα εἰδῆτε ὅτι ζωὴν ἔχετε).

This ties up too with the use of 'τέκνα Θεοῦ' by Jn. If in the Gospel John speaks of 'becoming' children of God (Jn 1:12), in the Epistle he speaks of the believers who 'are already children of God' (I Jn 3:2). In the Epistle he never speaks of 'becoming' children of God, but of the manifestation of being the children of God (ἐν τούτῳ φανερά ἐστιν τὰ τέκνα τοῦ Θεοῦ) (cf. I Jn 3:10). So the Epistle speaks of the believers as already 'begotten by God' and uses the Greek perfect tense of 'γεννᾶν' to express their present spiritual condition as children of God. They have been begotten by God at some time in the past, and as a consequence, they are now God's children.

Thus, in contrast to the use in the Epistle, the use of the aorist in the Gospel shows that the experience of the divine sonship of the believer has a definite point of beginning in each person, who really 'becomes' a child of God. It is this definite point of beginning that is marked by the aorist γεννηθῇ ἄνωθεν and γεννηθῇ ἐξ ὕδατος καὶ πνεύματος of Jn 3:3 and 5. Now it remains to be specified what the two complements 'ἄνωθεν' and 'ἐξ ὕδατος καὶ πνεύματος' mean.

b. Critical Problem of v. 5

Before proceeding to the analysis of the two phrases, we have to speak of the critical problem regarding the primitive text of v. 5 [20]. According to many authors, the words ὕδατος καί are not primitive. According to some, the words are a later ecclesiastical interpolation, after the ultimate redaction of the Gospel, in order to introduce a sacramental doctrine into it [21]. Others think that these words go back to the Evangelist himself, though not to Jesus, in his discourse with Nicodemus [22].

This second opinion seems to be the correct one, because to speak of Baptism at the beginning of the public life of Jesus would be an anachronism, as the mission of baptism is given after the resurrection (cf. Mk 16:16 and parallels), and because it is quite possible that the

---

[20] As this problem is treated in a masterly manner by P. I. DE LA POTTERIE, in his article " Naître ... " in *La vie selon l'Esprit*, pp. 31-63, we do not want to repeat it here. We give only an outline of the problem and its solution.

[21] Cf. J. WELLHAUSEN, *Das Evangelium Johannis*, Berlin, 1908, on Ch. 3:5 ; BULTMANN, *Evangelium*, p. 98, note 2 ; E. LOHSE, " Wort und Sakrament im Johannesevangelium ", *NTS* 7 (1960-61), 116-125.

[22] This is the opinion of many authors both Protestants such as Wendt, Bernard, Flemington etc. and Catholics such as Braun, Leon-Dufour, Feuillet, Van den Bussche, Mollat etc. For a complete bibliography on the matter, cf. I. DE LA POTTERIE, art. Naître, p. 40, note 2.

Evangelist added these words later, being conformable to the mind of Jesus, expressed in the post-resurrectional texts, and to the practice of the Church [23]. A literary analysis of the section and a comparative study with the Synoptics would be revealing in this matter [24]. We just give below certain points that appear to be decisive in the matter.

As we can see from the structure of the section Jn 3:2-10, the words that have a thematic function in the discourse such as ' οἴδαμεν ', ' δύναται ', ' γεννηθῆναι ', ' βασιλείαν τοῦ Θεοῦ ', ' ἐκ πνεύματος ', ' ἄνωθεν ', ' εἰσελθεῖν ' etc. occur repeatedly and form the movement of the argument in the structure, while the word ' ὕδατος ' remains isolated in the whole section. Hence, the words ὕδατος καί seem to be secondary and redactional from a literary angle [25].

A comparison with the parallel Synoptic texts such as Mk 1:15; 10:15; Mt 4:17; 18:3; Lk 18:17 points to the same [26]. The fact that the words ' Kingdom of God ' and ' Enter the Kingdom of God ' are ' hapax ' in Jn, and are frequent in the Synoptics shows this parallelism with those Synoptic texts. Now, in none of these Synoptic texts speaking of entry into the Kingdom of God, do we find Baptism mentioned. So it seems probable that the earlier text of Jn did not speak of Baptism either. So the earlier text seems to have had only ' ἐκ πνεύματος ' as in v. 8c.

Having settled the text, we come to the interpretation of the two phrases. First of all we speak of ἄνωθεν as parallel to ἐκ πνεύματος, and then we will try to see the specific signification of the more redactional formula ' from water and Spirit '.

---

[23] It is commonly admitted that in the present text ὕδατος indicates the Christian Baptism. There are only very few, who do not admit this such as H. W. BATES, who refers it to the Word (cf. art. " Born of Water ", BS 85 (1928), pp. 230-236) and J. W. CARPENTER, who applies it to the physical birth (cf. art. " Water Baptism in Jn 3:5 ", RExp 54 (1957), pp. 59-66).

[24] Cf. I. DE LA POTTERIE, art. " Naître ", pp. 41-53, where he makes a study of the same and decides himself for this second opinion.

[25] It is true that we can integrate the present formulation in the actual interpretation of the passage as such. But this is not an excuse to overlook the secondary nature of the words as done by G. GAETA in his book (cf. op. cit., p. 66).

[26] Different authors recall these Synoptic texts as parallel to Jn 3:3,5. Cf. the Commentaries of Hoskyns, Bernard etc. Cf. specially J. JEREMIAS, Infant Baptism in the First Four Centuries, 2nd ed., London, 1964, pp. 48-55; K. ALAND, Die Säuglingstaufe im Neuen Testament und in der alten Kirche, München, 1961, pp. 67-71.

c. The Meaning of ἄνωθεν

The word 'ἄνωθεν' in itself can have different meanings according to whether it is local or temporal such as 'from above' (Mt 27:51), 'from the beginning' (Act 26:5; Lk 1:3), 'again' (Gal 4:9) and 'for a long time' [27]. From the very beginning there was difference of opinion as to the meaning here. Some prefer the meaning 'again' [28], while others favour 'from above' [29]. Again some others think that in this word we have a purposely ambiguous use expressing both meanings 'from above' and 'again', because the divine begetting is both new and supernatural [30].

The primary meaning of 'ἄνωθεν', is 'from above' both in classical and hellenistic usage [31]. And in the other Johannine texts themselves, 'ἄνωθεν' is always used in the sense of 'from above' (cf. 3:31; 19:11,23) [32]. Moreover, Jn never speaks of an 'ἀναγεννηθῆναι', and whenever he speaks of the divine begetting, he describes it in terms of its origin, always accompanied by 'ἐκ' [33]. Since it is resumed in v. 5 with 'from water and Spirit' it shows that in 'ἄνωθεν' we have more a question of origin [34], though the temporal meaning is not excluded.

The fact that in v. 4 Nicodemus interprets the 'ἄνωθεν' as 'δεύτερον' cannot be taken as an argument against the meaning

---

[27] Cf. W. BAUER, *A Greek-English Lexicon of the New Testament and Other Early Christian Literature*, tr. from the German by W. F. Arndt and F. W. Gingrich, Chicago, 1964, p. 76.

[28] So the ancient versions such as Vet. Lat., Vg, Sys, Copt, Syp and the Latin Ecclesiastical Writers as Justin (Apol. 61,4), Tertullian (De Bapt. XIII), Augustine, Jerome and many other modern Commentators.

[29] So the Harclean Syriac, Armenian and Gothic versions, and the Greek writers such as Origen, Cyril of Alexandria, Chrysostom and other modern Commentators such as Calmes, Tillmann, Lagrange, Braun etc.

[30] Cf. C. K. BARRETT, The Gospel according to St. John, London, 1962, pp. 171-172; A. ROLLA, " Il Dialogo con Nicodemo ", in *Cento Problemi Biblici*, Assisi, 1961, p. 365; O. CULLMANN, " Der johanneische Gebrauch doppeldeutiger Ausdrücke als Schlüssel zum Verständnis des Vierten Evangeliums ", *ThZ* 4 (1948), p. 365.

[31] Cf. E.C. HOSKYNS, *The Fourth Gospel*, p. 211.

[32] It is worth noting here that the NT usage is mostly in this sense. Out of the 13 instances, 10 are in this sense. Besides, in Jam 1:17 the new birth is said to be a gift ἄνωθεν that is coming down from the Father.

[33] Cf. ἐκ Θεοῦ (Jn 1:13; I Jn 2:29; 3:9; 4:7; 5:1,18), ἐκ τῆς σαρκός (Jn 3:6), ἐξ ὕδατος (Jn 3:5), ἐκ πνεύματος (Jn 3:8) etc.

[34] It is worth noting here that the underlying Aramaic word *mil$^{e‘}ēlā$'* has only this sense, and not the temporal sense. Cf. Str. Bill., vol. II, p. 420; BULTMANN, *Evangelium*, p. 96.

'from above'[35], because it could be explained in both interpretations. Besides, Nicodemus' misunderstanding depends not necessarily on the word 'ἄνωθεν', but on the whole idea proposed[36].

The response of Nicodemus could be better explained from his religious background, according to which one normally enters into the Kingdom, by being born into it by natural descent, through the Jewish race as a son of Abraham. Steeped as he was in Judaism, he could not conceive of any other way of entering the Kingdom. So there is no wonder that he construed Jesus' term ἄνωθεν to mean 'again' or 'a second time' rather than 'from above'. Nicodemus had characteristically looked at it from the merely physical side. He does not understand the difference between a 'second' and a 'different' beginning[37].

Also the term 'ἀναγεννᾶν' which is typically hellenistic and is found in the NT (I Pet 1:3,23; Tit 3:5) does not justify here the meaning of 'rebirth' in that sense, as it is still to be proved whether Jn has something in common with the hellenistic concept in this regard[38].

Another objection against taking ἄνωθεν in the sense of 'from above' is that it seems strange that the usual mode of expressing the begetting by God 'γενν. ἐκ τοῦ Θεοῦ' is abandoned here. If this is taken as an argument to deny the meaning 'from above' to ἄνωθεν, then we should say that the complete absence of the expression 'γενν. ἐκ τοῦ Θεοῦ' in the whole of ch. 3 would mean a denial of the theme itself of the divine begetting in ch. 3, which will hardly meet with the approval of scholars. So it does not constitute a valid argument in this respect[39].

Perhaps the very omission of the complement 'ἐκ Θεοῦ' will speak in favour of the meaning 'from above'. Discussing the Johannine usage of 'γεννᾶν' we saw how Jn makes a distinctive use of aorist and perfect in applying it to Christ and the believers respect-

---

[35] Cf. B. F. WESTCOTT, Gospel, p. 63 where he puts it forward as an argument for the meaning 'again'; cf. also W. TWISSELMANN, op. cit., p. 79.

[36] Cf. R. SCHNACKENBURG, The Gospel, p. 367; Str. Bill., vol. II, p. 421.

[37] Cf. M. R. VINCENT, Word Studies in the New Testament, vol. II, p. 91.

[38] Here it is good to note that even the terminology that is so characteristic of Hellenistic thought, found in the NT (cf. Tit 3:5) is not a guarantee for a similarity of concept. Cf. J. DEY, ΠΑΛΙΓΓΕΝΕΣΙΑ (Ntl. Abh. XVII, 5), Münster, 1937; R. SCHNACKENBURG, Das Heilsgeschehen bei der Taufe nach dem Apostel Paulus, München, 1950, pp. 8-14.

[39] The use of the word ἄνωθεν could be perhaps explained from the revelatory context of vv. 2-3. As Christ the Teacher and Revealer has come from elsewhere other than the earthly sphere, so also he who wants to enter this sphere of Christ (the Kingdom of God) must be born from above too.

ively. In keeping with this distinctive usage, it is quite normal to expect Jn to avoid the complement ' ἐκ Θεοῦ ' with γεννᾶν, when used of the believers in the aorist (though subjunctive), and to supply other equivalent terms to express the idea, so as to maintain the full distinction between the divine begetting of Christ and that of the believers.

Thus all the above considerations seem to support the meaning ' from above ' for ' ἄνωθεν ' as being equivalent to the other formulas as ' ἐκ πνεύματος ' in Jn 3, and ἐκ Θεοῦ elsewhere in Jn. So we take ' from above ' as the fundamental meaning here, referring to a principle that is coming from God, which communicates divine life to man.

d. Begetting from the Spirit

The formula ' γεννηθῇ ἐκ πνεύματος ' in the primitive stage of tradition, being equivalent to the formula γεννηθῇ ἄνωθεν is an elucidation or a making concrete of the latter. To understand well the import of this formula, first we give the background of the ' begetting from the Spirit ' in the OT, Judaism and in the Synoptic Gospels.

i. *The OT Concept of a Begetting from the Spirit*

The idea of the Spirit of Yahweh, compared often to the wind, as the source of life was a very ancient concept in Israel [40], and the doctrine of a pouring forth of the Spirit in an eschatological time was an important feature in the OT picture of the last days [41]. For Israel, the Spirit of Yahweh is parallel to the Word of Yahweh; both effect the same work in the same manner [42]. Note Ps 33:6 where *rûaḥ* and *dābār* are parallels and are put as equivalent terms [43]. Perhaps Gen 1:2f shows the Spirit entering in action through the divine Word [44]. So the activity of the Spirit through the Word of God, and the pouring out of the Spirit of God in eschatological times were ideas with which Nicodemus was familiar. So there is no wonder that Jesus makes use of these terms to explain to Nicodemus the conditions for entering the Kingdom of God.

As we saw when speaking of the OT concept of the divine sonship

---

[40] Cf. P. VAN IMSCHOOT, " L'esprit de Jahvé, source de vie dans l'Ancien Testament ", *RB* 44 (1935), pp. 481-501.

[41] Cf. Is 32:15 ; 44:3 ; Ez 36:25-26 ; Joel 2:28-29 etc.

[42] Cf. Is 11:4 ; 34:16 ; Ps 147:18 etc.

[43] It is interesting to note also that among the Babylonians and Egyptians of the OT time, the spirit (respiration) and the word from the mouth of a god were equivalent entities producing life. Cf. J. HEHN, " Zum Problem des Geistes im Alten Orient und im A. T.", *ZAW* 43 (1925), p. 218.

[44] J. HEHN, art. cit., p. 220.

of men, the divine sonship of Israel was the result of the making of the people of Israel through the Exodus and Covenant, and this is described, though rarely, as a begetting by God [45], while the Law, as a constituent element of the Covenant, has its role in this begetting.

Coming to the New Covenant, we saw the Spirit of Yahweh at work in the interiorization of the Law and the renewal of life (cf. Jer 31:31-34; Ez 36:26f; 37:9). Thus the Holy Spirit becomes the source of a new life according to the Spirit of Yahweh. But it is to be noted that while the formation of Israel as a people through the Exodus and Covenant was called a begetting by God, this beginning of a new life in each individual is called a new creation. Nevertheless the idea of a beginning of a new life according to the Spirit working through the Law was quite familiar to OT Judaism.

ii. *In Later Judaism*

The role of the Spirit in purifying and renewing the life of men ordained to the divine sonship through the truth and the law of God, was current also in Later Judaism of NT times [46]. The description of it as a birth through the Teacher (so through the word) and through the Spirit (power) of God is also an idea that is present in later Judaism [47].

So we see that the renewal of life of the individuals through the truth and law and the Spirit of God, and a birth of the community through the Teacher and the Spirit of God, were all concepts understandable to Nicodemus. But in none of these texts is mention made of a begetting or birth of the individual through the Holy Spirit. When it is a question of birth, it is the community that is mentioned, and when the individual is mentioned, it is a question of moral renewal of life. And it is precisely on the point of this individual birth that Nicodemus stumbles, because in the case of an individual he can conceive only of a physical birth into the community. Here we see the newness of Jesus' teaching in affirming the necessity of a birth of each individual from the Spirit. So we pass on to the parallel texts in the Synoptics, in order to understand this newness of the teaching of Jesus.

---

[45] Cf. Dt 32:15-18; Is 1:2; 45:9-11; Jer 2:26-27; Hos 2:1-24. Cf. our treatise on the OT pp. 23-24.

[46] Cf. I QS 3:4-9; 4:20f; 7:29-31; 9:30-36; 11:10-12; Jub 1:23-25 etc. For the notion of divine sonship contained in these contexts cf. our treatise on Later Judaism.

[47] Cf. our treatise on I QH 3:1-18 in the Later Judaism, pp. 38-42.

iii. *The Synoptic Teaching on the Matter*

As we have seen above, the primitive text has parallels in the Synoptics, and Mt 18:3 and parallels are specifically referred to in this case [48]. Whatever may be the connection of Jn 3:5 to the Synoptic parallel texts [49], the parallelism is evident. We give below the three formulas for the sake of comparison:

Mt 18:3   ἐὰν μὴ στραφῆτε κ. γένησθε ὡς τὰ παιδία οὐ μὴ εἰσέλθητε εἰς ...
Mk 10:15 & Lk 18:17   ὃς ἂν μὴ δέξηται τὴν βασιλείαν τοῦ Θεοῦ ὡς παιδίον, οὐ μὴ εἰσέλθῃ εἰς αὐτήν.
Jn. 3:3,5   ἐὰν μὴ τις γεννηθῇ (ἄνωθεν) ἐκ πνεύματος οὐ δύναται (ἰδεῖν) εἰσελθεῖν εἰς ...

Comparing the three formulas, we see that 'conversion' and 'becoming like a child' in Mt becomes a 'reception of the Kingdom as a child' in Mk and Lk and a 'birth from the Spirit' in Jn. The fact that the 'conversion' in Mt is changed to the 'reception of the Kingdom' in Mk and Lk shows that it is a conversion that is effected in faith [50]. The role of faith underlying this conversion is clear from the intimate connection of 'conversion' with 'faith' [51], and from the gradual replacing of the word 'μετάνοια' with 'πίστις' in the primitive Christian tradition [52].

If in the Synoptics this conversion effected in faith is compared to the disposition of a child, in Jn it is described as a 'being born into a child', a completely new beginning of existence itself. So the

---

[48] Cf. J. Jeremias, op. cit., p. 64 where he gives a synoptic table of the different parallel texts.

[49] Some say that both go back to one and the same word of Jesus (cf. K. Aland, op. cit., p. 70), while others say that Jn has reinterpreted the texts of Mk and Lk (cf. J. Jeremias, op. cit., p. 63). Some others again see two different pronouncements of Jesus regarding entrance into the Kingdom, but in similar terms (cf. I. de la Potterie, art. "Naître", p. 53).

[50] It is worth noting that in the Primitive Christian Tradition, the welcoming of the Gospel Message was the fundamental attitude required to enter Christianity. Cf. W. Grundmann, art. δέχομαι in *TDNT* II, p. 54, where he sees the use of δέχομαι in this connection as equivalent of faith.

[51] Cf. Mk 1:15 "μετανοεῖτε καὶ πιστεύετε ἐν τῷ εὐαγγελίῳ" in which the 'πιστεύετε ... εὐαγγελίῳ' is Mk's redactional work on Mt's μετανοεῖτε in Mt 4:17. The same connection is found also in Acts 11:17-18; 19:4; 20:21; 26:18-20 etc.

[52] Μετάνοια and μετανοεῖν occur in Mt 7 times, Mk 3 times, Lk 14 times, Acts 11 times, Paul 5 times and in Jn not at all, while πίστις and πιστεύειν occur in Mt 19 times, Mk 19 times, Lk 20 times, Acts 52 times, Paul 196 times and in Jn and I Jn 108 times.

life of faith is an entirely new life. Jn demands even more radically the same thing as the Synoptics, namely, the necessity of a change into a life of faith. The only difference is that, while the Synoptics consider this change from the point of view of man, Jn considers it from that of God, the Holy Spirit, without whose action such a conversion (faith) [53] would be impossible [54]. Thus in Jesus' teaching the Holy Spirit communicates and remains as the principle of an entirely new life, the life of faith. So the parallelism with the Synoptic passages shows that γεννηθῇ ἐκ πνεύματος in Jn 3:5 means essentially ' to be begotten into a new life ', a life of faith through the Holy Spirit. It is the communication of this vital principle, life in each individual, that was lacking in the teaching of the OT and Judaism.

iv. *The Johannine Vocabulary*

Now we come to the Johannine vocabulary itself, to see better the meaning of the phrase. In Jn πνεῦμα, Θεός, ἄνω are used as parallels in contrast to σάρξ, διάβολος, κάτω, κόσμος etc. This is clear from the formulas composed of ' γεννηθῆναι ἐκ ' [55] and ' εἶναι ἐκ ' [56], which give these two groups of synonyms in terms of contrast. So the ' πνεῦμα ' in Jn points to the gift of God. It is then this gift of God, the Spirit of God, opposed to the flesh (cf. Jn 3:5-6) that becomes the begetting principle in Jn 3:5 [57].

The fact that the Spirit becomes the begetting principle shows that the Spirit is the life-giving power in Jn, exactly what is expressed in Jn 6:63 where the πνεῦμα in contrast to the σάρξ is said to be the ' ζωοποιοῦν '. Now, life for John consists in knowing God (ἀληθινὸν Θεόν) and Christ (cf. Jn 17:3). So the Spirit should be life-giving, by imparting this knowledge, the knowledge that in Jesus God Himself has come into the world.

In the theology of Jn, the Spirit is the Spirit of Truth, who testifies to (I Jn 5:6), or makes present in us the Truth of Christ through faith [58], and who gives full knowledge of the Truth of Christ

---

[53] Cf. D. MOLLAT, " La conversion chez saint Jean ", *Lum et Vie* 47 (1960), p. 113.

[54] Cf. W. GRUNDMANN, in art. cit. in *TDNT* II, p. 54 speaks of the theological significance of δέχομαι and says : " Only when God speaks His word and opens the understanding through the Spirit, can man also decide ".

[55] Cf. Jn 1:13 ; 3:3, 6 ; I Jn 2:29 ; 3:9 ; 4:7 ; 5:1,4,18.

[56] Cf. Jn 8:23,42-47 ; 15:19 ; 17:14-16 ; I Jn 3:8,10 ; 5:19.

[57] Cf. R. E. BROWN, *The Gospel*, p. 140.

[58] See how in Jn 1:7 and 19:35 the ' witness ' is essentially directed to ' faith ' and in Jn 3:11-12,33,36 ; 10:25-26 ; I Jn 4:14-15 etc. ' to receive the witness ' and ' to believe ' are practically synonyms. For the relation between

(cf. Jn 14:26 ; 16:13-15). Thus the action of begetting (3:5) and life-giving (6:63) by the Spirit seems to consist in the action of bringing man to the life of faith.

On the other hand, the spiritual γεννᾶσθαι of men in Jn is always considered to be the result of faith [59]. In I Jn 3:9 the 'divine begetting' is attributed to the 'seed of God remaining in us', which is to be interpreted as the 'Word of God' accepted in faith, under the influence of the Spirit, and interiorized through the Spirit [60]. Also Jn 1:12, as we have seen, gives the divine sonship of men as the immediate result of faith. So it is quite understandable that Jn describes here the divine begetting of men as a begetting by the Spirit, as it is the Spirit who begets faith in man.

By speaking of a divine begetting through faith (Word of God) on the one hand, and a divine begetting through the Spirit on the other, Jn only allows us to have a comprehensive view of the divine begetting of men as interpreted in the primitive Christian tradition, in which we see two series of texts : one, speaking of the Word of God as the principle of this begetting (I Pet 1:22-23 ; 3:23 ; James 1:17-18), and the other, speaking of the Holy Spirit, as the principle of this begetting (Rom 8:15-16 ; Gal 4:6 ; Tit 3:5). In fact neither of these two interpretations, can be exclusive of the other. It is through the Word of God that the Holy Spirit works in us, and it is the Holy Spirit, who begets in us faith in the Word of God and gives efficacy to it [61].

The very context of Jn 3:5 favours this meaning of a begetting by the Spirit. As we have seen from the structure of the whole section, this section deals with the fundamental condition of passing from the imperfect faith of the Jews (2:23 – 3:2) to the authentic faith (3:11-21). So the 'begetting by the Spirit' is a begetting to the new life of authentic faith, that is to the life of the Children of God.

This condition is most suitably called a 'begetting', because the Kingdom of God and participation in it through the life of faith are

---

'witness' and 'faith' in Jn cf. I. DE LA POTTERIE, " La Notion Johannique de Temoignage ", *SacPag* II, Gembloux 1959, pp. 193-208.

[59] Cf. Jn 1:13 (if read as plural) ; I Jn 5:1,4-5 etc.

[60] Cf. I. DE LA POTTERIE, art. " L'impeccabilité du chrétien d'après I Jn 3,6-9 ", in *La vie selon l'esprit*, pp. 208-216 ; M.E. BOISMARD, *Quatre hymnes baptismales dans la première épître de Pierre*, Paris, 1961, p. 22.

[61] Cf. I. DE LA POTTERIE, art. " Naître ", p. 57, note 1, where he notes traces of the effort of a synthesis of these two lines of interpretation in the Mss tradition of I Pet 1:22, in which an important fraction of the Mss adds the words διὰ πνεύματος after τῆς ἀληθείας.

essentially of a different, higher and spiritual realm than the material, physical world. And the natural powers of man cannot apprehend that which is essentially spiritual — " That which is born of the flesh, is and remains flesh " (cf. Jn 3:6) [62]. There is no evolution from flesh to Spirit. So it requires a new beginning of life utterly dissociated from natural birth, which can come only from God, from the Spirit. Hence, the naming of it as a begetting by the Spirit, is well suited to the context.

2. *Begetting from Water and Spirit*

After examining the meaning of the text in its earlier form, we come now to examine what it means in its present form. But before proceeding to the analysis of the text, it will be interesting to glance over the history of the Exegesis of the text in its present form.

a. History of the Exegesis of Jn 3:5

With regard to the signification of ' water ' and its relation to ' Spirit ' in bringing about a spiritual begetting, we see various interpretations from the very beginning.

i. *The Signification of ' Water '*

Some find in the ' Water ' a reference to the baptism of John the Baptist, which Nicodemus ought to receive as a rite of penance, together with a receiving of the Holy Spirit promised by the Prophets recalling the preaching of John the Baptist in Jn 1:33 and placing side by side the baptism of water and the baptism of the Spirit [63]. Others say that it meant for Nicodemus the baptism of John the Baptist, while for the Evangelist it meant Christian Baptism [64]. For others, when Jesus declared that in order for a man to enter the Kingdom he must be born of water, he was making a positive allusion to the experience of repentance (as symbolysed in the OT and in the Baptism of John). So John is not teaching the necessity of the physical act for spiritual quickening, but he is teaching rather the absolute indispensability of a humble, contrite, repentant heart in the one who would be born anew and enter the Kingdom of God [65].

---

[62] Compare also Paul's comment: " The natural man receives not the things of the Spirit of God ... neither can he know them, because they are spiritually discerned " (I Cor 2:14).

[63] Cf. Th. ZAHN, *Das Evangelium*, p. 186 ; M. C. TENNEY, *John the Gospel of Belief*, Michigan, 1953, p. 87.

[64] Cf. WESTCOTT, *Gospel*, pp. 49-50 ; E.C. HOSKYNS, *The Fourth Gospel*, pp. 213-215.

[65] Cf. R. F. BAILEY, *The Gospel of St. John*, London, 1940, p. 65 ; W. F.

Dr Odeberg has advanced the theory, supported by numerous passages from Jewish mysticism and Gnostic Writings, that the phrase 'from water and the Spirit' belongs to a range of conception, according to which 'water' is used as a term for celestial 'seed', viewed as an outpouring from above, from God. For him 'from water' does not contain any essential allusion to baptism, but it calls up a whole world of ideas, such as water as a divine outpouring, celestial waters, waters from above, life-giving water, the divine gift coming down from on high, waters of eternal life, waters of eternal truth [66].

In the same line could be put Calvin and Grotius, who also deny to 'water' any reference to baptism and take it as a simple metaphor to designate the purifying action of the Spirit, which takes place without any exterior rite [67].

There are again some who take the 'water' for the 'Word' in the light of Eph 5:26; Jn 6:63 etc, and say that the Holy Spirit, using the Word symbolized by 'water', is the sole and only author of regeneration. According to them 'born of water' finds its explanation in I Pet 1:23 and James 1:18 [68]. In passing, we may mention also authors who see in the 'born of water' a physical birth [69].

It is quite understandable that scholars refer to the proselyte or Johannine baptism, as long as they take the words 'ὕδατος καί' as original and authentic in the discourse of Jesus with Nicodemus. But as we have seen above, these words have a secondary character in the discourse, and hence are a later addition by the Evangelist in the light of the post-resurrection teaching of Jesus. The interpretations that treat the term 'water' as simply figurative, descriptive of the cleansing power of the Spirit, without any reference to Baptism, are essentially defective, as it is against the usual manner of the Evangelist, who makes allusion to Baptism through water in other contexts (cf. Jn 19:34 and I Jn 5:6-8) and also against the latent interest of

---

HOWARD, *The Fourth Gospel in recent Criticism and Interpretation*, 3rd ed., London, 1945, pp. 206-209.

[66] Cf. H. ODEBERG, *The Fourth Gospel*, vol. I, Uppsala, 1929, pp. 48ff and 67.

[67] Cf. Corpus Reformatorum, vol. 47, p. 56; H. GROTIUS, *Annotationes in Novum Testamentum*, I, Halae, 1769, p. 969; cf. also M. BARTH, *Die Taufe - ein Sakrament?*, Zürich, 1951, p. 445; D. W. B. ROBINSON, "Born of Water and Spirit: Does Jn 3:5 refer to Baptism?", *RefTR* 25 (1966), pp. 15-23 where he holds the same opinion, and also speaks of the possibility of 'water' as referring to the OT religion.

[68] Cf. H. W. BATES, art. cit., pp. 235-236.

[69] Cf. J. W. CARPENTER, "Water Baptism", *RExp*, 54 (1957), p. 60; R. FOWLER, "Born of Water and Spirit (Jn 3:5)" *ET2* (1971), p. 159.

the Evangelist in the Sacraments [70]. If the word 'Spirit' is to be taken in a real sense, and not in a figurative, the same should be said also of 'water', as both are put in the same way and co-ordinated with καί [71]. It is worth noting that Jn 3:5 is in a context where Jn speaks often of baptism (cf. Jn 1:25-33 ; 3:22,23,26 ; 4:1-2). Besides, the figurative understanding of 'water' is opposed to the whole of tradition, which as we shall see, usually took it for granted, that 'water' here referred to Christian Baptism. Hence we take the word 'water' here as referring exclusively to Christian Baptism, and introduced by the Evangelist, as being in agreement with the teaching of Jesus.

ii. *The Relation between Water and Spirit*

Now we come to the second question. Supposing that the 'water' refers to Christian Baptism, what role does it play together with the Spirit, in bringing about the divine begetting ? In other words, what is the relation between Baptism and the Holy Spirit in effecting the divine begetting ? We do not intend to give a detailed history of the exegesis on this matter, but to limit ourselves to giving only the main trends [72].

In the course of History the majority of commentators have tried to co-ordinate the act of Baptsim with that of the Spirit in producing the effect of a new birth. But in doing so, we see two different trends : one, taking 'Spirit' as principal cause and 'Water' as instrumental cause, the other, taking both 'Water' and 'Spirit' as two main causes that are distinct and complementary [73].

(a) Water as Instrumental Cause

The defenders of this position are :
In ancient Times. Chrysostom [74], Theodore of Mopsuestia [75], Ammo-

---

[70] Cf. R. SCHNACKENBURG, " Die Sakramente im Johannesevangelium ", *SacPag* vol. II (1959), pp. 235-254.

[71] Cf. J. LOUW, " De Vraag naar de Beteekenis van ἄνωθεν, Johannes 3:3 " *NThSt* 23 (1940), 56 : " Wanner het tweede woord 'Geest' niet als beeldspraak is op te vatten, dan geldt dat ook voor het eerste woord (Water), wijl beiden eng en onmiddelbaar met elkander verbonden zijn ".

[72] Cf. I. DE LA POTTERIE, art. "Naître", pp. 32-39 where he gives a detailed account of the history of exegesis on the matter.

[73] There is another opinion that says that here the Spirit is conferred through Baptism. For the defenders of this opinion, cf. I DE LA POTTERIE, art. " Naître ", p. 33, note 1. This opinion is to be rejected, because it makes the Spirit an effect, while in the text the Spirit is not an effect, but the cause of begetting.

[74] Cf. PG 59, 148.

nius [76], Cyril of Alexandria [77], St Basil [78], Cyril of Jerusalem [79]. Chrysostom sees 'water' as instrumental to the working of the Holy Spirit, as soil was said to be instrumental to God in creation. The Fathers usually speak of 'water' as a maternal womb and the Holy Spirit as the active principle in this begetting [80]. The same comparison is taken up by other writers in subsequent ages. St. Cyril conceives 'water' as receiving the power to sanctify by the efficacy of the Spirit [81].

In the Middle Ages. Theophylactus [82], Euthymius [83], Albert the Great and Bonaventure [85]. Theophylactus compares the instrumentality of water in Baptism to the 'semen' by means of which man effects generation [86]. Euthymius and Bonaventure take up the comparison of water with the maternal womb in the regeneration, while Albert the Great describes the water as having the power of regeneration from the Holy Spirit [87].

In the Reformation and Post-Reformation Period. All the Catholic authors without exception held the instrumental causality of 'water' and expressed it differently, while the Protestant authors mostly held the metaphorical interpretation. Some take the comparison of human birth and attribute to 'water' the role of the mother, and to the Holy Spirit the role of the father [88]. Ribera [89] and Natalis [90] describe the Holy Spirit as the principal agent in the spiritual regeneration.

---

[75] Cf. CSCO 116, 47.
[76] Cf. PG 85, 1408-1409.
[77] Cf. PG 73, 244-245.
[78] Cf. PG 32, 129, 132.
[79] Cf. PG 33, 429.
[80] Cf. AMMONIUS in PG 85, 1408 : " τὸ ὕδωρ ἐν τάξει μήτρας ... τὸ δὲ πνεῦμα ἐν τάξει τοῦ διαπλάσσοντος Θεοῦ ".
[81] Cf. PG 73, 244-245.
[82] Cf. PG 123, 1203-1206.
[83] Cf. PG 129, 1163-1164.
[84] Cf. Opera Omnia, ed. Aug. Borguet, vol. 24, Paris, 1898, p. 119.
[85] Cf. Opera Omnia, ed. Quaracchi, vol. VI, Florence, 1893, 279-80.
[86] Cf. PG 123, 1204 : " ὥσπερ ... ἐπὶ τοῦ σωματικοῦ σπέρματος οὕτω καὶ ἐπὶ τοῦ βαπτίσματος ὕδωρ ... ἀλλὰ τὸ πνεῦμα τὰ πάντα ἐνεργεῖ ".
[87] " ... Ex aqua ut materia habente vim regenerativam et Spiritu Sancto regenerante " cf. Opera Omnia, vol. 24, p. 119.
[88] Cf. for example, J. MALDONATUS, *Commentarii in Quatuor Evangelistas*, ed. by C. Martin, vol. II : in Lucam et Joannem, 1863, p. 482 ; CORNELIUS A LAPIDE, *Commentaria in Quatuor Evangelia*, vol. IV, ed. Ant. Padovani, Turin, 1906, p. 74 ; A. CALMET, *Commentarius Literalis in Omnes Libros Novi Testamenti*, vol. II, Würzburg, 1787, p. 44.

In Modern Times. Many hold the same instrumental causality of 'water', though they usually leave out the father-mother image, so frequent among the ancient writers [91].

(b) Water and Spirit as distinct and Complementary Causes

In this explanation, 'water' and 'Spirit' are dissociated. 'Water' signifies Christian Baptism, and the 'Spirit' refers to faith and the practice of virtues. This exegetical tradition is also attested from earliest times.

In Ancient Times. Hermas [92], who in Sim IX, 12-16 is under the literary influence of Jn 3:5 [93], sees in the first part of Jn 3:5 two necessary conditions for entering the Kingdom of God, namely, 'water' and 'Spirit', though he expresses these conditions in different words. Instead of 'water', he puts phrases such as 'carry or receive the name of the son of God' (cf. Sim IX, 12:4,5,8; 15:2) [94], 'carry or receive the seal' (Sim IX, 16:3) [95], or 'ascend through the water' (Sim IX, 16:2). Instead of 'Spirit', he puts phrases such as 'to put on the habits of the virgins, their virtues and their spirits (Sim IX, 13:2,3), 'to carry their names' (Sim IX, 13:3) [96] and 'follow the

---

[89] Cf. F. RIBERA, *In Sanctum Jesu Christi Evangelium secundum Joannem Commentarii*, Lyon, 1623, p. 108.

[90] Cf. A. NATALIS, *Expositio Literalis et Moralis S. Evangelii Jesu Christi secundum Joannem*, Paris, 1743, p. 478.

[91] Cf. A. H. HALLER, " Der Begriff der Wiedergeburt nach der Schrift ", *NKZ* 11 (1900), p. 614; J. M. VOSTÉ, " De Spirituali Regeneratione ex Aqua et Spiritu ", in *Studia Joannea*, Rome, 1930, p. 129; E. K. LEE, *The Religious Thought of St. John*, London, 1950, pp. 188-190; R. SCHNACKENBURG, Die Sakramente im Johannesevangelium, p. 245; L. VILLETTE, *Foi et Sacrement*, I, Paris, 1959, p. 89.

[92] Cf. A. LELONG, *Les Pères apostoliques*, IV, Paris, 1912, pp. 254-272.

[93] Note the occurrence of the phrase ὄψεται τὴν βασιλείαν τοῦ Θεοῦ (Sim IX, 15:3) and εἰσελθεῖν εἰς τὴν βασιλείαν τοῦ Θεοῦ (Sim IX, 12:3,4,5,8; 15:2; 16:2,3) and that conditioned by Baptism.

[94] Cf. Sim IX, 17:4; 16:4(2,3), where it is clear that this phrase refers to Baptism. Cf. A. RESCH, *Aussercanonische Paralleltexte zu den Evangelien*, III, TU 10 (Leipzig 1897), p. 77.

[95] For σφραγίς referring to Baptism, cf. G. RESCH, " Was versteht Paulus unter der Vorsiegelung mit dem Hl. Geist ", *NKZ* 6 (1895), 991-1003; I DE LA POTTERIE, art. " L'Onction du Chrétien par la Foi ", in *La Vie selon l'Esprit*, pp. 110-118.

[96] Cf. Sim IX, 15:1-2 where the names of the virgins are enumerated as the different virtues.

commandments' (Sim IX, 14:5) [97]. The above references show that for Hermas, 'entering into the Kingdom of God' is conditioned by both Baptism and 'a life according to the Spirit', which naturally refers to Jn 3:5, presenting 'water' and 'Spirit' as two distinct and complementary causes of the new begetting [98].

There seems to be already an allusion to these two elements, working out our regeneration, by Clement of Rome in his Second Epistle to the Corinthians, which gives a text parallel to Jn 3:5. There we read " What confidence have we to enter the Kingdom, if we do not keep our Baptism pure and immaculate ? " [99]. Thus he refers to a life that begins in Baptism, a life that is pure and immaculate, which together with baptism gives the possibility of entering the Kingdom of God. Clementine Homily VII, 8 gives both Faith and Baptism, as means of regeneration [100].

St Justin, in his Dialogue with Tryphon 135:6 and 138:2 [101] and in Apol 61 [102] gives these two elements of Faith and Baptism as essential to the new birth. And the same could be said of St. Ireneus [103], Origen [104] and St. Augustine [105].

In the Middle Ages. Bede the Venerable makes allusion to the two elements, visible and invisible, at work in Baptism [106], which is taken up also by B. Alcuinus [107]. J. Scotus Erigena states these two elements clearly specifying the visible element as the visible sacrament of Baptism, expressed in the word 'water', and the invisible element as the invisible understanding of that which takes place in Baptism, expressed in the word 'Spirit' [108]. Speaking of Jn 1:13 he says that birth from God takes place in Baptism for those who believe, thus

---

[97] The fact that for Hermas there is a strict relation between the Spirit and the virtues, and that all these images are symbols of virtues, shows that all these stand for the 'Spirit'.

[98] Cf. E. MASSAUX, *Influence de l'évangile de saint Mattieu sur la literature chrétienne avant saint Irénée*, Gembloux, 1950, pp. 293-300.

[99] Cf. PG 1, 337.

[100] Cf. PG 2, 221 : " τῷ τῆς ἀληθείας μόνῳ πιστεύειν προφήτῃ, καὶ εἰς ἄφεσιν ἁμαρτιῶν βαπτισθῆναι, καὶ οὕτως ... ἀναγεννηθῆναι Θεῷ ".

[101] Cf. PG 6, 789 and 993.

[102] Cf. PG 6, 420-421.

[103] Cf. Frag. 33, ed. Harvey, II, pp. 497-498.

[104] Cf. Comm. de Mt 23:1-12, GCS ORIGENES, XI, 23,26-27.

[105] Cf. De Baptismo contra Donatistas, VI, 12,19 (CSEL 51, 310-311). For further details in this respect, cf. I DE LA POTTERIE, art. " Naître ", pp. 35-37.

[106] Cf. PL 92, 668 : " ... Videtur quidem, qui baptizatur ..., quid autem in illo lavacrum regenerationis egerit, minime potest videri ".

[107] Cf. PL 100, 779.

[108] Cf. PL 122, 316.

showing both elements of Faith and Baptism bringing about the birth from God [109].

Rupertus Abbatus [110] makes a distinction between ' nisi quis baptizatus fuerit ' and ' nisi quis renatus fuerit ex aqua et Spiritu Sancto ' and says that the second formula is used in Jn 3:5 precisely to show that it is not enough to be baptized externally. According to him, ' he who is reborn from water and the Spirit ' is ' baptized ' while ' he who is baptized ' is not necessarily ' reborn from the Holy Spirit ' [111]. So baptism, together with the action of the Spirit (faith) leading to the renewal of man, effects the new birth. This interpretation is taken up again by two works called ' Glossa Ordinaria ' [112] and ' Glossa Interlinearis ' [113]. St Thomas, though he attributes spiritual vision to the Holy Spirit, speaks of the infusion of the Holy Spirit in us through Baptism (lavacrum regenerationis) [114].

Reformation and Post-reformation Period. Luther in his sermons attributes regeneration to Baptism and Faith in the Word of God [115]. Like J. Scotus Erigena, Luther also insists on the aspect of development or progress in regeneration, namely, in the life of faith, that begins in the regeneration and in the fruits and good works of the Holy Spirit [116]. In the Reformation period, we do not see Catholic authors speaking in these terms. This may be due to the emphasis given to the sacramental efficacy of Baptism, as a reaction to the Protestant Reformation.

Modern Times. The great majority of Exegetes, both Catholic and Protestant, hold the instrumental causality of Baptism in the new birth. They seem to be still greatly influenced by the Post-Tridentinian sacramental emphasis in Baptism. But there are a few authors, both Catholic and Protestant, who see in the Spirit, a factor that

---

[109] Cf. PL 122, 297 : " Sed ex Deo nati sunt, per gratiam videlicet ' Baptismatis ', in quo incipiunt ' credentes in Christum ' ex Deo nasci ".

[110] Cf. PL 169, 313.

[111] Cf. ibid. where he describes him who is reborn from the Spirit as " Spiritu mentis suae renovatus, veterum hominem cum actibus ejus exuit et novum induit sanctitate ".

[112] Cf. PL 114, 336.

[113] Cf. Biblia Sacra cum Glossa Ordinaria, vol. V, Antwerpiae, 1617, pp. 1057-1058.

[114] Cf. S. THOMAS, *Super Evangelium S. Joannis Lectura*, ed. R. Cai, Roma, 1952, pp. 432-434.

[115] Cf. *M. Luthers Werke*, ed. Böhlau, Weimar, 1883-1912, vol. XLVII, pp. 1-28.

[116] Cf. ibid., XLVII, p. 13.

works through faith in Baptism, and thus brings about the new birth [117].

b. Interpretation of the Text

The very construction of the text suggests that the 'water' and 'Spirit' contribute equally to a spiritual begetting. Both words are equally governed by the preposition ἐκ and coordinated by the conjunction καί. Schematically it could be put in this way:

$$\dot{\varepsilon}\grave{\alpha}\nu\ \mu\grave{\eta}\ \tau\iota\varsigma\ \gamma\varepsilon\nu\nu\eta\vartheta\tilde{\eta}\ \dot{\varepsilon}\xi \begin{cases} \ \ddot{\upsilon}\delta\alpha\tau o\varsigma \\ \ \kappa\alpha\grave{\iota} \\ \ \pi\nu\varepsilon\acute{\upsilon}\mu\alpha\tau o\varsigma \end{cases}$$

So neither of the two words is subordinated to the other. Both 'water' and 'Spirit' are two principles of the new birth, principles that are distinct and complementary.

When speaking of the primitive formula with ἐκ πνεύματος we saw how it meant a begetting to the life of faith. By adding the words ὕδατος καί the Evangelist does not change anything in the primitive formula, but only adds another basic principle, namely, baptism that goes together with the faith engendered by the Spirit, to bring about the new begetting. So the present formula points to Baptism (Water) and Faith (Spirit) as the two basic principles of the divine begetting.

i. *The Pre-Johannine Doctrine on the matter*

This is in fact in perfect agreement with the common NT doctrine regarding the conditions to be saved, namely, faith and baptism [118]. The same doctrine is found in the practice of the primitive Church in demanding Faith before administering Baptism, as described in the Acts of the Apostles [119].

---

[117] Cf. E. SCHWEIZER, art. πνεῦμα, *TWNT* VI, p. 439 where he says that the birth from the Spirit signifies : " das Geschenk der Erkenntnis ... das im Ereignis des Glaubens Wirklichkeit wird "; cf. also E. A. ABBOTT, *Johannine Vocabulary*, London, 1905, no. 1494 ; S. SMALLEY, " Liturgy and Sacrament in the Fourth Gospel ", *EvQ* 29 (1957), 165 ; W. GRUNDMANN, " Die ΝΗΠΙΟΙ in der urchristlichen Parenese ", *NTS* 5 (1958-59), 199, note 1. Among the Catholic authors, cf. P. M. DE LA CROIX, *The Biblical Spirituality of St. John*, (trans. from the French ' L'évangile de Jean et son témoignage spirituel ') New York, 1966, pp. 282-285 ; I DE LA POTTERIE, art. " Naître ", pp. 57-63.

[118] Cf. Mk 16:15-16 (par. Mt 28:19) : " Go ..., he who ' believes ' and is ' baptized ' will be saved ".

[119] Cf. Acts 8:12,36-37 ; 16:14-15,30-33 ; 18:8 ; 19:4-5. Cf. above our treatise on the divine sonship of men in Paul, pp. 74-77.

The same juxtaposition of faith and Baptism is found also in Paul. Speaking of Paul's doctrine on the Christian sonship we saw how Gal 3:26-28 puts together the 'being baptized' and the 'putting on Christ', which is the formal explanation of becoming sons of God through faith. The seal of the Holy Spirit (Baptism) connected with the unction by God (faith) (cf. Eph 1:13 ; 2 Cor 1:21-22) points to the same doctrine [120]. These two principles of divine begetting are seen also in Tit 3:5, which, according to the more probable interpretation, speaks of a washing of regeneration (baptism) and a renewal in the Holy Spirit (faith), necessary for salvation [121].

ii. *The Relation between Faith and Baptism in Jn*

In Jn himself, we see a strict relation between Baptism and faith. This is clear from the scene of the piercing of the side of Christ in Jn 19:33-37 [122], where the flowing of water from the side of Christ seems to have a reference to Baptism, namely baptism as a prolonging of the efficacy of the death of Christ [123].

A structure of the section is enlightening in this respect.

V. 33 A   When they came ... saw ... they DID NOT BREAK HIS *legs*
  34 B   But one ... PIERCED HIS side ... and at once there came out *blood* and *water*
  35 C   And he who saw it has borne witness
               And his witness is true
               And he knows that he tells the true things
               that you also may believe
  36 A'   For these things ... not a *bone* OF HIM SHALL BE BROKEN
  37 B'   And again they shall *look*
               on HIM whom they PIERCED

In the structure we notice immediately the correspondence of the vv. 34 and 37 (BB'). In v. 34 two facts are expressed : ' the piercing

---

[120] Cf. I. DE LA POTTERIE, art. " Onction ", pp. 110-123.

[121] Cf. I. DE LA POTTERIE, " Le rapport de la foi et du baptême dans la mission d'après le Nouveau Testament ", p. 161.

[122] Vv. 33-37 form the main body of the pericope Jn 19:31-37, in which vv. 31-32 form the introduction.

[123] The position of G. RICHTER in " Blut und Wasser aus der durchbohrten Seite Jesu (Jn 19,34b) ", *Münch Theol Zeit* 21 (1970), pp. 1-21 that Jn 19: 34-35 has nothing to do with a sacramental symbolic meaning seems to be defective since he takes it for granted that vv. 34-35 are a secondary and later addition occasioned by John's polemic against Docetists. In fact these verses have a theological symbolism that is in perfect harmony with Johannine thought. Cf. R. E. BROWN, *The Gospel according to John* XIII-XXI, N.Y., 1970, pp. 944-956.

of the side' and the 'coming out of blood and water'[124]. Though apparently the 'looking' in v. 37 refers only to the first of these two facts, actually it refers to both, because they look not at the simple fact of piercing, but at the one who is pierced, namely, the event in its totality, piercing together with its whole effect expressed in the second fact. Hence the 'looking' corresponds to the whole saving event signified by the 'piercing of the side' and the 'flowing of blood and water', namely, to the death of Christ, together with its salutary effects prolonged in the Church through the Holy Spirit, concretely in the Sacrament of Baptism (and Eucharist)[125].

The correspondence between vv. 34 and 37 is reinforced by the OT context of the quotation in v. 37. In the text of Zach 12:10a which is quoted here, 'they shall look' indicates a 'look of conversion' to Yahweh with a contrite heart (12:10b – 14) and thus an approaching to the source of purification (13:1). There is a correspondence, therefore, between the source of purification and the 'look of conversion'[126]. In the same way, in Jn 19:33-37, we see a correspondence between the source (the salutary efficacy of the sacrifice of Christ operating in the Church through the Holy Spirit in Baptism) (v. 34) and the 'look of conversion' (Faith) (v. 37)[127]. So the 'looking' here is a historical look deepened in a vision of faith resulting in an adhesion to Christ. Jn 19:37 refers then to the faith that corresponds to and is operative in the concrete realization of Christ's

---

[124] Some Greek Mss as 579, 054 and versions such as e (vet. lat.), boh, and Fathers such as Apollinarius, Tatian, Eusebius of Caesarea, Epiphanius, Chrysostom, Theodoretus, Tertullian, Ambrose, Jerome and the like have the reverse order 'Water and blood' and is supported by M. E. BOISMARD (cf. " Problème de critique textuelle concernant le quatrième évangile ", *RB* 60 (1953), pp. 347-371). (On this point cf. also A. BARBERIS, " Sangue e Acqua od Acqua e Sangue ? (Giov 19,34) ", Sindon 10,11 (1967), pp. 31-33). But the order ' Blood and Water ' seems to be the correct one, as it is given by almost all the Greek Mss, and also because of the second place demanded by ' water ' which is symbolically more important than ' blood ' in Jn.

[125] Cf. B. VAWTER, *The Gospel according to John*, in The Jerome Biblical Commentary, London, 1968, p. 462 ; VAN DEN BUSSCHE, Jean, p. 532.

[126] Cf. P. LAMARCHE, *Zacharie IX-XIV, Structure literaire et messianisme* (Etudes Bibliques), Paris 1961, pp. 85-87, where he divides the pericope Zach 12:10 – 13:1 into four strophs arranged according to the scheme abb'a', in which 12:10a (a) corresponds to 13:1 (a') ; cf. also, C. TRAETS, op. cit., pp. 158-161.

[127] We have already seen how the theme of ' conversion ' is replaced by ' faith ' in John. Cf. D. MOLLAT, " Ils regarderont celui qu'ils ont transpercé. La conversion chez saint Jean ", *Lum et Vie* 9 (1960), p. 100 : " La scène de la Transfixion est ... la révélation saisissante de la grâce de conversion ... : baptême d'eau et de sang, que tous sont invités à recevoir dans la foi ...".

saving work through Baptism, indicated in Jn 19:34, which finally lead to the life of faith as affirmed in v. 35 [128].

This shows how for John, Baptism and Faith under the action of the Spirit go together and are the two fundamental conditions for entering the life of perfect faith, namely, the life of the Children of God.

The same connection between Faith and Baptism could be seen also in I Jn 5:6-8, where the Spirit is in strict relation to 'Water' and 'Blood', which point to the concrete situation of the Church referring to Baptism and Eucharist [129]. In vv. 6-8 there is a movement from the historical events to the concrete sacramental situation in the Church. If the aorist 'ὁ ἐλθών' and the 'water' and 'blood' without a definite article in v. 6a refer to the historical coming of Christ, from baptism to the death on the cross, considered as a fact [130], the change of διά into ἐν and the 'Water' and 'Blood' with the article refer also to the event mentioned in Jn 19:34, thus preparing the sacramental sense in v. 8 [131]. By introducing the Spirit as the one who testifies (at present), the author seems to refer to the witness of the Holy Spirit about Christ and about his Truths in the Church at large and in the life of each one, begetting Faith in them. And then he goes on to speak of 'Water' and 'Blood' as witnesses together with the 'Holy Spirit', thus explicitly referring to the concrete situation of the Church with the sacraments of initiation — Baptism and Eucharist.

The witnessing of the Spirit means to make known the Truth of Christ, and thus to beget Faith [132]. So the 'Spirit' coming just before and in strict relation and co-ordination to 'Water' and 'Blood', refers to Faith as a salvific experience, that accompanies the sacraments of Baptism and Eucharist. Thus I Jn 5:6-8 also shows that

---

[128] Note how v. 35 (C) stands in the centre of the section giving vv. 36 and 37 (A'B') as parallel to vv. 33 and 34 (AB).

[129] Cf. I. DE LA POTTERIE, "La notion johannique de temoignage", in SacPag II, Gembloux, 1959, pp. 203-204; R. SCHNACKENBURG, Die Sakramente im Johannesevangelium, p. 246; E. SCHWEIZER, Das johanneische Zeugnis vom Herrenmahl, EvTh 12 (1952-53), pp. 344-348.

[130] Cf. B. VAWTER, The Johannine Epistles, in The Jerome Biblical Commentary, p. 411.

[131] Cf. W. NAUCK, Die Tradition und der Character des Ersten Johannesbriefes, (WUNT 3), 1957, p. 151.

[132] Cf. I. DE LA POTTERIE, art. "La notion", p. 205; on the theme of 'witness' in John, see J. BEUTLER, Μαρτυρία, Traditionsgeschichtliche Untersuchungen zum Zeugnisthema bei Johannes. Frankfurter Theologische Studien 10, Frankfurt a. M. 1972.

for Jn the Spirit that begets Faith, and Baptism are intimately connected.

iii. *Begetting brought about by Baptism and Spirit working through Faith*

So in Jn 3:5 to enter into the Kingdom of God a new birth is required, which is to be brought about by the two elements: Baptism of water and the Spirit working through Faith. Thus Jn 3:5 presents the new birth as resulting from two fundamental agents, namely Baptism and the Holy Spirit. Both are equally necessary. The doctrine is, therefore, essentially the same as that of the Synoptics regarding the fundamental conditions to be saved (cf. Mk 16:15-16). The difference is that Jn speaks of the element of Faith from the point of view of God, because for him Faith is essentially an action of the Spirit. In this way Jn combines the divine and human elements working in the new begetting. The new begetting is not simply an effect of a rite, in which God operates and which man undergoes passively. He has also an active role to play in it, namely, through Faith, which remains at the same time a divine gift, because it is caused by the Spirit. It is true that John is positively theocentric in his approach. But this does not make of him, as some commentators seem to think [133], a fatalist or predestinarian. The 'begetting', as the word itself suggests, is exclusively an act of the begetter, namely, of God and the whole initiative rests with him [134]. But there is a human aspect in the experience of being begotten and thus becoming a child of God, which provides both the occasion and opportunity for divine activity in begetting men children of God. Or, to put it in another way, there are human conditions corresponding to the divine action. Though these human conditions themselves depend on God's activity, the fact remains that there are human conditions, whenever God begets spiritual children. While the initiative in the divine begetting is always with God, so also the realization of it is always inextricably connected with human conditions and response.

If this were not true, then divine begetting and sonship would be an imposed external relation for men, rather than an internal reality. And Jn, in describing the divine begetting in 3:5 as a 'begetting from Water and Spirit', brings to light both these aspects of divine initiative and human response to it, which together bring about the 'divine begetting', that takes place in the Sacrament of Baptism.

---

[133] Cf. J. MOFFAT, *The Theology of the Gospels*, New York, 1920, p. 196.
[134] Cf. J. C. RYLE, *Expository Thoughts on the Gospel* of St. John, vol. I, London, 1896, p. 123.

3. Begetting from the Spirit — a continued Life of Faith

It is remarkable that in Jn 3:5 the 'Spirit' comes after the 'water', contrary to the usual Johannine order [135], and this seems to be intentional [136], because here Jn does not put the 'Spirit' as a condition for 'Baptism', but both 'Baptism' and 'Spirit' as two coordinated elements that produce the new begetting. So the 'Spirit' here seems to refer to the 'life of faith' that should accompany Baptism. So it is not something that is fully realized at the moment of Baptism, but something that accompanies and then goes on progressing towards perfection. So it is quite normal that it is put after ὕδατος to signify this continued life of faith under the Holy Spirit [137].

This is indicated also by the use of the word γεννηθῆναι in the context. Note how the word is used till now in the inceptive aorist γεννηθῇ, γεννηθῆναι (vv. 3, 4, 5), while now it passes on to the use of the perfect tense τὸ (ὁ) γεγεννημένον(ς) (vv. 6, 8), which refers to the continued state of begetting that took place at the time of baptism. This emphasis on the continued life of the Spirit, indicated by the second place of πνεύματος in Jn 3:5 is perhaps suggested also by the fact that when Jn uses two words coordinated by καί usually the emphasis falls on the second [138].

a. The Holy Spirit — the Principle of Birth into this life of Faith

Though Faith is a condition to the communication of the life of the children of God, nevertheless, it is not the real principle of it. Speaking of the 'Begetting by the Spirit' in Jn 3:5, as a condition for entering the Kingdom of God, we saw how it points to Faith, but Faith which is caused by the Spirit.

Spirit and breath of life are interchangeable terms in Hebrew thought. Just as natural life has breath or spirit as its principle, so

---

[135] The usual order is found only in the Syro-Sinaitic version, which could be explained from the liturgical practice of the Church, which put the unction of the Spirit before Baptism, and which custom probably lies behind the text of I Jn 5:8.

[136] Cf. R. E. Brown, *The Gospel*, p. 144 where he takes this detail as an argument for the communication of the Spirit through Baptism, which is, however, a subordination of the Spirit to the 'Water', and hence not justifiable in the context.

[137] The words of Ruppertus Abbatus are interesting in this connection: "Illi autem qui ex aqua et Spiritu Sancto renati, regnum Dei p e r s e v e r a n t e r i n t r o e u n t" (cf. PL 169, 313). This shows the dynamism involved in this action of the Spirit.

[138] Cf. I. de la Potterie, art. "Naître", p. 60, note 1.

divine life has as principle the Spirit of God, and the 'begetting by the Spirit' in Jn 3:5 refers to the communication of the divine life, which marks the beginning of the life of a child of God [139]. The Holy Spirit, then, remains the principle of the life of the children of God, though for Jn this principle works mainly through faith.

i. " Holy Spirit that is Given to us " (I Jn 4:12-13 ; 3:23-24)

It is in the First Epistle that Jn takes upon himself the charge of explaining this aspect of the Spirit as the principle of the new life of the children of God. I Jn 4:13d gives the reason of our knowledge of communion with God, namely, of eternal life as the giving of the Holy Spirit in us [140]. Though in I Jn 4:13 and in 3:24 the Holy Spirit is considered in its effects, as the Spirit cannot be a visible criterion, nevertheless the Spirit is presented as a principle that is in the believer and that becomes an interior source of the life of the believer [141].

There are various indications that in these two verses Jn emphasized this role of the Spirit as an imparted principle of life in the believer. First of all, these are the only two places where πνεῦμα occurs in I Jn in the sections speaking of 'love', as the criterion of communion with God. In both these sections Jn begins to speak of communion with God from the point of view of divine sonship or divine begetting (cf. I Jn 3:10-12 and 4:7), and vv. 3:23-24 and 4:12-13, where he speaks of the Holy Spirit, are texts corresponding to 3:10-12 and 4:7 respectively [142]. In 4:12-13 as will be seen from the structure of the section, the 'indwelling of God in man' and the 'perfection of love in man' is a further explanation of the community of life designated by the expression 'begotten by God'. So this experienced knowledge of the presence of God is a knowledge of the divine sonship, namely, man knowing that he possesses the same life

---

[139] Note how in Lk 1:31 Jesus is called ' Son of God ' on account of the birth from the Holy Spirit.

[140] The ἐν τούτῳ of v. 13a, though it refers to what precedes, is further explained in the ὅτι sentence in 13d. Hence the knowledge of our communion with God is caused by the Spirit.

[141] Note the almost literal parallelism of 3:24 and 4:13 :

3:24 " In this we know that He dwells in us by the Spirit, which He has given us ".
4:13 " In this we know that ... dwell ... in us, for He has given us of His Spirit ".

[142] Note how 3:23-24 forms an inclusion with 3:10-12 with the literary parallels αὕτη ἐστὶν ἡ ἐντολὴ (ἀγγελία) ... ἵνα ... ἀγαπῶμεν ἀλλήλους. I Jn 4:12-13 corresponds to 4:7b-8 as can be seen from the structural division on p. 303.

as that of God, arrives at the knowledge of God as his Father. It is this filial knowledge of God as Father that is caused by the Holy Spirit [143]. So the Holy Spirit that is imparted to the believers becomes the principle of the divine life.

The same could be seen in 3:23-24. Here the invisible reality of abiding in God — communion with God — is known from the visible reality of keeping the commandments of God. The commandment is 'to believe' and 'to love' (v. 23). Now what is the role of the last phrase ἐκ τοῦ πνεύματος οὗ ἡμῖν ἔδωκεν? This can be better seen if we look at the structure of the section.

ii. The Structure of I Jn 3:23-24

V. 23   A   And this is HIS COMMANDMENT
       B   That WE should believe IN HIS SON JESUS CHRIST ... love...
       C   Just as HE HAS commanded US
   24   A'   Everyone who keeps HIS COMMANDMENTS
       B'   abides IN HIM and HE IN them ... HE abides IN US
       C'   by the Spirit which HE HAS given US.

In this structure, the expression, 'just as He has commanded us' (C) seems to add something more to the expression 'this is his commandment' (A), namely, it refers also to the source which enables one to keep his commandment of faith and love (AB). Though καθώς ordinarily expresses a comparison, when this comparison is founded on God or Christ, then it points necessarily to the very source [144]. Since A'B'C' is a further development of ABC, the expression 'by the Spirit which he has given us' (C') seems to refer similarly to the very source of the mutual communion (B') and its exterior manifestation of keeping the commandments (A') of faith and love, which is the concrete Christian life [145]. So the Holy Spirit that is given to us becomes the interior principle of the life of the children of God, manifested in faith and love [146].

iii. Love infused in us through the Holy Spirit

In Rom 5:3-5 the hope of glory of the children of God is based on the love infused in us through the Holy Spirit. So already in the

---

[143] Here it is interesting to note that in Rom 8:15 and Gal 4:6 it is the Holy Spirit that brings us to the knowledge of God as Father, in which we call 'Abba Father'.

[144] Cf. O De Dinechin, " ΚΑΘΩΣ : La similitude dans l'évangile selon saint Jean ", *RSR* 58 (1970), pp. 195-236.

[145] Cf. F. Mussner, " Eine neutestamentliche Kurzformel für das Christentum " *Trier Theol Zeit* 79 (1970), 49-52.

[146] That it is an interior reality in man, is indicated by the fact that the Holy Spirit is here said to be given to us.

Baptismal tradition, the Holy Spirit was connected with the divine sonship, because of the love infused in us. So there is no wonder that Jn makes use of the same baptismal elements connected with love, to insist on brotherly love, especially after the section 2:29 – 3:10, where he certainly makes use of the traditional baptismal elements [147]. We will see later how Jn begins the section on brotherly love in 3:10 by taking the motive of divine sonship, connected with love in the Baptismal tradition (cf. I Pet 1:22-23 ; Rom 5:3-5). In I Jn 4:7 too he begins his third section on brotherly love in the same way with the same motive of divine begetting. So it is quite natural that he brings in the role of the Holy Spirit in the corresponding texts.

The very expression 'the Spirit is given to us' points to the baptismal 'Sitz im Leben' of the context [148], and in I Jn ' πνεῦμα ' is used with ' διδόναι ' only in these two contexts. Note too the partitive signification of the preposition ἐκ with the genitive, indicating a fulness out of which something, as part of a whole, is given [149]. So the Spirit here seems to be a real object, something that is delivered by God to the believers, and which they possess within themselves [150], and which becomes the principle of their life as 'children of God'.

b. **Continuous Influx of the Parent source in the Life of Sonship**

Actually, Jn speaks of the divine begetting of men in the aorist only in Jn 3, speaking of it as a condition absolutely necessary to see or enter the Kingdom of God. On all the other occasions he makes use of the perfect tense γεγέννηται or γεγεννημένος. This phenomenon is indeed of far reaching significance. It shows that, unlike a human parent, God does not impart His own life to the begotten only once and for ever. He continues to strengthen it habitually by His divine influence. The life imparted is not developed in a separate and independent existence, but it is developed in its sustenance and

---

[147] Cf. W. NAUCK, op. cit., pp. 180-181 where he sees the traditional baptismal elements and the baptismal 'Sitz im Leben' in connection with the ideas of divine sonship and love of the Father together with giving of the Holy Spirit as Jn describes here in these contexts.

[148] Cf. Rom 5:5 ; II Cor 1:22 ; 5:5 ; Eph 1:14 ; Heb 6:4.

[149] Cf. F. ZORELL, *Lexicon Graecum*, col. 389 ; W. BAUER, *A Greek-English Lexicon*, p. 235. In 3:24 the Vulgate takes the pronoun οὗ as an attracted genitive and translates by the accusative " quem dedit nobis ". The sense is evidently the same as that of a partitive genitive.

[150] Cf. also Jn 20:22 ; 7:39 where Jn speaks of the Spirit as a gift which may be given and received.

growth upon the continuous influx of life from the parent source. The divine begetting, once carried out in germ, still goes on in its development.

This idea is well expressed in the Gospel illustration of the ' Vine and its branches ' (Jn 15:1-10). Truly, this analogy is apt to illustrate the peculiar characteristic of the divine begetting and life of the children of God. As the branches that are the children of a tree draw continually from the parent tree for their sustenance and growth, so the life in the children of God, begun by divine power, is also habitually sustained and fostered by the same divine power [151].

The metaphor of vine and branches implies, moreover, that the vitalizing union by which the influx of divine life is maintained in those who are begotten of God, consists of two reciprocal activities: God's abiding in us and our abiding in God. As the sap of the parent vine vitalizes all the branches, so does the divine germ vitalize the children of God through a mutual abiding [152].

c. **Permanent Communion of Life between the Father, the Son and the Children**

For Jn there is no life apart from union with the Son who is the life, and therefore ' to abide in the Son ' means ' to live by Him ' [153]. So a mutual abiding of God (Christ) and men means to have the permanent life-giving principle from the divine source, the initial act of which is the divine begetting [154]. It is this mutual

---

[151] Cf. R. LAW, op. cit., p. 199; A. M. DONATUS, art. cit., p. 21.

[152] Note how throughout the whole Johannine literature the verb μένειν occurs 67 times, while in the rest of the NT it occurs 50 times in all, which shows the characteristically Johannine note of this verb. Besides, in the Gospel itself out of the 21 occurrences of μένειν in the spiritual sense, 11 occur in Ch. 15 itself.

[153] Cf. F. MUSSNER, ZΩH. *Die Anschauung vom Leben im 4. Ev. unter Berücksichtigung der Johannesbriefe*, München, 1952, p. 151: " Wie die Bildanschauung ergibt, heisst μένειν ἐν ἐμοί nichts anderes als in Lebensverbindung mit Christus bleiben "; cf. also R. BORIG, *Der Wahre Weinstock. Untersuchungen zu Jn 15:1-10*, München, 1967, p. 202. Cf. Jn 6:56-67 where this parallelism between the mutual abiding of Christ and men, and ' living through Christ ' is expressed clearly (cf. also I Jn 5:11). Note how in the second part of the Gospel, the concept of ' abiding ' takes the place of the concept of ' life ', which is characteristic of the First part. μένειν occurs 7 times in Jn 1-12 and 14 times in Jn 13-21, while ζωή occurs 33 times in Jn 1-12 and 4 times in Jn 13-21.

[154] It is remarkable that while in the Epistle it is God who abides in us and we in Him, in the Gospel it is Christ who abides in us and we in Him. The latter has then its counterpart in Christ's abiding in the Father (15:10)

abiding of God the Father (Christ the Son) and men his children that is expressed in I Jn in the substantive form of κοινωνία (cf. I Jn 1:3,6,7) [155]. I Jn 1:3 which forms also an introduction to the whole Epistle, puts forth the leading idea of the Epistle, namely, that of having an intimate fellowship like that of a family, which is at once divine and human. On the human level it points to a fellowship among the members of the Christian community, which however grows out of a divine fellowship with God and His Son Jesus Christ. This fellowship is in the life of God, as is clear from I Jn 5:13, which forms an inclusion to I Jn 1:3, both expressing the purpose of the Letter. So it is a filial fellowship with God the Father, together with His Son Jesus Christ and with the other children of God, who participate in the same life of God.

Thus participating in the same divine life, the Father and the Son and the Children of God become really one, a concept expressed by Jn in the brief and absolute form ἕν εἶναι [156], and here the Johannine notion of fellowship with God and abiding in God reaches its culmination.

But the only way to arrive at this filial fellowship in which all become one, is by adhering in faith to the historically revealed Son of God, who is the 'Life' of God Himself, or the Revealed Word of Life (cf. I Jn 1:1-3) [157]. Note how the 'becoming one with the Father and the Son' is for those who believe in the Son (cf. Jn 17:20) [158]. The permanent life-giving principle, therefore, is the result of a permanent communion of life with Christ and through Him with God [159]. This is quite coherent with the Johannine concept of the divine be-

---

and the Father's abiding in Him (14:10 ; 17:23). But as, for Jn, Christ is the only way to the Father, it comes to the same.

[155] Compare H. SEESEMANN, *Der Begriff* κοινωνία *im NT*, in BZNT 14 (1933), pp. 92-99 ; cf. also R. SCHNACKENBURG, *Die Johannesbriefe*, p. 64, note 3 where he considers κοινωνία as " die substantivische Form des meist durch εἶναι ἐν, μένειν ἐν, u. a. ausgedrückten Joh. Gemeinschaftsgedankens ". Cf. also F. HAUCK, art. κοινωνός, *TDNT* III, pp. 807-808.

[156] Cf. Jn 17:21-23 where this oneness is expressed. Note the Formula : ἵνα καὶ αὐτοὶ ἐν ἡμῖν ἕν ὦσιν. On the theme of this oneness in Jn, cf. J. F. RANDALL, " The Theme of Unity in Jn 17,20-23 ", *ETL* 41 (1965), pp. 373-394.

[157] Cf. R. SCHNACKENBURG, *Die Johannesbriefe*, p. 65 where he puts the main thought of I Jn 1:3 as " Gemeinschaft mit Gott durch den Glaubensanschluss an den geschichtlich erschienenen einen und wahren Gottessohn Jesus Christus ".

[158] Here it is worth noting how in Gal 3:26-28 ' to be the sons of God through faith ' is parallel to ' be one in Christ '.

[159] Cf. F. MUSSNER, op. cit., p. 157 ; Compare A. WIKENHAUSER, *Das Evangelium nach Johannes übersetzt und kurz erklärt*, Regensburg, 1957 p. 221.

getting and sonship as the result of faith in Christ, without which we cannot have perfect communion with Him. It is also in perfect agreement with the Christological interpretation of the Kingdom of God, the entrance into which is an entrance into communion with Christ.

d. The Dynamism of the Divine Begetting

We saw how the divine element (Spirit) producing faith in us and human element (docility to the Spirit), work together in bringing about the divine begetting. So when we speak of permanent sustenance and growth of the life issuing from this begetting, it is the permanent working of these two elements that is implied in it. This permanent working together of the divine and human elements seems to be expressed also by the formula of 'God (Christ) abiding in us and we abiding in God (Christ)', which is again parallel to 'God's seed remaining in us' (cf. I Jn 3:6,9) [160].

The above considerations show how dynamic is the Johannine concept of divine begetting and the life of divine sonship resulting from it. The elements that are at work in the beginning, do not cease to work after bringing about the begetting. They go on working to contribute to the sustenance and growth of the life that is begotten. Hence the dynamism implied in the Johannine use of γεγέννηται (ὁ γεγεννημένος) ἐκ τοῦ θεοῦ (πνεύματος).

D. *The Nature of the one who is Born of the Spirit* (Jn 3:6-8)

After having described the divine begetting in the aorist as the condition for entering into the life of the children of God in Jn 3:3 and 5, he goes on to describe the nature of those who are thus begotten to the life of the children of God [161].

1. *Born of the Spirit versus Born of the flesh* (Jn 3:6)

In v. 6 describing the nature of those who are begotten of the Spirit in contradistinction to those who are begotten of the flesh, he illustrates once more the necessity of a begetting from God for entering into the life of the children of God.

In Johannine thinking, nature is determined by its origin as

---

[160] Note how here in I Jn 3:6,9 'our abiding in God' and 'God's seed remaining in us' are parallels and have the same effect of 'not sinning'. We will see how the 'remaining of God's seed in us' refers to the working of the Spirit in us through the Word of God (Faith).

[161] Note the perfect tense of γεγεννημένον(ς), which denotes the state of being begotten by God.

appears from the frequent use of εἶναι ἐκ, which affirms both the origin and the type of being [162]. Thus in v. 6 Jn distinguishes the two essentially different orders of being, deriving from their different origins. He who is begotten of the flesh, is essentially merely flesh, and he who is begotten of the Spirit is of the nature of the Spirit [163], 'Σάρξ' in Jn does not have the Pauline sense of a source of sin. Apart from the Eucharistic texts speaking of the flesh of Christ (6:51, 52,53,54,55,56) σάρξ in Jn is put in opposition to the sphere of God or Spirit (cf. Jn 1:13 ; 3:6 ; 6:63 ; 8:15) [164]. The flesh is to the Spirit, what the earthly is to the heavenly [165]. So the σάρξ here is the natural man as such, the non-regenerated man, who is not capable of entering the Kingdom (eternal life), which belongs to a completely different order (divine and supernatural) of being [166]. The absolute impossibility of the σάρξ to come to the life of the Spirit, is best expressed in Jn 6:63-64, where the Spirit is said to vivify and the σάρξ is said to be of no avail in this respect [167]. So in face of the divine life, σάρξ is of no use, and that which is begotten of σάρξ is always σάρξ. That which vivifies — makes the life of faith possible [168] — is the Spirit, and only that which is begotten of the Spirit is Spirit.

So here John reaffirms the necessity of a begetting from the

---

[162] Cf. 3:31 ; 8:23,44,47 ; 15:19 ; 17:14,16 ; 18:36ff ; I Jn 2:16,21 ; 3:8,10,12, 19 ; 4:1-3,4-6 ; 5:19 etc.

[163] Note how in certain Mss the thought is explained by the addition of ὅτι ἐκ τῆς σαρκὸς ἐγεννήθη after σάρξ ἐστιν. (cf. 161, it codd Syc Tert), 'quia Deus Spiritus est' (e a ff² j m z Syc) and 'et ex Deo natus est' (a j Syc) after πνεῦμά ἐστιν.

[164] The only exception is Jn 17:2 where the traditional form πᾶσα σάρξ is used to signify all men in general, without referring to the opposition with the Spirit. Cf. E. SCHWEIZER, art. σάρξ, TWNT VII, pp. 106, 138.

[165] Cf. X. LEON DUFOUR, art. "Chair", in Vocabulaire de théologie biblique, Paris, 1964, col. 114.

[166] Cf. E. SCHWEIZER, art. "σάρξ", TWNT VII, p. 139 : "σάρξ ist die menschlich-irdische Sphäre, die keine Gotteserkenntnis hat und darum auch keine vermitteln kann " ; cf. also F. ROUSTANG, " L'Entretien avec Nicodème ", NRT 78 (1956), 343, for whom the comparison with the flesh shows the radical newness of the second creation.

[167] Cf. J. PASCHER, " Der Glaube als Mitteilung des Pneumas nach Joh 6:61-65 ", ThQ 117 (1936), pp. 301-321. On p. 307 he says : " Nur der Geist verleiht übernatürliches Leben, wobei das Wort ' Leben ' die ganze Übernatur umfasst. Negativ wird zum Ausdruck gebracht, dass das Fleish, d. h., das rein Natürliche, nicht-Pneumatische zu dieser Lebensverleihung nichts beitragen kann ".

[168] That this vivifying refers to the life of faith is clear from the following verses 63b-64 of Ch. 6 where he speaks of the ' Word ' as ' Life ' and of those who do not believe.

Spirit, to enter the life of faith (Kingdom), from the very nature of that which is begotten of the Spirit, in contradistinction to that which is begotten of the flesh [169]. This is clear from v. 7 where he again repeats the absolute necessity of the begetting from above (δεῖ ὑμᾶς γεννηθῆναι ἄνωθεν) for all the non-regenerated Jews represented by Nicodemus [170].

2. Born of the Spirit is Spirit (Jn 3:8)

Having shown the nature of him who is begotten of the Spirit, in contrast to him who is begotten of the flesh, he now proceeds to describe better the nature of the one who is begotten of the Spirit in Jn 3:8. Since he said in v. 6 that which is begotten of the Spirit is Spirit, now he takes up the word ' Spirit ' and describes its nature to illustrate better the nature of the one who is begotten of the Spirit.

a. Use of πνεῦμα in the Context

Since πνεῦμα could be understood as ' wind ' or ' Holy Spirit ', we meet with the problem of how to understand πνεῦμα here. This problem has intrigued scholars from the very beginning. Some have understood it as ' wind ' [171], while others understood it directly as the Holy Spirit [172], while again some others understood both [173].

If we take the word πνεῦμα simply for the wind, we have here merely a comparison or parable. The adverb οὕτως may seem to point to this parabolic sense. But in Jn οὕτως seems to say something more than a mere comparison. In Jn οὕτως is used in a com-

---

[169] Cf. R. E. BROWN, " The Eucharist and Baptism in John ", in *New Testament Essays*, Milwaukee, 1965, pp. 92-93 ; R. SUMMERS, " Born of Water and Spirit ", in *Studies in Memory of Henry Trantham*, Texas, 1964, p. 126.

[170] Note the singular σοι and then the plural ὑμᾶς referring to all Jews, resuming the οἴδαμεν of v. 2 representing Jews, who being only σάρξ in themselves could not come to the authentic faith in Jesus, entering the Kingdom of God.

[171] Cf. CHRYSOSTOM, PG 59, 154-155 ; CYRIL OF ALEXANDRIA, PG 73, 245 ; THEOPHYLACTUS, PG 123, 1205 ; EUTHYMIUS, PG 129, 1165 ; among the modern authors, cf. LAGRANGE, *Évangile*, p. 77 ; BULTMANN, *Evangelium*, pp. 101-102 ; SCHNACKENBURG, *Gospel*, pp. 373-374.

[172] Cf. IGNATIUS OF ANTIOCH, Ad Philad., 7:1, SC 10, 114 ; AUGUSTINE, PL 35, 1486-1487 ; BEDE THE VENERABLE, PL 92, 669 ; GLOSSA ORDINARIA, PL 114, 367 ; among the modern authors, cf. BERNARD, *St. John*, I, p. 108.

[173] Cf. LOISY, *Évangile*, pp. 313-314; E.C. HOSKYNS, *The Fourth Gospel*, p. 215; BARRETT, *Gospel*, pp. 175-176 ; BROWN, *Gospel*, p. 131 ; O. CULLMANN, " Der johanneische Gebrauch doppeldeutiger Ausdrücke als Schlüssel zum Verständnis des Vierten Evangeliums ", *ThZ* 4 (1948), pp. 360-372.

parative construction only six times apart from 3:8. Out of these six times, four times it speaks of the relation between the Father and the Son (cf. 5:21,26; 12:50; 14:31), and in all these four cases, it shows not a mere comparison, but a comparison that implies a communion between the Father and the Son. In one of the other two cases, the οὕτως implies not only a comparison, but a typology (cf. Jn 3:14). In 15:4, the last case, it is certainly a comparison most similar to our case in Jn 3:8. But as could be seen from Jn 15:1 it is not a mere comparison, but also a real allegory. So practically there is no case in Jn, where we can find οὕτως in a purely comparative or parabolic sense.

A merely comparative sense would destroy the essential continuity and coherence required by the construction of vv. 6-8, which begin and end with ὁ (τὸ) γεγεννημένος(ν) ἐκ τοῦ πνεύματος forming thus an inclusion for the description of the nature of those who are begotten of the Spirit. Having said in the beginning that 'that which is begotten by the Spirit is Spirit' (v. 6), he passes on to the description of this Spirit in vv. 7-8, and then concludes in v. 8b resuming the phrase of introduction. This procedure requires that the πνεῦμα here be taken, not as a mere comparison, but as intimately connected with the πνεῦμα that is ὁ γεγεννημένος ἐκ τοῦ πνεύματος in vv. 6 and 8 [174].

b. Other expressions in the Context

The expressions πνεῦμα πνεῖ, τὰ ἐπίγεια etc. induce some authors to understand the πνεῦμα in a purely parabolic sense of the wind [175]. But the expression πνεῦμα πνεῖ is rare in the OT and NT. In the OT it occurs only in Bar 6:61 and Is 40:7 (Sm. and Th.), and in both contexts there is some allusion to the divine action [176]. In the NT Jn 3:8 is the only place where πνέω occurs with πνεῦμα and when it is used of the natural blowing of the wind, it is used with ἄνεμος [177]. The fact that Jn himself makes use of ἄνεμος with πνέω (Jn 6:18) when speaking of the wind, shows that here he thinks of something higher than merely the wind [178].

---

[174] This connection is emphasized by Toletus who says: " Dominus prius dixerat natum de Spiritu esse Spiritum ..., opportebat ergo probare et ostendere Spiritum esse eum qui natus est de Spiritu, quod certe non efficitur propter hoc quod natus de Spiritu similis est vento " (cf. F. TOLETUS, *In Sacrosanctum Joannis Evangelium Commentarii*, Romae, 1588, col. 272).

[175] Cf. for example, P. SCHANZ, *Kommentar über Das Evangelium des Hl. Johannes*, Tübingen, 1885, p. 171.

[176] In Is 40:7 it is called expressly πνεῦμα κυρίου.

[177] Cf. Mt 7:25,27; Jn 6:18; Apoc 7:1.

[178] Note that πνεῦμα is never used in Jn to signify the wind, but always used in a theological sense.

The τὰ ἐπίγεια and τὰ ἐπουράνια refer to the object of revelation[179], but not in the sense that τὰ ἐπίγεια refers to earthly things in contradistinction to τὰ ἐπουράνια as referring to heavenly things [180]. The term οὐρανός is used in Jn exclusively in relation to the revelation of the person and mission of Christ [181]. So it seems that τὰ ἐπουράνια refers to the revelation of the mystery of Christ, to be followed in vv. 14-18 in contradistinction to the τὰ ἐπίγεια referring to the supernatural birth concerning man who is earthly (v. 31). So τὰ ἐπίγεια also cannot be taken as an indication of πνεῦμα as referring to 'wind'.

Words such as θέλει, φωνή, and the phrase πόθεν ἔρχεται καὶ ποῦ ὑπάγει are all of theological importance in Jn. The verb θέλει is used either of the will of Christ in relation to His saving mission (Jn 5: 21 ; 17:24 ; cf. also 1:44 ; 7:1 ; 21:22), or of the will of men in relation to spiritual realities (cf. 5:35,40 ; 6:67 ; 7:17 ; 8:44 ; 9:27 ; 12:21 ; 15:7 ; 16:19 ; 21:18) [182].

The word φωνή [183] is always used in a supernatural sense [184]. When used with an article, it always refers to the voice of Christ, who is the spouse (3:29), the Son of God (5:25,28), the Good Shepherd (10:3,4,16,27) and King (18:37) or to the voice of others opposed to Christ the Good Shepherd (10:5) [185]. When used without an article, it refers to the celestial voice of the Father (5:37 ; 12:28) or to John the Baptist who is the voice in the desert (1:23). Thus φωνή is used in Jn almost exclusively in a supernatural sense.

---

[179] So it is understood by LAGRANGE (*Évangile*, pp. 79-80), E.C. HOSKYNS (*Gospel*, pp. 216-217), BARRET (*Gospel*, p. 177) A. SCHLATTER (*Der Evangelist Johannes, wie er spricht, denkt und glaubt*, Stuttgart 1930, pp. 92-93), etc.

[180] Cf. W. THÜSING, *Erhöhung und Verherrlichung ...*, pp. 254-259 where he refers τὰ ἐπίγεια to the revelation of Christ during His earthly life and τὰ ἐπουράνια to the revelation during His glorified state through the Holy Spirit. Cf. ibid. pp. 50-75 and Idem, *Herrlichkeit und Einheit*, Düsseldorf, 1962, pp. 23-27 ; 46-47 where he makes the same distinction between ' the work of Christ ' and ' greater works ' (Jn 5:20 ; 14:12 ; 17:4) and also between ' I made known your name ' and ' I shall make known ' (Jn 17:26).

[181] Cf. Jn 1:32,51 ; 3:31,35 ; several texts in ch. 6 ; 12:28 ; 17:1 etc.

[182] The few cases of θέλει with objects which have apparently nothing to do with a spiritual reality, are also always connected with some action or the Person of Christ (cf. Jn 5:6 ; 6:11,21 ; 7:44).

[183] Cf. M. R. VINCENT, *Word Studies in the New Testament*, vol. II, p. 94 where he takes the use of the noun φωνήν as an indication of reference to the wind.

[184] Out of the 15 occurrences of φωνή only one (11:43) speaks of it referring to the voice of Christ in a physical sense.

[185] The only exception is 12:30 which refers to the celestial voice as mentioned in 12:28.

The phrase πόθεν ἔρχεται καὶ ποῦ ὑπάγει occurs apart from here only in Jn 8:14 speaking of Christ. It seems to refer to the nature of Christ, which cannot be understood by those who judge according to the flesh (cf. Jn 8:15). In the light of the Johannine dualistic concept of flesh and Spirit, it should be referring to the nature of Christ resulting from the Spirit, which belongs to a completely different order of being than that of flesh. As it refers to the origin of Christ (πόθεν), it seems that here the reference is to the nature of Christ resulting from His birth from (God) the Spirit, and hence to Christ as Son of God (ὁ γεννηθεὶς ἐκ πνεύματος: cf. Mat 1:20)[186]. So it is, in his own measure, of every child of God who is begotten of the Spirit. So it refers to the quality of the Spirit which is shared by the one who is begotten of the Spirit.

c. **The Unfathomable character of the Divine Begetting**

All the above considerations urge us to favour the symbolic interpretation of the text referring both to the wind and to the Spirit. The relation between the wind and the Spirit in Jn is not one of mere comparison. It is much more real and concrete as can be seen from Jn 20:22 where Christ is said to have breathed on the disciples to give them the Holy Spirit[187].

So here Jn speaks of the working of the Spirit in terms of the wind. Men cannot in themselves fathom the operation of the Spirit, who is perfectly free in his operations[188]. In the same way the one who is begotten of the Spirit, sharing the quality of the Spirit[189], shares the unfathomable character of the Spirit. The existence of

---

[186] As we have remarked elsewhere, the origin in Jn points to the nature of a person expressed in his works and deeds. The origin is decisive of character. And we saw how for Jn if εἶναι ἐκ and γεγεννῆσθαι ἐκ are used to denote the origin of the believers, ἐξέρχεσθαι ἐκ or εἶναι παρά are used to denote the origin of Christ. Note the special Johannine use of (ἐξ)έρχεσθαι ἐκ to express the temporal generation of Christ, as we explained elsewhere, on p. 125 which corresponds to the πόθεν ἔρχεται of 8:14.

[187] Cf. also Acts 2:2 where the Holy Spirit is said to have manifested himself in the rush of a mighty wind. Cf. O. CULLMANN, art. " Der johanneische Gebrauch ...", in ThZ 4 (1948), p. 364.

[188] Here it is to be noted that this freedom is not in opposition to the working of the Spirit through definite elements such as the Word of God. It expresses only the unfathomable character as explained in the subsequent phrase; cf. H. SCHLIER, " Zum Begriff des Geistes nach dem Johannes evangelium ", Besinnung auf das Neue Testament, Herder, 1964, p. 270, note 21.

[189] Cf. Jn 3:6 " He who is begotten of the Spirit is Spirit ", which shows that there is a community of nature resulting from birth.

him who is begotten of the Spirit is a reality, though mysterious. The nature itself of this state of being begotten by the Spirit cannot be perceived by men except in its effects. One can see those who are begotten from above through the Spirit, those who have believed in Jesus and lives the life of faith, without seeing just when or how this Spirit begets them, and without knowing why one is begotten and the other is not [190].

At this point Jn seems to make a transition to his manifold affirmations in the First Epistle regarding the criteria of having been begotten by God, namely, Justice and impeccability (I Jn 2:29 – 3:10), brotherly love (I Jn 4:7) and Faith (I Jn 5:1). These are the outward criteria, by means of which one comes to know who is begotten of God [191].

Nicodemus is asked not to wonder at the demand Christ is making about this new begetting. The fact that the nature of the begetting in itself is mysterious and not perceptible to the human mind, does not mean it is non-existent, and does not justify his scepticism regarding it. Θαυμάζειν in Jn always refers to a wonder that arises from not being able to understand something (cf. Jn 4:27; 5:20,28; 7:15,21; I Jn 3:13). Nicodemus is in the same situation. And Jesus warns him not to wonder in face of the mysterious character of the working of this begetting by the Spirit and he calls for faith in His words.

E. *The Kingdom of God and the Divine Sonship of Men* (Jn 3:3,5,15)

1. *See (enter) the Kingdom of God* (Jn 3:3,5)

The result of the new begetting is described by Jn as 'seeing' and 'entering' the Kingdom of God. In Jn the phrase 'Kingdom of God' occurs only in this dialogue, while it is frequently employed by the Synoptics, often in the form 'Kingdom of heaven' [192]. As to

---

[190] The reference is not to the one who is begotten of the Spirit confronting the working of the Spirit in himself, as some say (cf. TH. ZAHN, *Das Evangelium*, ad loc.; R. SUMMERS, "Born of Water and Spirit", pp. 126-127), but to others confronting the working of the Spirit in the one who is begotten of the Spirit (cf. LAGRANGE, *Évangile*, p. 77). Note v. 7 warning others (represented by Nicodemus) of the marvel of the working of the Spirit.

[191] Note the perfect tense of γεγεννημένος(ν) that is used here, which is constantly used in the Epistle. Here it is to be observed that E. SCHWEIZER is not perfectly right when he says that "the being born of the Spirit is unobservable whether in its activity or its appearance (cf. art. πνεῦμα, TWNT VI, p. 439).

[192] Codex Bezae and some other Western witnesses such as 245, 472, 0141 e Justin, Ireneus, Tertullian and Eusebius and also the critical edition of

the meaning of the phrase here, we have different interpretations among critics.

a. Different Explanations

Some understand it in the same sense as that in the Synoptics, namely, as referring to the eschatological salvation, that is actualized in the realization of the Kingship and power of God [193]. In this interpretation, ἰδεῖν of v. 3 and εἰσελθεῖν of v. 5 are taken as synonyms. This idea of the Kingdom of God is considered more specifically by others as the Church, the type of the future universal reign of Christ [194], or as the heavenly realm on high, to which the divine envoy leads us [195].

Others give a Christological interpretation, connecting the Kingdom of God immediately with the person of Christ [196]. This is supported by the Ancient Ecclesiastical Writers such as Chrysostom [197], Theophylactus [198], Euthymius [199], Cyril of Alexandria [200], J. Scotus Erigena [201], Glossa Ordinaria [202] and Glossa Interlinearis [203]. Certain expressions of these writers are very interesting in this respect. Chrysostom explains the phrase in Jn 3:3 as " ... you cannot arrive at a right opinion about me unless ...". Cyril of Alexandria identifies 'to see the Kingdom' with 'believe' (τὸ πιστεύειν). J. Scotus Erigena explains it as 'to know the truth' (hoc est veritatem cognoscere). Theophylactus and Glossa Ordinaria connect it with the sonship of Christ and Christians [204].

Tischendorf read 'Kingdom of Heaven' in v. 5. Lagrange accepts this reading on the ground that 'God' is a harmonization with v. 3 (cf. *Évangile*, p. 76). But for Bultmann it is a remodelling of the verse imitating Mt 18:3 (cf. *Evangelium*, p. 98, note 1).

[193] Cf. LAGRANGE, *Évangile*, pp. 74-76; BERNARD, *St. John*, I, pp. 101-102; BULTMANN, *Evangelium*, p. 95, note 3; BARRETT, *Gospel*, p. 173.

[194] Cf. WESTCOTT, *Gospel*, p. 49.

[195] Cf. R. SCHNACKENBURG, *Gospel*, pp. 366-367.

[196] Cf. L. BOUYER, *Le quatrième évangile - Introduction et commentaire*, Tournai, 1955 (2nd ed.), pp. 90-91; H. VAN DEN BUSSCHE, *Jean*, pp. 162-163; C. Traets, op. cit., pp. 128-130.

[197] Cf. PG 59, 146.

[198] Cf. PG 123, 1203.

[199] Cf. PG 129, 1159.

[200] Cf. PG 73, 241.

[201] Cf. PL 122, 315.

[202] Cf. PL 114, 366.

[203] Cf. Biblia Sacra cum Glossa Ordinaria, Antwerpen, 1617, cols. 1061-1062.

[204] THEOPHYLACTUS says that, as the Son is the wisdom of God, so He is

b. The Kingdom of God and the Person of Christ

It is true that the term in itself indicates the eschatological salvation realized by God exercising His sovereignty [205]. But it seems that in Jn it is strictly connected with the Person of Christ, almost bordering on an identification.

This is not absolutely foreign to the Synoptics. The 'seeing the Kingdom' in Mk 9:1 and Lk 9:27 is transferred by Mt 16:28 to 'seeing the Son of Man coming with His Kingdom'. Mt 19:29 with Mk 10:29 and Lk 18:29 puts Christ and the Kingdom of God as parallel [206]. The same parallelism is found also in Mk 11:10 and Lk 19:38. In the Acts of the Apostles too the Kingdom of God and the Person of Jesus are linked [207]. It is in the Person of Christ that the Kingdom of God is realized, initially during his public ministry, and decisively in his saving work as it moves towards its consummation [208]. This realization of the Kingdom of God in the Person of Christ is indicated by the fact that the miracles worked by Christ are signs that the Kingdom has come [209].

The very Johannine use of the phrase favours this interpretation and seems to speak in a more specifically Christological sense than the Synoptics. The Only other place in Jn where the term βασιλεία occurs is Jn 18:36-37. Here the Kingdom and Kingship of Christ [210] are parallel to his 'coming into the world to witness to the truth', and he affirms the necessity of being 'of the truth', to hear his

---

said to be also the Kingdom of God (cf. PG 123, 1204). Glossa Ordinaria says: "Ideo incoepit eum (Nicodemum) instruere Jesus de secunda regeneratione, qua intelligit eum Filium Dei, et se posse Filium Dei fieri" (PL 114, 366).

[205] Cf. K. L. SCHMIDT, art. βασιλεία, *TDNT* I, 581-592; R. SCHNACKENBURG, *Gottesherrschaft und Reich*, Freiburg, 1959.

[206] "And everyone who has left for my name's sake (Mt 19:29), for my sake (Mk 10:29), for the sake of the Kingdom of God" (Lk 18:29).

[207] Cf. also Apoc 12:10 where it is said: "Now the salvation and the power and the Kingdom of our God and the authority of His Christ has come ...".

[208] Cf. R. SCHNACKENBURG, *Gottesherrschaft ...*, pp. 79-148.

[209] Cf. Mt 12:28 = Lk 11:20: "If it is by the Spirit of God that I cast out the devils, then the Kingdom of God has come upon you". Cf. also Mt 4:23; 9:35; 10:7-8 = Lk 9:2-11; 10:9 where the miracles of Christ are connected with the Kingdom of God. Cf. A. RICHARDSON, *Introduction to the Theology of the New Testament*, London, 1966, pp. 95-100.

[210] Though the terminology is different, 'Kingdom of God' and 'Kingdom of Christ' are identical. Cf. K. SCHMIDT, art. cit., pp. 581-582.

voice. In other words he affirms the realization of his Kingship, in the measure in which one lives a life of faith in Him [211].

The same idea is indicated also by the context of Jn 3:3 in which vv. 2-3 form a concentric unity.

Note the following structure:

V. 2   a   We *know* (οἴδαμεν) that you ... come from GOD, for
      b   None CAN do these things that you do
      c   UNLESS God is with him ... Jesus ...
  3   c'   UNLESS one is begotten *from above*
      b'   HE CANNOT
      a'   *See* (ἰδεῖν) the Kingdom of GOD.

As we can see from the above structure, in this unity, " we know that you are a teacher come from God " (a) is parallel to " see the Kingdom of God " (a').

A further proof is provided by the parallelism between the ' kingdom of God ' and ' Life ', ideas identified already by the Synoptics [212]. The same parallelism is found between Jn 3:3 and 3:36 (See the Kingdom of God', and ' See the Life '), and in 3:36 the ' seeing Life ' is immediately connected with faith in the Son [213].

Here it is worth noting that out of the many references to the Kingdom of God in the Synoptics only one text speaks of ' seeing the Kingdom of God ' (cf. Mk 9:1 = Lk 9:27), and this is in Mt 16:28 explicitly referring to ' seeing the Son of Man coming in his Kingdom '. So in Jn, in whom the verb ' seeing ' has a much more theological sense than in the Synoptics, one connected with faith [214], the formula ' to see the Kingdom of God ' is to be taken in a specifically Christological sense. Hence the ἰδεῖν of v. 3, which resumes and perfects the θεωροῦντες of 2:23 and the οἴδαμεν of 3:2, seems to refer to a deep vision of faith in Jesus.

---

[211] Cf. M. DE JONGHE, " Jewish Expectations about ' Messiah ' according to the Fourth Gospel ", NTS 19 (1973), pp. 246-270.

[212] Cf. Mk 9:43,45 where ζωή is used while in v. 46 βασιλεία τοῦ Θεοῦ is used parallely referring to the same for which Mt 18:9 retains the ζωή. Cf. also Mk 10:17,23 and parallels Mt 19:16,23 and Lk 18:18,24 where both ζωή and βασιλεία τοῦ Θεοῦ are used interchangeably.

[213] Note I Jn 5:12 where " to have life ' is ' to have the Son '.

[214] Cf. O. CULLMANN, " Εἶδεν καὶ ἐπίστευσεν. La vie de Jesus, objet de la ' vue ' et de la ' foi ' d'après le quatrième évangile ", in Aux sources de la tradition chrétienne. Mél. M. Goguel, Neuchâtel, 1950, pp. 52-61 ; Cf. G. L. PHILIPS, *Faith and Vision in the Fourth Gospel*, London, 1957, pp. 83-96.

c. Seeing and Entering

Most of the Exegetes consider ἰδεῖν of v. 3 and εἰσελθεῖν of v. 5 as synonyms [215]. It is also to be remarked that the majority of the Ancient writers make a similar identification, so that they did not even trouble to explain the phrase in v. 5, having spoken of it in v. 3. Only a few distinguish between the two phrases and see in ἰδεῖν an outward apprehension of the Kingdom, and in εἰσελθεῖν a real participation in (becoming a citizen of) it [216].

Though we cannot speak of a substantial difference between ἰδεῖν and εἰσελθεῖν in this case [217], the two different words used point nevertheless to some kind of specification. If ἰδεῖν brings out more clearly the relationship of the Kingdom to the revelation brought by Christ, revelation that has to be seen, accepted and believed, and so emphasizes the aspect of faith, εἰσελθεῖν expresses the concept of experience or participation in that which is brought by Christ, and so it emphasizes more the aspect of communion. The ἰδεῖν necessarily leads to εἰσελθεῖν and the εἰσελθεῖν necessarily implies ἰδεῖν. So both are inseparably united, but at the same time they give emphasis to one and the other aspect of the substantially same event.

This is quite consistent with the Johannine doctrine that those who believe in Christ also participate in that which is Christ. It is the same doctrine that we saw in Jn 1:12-13, where those who believe in Christ, who are begotten by God, also participate in His divine begetting — divine sonship. This description of Jesus as the means and the end, as the object of faith through which one arrives at communion, is illustrated also in the parables of the Good Shepherd, where he is not only the door, but also the fold; not only the 'Way' but also the 'Life' (cf. Jn 10:7-9; 14:6) [218]. So to 'enter into the Kingdom of God' means for Jn to enter into communion with Christ.

---

[215] Cf. BERNARD, *St. John* I, pp. 102-103; BULTMANN, *Evangelium*, p. 95; BARRETT, *Gospel*, p. 173; J. DUPONT, *Essais sur la christologie de saint Jean*, Bruges, 1951, p. 167.

[216] Cf. WESTCOTT, *Gospel*, pp. 48-49; HOSKYNS, *Gospel*, p. 203; cf. also C. TRAETS, op. cit., p. 129 where he is more inclined to this opinion.

[217] Note that the condition for both is the same — birth from above (the Spirit), and in other contexts where John uses the verb ἰδεῖν as in 3:36; 8:51 etc, it has really a sense of experiencing or participating in.

[218] Cf. I. DE LA POTTERIE, *Je suis la voie, la verité et la vie*, (Jn 14:6), Rome, 1966, p. 14; cf. also BULTMANN, *Evangelium*, p. 466; H. SCHLIER, "Meditationen über den johanneischen Begriff der Wahrheit", in *Besinnung auf das Neue Testament*, Freiburg, 1964, p. 274.

2. *"... have eternal Life in Him"* (Jn 3:15)

This Christological interpretation of 'seeing' and 'entering' the Kingdom of God is favoured by the subsequent vv. 11-21, which form the third section of the passage, and which gives the content of the life of authentic faith, announced in these two phrases of vv. 3 and 5 [219]. One is led to this authentic faith through the supernatural birth described in vv. 3-10. A look at the thematic structure of the section would be enlightening.

a. The Structure of the Section Jn 3:11-21

V.			
11	A	Amen ... WE SPEAK ... BEAR WITNESS ... You DO NOT RECEIVE ..
12	B	If ... you DO NOT BELIEVE, how YOU BELIEVE ...
13	C	No one has ... he who descended from heaven SON OF man
14	D	And ... Moses ... so must the SON of Man be lifted up
15	E	That WHOEVER BELIEVE MAY HAVE ETERNAL LIFE IN HIM.
16	D'	For God ... gave his only SON that ... may have ... life
17	C'	For God sent the SON into ... world ... might ... him
18	B'	He who BELIEVES is not ... he who DOES NOT BELIEVE ...
19-21	A'	This ... the Light has come ... men ... does not come to ... Light ...

The importance of faith in this section is clear from the frequent occurrence of the verb 'πιστεύειν' [220] and also from the fact that the theme of faith forms a framework for the section [221]. The whole passage is built up with the three basic themes of John:

(1) The salvific revelation in Jesus Christ (ACDD'C'A);
(2) The response to it on the part of man (ABB'A') and
(3) The result of the positive response (E, taken up again in D').

---

[219] Cf. C. TRAETS, op. cit., p. 128. Cf. also what we said above on the general structure of the whole section on pp. 163-164.

[220] The verb πιστεύειν occurs 7 times, while the equivalent expressions λαμβάνετε μαρτυρίαν occurs once and ἔρχεται πρὸς τὸ φῶς occurs two times.

[221] Cf. AB and B'A' which begin and conclude the section.

As it can be seen from the structure, these themes occur in a repetitive and parallel manner and at the same time moving towards the central statement about the result of the positive response to Christ, namely, the eternal Life in Christ (E = v. 15) [222]. Thus we have here the unfolding of the theme announced in Jn 3:3,5 ' seeing and entering the Kingdom of God ' [223].

The structure of the passage reminds us of the different stresses, we noted in the use of ἰδεῖν and εἰσελθεῖν in vv. 3 and 5. If ἰδεῖν corresponds to the beginning and concluding parts of this section, emphasizing the revelatory aspect, εἰσελθεῖν corresponds to the central part emphasizing the aspect of communion in the life of faith, though both go together and are complementary. This progress towards the centre is indicated also by the use of πιστεύειν, which in the introductory part (vv. 11-13) is used absolutely, while in the central part (vv. 14-18) it is used with εἰς and the accusative pointing towards that life of faith which is the newly begotten life of the children of God, which is called also eternal life [224].

b. The Kingdom of God and Eternal Life

The parallelism between the Kingdom of God and Divine Sonship is all the more impressive when we see that in Jn 3:11-21 the idea of ' entering into the Kingdom of God ' is expressed in terms of ' having eternal life in him ' (Jn 3:15), and it is precisely the result of a begetting. The notion of a ' begetting ' essentially implies the communication of life from the parent to its child. The same, though in an analogous manner, must be said to happen with regard to the divine begetting of the children of God. So ' having eternal life ' parallel to ' participation in the Kingdom of God ' as a result of the divine begetting (by the Spirit) certainly puts the ' Kingdom of God ' and ' Divine sonship ' on the same footing.

The word ζωή is truly peculiar to Johannine vocabulary [225]. The

---

[222] For other indications for a concentric structure of Jn 3:11-21, cf. G. GAETA, op. cit., pp. 99-105.

[223] Note v. 15 the central statement, where this aspect of communion is expressed in the ἐν αὐτῷ ἔχῃ ζωὴν αἰώνιον. The best attested reading is ἐν αὐτῷ (B, p. 75 etc.) and not εἰς αὐτον attested by some Mss, and this ἐν αὐτῷ should go with the following, because πιστεύειν ἐν αὐτῷ would be strange in Jn.

[224] Cf. A. JAUBERT, " ' Croire ' dans l'Evangile de Jean ", Vie Spir 118 (1968), p. 146 : " ... ' Croire ' se charactérise non par l'adhésion à des concepts, mais par la réalité de la nouvelle naissance en Dieu ".

[225] In the Gospel it occurs 36 times, while in the three Synoptics only 16 times in all, and in I Jn it is met with 13 times. The verb ζάω occurs 17

very fact that the aim of the Johannine Gospel and Epistle is expressed as 'to have life' (Jn 20:31) and 'to know of having the eternal life' (I Jn 5:13), shows that the word ζωή gives by itself a synthesis of the whole Johannine theology.

c. Eternal Life — Life of the Children of God

Unlike the other NT Writers, who make use of ζωή to signify the natural life of man (cf. for example, Lk 12:15 ; 16:25), Jn makes use of ζωή always and only to refer to the spiritual and moral order[226]. In Jn it is often accompanied by the adjective αἰώνιος which usually refers to the future and thus would seem to refer to the eternal beatitude of after life [227], and is something that will be possessed only in the world to come (cf. Mt 19:29 ; Mk 10:30 ; Lk 18:30). Actually some scholars do not hesitate to see the same eschatological concept of 'Life' in Jn [228]. But a comparison of the Johannine passages speaking of 'Life' shows that Jn uses both forms interchangeably (cf. Jn 3:36 ; 5:24,39f ; 6:53f, 57f ; I Jn 5:12f etc.). The original idea of duration and futurity expressed by αἰώνιος have become in Johannine usage only one element, and that not the primary element in its significance [229].

In the First Epistle and generally also in the Gospel there is no passage where 'Life' with or without the adjective 'eternal' does not primarily signify a present state rather than a future immortal bliss [230], though the latter is always implicitly included. So 'Life' is regarded in Jn as a present reality [231]. The adjective 'eternal' is added even when the reference to its present possession is most em-

---

times in the Gospel and once in I Jn, while ζωοποιέω occurs 3 times in the Gospel.

[226] Out of the 56 passages speaking of life, only 3 restrict the sense to a purely human existence (cf. Jn 4:50,51,53), and all these three cases use the verb ζάω and not the noun. Whenever John speaks of life in the physical sense, he makes use of ψυχή (cf. Jn 10:11,15,17,24 ; 12:25,27 ; 13:37ff ; 15:13 ; I Jn 3:16).

[227] It is in this sense that the Synoptics usually understand it, according to whom, life everlasting denotes mostly the final phase of the Kingdom of God (comp. Mt 5:20 ; 7:21 with Mt 18:8,9 ; 19:17 and Mt 25:34 with 25:46).

[228] This equivalent use of 'life' and 'eternal life' once more confirms the spiritual and divine character of this life. Cf. N. LAZURE, op. cit., p. 259.

[229] Cf. R. LAW, *Tests of Life*, Edinburgh 1909, p. 189.

[230] I Jn 2:25 may be the only exception to this rule, which just means that the concept of duration and futurity is not completely absent in the Johannine usage.

[231] Note the verb ἔχειν and the verb δίδωμι in the present tense accompanying ζωή (cf. Jn 3:15,16,36 ; 5:24,40 ; 6:40,47 etc.).

phatic [232]. This present possession of 'eternal Life' is still sharply marked by the use of the perfect tense, speaking of our having been already transferred from death to life in I Jn 3:14. So it is a 'Life' that is present and continues into eternity [233].

The emphasis in the adjective 'eternal' is on 'quality' and not on 'duration' [234]. 'Eternal Life' is one kind of 'Life', the divine kind of Life, irrespective of its duration. But it is impossible to conceive of a divine Life which is liable to interruption. So it is a kind of Life similar to that of God, the Father, already possessed by the believers [235], who are His children.

d. Member of the Kingdom — A Child of God

In the light of the above considerations, we are confronted with a quasi-identification of the 'life of divine sonship' and 'membership in the Kingdom of God'.

i. The Synoptic Teaching on the Matter

We find the Synoptics already bordering on a kind of identification between the 'members of the Kingdom' and the 'sons of God' [236]. Mt's Gospel which is preeminently the Gospel of the Kingdom, seems to give special emphasis to it. The only two texts in Mt that speak explicitly of the divine sonship of men (Mt 5:9,45), come in the section Mt 5-7, known as the 'charter of the Kingdom of heaven'.

The divine sonship in Mt 5:9, is one of the eight beatitudes, which begin and end with the promise of the Kingdom of heaven.

---

[232] Cf. I Jn 3:15: "You know that no murderer hath eternal life abiding in him".

[233] Cf. J. SLIPYJ, *Die Auffassung des Lebens nach dem Evangelium und I Briefe des Hl. Johannes*, Rom, 1965, pp. 45-53 where he analyses the relevant texts and concludes: "Dass Johannes mit ζωή αἰώνιος das übernatürliches Leben im diesseits bezeichnet, das in die Ewigkeit fortdauert".

[234] Cf. SCHNACKENBURG, *Gospel*, p. 389; on the significance of the attribute, cf. H. SASSE, art. αἰώνιος, *TDNT* I, p. 208ff; F. MUSSNER, op. cit., pp. 177ff.

[235] We do not discuss here the complex question regarding the origin of the concept of life in Jn, which many attribute to Hellenistic influence (cf. J. LINDBLOM, *Das ewige Leben, Eine Studie über die Entstehung der religiösen Lebensidee im Neuen Testament*, Uppsala-Leipzig 1914; C. H. DODD, *The Interpretation of the Fourth Gospel*, pp. 144-150). We limit ourselves to say that, whatever be the soil that favoured the growth of the Johannine concept of Life, it is deeply rooted in the teaching of Jesus regarding the realization of the Kingdom of God in His person (cf. A. FEUILLET, "La participation ..." *StEv*, TU 73 (Berlin 1959), pp. 295-308).

[236] Cf. our treatise on the divine sonship of Christians in the Synoptic Gospels, on pp. 53-68.

This promise of the kingdom of heaven, forming an inclusion to all the beatitudes, shows that they are all a living description of the Kingdom of heaven [237]. So the 'divine sonship' in Mt 5:9 seems to be identified with 'membership in the Kingdom of heaven'.

ii. Development of the Doctrine

Certainly the Kingdom, as preached by Jesus is primarily an inward experience of living under the rule of God who is the Father [238]. Phrases like " It is the Father's good pleasure to give you the Kingdom ", " in my Father's Kingdom ", " our Father ... Thy Kingdom come " are of the essence of Christ's teaching [239]. So the ideal life in the Kingdom is that of subject-sonship, obedient trust and trustful obedience to the rule of the Father — to the revealed Will of the Father [240], and this experience of 'membership in the Kingdom' is described as 'Life' and 'salvation' [241].

But in fact men, being neither obedient nor trustful, had become 'lost', deliberately spurning the Father's love, so that Jesus' task was to call sinners back to repentance, to seek and to save those who were lost. This being the universal situation, the way of entrance into 'subject-sonship' in the Kingdom could only be by a radical change of attitude towards God the Father. Thus the call to 'repentance' and 'faith' is addressed to all men as the terms upon which alone they may exchange their state of being 'lost' for that of 'Life' and 'salvation', namely, for subject-sonship in the Kingdom of their Father.

In so describing the steps by which men may enter upon 'subject-sonship' in the Father's Kingdom, Jesus makes use of the metaphor of a 'child', which became important in later baptismal doctrine (cf. Mt 18:1-4; Mk 10:14f; Lk 18:17), and this child-figure provides an easy link with the Fourth Gospel's association of the 'New Begetting' with 'Baptism', and thus with the doctrine of Baptismal regeneration [242].

---

[237] Cf. Th. ZAHN, *Das Evangelium des Matthäus*, Leipzig 1922, p. 194. For the identification of the 'Kingdom of Heaven' and the 'Kingdom of God', cf. J. F. WALVOORD, " The Kingdom of Heaven ", *BS* 124 (1967), pp. 195-205.

[238] Cf. T. W. MANSON, *The Teaching of Jesus*, Cambridge 1931, pp. 134-135; H. W. ROBINSON, *The Christian Doctrine of Man*, New York 1911, pp. 66, 83ff.

[239] Cf. H. W. ROBINSON, *Christian Doctrine of Man*, pp. 78ff.

[240] For 'doing the divine will' as essential to membership in the Kingdom, cf. Mt 7:21; 21:28-32; 12:46ff; Mk 3:31ff; Lk 8:19.

[241] For this experience as 'Life', cf. Mt 7:14; 18:8; 19:16,29; 25:46; Lk 10:25, and as 'salvation' cf. Mt 10:22; Lk 7:50; 19:9.

[242] Cf. R. E. O. WHITE, *The Biblical Doctrine of Initiation*, London, 1960,

Thus we see the evolution of the two concepts of the 'Kingdom of God' and 'divine sonship' side by side, until they reach in Jn their culmination, where entrance into the 'subject-sonship' in the Kingdom of God the Father takes place properly through a 'begetting by God' (Spirit) (cf. Jn 3:3,5) [243]. So the Johannine identification of the 'divine sonship' and 'membership in the Kingdom' is not a completely new phenomenon, but the result of a homogeneous and progressive development of the Teaching of Jesus.

iii. The Johannine Teaching

According to Jn 3:11-21 the Kingdom of God is realized in Christ as Son of God [244]. Apart from the Prologue, this passage is the only Gospel text in which Jn uses the term μονογενής. Here it occurs twice, and in v. 18 it occurs in the typical Johannine formula πιστεύειν εἰς τὸ ὄνομα τοῦ μονογενοῦς υἱοῦ τοῦ Θεοῦ. Thus imperfect faith expressed with a similar formula in 2:23, passing through the supernatural begetting described in 3:3-10, is transformed into authentic faith expressed in 3:18. So with faith in Christ as the only Begotten Son of God, one sees the Kingdom of God realized (v. 3) and enters into it (v. 5). So entering into the Kingdom of God means for Jn entering into a life of faith in, and communion with, Christ who is the Son of God, namely, to become children of God participating in His sonship.

The only other place where the formula πιστεύειν εἰς τὸ ὄνομά τινος occurs, apart from this section, is in the Prologue, and there the object of faith is Christ in His quality of being Begotten by God (cf. Jn 1:12-13). There the result is 'becoming children of God'. This reinforces the parallelism in Jn between 'becoming children of God' and 'entering upon a Life of faith in the Son of God', which is for Jn 'entering the Kingdom of God'. Thus by entering the Kingdom of God, men become children of God. In other words, it is the children of God who are members of the Kingdom.

---

pp. 114-115. Cf. also what we said about the Johannine faith that takes the place of the Synoptic 'conversion' on pp. 176-177.

[243] Note how the vestiges of the Synoptic description of membership in the Kingdom as 'Life' and 'salvation' in opposition to the 'being lost' reappear in the very context where John speaks of this begetting into the Kingdom of God (Jn 3:15-18).

[244] Note how in the 5 verses (vv. 13-18), the word υἱός occurs 5 times, and nowhere else in the whole section 2:23 – 3:21.

III. The Divine Sonship of the Believers through the Death of Christ (Jn 11:52)

The manifestation of the Life of God in Christ was consummated in his death on the cross, which is the supreme revelation of God who is Love (I Jn 4:8,16), and which channels the divine Life to man [245]. This is indicated in Jn 3:14-15, where the 'lifting up of the Son of Man' is said to lead those who believe to Life eternal [246]. This imparting of divine Life to men putting them in a filial relationship with God, through Christ's death on the cross, seems to be implied in the declaration of Jn 11:52, where the death of Christ is said to 'gather together the dispersed children of God into one'.

A. *History of the Exegesis*

In the course of the history of exegesis the identity of these τὰ τέκνα τοῦ Θεοῦ has been the object of discussion among scholars. The great majority of scholars, ancient and modern, identify them with the Gentiles, namely, all those who are outside the Jewish people [247]. Origen sees in the expression the Jews of the dispersion [248], while for Cyril of Alexandria, the 'children of God' are all men created by God, but scattered through original sin [249].

---

[245] It is worth noting here how John defines God in I Jn 4:8 as Love and goes on describing the manifestation of this love in sending His only Begotten Son (v. 9).

[246] Note that all three times that Christ predicts his death on the cross, he expresses it by the verb ὑψωθῆναι. Cf. A. VERGOTE, "L'exaltation du Christ en Croix", *ETL* 28 (1952), pp. 6-7. It is quite natural that this communication of life takes place through the expiatory death on the cross, because the sin is considered by John as death (I Jn 3:14-15) and as the great obstacle to Life (cf. J. LINDBLOM, op. cit., p. 222; J. SLIPYJ, op. cit., p. 29). Note the opposition between sin and life in I Jn 4:9-10. Cf. also I Jn 1:7; 2:2; Jn 1:29 where this aspect of the revelation of Christ is stressed.

[247] Cf. CHRYSOSTOM, PG 59, 361; THEOPHYLACTUS, PG 124, 109; NONNUS PANOPOLITANUS, PG 43, 848; AMMONIUS ALEXANDRINUS, PG 85, 1472; EUTHYMIUS, PG 129, 1353; AUGUSTINE, PL 35, 1758; B. ALCUINUS, PL 100, 904; BEDE THE VENERABLE, PL 92, 782; RUPERTUS ABBATUS, PL 169, 646-647; GLOSSA ORDINARIA, PL 114, 401; St. THOMAS, *In Jo Lectura*, p. 295; MALDONATUS, *Commentarius* II, pp. 777-778; Among the modern authors, cf. the Commentaries of Schanz, Knabenbauer, Loisy, Calmes, Bauer, Zahn, Lagrange, Schlatter, Lightfoot, Brown, Van den Bussche etc.

[248] Cf. GCS 28, 184-185.

[249] Cf. PG 74, 69; among the modern authors, cf. WESTCOTT, *Gospel*, p. 175.

The interpretation that would identify the 'children of God' with the Gentiles, shows Jn transferring the OT theme of the 'scattered children of God', the dispersed Jews, to the Gentiles [250]. This is quite possible, as it is conformable to the Johannine method of replacing Jewish institutions and notions with those that are Christian. But in this matter it does not seem compatible with the Evangelist's outlook. John makes it clear that men become children of God solely through faith in Christ (Jn 1:12-13) and birth from Water and Spirit (Jn 3:3,5), whether they be Jews or Gentiles. So an interpretation that limits the concept of the 'children of God' to the Gentiles is foreign to Jn [251].

The interpretation that identifies the children of God with all men created in the image of God, may go well with the Stoic belief in a σπερματικὸς λόγος, which is believed by some to underlie John's thought. But this also would be a concept that is strange to the Johannine notion of the 'children of God' [252].

It would seem then that the 'children of God' should be all those who believe in Christ. In fact those who limit the term 'children of God' as used here to the Gentiles, see in it those Gentiles who are to believe in Christ. Thus they speak of 'gathering into one flock and one faith' (εἰς ἕν ποίμνιον, εἰς μίαν πίστιν) [253], of 'gathering the faithful from the Gentiles' (τοὺς πιστοὺς ... τοὺς ἐξ ἐθνῶν) etc. [254]. But how could John call those, who had not yet believed, 'children of God'? The question has intrigued Commentators from the beginning, and almost all of them speak of calling τέκνα Θεοῦ here by way of anticipation [255] or predestination [256].

B. *A Prophecy after the Event*

An absolute anticipation or predestination is not necessary here when we consider that the hand of the Evangelist is working behind

---

[250] Note that this theme runs all through the OT. Cf. Dt 30:1-3; Is 43: 5; 60:4; Jer 23:1-3; Ez 20:34; 34:11-13; 37:21ff. Note specially Jer 31:8-11 where the gathering of the dispersed Jews is associated with the Fatherhood of God.

[251] Cf. J. L. D'ARAGON, " La notion johannique de l'unité ", ScE 11 (1959), pp. 115-116, note 8.

[252] Cf. BARRETT, *Gospel*, p. 340.

[253] Cf. EUTHYMIUS, PG 129, 1353.

[254] Cf. AMMONIUS ALEX., PG 85, 1471.

[255] Cf. for example THEOPHYLACTUS, PG 124, 109; EUTHYMIUS, PG 129, 1353.

[256] Cf. for example St. AUGUSTINE, PL 35, 1758; BEDE THE VENERABLE, PL 92, 782; B. ALCUINUS, PL 100, 904; GLOSSA ORDINARIA, PL 114, 401; CORNELIUS A LAPIDE, *Commentarius*. p. 291; BARRETT, Gospel, p. 340 etc.

this section, and that he is writing in the light of his experience of the early missionary activity of the Church, which taught him that there are men from all nations, both Jewish and Gentile, among the believers who are children of God. Whether the section is completely of Johannine creation [257], or of Johannine rehandling of the material that goes back to early Jewish Christianity [258], the Johannine character of the section is evident from the vocabulary such as ποιεῖν σημεῖα [259], πιστεύειν εἰς [260], ἀφ' ἑαυτοῦ [261], and the peculiar constructions with ὅτι (v. 47), ὧν (v. 49), τοῦτο δὲ εἶπεν (v. 51), οὐκ ... ἀλλά (vv. 51 and 52), ἀλλ' ἵνα (v. 52) etc.[262]. Besides, the verse speaking of the children of God is part of the Evangelist's reinterpretation of the High Priest's saying. So it seems to be a prophecy after the event.

C. *Imparting the Divine Sonship and 'gathering into one'*

Nevertheless we cannot deny some sort of anticipation, because he speaks of the ' children of God ', who are in a state of dispersion [263], and for Jn ' to be children of God ', and ' to be in the state of dispersion ', seems to be a contradiction in terms. For Jn ' to be children of God ', means to have been begotten to the divine life [264], and to participate in the divine life means for him to enter into communion with the Father and Son (Jn 17:21-23) [265]. For Jn there is no ' Life ' apart from union with the Father and the Son [266]. So

---

[257] Cf. J. TINEGAN, *Die Überlieferung der Leidens- und Auferstehungsgeschichte Jesu*, in BZNW 15 (1934), p. 40f; BULTMANN, *Evangelium*, p. 313, note 2.

[258] Cf. C. H. DODD, " The Prophecy of Caiaphas, John XI, 47-53 ", in *Neotest. et Patr.* (Supplement to Novum Testamentum VI), Leiden 1962, pp. 134-143; cf. also M. GOGUEL, *Introduction au Nouveau Testament*, Paris 1923, II, pp. 403ff.

[259] It occurs 14 times in Jn, while nowhere else in the Gospels.

[260] Cf. what we stated above on the concept of faith in John, where we saw the Johannine character of this formula on pp. 143-145.

[261] It occurs 6 times in Jn and mostly with λέγειν, εἰπεῖν, λαλεῖν and once in Lk (12:57), while otherwise it is unknown in the NT.

[262] Cf. BULTMANN, *Evangelium*, p. 313, note 2.

[263] Note the perfect tense of διεσκορπισμένα which points to the actual state of being dispersed.

[264] Note the parallelism between the τέκνα Θεοῦ and ὁ γεγεννημένος ἐκ τοῦ Θεοῦ in the different contexts in John such as I Jn 2:29 – 3:2; 5:1-2.

[265] Note how I Jn 5:13 speaking of ' having eternal life ' forms an inclusion with I Jn 1:3 speaking of communion with the Father and the Son together with all the believers.

[266] Note how Jn 17 which contains the clearest and most important texts on the Johannine concept of unity speaks of it as a unity of mutual knowledge, love and indwelling (Jn 17:21-26), and life is said to consist in this

the 'gathering together into one' mentioned here, should point to this unity, that results from becoming children of God, participating in the same divine life. Out of the seven texts speaking of this unity in Jn, making use of the neuter singular ἕν [267], only two are accompanied by the preposition εἰς, namely, 11:52 and 17:23. And as we saw above, the unity in 17:23 goes with the possession of eternal life. So the very fact of becoming 'children of God', results in the unity mentioned in 11:52 [268].

This idea of unity is clear also from the fact that it is faith that brings men to this unity [269], and, as we saw above, for Jn it is faith that brings men to eternal life and divine sonship: It is worth noting that in Jn 10:16, which forms a parallel to our text, it is all those who hear the voice of the Shepherd that form one flock (μία ποίμνη), and not exclusively the Jewish nation which is of the fold (ἐκ τῆς αὐλῆς ταύτης) nor those who are not of the fold.

All the above considerations show that the 'children of God' here are all those who believe in Christ, whether Jew or Gentile, and they are made children of God as a result of the death of Christ. And it is because they are made children of God that they are gathered into one [270]. So John, though, he writes in the light of his present experience, presents it as a prophecy looking forward to the future; he links it with the death of Christ, that makes men 'children of God' and effects the unity contemplated by him in different contexts. This is confirmed by the structure and vocabulary of the section 11: 47-53.

1. *The Structure of Jn 11:47-53*

V. 47   A   The CHIEF PRIESTS ... *gathered* ... and SAID ...
   48   B   What ... for THIS MAN performs many signs
        C   If we let ... A l l   w i l l   b e l i e v e   i n   H i m
            and the Romans will ... DESTROY ... THE NATION

---

knowledge of the Father and the Son (17:3). For this concept of Unity, cf. J. L. D'ARAGON, art. cit., pp. 111-119.

[267] Cf. Jn 10:16,30; 11:52; 17:11,21,22,23.

[268] Some authors understood this unity in a merely local or national sense (cf. for example, MALDONATUS, *Commentarius*, pp. 777-778), which is certainly not Johannine.

[269] Cf. Jn 17:11,20-23 where it is those who believed or will come to believe, that are the participants of this unity. Cf. J. F. RANDALL, "The Theme of Unity in John 17:20-23", *ETL* 41 (1965), pp. 373-394, specially pp. 390-391.

[270] To postpone this 'gathering into one' to a more distant future than that of becoming children of God, as suggested by some authors (cf. for instance, BERNARD, *St. John* II, p. 406) does not seem to go well with the Johannine concept of Unity.

49 A'   One of them ... Caiaphas WHO WAS HIGH PRIEST THAT
                                              YEAR ... SAID
50 B'   It is expedient ... ONE MAN SHOULD DIE
   C'   for the people
        and that THE NATION should not PERISH
51 A²   He SAID ... BEING HIGH PRIEST THAT YEAR ...
   B²   That JESUS SHOULD DIE
52 C²   for THE NATION ... not for THE NATION only
        but that the Children of God may be
        gathered into one.
53 A³   From that day *They took counsel* how ... to kill him.

Here we have a parallel and repetitive structure giving three elements:
(1) The counsel of the chief priest(s) (AA'A²A³);
(2) The acts or the death of Jesus (BB'B²) [271] and
(3) The result of these acts or death of Jesus (CC'C²).

As we can see, the result is presented on two levels: one, on a broader level, expressed by the words 'all who believe' (πάντες) (C), 'the people' (λαός) (C') and 'the children of God' (τὰ τέκνα τοῦ Θεοῦ) (C²); and the other, on a restricted level of the Jewish nation expressed by the word 'the nation' (ἔθνος) (CC'C²). Thus in three progressive developments Jn describes the (action) death of Christ with its effect culminating in the affirmation of the 'gathering into one the scattered children of God' (the divine sonship of the believers).

To understand this parallel and progressive development in three stages, we have to examine the parallelism between πάντες, λαός and τὰ τέκνα τοῦ Θεοῦ in contradistinction to ἔθνος. It is not difficult to see the parallelism between πάντες πιστεύσουσιν εἰς αὐτόν and τὰ τέκνα τοῦ Θεοῦ ... συναγάγῃ εἰς ἕν [272]. But the parallelism of these with λαός in contradistinction to ἔθνος is much more difficult to understand, specially because here Jn resumes the very words of Caiaphas, substituting ἔθνος for λαός.

2. *Vocabulary*

In the History of exegesis the great majority of exegetes, ancient and modern, identify the two words λαός and ἔθνος applying both

---

[271] The paralleliam between B and B'B² is supported by the fact that the death and resurrectian of Jesus was the supreme sign towards which all his signs were tending.

[272] Here it is enough to recall what we said regarding the role of faith in the making of the children of God, and in the Johannine concept of Unity.

terms to the Jews. We find only Origen and Lightfoot, who try to make a distinction here, Origen applying λαός to the Jews and ἔθνος to the Gentiles [273], and Lightfoot applying ἔθνος to all men [274].

Even more recent commentaries have paid little attention to this. Bultmann and Barrett simply put ἔθνος and λαός as synonyms [275]. Some apply both terms to the Jews, but make a distinction that λαός applies to the theocratic people, whereas ἔθνος indicates the civil organization [276]. But even they do not explain why Jn passes from one term to the other.

An examination of the notion of these two terms in Jn and their use in this context, would lead us to a better identification of the ' children of God ', and of their ' gathering into one ' as mentioned here.

a. Λαός and Ἔθνος in the LXX

In the LXX ' λαός ' corresponds to the Hebrew word *'am* and is used mostly in the singular [277], and becomes a specific term for Israel, expressing their special and privileged position as the people of God. The continual recurrence of the phrase λαός Θεοῦ gives colour to the special use of the simple λαός for Israel. The decisive point that brings about this specific meaning in the LXX seems to be the fact that λαός usually does not mean people in the sense of a mere crowd or population as such, but in the sense of a people as a union [278], though in contradistinction to the governing body.

The relation expressed in ' Israel ' as the ' People of God ' is the Covenantal relation of reciprocal obligation, faithfulness and love. Speaking of the divine sonship of Israel, we saw how the Covenant relation, in which Israel becomes a people of God, results in a father-son relationship between Yahweh and Israel, which is explicitly ex-

---

[273] Cf. *Comm. in Jo*, GCS 28, 169-170.

[274] Cf. R. H. LIGHTFOOT, *St. John's Gospel. A Commentary with the Revised Version Texts*, London, 1956, p. 230 : " On Caiphas' lips the expressions 'the people ' and ' the whole nation ' will have carried the same meaning. But in the light of 11:51-52 the reader is meant to perceive that, while the reference in the ' people ' is to the chosen people, the Jews, ' the whole nation ' signifies ultimately all men ".

[275] Cf. BULTMANN, *Evangelium*, p. 313, note 10 ; BARRETT, *Gospel*, p. 339.

[276] Cf. SCHANZ, *Evangelium*, p. 423 ; WESTCOTT, *Gospel*, pp. 174-175.

[277] Out of the 2000 occurrences of the term, the plural occurs only some 140 times.

[278] Cf. Gen 34:22 where the Schechemites and the family of Jacob are to intermarry ὥστε εἶναι λαόν ἕνα. This use corresponds to the Heb. *'am* to the degree that *'am* was originally a term of relationship. Cf. H. STRATHMANN, art. λαός, *TWNT* IV, p. 33, note 16.

pressed in texts such as Dt 14:1-2 ; Is 63:8 ; 64:8 ; Hos 2:1 ; Mal 3: 17. This shows how the term λαός in biblical usage came to be intimately connected with the father-son relationship between God and man.

The term ἔθνος in LXX corresponds to the Hebrew Word *gôi* and becomes a technical word to describe all the individuals who do not belong to the chosen people. This differentiation of ἔθνος from λαός can be perceived in different contexts. Thus in Ex 33:13 ἔθνος is used for people in general, whereas λαός denotes the chosen people. In Dt 7:6 the LXX sharply distinguishes between ' ἔθνη ' = gentiles and ' λαός ' = the people of God [279]. So the LXX gives ἔθνος as a term indicating the people as opposed to λαός, which indicates the chosen people of God [280].

b. Λαός and Ἔθνος in the NT

The use of λαός in the NT is strongly conditioned by its use in the LXX. This is so true that λαός, even in its ordinary meaning, always refers to a group or crowd of Israelites [281]. In the technical sense, it is always used in reference to Israel [282]. The newness of the NT usage of λαός is that it identifies the Christian community as the ' λαός τοῦ Θεοῦ '. Thus in Rom 9:25-26 the writer applies to the Christians coming from the Gentiles, Hos : 1 : 10 and 2 : 25 speaking of ' my people '. In II Cor 6:14f he applies similarly Lev 26:16, speaking of the ' people of God ', to the Christians. Tit 2:14 goes further and applies λαός περιούσιος (Ex 19:5,23 ; Dt 7:6 ; 14:2) to the Christian community. This appropriation of the honorific title λαός τοῦ Θεοῦ by the Early Church is so characteristic that, in many texts, the ἔθνη are no longer the ' non-Jews ', but the ' Non-Christians ' [283]. This distinction is kept up also in Acts 15:14 and 18:10 taking λαός for the Christian community, but without excluding Israel, or questioning the status of Israel as ' people of God ' [284]. The interpretation of Strathmann [285] and Dupont [286] to the exclusion of Israel

---

[279] Cf. also Ex 34:24 ; Lev 18:24 ; 25:44 ; Num 14:15 ; Dt 4:27 etc., where ἔθνη is used about the nations that are inimical to Israel.

[280] G. BERTRAM, art. λαός, *TDNT* II, pp. 364-369.

[281] Cf. H. STRATHMANN, art. λαός, *TDNT* IV, p. 52.

[282] Cf. Lk 1:68,77 ; 2:10,32 ; 7:16 ; 24:19 ; Mt 1:21 ; 2:6 ; 13:15 ; 15:8 ; Acts 4:10 ; 7:24 ; 13:17 ; 26:17,23 ; 28:27,28.

[283] Cf. I Cor 5:1 ; 12:2 ; I Thes 4:5 ; I Pet 2:12 ; III Jn 7.

[284] Cf. N. A. DAHL, " A People for His name ", (Acts XV:14), *NTS* 4 (1957-58), pp. 319-327.

[285] Cf. art. λαός, *TDNT* IV, p. 53.

[286] Cf. J. DUPONT, art. " λαὸς ἐξ ἐθνῶν (Acts 15:14) ", *NTS* 3 (1956-57), pp. 47-50.

does not seem to be correct, because elsewhere in Luke-Acts the conversion of the Gentiles is seen as a fulfilment of God's promises to Israel [287].

As for ἔθνος it is applied to Israel only eight times [288]. In all these cases the word is either used by the Non-Jews (Acts 10:22) or in speeches before Non-Jews (Lk 23:2 ; Acts 24:2,10,17) or in passages which refer to the attitude of Non-Jews (Lk 7:5) [289]. And this use is understandable, because a Gentile would not normally distinguish between the nation as a 'theocratic people' and as a 'civil organization'.

But in most of the cases (100 out of 160) ἔθνη, like the corresponding *goîm* in the OT, is undoubtedly used as a technical term for the Gentiles as distinct from the Jews or Christians [290]. This is reinforced by the fact that about 40 occurrences of ἔθνος are quotations from the OT, and that there are many other more or less clear reminiscences or echoes of the OT usages.

c. Johannine use of ἔθνος and λαός

Jn uses both words very sparingly. Both are found in Jn 11: 48-52, λαός once and ἔθνος 4 times. Both appear only once more in the Gospel, λαός in Jn 18:14 and ἔθνος in Jn 18:35. Unlike the other NT Writers, Jn does not use the word ἔθνος for Gentiles. It is interesting to note that Jn uses ἔθνος only in the singular, and that with a definite article. The term ἔθνος in the singular occurs in the NT 29 times, and out of these, 15 are with the definite article, and outside John it always refers to the Jews, accompanied by possessive pronouns as ἡμῶν (Lk 7:5 ; 23:2), μου (Acts 24:10,17 ; 28:19) or a demonstrative pronoun τούτῳ (Act 24:3,10) or explicitly spoken of as τὸ ἔθνος τῶν Ἰουδαίων (Acts 10:22) [291]. In Jn too ἔθνος in 11:48 and 18:35 is accompanied by the possessive pronouns ἡμῶν and σόν respectively, and clearly designates the Jewish people. This seems to show that the other uses in Jn 11:50,51,52 refer to the Jewish People, specially because these repeat the ἔθνος in 11:48 [292]. The fact that

---

[287] Cf. Lk 2:29-32 ; Acts 2:39 ; 3:25 ; 13:47 etc.

[288] Cf. Lk 7:5 ; 23:2 ; Acts 10:22 ; 24:2,10,17 ; 26:4 ; 28:19.

[289] The only case that is a little strange is that of Acts 28:19. But it is under the influence of the foregoing speech and refers back to Acts 24:17 and 26:4. Cf. H. STRATHMANN, art. cit., pp. 51-52.

[290] Cf. K. L. SCHMIDT, art. ἔθνος, *TDNT* II, p. 370.

[291] Two cases make exception to this, namely, Acts 7:7 which is a quotation from Gen 15:14 and Acts 8:9 referring explicitly to the people of Samaria.

[292] Note the mutual correspondence of these passages in the proposed

Jn does not use ἔθνος for the Gentiles, and for him ἔθνος is exclusively the Jews, may be explained from the polemics with the Jews, who in their obduracy to the message of Jesus ceased to be the 'people of God', and have become a nation like any other nation [293].

The term 'λαός' occurs in Jn only twice: here in Jn 11:50 and in 18:14 [294]. As we saw above, many scholars treat λαός and ἔθνος as synonyms. But the LXX usage and that of the rest of the NT does not seem to support such a conclusion. Since λαός and ἔθνος in Biblical Tradition always keep up the specific distinction we can presume the same here, though in a manner characteristic of Jn. On the one hand, we saw how 'λαός' in the NT slowly comes to be applied to the New Israel, the Christian Community. On the other hand, we saw how in Jn 'ἔθνος' came to be applied exclusively to the Jews. This points to λαός in Jn as having a meaning that is in contradistinction to ἔθνος the Jews.

Besides, it is rather strange and surprising to see Jn substituting ἔθνος in v. 51 for the λαός in v. 50, if both were synonyms. This is all the more so, since he gives such importance to these words and repeats them later on in the Gospel, this time using the selfsame word λαός and not ἔθνος (cf. Jn 18:14). It is to be noted also that when Jesus is said to die for the λαός (11:50; 18:14), nothing further is added. But when he is said to die for the ἔθνος, the Evangelist immediately adds " not only for the nation ... etc. " (Jn 11:51b-52). So for Jn λαός has a highly technical meaning much superior to ἔθνος, and a meaning that is sacred, referring to the ' New People of God ' for whom Jesus died [295].

---

structure of the passage. The explanation of ἔθνος here by ORIGEN (cf. *GCS* 28, 169-170) and LIGHTFOOT (*Gospel*, p. 230) as Gentiles or all men seem to be dictated by an effort to explain the transition from λαός to ἔθνος, which, as we will see below, could be otherwise explained.

[293] Cf. K. L. SCHMIDT, art. ἔθνος, *TDNT* II, p. 371; WESTCOTT, *Gospel*, p. 175.

[294] The omission of the phrase ὑπὲρ τοῦ λαοῦ is attested by some Ecclesiastical Writers such as CHRYSOSTOM (PG 59, 361), THEODORETUS (PG 81, 245), St. JEROME (PL 30, 583) and by some Mss of the Ethiopian version (cf. the Mss 515 of British Museum and 33 of the National Library of Paris) and is favoured by F. BLASS (cf. *Evangelium secundum Johannem cum variae lectionis delectu*, Leipzig 1902, pp. 39-40) and M. E. BOISMARD (cf. " Problèmes de Critique Textuelle concernant le Quatrième Evangile ", *RB* 60 (1953), pp. 352-353). Though the expression implying a theology of redemptive and expiatory death of Christ may not be original in the mouth of Caiaphas, there is no reason to deny its existence in the primitive text of the Gospel.

[295] Cf. S. PANCARO, " ' People of God ' in St. John's Gospel ", *NTS* 16 (1969-70), pp. 114-129. Note that elsewhere when Jn explicitly speaks of the

3. 'Dying for the People' and 'Gathering the scattered Children of God'

In the light of the above considerations the parallelism of the death of Christ for λαός in v. 50 with ' all believing in Him' of v. 48 and ' the gathering of the scattered children of God into one' of v. 52 becomes clear. By the words ' one man should die for the λαός' Caiaphas meant the Jewish nation according to the classical usage of OT and Judaism [296]. But he said λαός. And for the Evangelist it meant the ' people of God', comprising all those who believe (both Jews and Gentiles), the children of God [297]. Thus without realizing it Caiaphas prophesied, that Jesus would die for the people of God (v. 50 – B' C'), who, believing in Him (v. 48 – B C), will be made children of God, and thus brought to the unity contemplated by Jn (vv. 51b-52 – B² C²).

The second part of the prophecy ' and that the whole nation should not perish' (v. 50b – C') corresponding to the temporal destruction of the nation (v. 48b – C) and Jesus dying for the nation (v. 51b – C²) goes well with the above explanation. The Jewish nation as such would be destroyed by the Romans. But this destruction is not a complete destruction, a destruction in every sense. It is only a physical destruction. This would not mean a spiritual destruction [298], because Jesus dies for the nation.

Jesus dies for the people of God (λαός), in which, part of the Jewish nation is included (μὴ ὅλον τὸ ἔθνος ἀπόληται) because He is dying for the Jews too (ὑπὲρ τοῦ ἔθνους). Therefore the Evangelist could specify that Jesus dies not only for the Jewish nation (καὶ οὐχ ὑπὲρ τοῦ ἔθνους μόνον), but for all who would be made ' children of God' [299]. ' To gather into one the scattered children of God ' of v. 52

---

purpose of Christ's death, this purpose is always the salvation of the whole world, of all those who believe. Cf. Jn 3:14f; 10:1-21; 12:23,24,32-33; 19:37 etc.

[296] Cf. what we said above on the classical use of the word λαός in the OT and Judaism on pp. 219-220.

[297] For this usage of double-meaning-expressions in Jn, cf. O. CULLMANN, " Der Gebrauch ...", *ThZ* 4 (1948), pp. 360-372.

[298] Note that in Jn the word ἀπόλλυμι is used 10 times, and out of these, 8 speak of a destruction that is opposed to eternal life (cf. Jn 3:16; 6:27, 39; 10:10,28; 12:25) and the unity that results therefrom (cf. Jn 11:50; 17:12).

[299] The καί after ἵνα in v. 52 seems to put ἔθνος and τὰ τέκνα τοῦ Θεοῦ in opposition. It expresses a kind of opposition in the sense of contradistinction, but not in the sense of an exclusive opposition. This is perhaps suggested by the omission of this καί in different Mss such as It Vg Arm, Tatian's Diatessaron etc. and also unanimously in the Latin Patristic Tradition. Cf. AUGUSTINE, PL 35, 1758; BEDE THE VENERABLE, PL 92, 782; B. ALCUI-

restates and clarifies 'for the people' in v. 50. So the death of Jesus for the people in v. 50 means, for the Evangelist, the 'giving birth to the new people of God', by means of imparting the divine sonship and thus creating a family unity of all these children of God, resulting from the divine life imparted to them (v. 52). And this takes place through faith in Christ, which is hinted at in v. 48 being parallel to vv. 50 and 52. So the divine sonship of the believers is made possible through the death of Christ.

Conclusion

In Jn 3 the life of divine sonship of the believers is considered with special reference to its beginning, namely, to the birth that introduces one to the life of sonship. A spiritual birth is an indispensable condition for the life of sonship, because, man, left to himself, is in a condition of absolute and radical inability to enter into the life of the children of God (life of faith) which belongs to the sphere of the Spirit ... This spiritual birth marks the definite beginning indicated by 'ἔλαβον' and 'ἔδωκεν ἐξουσίαν' of Jn 1:12. This spiritual birth is indicated by Jn 3 as a birth 'from above' (v. 3) and a birth 'from the Spirit' (v. 5 in its earlier form). These two formulas refer to the principle coming from God, which communicates divine life to man. This principle that is communicated is the Holy Spirit, which remains as the permanent principle of the new life of faith – life of sonship.

In the present text of Jn 3:5, he presents Baptism and Faith (through the Spirit) as the two basic conditions of the divine begetting which is quite coherent with the Pre-Johannine and Johannine traditions in which Baptism and Faith are intimately related in view of salvation. By putting Baptism and Faith (Spirit) as the two basic conditions of divine begetting, Jn shows that, while the initiative in the divine begetting lies with God, the realization of it is always inextricably connected with human conditions and response.

Though Baptism and Faith are the two basic conditions of the divine begetting, the Holy Spirit remains the principle of this birth into the life of the believers. The indispensability of this principle for the life of the children of God is proved also from the nature of the life begotten of the 'Spirit' in contradistinction to the life begotten of 'flesh' (Jn 3:6). The usage of the perfect tense shows that, unlike the human begetting, the elements that are at work in the

---

NUS, PL 100, 904; RUPERTUS ABBATUS, PL 169, 646; GLOSSA ORDINARIA, PL 114, 401. Cf. also NONNUS PANOPOLITANUS, PG 43, 848.

beginning go on working to contribute to the sustenance and growth of this life that is begotten.

The state of being begotten of the Spirit is a reality. But its nature cannot be perceived except in its effects (Jn 3:8), of which Jn speaks elaborately in his First Epistle. The spiritually 'reborn' shares in the unfathomable character of the Spirit Himself.

The 'seeing and entering the Kingdom of God' which describes the effect of the begetting refers to the life of the children of God consisting in a 'life of Faith', and resulting in communion with Christ the Son of God. This Johannine identification of the 'life of sonship' with the 'life in the Kingdom' is in line with the teaching of Jesus in the Synoptics, where the 'sons of God' are identified with the 'members of the Kingdom'.

Though God the Father is the ultimate source of Life in the Children of God, for Jn Christ, possessing the Life in its fulness, becomes the only mediator of this Life. This takes place through the revelation of the Father in Christ's person and work, culminating in his death on the cross. This is illustrated in Jn 11:52 where the death of Christ is said to 'gather together the scattered children of God into one'. It is 'Faith' that brings men to unity in Jn, and it is 'Faith' that makes men children of God. So all those who come to believe in Christ, the revelation of the Father, are 'made children of God' and are thereby 'gathered into one'.

CHAPTER VIII

Righteousness: Criterion of the Life of the Children of God
(I Jn 2:29 – 3:10 ; Jn 8:31-47)

In the preceding exposition we have tried to see the Johannine concept of 'who are the children of God' (Jn 1:12), and 'how one becomes a child of God' (Jn 3:3,5). In Jn Ch. 3 we discovered how Jn conceives of the divine begetting, not only as a means of entering into the condition of the children of God, but also as something that continues during the life of the children of God [1]. Actually, the First Epistle of Jn, speaking of the divine begetting of the children of God, constantly makes use of the perfect tense of γεννᾶσθαι [2], which points to the present condition of the children of God, in whom the divine begetting still persists in its abiding power.

Also in the use of τέκνα Θεοῦ Jn seems to show the same procedure. Jn who speaks of a 'becoming children of God' in the Gospel (1:12), speaks of those who are already children of God in the Epistle (I Jn 3:1-2). Moreover, in the Prologue itself, where he mentions for the first time the theme of the divine sonship of men, he speaks of those who 'become' children of God, which also points to a stage of development following the divine begetting.

Therefore in the coming chapters we consider the life itself of the children of God, which is manifested in a concrete life of 'righteousness' which is the 'criterion' and 'fruit' of the divine sonship. Then we will try to specify better the nature of this life and experience of sonship, which grows into its eschatological development. Before entering into the exegetical analysis of the text speaking of 'righteousness' as the criterion of sonship, we present certain preliminary observations regarding the Johannine presentation of the life of divine sonship.

---

[1] Note what we stated above on p. 191 of John using the aorist of γεννᾶσθαι when speaking of the begetting as a condition for entering the Kingdom (Jn 3:3,5), and then proceeding to the use of the perfect tense of γεννᾶσθαι to describe the nature of the one who is begotten.

[2] Cf. I Jn 2:29 ; 3:9 ; 4:7 ; 5:1,4,18.

I. The Divine Sonship in Two Stages

John presents the theme of divine sonship and begetting in two stages: one, in the initial stage of 'being begotten by God (Spirit)' (Jn 3:3,5), and two, in the progressive stage of 'having been begotten by God (Spirit)' (Jn 3:6,8; I Jn 2:29; 3:9; 4:7; 5:1,4,18). This latter stage indicated by the perfect γεγέννηται seems to correspond to the use of τέκνα Θεοῦ in the Epistle [3].

A. Witness of the Ecclesiastical Writers

Long ago the Ancient Ecclesiastical Writers distinguished two ways of being children of God, and begotten of God in the Johannine Writings. Thus Maximus Confessor spoke of a twofold birth from God: one, that by which the grace of sonship in us is in 'potentia' (δυνάμει) and the other, that by which the grace of sonship is in us in its 'efficacy' (κατ' ἐνέργειαν ὅλην) [4]. Photius, trying to make a compromise between the fact of sin committed by those who are children of God and the impeccability of the children of God affirmed in the Scriptures, also distinguished two sorts of sonship: one, consisting only in the gift of God who adopts, and the other, joined with one's own effort in practising virtues (τῶν ἀρετῶν ἐργασία) conducting himself as a child of God, and thus possessing the unchangeable sonship (ἀμετακίνητον τὴν υἱοθεσίαν) [5].

Theophylactus spoke of the divine seed in I Jn 3:9 as the Holy Spirit or Christ who remains in the faithful and makes them sons of God, and hence of a sonship that is distinct from the initial sonship at the reception of the seed [6].

B. The Synoptic Teaching on the matter

This distinction between the two stages of the divine sonship is not something entirely new and of Johannine creation. We find

---

[3] Note how in I Jn 2:29 – 3:2 τέκνα Θεοῦ ἐσμεν is used parallel to ἐξ αὐτοῦ γεγέννηται.

[4] Cf. *Questiones ad Thalassium* VI, PG 90, 280. Also SEVERUS OF ANTIOCH expresses himself in similar terms (cf. J. A. CRAMER, *Catenae Graecorum Patrum in Novum Testamentum*, VIII, Oxford 1844, pp. 124-125.

[5] Cf. *Ad Amphilochium Quaestio VIII*, PG 101, 113. He explains in the same way Jn 1:12 exhorting the believers to remain as children of God. Cf. J. REUSS, "Die Erklärung des Johannes-Evangeliums durch den Patriarchen Photius von Konstantinopel", BZ 6 (1962), p. 281.

[6] Cf. PG 126, 33 : " ὅς, ἐνοικῶν ἐν τοῖς πιστοῖς ποιεῖ αὐτοὺς γενέσθαι υἱοὺς Θεοῦ ; cf. also J. A. CRAMER, *Catenae Graecorum ...*, VIII, p. 127.

traces of it, already in the Synoptics, who conceive of the divine sonship as eschatological, to be realized gradually [7]. Lk 20:36 identifies the 'sons of God' with 'sons of the resurrection'. When dealing with the Synoptics we saw how the sons of God are identified with the 'sons of the Kingdom'. So men become sons of God the moment they enter into the possession of the Kingdom [8].

C. *In the Specific Johannine Context*

St. John only anticipates this eschatological sonship in his specific view of realized eschatology. He sees this developed or progressive stage of sonship, not in the final eschatological time, but already at present in the full life of faith. And it is for this second progressive stage of being the children of God that Jn makes use of the formula " γεγέννηται ἐκ τοῦ Θεοῦ ".

1. *Presentation of the Epistle*

The very fact that the purpose of the Epistle is to show the criteria by means of which one arrives at the knowledge of the 'Life' of the believers (cf. I Jn 1:4 ; 5:13), shows that the Epistle presents the life of the children of God as actually possessed and manifested. Indeed, the subject-matter of the Epistle seems to consist chiefly of the delineation of the ideal Christian life, which naturally answers to the dignity of the Christian as a 'child of God' [9]. And this accounts for the constant use of the perfect γεγέννηται in the Epistle when speaking of the children of God, and for the specific Johannine structure found throughout when presenting the invisible reality of the life of the believers (children of God) as manifested by a visible reality such as Righteousness, Love, Faith etc. [10].

This knowledge-giving rule regarding the children of God is already anticipated by Jn 3:7, where he compares the one who is begotten of the Spirit to the Spirit (wind), whose existence is manifested and is known through its actions. The child of God shows by deed and word that an invisible influence has moved and inspired him [11]. But its development is a common theme in the Epistle. If in the Gospel the author contemplates the germ and the first principle of this new

---

[7] Cf. the future υἱοὶ Θεοῦ κληθήσονται of Mt 5:9 and the ὅπως γένησθε υἱοὶ τοῦ πατρὸς ὑμῶν of Mt 5:45.

[8] Cf. J. Dupont, *Les béatitudes*, p. 290.

[9] Cf. M. E. Boismard, " La connaissance de l'alliance nouvelle d'après I Jean ", *RB* 56 (1949), pp. 374ff.

[10] Cf. I Jn 2:29 ; 4:7 ; 5:1 etc.

[11] Westcott, *Gospel*, p. 51.

life, in the Epistle he contemplates this new life with its fruits issuing from the new begetting [12].

2. *The use of* εἶναι ἐκ τοῦ Θεοῦ

The use of εἶναι ἐκ τοῦ Θεοῦ in Jn seems to favour this interpretation. Speaking of the Johannine phraseology, we saw how εἶναι ἐκ τοῦ Θεοῦ refers to the father-son relationship between God and the believers, in which the being of God fully determines the being of the children of God and their actions proceeding therefrom. So the formula ' to be of God ' is specially related to the second progressive stage of the divine sonship of men characteristic of Jn [13]. This is perhaps suggested also by the fact that the formula εἶναι ἐκ τοῦ Θεοῦ occurs mostly in the Epistle [14], in which this specifically Johannine concept of divine sonship is brought to light.

We find in Jn three formulas that practically correspond to each other: namely, τέκνον Θεοῦ εἶναι, ἐκ τοῦ Θεοῦ εἶναι and ἐκ τοῦ Θεοῦ γεγέννηται (γεγεννημένος εἶναι). The parallelism of these three formulas is clear just from the section I Jn 2:29 – 3:10, which speaks of the life of the children of God manifested in the practice of righteousness in opposition to the life of the children of the devil, manifested in committing sins [15].

The fact that Jn makes use mostly of the perfect tense of γεννᾶσθαι to express the divine begetting of men [16], shows that for him what is important is the actual state of life or manner of being the children of God, under the influence of the vital communication that took place at the divine begetting [17].

---

[12] N. ALEXANDER, *The Epistles of St. John*, London, 1962, p. 328 : " The Fourth Gospel refers principally to the new birth ... ; the Epistle of St. John refers principally to the new life ".

[13] Note that the very formula εἶναι ἐκ τοῦ Θεοῦ is exclusively Johannine, which coincide with this characteristically Johannine concept of divine sonship.

[14] Out of the 11 occurrences of the phrase, only 3 occur in the Gospel.

[15] Note the three phrases occurring parallely in I Jn 2:29 ; 3:1 and 3:10 forming thus an inclusion of the whole section.

[16] Note that out of the 17 occurrences of γεννᾶσθαι in connection with the divine begetting of men 11 occur in the perfect tense.

[17] Here it is worth noting that the exclusive and frequent use of εἶναι ἐκ (52 times) in the Johannine Writings is indicative of this interest of John.

II. The Twofold Johannine scheme in the manifestation of the Sonship

As we said above, this interest of Jn accounts for the specifically Johannine structure in the Epistle, presenting the visible realities of righteousness, love and faith as manifestations of the invisible reality of being the 'children of God' or of 'having been begotten of God', or again of 'being from God'. Treating of this specifically Johannine scheme, we have to note a twofold procedure in Jn to describe the relation existing between the visible and invisible realities, namely: one, from the exterior reality to the interior reality (ab extra ad intra), which could be called a 'criterion scheme' and the other, from the interior reality to the exterior reality (ab intra ad extra), which could be called a 'fruit scheme'. Usually scholars speak of the 'criterion scheme' found in Jn [18], but ignore the 'fruit scheme', which is also of equal importance for Jn.

In fact, the very literary construction used by I Jn illustrates this twofold scheme, according as the exterior or interior reality is put first. We give below examples of the two series of texts representing this twofold scheme:

1) *Ab extra ad intra* — *Criterion scheme*

        Exterior reality   Interior reality
He who does righteousness is begotten of God (I Jn 2:29)
He who loves is begotten of God (I Jn 4:7)
He who believes that ...... is begotten of God (I Jn 5:1)

2) *Ab intra ad extra* — *Fruit scheme*

        Interior reality   Exterior reality
He who is begotten of God does not sin (I Jn 3:9; 5:18)
He who remains in Him does not sin (I Jn 3:6)
That which is begotten of God conquers the world (I Jn 5:4)

Examples of this twofold scheme could be multiplied. In fact these two schemes are inseparable, because if the 'fruit scheme' shows the interior reality as the source that produces the exterior realities that are its fruits, the 'criterion scheme' shows these very fruits produced by the interior reality, as the criteria leading to the knowledge of the same interior reality. This is seen from the typically Johannine way of putting both schemes in a well-knit literary frame.

Cf. for example, I Jn 3:6:
A   Everyone who remains in Him

---

[18] Cf. M. E. BOISMARD, art. " La connaissance ...", pp. 365-390.

```
B                        does not sin              ab intra ad extra
B'         Everyone who does sin
A'    Did not see Him nor knew Him              ab extra ad intra.
```

This twofold and inseparable scheme of I Jn warns us against considering the divine sonship of Christians merely as something that is in some way defined by external criteria [19], or even as a mere moral and psychological predisposition, naturally manifesting itself by external actions [20]. For Jn the interior reality of the divine sonship is the foundation and the source of its outward manifestations. The believers can perform good actions, just because they have been begotten of God [21]. Thus to the Christian, his morally good actions (exterior realities), being the effect of his generation from God, prove and testify that he is really a child of God (interior reality).

III. The Literary Criticism of I Jn 2:29 – 3:10

After presenting in general terms the specific character of the Johannine concept of the divine sonship of Christians contemplated in the progressive stage of a real life of sonship manifested in external realities, we pass on to the interpretation of the texts that explicitly present this Johannine concept. In this chapter we deal mainly with the section I Jn 2:29 – 3:10 where the divine sonship of the believers is connected with ' doing righteousness '. First of all, we give a literary criticism of the section.

A. *Different Attempts on the History of Redaction*

In the first half of this Century, the literary character of the First Epistle of St. John had been the object of much discussion. We cannot give here all the different opinions regarding the matter [22], nor is it within our scope. However, something should be said about the various attempts at solutions, especially because our present sec-

---

[19] Cf. A. M. DONATUS, art. cit., p. 61 where he interprets I Jn 3:8 " He who sins is of the devil " in this sense.

[20] Cf. St. AUGUSTINE, *In Epist. Jn*, PL 35, 2015 where he gives a similar interpretation to I Jn 3:10,12 ; cf. also A. M. DONATUS, art. cit., pp. 61-62 where he interprets Jn 8:47 similarly.

[21] Cf. G. B. STEVENS, *The Johannine Theology*, London, 1894, p. 245 : " The divine begetting is the logical ' prius ' of the spiritual life and all its fruits ".

[22] For a detailed study of the different attempts of solution in the matter, cf. W. NAUCK, *Die Tradition und der Charakter des Ersten Johannesbriefes*, (WUNT 3), Tübingen, 1957.

tion had been precisely the object of discussion among the critics, and because a clear vision of the literary background is of utmost importance for the exegesis of the relevant texts.

Some find in the Letter two series of propositions, which are of a different nature, and hence they attribute them to two different sources, namely, a primitive written document (Vorlage) and later commentative additions (Bearbeitung). E. V. Dobschütz [23] analyses our section I Jn 2:29 - 3:10 and finds there four series of 2 verses which are constructed in antithetical parallelism and show a 'lapidarer Stil' of different categorical affirmations. These verses are: 2: 29b, 3:4a,6b,7b,8a,9a, and 10b. According to him these verses form the 'Vorlage' and are of an ethical character, while the rest are additions forming the 'Bearbeitung', and are of a physical character. Bultmann distinguishes in the same way between the 'Vorlage' and 'Bearbeitung' in the whole Epistle. According to him the 'Vorlage' belongs to the 'Offenbarungsreden' as in the Gospel, having its origin in Gnosticism, while the 'Bearbeitung' are homiletical and parenetical additions made by the author [24]. He also finds certain later interpolations in the Epistle, made in the church, in order to make it more conformable to the common doctrine [25]. H. W. Beyer [26], H. Preisker [27] and H. Braun [28] give explanations similar to that of Bultmann. Preisker suspects another additional 'Vorlage', that belongs to an eschatological text, and to it he attributes vv. 2:28;3:2,13f,19-21;4:17 and 5:18f.

The above theories are refuted by both Catholics and Protestants [29]. Nauck recently gave a new orientation to this problem, con-

---

[23] Cf. E. von Dobschütz, "Johanneische Studien I", *ZNW* 8 (1907), pp. 1-8.

[24] Cf. R. Bultmann, "Analyse des Ersten Johannesbriefes", in *Festgabe für A. Jülicher*, Tübingen, 1927, pp. 138-158. In 'Die drei Johannesbriefe', Göttingen, 1967, p. 49 he reconstructs the 'Vorlage' of I Jn 2:29 - 3:10 comprising the verses 2:29; 3:4,6,7,8,9, and is slightly different from that which is given in 'Festgabe für A. Jülicher', pp. 157ff.

[25] Cf. R. Bultmann, "Die kirchliche Redaktion des I. Johannesbriefes", *In Memoriam Lohmeyer*, Stuttgart, 1951, pp. 189-201.

[26] Cf. H. W. Beyer, "Bespr. Festgabe für A. Jülicher", *TLZ* 54 (1929), pp. 606-617.

[27] Cf. H. Windisch, *Die katholischen Briefe*, (HNT 15), 3rd ed., Tübingen, 1951, pp. 168-171.

[28] Cf. H. Braun, "Literaranalyse und theologische Schichtung im Ersten Johannesbrief", *ZTK* 48 (1951), pp. 262-292.

[29] Cf. R. Schnackenburg, *Die Johannesbriefe*, Freiburg, 1963 (2nd. ed.), pp. 11-14; A. Feuillet, *Les épîtres johanniques*, in Introduction à la Bible II, Tournai, 1959 (2nd ed.), pp. 690-694; E. Käsemann, "Ketzer und Zeuge. Zum johanneischen Verfasserproblem", *ZTK* 48 (1951), pp. 292-311; O. Piper,

necting the traditional element of the Epistle to the Primitive catechetical teaching [30]. He also admits the distinction between the 'Vorlage' and the 'Bearbeitung', but both are attributed to the same author. The 'Sitz im Leben' of the Epistle is, according to him, the Judaic tradition and later the baptismal tradition of the Primitive Christian Community. Though the pre-existence of a written document is still to be proved, the catechetical elements, and specially elements of a baptismal catechesis are certainly found in the Epistle as a whole, and in our section in particular [31]. Hence a consideration of these elements is of great importance.

B. *The Baptismal Tradition in I Jn*

First of all we see in general certain expressions that are most expressive of this baptismal catechetical character. The frequent reference of the author to that which they heard (ἠκούσατε) (cf. 2:7, 18,24; 3:11; 4:3) points in this direction [32]. Specially the combined use of phrases such as 'the word that you heard', 'what you heard from the beginning' etc. certainly remind us of the initial Christian instruction. The term 'from the beginning' "ἀπ'ἀρχῆς" becomes almost stereotyped in the Epistle (cf. 1:1; 2:7,13,24; 3:8,11 etc.). This beginning is in many texts the beginning of the Christian life. The frequent use of the word 'οἴδαμεν' and 'οἴδατε' refers to the knowledge of faith possessed by the Christians from the beginning [33]. Out of the 15 texts, 12 give the verb in the above mentioned form (cf. 2:20,21; 3:2,5,14,15; 5:15,18,19,20). The repeated mention of the confession of faith ὁμολογεῖν (cf. 2:22,23; 4:2,3,15 etc.) is a reminiscence of the baptismal confession of faith [34]. The Epistle to the Hebrews 3:1; 4:14; 10:23 also reminds the readers of the baptismal confession of faith through this homology [35]. These few remarks are

---

"I Jn and the Didache of the Primitive Church", *JBL* 66 (1947), pp. 437-451; F. BÜCHSEL, "Zu den Johannesbriefen", *ZNW* 28 (1929), pp. 235-241.

[30] Cf. W. NAUCK, op. cit., passim.

[31] Cf. M. E. BOISMARD, "Une liturgie baptismale dans la Prima Petri I: Son influence sur Tit, I Jn et Col", *RB* 63 (1956), pp. 200-204.

[32] For the Kerygmatic character of this word, cf. Rom 10:14,17.

[33] For the special characteristic of the verb οἶδα in connection with the knowledge of faith, cf. I. DE LA POTTERIE, art. "οἶδα et γινώσκω — Les deux modes de la connaissance dans le quatrième evangile", *Bib* 40 (1959), pp. 709-725; cf. also R. BULTMANN, art. cit., in *Festgabe für A. Jülicher*, p. 146 where he says that in the use of οἴδαμεν and οἴδατε we have 'eine Berufung auf den Glauben der Gemeinde'.

[34] Cf. Acts 8:36-37 where the same confession of faith precedes Baptism.

[35] Cf. G. BORNKAMM, "Das Bekenntnis im Hebräerbrief", *ThBl* 21 (1942), pp. 56-66.

sufficient to show the underlying baptismal tradition of the Epistle in general [36].

C. *The Baptismal Liturgy underlying the section*

Having seen the baptismal character of the underlying tradition in I Jn in general, now we come to examine closely our particular section. A comparison of our section with the other parts of the NT reproducing the traditional baptismal liturgy is quite enlightening. We present a comparison of our section with I Pet 1:3-23 which is so close to our passage literally and thematically [37].

I Pet.	I Jn
1:3 Blessed ... *Father* ... by his m e r c y ... we have been *born anew*	2:29 ... *is born of Him* 3:1 ... l o v e *the Father* gave us we called c h i l d r e n of G o d
to a life of *hope*	2 Now we are c h i l d r e n of G o d *is not yet revealed* what we shall be
4 to an incorruptible inheritance kept in heaven	
5 for the salvation ... *to be revealed* ... last hour ... glory	When *he is revealed* we shall be like Him
7 in *revelation of Jesus* whom not seeing ... love and believe	for we shall see him as He is
13 Put *your hope* for good ...	3 Who has this *hope*
15 *As He is* h o l y so y o u [38] must be h o l y too	purifies himself *as He is* p u r e
	7 Who does j u s t i c e *as He is* j u s t
18 *Knowing that* you are redeemed from the futile	5 *You know that He appeared* to take away sins
19 by ... Christ lamb *unblemished*	and *sin is not in Him*
20 *He appeared* at ... of ages for your sake	8 *The Son of God appeared* to undo the devil's deeds
22 *brotherly love* ...	
23 You *are born anew* by an incorruptible *seed* ... word *of God*	9 Who *is born of God* does ... The *seed of God* remains in him
	10 Who ... *love his brother.*

---

[36] For a detailed study on this point, cf. W. NAUCK, op. cit., pp. 84-98.
[37] Cf. M. E. BOISMARD, " Une liturgie baptismale ...", pp. 200-204.
[38] Note that Jn speaks of imitating Christ unlike I Pet who speaks of imitating God.

As we can see from the above comparison, I Jn follows the same order and gives the same themes as that of I Pet. Both follow the usual homiletic scheme acknowledged by all, namely, i) The eschatological vocation of a Christian (I Pet 1:3-5 = I Jn 3:1-2); ii) Change of life demanded by this vocation I Pet 1:13-20 = I Jn 3:3-10b); iii) Particular obligations of a Christian (I Pet 1:22f = I Jn 3:10cf)[39].

Both begin with an affirmation of our birth from God and our divine sonship (I Pet 1:3 = I Jn 3:1-2)[40]. Both attribute the fact of our birth to the love of God the Father. I Pet uses ἔλεος. Jn never makes use of this word either in the Epistle or in the Gospel and has a preference for ἀγάπη, which he uses 18 times in the Epistle itself. In spite of this difference in words, the idea remains the same in both. The distinction between the two stages of our eschatological redeemed condition is given by both, namely, the present state of hope (I Pet 1:3,13 = I Jn 3:3), because the real state is hidden for the moment (I Pet 1:4 = I Jn 3:2ᵃ), and the revealed state to be manifested on the last day (I Pet 1:5 = I Jn 3:2b). This hope becomes the motive of sanctifying oneself in both (I Pet 1:13-16 = I Jn 3:3,7). Both remind us of the redemptive work of Christ the innocent, to take away sins — to destroy the works of the devil (I Pet 1:18-20 = I Jn 3:5,8). Finally birth from God is attributed by both to an incorruptible seed that remains in man, which makes him impeccable and capable of observing the commandments, the greatest of which is love (I Pet 1:22-23 = I Jn 3:9-10)[41]. These literary and thematic convergences in I Pet and I Jn cannot be explained unless we admit some common ground for both. And since I Pet 1:3-23 certainly takes up a baptismal liturgy, we could suppose the same baptismal liturgy as the background for I Jn too[42], which, however, he puts in

---

[39] Cf. M. E. BOISMARD, art. " Pierre, première épître de ", in DBS VII, p. 1447.

[40] John anticipates the idea of birth from God, and uses τέκνα Θεοῦ connected with the love of the Father, for the special structure intended by John, in which the idea of birth from God and the divine sonship with doing righteousness introduces and concludes the section forming thus an inclusion (cf. I Jn 2:29 and 3:10).

[41] The inversion of the themes of divine birth and fraternal love in John is also to be explained by the structural intention of John, in which vv. 6 and 9 correspond to each other and v. 10 forms a transition to the next section speaking of love.

[42] Cf. M. E. BOISMARD, art. " Une liturgie baptismale ...", p. 204 where he says : " Cette séquence de thèmes semblables, et dont certains ne se retrouvent pas ailleurs dans le NT, ne peut être l'effet du hasard. Puisque, on l'a vu, I Pet 1,3-5 ; 1:13 - 2:10 reprend une liturgie baptismale, le mieux est de supposer que l'auteur de la Prima Johannis s'est inspiré de la même liturgie

the frame of his special literary structure. The elements of this baptismal parenesis also are found in the Epistles of St. Paul, to which we will refer below occasionally.

D. *Eschatological and Dualistic Context*

The fact that the baptismal texts speak of the eschatological vocation of the Christian shows the eschatological context of our section too. Besides, the Johannine texts themselves give evidence of this. The ending of the previous section is strongly eschatological, where he begins with his new theme [43]. This eschatological situation of the Christian is presented by Jn under the aspect of the divine sonship and frames it in a dualistic eschatological opposition. This is clear from the words of inclusion in the section [44]. In v. 10 the author concludes the whole passage with the words: " In this is manifested the children of God and the children of the devil" which actually contains the theme of the section. So the whole section brings out the eschatological opposite situation and its criterion regarding the children of God and the children of the devil. This is done by Jn keeping the traditional baptismal scheme, as we have seen above, with the necessary repetitions and rearrangements to fit in to his eschatological dualistic structure. Jn makes this opposition mainly by introducing two formulas regarding ' righteousness ' and ' sin ' (ὁ ποιῶν τὴν δικαιοσύνην and ὁ ποιῶν τὴν ἁμαρτίαν which are the criteria of the interior reality of ' being begotten of God ' and ' being of the devil ', or of ' being children of God ' and ' children of the devil ' respectively. The following table will show this:

	I Pet		*I Jn*
A		A	Does righteousness – He is righteous
	Father – mercy – begetting		Father – love – begetting
B		B	Children of God and the World
	Heritage to be revealed		Sonship to be revealed
	Now not seeing Him		Will see Him

baptismale qu'il a adaptée à son propre dessein ". In his book' *Quatre hymnes baptismales dans la première épître de Pierre* ', Paris, 1961, on p. 130 he modifies the above opinion and makes I Jn depend on I Pet. Whatever be the interdependence of I Jn and I Pet, it is undeniable that the baptismal liturgy lies behind I Jn 2:29 – 3:10.

[43] It is interesting here to note that the technical term παρουσία comes only here in the whole Johannine Literature.

[44] Cf. I Jn 2:29 " Who does justice, is begotten of God ", and 3:10 " who does not do justice ... is not from God ".

C	With hope ... be holy	C	With hope ... purify oneself
		D	Who sins ... commits iniquity
E	Christ appeared to save	E	He appeared to take away sins
		F	He who remains in Him does not sin
C'	Sanctify your souls	C'	Does justice – He is just
		D'	He who sins is from the devil
		E'	Son of God appeared ... devil
	Brotherly love		
F'	Born again ... seed of God	F'	Born of God – seed of God – not sin
		B'	Children of God – children of the devil
		A'	Does not do righteousness – not from God.

The above table shows the new elements in I Jn and the rearrangement of the traditional elements in the new structure of I Jn.

E. *Locating the section in the frame of the Baptismal Parenesis*

As we have seen above speaking of the baptismal parenesis underlying this section, the first part (I Jn 2:29 – 3:2) reminds the Christians of their eschatological vocation. This eschatological vocation is considered by Jn under the aspect of divine sonship and divine begetting. Actually all the parallel texts giving the baptismal parenesis consider this eschatological vocation under the aspect of a 'rebirth' effected by God (cf. I Pet 1:3,23 ; Tit 3:5) or of 'divine sonship' (cf. Gal 3:26 ; 4:4-6 ; Rom 8:14-17), though it is only Jn who combined both. All these texts have the following elements in common, namely, the starting point, a present state of hope that is hidden, and a future state that is revealed or manifested, and all these three stages are experienced in solidarity with Christ. The starting point is described as 'born of God' (I Jn 2:29), 'regenerated' (I Pet 1:3) through the washing of regeneration (Tit 3:5), faith and baptism (Gal 3:24-27), Spirit of adoption (Rom 8:14) and death and resurrection with Christ (Col 3:1-2). The present state is described as 'Children of God ' (I Jn 3:1 ; Gal 3:26 ; 4:6 ; Rom 8:14,16), ' heirs ' (I Pet 1:4 ; Tit 3:7 ; Gal 3:29 ; 4:7 ; Rom 8:17) and ' life hidden ' (Col 3:3). The idea that it is hidden and of the hope of being once manifested is also mentioned by all (cf. I Jn 3:2 ; I Pet 1:4-5 ; Tit 3:7 ; Gal 3:23 ; Rom 8:17-21 ; and Col 3:4).

These fundamental elements of the eschatological vocation of a Christian help us to see the texts of I Jn 2:29 – 3:2 in its true perspective. Thus we could place these texts in general in the following way :

2:29 — The condition of the Christian with special reference to the beginning
3:1 — ” ” ” ” ” with reference to the present
3:2 — ” ” ” ” ” with reference to the future

As we have said above, Jn frames the scheme of the baptismal parenesis in his perspective of realized eschatology and eschatological dualism. Some have tried to exclude all eschatology from the writings of Jn [45]. But scholars generally speak of an eschatological outlook of Jn in a state of tension between the present and future [46]. In our context the children of God already possess the divine life by their divine birth [47]. But beside this realized eschatology, there exists a tension towards the future manifestation of it [48]. So Jn giving special emphasis to the present condition of the children of God (3:1), looks back to the past communication of the filial life which remains dynamic throughout (2:29) and its future manifestation (3:2).

Besides as we have seen, he introduces the dualism, which is essentially connected with his eschatology [49]. All these things he does

---

[45] Cf. R. BULTMANN, art. ζάω, *TDNT* II, p. 870 : " The promises in the future tense do not refer to a later eschatological future ... In the Gospel there are no express references to an eschatological future in the sense of Jewish and early Christian eschatology and of Pauline Teaching ...".

[46] Cf. N. LAZURE, *Les valeurs morales de la théologie johannique*, Paris, 1965, p. 23 ; L. VAN HARTINGSVELD, *Die Eschatologie des Johannesevangeliums*, Assen, 1962 ; M. E. BOISMARD, " L'Evolution du thème eschatologique dans la traditions johannique ", *RB* 68 (1961), pp. 507-524 ; G. EICHHOLZ, " Erwählung und Eschatologie im I Johannesbrief ", *EvTh* 5 (1938), 1-28 ; G. STÄHLIN, " Zum Problem der johanneischen Eschatologie ", *ZNW* 33 (1934), pp. 225-254. P. RICCA, *Die Eschatologie des Vierten Evangeliums*, Zürich, 1966.

[47] Note the perfect tense of γεγέννηται in 2:29 and the present tense of ἐσμέν in 3:1-2.

[48] Note the future tense of ἐσόμεθα and ὀψόμεθα in 3:2.

[49] Cf. I. DE LA POTTERIE, art. " L'impeccabilité du chrétien ..." p. 208. Note the opposition between the ' children of God ' and ' children of the

subjected to his general purpose of bringing the believers to the knowledge of their status as Christians [50], and in our context specifically as children of God [51].

IV. The Structural and Grammatical Considerations

A. *The Structure of I Jn 2:29 – 3:10a*

We now present a structure of I Jn 2:29 – 3:10a, which will show better the eschatological and dualistic presentation of the theme of the life of the children of God and its outward manifestation.

2: 29 A   If ... HE IS RIGHTEOUS ... EVERYONE WHO DOES RIGHTEOUSNESS IS BORN OF HIM.

3:1-2 B   See ... we ... CHILDREN OF GOD ... t h e   w o r l d
                    DID NOT KNOW HIM ... APPEARED ... WE SHALL SEE HIM ...

3   A'a   EVERYONE WHO ... purifies himself AS HE IS PURE
4   b   EVERYONE WHO COMMITS SIN COMMITS INIQUITY ... SIN ...
5   c   You know ... HE APPEARED TO take away sins ...
6   d   EVERYONE WHO REMAINS IN HIM DOES NOT SIN
      B'   Everyone who sins DID NOT SEE HIM ... NOT KNOW HIM ...

7   A²a' HE WHO DOES RIGHTEOUSNESS IS RIGHTEOUS AS HE IS RIGHTEOUS
8   b'   HE WHO COMMITS SIN is of the devil ... SINS ...
      c'   For this Son of God APPEARED TO undo devil's deeds
9   d'   EVERYONE WHO IS BORN OF GOD DOES NOT SIN
             because the seed of God REMAINS IN HIM ... cannot SIN
             because he IS BORN OF GOD

10   B²   In this APPEAR the CHILDREN OF GOD ... c h i l d r e n   o f   t h e   d e v i l

     A³   EVERYONE WHO DOES not DO RIGHTEOUSNESS IS n o t   o f   G o d.

---

devil' (3:10) ' world ' (3:1) ; ' he who does justice ' and ' he who commits sin ' (2:29 ; 3:4,7,8,10) ; ' Son of God ' and ' devil ' (3:8) etc.

[50] Cf. I Jn 1:4 (the prologue) and 5:13 (Epilogue), where the aim of writing the letter is expressed, and says that " he writes this so that they may know that they have eternal life — the communion with God, and thus knowing they may rejoice, and that their joy may be full ".

[51] Note 2:29 " If you know ... you may be sure ", which points explicitly to this purpose in our context.

The clear literary inclusions such as ' he who does righteousness ', ' is born of God ', and ' children of God ' certainly frame the section. The expressions ' being born of God ', ' being from God ' and ' being children of God ' are characteristic of this section, because none of these expressions occurs in the preceding sections, and in the following section of the second part of the Epistle (I Jn 2:29 – 4:6) [52], these three expressions do not occur as parallels to express communion with God, as they occur here. In the second part of the Epistle itself, the two expressions ' being born of God ' and ' being children of God ' occur only in this section. Likewise, the expression ' he who does righteousness ' is found nowhere in the Epistle except here as the criterion of Communion with God. In the same way, ' he who commits sin ' as opposed to ' he who does righteousness ' with the present participle ' ποιῶν ' is also confined to this section. It is also worth noting here that out of the 26 instances of ' ἁμαρτία ' 10 occur in this section alone. As we have seen above, the distinctive redactional elements of I Jn in our section are precisely these two opposites.

The very structure of the section shows the movement of the argument. In v. 29 (A) the author introduces the theme of the passage with all the three elements belonging to the general structure of the Epistle presenting the idea of the spiritual reality of Christian life that is invisible, manifested by an external sign, found throughout the Epistle [53]. These elements are :

1) Communion with God — ' are born of Him '
2) The Criterion — ' everyone who does righteonsness '
3) The Basis — ' He is Righteous '

Note A³ that takes up the same elements forming thus an inclusion to the section. In the rest of the section he developes the same theme following the same structure introducing the dualistic opposition

---

[52] Several divisions have been proposed for the Epistle by authors. Cf. T. HÄRING, *Gedankengang und Grundgedanke des Ersten Johannesbriefes*, Freiburg, 1892 ; E. NAGL, " Die Gliederung des I. John. ", *BZ* 16 (1924), pp. 77-92 ; H. LOHMEYER, " Über Aufbau und Gliederung des Ersten Johannesbriefes ", *ZNW* 27 (1928), pp. 225-267 ; C. C. OKE, " The Plan of the First Epistle of John", *ET* 51 (1939-40), pp. 347-350 ; R. SCHWERTSCHLAGER, *Der I Joh. in seinem Grundgedanken und Aufbau*, Coburg, 1935. But all of them have their drawbacks. For an exposition of their theories, cf. A. FEUILLET, *Introduction à la Bible* II, pp. 687-690. We adopt the following division of the Epistle : Prologue 1:1-4 ; Three expositions of criteria of our communion with God 1:5 – 2:28 ; 2:29 – 4:6 ; 4:7 – 5:12 ; Epilogue 5:13 -21, based on the so-called spiral mode of thinking and writing found in I Jn (cf. R. LAW, *Tests of Life*, p. 5) and on the literary criteria.

[53] Cf. M. E. BOISMARD, art. " La connaissance ...", pp. 365-380.

between 'sin' and 'righteousness' [54]. In BB² he already introduces the opposite elements 'children of God' and 'world' (children of the devil). The A' (abcd) and A² (a'b'c'd') show the particularized and dualistically opposite development of the theme introduced in A, in two parallel resumptions. In between these two parallel developments we see B', also a resumption of B, but this time taking up only the opposite element 'he who sins'.

B. *The Scheme of the Structure*

As we see from the structure, the whole passage is a repetitive development of the same basic elements introduced in I Jn 2:29 with more specifications and with dualistically opposing elements. The different parallelisms in the section could be better seen in the following scheme:

	Basis	Visible Reality (criterion or fruit)	Invisible Reality (Communion)
2:29	He is righteous	He who does righteousness	born of God
		CHILDREN OF GOD	
3:1-2			We are children of God We shall be like Him We shall see Him as He is
3:3	He is pure	He who purifies himself	has this hope in Him
5-6	He appeared to take away sins In Him there is no sin	He does not sin	who remains in Him
7	He is righteous	He who does righteousness	is righteous
8-9	Son of God appeared to destroy the work of the devil	Does not sin He cannot sin	who is born of God God's seed remains in him He is born of God

---

[54] 3:1-2 (B) may seem to interrupt the structural presentation of the theme, as a contemplation of the future glory of the spiritual reality of divine sonship. But it is only a repeated affirmation of the same spiritual reality, mentioned in 'A' with special reference to growth and development towards perfection, in order to come back with added emphasis (v. 3) to the same structural procedure. Besides, B and B² also speak of the manifestation of the divine sonship, both eschatological (B) and present (B²).

10			Children of God
	CHILDREN OF THE DEVIL		
3:1-2			The world did not know Him
4	Sin is iniquity	Who commits sin	commits iniquity
6		Who commits sin	did not see nor know Him
8	The devil has sinned from the beginning	Who commits sin	is of the devil
10		does not do righteousness	children of the devil is not of God

From the above scheme we see that on the one side Christ, the meeting point of the invisible and visible realities, stands as righteous in his quality of being pure, in whom there is no sin, and of having conquered sin, the works of the devil. This shows the triumphant and salvific character of his righteousness. The children of God are compared with Christ the Righteous, and they stand united with Him, and therefore their life is manifested in doing righteousness by purifying themselves and by not committing sin. Thus righteousness becomes the criterion of their sonship. A child of God is the one who is born of God and who remains in Him. He has a hope of total resemblance to Him in future (I Jn 3:2).

On the other hand, the meeting point of the opposite visible and invisible realities is the devil as the one who sins from the beginning. The children of the devil are compared with him and they stand united with him being under his influence, by committing sin and by not doing righteousness. Therefore a life of sin is the criterion of their diabolic sonship. The children of the devil are from the devil, namely, the power working in them is diabolic.

C. *Evaluation of the tenses of the verbs in 2:29*

The particle ἐάν with εἰδῆτε subjunctive (pf) present forms a conditional clause, and usually denotes what is expected to occur under certain circumstances from a given standpoint in the present [55]. But here it is not merely conditional, as it is a knowledge of faith. It seems to have a causative force also and here ἐάν seems to stand

---

[55] Cf. W. BAUER, *A Greek-English Lexicon*, p. 210.

for εἰ (ἐπεί)[56]. Hence it assumes the value of a causal indicative present[57].

The form 'γινώσκετε' could be indicative or imperative. Both renderings are found in early Latin authorities. For those who take the v. 29 as a general reason for the command of 'abiding in Him' of v. 28, naturally the indicative would be preferable[58]. But as we have seen above, the section 2:29 – 3:10b forms a separate unity literally and thematically, and hence v. 29 should be seen rather in relation to what follows. Another reason that favours the indicative could be the conditional force of ἐάν εἰδῆτε. But as we have seen above, it has more of a causative force, which will be clearer below in our detailed study too. As it stands between the two imperatives μένετε (2:28) and ἴδετε (3:1) the parallelism favours the imperative. Besides, the consideration of a divine quality is usually brought in as a motive of doing something or in a parenetical context (comp. 4:7, 11). Moreover, γινώσκειν usually refers to a knowledge that derives from experience of life[59]. Hence, the imperative seems to be more in accordance with the context, namely, St. John charges his readers to apply practically the truth which they know by faith rather than appealing to them as having already done this.

The term ποιῶν being a present participle, the ordinary significance is a continuous action without any specification of time.

The perfect tense γεγέννηται indicates something that took place in the past, but considered in its abiding power. So Jn appeals to the knowledge of the readers regarding God or Christ as 'righteous', in order to bring them to the knowledge of their status of being born of God, through the continuous realization in their life of that righteousness that corresponds to the righteousness of God or Christ.

---

[56] Cf. BLASS-DEBRUNNER, *Grammatik des neutestamentlichen Griechisch*, 9th ed., Göttingen, 1954, 372, 1a: "So wie, so bald ... so wisst auch ..."; cf. WESTCOTT, *Epistles*, p. 82: "Knowledge which is absolute (εἰδῆτε) becomes the basis of the knowledge realized in observation (γινώσκετε)'.

[57] Cf. J. CHAINE, *Les épîtres catholiques*, 2nd ed. Paris, 1939, p. 177, where he translates: "Puisque vous savez qu'il est juste, vous connaissez ...". Cf. also F. M. ABEL, *Grammaire du grec biblique*, Paris, 1927, p. 287.

[58] F. BÜCHSEL, *Die Johannesbriefe*, Leipzig, 1933, p. 44; CHAINE, *Les Epîtres*, p. 177; BULTMANN, *Die Johannesbriefe*, p. 49, note 3; SCHNACKENBURG, *Die Johannesbriefe*, p. 167, note 2 where he says that the introductory sentence conditions a sequence which consists in an acknowledgement, and that such acknowledgements are in other places as assertions, and quotes as examples 2:3,5; 3:16,19,24; 4:2,6,13; 5:2. But all these examples are accompanied with ἐν τούτῳ, which is, however, wanting here.

[59] Cf. I. DE LA POTTERIE, art. "οἶδα et γινώσκω ...", pp. 710-712.

V. Vocabulary

A. εἰδῆτε and γινώσκετε

Now we proceed to the semantic study of the versicle. First of all we take the two verbs εἰδῆτε and γινώσκετε [60]. These two verbs of knowing are used by Jn in different ways and hence have a difference of signification in Jn. While οἶδα is a knowledge of absolute character, γινώσκω is a knowledge of acquisition. When speaking of religious knowledge, οἶδα always refers to the knowledge of faith either negatively, namely, the incapacity of men to understand the things of faith (cf. Jn 1:31,33 ; 4:10,32 ; 14:5 ; 20:9,14 ; 21:4), or positively, namely, the absolute certitude deriving from faith (cf. Jn 11:22, 24 ; 19:35 ; 21:12,24). On the other hand γινώσκω signifies the gradual acquisition of knowledge, through experience (cf. Jn 8:28 ; 14:20 ; 17:8,25 etc.) or teaching (cf. Jn 15:18) [61]. Often the condition required for this knowledge on the part of the disciples is faith (cf. Jn 6:69), which, in a sense, being anterior to knowledge, leads them to it (cf. Jn 8:32 ; 15:7,8) [62]. It is the same use that we find also in the Epistle. οἶδα is exclusively employed for the knowledge of faith, such as the knowledge of truth (I Jn 2:20-21), of eternal life (I Jn 3:14 - 15 ; 5:13) and the revelation of Christ as Saviour (cf. I Jn 3:2,5 ; 5:20), while γινώσκω signifies mostly a derived knowledge with ἐν τούτῳ or ὅθεν etc., pointing to the origin of the knowledge [63].

In addition οἶδα signifies a knowledge that one already possesses and a certain conviction that proceeds from this knowledge. For example, in I Jn 5:15 he appeals to faith, presented as a conviction that God will hear us. The same could be said also of other texts. On the other hand γινώσκω signifies a dynamic knowledge 'in fieri' and is used for the knowledge of the signs of a higher reality [64].

So in our context Jn appeals to the conviction derived from the knowledge of faith of the believers regarding God or Christ (because you know that He is righteous) in his quality of righteousness, and he invites them to arrive at the knowledge of their own divine birth by 'doing righteousness' which corresponds to the nature of God as

---

[60] Cf. I. DE LA POTTERIE, art. " οἶδα et γινώσκω ...", pp. 709-725 where he makes a complete study of the Johannine usage of these two verbs.

[61] Cf. I. DE LA POTTERIE, art. cit., pp. 713-725.

[62] It is worth noting here that if Jn 6:47 and 10:38 say " he who believes has eternal life ", Jn 17:3 says that " eternal life is to know ...". Cf. BULTMANN, art. γινώσκω, TDNT I, p. 712.

[63] Cf. I Jn 2:3,5,18 ; 3:16,19,24 ; 4:2,6,13 ; 5:2.

[64] Cf. for example, I Jn 2:3.

Father or Christ as Son. The καί in 2:29b implies a certain comparison between 'He who is righteous' and 'he who does righteousness'.[65]

B. δίκαιος God or Christ?

Scholars are not unanimous in answering this question. Many authors as Loisy[66], Vrede[67], Büchsel[68], Chaine[69] say that it refers to God. Their main argument is that it should refer to the same person of whom it is said in v. 29c 'born of Him', and that this 'Him' can only be God. But the phrase 'born of Him' comes later and hence could not be present to the readers' mind as the subject of δίκαιος. It is more natural to suppose Christ as subject of δίκαιος, He being the subject of the immediately preceding v. 28[70], since no personal pronoun is introduced in v. 29, and in 3:1 the new subject 'Father' is explicitly mentioned. The ἐξ αὐτοῦ γεγέννηται is not to be explained simply as a sentence belonging to the written source, which Jn used[71]. But it could be explained from the intention of the author to introduce the new theme of the divine sonship of men, taken from the baptismal parenesis common to the other NT Epistles, and hence anticipating it with an expression that is characteristic of him, while speaking of this theme.

1. Comparison with I Jn 3:7

Also a comparison with I Jn 3:7 points to Christ as the subject of δίκαιος. In 3:7 He is called ἐκεῖνος. This word occurs in Jn only six times (cf. 2:6; 3:3,5,7,16 and 4:17), and every time it refers to Christ. The value of this comparison with 3:7 is reinforced by the fact that in the literary structure of the section 3:7 corresponds to 2:29 too. (Cf. A A² in the structure).

---

[65] Cf. I Jn 3:7b where this comparison is explicitly brought out: " he who does righteousness is righteous as He is righteous ".
[66] Cf. *Le quatrième évangile, Les épîtres dites de Jean*, Paris, 1921, p. 550.
[67] Cf. *Der Erste Brief des hl. Johannes*, Bonn, 1916, p. 183.
[68] Cf. *Die Johannesbriefe*, p. 44.
[69] Cf. *Les épîtres catholiques*, p. 177.
[70] Cf. R. SCHNACKENBURG, *Die Johannesbriefe*, p. 166.
[71] Bultmann and BRAUN try to solve the problem from such a diversity of sources. Cf. BULTMANN, *Analyse* ... p. 146 ; BRAUN, *Literaranalyse* ..., p. 269. But no solid argument is brought forward. Besides, the construction ἐάν ... and γινώσκετε, ὅτι are characteristic of the author. Cf. SCHNACKENBURG, *Die Johannesbriefe*, p. 167, note 1.

2. The Use of δίκαιος in Jn

Also the general use of δίκαιος in Jn justifies its attribution to Christ. It is attributed to God only once in I Jn 1:9 [72], and that as a by-name " πιστός καὶ δίκαιος " in as much as he saves men from sin through Christ [73]. And Christ is really called δίκαιος as the redeemer from sin in I Jn 2:1 [74], and it is only Christ who is, as 'righteous', presented as a moral exemplar or model for the imitation of Christians (cf. 3:7) [75].

3. Transition from Christ to God

The transition from Christ in v. 29a to God in v. 29c, without explicitly mentioning the change of subject can be explained easily, if we consider the inseparability of Christ and God the Father in Johannine thought when considering the work of salvation. For Jn God appears to us always in Christ [76], and works always through Christ [77]. In the Epistle itself, 'the charity that God has and is' (cf. 4:16) is manifested in Christ (cf. I Jn 3:16). The same charity that is described in the second part of the Epistle in its revelation in Christ (3:16) goes back to its source, God, in the third part of the Epistle (4:16). So the transition from Christ to God or *vice versa* is so easy in Jn [78]. And since for Jn Christ is God revealed to men, if δίκαιος is primarily applied to Christ, by that very fact it is also applied indirectly to God. This transition from God to Christ is all the more clear specially in I Jn 1:9 – 2:2 where the very adjective δίκαιος is attributed to God and Christ in the same way in connection with forgiveness and expiation of sins. If in 1:9 God is righteous, because he liberates us from sins, in 2:1 it is Christ who is righteous, because he is the expiation for our sins, and it is through Christ that the Father liberates us from sins. So for Jn, the Father who is righteous is revealed in Christ who is himself righteous.

---

[72] In the Gospel also God is called once righteous (Jn 17:25), but only as vocative πάτερ δίκαιε without any development of thought.

[73] Note its parallelism with 1:7 where Christ is said to be the redeemer.

[74] Compare also I Jn 3:5 and 8.

[75] Compare also I Jn 2:6; 3:6,16; 4:17 etc. where Christ is presented as a model for the moral conduct of Christians.

[76] Cf. for example, Jn 14:9 " He who sees me sees the Father ".

[77] Cf. Jn 14:10 " The Father remaining in me does His works ".

[78] If here the transition is from Christ to God, in 3:1-4 the transition is from God to Christ (τέκνα Θεοῦ ... καθὼς ἐκεῖνος). Cf. WESTCOTT, *Epistles*, p. 83.

C. Christ as Righteous

Outside the section I Jn 2:29 – 3:10 Jn uses δικαιοσύνη only once, and that is in Jn 16:8-10, speaking of the righteousness of Christ [79]. Therefore this text will throw light on Christ as Righteous.

1. Christ's Righteousness in Jn 16:8-10

The Commentators are usually of two opinions regarding the nature of this righteousness, namely, some speak of a juridical righteousness (righteousness of the cause of Christ) [80] and others speak of a moral righteousness (sanctity of Christ) [81]. In the juridical sense, righteousness is usually applied to the judge and judgement [82]. But Christ is here the one who is judged, and the innocence of a party is rarely called δικαιοσύνη. Besides, it would be strange that such a righteousness be mentioned separately and immediately before the judgement as is the case here. So the moral sense seems to be better here. It agrees better too with the antithesis between 'sin' and 'righteousness' here, as is also the case in I Jn 2:29 – 3:10.

But it seems to speak of something more than a merely moral sanctity. It is a righteousness that is a victory over sin [83]. If sin separates man from God (did not believe in Christ), righteousness unites man with God (Christ united with the Father). So the righteousness of which the world will be convicted to its shame is the triumphant righteousness of Christ, which is manifested in his going to the Father, namely, in the fulfilment of his victorious redemptive work over sin, making the same righteousness accessible to everyone who believes in him [84]. The victory over sin (righteousness) which

---

[79] Some Fathers and Reformers of the 16th Century attributed this righteousness to the Christians. Cf. M. F. BERROUARD, " Le Paraclet, défenseur du Christ devant la conscience du croyant Jn 16,8-11 ", *RScPhTh* 33 (1949), pp. 364, 381ff. But the words 'because I go to the Father ...' show that Jesus is the subject of righteousness here.

[80] Cf. J. MALDONATUS, *Commentarius*, pp. 1791-1795; Th. CALMES, *L'évangile*, pp. 404-405; LOISY, *Évangile*, pp. 430-432; BULTMANN, *Evangelium*, pp. 432-437; VAN DEN BUSSCHE, *Jean*, p. 437; T. PREISS, 'La Justification dans la pensée Johannique. Hommage et Reconnaissance. Recueil de Travaux publiés à l'occasion du soisantième anniversaire de Karl Barth, Paris, 1946, pp. 100-118.

[81] Cf. CHRYSOSTOM, PG 59, 421-422; EUTHYMIUS, PG 129, 1424-1425; THEOPHYLACTUS, PG 124, 209-212; B. WEISS, *Evangelium*, pp. 440-443; WESTCOTT, *Gospel*, 227-230; LAGRANGE, *Évangile*, pp. 418-420.

[82] Cf. Jn 5:30; 7:24; cf. also Acts 17:31; Apoc 19:11.

[83] Cf. A. DESCAMPS, *Les justes et la justice dans les évangiles et le christianisme primitif*, Louvain, 1950, p. 91.

[84] The idea of a triumphant righteousness is also more conformable to the

was effected by Christ through His death, resurrection and ascension (fulfilment of redemptive work) becomes that of the Christian being united with Christ in faith, which is the pledge of glory [85].

2. *Christ the Righteous in I Jn 2:1-2*

The same idea is brought out in I Jn 2:1-2, where Christ is pictured as the 'advocate' and 'expiation' of sin in his quality of being righteous [86]. In Christ who is righteous, who is unstained by sin, and has conquered sin, the Father sees His own essential righteousness revealed [87]. Christ as righteous stands before God as the divine ideal of humanity, and thus is qualified to undertake the cause of mankind before the righteous Father (cf. Heb 7:26,27). Christ is the propitiation for our sins. Christ's prerogative of advocacy is founded on the fact that he was made a propitiation for the sins of the world, and it is by Christ's advocacy that the propitiation becomes actually operative. The two acts are not only united in one person, they constitute the one reconciling work, by which there is abiding fellowship between God and man [88]. Note the very structure of the two verses which presents Christ the righteous as combining both concepts of advocacy and propitiation:

2:1 a   If anyone does sin
    b   We have an a d v o c a t e with the Father
      c   Jesus *Christ the righteous* [89]
2   b'   And he is e x p i a t i o n
    a'   for our sins.

So it is as the one who is not tainted by sin and has triumphed over the sin, that Christ is described as 'righteous'.

Biblical tradition, in which the victory of God in war is a work of righteousness (Is 41:10). The frequent combination of peace and righteousness (cf. Is 32:17; Mt 12:20; Jam 3:18; Apoc 19:11) also points to the same. For this nuance of the vocabulary of righteousness, cf. BULTMANN, *Evangelium*, p. 434, note 7.

[85] Cf. I Jn 5:4ff "And this is the victory that overcometh the world, our faith".

[86] Note the absence of the article for δίκαιον, which emphasizes the quality of the righteousness of Christ.

[87] The righteousness of Christ as presented here answers to the righteousness of the Father in I Jn 1:9. Cf. WESTCOTT, *Epistles*, p. 43.

[88] Cf. R. LAW, *Tests of Life*, p. 171.

[89] Note that the adjective δίκαιον is not a simple epithet, but marks predicatively (being as He is righteous) that characteristic of Christ which gives efficacy to His advocacy of man. Cf. WESTCOTT, *Epistles*, p. 43.

Also the section I Jn 2:29 – 3:10 presents Christ as righteous (2:29; 3:7) in his quality of being pure, and having no sin in him (cf. 3:3; 3:6), and as the one who took away sins (3:5-6), and undid the devil's deeds (3:8). This Christ, the righteous is presented here as the ideal for the Christian (cf. 3:7). So Christ as righteous stands in the section, both as source and exemplar of the righteousness of Christians [90].

3. Christ as Righteous in filial relationship with God

As we saw, I Jn 2:29 – 3:10 puts 'righteousness' and 'sin' as representing two diametrically opposite spheres. If he who does righteousness is 'born of God' (2:29), he who commits sin is 'from the devil' (3:8). So the righteous and the sinner are controlled by the spheres of God and the devil respectively, and consequently stand in a filial relation to God or to the devil [91]. Now for Jn Christ stands out as the one and only 'Righteous' who is untainted by sin and has triumphed over sin, and this is precisely because he stands preeminently in a filial relation to God [92].

a. The Pre-Johannine Teaching on the matter

This relationship of divine sonship and righteousness in Christ is not an entirely Johannine creation. Already in the Synoptics we have references to it. In the few Synoptic passages in which Jesus speaks of himself as Son of God or simply as 'Son' two aspects always appear: first, the obedience of the Son in fulfilment of the divine plan; second, the constant awareness and experience of his unique relation to God in executing his obedience [93].

Specially in Mt, in whom the word δικαιοσύνη is characteristic [94], and means a right relation to God [95], Jesus is called ὁ υἱός μου ὁ ἀγαπητός as he is baptized to 'fulfil all righteousness' (cf. Mt 3:15,17), and which he proves to be in the temptation immediately following, without yielding to the contrary suggestions (cf. Mt 4:3-11). The

---

[90] Cf. SCHNACKENBURG, *Die Johannesbriefe*, p. 166; compare also I Jn 2:6; 3:6,16; 4:17 where He is described as exemplar for Christians.

[91] Cf. H. SEEBASS, art. "Gerechtigkeit", *TBLNT* I, p. 505.

[92] Cf. the Parallel scheme of the section 2:29 – 3:10, in which Christ as righteous and pure stands parallel to Christ as 'Son of God' (v. 8).

[93] For an evaluation of all the relevant passages in the Synoptic Gospels, cf. J. BIENECK, *Sohn Gottes als Christusbezeichnung der Synoptiker*, Zürich, 1951, in which he shows these aspects of Christ's sonship.

[94] Mt makes use of it 7 times, while Lk only once and John twice.

[95] Cf. A. DESCAMPS, op. cit., pp. 158-206.

very word ἀγαπητός seems to point to this aspect of his sonship [96]. His unique relation to the Father is emphasized also in Mt 11:27 and 14:23. In the Transfiguration too, as in the complex composition of 'Baptism' and 'Temptation', the obedient fulfilment of the will of God is emphasized [97]. In Mt 26:63f, perhaps the most important of all texts, since here Jesus himself gives a positive answer to the question about his 'mission' and 'sonship' for the first and only time, and that before the highest representatives of the people, he refers to himself as 'Son of God' identified with the Son of Man, thus referring to his passion as an obedient fulfilling of the will of God, and as the way to his enthronement. Jesus is shown then as the 'Son of God', being obedient to the will of God from his baptism to the cross. So there is no wonder that Jn describes him as 'Son of God' in 'being righteous' through his sinlessness and triumph over sin.

b. In the Johannine Texts

In fact, we see that the righteousness of Christ as presented in I Jn 2:1 answers to the righteousness of the Father in 1:9, because Christ accomplishes perfectly all that is set forth in the revelation of the Father's nature [98]. Here it is worth noting that the righteousness of Christ in Jn 16:10 is grounded on the fact that He goes to the Father, and as we saw above, it meant the triumphant righteousness over sin through the work of redemption. All these considerations induce us to see in Christ the Righteous his filial relation to God [99].

---

[96] Cf. Th. DE KRUIJF, *Der Sohn des lebendigen Gottes*, Rome, 1962, pp. 124ff, where he translates it as 'unique', referring to his unique obedience.

[97] See how the declaration of Christ's being the Son of God is framed by the two passion sayings (Mt 16:21-23 = 17:1-8 = 17:22-23) which already suggests that the sonship of Christ as an obedient fulfilling of the will of God (righteousness) is culminating in the Passion and Resurrection. Note the variant reading of Lk 23:47 δίκαιος instead of the υἱὸς Θεοῦ of Mt 27:54 and Mk 15:39.

[98] Note that the thought of righteousness as a divine attribute belongs peculiarly to John (cf. Jn 17:25; I Jn 1:9). Note also the words πρὸς τὸν πατέρα in Jn 2:1, which are significant there, because the advocacy of Christ as righteous for man is addressed to God in that relation of fatherhood, which has been fully revealed in the Son (cf. WESTCOTT, *Epistles*, p. 43).

[99] Here we may recall the difficulty in I Jn 2:29 as to who is righteous. In fact, for John Christ is righteous as the revelation of the Father.

D. 'Everyone who does righteousness'

The ποιῶν of men in John shows the origin and is the proof of sonship, so that the nature of the ποιεῖν points to the father from whom one is born [100]. This is clearly brought to light in Jn 8:31-47 [101]. The ποιεῖν of man depends on what kind of a father he has or whose son he is or what he heard from his father (cf. Jn 8:38,39, 41,44), so that the ἁμαρτίαν ποιεῖν is the sign of his wrong origin, of his slavery (Jn 8:34), which is clear from the origin, not from Abraham, nor from God, but from the devil (Jn 8:41,44) and the deeds of the Jews. It is interesting to note that this is the only other place in John where he uses the expression ὁ ποιῶν τὴν ἁμαρτίαν (v. 34) outside I Jn 2:29 – 3:10a, the exact opposite term of ὁ ποιῶν τὴν δικαιοσύνην, and connecting it with the theme of a spiritual father-son relationship. As in I Jn 2:29 – 3:10a ὁ ποιῶν τὴν δικαιοσύνην and ὁ ποιῶν τὴν ἁμαρτίαν are the two distinct elements in the Johannine structure of the section, and they are the criteria of the divine and the diabolic sonship respectively. An examination of the section Jn 8:31-47 increases our understanding of the divine sonship of men manifested in 'doing righteousness'.

1. *Comparison between I Jn 2:29 – 3:10 and Jn 8:31-47*

In fact, a comparison of I Jn 2:29 – 3:10 with Jn 8:31-47 betrays striking similarities in thought and expressions.
Note the expressions that are literally identical, such as: ὁ ποιῶν τὴν ἁμαρτίαν (8:34 = I Jn 3:4,8); ἐκ τοῦ Θεοῦ οὐκ ἐστέ (8:47 = I Jn 3:10); ἐκ τοῦ ... διαβόλου (8:44 = I Jn 3-8) and also expressions that are thematically identical, such as: ὁ λόγος ... χωρεῖ ἐν ὑμῖν (8:37 = I Jn 3:9); τίς ἐξ ὑμῶν ἐλέγχει με περὶ ἁμαρτίας (8:46 = I Jn 3:5). Though

---

[100] Cf. H. BRAUN, art. ποιέω, *TWNT* VI, p. 480 where speaking of the Johannine concept of ποιεῖν says: " Das menschliche Tun wird deshalb in Frage gestellt, weil es unausweichbar aus dem Woher des Menschen entspringt". It is worth noting here that speaking of ποιεῖν of Jesus in the first part of the Gospel (the Book of Signs), it is almost always connected with σημεῖον explicitly or implicitly (21 out of 30), so that the ποιεῖν of Jesus was always a testimony to His divine origin.

[101] Jn 8:31-47 is the first part of the great section 8:31-59 in which we can notice a transition in v. 47 concluding the theme treated up to that verse. (Cf. C. H. DODD, " A l'arrière – plan d'un dialogue johannique ", *RHPR* 37 (1957), p. 6). We will see the literary unity of the section 8:31-47 also from the structure given below on p. 253. W. KERN, " Der symmetrische Gesamtaufbau von Joh 8:12-58 ", *ZKT* 78 (1956), pp. 451-454 attempts a much more elaborate analysis of the poetic structure of vv. 12-59, which R. E. BROWN in his Commentary, p. 342 qualifies as a 'tour de force' of the investigation, rather than the plan of the Evangelist.

the distinction between the τέκνα τοῦ Θεοῦ and the τέκνα τοῦ διαβόλου (I Jn 3:1,10) is less explicit in the Gospel, nevertheless this distinction lies behind the Jews having the devil for their father (v. 44), in contrast to those who are truly disciples (ἀληθῶς μαθηταί - 8:31) [102].

2. *The Structure of Jn 8:31-47*

A structure of the section will help us to see the real import of the sonship that is affirmed here:

Vv. 31-32 A IF YOU remain in MY WORD, YOU WILL BE TRULY MY DISCIPLES ... YOU WILL KNOW THE Truth, and
The *Truth* will SET YOU FREE.
33 B We are the SEED OF ABRAHAM ... not slave ... but free
34 C Everyone w h o c o m m i t s s i n is a slave to sin ...
35 D T h e S o n remains for ever
36 A′ IF the *Son* SETS YOU FREE, YOU WILL BE TRULY FREE
37 B′ I know ... You are the SEED OF ABRAHAM
C′ But YOU SEEK TO KILL ME ...
M y W o r d d o e s n o t r e m a i n i n y o u
38 D′ I SPEAK what I s a w FROM MY FATHER
A² YOU DO what YOU HEARD from YOUR FATHER ...
39 B² Our FATHER IS ABRAHAM
C² Jesus ... If ... do the works ...
But YOU SEEK TO KILL ME
40 D² Man who SPOKE THE TRUTH ... h e a r d FROM GOD ...
A³ YOU DO YOUR FATHER'S works
41 B³ They ... we are not born ... we have one FATHER, GOD
42 C³ He said ... if God ... Y o u w o u l d l o v e me
D³ For I c a m e FROM GOD ... He sent me
43 A⁴ YOU DO not ... cannot HEAR MY WORD ...
YOU are from YOUR FATHER the devil
Your will is to DO YOUR FATHER'S desires
44 B⁴ He was a murderer ... a liar ... father of lies
45 C⁴ If I speak ... Y O U d o n o t b e l i e v e me
46 D⁴ Who will ... me of sin ... I SPEAK THE TRUTH to you why don't you believe me
47 A⁵ He w h o i s f r o m G o d
HEAR THE WORDS of God
You DO NOT HEAR,
because Y o u a r e n o t f r o m G o d.

---

[102] Cf. F. M. BRAUN, *Jean le théologien, sa théologie. Le mystère de Jésus Christ*, Paris, 1966, p. 129.

Here we have five small sections repeating the same arguments with certain modifications. Note the literary parallels in the corresponding sections. The structure in this case is based not only on literary parallelism but also on thematic parallelism. Thus A stanzas speak of the sonship of men (represented by the believing Jews) [103]. If in A and A' John speaks of real sonship and the discipleship and freedom proper to it attained through the Truth, the Son, in A² A³ and A⁴ he speaks of the diabolic sonship manifested in deeds, specifically in not hearing the Word–Truth [104]. In A⁵ which rounds off the section [105], he speaks of both divine and diabolic sonship in the form of 'being (or not) from God' [106].

It is interesting to note the progress of the argument regarding sonship. If in A and A' it is the question of becoming truly disciples and obtaining the freedom proper to the divine sonship, namely, the deepening and progression in the life of the children of God through the remaining in the Word of God [107], on the contrary, in A², A³ and A⁴ it is a question of the manifestation of the actual diabolic sonship which they possess [108]. Finally in A⁵ concluding the section, he presents both divine and diabolic sonship in the form of εἶναι and οὐκ εἶναι ἐκ τοῦ Θεοῦ which already refers to the abiding result of the vital communication from God, which influences the whole conduct of the children of God. Thus he takes up again the introductory aspect of the dynamic development of the life of the children of God.

That Jn refers here to the divine sonship and begetting is clear from the fact that εἶναι ἐκ τοῦ Θεοῦ is attributed to men only here in v. 47 in the whole Gospel, and in the Epistle it is used parallel to γεγέννηται ἐκ τοῦ Θεοῦ (cf. I Jn 3:10 ; 5:19). This is, perhaps,

---

[103] Cf. v. 30 that says that : " many believed in Him ", and v. 31 in which Jesus addresses his speech to the πεπιστευκότας αὐτῷ 'Ιουδαίους. This may suggest that the ' Sitz im Leben ' of this dialogue was the controversy with the Jewish Christians in the Primitive Church, traces of which are found in the Acts of the Apostles (cf. 10:45 ; 11:2 ; 15:5 ; 21:20 etc.) and in the polemics of St. Paul (cf. Gal 3:17-18,26-27 ; 4:1-10,21-31 ; 5:1-14). For a detailed study on the matter, cf. C. H. DODD, art. cit., " A l'arrière — plan ...", pp. 5-17.

[104] Cf. vv. 43-44 (A⁴) where the 'doing the desires of the devil their father' consists specifically in 'not hearing the Word'.

[105] Note the parallelism with A : ' hear (remain in) the Word ', ' you will be (are- ἐστέ) my disciples ' + ' not from God '.

[106] Cf. above what we spoke of εἶναι ἐκ Θεοῦ as being parallel to γεγεννῆσθαι ἐκ Θεοῦ on pp. 96-97.

[107] Note the future tense of the verbs γνώσεσθε, ἐλευθερώσει, γενήσεσθε, ἔσεσθε, in vv. 31-37 which indicates the end towards which the life of the believers progresses.

[108] Note the present tense of ποιεῖτε and θέλετε ποιεῖν so frequent here.

prepared by previous statements regarding the pretended sonship of the Jews as a begetting (ἡμεῖς ἐκ πορνείας οὐ γεγεννήμεθα) and their diabolic sonship as ' being from the devil ' (v. 44) and also as regards the sonship of Christ presented as a ' coming from God ' [109].

Another thing to be noted is that in this concluding section the norm is reversed. If in the preceding A^2, A^3, A^4 deeds are presented as the criterion of sonship, in A^5 the ' hearing of the word ' is presented as the result or fruit of the sonship [110]. This procedure corresponds to the general Johannine presentation of the theme of divine sonship in the second stage and the presentation in the double (criterion and fruit) scheme mentioned at the beginning of this chapter.

B stanzas speak of the pretended claim of the Jews to be the seed of Abraham (vv. 33, 37 – B, B′) and to have Abraham or God as father (vv. 39, 41 – B^2, B^3), which is actually disproved by showing the nature of their real father the devil (murderer, liar) (vv. 44 – B^4). The C stanzas speak of the actual position of the Jews. In C he expresses this position in generic terms as ' the one who does sin '. In the following C′, C^2, C^3, C^4 this sin is expressed concretely as the rejection of Christ and his message. The D stanzas speak of the position of Christ in contradiction to the position of the Jews. In D he is qualified explicitly as ' Son ', while in the following D′, D^2, D^3, D^4, he is presented as the one ' who speaks the Truth from the Father ', or ' coming from the Father ', which certainly point to His sonship [111].

The parallel procedure of the themes could be presented thus schematically:

A A′ A^2 A^3 A^4 A^5	— Real sonship of men manifested in deeds
B B′ B^2 B^3 B^4	— Pretended sonship of the Jews
C C′ C^2 C^3 C^4	— Denial of the pretended sonship through their sinful position
D D′ D^2 D^3 D^4	— Sonship of Christ.

The controversy constituted by these four elements brings to light the real nature of divine sonship.

---

[109] Cf. v. 42 ἐγὼ γὰρ ἐκ τοῦ Θεοῦ ἐξῆλθον καὶ ἥκω. Cf. what we said about the parallelism between the coming of Christ and the divine begetting of Christ speaking of Jn 1:13 on pp. 125ff.

[110] Cf. v. 47 " He who is from God hears the word of God ...".

[111] Cf. above what we said of the sonship of Christ as the revelation of the Father, and his divine begetting as parallel to His coming from the Father on pp. 125-126.

3. *Sonship manifested in conduct*

The Jews thought of sonship as a relationship established and maintained by dint of natural lineage through Abraham [112]. But Jesus insisted that true sonship is a relationship revealing spiritual lineage and characterized by action that expresses moral and spiritual likeness to the one who is claimed as father (v. 39). And he illustrates this by putting his sonship manifested in his actions in contrast to their claimed sonship [113]. The sonship of Jesus is the test for the sonship of the Jews. His sonship is manifested in His speaking and doing what he saw and heard from the Father, so reproducing the Father's life in himself [114]. If the Jews too had God as their father, then they would recognise and love him and hear his word. The divine sonship would have given them a connaturality towards him who is sent by God, and they would have been able to recognise his language (v. 43) and they would believe in Him [115].

4. *Diabolic Sonship manifested in committing sin*

But, in fact, they do not believe in Him and even seek to kill Him. So, evidently this conduct points to their filial relation to a father who is different and hostile to God, namely, the devil (v. 44). Just as Jesus had manifested his unique sonship to the Father by unhesitating and unvarying obedience (vv. 38, 40, 42, 45), so the Jews, in contrast, were revealing their diabolic sonship by their consistant imitation of the evil example and deadly lusts of the devil (vv. 34, 37, 39, 42, 45).

This contraposition of Jesus' sonship with that of the Jews can be seen in the structure:

	Jesus		*Jews*
D	Son remains in the house ... free	C	He who does sin is a slave of sin
D'	Speaks what he heard from father	$C'A^2$	Seek to kill ... heard from father
D^2	Speaks ... heard from God	C^2A^3	Seek to kill ... their father's work

---

[112] Note that even their claim of having God as Father rests on this natural lineage through Abraham, because it is through this natural lineage that they become members of the people of God, and sons of God.

[113] Note the parallel developments of C and D stanzas in the section.

[114] Note the parallelism of the D stanzas all manifesting His sonship, as one who comes from God, speaks the Truth — as the revelation of the Father.

[115] Cf. A. VANHOYE, " Notre foi, oeuvre divine d'après le quatrième évangile ", *NRT* 86 (1964), pp. 337-354, where he illustrates that faith in Christ is the work of the Father and manifests the sonship to the Father.

D³	Came from God	C³A⁴	From their father ... devil
D⁴	Speaks the truth	C⁴A⁵	Do not believe, do not hear.

So, diabolic sonship is manifested in 'doing sin'. To speak of doing sin, in general, is not characteristic of the Gospel [116]. It is the Epistle that speaks of sin in general, and 'doing sin' as a mode of existence that is incompatible with Christian existence. We saw how the expression ποιεῖν τὴν ἁμαρτίαν occurs apart from Jn 8:34 only in I Jn 3:4,8,9. So the concept of sin in the section I Jn 2:29 – 3:10 and in Jn 8:34 should be mutually explanatory.

a. The concept of sin in concrete

The correspondence of the C stanzas in Jn 8:31-47 shows that the ποιεῖν τὴν ἁμαρτίαν refers concretely to the Jews who do not believe in Jesus and who try to kill him. So, practically, Jn identifies the 'sin' here (note the article) with their 'unbelief'.

Also the concept of sin in I Jn 2:29 – 3:10 confirms this idea. The exhortation in v. 7 " Little children, let no one deceive you, he that doeth righteousness ..." seems to imply that there were persons who pretended to be righteous apart from the 'doing' of righteous deeds, and that on the other hand, the mere doing of sinful acts is no disproof of inward spirituality [117]. So, the sin from which Jn wants to preserve the faithful is the manner of acting of the false teachers[118].

The very emphatic formula " ὁ ποιῶν τὴν ἁμαρτίαν " (with the article) shows that here it is a question of a particular sin that is well-known, and in the eschatological and dualistic context of our section, it cannot be other than the well-known sin of the 'Anti-Christs' who reject Christ — The Son of God (cf. I Jn 2:22-23) [119]. So, it is this sin of rejection of Christ, this sin of unbelief, which

---

[116] The Gospel usually speaks of sin, not in itself, but as realized in particular persons such as the pharisees (8:21,24), Pilate (19:11) etc. Cf. N. LAZURE, Les valeurs morales ..., p. 289. This also points to the correspondence of this phrase to the stanzas speaking of the concrete sin of the Jews.

[117] Cf. R. LAW, Tests of Life, p. 219, where he finds in this affirmation the disclosure of the polemical import, which is the clue to discover the precise significance of the phrase ὁ ποιῶν which is so characteristic of the paragraph (2:29 ; 3:4,7,8,9,10).

[118] Note the parallel section I Jn 1:5 – 2:2 where the exhortation regarding sin seems to be inspired by the pretension of false teachers, who believed themselves to be without sin. Cf. I. DE LA POTTERIE, art. " Le péché, c'est l'iniquité ", in La vie selon l'Esprit, p. 77.

[119] Note that it is this sin of unbelief that is described in Jn as 'the sin of the world' (cf. Jn 16:11 ; comp. 1:10-11 ; 8:21,24,46 ; 15:21-22). Cf. I. DE LA POTTERIE, art. " Le péché ", p. 78.

gives origin to all other sins, that Jn calls 'the sin' in the section as in Jn 8:34.

b. The Specific Character of Sin in the context

Jn himself gives a definition of sin in I Jn 3:4 "ἡ ἁμαρτία ἐστὶν ἡ ἀνομία". Usually the commentators translate ἀνομία as 'lawlessness' or 'violation of law' according to the usage of ἀνομία in classical Greek and LXX [120]. But the context does not favour this interpretation [121], and for a correct interpretation of the passage, one has to see the usage of the word in NT times [122]. As it is clear from the article of I. de la Potterie, ἀνομία has a sense of 'diabolic power', a state of enmity to God under the power of the devil, with an eschatological orientation [123].

In fact, the context of I Jn 2:29 – 3:10 itself gives evidence for this sense of ἀνομία. We saw above how I Jn 2:29 introduces the theme of the section following the structure of describing the interior reality of communion as manifested in the exterior reality, and how the whole section is a development of the same theme. The parallelism in the antithetical structural development shows that the phrase 'he commits iniquity' comes under the series expressing the interior reality as seen in the following scheme:

v. 4   He who commits sin   — commits also iniquity
v. 6b He who commits sin   — has not seen ... known Him
v. 8   He who commits sin   — is of the devil
v. 10 He who does not do righteousness — is not of God.

So the term ἀνομία belongs to the series of expressions that describe the interior situation of the sinner, rather than the act itself.

This interior situation is again a synonym for 'being of the devil' [124], and 'not being of God' as seen from the parallelism. This

---

[120] Cf. for instance, P. GALTIER, "Le chrétien impeccable (I Jn 3,6 et 9)", *MélScRel* 4 (1947), p. 149; M. E. BOISMARD, art. "La connaissance ...", p. 379; cf. also the Commentaries of Calmes, Loisy, Chaine, Bonsirven, Windisch, Büchsel, Westcott, Brooke etc.

[121] For an evaluation of the drawbacks of this interpretation, cf. I. DE LA POTTERIE, art. "Le péché", pp. 66-67.

[122] Cf. I. DE LA POTTERIE, art. "Le péché", pp. 68-73 where he traces the semantic evolution of the term in LXX, Judaism and the Synoptic Gospels.

[123] Cf. also W. NAUCK, *Die Tradition und der Character* ..., p. 16f; R. SCHNACKENBURG, *Die Johannesbriefe*, pp. 185-187.

[124] Note the parallelism of vv. 5 and 8b where the 'sins' are synonymous with the 'works of the devil'. Cf. E. J. COOPER, "The Consciousness of Sin in I John", *LavThéolPhil* 28 (1972), pp. 237-248.

means that for Jn 'to commit sin' is the expression of being actually under the influence of the diabolic power [125].

The antithetical parallelism of ὁ ποιῶν τὴν ἁμαρτίαν with ὁ ποιῶν τὴν δικαιοσύνην in I Jn 2:29 – 3:10 induces us to see in the notion of sin also an opposition to the will of God (I Jn 2:17). For I Jn ἁμαρτία is not only ἀνομία but also ἀδικία [126]. So the concept of sin in I Jn seems to combine both notions of an eschatological diabolical power and a transgression of the will of God [127].

This combined notion of sin seems to be supported by the parallel section Jn 8:31-47. First of all Jn 8:34 speaks of the 'one who commits sin' as being a slave to sin [128]. As the section 8:31-47 contains different expressions that remind us of the Jewish theology [129], the Jewish concept of freedom and sin seems to lie behind this versicle [130].

---

[125] Cf. R. LAW, *Tests of Life*, p. 129, note 1 where he distinguishes the different Johannine uses of ἁμαρτία and describes ἡ ἁμαρτία in singular with article as signifying sin in its constitutive principle (3:4,8) in direct antithesis to ἡ δικαιοσύνη (2:29 ; 3:7), and thus ὁ ποιῶν τὴν ἁμαρτίαν as expressing in actual deed the essential principle of sin. Cf. also W. R. COOK, " Hamartiological Problems in First John ", *BS* 123 (1966), 250, note 2 where he says that the statement 'sin is lawlessness' is a convertible one because of the use of the definite article with both substantives and thus is probably the most definite Biblical statement regarding sin.

[126] Cf. I Jn 1:7,9 ; 5:17 where the words 'sin' and 'unrighteousness' are used interchangeably.

[127] Cf. A. CHARUE, *Les épîtres de saint Jean*, Paris, 1938, p. 537, where he combines both these meanings for the phrase 'the sin is iniquity' ; cf. A. SKRINJAR, " Errores in Epistola I Jo impugnati ", *VD* 41 (1963), p. 67 : " Esto tamen in hoc diabolico quid aliud magis eminet quam oppositio et rebellio adversus Deum ejusque sanctam voluntatem ? ". Cf. also N. LAZURE, op. cit., pp. 308-309. The very fact that Jn alludes concretely to the sin of unbelief favours this interpretation, because faith is clearly presented by Jn as an exigence of the will of the Father (cf. Jn 6:29 where faith is described as the work demanded by God). I Jn 3:23 says : " This is his commandment, that we believe ...".

[128] Note that the words τῆς ἁμαρτίας are omitted by D, b, 1a, Syr sin, and Clement of Alexandria. This strong combination of witnesses perhaps suggests that it is an addition from Rom 6:17-20 (cf. R. E. BROWN, *Gospel*, p. 355 ; N. LAZURE, op. cit., p. 296, note 32). Anyhow it is fitting into the Johannine concept of sin.

[129] Cf. N. LAZURE, op. cit., p. 296 ; cf. also H. ODEBERG, *The Fourth Gospel*, Uppsala, 1929, p. 301 : " It might be urged that the utterances in the present section (8:30-59) laid in the mouth of the Jews, not only reproduce exactly the early Rabbinic conceptions, but also constitute a picture artistically drawn of the Rabbinic mode of reasoning ".

[130] For the interpretation of the text in the light of the Rabbinic parallel texts, cf. H. ODEBERG, *The Fourth Gospel*, pp. 296-310.

In Jewish theology, the one who sins shows that he is dominated by, namely, a slave to his bad inclinations (*Yēser hā-ra*) [131], and only the just, who is faithful to the accomplishment of the divine will really enjoys freedom from this slavery, and merits to be called a child of God. This Yeser ha-ra is connected or even identified with Satan, and its activity is directed towards man's destruction: he is a man-slayer [132]. All these indicate the sin in Jn 8:34 as a diabolic power which dominates the life of the sinner [133].

On the other hand, the fact of the sin is qualified as a carrying out of the wishes of their father, the devil, and this is put in contrast to Jesus who, being without sin, (v. 46), carries out what he saw and heard from His Father (vv. 38, 40, 42) [134]. It is interesting to note here that in the Gospel the word ἀδικία is used only once (7:18) and it says that there is no 'injustice' in him (Jesus), because He seeks the glory of the One who sent Him and is consequently ἀληθής. Also in our section Jesus declares that He has no sin in Himself (v. 46) and this is parallel with his speaking the truth, seen and heard from the Father (vv. 38, 40, 45, 46), who sent Him (v. 42) [135]. So, not having injustice certainly includes acting according to the will of God [136].

So, 'to commit sin' is for Jn 'to let oneself be dominated by the diabolic power' that sets itself against the will of God, which concretely and fundamentally takes place in the rejection of Christ, namely, unbelief. And this is the criterion for 'being children of the devil' (Jn 8:44; I Jn 3:10) and 'being from the devil' (Jn 8:44; I Jn 3:8) and for 'not being from God' (Jn 8:47; I Jn 3:10).

---

[131] On the Rabbinic concept of Yéser hara cf. Str. Bill. IV, pp. 466-483; F. C. PORTER, 'The Yéser hara. A Study of the Jewish Doctrine of sin' in *Biblical and Semitic Studies*, New York, 1901, pp. 93-156.

[132] Cf. H. ODEBERG, *The Fourth Gospel*, p. 300; Note that also Jn speaks of the devil as a 'man-slayer' from the beginning (Jn 8:44).

[133] Note the parallel expression in v. 44 ὑμεῖς ἐκ τοῦ πατρὸς τοῦ διαβόλου ἐστέ which points to the diabolic power that determines the life and actions of the Jews who are slaves to sin.

[134] Note the parallelism between the sections DA, D'A², D²A³, and D³A⁴. The fact that several texts of the Fourth Gospel speak of sin, addressing a Jewish audience, warns us against excluding from the Johannine concept of sin all Jewish notion, which always contained the idea of disobedience to the ordinances of God (cf. G. F. MOORE, *Judaism in the First Centuries of Christian Era*, II, Cambridge, (1927-30), p. 319). For the notion of the diabolic sonship manifested in the conduct of the Jews as expressed in this section, cf. E. GRÄSSER, *Die Juden als Teufelssöhne nach Joh 8,37-47*, Abh. z. Christl. Jüd. Dialog 2 (Mü. 1967).

[135] Note the parallelism of D stanzas in the structure of the section.

[136] Cf. also Jn 4:34; 6:38; 8:29,55.

VI. Divine Sonship manifested in 'doing righteousness'

If the 'ποιεῖν τὴν ἁμαρτίαν' is the criterion of the diabolic sonship, it is quite understandable that I Jn 2:29 brings the 'ποιεῖν τὴν δικαιοσύνην' as the criterion of one's divine origin and sonship, of being born of God.

A. *Sonship of Christ and Sonship of Christians*

If Christ in his quality of being 'Righteous' stands in a filial relationship to God, it is quite natural that those who do righteousness also stand in such a filial relationship to God. The καί before πᾶς places the 'one who does righteousness' in the same line as Christ the Righteous. Thus the righteousness of the believer is not only moral, though it is of moral character. It is the very righteousness of Christ, the sinlessness and triumph over sin, that is shared by the believer, and which is active in him throughout his life [137], and which becomes a real criterion of his divine sonship.

This solidarity between Christ and the believer shows that the divine sonship of man is essentially dependent on Christ's sonship. As Christ, by his victory over sin, was established as the 'Son of God' at the resurrection (Acts 13:33; Rom 1:3-4), so the believer who participates in this righteousness is also begotten of God, a child of God, whose sonship will also come to perfection at the resurrection (I Jn 3:1-2) [138].

B. *Likeness of Conduct in the Children of God*

The 'αὐτοῦ' in the phrase 'ἐξ αὐτοῦ γεγέννηται' grammatically should refer to Christ. But in Jn there is no mention of a sonship or birth from Christ. So, here he speaks of birth from God, though the idea of Christ as Son is implicitly included in it. The term 'γεγέννηται' in Jn, as we have seen, is always used together with an expression that indicates origin [139]. The phrase 'to be begotten of

---

[137] Note what we said above on Christ the Righteous as both the source and the model of the righteousness of Christians on pp. 248ff.

[138] It is worth noting here that as is clear from Jn 8:31-47, in both instances of sonship (divine and diabolic), the kind of sonship which men possess is inextricably connected with their relation to the Son of God. In the case of the children of God, their sonship originates from or follows upon their personal reception of the Son and His revelation (Jn 8:31-32,36,46; 1:12). In the case of the children of the devil, their sonship is manifested by their rejection of the Son of God (Jn 8:34,37,39,42,43-45).

[139] Note the expressions such as ἐκ τοῦ Θεοῦ — ἐξ αὐτοῦ (I Jn 2:29; 3:9;

God' is employed usually in the perfect tense (γεγέννηται, γεγεννημένος) showing thereby that the initial communication of the divine life is regarded in its abiding power. Hence it shows the abiding and permanent dynamic character of the divine principle of Life once received. In this verse under our present consideration it indicates, therefore, the father-son relationship created by this birth from God, and thus the community of nature between God and man that is the principle of his moral life expressed in ' ποιεῖν τὴν δικαιοσύνην'.

Already Jn 8:31-47 both tacitly and expressly emphasizes the truth that a true son has a moral and ethical likeness to his father. By the strong contrast between the Jews and Jesus, it is made clear that the genuine child of God is like the Son of God, who is speaking and reasoning with them. The measure of sonship to God is the life of sonship in Christ.

Sonship in the case of Jesus in our present section is manifested in His righteousness, which is actually the revelation of the righteousness of the Father. So, in the measure in which they do righteousness, the believers participate in the righteousness of Christ, and thus possess the moral and ethical likeness to God as His children.

Conclusion

John presents the theme of divine sonship and begetting in two stages, namely, in the initial stage of ' being begotten of God ' and in the progressive stage of ' having been begotten of God '. In the johannine view of realized eschatology, he sees this progressive stage of sonship already at present in the full life of faith. This is indicated by his vocabulary regarding ' being born of God ', ' being children of God ' and ' being of God '. So in the Epistle it is not the origin of the sonship that is of interest, but the actual state of being children of God.

In the Epistle of John we see a twofold scheme related to this life of sonship, namely, a ' criterion scheme ', which shows the external criteria leading to the knowledge of the interior reality, and a ' fruit scheme ' which shows the interior reality as the source that produces the external realities that are the criteria. Following the criterion scheme, Jn puts forward ' doing righteousness ' as the criterion of ' being born of God ' (I Jn 2:29 – 3:10), the doing of man being for Jn the proof of origin and sonship. This he does presenting Christ as the ' Righteous ' par excellence standing in filial relationship to the Father and as exemplar of the believers. Jn also proves it by

---

4:7 ; 5:1,4,18 ; Jn 1:13), ἐκ πνεύματος (Jn 3:5,6,8), ἐξ ὕδατος (Jn 3:5), ἐκ τῆς σαρκός (Jn 3:6), ἐκ θελήματος (Jn 1:13), ἄνωθεν (Jn 3:3,7).

bringing the dualistic opposite element of ' committing sin ' as the criterion of the diabolic sonship.

The sonship, according to Jn, is manifested in conduct that shows moral and spiritual likeness to the one who is claimed as father. ' To commit sin ' is concretely ' to reject Christ who bears witness to the Truth ', and therefore, sin is the criterion of the diabolic sonship, because it manifests a conduct showing moral likeness to the devil, who is a murderer from the beginning and a liar. On the contrary, ' to do righteousness ' is the criterion of the divine sonship, because, it entails a dynamic adherence to Christ, who in his triumphant righteousness stands in a filial relationship with God, and hence implies a sharing in his sonship. As Christ the Righteous is the revelation of the Father who is Righteous, the ' doing righteousness ' in the children of God shows also a likeness to God their Father, derived from the communication of Life which remains active throughout their filial life, and is manifested in their conduct.

CHAPTER IX

Impeccability: Fruit of the Life of Divine Sonship
(I Jn 3:9; 5:18-20; Jn 8:31-36)

We have already seen that 'doing righteousness' is in the context a condition of sinlessness and victory over sin. Now Jn goes so far as to speak of an impeccability of the Divinely Begotten: "Everyone who is born of God does not sin... and he cannot sin, because he is born of God" (I Jn 3:9)[1]. This comes under the 'fruit scheme', which points to impeccability as a fruit of the condition of being born of God.

I. The Notion of impeccability in I Jn 3:9

A. *Different Interpretations*

The affirmation of the impeccability of the divinely born, which seems to be diametrically opposed to the affirmations in I Jn 1:8, 10[2], has intrigued scholars at all times. Some understand this categorical affirmation as a merely moral exhortation not to sin[3]. Though the parenetical aspect is not to be denied, the antithetical confrontation of the 'children of God' with the 'children of the devil' shows impeccability as the distinguishing mark, that belongs to the nature of the 'children of God', as different from the nature of the 'children of the devil'[4]. Others have tried to interpret it as referring to cert-

---

[1] On this problem of impeccability of the divinely begotten, besides the commentaries, cf. P. GALTIER, art. cit., in *Mél. Sc. Rel.* 4 (1947), pp. 137-154; I. DE LA POTTERIE, art. "L'impeccabilité" in *La Vie selon l'Esprit*, pp. 197-216; O. PRUNET, *La morale chrétienne d'après les écrits johanniques*, Paris, 1957, pp. 87-94.

[2] Cf. I Jn 1:8 "If we say that we have no sin... the truth is not in us"; 1:10 "If we say that we have not sinned, we make Him out to be a liar".

[3] Cf. O. CLEMEN, *Die christliche Lehre von der Sünde*, I, Göttingen, 1897, pp. 121ff; J. E. BELSER, *Die Briefe des hl. Johannes*, Freiburg, 1906, pp. 77-79; CHAINE, *Epître*, p. 185 explains it as an exaggerated way of speaking in imitation of the manner of stoic philosophy.

[4] Cf. I Jn 3:8-9 which point to this character of sin related to the nature

ain particular sins, such as sins against charity [5], impurity [6], or a wilful refusal of Christ [7], or of capital sins [8]. But we have no indication in the context of a particular sin that is meant here. The statement is quite general. Again some others have understood it as habitual sin or the general tendency to sin, and not as actual sins [9]. A better explanation is brought forward by some who say that we become incapable of sin in the measure in which we submit ourselves to grace [10]. This is inspired by the Greek Patristic tradition, which sees the ' seed of God ' in I Jn 3:9 as an interior force, by the action of which the divinely begotten lets himself be guided by its dynamism and thus becomes incapable of choosing the evil [11].

All these explanations are based on the text itself, and try to give a logical and psychological explanation, without taking account of the historical and literary context. Recently certain authors have tried to place the text in its true context, that is, eschatological and sapiential [12].

B. *Impeccability in the Johannine Context*

First of all, we have to note that the affirmation of sin in the Christian is in a kerygmatic context (cf. I Jn 1:5) and in the Primitive Kerygma the role of Christ in obtaining the remission of sins was always emphasized [13]. On the contrary, the context of the affirmation of impeccability of the God-begotten is theological, and it is a context

---

of the one who sins or does not sin. Cf. R. SCHNACKENBURG, *Die Johannesbriefe*, p. 283.

[5] Cf. St. AUGUSTINE, PL 35, 2013 ; BEDE THE VENERABLE, PL 93, 101-102 ; GLOSSA ORDINARIA, PL 114, 679.

[6] Cf. J. E. BELSER, *Die Briefe des hl. Johannes*, pp. 77-79.

[7] Cf. P. GALTIER, art. cit., pp. 137-154.

[8] Cf. J. BONSIRVEN, *Epîtres*, pp. 174ff ; cf. also W. R. COOK, art. cit., p.255, where he explains the impeccability in I Jn 3:6,9 as : " the true disciple of Christ cannot, in the nature of the case, lead a life characteristically sinful, although he still commits acts of sin ".

[9] Cf. BROOKE, *Epistles*, pp. 89-90 ; C. H. DODD, *Epistles*, p. 79.

[10] Cf. A. CHARUE, *La Saint Bible* XII, Paris, 1938, pp. 537-538.

[11] Cf. SEVERUS OF ANTIOCH, in J. A. CRAMER, *Catenae Graecorum Patrum*, pp. 124-127 ; MAXIMUS CONFESSOR, PG 90, 279-289 ; PHOTIUS, PG 101, 112-113 ; OECUMENIUS, PG 119, 684 ; THEOPHYLACTUS, PG 126, 33 and 65.

[12] Cf. I. DE LA POTTERIE, art. " Impeccabilité ", pp. 199-208 where he analyses both these contexts. The eschatological context had been noted also by H. WINDISCH, *Die katholischen Briefe*, pp. 121-122 ; DODD, *Epistles*, 78-81 ; SCHNACKENBURG, *Die Johannesbriefe*, pp. 281-288.

[13] Cf. Acts 2:38 ; 3:19-26 ; 5:31 ; 10:43 ; 13:38 etc.

of eschatological dualism, where the 'children of God' and the 'children of the devil' are opposed [14].

Impeccability through knowledge of God and Life by means of the active presence of the Spirit and Truth (Wisdom) and the Law in the heart of men, was an eschatological theme both in biblical and judaic tradition [15]. So there is no wonder that this eschatological theme was resumed by Jn in his characteristically dualistic and realized eschatological presentation of the divine sonship. Impeccability and triumph over sin, like all the other eschatological gifts, were realized in Christ (cf. I Jn 3:5,8); and by adhesion to Christ through faith, one participates in all of them. Thus participating in the sonship and impeccability of Christ, the Christian also becomes 'begotten of God' and 'impeccable', namely, he possesses these gifts by virtue of Christ.

In his dualistic eschatology, Jn divides the children of God and the children of the devil, considering them according to their theological reality. And in this theological reality, the children of God are impeccable as Christ himself was, because their nature is an extension of the nature of Christ himself as 'begotten of God' and 'impeccable', while the absence of this nature in the children of the devil shows their diabolic nature in sin, because the devil sins from the beginning (3:8).

However, the children of God with their nature opposed to the hostile children of the devil, live still in a condition, where there is danger of losing it again. But they have in Christ the power to stand against sin, and to preserve their sonship and impeccability (I Jn 5:4, 18). But that is guaranteed only by a dynamic adherence to Christ. Hence the manifold exhortations in I Jn [16]. The divine sonship and the impeccable nature of this sonship which they possess initially, should be kept up and realized fully, progressing towards the eschatological perfection. So the divine sonship and impeccability are in a tension between 'being' and 'becoming'. This shows once again the dynamic character of the divine sonship in Jn.

---

[14] Cf. N. LAZURE, op. cit., p. 319 : " Au chapitre premier, l'auteur s'intéresse à la vie concrète de ses lecteurs tandis que dans la deuxième série de textes il se place au niveau de l'être du Chrétien considéré en lui même ".

[15] Cf. I. DE LA POTTERIE, art. " 'impeccabilité ", pp. 194-204. As it is well treated there, we do not intend to repeat the same here.

[16] This keeps the Johannine doctrine of divine sonship and impeccability away from a false determinism. Cf. P. FEINE, *Theologie des Neuen Testaments*, Leipzig, 1922 (4th ed.), pp. 366ff; A. AUGUSTINOVIC, *Critica Determinismi Joannei*, Jerusalem, 1947; J. HERKENRATH, 'Sünde zum Tode (I Jn 5:16)', in *Aus Theologie und Philosophie*, Fs. für F. Tillmann, Düsseldorf, 1950, pp. 119-138.

II. Impeccability of the one who is born of God (I Jn 3:9)

I Jn 3:6 and 9 speak of 'freedom from sin' or impeccability of the children of God, precisely as the result of both 'remaining in God' and of the 'remaining of the seed of God in man'.

A. *The Structure of I Jn 3:9*

In the structure of v. 9 'the remaining of the seed of God in man' runs parallel to 'being born of God':

A   Everyone who IS BEGOTTEN OF GOD
B   Does NOT commit SIN
C   *Because His seed dwells in him*
B'   And he is NOT able to SIN
A' Because he IS BEGOTTEN OF GOD

Thus impeccability is attributed to a twofold cause: the remaining of the seed of God in man and his new birth from God. This is of particular significance, because the condition of being born of God (in perfect tense) corresponds to the progressive stage of divine sonship of men as conceived by Jn, and hence impeccability seems to be an effect of the dynamic condition of the progressive stage of sonship, made dynamic through the remaining of the seed of God.

B. *Different interpretations of* σπέρμα

Various interpretations have been given to the σπέρμα. Some have taken it as a collective noun for the 'offspring' of God as the 'seed of Abraham' in Jn 8:33,37 [17]. This would give good sense to the verse being parallel to v. 6 and keeping the usual meaning of the expression 'remain in him' and also has the advantage of reading the same person of God in both αὐτοῦ and αὐτῷ of v. 9 instead of reading the first one of God and the second one of the Christian. But there are many reasons that go against this interpretation. First of all, the expression 'seed of God' in this sense is never found in the NT. Besides, in this case σπέρμα should have an article, which is lacking here. Moreover, if the seed of God is simply a synonym for the 'one who is born of God', then there is an unnecessary tautology. Besides, it makes the following clause difficult both in grammar and sense [18]. So it seems better to interpret it as a divine

---

[17] Cf. A. W. ARGYLE, "I Jn 3:4", in *ET* 65 (1953), pp. 62-63.
[18] Cf. R. LAW, *Tests of Life*, p. 389 where he says that "so understood,

principle that remains and is operative in the one who is born of God.

But even those who understand it in this sense, differ in opinion as to how to understand this divine principle. Many of the authors understand it as the Holy Spirit [19], while others understand it as the Word of God [20]. Nor are the Fathers unanimous on this point. Theophylactus [21], and Ps. Oecumenius [22] see in the 'seed' the Holy Spirit or Christ, while Dydymus Alexandrinus [23] sees in it the power or the spirit of adoption of sons. Many others as Clement of Alexandria [24], Photius [25], St. Augustine [26] and Bede the Venerable [27] say that the seed of God is the Word of God.

The reason that favours understanding it as the Holy Spirit is that in Jn the thought of the Holy Spirit is predominant and it is the principle of the divine life in man (Jn 3:6). But it is to be noted that in the whole NT the principle of the divine life is never compared to a 'seed'. Besides, the relation of the Spirit with the one 'born of the Spirit' is described in Jn 3:6 as 'that which is born of the Spirit is Spirit', hence a kind of identification with the Spirit Himself. In I Jn 3:9 the one who is born of God is not the seed itself, but the seed of God only remains in him, who is born of God. So it seems to be a reality that is different from the Spirit. Here it is worth noting that none of the Fathers saw exclusively the Holy Spirit in the 'seed'.

C. *Source of Impeccability in the Jewish and Primitive Christian Tradition*

Actually in the Jewish and primitive Christian tradition impeccability was attributed to the Law or the Word of God or Wisdom

---

the whole sentence becomes singularly lame " and that " on this interpretation the last clause must have been ' and they cannot sin, because they abide in Him ' ".

[19] Cf. R. SCHNACKENBURG, *Die Johannesbriefe*, pp. 190-191; A. E. BROOKE, *Epistles*, p. 89.

[20] Cf. DODD, *Epistles*, pp. 75-78; I. DE LA POTTERIE, art. "'impeccabilité", pp. 208-215.

[21] Cf. PG 126, 38.
[22] Cf. PG 119, 651-654.
[23] Cf. PG 39, 1785.
[24] Cf. *Adumbrationes in I Epist. Johannis*, GCS III, 214; PG 9, 738.
[25] Cf. PG 101, 112.
[26] Cf. PL 35, 2016.
[27] Cf. PL 93, 102.

interiorized [28], truth and knowledge of God [29]. Ez 36:25-27 puts the Spirit as the principle of impeccability. But as we saw, most of the texts speak of the interior reality that remains in the heart of men and is operative under the Spirit, such as the Word of God, Law, Truth etc. IV Esdr 9:31 uses the very metaphor of 'seed' for the Law that remains in the hearts.

In the teaching of Jesus, the Word of God is represented as a seed, as is seen from the parable of the sower (Mt 13:3-8,19-23). That the primitive Christians were familiar with this is clear from the fact that in the parallel texts of the baptismal parenesis regeneration is closely associated with the Word of God. In I Pet 1:23-25 we are said to be born anew of immortal, not mortal, seed (σπορᾶς), by the living and abiding Word of God, which is further identified with the Word of the Gospel [30]. Paul, in I Cor 4:15, speaks of having begotten the faithful through the Gospel. Note the similarity of I Cor 4:15 with I Pet 1:23-25 ; I Cor 4:15 " διὰ τοῦ εὐαγγελίου ὑμᾶς ἐγέννησα "; I Pet 1:23-25 " διὰ λόγου ... τὸ ῥῆμα τὸ εὐαγγελισθὲν ... ἀναγεγεννημένοι " [31].

In Jam 1:18,21 the Father of lights has begotten us λόγῳ ἀληθείας and the λόγος is ἔμφυτον (implanted) [32]. All these show how the idea of a new birth through the Gospel as a 'seed' belongs to the catechetical teaching of the primitive Church [33]. Hence we may be justified in seeing the same as background in I Jn 3:9.

---

[28] Cf. Jer 31:33-34 ; Ps 37:31 ; 119:11 ; Eccl 24:26 ; Prov 9:6 ; IV Esdr 9:31 ; Bar Syr 48:24 ; Hen 6:8.
[29] Cf. Test of Levi 18:9 ; I QS 4:20-23.
[30] Note the perfect tense of ἀναγεγεννημένοι and the adjectives of λόγος, ζῶντος and μένοντος which are certainly corresponding to I Jn 3:9.
[31] Cf. St. AUGUSTINE, PL 35, 2016 where he actually connects these two texts : " Semen Dei, id est, verbum Dei : unde dicit Apostolus, ' per Evangelium ego vos genui ' (I Cor 4:15) ".
[32] Cf. St. THOMAS, Super Ep. Lectura, ed. R. Cai, Roma, 1953, p. 275, where he, commenting on I Cor 4:15, connects it with Jam 1:18 " Generatio est processus ad vitam-homo vivit in Christo per fidem (Gal 2:20). Fides ex auditu, auditus per Verbum (Rom 10:17). Unde Verbum Dei est Semen, quo Apostolus eos genuit in Christo, unde Jam 1:18 ".
[33] The parallelism between the two texts of Peter and James belonging to the baptismal catechesis is very well brought out by M. E. BOISMARD, in Quatre hymnes baptismales dans la première épître de Pierre, Paris, 1961, p. 105.

D. *Source of Impeccability in Jn*

In Jn we actually find a connection between the word of God and purification from sins [34]. As we have mentioned above, Jn 8:30-47 repeatedly speaks of the truth that is his Word; and it was the refusal to accept him and remain in his word, that hindered them from becoming children of God. II Jn 2 also speaks of the 'truth that remains in us'. Besides, in Jn the Spirit is never said to remain in man [35], while the λόγος is explicitly said to be remaining in man (I Jn 2:14,24 ; II Jn 2).

1. *Dwelling of the Word of God and Victory over the evil one*: (*I Jn 2:12-14*)

In I Jn 2:14 the dwelling of the Word of God is put parallel to being victorious over the evil one, and from I Jn 5:18 we know that 'victory over the evil one' means to be free from sin: "Everyone who is born of God does not sin ... the evil one does not touch him".

The parallelism is better seen in the following structure:

V. 12 A   I WRITE TO YOU CHILDREN
           Because your sins have been forgiven
   13 B   I WRITE TO YOU FATHERS
           BECAUSE YOU KNEW HIM WHO IS FROM THE BEGINNING
      C   I WRITE TO YOU YOUNG MEN
           Because YOU HAVE BEEN VICTORIOUS OVER THE EVIL ONE
   14 A'   I have WRITTEN TO YOU CHILDREN
           Because you know the Father
      B'   I have WRITTEN TO YOU FATHERS
           BECAUSE YOU KNEW HIM WHO IS FROM THE BEGINNING
      C'   I have WRITTEN TO YOU YOUNG MEN
           Because the Word of God dwells in you
           And YOU HAVE BEEN VICTORIOUS OVER THE EVIL ONE.

Note how in AA' the 'knowledge of the Father' is parallel to 'freedom from sins', which is again parallel to CC' the 'victory over the evil one', which is put as concomitant to the 'dwelling of the Word

---

[34] Cf. Jn 15:3 which says : " You are purified through the (διά) word, which I spoke to you ".

[35] In Jn 14:17 is said παρ' ὑμῖν μένει καὶ ἐν ὑμῖν ἔσται but not ἐν ὑμῖν μένει.

of God in us ' [36]. In the section I Jn 2:29 – 3:10 the ' one who sins ' and the ' world ' have not known God (cf. I Jn 3:1,6), while the ' one who is born of God ' and ' in whom the seed of God dwells ', does not sin, and hence knows God and is ' victorious over the world '.

2. *Faith*: *Victory over the World* (*I Jn* 5:4)

The victory over the evil one is for Jn also the victory over the world, because the whole world is in the power of the evil one (I Jn 5:19). And I Jn 5:4 puts the ' victory over the world ' parallel to ' faith ' and to ' being born of God ' :

A Everyone who *is born of God*
B   IS VICTORIOUS OVER THE WORLD
B'   And this is the VICTORY that IS VICTORIOUS OVER THE WORLD
A' Our *Faith*.

In I Jn 5:1 it is said that " everyone who believes that Jesus is the Christ, is born of God ". The faith certainly refers to the Word of God received in faith, and ' ὁ πιστεύων ' in the present participle certainly refers to the ever dynamic working of the Word of God, received in faith. Hence the relation of this ' faith ' and ' victory over the world ' together with the ' being born of God ' to the impeccability affirmed in I Jn 3:9, which comes in a section (I Jn 2:29 – 3:10) speaking of the birth from God related to an adherence to Christ's righteousness (also victory over the world) through faith. All these seem to indicate that it is the ' Word of God ' that is meant by the ' seed of God ' in I Jn 3:9.

3. *Sinlessness*: *Effect of a Mutual Dwelling* (*I Jn* 3:6,9)

As we have seen in the structure of 2:29 – 3:10, v. 6 is parallel to v. 9 (A'd A²d'). If in v. 6 ' sinlessness ' is attributed to ' our dwelling in Him ', in v. 9 it is attributed to the ' seed's dwelling in us '. Here we meet with the newness of the Johannine doctrine. Impeccability in Jn is not only due to the ' presence ' of the Word of God in us, but also due to the ' remaining ' of the Word of God

---

[36] Note that the OT texts of the New Covenant, specially Jer 31:33-34, traces of which are found in I Jn 2:12-14 connect the knowledge of God with purification from sins. For a study of this theme of knowledge of God in I Jn 2:12-14 in the light of the New Covenant texts of the OT, cf. I. DE LA POTTERIE, " La Connaissance de Dieu dans le Dualisme eschatologique d'après I Jn 2:12-14 " in *Au service de la parole de Dieu*, Mélanges offerts à Mgr. A. M. Charue, Gembloux, 1969, pp. 77-79.

in us, which supposes ' our remaining in God ' (I Jn 3:6) or in the Word of God (Jn 8:31). The correspondence of this mutual dwelling is seen from I Jn 2:24 :

" Let what you heard from the beginning
  dwell in you.
  If there dwells in you
What you heard from the beginning
  You yourselves will dwell in the Son and in ...
                                                Father ".

So our dwelling in God is conditioned by the dwelling of the Word of God in us. The mutual correspondence of both these dwellings is of great significance. This brings out the full meaning of the verb μένειν namely, the dynamic and constant presence of the Word of God in us, and its influence on ' our remaining in God '[37]. Here enters the role of the Holy Spirit which vivifies the Word of God in us, or in other words, gives the μένειν to the Word of God in us, leading to impeccability. This is due to the specifically Johannine concept of the divine sonship (begetting) in the progressive stage. It is the man who is in the progressive stage of sonship, namely, he who lets himself be constantly led by the Spirit through the Word of God, and thus aquires a connaturality with the Spirit [38], who is impeccable. The very way of putting parallel ' he has been born of God ' (perfect) and ' the seed of God dwells in him ' in I Jn 3:9 points to the same. If μένει expresses the objective aspect, γεγέννηται (perfect) expresses the subjective aspect of this working of the

---

[37] For a study of the Johannine use of μένειν, cf. G. PECORARA, " De Verbo ' manere ' apud Johannem ", *DThom* 40 (1937) pp. 159-171 ; J. HEISE, *Menein in den Joh. Schriften*, (HermUnt NT 8) Tübingen, 1967 ; cf. also, DODD, *Interpretation*, pp. 187-200 ; B. LAMMERS, *Die Menein-Formeln der Johannesbriefe*, Diss. Greg. Rome, 1954 ; SCHNACKENBURG, *Die Johannesbriefe*, pp. 91-95 ; E. MALATESTA, *Interiority and Covenant*, Rome, 1974.

[38] Cf. Jn 3:6 " He who has been born of the Spirit (in perfect tense) is Spirit ". Here we may recall the concept of freedom proper to the sonship, which means not a lack of determination by someone or something, but a true self-determination, namely, a determination by the Spirit of sonship. Actually, in the OT too the freedom of Israel from the slavery in becoming sons of Yahweh was a freedom to serve Yahweh (cf. Exod 4:22-23 " let my son go (free), so that he may serve me "), and this concept of freedom proper to the sonship continues to be also in the NT. Cf. S. LYONNET, " La libertà dei Figli di Dio ", *Humanitas* (nuove serie), 1 (1969), pp. 76-94 ; cf. also M. F. CLIFFORD, " Aspects of Freedom in the Writings of John and Paul ", *BiTod* 29 (1967), pp. 2035-2039.

Holy Spirit through the Word of God in men, in producing impeccability.

a. The Johannine usage of μένειν

The very Johannine usage of μένειν points to this twofold aspect (subjective and objective) of impeccability connected with sonship. In Jn we find a twofold usage of μένειν; one, exhortative and conditional, and the other, declarative and absolute [39]. In the exhortative series, when it is question of impersonal realities, the verb has always as object the Word of Christ or charity (cf. I Jn 2:24; II Jn 9; Jn 8:31-32), while in the declarative series, it has always as object the Spirit of truth (Jn 14:17), the Word of God (I Jn 2:14), the truth (II Jn 2), the seed of God (I Jn 3:9) or the unction (I Jn 2:27), hence always connected with the Word of God or teaching of Christ. So, on the one hand, we have the supernatural reality of the Word of God remaining in us with its permanent power of sanctification (declarative use) while on the other, it needs our cooperation letting ourselves be permanently guided and determined by it (exhortative – conditional use). So impeccability is the result of both the remaining of the seed (Word) of God in us (I Jn 3:9) and our remaining in Him (I Jn 3:6) or letting ourselves be determined by Him (his Word) (Jn 8:31). This shows the dynamism involved in the state of being born of God, which is always a component of divine and human, objective and subjective, once given and continually to be possessed, realities.

b. The χρῖσμα in Jn

So too the concept of χρῖσμα in Jn confirms this sense of the 'seed of God', because it is the Word of God interiorized in faith and vivified by the Holy Spirit, that is called by I Jn χρῖσμα and is said to be remaining in us (I Jn 2:27) [40]. That χρῖσμα means this interiorized Word of God is suggested by the fact that both vv. 20

---

[39] Cf. I. DE LA POTTERIE, art. "L'impeccabilité", pp. 210-211.

[40] Cf. I. DE LA POTTERIE, "L'onction du chrétien par la foi", pp. 126-136. Some identified it with the unction of the Spirit (cf. J. MICHL, "Der Geist als Garant des Rechten Glaubens", in *Vom Wort des Lebens* : Fs. für Max. Meinertz, 1951, p. 144; W. NAUCK, op. cit., p. 94). Others identified it simply with the Word of God (cf. R. REITZENSTEIN, *Die hellenistische Mysterienreligionen*, 1927, pp. 396-397; DODD, *Epistles*, p. 62f). Others speak of an illumination or interior teaching of the Holy Spirit (cf. the Commentaries of Bonsirven, Charue and Schnackenburg), while again some others understood it as a sacramental rite of confirmation (cf. the Commentaries of Belser, Vrede, R. A. Knox etc.).

and 27 of I Jn 2, where the word χρῖσμα occurs exclusively, speak of the teaching and knowledge of Christians. The baptismal catechetical terminology of the 'homology' (2:22-24) and of 'ὃ ἠκούσατε ἀπ'ἀρχῆς' (2:24) which are part of this section where the word χρῖσμα occurs, point to the beginning of faith, when the Word of Christ (χρῖσμα) is received by Christians [41]. The identity of the χρῖσμα with the Word of Christ could be seen also by a comparison of the different texts speaking of the knowledge of truth:

Jn 8:31-32   "If You REMAIN in m y W o r d .....
                                    You will KNOW THE
                                              TRUTH"
II Jn 1-2   "All who KNOW THE
                                    TRUTH because of
          t h e T r u t h which REMAINS in us"
I Jn 2:20-21 "You have an U n c t i o n f r o m t h e H o l y O n e
(v. 27)   ... which REMAINS in you ... — You KNOW THE TRUTH"

The three words 'the Word of Christ' (Jn 8:31-32), 'the truth' (II Jn 1-2) and 'the unction' (I Jn 2:20-21), which are parallel here point to the same reality leading to the knowledge of Truth. So the χρῖσμα that dwells in us indicates the Word of Christ, which is perceived in the light of faith, and is the source of our interior instruction [42]. Note also the parallelism between the two 'remainings' in the knowledge of Truth. If the 'knowledge of Truth' is the result of 'our remaining in the Word' in Jn 8:31-32, in II Jn 1-2 it is the result of the 'remaining of the Truth in us'. Thus the mutual remaining results in the 'knowledge of the Truth' (Communion with the Truth — the Son), which, in its turn, gives us the freedom from sin proper to the divine sonship.

---

[41] Note the regular use of ἀπ' ἀρχῆς by I Jn in the contexts in which he reminds the Christians of the moment of their conversion. Cf. W. NAUCK, op. cit., pp. 84-86, who refers it to the moment of Baptism, while I. DE LA POTTERIE, art. " L'onction " pp. 128-129 refers it to the moment of announcement of the Word of God-Gospel.

[42] Cf. R. BULTMANN, *Theologie des NT*, Tübingen, 1958, p. 406 where he describes the χρῖσμα of I Jn as " das machterfüllte Wort " and on p. 435, note 1 as " den Geist als Kraft der Wortverkündigung ". Cf. also SCHNACKENBURG, *Die Johannesbriefe*, p. 161 where he says : " Nur geht mit dem Hören, dem gläubigen Aufnehmen der von Anfang an verkündeten Christusbotschaft, die innere Belehrung durch den Heiligen Geist Hand in Hand ...".

III. Impeccability of the Children of God through the Son of God: (I Jn 5: 18-20)

I Jn 5:18-20 speaks of a triple certitude of the 'children of God' in being free from sin (v. 18), being determined by (v. 19) and being in communion with (v. 20) God the Father through the Son. Actually in I Jn 5:18 the author takes up again the theme of the divine begetting, and attributes to those 'begotten of God' the freedom from sin, which was also the theme in I Jn 3:4-10 [43].

A. Textual Criticism of I Jn 5:18

1. External Criticism

In I Jn 5:18 there are two different readings. Some Mss read ἡ γέννησις instead of ὁ γεννηθείς ... Θεοῦ [44] and ἑαυτόν instead of αὐτόν [45]. But many important Mss and almost the whole Greek Patristic Tradition have the reading ὁ γεννηθεὶς ἐκ τοῦ Θεοῦ [46]. The word αὐτόν is also attested by important Mss [47]. The different readings have probably their origin in the difficulty to understand the verse with ὁ γεννηθείς and αὐτόν. If by ὁ γεννηθείς the same as ὁ γεγεν-

---

[43] Here we do not intend to discuss the redactional problem of the section 5:13-21, which is examined by W. Nauck in detail. After a detailed analysis of both formal and theological elements of the section, he arrives at the conclusion that I Jn 5:13-21 is written by the same author as that of the other parts of the Epistle. (Cf. W. NAUCK, op. cit., pp. 135-146). Whether the pericope begins with v. 13 (cf. Commentaries of Brooke, Schnackenburg) or with v. 14 (cf. Commentaries of Dodd, Bultmann) is not very decisive for our purpose, nor is it easy to decide, because if v. 13 forms a conclusion to the Letter, it forms also an introduction and transition to the Epilogue (vv. 14-21).

[44] Thus 2138 (1852) p r Vg Syh and other Latin Mss read 'generatio Dei'. Among the Ancient Ecclesiastical Writers who adopt this reading could be mentioned JEROME (C. Pelag. 1,13); CHROMATIUS OF AQUILEJA, PG 20, 359; BEDE THE VENERABLE, PL 93, 119. Among the modern Authors, cf. A. v HARNACK, " Zu Textkritik und Christologie des Schriften des Johannes ", in *SitzAW*, Berlin, 1915, pp. 534-542; M. DIBELIUS, *Aufsätze zur Apostelgeschichte*, Berlin, 1953, p. 57, note 2.

[45] Cf. S, Textus receptus and other editors as Weiss, Von Soden, Merk and Vogels. Among the Eccl. Writers, cf. DYDYMUS ALEX., PG 39, 1805; THEOPHYLACTUS, PG 126, 65; OECUMENIUS, PG 119, 681-682. Among the modern authors, cf. J. H. THAYER, *A Greek English Lexicon of the NT*, Edinburgh, 1956 (4th ed.).

[46] Except the Mss mentioned in note 44 all the other Mss give this.

[47] Cf. B, A, p, r, Vg. Among the Editors, Tischendorf, Westcott-Hort, Nestle and the Greek New Testament.

νημένος is meant, then it is difficult to understand, what it means to say 'the Christian keeps him'. Hence it is quite understandable why the above mentioned variants have been introduced to make the text more intelligible. On the other hand, if the original reading was ἑαυτόν it is difficult to see why it should ever have been altered into αὐτόν.

2. *Internal Criticism*

As to the reading with ἑαυτόν the internal reasons are not favourable. In similar uses of τηρεῖν ἑαυτόν it is usually followed by a qualificative or circumstantial complement such as ἐν ἀγάπῃ Θεοῦ (Ep. Jud v. 21), ἀβαρῆ (II Cor 11:9), ἁγνόν (I Tim. 5:22), ἄσπιλον (Jam 1:27) [48]. If ἑαυτόν is admitted here, this would be an isolated case in the whole NT. Moreover, the Johannine Writings which have a marked predilection for this verb τηρεῖν [49], makes use of it always in the active sense of keeping or preserving something or someone. Hence the reflexive use as here with ἑαυτόν is not Johannine. Besides, the expression 'One who is born of God, keeps himself, and the evil one does not touch him' sounds irreligious [50].

The only internal reason that is brought forward for the reading with ἡ γέννησις is the parallelism with I Jn 3:9 where the 'remaining of the seed of God' is the basis or reason for not committing sin of the one who is begotten of God [51]. This comparison may be valid on the level of speculation [52]. But philologically and grammatically the comparison is not valid. Note the construction of the two sentences:

5:18 πᾶς ὁ γε ... ο ὐ χ ἁμαρτάνει, ἀ λ λ ' ὁ γεν ... ἑαυτόν
3:9 πᾶς ... ἁμαρτίαν ο ὐ ποιεῖ, ὅ τ ι σπέρμα ... μένει

While in I Jn 3:9 with οὐ ... ὅτι, the ὅτι clause gives the reason of the οὐ clause, in I Jn 5:18 the ἀλλά clause shows a contrast or opposition to what precedes in the οὐ clause. After a negative ἀλλά always indicates a contrast which is nearly equal to contrariety [53].

---

[48] Cf. A. v HARNACK, art. cit., " Zur Textkritik ...", p. 536 ; A. SEGOND, " Ire épître de Jean, Chap. 5:18-20 ", *RHPR* 45 (1965), p. 350.

[49] Out of the 70 occurrences in the whole NT John alone makes use of it 25 times (18 times in Jn and 7 times in I Jn), while it occurs in Mk once, Mt 6 times and Lk ignores it.

[50] Cf. A. v HARNACK, art. cit., p. 536.

[51] Cf. A. v HARNACK, art. cit., pp. 539-540.

[52] It is worth noting here that also the Ancient Eccl. Writers who adopt ὁ γεννηθείς often make use of I Jn 3:9 to explain I Jn 5:18. Cf. DYDYMUS ALEX., PG 39, 1805.

[53] Cf. BLASS-DEBRUNNER, *A Greek Grammar of the New Testament and*

So here the fact of the preservation accorded to the 'one begotten of God' is not directly mentioned as the reason of 'not committing sin' but as a fact that is contrasted or contrary to the fact of committing sin.

The very Johannine use of the construction οὐ ... ἀλλά in I Jn 2:27; 4:1,10,18 confirms this ordinary sense of contrast natural to it. The logical connection is rather to the following clause connected with καί: "the ὁ γεννηθείς keeps him and consequently the evil one does not touch him". This does not mean a denial of connection between 18a and 18b on the theological level. But the acceptance of a text, that is attested by so few Mss, solely on the basis of comparison on the theological level, cannot be justified. Moreover the reading ὁ γεννηθείς and αὐτόν being 'lectio difficilior' has more probability of being the original one. Hence with the majority of the Commentators, we would prefer to take the text with ὁ γεννηθείς and αὐτόν [54].

B. *Analysis of the Expressions*

1. *" ... He who was Begotten of God keeps him ..."*

Having fixed up the text with ὁ γεννηθείς and αὐτόν we come to the interpretation of it. Here too we find two main currents of interpretation, one, applying the ὁ γεννηθείς to Christ and the other, applying it to Christians. Some have understood the αὐτόν for God and have tried to explain it so, meaning thereby that "one who is once begotten of God, holds fast on Him (God)", thus giving to τηρεῖν a sense equal to that of ἔχειν τὸν Θεόν [55]. But the expression τηρεῖν τὸν Θεόν is singular in Jn, because Jn in similar cases makes use of ἔχειν τὸν Θεόν (cf. I Jn 2:23; 5:12; II Jn 9). Besides, τηρεῖν with an accusative of person has always in the NT a sense of watching or guarding in a friendly or hostile manner [56].

Again some of those, who apply ὁ γεννηθείς to Christians, see God as subject of τηρεῖν and consider it as implicit here or omitted

---

other Early Christian Literature (trans. from German), Chicago, 1961, nos. 447, 448; W. BAUER, *A Greek English Lexicon*, p. 37.

[54] Cf. BROOKE, *Epistles*, pp. 148ff; WESTCOTT, *Epistles*, p. 194; J. BONSIRVEN, *Epîtres*, p. 273; SCHNACKENBURG, *Die Johannesbriefe*, pp. 272-281; J. C. O'NEILL, *The Puzzle of 1st John*, London, 1966, p. 62; DODD, *Epistles*, p. 138.

[55] Cf. W. BAUER, *Wörterbuch zum Neuen Testament*, Berlin, 1958, col. 1613; also J. HERKENRATH, art. cit., p. 127.

[56] Cf. BROOKE, *Epistles*, p. 149. Besides, it does not respect the parallelism of this verse in the structure (see below on p. 282).

by the copyists and translate: " He who is begotten of God, him (God) keeps, and the evil one does not touch him "[57]. As in Jn 17:2 such a construction is possible. But as this verse is liable to many interpretations it cannot be taken for granted that here we have a semitism, unless it is proved by the very context of the verse. And in the context we meet with serious difficulties in taking the ὁ γεννηθείς for the Christian rather than for Christ.

a. The Context

First of all, if ὁ γεννηθείς is the same as ὁ γεγεννημένος the repetition of the subject is quite unnecessary here. In that case the author would write quite spontaneously: " ὁ γε ... ἐκ τοῦ Θεοῦ οὐχ ἁμαρτάνει, ἀλλὰ τηρεῖ ἑαυτόν. Besides, the believer is never called in Jn ὁ γεννηθείς ἐκ τοῦ Θεοῦ in aorist, but ὁ γεγεννημένος ἐκ τοῦ Θεοῦ in the perfect. Hence the aorist coming just after the usual ὁ γεγεννημένος is quite embarrassing if applied to the same person [58], unless the motive of changing the tense is clear from the context [59]. Moreover, if applied to the same person, then γάρ would be much more fitting in the place of ἀλλά [60].

On the contrary, there are many reasons that favour the application of ὁ γεννηθείς to Christ [61]. First of all, it avoids the tension between the two different tenses used for the same person, in the same sentence, namely, aorist ὁ γεννηθείς in close juxtaposition with the perfect ὁ γεγεννημένος.

Understanding ὁ γεννηθείς for Christ, makes it also easy to take both αὐτόν in v. 18b and αὐτοῦ in v. 18c as referring to the same person.

---

[57] Cf. A. SEGOND, art. cit., p. 350; cf. also K. L. BEYER, *Semitische Syntax im Neuen Testament*, p. 216f; SCHNACKENBURG, *Die Johannesbriefe*, pp. 280-281; recently also P. COUTURE, *The Teaching Function in the Church of I John*, Rome, 1968, p. 11.

[58] Cf. ORIGEN, Comm. in Joh XX, 15 in *Das Evangelium nach Johannes*, ed. Preuschen (GCS), Leipzig, 1903, p. 346, 10ff, where he writes " καὶ ἐν τοῖς ... ὅτι πᾶς ὁ γεγενν .... ἀλλὰ ὁ γεγεννημένος ἐκ ... τηρεῖ ..." which shows that he also felt this difficulty.

[59] The attempt of B. WEISS to explain it as a process of becoming from a ὁ γεννηθείς to a γεγεννημένος (cf. *Die Drei Briefe des Apostel Johannes*, Göttingen, 1899 (5th ed.), pp. 155-156) does not have any solid basis on the text, and hence not satisfactory (cf. HARNACK, art. cit., p. 535).

[60] Cf. What we said above on the construction οὐκ ... ἀλλά, on pp. 277-278.

[61] In favour of applying ὁ γεννηθείς to Christ, cf. BULTMANN, " Die kirchliche Redaktion des Ersten Johannesbriefes ", in *In Memoriam E. Lohmeyer*, Stuttgart, 1951, p. 195; W. NAUCK, op. cit., p. 139; G. WOHLENBERG, " Glossen zu I Jo ", *NKZ* 13 (1902), p. 240; also Commentaries of Brooke, Windisch, Dodd, Bonsirven and Westcott.

b. The Vocabulary

(1) Ὁ γεννηθεὶς ἐκ τοῦ Θεοῦ

The Johannine vocabulary itself favours taking the ὁ γεννηθείς for Christ. Speaking of the use of γεννάω in Jn to signify the supernatural birth, we saw how γεννάω is used in Jn always in the perfect or aorist subjunctive to signify the supernatural birth of Christians, and not in the aorist indicative or aorist participle. The only real objection that the authors usually bring against taking ὁ γεννηθείς for Christ, is that the expression γεννᾶσθαι ἐκ Θεοῦ is not used of Christ elsewhere in the Johannine Writings [62]. But in our textual criticism of Jn 1:13 we saw how the application of a birth from God to Christ in the aorist is with all probability to be maintained in the Johannine Writings.

Besides, the expression ὁ γεννηθείς in the aorist as against the πᾶς ὁ γεγεννημένος in the perfect points to the one who is uniquely begotten of God as against those who are begotten of God, through a begetting that is common to all, indicated by the πᾶς. This difference compels the readers to search after another subject in ὁ γεννηθείς other than that of ὁ γεγεννημένος and also to emphasize the sense of the verb as such. The article points to the well known Son of God – Begotten of God [63].

The very use of the perfect participle of γεννάω in Jn favours this distinction. It is interesting to see that Jn makes use of ὁ γεγεννημένος in the masculine always with πᾶς (cf. Jn 3:8; I Jn 3:9; 5:18). When he uses the γεγεννημένος without πᾶς then it is always in the neuter, emphasizing thus the nature rather than the person (cf. Jn 3:6; I Jn 5:4) [64]. Hence aorist participle ὁ γεννηθείς seems to refer to Christ, the uniquely begotten Son of God.

(2) Τηρεῖ

Also the use of τηρεῖν in Jn favours this interpretation. The verb τηρεῖν in the Johannine Writings is almost exclusively connected with τὰς ἐντολάς, τὸν λόγον or τὸ σάββατον. The only place where

---

[62] Cf. A. v HARNACK, art. cit., pp. 538-539. It is worth noting that the same Harnack defends the singular reading ἐγεννήθη in Jn 1:13 and that in the same article pp. 542-552; cf. also R. SCHNACKENBURG, *Die Johannesbriefe*, p. 281; B. WEISS, op. cit., p. 156; A. SEGOND, art. cit., p. 350.

[63] Cf. G. WOHLENBERG, art. cit., p. 239.

[64] The only time he makes use of γεγεννημένος in the masculine without πᾶς is in I Jn 5:1 where it is in the accusative, and the emphasis put on the nature rather than on the person is clear from the context. Besides, here there is no chance of understanding it for anybody else other than Christians. Actually there is a variation for it in the neuter given by the Mss S 69 1319.

it is used with a personal pronoun in the accusative (αὐτούς) is in Jn 17:11,12,15. And here it is God or Christ who is keeping the faithful, from the evil one (ἐκ τοῦ πονηροῦ). Besides, we see too the antithesis between the faithful who are not of the world, and the world that hates them, which certainly reminds us of I Jn 5:18, where also we find the same antithesis between the faithful who are of God and the world that lies in the evil one. So, also in I Jn 5:18, ' the one who keeps ' seems to be God or Christ. And in I Jn ' he who comes against the evil one ' is usually Christ [65]. Hence the ὁ γεννηθείς here seems to refer to Christ.

c. The Structure of I Jn 5:18-20

The structure of the section 5:18-20 seems to favour this interpretation. As all the three verses begin with οἴδαμεν ὅτι, the section forms a threefold rhythmic unity in which vv. 18 and 20 are composed of 3 rhythmic statements and v. 19, of 2 rhythmic statements[66].

(1) The Literary Unity of the Section

In the section 5:14-21, in these three verses alone occur the formulas of communion such as ὁ γεγεννημένος ... Θεοῦ, ἐκ τοῦ Θεοῦ ἐσμέν, γινώσκειν τὸν ἀληθινόν and ἐσμὲν ἐν τῷ ἀληθινῷ. Perhaps the v. 17 with πᾶσα ἀδικία ἁμαρτία ἐστιν reminded the author about 2:29 – 3:10, where he opposed righteousness to sin and described it as the criterion of the divinely begotten, and thus caused the composition of these three rhythmic verses, which have different parallels with 2:29 – 3:10, as could be seen from the comparison given below. The fact that the idea of communion with God (birth from God) in v. 18 is resumed in v. 19 as ' being from God ' and in v. 20 as ' being in God ' also shows the literary unity of this section [67]. The structure of the section could be seen better after a comparison of the different elements of this section to those in 3:5 – 10, to which it has several literary contacts :

(2) Comparison between 5:18-20 and 3:5-10

5:18 a Everyone who is born of God does not sin   3: 9 Everyone who is born of God does not sin

---

[65] Cf. I Jn 3:8 where the appearance of Christ is connected with the destroying of the works of the devil, and that connected with not committing sin.
[66] Cf. W. NAUCK, op. cit., p. 134.
[67] Cf. W. NAUCK, op. cit., pp. 134-135.

b He who was born of God keeps him ... the evil one... not touch

8 The Son of God appeared to undo the devil's deeds

19 a We are of God

10 Children of God + Children of the devil-not of God

b World in power of evil one

8 Who sins is of the devil

20 a The Son of God has come

5-8 He (Son of God) appeared

b gave understanding to know the Truthful one

6 Who sins (v. 1 World) did not know Him.

c We are in the Truthful One

6 Who dwells in Him does not sin.

(3) The Structure

In the light of this parallelism, the structure of I Jn 5:18-20 becomes clearer:

V. 18   A   We know that Everyone who i s b o r n OF G O D does not sin

      B   BUT (ἀλλά) H e w h o i s B e g o t t e n OF GOD keeps him

      C   And THE EVIL ONE does not touch him

19   A'   We know that WE ARE OF GOD

      C'   And the whole world is laid in THE EVIL ONE

20   B'   BUT (δέ) we know that t h e S o n OF GOD came... gave understanding to know Him who is True

      A"   And WE ARE i n H i m who is true ... in His Son Jesus Christ.

In A A' A" are given elements that express communion with God. The three expressions ' born of God ', ' be from God ' and ' be in God ' are interrelated and are connected with the fact of not committing sin [68]. Note the literary parallelism in C and C', namely, πονηρός. The evil one and the world are, as we have seen, the sinful world, that stands opposite to the children of God in communion with God (cf. I Jn 3:16,10) [69]. Hence C and C' corresponding to each

---

[68] Cf. I Jn 3:6 ' who dwells in Him does not sin ' and 3:8 ' who commits sin is of the devil ', namely, not from God (3:10). Thus the two phrases ' to be from God ' (v. 19) and ' to be in God ' (v. 20) form here really a parallel to the phrase ' be born of God ' (v. 18). Hence the parallelism of A A' A".

[69] ' The world is laid in the evil one ' means that it is fully under the control of the evil one, the devil, and hence is identified here with the devil inimical to the children of God.

other, give the opposite elements of those who are in communion with God in A A' A''[70]. This naturally points to the probability of the mutual correspondence between B and B'. In B' the Son of God gives those who are in God 'the understanding to know the truthful one', while in B the ὁ γεννηθείς gives to those who are born of God protection, so that they do not sin. 'To know God' and 'to avoid sin' are really parallels in I Jn 3:6. In 3:1 the κόσμος (sinful world) is said to have not known God[71]. This means that the giving of understanding to know God in v. 20 (B') is parallel to the giving of protection (from sin) in v. 18 (B). This naturally compels us to take the ὁ γεννηθείς in v. 18b as referring to Christ, being parallel to 'the Son of God' in v. 20a. This is reinforced by the fact that ὁ γεννηθείς stands here in contraposition to the evil one, as is also the case in 3:4-10.

Thus here the author speaks of three parties — the faithful, the Son of God, and the evil one (together with the world) — that are involved in the process and proceeds in a quasi-concentrical structure, but in three rhythmic developments marked by οἴδαμεν. The second rhythmic development resumes the first and the third elements of v. 18 (A and C), while the third rhythmic development resumes the second element of v. 18 (B) concluding it by going back to the first element of v. 18 (A). Hence the threefold procedure marked by οἴδαμεν is not destroyed in this quasi-concentric structure. At the same time we have to remark that the third οἴδαμεν is not exactly parallel to the other two οἴδαμεν because it introduces a contrast to the preceding, with οἴδαμεν δὲ ὅτι while the other two are simply οἴδαμεν ὅτι. Thus philologically the B' (with δέ) is parallel to B, starting with ἀλλά[72].

Hence, the ὁ γεννηθείς in v. 18b refers to Christ, who precisely in His quality of being Begotten of God keeps the children of God (all those who are begotten of God). Hence the evil one has no power over them, and as a consequence of it they do not sin.

This designation of Christ as ὁ γεννηθείς here in close juxtaposition with ὁ γεγεννημένος in connection with freedom from sin is quite significant. It shows once more the special characteristic of freedom from sin in the divinely begotten children of God.

---

[70] Note that if the evil one is put in C in his relation to the children of God, in C' he is put in his relation to the world.

[71] Cf. also I Jn 2:12-14 where the three elements of 'knowledge of the Father' 'freedom from sin' and 'being victorious over the evil one' are parallels, which parallelism is seen also in 5:18-20.

[72] Cf. B. WEISS, *Die drei Johannesbriefe*, p. 157, where he admits: " dass die drei οἴδαμεν keineswegs parallel stehen ".

2. "... has given us understanding ..."

We have already seen that the freedom from sin of the children of God is effected by means of a mutual dwelling of us in His Word (Jn 8:31) and of His Word (seed of God) in us (I Jn 3:9). Here again Jn takes up the same theme of 'freedom from sin' of those who are born of God, effected by Christ in His quality of 'Begotten of God', making it possible through a communion with God (knowledge of the Truthful One — v. 20).

As we have seen from the structure, v. 20 explains B (v. 18b), namely, the role of Christ, in effecting this freedom from sin (keeping the children of God). Thus the role of the Son of God in keeping those who are begotten of God is illustrated by the following analysis of v. 20.

Here Christ's mission as Son of God is described as a giving διάνοια [73], which brings men to the knowledge of the Truthful One. This is the only place where John uses the word διάνοια. Usually Commentators give to διάνοια a meaning close to that in Greek Anthropology, though some of them admit a 'New Covenant' context [74]. The context here, however, seems to be placed in a Covenant perspective [75]. The LXX almost always translates with διάνοια the Hebrew word ' lēb ' or ' lēbāb ' [76], by which the very centre of the personality affecting the whole interior life of man is indicated. So it means a faculty for a knowledge of God that affects the whole life of man [77]. Here Jn seems to refer to the fulfilment of what is said in the Covenant texts of Jer 31:31-34 and Ez 36:25-27 regarding the giving of a new heart and a new Spirit, and writing the laws on the heart of Israel, so that they may know God and walk in the ways of the commandments of the Lord and be free from sin [78].

---

[73] Cf. P. COUTURE, op. cit., in which he makes a detailed study of διάνοια in this context. Cf. also LIDDELL-SCOTT, *A Greek English Lexicon*, Oxford, 1961, p. 405; W. BAUER, *A Greek English Lexicon*, p. 186; J. BEHM, art. νοέω, *TWNT* IV, pp. 961-965; H. A. A. KENNEDY, "The Covenant Conception in the First Epistle of John", *ET* 28 (1916), pp. 23-26; N. LAZURE, op. cit., p. 115.

[74] Cf. DODD, *Epistles*, p. 139; M. KOHLER, *Le cœur et les mains*, Neuchâtel, 1962, p. 198; BONSIRVEN, *Epîtres*, p. 245; SCHNACKENBURG, *Die Johannesbriefe*, pp. 272, 290.

[75] For details on the matter, we refer the reader to P. COUTURE, op. cit. Cf. also M. KOHLER, op. cit., p. 198; M. E. BOISMARD, art. " Connaissance ...", pp. 365-391; Idem, art. " Je ferai avec vous une alliance nouvelle ", *Lum et Vie* 8 (1953), pp. 94-109; H. A. A. KENNEDY, art. cit., pp. 23-26.

[76] Out of the 45 occurrences 38 translate with διάνοια.

[77] Cf. Jer 24:7 " I will give them a heart, that they may know that I am the Lord ".

[78] Cf. M. E. BOISMARD, art. " La Connaissance ..." pp. 365-390. Note that

In these Covenant texts there is a striking parallelism between διάνοια and καρδία (Jer 31:31-34)[79], between καρδία and πνεῦμα (Ez 36:26-27) and between νόμος and πνεῦμα (Comp. Jer 31:33 with Ez 36:27; cf. also Is 59:21)[80]. It is to be noted here that the Spirit and the Word of Yahweh are closely related in the OT[81].

Speaking of the notion of the divine sonship of men in the OT, we saw how the Law, the revealed will of God, enters as a constituent element into the Covenant and therefore into becoming children of God. And in the New Covenant this Law becomes interiorized through the Spirit and leads to the knowledge of God and purification from sins (Jer 31:31-33; Ez 36:26-27). The association of all these elements seems to have persisted in the Johannine conception of διάνοια where it leads to the knowledge of the Truthful One (v. 20), and freedom from sin (v. 18). So in Jn διάνοια implies the ' Word of God '[82], interiorized through the Spirit, which leads men to communion with God or Christ, (knowledge of the Truthful One)[83], and to freedom (from sin) proper to those who are begotten of God. So it is concretely by giving this διάνοια that the Son of God (ὁ γεννηθείς) ' keeps ' the child of God, and thus the child of God (ὁ γεγεννημένος ἐκ ... Θεοῦ) does not sin.

The aspect of Communion implied in this knowledge of God[84] is explicitly expressed in v. 20c (A'') ' and we are in the truthful One '. The phrase ' in His Son Jesus Christ ' shows that it is in virtue of

---

the word διάνοια occurs in Jer precisely in this New Covenant text and nowhere else.

[79] That καρδία and διάνοια cover the same ground and are convertible is shown in the Greek text where there is often wavering between the two (e. g., Dt 28:47; Jos 14:8; Prov 4:4; 27:19).

[80] For the parallelism between Jeremiah and Ezechiel on these New Covenant texts, cf. J. W. MILLER, *Das Verhältnis Jeremias und Ezechiels sprachlich und theologisch untersucht*, Neukirchen, 1935, pp. 97-100.

[81] For a detailed study on the parallelism of these elements in the Covenant texts affecting the notion of διάνοια, cf. P. COUTURE, op. cit., pp. 29-33.

[82] Note that in the NT the Word of God (Revelation in Christ) takes the place of the Law (revealed will of God).

[83] The γινώσκομεν (indicative) is preferable (A B L P 98 101 180 etc.) than γινώσκωμεν (subjunctive) (B³ K) and ἵνα seems to be epexegetical, explaining διάνοια. Cf. BLASS-DEBRUNNER, A Greek Grammar ..., no. 394; BONSIRVEN, *Epîtres*, p. 246, note 2; H. RIESENFELD, " Zu den Joh. ' hina ' Sätzen ", *StTh* 19 (1965), pp. 213-220.

[84] We take ἀληθινός as referring to God but as revealed in Christ, because in Jn ἀλήθεια has essentially a revelatory sense, and in the Biblical Tradition ὁ ἀληθινός Θεός is used for God in opposition to idols who are vain (cf. Is 65:16; III Mach 6:18; I Thes 1:9; I Jn 5:21. In Jn ὁ ἀληθινός is used both for God (8:2; 17:3) and for Christ (Apoc 3:7,14; 19:11).

our relation to Christ and our communion with Him that our communion with God is realized [85].

In the light of the above analysis the meaning of the whole passage (vv. 18-20) becomes clear. If A A' A'' describe the communion with God ('being born of God', 'being of God' and 'being in God'), which produces freedom from sin, B B' describe the role of Christ in making this communion operative by keeping the child of God, and by giving 'διάνοια'. Finally, C C' give the antithetical elements as usual in Jn: the evil one who is operative in the world that is completely determined by him, in contrast to those 'born of God', who are completely determined by God (ἐκ τοῦ Θεοῦ ἐσμέν). Thus once more John takes up the dynamic and operative character of the progressive stage of the divine sonship, which results in impeccability. At the same time, he underlines the solidarity of those who are 'born of God' with the One who is 'Begotten of God', and who makes this dynamic and progressive sonship possible.

IV Freedom proper to the Divine Sonship (Jn 8:31-36)

Jn 8:31-36 illustrates further the nature of this impeccability of the children of God. There Jesus speaks of a freedom that is opposite to the 'slavery of sin' and hence freedom that consists in 'being righteous' [86] and which is effected through Christ who is 'the Son'.

A. The Structure of Jn 8:31-36

A particularized structure of the section speaking of this freedom should be rewarding:

V. 31	A	IF YOU abide in my Word, YOU WILL BE TRULY my disciples
32		YOU will know the Truth and the Truth WILL MAKE YOU FREE
33	B	They replied, we are the Seed of Abraham
	C	and never have been SLAVES OF anyone
(A)	D	How do you say that YOU WILL BECOME FREE ?
34	C'	Everyone who commits sin is a SLAVE OF sin

---

[85] Cf. DODD, *Epistles*, p. 140. It is worth noting here how in Jn 8:31-36 the Knowledge of Truth (Son) leads to freedom. If the Gospel is Christocentric, the Epistle is more Theocentric.

[86] Cf. the dualistic opposition of sin and righteousness in I Jn 2:29 – 3:10. About the notion of freedom in this section, cf. J. O. T. VANCELLS, *La Verdad os hará libres (Jn 8,32)*. Barcelona, 1973.

35	B′	The slave does not remain in the house forever
		The Son remains for ever
36	A′	IF therefore the Son WILL MAKE YOU FREE YOU WILL BE TRULY Free.

Here we have a concentric structure in which the question of the Jews as to the 'how' of becoming free stands in the centre (D), moving backward and forward towards the reply of Jesus in A and A′ with the affirmation of the nature of the true freedom obtained through the 'Truth' and the 'Son'. The correspondence of A and A′ with D as answer to the question is confirmed by the literal parallelism indicated by (A). In B and C we have the position claimed by the Jews, while in C′ and B′ we have the actual position of the Jews in contrast to the position of Jesus with regard to 'sonship' and 'freedom' [87].

B. Vocabulary

1. 'Son' and 'Slaves'

As we have already seen, here it is a question of freedom from the sin of unbelief, implying a domination of the diabolic power of sin [88]. Slavery of sin, therefore, means diabolic sonship [89], and consequently, is absolutely contradictory to the condition of divine sonship. Slavery and sonship are mutually exclusive. He who is a slave

---

[87] The ὁ δοῦλος in v. 35 (B′) is not exactly parallel to the δεδουλεύκαμεν and δοῦλος of v. 33 and 34 (CC′), because in v. 35 the contrast has changed from that between 'free' and 'slave' of vv. 33 and 34 to one of gradation in the household between 'slave' and 'son'. Cf. R. E. BROWN, *The Gospel*, p. 355, taking v. 35 as a parenthetical insertion of a once independent Johannine saying. Cf. also DODD, *Interpretation*, pp. 380-382, where he interprets v. 35 as a short parable of the slave and the son different in character from the rest of the section.

[88] Cf. what we said above on the character of sin in this context on pp. 258ff. Cf. also Jn 16:8-9 where the sin is actually defined as unbelief: "The Spirit would convict the world of sin, because they believe not in me". The fact that Jesus speaks to the believing Jews does not go against seeing this sin as the sin of unbelief, because it is not the authentic faith demanded for becoming disciples and true children of God. Note the formula τοὺς πεπιστευκότας αὐτῷ (dative) and πολλοί the subject of ἐπίστευσαν εἰς αὐτόν which all point to imperfect faith.

[89] Note the parallelism of this condition of the Jews with the other stanzas in the whole section, in which their sinful conduct manifests the devil as their father (vv. 38, 40, 43-44) and their condition of not being from God (v. 47), and being from the devil (v. 44).

in the household cannot be a son. The slave has no permanent status and may be dismissed at any time. But the son is free and belongs to the household, having a permanent relationship to the father. The sinner, whatever his ancestry is, is a slave to sin and is not free.

When introducing this metaphor of 'son' and 'slave', Jn thinks concretely of the condition of Jesus and Jews respectively [90]. Jn, introducing v. 35 parallel to v. 33, thus putting the Son parallel to the Seed of Abraham (in the singular) seems to indicate that Jesus is the real Seed of Abraham, while mere physical descent from Abraham is equal to slavery [91]. So in the parallel verses 33a and 34-35 Jesus disproves the claim of the Jews to be the 'Seed of Abraham', and to have the freedom proper to the son in the household, and he says that their sinful conduct is a proof of their being in the position of slaves and so of not having the freedom proper to the son in the household. Moreover, Jesus presents himself as the 'Son' who enjoys real freedom, having a permanent place in the household of the Father. Putting the Jews as being slaves to sin (sons of the devil), in contrast, he presents himself as perfectly exemplifying the filial relation to God, and thus enjoying the real freedom proper to a Son of God.

2. *"If the Son makes you free, you will be free indeed"* (v. 36)

After setting this contrasting position of Himself as the Son and the Jews as slaves, in vv. 31 and 36 he presents the true freedom proper to the sons in the household of their Father, which will be obtained through Himself who is the only one who can impart this sonship and freedom, because He is the only One, who has in His own being this condition of sonship [92]. So it is in the measure in which we participate in the condition of Christ as Son of God that men are going to be really 'free' [93]. This shows that it is a freedom gained by becoming sons of God, and that it is in strict dependence on the sonship of Christ [94].

---

[90] The opinion of Dodd that v. 35 contains a mere parable seems to be defective, because in v. 36 Jesus is concretely spoken of as 'Son', and it is the same Son who stands in v. 35 in contrast to the slave.

[91] Note the parallelism of B B' in the structure.

[92] Note how the condition for obtaining the real freedom proper to the sons of God is that "the Son will set you free" (v. 36).

[93] Note what we said above on impeccability as an eschatological good realized in Christ and participated in by those who are begotten of God on pp. 266-267.

[94] Cf. W. M. MILLIGAN, and W. M. F., *Commentary on the Gospel of St. John*, Edinburgh, 1898, p. 107: "One only can give this freedom, for one only can give this sonship — He who is the Son (see ch. 1:12)".

a. Freedom from sin

The fact that the slavery of diabolic sonship is manifested concretely in 'doing sin' (Jn 8:34) shows that the freedom of the divine sonship is manifested in 'doing righteousness' (I Jn 2:29; 3:10). So the freedom proper to the Son seems to be manifested in the righteousness of Christ. We saw above that the righteousness of Christ consists in 'being sinless' and 'being victorious over sin'. So the freedom that accompanies the divine sonship in men should also be, first of all, a 'freedom from the bondage of sin'.

b. Freedom inherent to the nature of sonship

But it is not only a freedom from actual sins. It is a freedom proper to the 'son' having a permanent standing in the household of the 'Father'. The attachment of the sons to the household of the Father is not merely external, like that of slaves, but a thing of nature. So the freedom from sins should have in the sons of God a permanent character, namely, it should be based on the life imparted to the sons by the Father, and hence it should be the fruit of a permanent life possessed by the sons [95]. The freedom from sin of the children of God, therefore, is the result of the imparted Life of God the Father Himself who is righteous (I Jn 1:9) and of the participation in the life of the Son, who is equally righteous (I Jn 2:1,29; 3:7).

The confrontation of Jesus as the Son who remains in the house for ever, with the Jews as the slaves who do not remain in the house for ever [96], suggests here a freedom that is much more significant than a mere freedom from actual sins [97]. It is manifestly a special freedom, freedom gained by becoming sons, and thus gaining all that belongs to the position of sons, retaining for ever a connection with the Father's house.

The figure of the 'house' (οἰκία and cognates) is one of the most frequent metaphors in the New Testament for the believer's place in the domestic domain of God (Acts 9:31; Rom 8:9,11; 14:19; 15:21; I Cor 3:9,16; 8:1; 10:23; 14:3-5). The 'Father's House' is God's

---

[95] Here it is worth noting that I Jn 3:9 and 5:18 speaking of the sinlessness of the begotten of God in the 'fruit scheme' imply thereby this special characteristic of freedom proper to sonship.

[96] Note the parallelism of B' (Jesus as Son in contrast to slave) with B (Jews claiming to be the seed of Abraham).

[97] Note what we said above on p. 287 on the difference of perspective in the idea of slavery in v. 35 from that in vv. 33b and 34. This difference may also explain the omission of the phrase 'the Son has a place there for ever' by some Mss.

household or family ⁹⁸, and therefore the freedom of the son in the house refers to the freedom of the children of God resulting from the abiding communion with the Father and the Son.

c. True Freedom: True Self-Determination

True freedom means true self-determination. And it is only a child of God, having the filial relation to the Father, enjoys this true self-determination. As the one who is determined by the nature of the Father, he is always pleased to do what is pleasing to the Father and thus he always does what he pleases. This is the true freedom of Christian sonship. And as it is Christ the Son of God ' par excellence ' who enjoys this freedom, and has consequently a permanent standing in the household of the Father, the one who is incorporated with him or is in communion with him possesses the same freedom and has the security of a permanent position in the family of God.

Whoever is determined by another power opposite to the nature of the Father ⁹⁹, has not really the power of true self-determination, and hence is not really free with the freedom of the divine sonship. The position of sonship claimed by the Jews (seed of Abraham) was artificial, because, being slaves to sin, being inimical to the real Son of God, they had no communion with the Son, and hence they had no permanent position in the household of the Father together with the Son. So only bondage and fear could be their lot and prospect. The child of God instead enjoys the power of true self-determination, and has thus the joy of Christian freedom, the freedom of the children of God.

3. " *You are truly my disciples and ... the Truth will make you free* " (vv. 31-32)

In the context, as the parallelism shows, it is a freedom that is identified with ' discipleship ' ¹⁰⁰. Hence ' to be free ' is not simply to be free from sins, but ' to be a disciple '.

---

⁹⁸ Cf. R. H. GUNDRY, " In my Father's House are many μοναί " (Jn 14: 2), *ZNW* 58 (1967), pp. 68-72.

⁹⁹ Note the diabolic sonship of the Jews expressed in v. 44 ὑμεῖς ἐκ τοῦ πατρὸς τοῦ διαβόλου ἐστε and in v. 47 ἐκ τοῦ Θεοῦ οὐκ ἐστέ, which brings to light this opposite diabolic power that determines the nature of those who are not sons of God.

¹⁰⁰ Note the parallelism between A and A' : " you will be truly my disciples " and " you will be truly free ".

a. Freedom of the children of God and discipleship

The term μαθητής is a favourite word in the Gospel of John to express the relation of the believer to Jesus [101]. It is mostly used with the definite article referring to the twelve who accompanied Him. The word occurs without the article, hence referring to the nature of being a disciple only 6 times [102]. These 6 texts show that it is a spiritual dependence that makes one a disciple of another, and not the material participation in the terrestrial life [103]. Out of these six texts, three are of special importance for our understanding of the meaning of discipleship in Jn, as they speak of 'being' and 'becoming' real disciples of Christ (Cf. Jn 8:31; 13:35; 15:8).

Jn 13:35 shows discipleship as manifested not in some special function, but in fraternal love, based therefore on a spiritual union between men manifested in fraternal love. This points already to discipleship as a spiritual family relation. Jn 15:8 speaks of 'becoming' (γενήσεσθε) a disciple and so helps us to see the source of this family relation. Here the glory of the Father is connected with two facts that go together, namely, the 'producing of fruits' and 'becoming disciples' [104]. The actual context of the allegory of the 'vine and branches' and the exhortation to remain in Jesus shows that it is the communion with Christ that enables them to 'bring forth fruits' and 'become disciples'. This communion with Christ is in his divine sonship, because as we saw above, it results in the spiritual family relation. Besides, the future tense of γενήσεσθε shows also the dynamic growth of this communion in the filial life of the Son, that produces fruits and culminates in discipleship. So 'to become disciple' is to enter upon a new existence itself, an existence that results from being incorporated to the divine and filial life of Jesus [105]. So in practice

---

[101] It occurs 78 times in Jn, while I Jn completely ignores it. Note also that the term 'disciple' occurs only in the Gospels and Acts in the whole NT.

[102] Cf. Jn 8:31; 9:27,28; 13:35; 15:8; 19:38.

[103] Note how in Jn 9:27 the pharisees are said to be the disciples of Moses and in 9:28 the blind man is said to be the disciple of Jesus. In the same way, in Jn 19:38 it is his spiritual attachment to Jesus that makes Joseph of Arimathea a disciple of Jesus.

[104] The second clause γενήσεσθε ἐμοὶ μαθηταί seems to depend on ἵνα though it is in future. Cf. M. ZERWICK, *Analysis Philologica Novi Testamenti Graeci*, 2nd ed., Rome, 1960, p. 241; Note that in the NT ἵνα can govern both subjunctive and future indicative (cf. M. ZERWICK, *Biblical Greek illustrated by examples*, Rome, 1963, no. 340).

[105] Cf. O. PRUNET, *La morale chrétienne ...*, p. 105 where he emphasizes the eschatological character of the discipleship as the participation of that

the state of 'being a disciple' is the advanced stage of being the children of God, producing fruits characteristic of the life of divine sonship.

In the light of the above considerations, we can see the real meaning of the freedom in Jn 8:31-36. 'To be free' which is equivalent to 'being the disciples of Christ', points to that special freedom that is proper to the state of being children of God, resulting from communion with Him who is the Son of God. Note the emphatic expression 'ὄντως ἐλεύθεροι ἔσεσθε'. The ὄντῶς, which is used nowhere else in the Writings of John, seems to underline this special character of the freedom mentioned here, freedom that can come only from the One who is the Son and who alone remains in the house of the Father for ever [106].

b. Freedom of the Children of God through the Truth

(1) Jesus - the Truth in his Sonship

The freedom that is proper to the sonship is obtained by means of 'knowing the Truth' (Jn 8:31-32). In the context, the 'Truth' is the 'Son' and so is identified with the person of Christ [107]. It is then in the quality of the 'Son of God' that Jesus is 'Truth'.

The very contrast between the divine sonship and the diabolic sonship in Jn 8 illustrates this. The devil who is a 'liar' and 'the father of lies' does not stand in the Truth, and has no Truth in him (Jn 8:44). Falsehood is of his very nature. And the Jews by trying to kill Him who spoke the Truth do the works of their father the devil, and thus show their diabolic sonship, having affinity and likeness of nature with the latter. In contrast to this, Jesus, who speaks the Truth that he saw and heard from the Father, stands in a filial relation to God, showing affinity and likeness of nature with Him who is 'ἀληθής' (8:26). So Jesus is 'Truth' in his Sonship, as the self-revelation of the Father.

(2) Knowledge of the Truth : Communion with the Truth (Son)

It is the knowledge of this Truth, Jesus the Son, that is described as the means to obtain the freedom proper to the divine sonship which is in Christ, and as something that determines the very being of the believer.

[106] Cf. W. M. MILLIGAN and W. M. F., *Commentary on the Gospel of St. John*, p. 107 where he says that " it is designedly employed in order to bring out that closeness of relation between the sons of God and the Son which is so striking a part of the teaching of this chapter."

[107] Note the parallelism between the ἡ ἀλήθεια and ὁ υἱός in vv. 31 and 36 (AA'). Compare also Jn 1:17 and 14:6.

of men. The word γινώσκειν is of special importance in the Gospel of John [108]. It is already admitted by the authors that the theme of religious knowledge in Biblical usage has often a profound meaning of communion between the one who knows and the object of ones knowledge. This is true of both the Old Testament [109] and the Later Jewish Literature [110]. We see the same profound sense too in the Johannine usage of γινώσκειν. Many passages in Jn use the word γινώσκειν to describe the personal relations between the Father and the Son [111]. Jn 8:32 likewise seems to emphasize the aspect of a vital experience of entering into communion with the Truth [112]. So the means of having the freedom of sonship through the Son (Truth) is to be in communion with Him, which again confirms the closeness of relation between the sons of God and the Son of God in possessing this freedom proper to sonship.

4. "If you remain in my word ..."

It is the 'remaining in the Word of God (Christ)' that makes the communion with the Truth (Son of God) and the consequent freedom of the children of God possible. As we saw, while discussing Jn 8:31-47, it was the refusal to accept Jesus and His Word (Truth) that hindered the Jews from becoming children of God. In the Johannine usage of μένειν this belongs to the series of exhortative or conditional usages and hence stresses the necessity of our co-operation by letting ourselves be constantly guided and determined by the

---

[108] We do not want to make a detailed study of the verb here. For studies on the use of γινώσκει in Jn, cf. R. BULTMANN, art. γινώσκειν, *TDNT* I, pp. 711-713; A. CAMPITELLI, *Il Valore del Conoscere religioso in S. Giovanni*, Diss. Rome, 1962; DODD, *Interpretation*, pp. 151-169; M. R. ELY, *Knowledge of God in Johannine Thought*, New York, 1925; I. DE LA POTTERIE, art. cit., "οἶδα et γινώσκω", in *Bib* 40 (1959), pp. 709-725; G. TIETZE, "Knowledge of God in the Fourth Gospel", *JBR* 22 (1954), pp. 14-19; E. VIAU, "Connaître Dieu. Une expression johannique", *Vie Spir* 77 (1947), pp. 324-333.

[109] Cf. E. BAUMANN, "Yada und seine Derivate", *ZAW* 28 (1908), pp. 22-41; 110-141; G. BOTTERWECK, '*Gott erkennen*' *im Sprachgebrauch des Alten Testaments*, Bonn, 1951.

[110] Cf. J. DE CAEVEL, "La connaissance religieuse dans les Hymnes d'action de grâce de Qumran", *ETL* 38 (1962), pp. 435-460; F. NÖTSCHER, *Zur theologischen Terminologie der Qumran, Texte*, Bonn, 1956, pp. 38-79.

[111] Cf. Jn 7:29; 8:55; 10:15; 17:25.

[112] Note the future tense of γνώσεσθε which points to this knowledge of truth as something that is realized as a consequence of a permanent abiding in the Word of God (ἐὰν ... μείνητε ἐν τῷ λόγῳ ... γνώσεσθε). We will see better this aspect of communion in the Knowledge of God and its relation to the divine sonship, when speaking of the texts in the Epistle.

Word of God (Christ) in order to obtain the freedom proper to the children of God.

This freedom consists essentially in the sonship that is communicated by the Son [113] which is again put as parallel to discipleship in Jn 8:31-32. Although they believe in Jesus (v. 31), men have still to 'become' disciples (sons), and thus obtain the freedom proper to the sonship. A disciple is one who lets himself be really instructed and guided by the Master. This attitude of perfect docility is obtained only gradually and progressively as 'His Word remains in us' and 'we remain in His Word'. This shows again the dynamism implied in obtaining the freedom proper to the children of God.

Conclusion

If 'righteousness' is the criterion of the divine sonship, because it is its spontaneous result. Therefore, following the 'fruit scheme' Jn puts impeccability as the fruit of the life of the children of God. Impeccability, like the other eschatological gifts, was realized in Christ as Son of God (I Jn 3:5,8) and by adhesion to him through faith, the children of God share in his impeccability too. So in their theological reality, the children of God are impeccable in opposition to the children of the devil (I Jn 3:9; 5:18). But as they still live in a condition where there is danger of losing it, this impeccability is guaranteed only by a constant and dynamic life of faith and communion with Christ. This is made possible through the mutual remaining of the seed (Word) of God in us (I Jn 3:9) and our remaining in Him (I Jn 3:6), letting ourselves be constantly determined by His Word (Jn 8:31). So impeccability is a fruit of the dynamic condition of the progressive stage of sonship.

This impeccability of the children of God is effected through Christ in his quality of being Begotten of God. He does it concretely by giving them understanding and knowledge of the Truthful One by means of His Word interiorized through the Spirit (I Jn 5:18-20).

Though this condition of the children of God is above all a condition of freedom from the bondage of sin, it is a freedom proper to the son having a permanent standing in the household of the Father. Therefore it is a freedom of the children of God resulting from an abiding communion with the Father and the Son, and hence a freedom that determines their nature, and thus allows a true self-determination of the children of God.

---

[113] Note that it is the Son and not the Father who is represented as giving freedom, in so far as he communicates to others that which is his own. Cf. B. F. WESTCOTT, op. cit., p. 134.

Chapter X

Love: The Expression of the Life of Divine Sonship
(I Jn 3:10-12; 4:7-8)

I. Brotherly Love — Manifestation of the Divine Sonship (I Jn 3:10-12)

Having spoken of 'doing righteousness' as the visible reality manifesting the invisible reality of the divine birth and sonship of men in I Jn 2:29 – 3:10b, in v. 10c Jn passes on to speak of brotherly love as the visible reality manifesting the same divine sonship.

A. *Tradition and Redaction*

As we saw above speaking of the traditional baptismal elements underlying I Jn 2:29 – 3:10, brotherly love was connected with divine birth already in the baptismal tradition (cf. I Pet 1:22-23). In the rearrangement made by John, we saw how he changes the position of the element of brotherly love to the end, in order to speak of it 'ex professo' separately and elaboratly, as it is one of the main themes of his Epistle [1]. Here the connection between the divine sonship and brotherly love becomes a starting point for him to speak anew of his favourite theme of brotherly love, and he introduces this theme by making use of the divine sonship as motive.

B. *Brotherly Love and Righteousness*

Though brotherly love and righteousness are presented in I Jn as parallels as regards their relationship to divine sonship, brotherly love seems to give a further specification to the divine sonship.

1. *Brotherly love and Righteousness as parallels*

a. In the construction of v. 10

V. 10 " In this are manifested   the children of God and
                                 the children of the devil,
    everyone who does not do righteousness — is not of God
    nor who does not love his brother ".

---

[1] Cf. the three sections of I Jn 2:3-11; 3:10-24 and 4:7-21 where he speaks of charity progressively, and that introducing various motives.

As we see from the construction of the verse, the 'Children of God', 'Children of the devil' and 'being from God' indicate the invisible realities, while 'doing righteousness'[2] and 'brotherly love', being parallel to it, indicate the visible realities manifesting those invisible realities in man. To put it more concretely, in v. 10c 'brotherly love' being parallel to 'doing righteousness', becomes the sign of 'being from God', and hence the sign of divine sonship, since v. 10b is the explanation of v. 10a speaking of the way in which the children of God and children of the devil can be recognised.

b. In the whole context of the Epistle

Now, love here for Jn is not something entirely different from 'righteousness'[3]. As in the first part (2:7-11) where brotherly love made concrete and contained in itself the observance of the commandments (2:3-6), so here in the second part, brotherly love expresses in a concrete fashion and embodies 'doing righteousness' (2:29 – 3:10), and thus becomes the decisive mark of the children of God[4]. Speaking of 'doing righteousness', we saw how for Jn 'to do righteousness' means a dynamic adherence to Christ's triumphant righteousness, participating in his sinlessness and triumph over sin, which is the basis for the fulfilment of all righteousness. This righteousness in Christ (Christ's saving work) took place concretely through the revelation of God as 'Love' (I Jn 4:8,16), and hence also our 'doing righteousness' should take place concretely and basically in Love.

2. *The Specific relation of Brotherly love to divine sonship*

Though the fundamental reality in righteousness and love is the same, brotherly love shows a different aspect of this reality. If in 'righteousness' our relation to God the Father is emphasized, in brotherly love more emphasis is placed on our relation to the other children of God. The relation of brotherly love with the divine sonship is seen better in the light of the following vv. 3:10-12.

---

[2] The reading ὁ μὴ ὤν δίκαιος attested by Vg and other Latin Writers is not to be accepted, since Jn bases the sonship on the 'doing' of righteousness, and also because the literary inclusion requires the current reading.

[3] Cf. R. LAW, *Tests of Life*, p. 237, note 2 where he takes 'he that loveth not his brother' in the second place as a further definition of 'whosoever does not do righteousness', the καί meaning 'namely'.

[4] Cf. WESTCOTT, *Epistles*, p. 109: "Righteousness involves the fulfilment of all law, of relations to God and to man both personally and socially. The love of Christian for Christian resting on the sense of a divine fellowship (cf. ch. 1:3) carries forward to its loftiest embodiment the righteousness which man can reach.

a. Grammatical Considerations

In v. 11 Jn begins solemnly to speak of the important theme of love, reminding Christians of their reception of the Christian message in the beginning [5]. The command to love one another, introduced by ἵνα is not simply the content of the message of the Gospel, but also the aim and purpose of it [6]. The message of the Gospel is Christ's life of salvific work. This Gospel message is at the same time connected with v. 10c with ὅτι, thus making it the basis of brotherly love, which is the sign of 'being from God' — 'child of God'. A right interpretation of this connection is of importance here for a right understanding of the relation between 'brotherly love' and 'sonship'.

b. Analysis of the Expressions

(1) "... for this is the message ..." (v. 11)

As we have seen above "εἶναι ἐκ τοῦ Θεοῦ" expresses the essential connection of a community of life existing between God and men as Father and children. The Gospel message, namely, Christ's life and saving work, was nothing but the revelation of the life of God, who is Love (cf. I Jn 4:8,16). In this connection, it is interesting to note that the word "ἀγγελία" [7] is found, apart from here, only in I Jn 1:5, where the object of the message is 'God is Light'. There are various opinions regarding the meaning of this definition. Some have given a purely rationalistic interpretation, trying to explain it from the religious syncretism of the time, perhaps following the example of the Fathers such as Oecumenius [8], Theophylactus [9] etc., who

---

[5] Note the words ἦν ἠκούσατε, ἀπ' ἀρχῆς all of which belong to the baptismal terminology. The ἀγγελία in I Jn 1:5 refers to the words of Jesus. But for John both come to the same. Cf. J. SCHNIEWIND, art. ἀγγελία, *TDNT* I, p. 59.

[6] Though the declarative or definitive use of ἵνα to introduce the contents of a command or the like, specially when preceded by αὕτη referring to the ἵνα clause, is characteristic of John (cf. BROOKE, *Epistles*, pp. 19-20, where he has collected the Johannine texts exemplifying this use of ἵνα), the context makes it clear that the ἵνα here keeps up the final sense too. Note the exhortatory tone of the whole section 3:11-24 and the description of the obligation of brotherly love as a consequence of Christ's laying down His life for men (v. 16).

[7] Some Mss such as X C P Ψ 1739 al Syh etc. give ἐπαγγελία instead of ἀγγελία. But ἐπαγγελία is never used in the NT to introduce a precept, while ἀγγελία here gives good sense to the text. Besides, ἐπαγγελία occurs only once in the Johannine Writings (I Jn 2:25), while it occurs 51 times in the NT. On the other hand ἀγγελία occurs only in I Jn.

[8] Cf. PG 119, 623-628.

[9] Cf. PG 126, 15-19.

were influenced by this rationalistic concept [10]. But in Jn the concept of 'Light' is quite different from the mere intellectual or quasi-physical concept of 'light' found in the Hellenistic philosophy and Gnosticism. Others have given a purely moral interpretation of the definition, taking the light for the perfect sanctity of God [11]. But in Jn the word "φῶς" is never used to designate sanctity as such. 'Light' for Jn is the revelation of the Father in Christ, which is the object of faith and the norm of life for Christians [12]. Hence "φῶς" is an image to designate revelation or God revealing Himself [13].

In the same context of I Jn 1:5 note the parallelism between v. 2 and v. 5, which is introduced by "καί", giving thus further explanation of what is said before:

V. 2 "... and proclaim to you that *life eternal* which was with the Father *appeared to us*"

V. 5 "... and proclaim to you that *God is light*".

So, if 'God is light' signifies the 'self-revelation of God', this corresponds perfectly to the other definition 'God is love', because this 'self-revelation of God' is the 'revelation of the love of God'. The Gospel message then is the self-revelation of God, who is Love, in Christ. And as the ἵνα clause implies, the aim and purpose of this revelation was naturally to create and strengthen the same love in men, through participation in this revealed love of God (cf. Jn 17:26; I Jn 3:1). And it is this revelation of God as 'Love' that is the basis of brotherly love, and love becomes the spontaneous manifestation of the 'divine sonship' and 'being from God'.

For Jn, therefore, the life of the children of God should be characterized by love, because the life of the children of God is a participation and extension of the life of the Father: God who is Light (the revealed love) [14]. So if one does not have this divine love in

---

[10] Cf. F. N. KLEIN, *Die Lichtterminologie bei Philon von Alexandrien und in den Hermetischen Schriften*, Leiden, 1962.

[11] Cf. for example, AUGUSTINE, PL 35, 1980-1981; BEDE THE VENERABLE, PL 93, 87; J. DUPONT, *Christologie de S. Jean*, Brugges, 1951, p. 74.

[12] Cf. Jn 1:9; 3:19-21; 12:35-36,46 etc. Φῶς in the important baptismal texts of the NT designates illumination through baptismal instruction of the message of the Gospel (cf. II Cor 4:4-6; Eph 1:18; 5:8-9,13-15 etc.).

[13] Cf. O. SCHAEFER, "Gott ist Licht", *TSKrit* 105 (1933), pp. 467-476; R. LAW, *Tests of Life*, p. 58.

[14] On the relation between 'Light' and 'Love' in I Jn, see J. CHMIEL, *Lumière et Charité d'après la première épître de Saint Jean*, Rome 1971. Note the pres. participle ὁ μὴ ἀγαπῶν in I Jn 3:10, which has the value of a substantive (cf. BLASS-DEBRUNNER, *A Greek Grammar of the New Testament*, 413),

him, and hence the community of life with God, he is not from God, and therefore is not a child of God.

(2) " ... love his brother ..." (v. 10)

Note the expression 'love his brother', which points to the Christian community as a family, of which God is the Father, and in which Christians are brothers among themselves. It is interesting to note that out of the 15 usages of the noun " ἀδελφός " in the whole of the Epistle, 8 are in this section alone, which begins with the divine sonship as the motive for brotherly love [15]. The author is obviously thinking of the members of the Christian society, who form the children of God, and hence of brotherly love which should exist in these children of God [16].

But this he does without excluding those outside the Christian community. This is clear from the following vv. 13-15. There the 'world' hates the Christians. And the hatred of the world towards the Christians is qualified by Jn as " ὁ μισῶν τὸν ἀδελφόν " and this is compared to the fratricide of Cain. So the world and the Christians were destined to be, at least in principle, in a fraternal relation. Hence Jn does not restrict brotherly love exclusively to the Christian community, though he actually thinks of brotherly love among the Christians. In fact the texts of I Jn regarding fraternal love present an ambivalent use in this regard. While texts such as I Jn 3:13; 4:5-6; 5:1-2,16 etc. convey a restricted sense applying what is said to the members of the Christian community [17], texts like I Jn 3:14,17; 4:20-21 seem to go against such a view of exclusively referring to the Christian community [18].

Here we have perhaps a hint of the universality of divine sonship in Jn, namely, the possibility of those who are actually Christians falling away from the state of being 'children of God' to being 'chil-

---

and shows that the brotherly love here is not an act, but a permanent quality, which is at the same time incessantly active or dynamic.

[15] It is remarkable that in the Epistle, which speaks of the life of the children of God, the use of the expression ἀδελφός is considerably frequent. There we find the word 15 times, while in the Gospel it is found in this specific Christian sense only twice (20:17; 21:23). Besides, while ἀδελφός is never used in the Gospel in direct relation to the verb ἀγαπᾶν, in the Epistle, out of 15 times, 13 are used in connection with the verb ἀγαπᾶν. On the theme, cf. J. RATZINGER, *Die christliche Brüderlichkeit*, München, 1960; M. BOUTTIER, " La Notion de Frères chez S. Jean ", *RHPR* 44 (1964), pp. 179-190.

[16] Cf. M. BOUTTIER, " La notion de frères chez saint Jean ", *RHPhRel* 44 (1964), pp. 179-190.

[17] Cf. III Jn 3, 5,10 which certainly support this view.

[18] Cf., the Commentaries of Brooke, Dodd, Schnackenburg and Bultmann.

dren of the devil' (world), and the possibility of those who are not actually Christians, becoming the children of God [19] and thus entering into this communion of brotherly love.

Hence the brotherly love is the very expression of the communicated divine life which unites the children of God into one family of God, which, though actually realized in the Christian Community is virtually and dynamically oriented to the whole mankind through Christ.

C. *Lack of Brotherly Love*: *Manifestation of the Diabolic Sonship*.

In v. 12 Jn brings in the example of Cain as the one who does not love and hence is not from God [20]. Abel was murdered by Cain who being from the evil one — the devil, represents the children of the devil, who do not love, not being from God. The murder was the expression of his being determined by the evil one. This condition of Cain is explained in the expression "ἐκ τοῦ πονηροῦ ἦν". Moreover, the evil works of Cain, that caused the murder also point in this direction, because for Jn works are always the expression of the origin that determines one's nature [21].

1. *The Structure of I Jn 3:10-12*

The parallelism between 'not being from God', 'being from the evil one' and 'doing of evil works' could be seen from the structure of the section I Jn 3:10-12.

V. 10 A   By this ... t h e   C h i l d r e n   o f   G o d
       B   and the children of the devil ... who does not do righteousness i s   n o t   o f   G o d, nor is he who does not love ...
11   C   Because this is the message ... that we should love one another

---

[19] In this connection it is worth noting that perhaps we have a hint to this universality of the divine sonship in the expression πᾶς ὁ ἀγαπῶν of I Jn 4:7, where the only condition for divine birth in authentic love, without any further restriction.

[20] The construction οὐ καθὼς ... is singular, being irregular and elliptical. The clause without the negative would have run on naturally with v. 10: "He who does not love ... even as Cain ...". But the insertion of v. 11 leads to this negative construction (cf. WESTCOTT, *Epistles* p. 110).

[21] Note that the same expression is used by John to describe the attitude of unbelief and hatred towards Jesus (cf. Jn 3:19; 7:7). Again in Jn 8:40 he qualifies this attitude of the Jews, as 'doing the works of their father' — the devil.

12   B'   not like Cain who ...
        ... b e i n g o f t h e e v i l o n e murdered his brother
        because   h i s   d e e d s   w e r e   e v i l
    A' And his brother's   r i g h t e o u s.

2. *Cain and Abel*: *Prototypes of Sonship*

Note how in the structure Cain who is ' of the evil one ' and whose ' deeds are evil ' (B') stands parallel to the ' children of the devil ' who ' are not of God ' (B). So, certainly Jn finds in Cain a type of the children of the devil, while in Abel, whose works were righteous, he finds a type of the children of God [22]. The antithetical parallelism intended by John between A A' and B B' is indicated in the fact that he does not give the motive of the murder as simply ' because he hated him ' (cf. v. 15), but in two antithetically parallel phrases contrasting the ' doing of evil ' of Cain with that of ' righteous deeds ' by Abel, thus referring to the sonship that lies behind the deeds [23].

This is also clear from its parallelism to 3:7-8. Jn, speaking of the sin of Cain, sees the diabolical aspect of it and hence its origin in the action of the devil in Paradise [24], and he pictures Cain as the ' one who sins ' and ' is of the devil ' (v. 8) [25], and hence a child of the devil, and Abel as the one who does righteousness and is righteous (cf. v. 7) and hence a child of God.

V. 13 itself, where the world represented by Cain hates the brothers who love, whom Abel represents, also points to Cain and Abel as types of the children of the devil and children of God respectively [26].

---

[22] The mere psychological explanation for the murder of Cain given by authors like Bultmann, Westcott etc. does not do full justice to the meaning of the text.

[23] Cf. BULTMANN, *Die Johannesbriefe*, pp. 59-60 where he sees this motive and says : " ... der Gegensatz von bösem und gerechtem Tun dem Gegensatz von Gotteskindschaft und ' Welt ' entspricht ".

[24] Cf. I Jn 3:8 : " because the devil has sinned from the beginning ".

[25] The expression ἐκ τοῦ πονηροῦ instead of ἐκ τοῦ διαβόλου seems to have been adopted here in order to show the parallelism between ' being of the evil one ' and ' his deeds were evil ', both of which point to the same reality parallel to ' being not of God ' in the structure BB' of the section. Note the phrase ' because his deeds were evil ', as the cause of the murder committed by Cain, and hence designating the eschatological and diabolical reality that produces the moral actions, rather than the actions themselves, which is quite coherent with the usual Johannine usage of ἔργα πονηρά.

[26] The opposition between Cain and Abel was already taken up in the Judaic tradition to represent the dualistic division between the just and evil (cf. W. BOUSSET, *Die Religion des Judentums im späthellenistischen Zeitalter*,

Cain, determined by the devil in his moral conduct (ἐκ τοῦ πονηροῦ), stands in a filial relation to the devil, and the murder of his brother was the manifestation of his diabolic sonship. By this Jn illustrates what he said in v. 10 that the lack of brotherly love is the criterion of the lack of filial relation to God.

3. *The Diabolic Sonship — Source of hatred*

In I Jn 3:10-12 we see a progress of argument too. If in v. 10 (B) diabolic sonship is only manifested by the lack of 'doing righteousness' and 'love', in v. 12 (B') diabolic sonship ('being of the evil one' and 'doing of evil deeds') is said to be the cause of the lack of brotherly love (murder)[27]. This is not something entirely new in Jn. Already in Jn ch. 8 we saw how the development of thought in vv. 31-47 leads to a climax in which the divine and diabolic sonship stand as the cause of the Jews 'hearing' or 'not hearing' the Word of God respectively[28].

The phrase "εἶναι ἐκ" that is used in both these contexts is indicative of this. As we saw above, it refers to the condition in which one is determined by someone or something in his moral life, and this someone or something becomes the source of his moral conduct. This corresponds to the 'fruit scheme' found in Jn when speaking of the divine sonship, though the essential difference between the divine sonship and diabolic sonship is to be kept up in this regard; for, while the divine sonship supposes a vital communication of life that produces righteous deeds in the children of God, this element of vital communication of life is wanting in diabolic sonship[29]. Nevertheless diabolic sonship remains as something that determines the conduct of the children of the devil.

II. ὁ ἀγαπῶν : **The Existential Definition of a Child of God (I Jn 4:7-8).**

I Jn 4:7 identifies the one 'who loves' with the one who 'is begotten of God', and it is part of a long section I Jn 4:7-21, which

---

3rd ed., by Gressmann, 1926, p. 183 ; G. F. MOORE, *Judaism*, I, p. 494) and later also in the NT (cf. Mt 23:35 ; Heb 11:4). In John this opposition assumes a profound sense of referring to the deeds as revealing the very nature (cf. K. G. KUHN, art "Αβελ–Κάϊν *TDNT* I, pp. 6-8).

[27] Note the expressions ἐκ τοῦ πονηροῦ ἦν and ὅτι τὰ ἔργα ... πονηρὰ ἦν.

[28] Cf. Jn 8:47 "He who is of God hears the word of God ; the reason why (διὰ τοῦτο) you do not hear them, is that you are not of God".

[29] Note above what we said, speaking of the Johannine phraseology on γεγέννηται ἐκ τοῦ Θεοῦ which gives the distinctive note to εἶναι ἐκ τοῦ Θεοῦ in respect to εἶναι ἐκ τοῦ διαβόλου.

speaks of love for the third time and corresponds to the other two sections 2:3-11 and 3:10-24, which also speak of charity[30]. But there is also a progress of idea in these three sections. In the first section (2:3-11) charity was considered as a mere precept to be observed, while in 3:10-24 the example of Christ, the revealed Love, is brought forward as model. In 4:7-21 the author ascends to God, the very source of charity. Moreover, in this last section he describes charity rather as a need of the nature of those begotten of God[31], than as an arbitrary obligation or fidelity to the commandment or even as a spirit of charity[32]. God is love. He has begotten the Christians, communicating to them the principle of the divine life, the Spirit of love. So His children cannot but love as their heavenly Father does. Consequently, brotherly love is something more than a mere criterion of ' having been begotten of God '.

A. The Literary Unity and Structure of the section 4:7-21

The following structural division of the section will show the position of our text in the section, which will, in turn help us to interpret it in the light of the whole section.

V. 7a	A	Beloved, Let US LOVE ONE ANOTHER ... LOVE is of G o d ...
7b-8	B	He who LOVES is b o r n o f G o d and knows God ...
9-10	C	In this was shown GOD'S LOVE in us that his ONLY SON God SENT into THE WORLD ...
11	A'	Beloved, if God so LOVED US, WE ought to LOVE ONE ANOTHER
12-13	B'	If we LOVE ... G o d d w e l l s i n u s and His LOVE IN US IS PERFECTED ... of His own Spirit
14-16	C'	And we ... Father HAS SENT THE SON as ... of THE WORLD if ... know and believe ... LOVE which GOD has in us
17-18	B''	In this is LOVE PERFECTED IN US ... confidence ...
19-21	A''	WE LOVE because He LOVED US ... loves God ... LOVES also h i s b r o t h e r.

---

[30] See how the word ἀγάπη or ἀγαπάω comes almost exclusively in these sections. Note also the importance of the theme in this third section. Out of the 18 occurrences of ἀγάπη 12 occur in this section alone. In the same way, out of the 28 occurrences of ἀγαπάω 15 occur here itself.

[31] Cf. C. SPICQ, Agapé dans le Nouveau Testament, Analyse des Textes, III, Paris, 1959, p. 270.

[32] It is interesting to note here that the word ἐντολή occurs in the first section 6 times and in the second section 4 times, while in the last section it appears only once.

Note the literary parallels in the corresponding sections, and also the thematic parallels. In A and A' the Apostle exhorts them to love giving the reason for it. If in A the reason is that love is from God, in A' the reason is the manifestation of this love of God towards us. In B and B' he shows us love as the manifestation of communion with God. In B this communion with God is given under the aspect of 'birth from God' and 'knowledge of God' while in B' it is under the aspect of the mutual dwelling of God and man, and the perfection of love in man [33]. In C and C' the revelation of God as love in Christ is described [34]. In the conclusion (A'') he recapitulates the exhortation to love one another, based on the love of God and the love for God, which will form also a transition to the next section. So our text comes under B where he speaks of love as the manifestation of communion with God, and speaks of it under the aspect of 'birth from God'.

B. *The Structure of I Jn 4:7-8* [35]

The structure of the verses could be given as follows:

Exhortation: v. 7a   Beloved, let us love one another
Motive: 7b   A   because the LOVE IS of GOD
    7c   B   and HE WHO LOVES, is born of God ...
                                                                         KNOWS GOD
    8a   B'   HE WHO does not LOVE did not KNOW
                                                                           GOD
    8b   A'   because GOD IS LOVE.

---

[33] Note how in B'' the same element of communion with God under the aspect of perfection of love in man (B') is resumed, though here it becomes more eschatological.

[34] Note that in C' is added the element of faith in this revealed love of God in Christ. It is interesting to note that already in I Jn 3:10-12 the love was presented as an object of revelation that is preached, and not simply as a commandment (cf. P. A. SISTI, "La Carità dei Figli di Dio", *BibOr* 9 (1967), p. 81.

[35] Bultmann finds in this verse too, as usual, a 'Vorlage', that is worked out by the author in his homiletic rearrangement (cf. R. BULTMANN, *Die Johannesbriefe*, p. 70). Thus he reconstructs the 'Vorlage' as the following:

4:7b πᾶς ὁ ἀγαπῶν ἐκ τοῦ Θεοῦ γεγέννηται
8a ὁ μὴ ἀγαπῶν οὐκ ἔγνω τὸν Θεόν

But as we have remarked above, there is not sufficient proof for such a 'Vorlage' made use of by John. Moreover the mixing up of theological and parenetical elements is characteristic of John (cf. R. SCHNACKENBURG, *Die Johannesbriefe*, p. 227).

Note the literary parallels in the corresponding parts of the verses. Though the author begins with the exhortation to brotherly love, his main concern is to give the motive for it, namely, by explaining the nature of love in itself and by showing it as the manifestation of communion of men with God. And when he speaks of this communion with God, he speaks of love absolutely, without specifying it [36]. So, Jn describes here the supreme revelation of the NT agape and its working in the Christian, rather than its application to others, though that is understood here, since love cannot exist without an object [37]. If in A and A' Jn speaks of the nature of love, in B and B' he speaks of the nature of communion in those who love. The love that is dynamic, namely, a permanent quality or nature, always tending towards action [38], becomes the manifestation of the invisible reality of our communion with God, namely, of our 'birth from God' and 'knowledge of God'. Hence the three elements that are interrelated in these verses are, 'Love', 'birth from God' and 'knowledge of God'. Now we have to see the relation between these three elements.

The interrelation of these three elements has been construed by authors in a bewildering variety of ways. Some take the 'loving' as a condition of the 'birth from God' and 'knowledge of God' [39]. This naturally goes against the usual Johannine scheme of putting the 'loving' (visible reality) as the fruit and criterion of 'birth from God' (invisible reality). Others take 'loving' as the consequence of 'birth from God' and 'birth from God' as the consequence of the 'knowledge of God' [40]. But as we have seen above, in Jn 'knowledge of God' and 'birth from God' are two terms that express the same reality of communion with God, though emphasizing different aspects. Besides, in the verse it is put parallel to 'birth from God',

---

[36] Note the four absolute usages of ἀγάπη and ἀγαπάω in vv. 7-8, while there is only one use specifying it as brotherly love. In the whole section 4:7-21 the absolute usage occurs 12 times, while the specified usage of brotherly love occurs only 5 times. The restrictive tendency of Codex A adding τὸν Θεόν and of the Old Latin Mss p r adding 'fratrem' in v. 7c seems to be out of context.

[37] Cf. A. NYGREN, *Eros et Agape*, Aubier, 1944, p. 134 : " Nous trouvons ici le plus haut point de la conception Johannique de l'Agapé. L'Agapè comme telle — quel qu'en soit l'objet — est une participation de la vie de Dieu. L'Agapè est née de Dieu ".

[38] Note the present participle ἀγαπῶν which points to this qualitative aspect of love.

[39] DE WETTE, *Kurze Erklärung des Evangeliums und der Briefe Johannis*, Leipzig, 1852, p. 357.

[40] Cf. B. WEISS, *Briefe*, p. 119.

co-ordinated with "καί". Only a detailed analysis of the text in its context will show the interrelation of the three elements in question.

C. *Evaluation of the tenses*

The expression 'ὁ ἀγαπῶν', the present participle, which has the value of a substantive, does not express time, but only the aspect [41]. Hence 'love' here is not an act, but a permanent quality or nature, with emphasis put on the manifestation of it, namely, it is a quality or nature that is incessantly active.

The term 'γεγέννηται', in the perfect tense, indicates something that took place in the past, but is regarded in its abiding power. So the begetting from God is a fact that already took place, but which created a permanent state, that continues to be dynamic. So love becomes the expression of this permanent state of being 'born of God'.

The verb γινώσκει, in the present tense, indicates the active and progressive character of this knowledge. As γινώσκειν usually refers to a knowledge that is acquired from experience, the present tense here describes not only the knowledge in itself, but also the progressive acquisition of it. While the combination of the perfect γεγέννηται with the present γινώσκει shows that the living knowledge is regarded in its present activity [42], the present tense of both γινώσκει and ἀγαπῶν shows that this living knowledge of God is concomitant to the quality of love that is incessantly active, and that this love contributes to the development and progress of this knowledge.

The οὐκ ἔγνω of v. 8a being in the aorist indicative, as such refers to the fact of not knowing God in the past, without further specification. But, as here it stands opposite to the present γινώσκει, it means that even the beginning of this progressive acquisition of the knowledge of God did not take place in the one who does not have this love [43].

D. *Analysis of the Expressions*

1. *'Love is of God'*

The two clauses 'love is of God' and 'everyone who loves is born of God' are so interrelated that one explains the other. First of all, note the absolute use of ἀγάπη and ἀγαπάω. This absolute use

---

[41] Cf. M. ZERWICK, *Biblical Greek*, no. 371.
[42] Cf. WESTCOTT, *Epistles*, p. 148.
[43] Cf. BROOKE, *Epistles*, p. 118 : "he shows by his want of love, that the process of knowledge never even began in him".

of ἀγαπᾶν is characteristic of John [44] and as we saw above, particularly of this section which speaks of the nature of love itself, ascending to its source. This shows the profound theological view of love presented by Jn. The fact that he calls the Christian " ὁ ἀγαπῶν " shows that he presents love here under the aspect of a vital movement, a form of existence, and actualization of God in the life of a Christian [45].

' Love is of God '. The expression εἶναι ἐκ shows the origin that determines the nature of the thing [46]. So this formula expresses the divine character of love, and therefore probably it denotes also the infused character of this love. So, when Jn says that he who loves is born of God, he means this love of divine character, that is infused in him and becomes the source of action in him. And the infusion of this love which makes man a child of God is described by Jn himself in I Jn 3:1.

2. ' *God is Love* '

The corresponding affirmation in v. 8b ' God is Love ' [47], which identifies love with God Himself, comes to illustrate better the relation between ' love ' and ' divine birth '. Together with other similar definitions of God in Jn such as " πνεῦμα ὁ Θεός " (Jn 4:24), ὁ θεός φῶς ἐστιν (I Jn 1:5), this defines one of the essential properties of God. On the other hand, the absence of the article for ἀγάπη avoids a deification of ἀγάπη. The fact that Jn arrives at this definition by contemplating the manifestation of God in Christ and his saving work (cf. I Jn 4:9f), shows that it is not an abstract definition of the divine nature, but that it refers to the life of God as ' Love ' that is revealed in Christ and in his saving work [48]. At the same time it tells us

---

[44] Apart from John we find it only in Lk 7:47-48. There too love is taken as a reality that is infused or communicated to the one who is justified, and which should animate his life afterwards.

[45] Cf. E. STAUFFER, art. ἀγάπη, *TDNT* I, p. 53 ; C. SPICQ, *Agapè dans le Nouveau Testament*, III, p. 248 where he sees ὁ ἀγαπῶν as a definition of the Christian.

[46] The designation of the origin as the sign of the essence is characteristic of John (cf. Jn 3:6,31 ; 8:23 etc). Cf. R. BULTMANN, *Evangelium*, p. 98, note.

[47] On this definition of God, cf. R. SCHÜTZ, *Die Vorgeschichte der johanneischen Formel* : ὁ Θεὸς ἀγάπη ἐστίν, Göttingen, 1917 ; C. SPICQ, *Agapè...*, III, pp. 273-278 ; Among the Commentators, see specially DODD, *Epistles*, pp. 106-110 ; SCHNACKENBURG, *Die Johannesbriefe*, pp. 206-213 ; A. FEUILLET, " Dieu est amour ", *EspVie* 81 (1971), pp. 537-548.

[48] This revelatory character of ἀγάπη is seen from the fact that Jn presents it as the object of knowledge and faith. Cf. I Jn 3:16 ἐγνώκαμεν τὴν ἀγάπην and 4:16 ἐγνώκαμεν καὶ πεπιστεύκαμεν τὴν ἀγάπην. This seems to be suggested also in the insistence of Jn in the section that ' no one has seen

something about the very being of God himself, because Jn says not that 'love is in God' or 'God loves us', but 'God is love'.

So 'God is love' in this revelatory context means that all His activity is a loving activity [49]. All that He does is the expression of His nature which is love. And this expression takes place, not in anybody or in any manner whatsoever, but precisely in Christ, in His quality of being the 'Only Begotten Son [50], which shows that the 'Love' that defines God refers to the very life of God, and this determines the relation between the Father and the Son. So ἀγάπη here defines God, in as much as God the Father loves the Son and thus communicates Himself to the Son and through Him loves the believers and communicates Himself to them [51]. The fact that this relation of Love refers to the Father – Son relationship between God the Father and Christ the Son, and that the communication of this Love to men results in their becoming children of God [52], shows that the definition 'God is love' refers specially to the life of God as Father [53].

This leads us to the conclusion that 'Love' that is of God and is God is the very Trinitarian Life of God, and it is this Life that is manifested and is communicated to us [54]. This makes the affirmation of the text regarding the connection between 'loving' and 'birth from God' quite understandable. 'To be born of God' means to receive the communication of the divine life that is essentially Trinit-

---

God' (v. 12) and that 'we have seen and witnessed that the Father has sent the Son'. Cf. the antithetical parallelism οὐδεὶς τεθέαται ... ἡμεῖς τεθεάμεθα.

[49] Cf. W. D. HOWARD, *Christianity according to St. John*, p. 62 where he says that in identifying love with God John has described God in His essential nature in terms of divine action.

[50] Cf. I Jn 4:9-10 and also Jn 1:18.

[51] Cf. C. SPICQ, *Agapè* ..., III, p. 321 : " Or qu'il s'agisse des relations de Dieu avec Jésus et avec les hommes ou des relations du Fils de Dieu avec son Père et avec les siens, c'est l'agapè qui résume tout, qui est l'explication exhaustive de ses rapports ".

[52] Cf. I Jn 3:1 and also 4:9 where the revelation of the love of God through the Only Begotten Son results in a communication of life.

[53] Note that in John 'agape' is uniquely and exclusively applied to the Father or God, while ἀλήθεια is applied exclusively to Christ or the Spirit, being the revelation of the Father, which also points to this character of 'agape'. Cf. also v. 9 where this love is said to be manifested in sending *His Son*.

[54] Cf. J. BONSIRVEN, *Epîtres*, p. 33 : " ... ce terme (ἀγάπη) définit admirablement Dieu comme principe de Procession, comme celui qui se donne : il manifeste son amour aux hommes en les constituant ses enfants, semblables à lui, participant à sa nature divine (3:1-2), et aussi en leur envoyant son fils pour leur donner la vie (4:9) ".

arian. If this Trinitarian Life of God is defined by Jn as 'Love', the communication of this Life means communication of 'love' that makes men 'born of God' and 'children of God' [55]. So, if 'birth from God' and 'divine sonship' consists in this participated Life of God, Who is 'Love', then naturally the fact of 'being born of God' should manifest itself in a 'life of love' (I Jn 4:7), which becomes an existential definition of 'being born of God'.

E. Love – Means of growing in the Life of Divine Sonship

1. 'To Know God' and 'To be Born of God'

I Jn 4:7-8 puts 'birth from God' as parallel to 'knowledge of God', and 'love' as the manifestation of both the realities. The expression 'to know God' comes 6 times in I Jn [56], and always in strict connection and parallelism with other expressions indicating Communion with God such as 'remain (be) in God', 'be of God' and 'born of God'. Note this parallelism in I Jn 2:3-6; 3:6,9; 4: 6-8.

The special relation of 'birth from God' with 'knowledge of God' is seen in the light of the relation between God the Father and the Son expressed in similar terms by Jn.

In the Gospel, Christ the Only Begotten Son of God (Jn 1:1-18) stands in a singular union with the Father [57] and to this corresponds mutual knowledge [58] and love [59] between the Father and the Son. The obedience of Christ to the commandment of the Father expressed in giving His life for men is the result of this mutual knowledge and love [60]. All these constitute the intimate and vital communion of the Son with the Father, based on His divine sonship.

---

[55] Cf. I Jn 3:1. Cf. E. MERSCH, " Filii in Filio ", *NRT* 65 (1938), p. 563, where he, speaking of Jn 17:26 " ... that the love with which Thou hast loved me may be in them ...", says : " Assurément, c'est de la vie trinitaire qu'il s'agit ici ...".

[56] Cf. 2:3,4 ; 3:6,7,8. The Johannine preference for the verb γινώσκειν could be seen in the frequency of its occurrence in John in relation to other NT Writings : Mt 20 times, Mk 13, Lk 28, Acts 18, Paul 50, while in the Johannine Writings 86 times.

[57] Cf. Jn 10:30 " I and the Father are One " ; 10:38 " ... the Father is in me and I am in the Father " ; cf. also Jn 5:17,19,21,23 ; 8:28,29 ; 14:10,11,20 etc.

[58] Cf. Jn 1:18 " No one has ever seen God, but the Only Son ... he has made Him known " ; cf. also Jn 6:46 ; 7:29 ; 8:55.

[59] Cf. Jn 3:35 " The Father loves the Son ..." ; 5:20 ; 10:17 ; 14:31 " ... that I love the Father " ; 15:9 ; 17:23,26.

[60] Cf. Jn 10:15 " As the Father knows me and I know the Father, and I lay down my life for the sheep " ; cf. also Jn 13:1 ; 14:31 ; 15:9,12.

It is a participation in this filial relationship of Christ to the Father that we find in the children of God, who receive the power to become children of God from the Son of God (cf. Jn 1:12). By means of a similar relation of mutual communion (Jn 17:21,23,26; 14:20) realized in a mutual knowledge (Jn 10:3,4,14,26,27) and Love (cf. Jn 13:1,34; 14:21; 15:12,17; 10:11,15) between Christ and the believers, and expressed in obedience to the command of Christ (cf. Jn 10:27; 14:21,23), the children of God arrive at a similar relation of communion with the Father (Jn 14:7-9) [61].

2. *An Experiential Knowledge of faith and love*

This shows that the knowledge of God described in I Jn is exclusively proper to the children of God, based on their birth from God also realized in Faith and love (cf. I Jn 5:1 and 4:7). This knowledge of God, identified with birth from God, is realized in faith, because this knowledge is not a mere speculative knowledge, nor a mystic vision independent of all historical determinations, but a knowledge that is concrete and essentially connected with the history of salvation [62]. It is realized in love, because it is an experiential knowledge of the presence of God in salvation history, and it is as love that this presence of God is experienced (cf. Jn 3:16; I Jn 4:9 etc.), which calls for a corresponding fidelity to His ways for men expressed in the work of salvation, which could also be summed up as love [63].

The relation of the 'knowledge of God' with 'love' and 'faithfulness to his commandments' is seen clearly from the parallelism of the Johannine texts themselves:

---

[61] Cf. also what we said on I Jn 5:20 how the Son of God makes it possible for us to arrive at the 'knowledge of God' — communion with God.

[62] Note how I Jn 3:16 and 4:16 put the love that is the revelation of God in the work of salvation as the object of knowledge of faith.

[63] In fact this is in perfect conformity with the OT concept of the knowledge of God, which was necessarily a result of practical experience of the presence of God in the history of salvation, and meant to acknowledge Him and His reign, to adhere to Him with love and to serve Him faithfully (cf. A. SUITBERTUS, art. cit., pp. 457-462). Thus in Hosea 4:1 the three expressions 'knowledge of God' 'love' and 'faithfulness' are put as parallels and in Hos 6:6 'knowledge of God' is practically identified with 'love'. Cf. M. E. BOISMARD, art. " La connaissance ...", in which he brings out all these characteristics of the knowledge of God in I Jn specially in the light of the New Covenant texts of the OT; cf. also J. MOUROUX, " L'Experience Chrétienne dans la Première Epître de S. Jean ", *Vie Spir* 78 (1948), pp. 401-403; R. SCHNACKENBURG, *Die Johannesbriefe*, pp. 95-101; R. BULTMANN, art. γινώσκω, *TDNT* I, pp. 688-791 also admits a relation of the concept of knowledge of God in I Jn to that in the OT, though he sees an admixture of Hellenistic concept.

I Jn 2:3 If we keep His commandments — we know Him
4:7 Everyone who loves is born of God — and knows God
He who does not love — did not know God
3:6 Everyone who sins — has not known Him.

If ' to love ' is to ' keep his commandments ' and is the expression of the knowledge of God, ' not to love ' is ' to sin ', and is the expression of not knowing God [64]. At the same time, we have to note the new aspect given to the faithful observance of the commandments in John, namely, in John the observance of the commandments is the observance of the Word [65], and hence seems to be reduced to faith [66]. Besides, in I Jn the whole commandment is reduced to ' faith ' and ' love ' [67]. This again takes us back to the conclusion that for Jn, just as Christ's sonship is realized in mutual knowledge and love between the Father and the Son, so a Christian's sonship to God is realized in ' faith ' and ' love '.

3. Γινώσκει

But ' love ' has a meaning and function in the ' knowledge of God ', much more profound than the mere keeping of the commandments, because love is identified with the life of God that is shared by us (I Jn 3:1) and is perfected in us (I Jn 4:12) [68]. So, if God is love, active participation in this love brings us closer to the knowledge of the real nature of God [69]. As the present tense itself indicates (γινώσκει) knowledge of God is active and progressive. Hence the one who leads a life of authentic and active love, a life proper

---

[64] Note what we said above about love that expresses in concrete fashion the observance of commandments and ' doing righteousness '. Cf. A. SKRINJAR, " Theologia Primae Epistolae Joannis ", *VD* 42 (1964), p. 9 : " Johannes cum suo conceptu cognitionis Dei non fit gnosticus, sed manet, prasertim in I Jn Apostolus caritatis ".

[65] Note the parallelism in I Jn 2:4-5 :
" He who says ' I have known Him ' and does not keep His commandments
is a liar and the truth is not in him.
But whosoever keeps his word, in him truly the love of God is perfect ".

[66] Note the expression ' truth is not in him ' referring to faith.

[67] Cf. 2:23 " And this ... commandment that ... believe ... and love ...".

[68] Many authors give to ἀγαπῶν only a moral value and see it as a mere criterion. Cf. BULTMANN, *Die Johannesbriefe*, p. 41.

[69] Note the parallelism between ' knowledge of God ' and ' perfection of love in us ' in I Jn 2:4-5 and also in I Jn 4:7-21 (cf. the structure). Cf. also C. CHARLIER, " L'Amour en Esprit " (I Jn 4:7-13) ", *BiViChr* 10 (1955), p. 61 : " Paradoxe suprême : ce n'est pas la connaissance qui conduit à l'amour, mais l'amour qui fait connaître ".

to the children of God, acquires gradually a deeper and closer perception of what God really is, because God is 'Love'. Thus the 'love' which is the 'expression' and 'fruit' of birth from God and knowledge of God, is also a 'means' of preserving and developing this birth from God and knowledge of God.

III. Analysis of Related Texts

A. "... *His Love is perfected in us* ..." (*I Jn 4:12-13*)

In vv. 12-13 which is parallel to vv. 7-8 of I Jn 4, our communion with God is expressed in terms of 'God's dwelling in us and our dwelling in God' and 'a perfection of His love in us' and is related again to 'brotherly love'. If God is Love and birth from God supposes a participation in this love by His children, love becomes the common possession of the Father and of the children, and hence it creates a communion of being and life, a mutual dwelling of God and his children [70].

Again, this is called a 'perfection of His love in us'. The 'αὐτοῦ' here is neither subjective genitive [71], nor objective genitive [72], but a qualitative or determining genitive, namely, the love that is divine and has its origin in God and is communicated to us by Him [73]. The periphrastic construction 'τετελειωμένη ἐστίν' instead of 'τετελείωται' seems to emphasize the stable and permanent condition of the participated love [74], that remains active in the children of God, constituting the very source of their life of sonship. So the love that is communicated to us is made perfect in all its dimensions, when it creates in us a communion of being and life with God the Father and constitutes the source of our life of sonship expressed in 'loving one another' [75].

---

[70] Cf. C. Spicq, *Agapè* ..., III, pp. 258-286.

[71] Cf. the Commentaries of Brooke, Bonsirven and Büchsel, and also R. Schütz, op. cit., pp. 4-6 for whom it means the love of God for us.

[72] Cf. the Commentaries of Dodd, Belser, Windisch, Chaine, and J. Moffat, *Love in the New Testament*, London, 1929, p. 299, for whom it means our love for God.

[73] Cf. M. Zerwick, *Analysis Philologica* ..., p. 559; R. Schnackenburg, *Die Johannesbriefe*, p. 241; V. Warnach, *Agape. Die Liebe als Grundmotiv der neutestamentlichen Theologie*, Düsseldorf, 1951, p. 150, note 1; cf. also p. 251 where he sees agape as an 'aion', as a sphere in which the redeemed exist.

[74] Cf. M. Zerwick, *Analysis Philologica* ..., p. 559.

[75] The interpretation of this perfection of love simply as a finality reached by the love of God (cf. N. Lazure, op. cit., pp. 236-237) does not seem to do full justice to the text.

The affirmation that 'no one has ever seen God' insists on brotherly love which should be the infallible expression of this life of sonship [76], arising from the communion of being and life with God, namely, the mutual relation of life — love — between God and His children [77].

All these considerations come to illustrate the import of 'love' in relation to divine birth in 4:7. The ὁ ἀγαπῶν, namely, the one in whom the divine and infused (ἐκ τοῦ Θεοῦ) love which is the very life of God (ὁ Θεός ἀγάπη ἐστίν) is perfected in all its dimensions, and expresses itself in brotherly love that is incessantly active, is certainly 'born of God'. Brotherly love is thus not only a 'manifestation' and 'fruit' of the divine birth, but it defines the very life of the one who is begotten of God.

B. " See what love the Father has given us that ... children of God " (I Jn 3:1)

The communication of divine love and the resulting divine sonship of men is best illustrated by I Jn 3:1 where Jn speaks : " See what love the Father has given us, that we should be called children of God " [78]. Among the texts reproducing the primitive baptismal liturgy, only Jn speaks of ἀγάπη that is given to us.

1. Ἀγάπη

In Jn ἀγάπη is always and distinctly a descending love [79], a heavenly reality that comes down to the world and remains in the world of Christ and the Christians as the principle of their lives. Thus Jn always speaks of the love of the Father for the Son (Jn 3:35 ; 10:17 ; 15:9) and for men in the world (Jn 3:16 ; I Jn 4:9f) or of the love of God for the disciples, which comes through Christ (Jn 17:23f ; 14: 21f ; I Jn 4:19 etc). Only rarely does Jn speak of the love of Jesus

---

[76] It is worth noting here that conditional prepositions beginning with ἐάν is one of the ways in I Jn for expressing the external criteria pointing to the internal realities. Cf. J. ALFARO, art. " Cognition Dei et Christi in I Jo ", p. 83.

[77] Note v. 20 " He who does not love his brother whom he has seen, cannot love God whom he has not seen ". The explanation given by some (cf. WESTCOTT, Epistles, p. 151 ; R. SCHNACKENBURG, Die Johannesbriefe, pp. 240-241 ; C. SPICQ, Agapè ..., III, pp. 285-286), applying it to the invisibility of God in contrast to the indwelling of God seems to be out of context.

[78] Note the perfect tense of the verbs δέδωκεν and τετελειωμένη ἐστίν in both contexts, which refer to the permanent character of the gift.

[79] On the Johannine theology of love, see A. FEUILLET, Le mystère de l'amour divin dans la théologie Johannique. Études Bibliques, Paris 1972.

for the Father (Jn 14:31) or of men for the Father (I Jn 4:20-21; 5:1-2), and that only to insist on brotherly love. Moreover, brotherly love is based on the love of God for us (I Jn 4:19; Jn 13:14; 15:12). So the ἀγάπη is for Jn the heavenly reality — God himself — who is working in the world in the form of love, and is the principle of the divine life in the life of the Christians [80]. Thus ἀγάπη in Jn becomes an objective reality, a form of existence, a concrete expression of the life of God in this world. Note the absolute use of ἀγαπᾶν and ἀγάπη without any subjective or objective specification in I Jn 3:16; 4:7,8, 10,16,17,18 etc. [81].

2. Δέδωκεν ἡμῖν

The verb 'δέδωκεν' in the perfect tense shows that the result of this received love is permanent and abiding. The perfect tense is often used in Jn to signify the permanent aspect of the work of salvation [82]. The verb 'δίδωμι' in Jn has a special meaning referring to the heavenly gifts of God. The existence of Jesus as such (what Jesus is) is through the giving of God. The objects of God's giving are the works of Jesus (Jn 5:36), the disciples of Jesus (6:37,39), the name of God (Jn 17:11), in short, everything that took place in Christ (cf. 3:35). In fact, for Jn Christ and the whole redemptive work of Christ is a giving of God [83]. Thus the δέδωκεν ἡμῖν of I Jn 3:1 also signifies the character of an undeserved and saving gift of God, contained in the realization of the divine sonship of the believers [84]. Thus we have here a description of the actual participation of the believers in the life of God, manifested as love in the redemptive work of Christ, and hence, the description of the divine sonship of the believers.

3. "... that we should be called children of God..."

The ἵνα clause shows in what this gift of the love of the Father results, namely, in being called children of God. The ἵνα here is not simply epexegetic [85]. The very meaning of the preceding part and its

---

[80] Cf. N. LAZURE, *Les valeurs morales de la théologie johannique*, Paris, 1965, p. 237.

[81] Out of the 18 occurrences of ἀγάπη in I Jn, 11 are used so absolutely.

[82] For the use of perfect tense in John, cf. M. S. ENSLIN, "The Perfect tense in the Fourth Gospel", JBL 55 (1936), pp. 121-131.

[83] Cf. F. BÜCHSEL, art. δίδωμι, *TDNT* II, p. 166.

[84] Note that Jam 1:17-18 which is also parallel to I Jn 3:1-2 and I Pet 1:3,23 speaks of God's begetting us as a perfect gift of the Father " πᾶσα δόσις ... καὶ πᾶν δώρημα τέλειόν ἐστιν ἀπὸ τοῦ πατρὸς ... ἀπεκύησεν ἡμᾶς ".

[85] Bultmann in his commentary on I Jn says that this ἵνα is epexegetic

relation to the second part of 'being called children of God' show that it has a consecutive meaning. The fact of being called children of God is the result of God imparting His life expressed in love [86].

According to scriptural usage, 'to be called' or 'to have the name' signifies also 'to be' what is signified by the name. The only other usage in Jn of this verb in the sense of 'being named' is Jn 1:42, which really applies to the special position of Peter in the Church. But there are other examples of this usage in both Old and New Testaments (cf. Is 7:14; Lk 1:32,35,36 etc.). So the participation in divine love results in the divine sonship [87].

The above analysis shows that the brotherly love which manifests the divine sonship is the natural outcome and expression of the divine love which is communicated to us and which becomes the permanent source of our life as 'children of God'.

Conclusion

As 'brotherly love' concretizes and embodies the 'doing righteousness' (2:29 – 3:10), it becomes also the decisive mark and expression of the divine sonship (I Jn 3:10-12), while the lack of brotherly love is the manifestation of the diabolic sonship. The diabolic sonship is presented also as a source of hatred towards the brothren and that is proved by John's example of Cain who was really the type of the children of the devil (I Jn 3:12).

On the other hand, the divine sonship is not only manifested in love but is, in a way, defined by 'love' (I Jn 4:7f). John arrives at this conclusion by defining God as 'Love', and this he does by contemplating the manifestation of God in Christ and his salvific work as the Only Begotten Son of God (I Jn 4:9f). 'Love' means for Jn the very life of God determining the relation between the Father and the Son. It is the communication of this 'Love' — 'Life' — to men (I Jn 3:1) and its perfection in them (I Jn 4:12) that results in their

---

and that it makes the divine sonship and divine begetting of the same significance (gleichbedeutend).

[86] For examples of such a consecutive ἵνα in Jn himself, cf. Jn 9:2.

[87] The very omission of the following καὶ ἐσμέν by certain Mss as K L etc. shows that it seemed to be a rather awkward parenthesis after the verb κληθῶμεν since this verb already included the meaning 'to be'. The Vg that translates 'et simus' connecting it to the ἵνα does not do full justice to the meaning of κληθῶμεν. The καὶ ἐσμέν in the indicative attested by the principal Mss is preferable and it insists on the reality that is contained in the κληθῶμεν.

being children of God. So a life of love is a sort of existential definition of 'being born of God'.

As 'love' is a participation of the life of God, a life of love makes one know God more and more, because 'God is Love'. The parallelism between 'birth from God' and 'knowledge of God' in relation to 'ὁ ἀγαπῶν' shows that this knowledge of God is proper to those who are begotten of God and grows parallel to sonship. Thus love becomes not only an expression of one's divine sonship and knowledge of God, but also a means of growing in the life of divine sonship.

CHAPTER XI

Life of Divine Sonship: A Life of Faith (I Jn 5:1-4)

I. **The Literary Criticism**

A. *The Context of I Jn 5:1-4*

In I Jn 5:1-4 the author speaks again of the divine begetting and sonship of men. It is not easy to situate these texts in clear - cut divisions because of the repetitions of the themes of faith and love intermingled. For example, the section about charity in 4:7-21 speaks also of faith (cf. vv. 14-16), while the section 5:1-12 which speaks mainly of faith, speaks also of charity (cf. vv. 1-3) [1]. But the fact that 5:1a is a perfect parallel to 4:7 seems to show that here the author enters upon a new section, though not entirely independent of the former one. For, if the author spoke of 'love' as the expression of divine birth in 4:7-21, in 5:1-12 he speaks of faith as the expression of this divine birth, faith being the basis of love itself. And it is in this connection that he speaks of love in the section under review, 5:1-4.

The connection between 'faith' and 'charity' proposed by the author in the whole Epistle, explains the text on charity in this section on 'faith'. Speaking of charity for the first time in 2:7-11, he does not connect it with faith, of which he speaks in 2:12-28. Speaking of charity for the second time in 3:10-24, he connects it with faith, namely, with the knowledge of love manifested in Christ (cf. 3:16) and making faith and love the same one commandment (cf. 3:23). Already there he makes faith the reason of love. Speaking of charity for the third time in 4:7-21, this connection with faith appears more developed, namely, love is rooted objectively in the

---

[1] This alternate occurrence of love and faith caused the different ways of division proposed by the authors. Thus when some bring 5:1-4 under the section on love together with the previous part 4:7-21 (cf. SCHNACKENBURG, *Die Johannesbriefe*, p. 251; A. FEUILLET, *Introduction à la Bible*, II, p. 690; R. BULTMANN, *Die Johannesbriefe*, pp. 78-82), others bring it under the section on faith, distinct from the previous 4:7-21 (cf. BROOKE, *Epistles*, p. 127; WESTCOTT, *Epistles*, p. 176; CHAINE, *Epîtres catholiques*, p. 209).

revelation of the love of God (4:9,14) and hence in faith (cf. 4:16). Faith and love become inseparable. So there is no wonder that Jn, speaking for the last time of faith, and thus concluding the letter in 5:1-12 resumes what he said before about charity. The fact that he speaks of charity using the expressions " ἀγαπᾶν τὸν γεννήσαντα ", " τὸν γεγεννημένον " " τὰ τέκνα τοῦ Θεοῦ " and not ἀδελφόν or ἀλλήλους shows that his main purpose here is not to exhort us to brotherly love, but to show the root of brotherly love, namely, faith and divine sonship [2].

B. *The Literary Unity and Structure of the Section*

Bultmann reconstructs the 'Vorlage' here with vv. 1a and 4b as follows:

πᾶς ὁ ἀγαπῶν τὸν ἀδελφὸν αὐτοῦ
ἐκ τοῦ Θεοῦ γεγέννηται
καὶ πᾶν τὸ γεγεννημένον ἐκ τοῦ Θεοῦ
νικᾷ τὸν κόσμον

This he does because he finds it strange that faith is brought in as the basis or condition to enforce love [3]. But these two verses as he presents them, do not stand in any antithetical relation, which should be the case for such a 'Vorlage' [4]. But, if we take it as a new section dealing with faith [5], which resumes the doctrine on charity already dealt with, this section could be better understood in this context.

5:1 A   EVERYONE WHO BELIEVES THAT JESUS IS Christ
    B   is BORN OF GOD
    C   Everyone who LOVES h i m w h o b e g o t
    D   LOVES also the o n e b o r n o f H i m
2   D'   In this we know ... we LOVE the C h i l d r e n o f G o d
    C'   When we LOVE G o d and keep ... commandments

---

[2] Here it is worth noting that the connection between 'love of God' and 'love of the brother' in 4:21 forms a transition to the new section 5:1-4, which explains this connection through faith and divine sonship (birth).

[3] Cf. BULTMANN, *Analyse* ..., p. 154; WINDISCH, *Die katholischen Briefe*, p. 136 where he attributes the whole section 5:1-12 to a redactional re-editing of the Letter, as also other 'antiheretical' sections such as 2:18-27; 4:1-6.

[4] Cf. W. NAUCK, op. cit., p. 75, note 8.

[5] Note that the word πιστεύειν occurs 7 times in the section 5:1-12, while it occurs only once in 4:7-21.

3   for this is the LOVE of God ... keep commandments ...
4   B'   Everyone who is BORN OF GOD ... victorious over the world
5   A'   This is the victory ... our faith ... victorious over ...
          HE WHO BELIEVES THAT JESUS IS the Son of God

Note the literary parallels, which shows the structure of the section, that proceeds in A B C D D' C' B' A'[6]. If A and A' speak of faith with its content, B and B' speak of birth from God, of which faith is the expression. C and C' speak of love of (for) God while D and D' speak of love of (for) the children of God (brotherly love), of which the basis is the love for God[7]. So the main theme of the section remains 'faith', and its implications in the life of the 'divinely begotten', with special reference to their mutual relation of love. Faith is the basis of the divine birth and the consequent relation of mutual love between the begotten[8].

In the course of the development of the section, we see also certain specifications of the different elements contained in the section. Thus, if in A B 'faith' is said to be the expression of being born of God, in B' A' faith seems to be identified with birth from God that produces victory over the world. If C speaks of love for God, C' specifies this love for God as practically consisting in observing the commandments of God. Finally D' specifies as 'children of God' the τὸν γεγεννημένον ἐξ αὐτοῦ of D. Besides, if C D presents the love for the children of God as the natural consequence of the love for God the begetter, D' C' presents the love for God and keeping the commandments as the criterion of the love for the children of God.

II. Experience of Sonship: A Faith Experience

I Jn 5:1a being parallel to the assertions in 2:29 and 4:7 gives faith as the criterion of 'being born of God'. In this sense, faith in Christ, which is ever active (note the pres. ptc.) is the criterion of the divine birth of man, which has already taken place and remains in its abiding power (perfect). But as we have seen above from the

---

[6] Note the elements of faith ὁ πιστεύων, ἡ πίστις and divine begetting ἐκ τοῦ Θεοῦ γεγέννηται, γεγεννημένον ἐκ τοῦ Θεοῦ in vv. 1a and 4-5 (ABB'A') that make an inclusion of this small section.

[7] Note what we said above on pp. 317-318 to the effect that John brings in the theme of love here, only to base it on the love for God in his position of Begetter.

[8] Cf. CHAINE, Epîtres, p. 210 where speaking of this section he says: "Sans la foi pas de filiation et donc pas de charité. Ainsi ... la charité dépend de la foi ... dans son existence même".

parallel statement in vv. 4-5, faith has something more to do with the divine begetting than being simply a criterion [9].

A. Faith: *The Concrete form of the Life of Sonship*

The 'πιστεύειν' as the criterion of the communion with God comes already in 3:23. But there it is as the fulfilment of the commandment that it becomes the criterion of the communion. Moreover, the formula 'πιστεύειν with the dative' is not the same as 'πιστεύειν εἰς with the accusative', and expresses the conviction of a revealed truth and in this case, it means to believe that Jesus is that which His name implies him to be. It is, so to say, a compressed creed [10], and refers to the external confession of this creed, as seen from 4:1-6 to which 3:23-24 forms a transition, while in the fifth chapter 'πιστεύειν' is used in a fuller and more definite sense. If in the former chapters faith was more an element of recognition of communion with God [11], in the fifth chapter, it seems to be an element which belongs to the essence of the communion with God [12].

Also the use of 'ὁμολογεῖν' which is inseparable from faith, shows the progressive use of 'πιστεύειν' in I Jn. While Jn uses 'πιστεύειν' for faith in Christ only once in the first four chapters (cf. 3:23) [13], in the fifth chapter he uses it six times. At the same time, 'ὁμολογεῖν' which shows more the external confession of faith is used 4 times in the first chapters (cf. I Jn 2:23; 4:2,3,15), while it does not occur at all in the fifth chapter [14]. This also points to the interior aspect of faith that is emphasized here [15].

---

[9] Note that the usual formula of criterion "ἐν τούτῳ γινώσκετε ὅτι" is not found in the case of 5:1 as also in that of 4:7.

[10] Cf. BROOKE, *Epistles*, p. 105; WESTCOTT, *Epistles*, p. 120.

[11] Note the use of πιστεύειν in plural and ὁμολογεῖν which shows more the external confession of faith, in the former chapters, while πιστεύειν is used in the singular in ch. 5.

[12] Bultmann's identification of ὁμολογεῖν in 2:23; 4:2,15 with πιστεύειν in Jn (cf. *Die Johannesbriefe*, p. 82) does not seem to be justifiable.

[13] The other two occurrences are in connection with distinguishing the spirits (I Jn 4:1) and with love of God (I Jn 4:16).

[14] Note also the exclusive use of πιστεύειν εἰς with accusative in the 5th chapter, which signifies an adhesion to the person of Christ himself, and is characteristic of John to express the concept of faith in all its dimensions.

[15] Note the use of πίστις in our context in v. 4, which runs parallel to v.1a which shows that ὁ πιστεύων in v. 1a indicates rather the plenitude of Christian faith. It is worth noting that ἡ πίστις ἡμῶν here is 'hapax legomenon' in John. Cf. WESTCOTT, *Epistles*, p. 176 where he says that the verb πιστεύειν is here (5:1a) used for the first time in the Epistle in its full and definite sense.

The very use of the word πιστεύειν in ch. 5 is indicative of this. In Ch. 5 we see a progressive usage of πιστεύειν from v. 1 to v. 13. If in vv. 1 and 5 we have πιστεύειν with ὅτι, in vv. 10 and 13 we have πιστεύειν with εἰς and accusative. In v. 13 John gives the formula πιστεύειν εἰς τὸ ὄνομα τοῦ υἱοῦ τοῦ Θεοῦ which denotes in Jn the most complete and perfect life of faith that is the concrete form of the life of sonship [16]. This is clear from the context where to 'have the Son' and 'to believe in the Son' are parallels:

v. 10 He who believes in the Son of God has the witness in Him
v. 12 He who *has the Son has the Life*
v. 13 You who *believe in* the name of the *Son of God* have eternal life [17].

The formulas like 'have the Son', 'have the Father' (I Jn 2:23) are characteristically Johannine and denote a living personal fellowship with the Son and the Father respectively [18]. So the faith here becomes identical with a living personal fellowship with the Son, which is actually the life eternal. Hence the faith here denotes the very life of the children of God in living fellowship with the Son of God. It is this faith that is already anticipated in I Jn 5:1-5 speaking of the birth from God [19].

All these considerations make it clear, that the faith here belongs to the very essence of the life of the children of God, and hence is the normal expression of the life of sonship.

B. *Faith in Jesus as Christ and Son of God*

The parallelism between vv. 1 and 5 (A A') shows that the object of faith (Christ) that goes with the divine birth is to be taken in its full sense, namely, including the divine sonship and the whole saving work of Christ. Jn was deeply concerned about the object and nature of faith that should characterize the child of God [20]. The content of

---

[16] Cf. what we said in Ch. VI on p. 150 on the power to become children of God as concretely consisting in a life of faith, expressed in similar terms.

[17] Note how in v. 11 the witness is said to be the same as the Life that is in the Son given by God.

[18] Cf. H. HANSE, art. ἔχω, *TDNT* II, p. 823.

[19] Note how in v. 4 which is parallel to v. 1 the faith is identified with the very fact of being born of God.

[20] This is quite understandable in the circumstance in which he had to preserve the faithful from the false teachers who were spreading false doctrine specially in the matter of the content of faith (cf. I Jn 2:18-26; 4:1).

Christian faith is identified with the fact and the purpose of the Incarnation. The whole Gospel centers on the thesis, that the Word was made Flesh, that the divine life has imparted itself to men through a human life. The new birth itself was a consequence of the fact that Jesus is the Christ. Apart from Jesus Christ, the new birth could not have taken place (cf. I Jn 4:9 and 5:11-12). Since for Jn faith in Christ makes men participate in that which is Christ Himself, the presence or absence of faith in Jesus as Christ (Son of God) necessarily reveals the presence or absence of sonship to God in any individual. To believe in Christ as Son and Saviour is to reveal the fact that the life of divine sonship is one's personal experience in Christ. The full life of faith in Jesus as Christ and Son of God is characteristic of the new-born, because it is concomitant to the divine begetting, in which the new birth originates [21]. So Christian faith is a power bestowed by the divine begetting, a function of the divine life which is imparted to men [22]. So faith in the Son of God Incarnate is, besides being a positive and indispensable criterion of sonship, the normal expression and manifestation of the very life of sonship.

C. Faith as a Baptismal Experience

1. The Baptismal Formula

The formula " ὁ πιστεύων ὅτι Ἰησοῦς ἐστιν ὁ Χριστός " seems to point also to the baptismal experience of the Christians. The parallelism with 5:5 and with the formulas of ὁμολογεῖν in 2:22-23 and 4:2,3, 15 [23] shows that for Jn ὁ Χριστός here means the same as " ὁ υἱὸς τοῦ Θεοῦ ". The confession of faith in the Son of God belongs to the oldest Christian baptismal confession [24]. This is shown especially by Acts 8:36f where, in the opinion of Cullmann, we can see probably ' das älteste Taufritual ' [25]. The fact that this faith in the Son of God

---

[21] Cf. what we said above in Ch. VI on p. 150 about the power of becoming children of God as concretely consisting in a genuine life of faith in Him who is begotten of God (Christ and Son of God) and also in Ch. VII about the new birth that is the condition of the life of faith (see and enter the Kingdom of God), which is the life of the children of God on p. 167.

[22] Cf. R. Law, Tests of Life, p. 262.

[23] Note that if ὁμολογεῖν means to confess something in faith, ἀρνεῖσθαι (the opposite of ὁμολογεῖν — cf. I Jn 2:22-23) means to deny this confession in unbelief (cf. O. Michel, art. ὁμολογέω, TDNT V, pp. 209-212.

[24] For a detailed study on the matter we refer the reader to W. Nauck, op. cit., pp. 86-88 ; cf. also G. Bornkamm, " Das Bekenntnis im Hebräerbrief ", ThBl 21 (1942), pp. 56-66 ; A. Seeberg, Der Katechismus der Urchristenheit, München, 1966, pp. 145ff.

[25] Cf. O. Cullmann, Die Tauflehre des Neuen Testaments, Zürich, 1948,

introduces the next section 5:5-12, which certainly speak of Baptism [26], shows also the connection of this formula with baptism.

The idea of victory (νίκη) in this context (vv. 4-5) also points to the event of baptism. W. Nauck brings two texts from Apoc 3:12 and 21:6 to prove the baptismal character of this victory [27]. The fact that it is connected with divine birth and with faith in the Son of God (I Jn 5:4-5), introducing the texts speaking of baptism, shows certainly that it is a victory connected with baptism [28].

2. *The Baptismal Tradition*

The very baptismal elements in I Pet 1:3-22, which Jn probably used in I Jn 2:29 – 3:10 to describe the divine sonship also connect the divine sonship with faith. Comparing I Jn 3:2 with I Pet 1:6-9 the ' seeing Christ ' is seen as the attainment of perfection of faith in Christ (... Χριστοῦ ὅν ... μὴ ὁρῶντες πιστεύοντες).

All these considerations seem to point to faith here as an experience that had its beginning in Baptism. Faith in Christ, namely, faith in his divine sonship (cf. 5:5) and in his salvific work (cf. 5:6) was the beginning of Christian life through baptism. This faith at the beginning of Christian life brought with it the divine birth and is ever active in him who remains begotten of God (cf. Jn 1:12-13). A man remains begotten of God, in the abiding power of this divine begetting (γεγέννηται) as long as this faith remains ever active (ὁ πιστεύων) in him. This leads us to the conclusion that the relation between faith and divine sonship (birth) is not merely a relation between a visible reality and an invisible reality that is manifested

---

pp. 65-73 ; cf. also Idem, *Die ersten christlichen Glaubensbekenntnisse*, Zürich, 1949, pp. 49-57.

[26] Cf. W. NAUCK, op. cit., p. 88 and pp. 147-182 ; also the majority of the Exegetes admits this baptismal reference of the following section ; cf. WESTCOTT, *Epistles*, p. 182 ; DODD, *Epistles*, p. 131.

[27] Cf. W. NAUCK, op. cit., pp. 88-89.

[28] It is worth noting here that in Rev 21:6 the ideas of heritage and sonship which already belong to the baptismal tradition (Rom 8:17 ; Gal 4:7 and Tit 3:7) are connected with this victory (... ὁ νικῶν κληρονομήσει ... ἔσται μοι υἱός). However, the frequent use of νικάω in perfect tense in I Jn and that referring to the victory over the antichrists (2:13-14) shows that for John this victory is concretized in constantly overcoming the false prophets. Note also that in I Jn the frequent recalling of the baptismal event is in order to warn the believers against the false teachers. Cf. W. NAUCK, op. cit., p. 89.

[29] Note that out of the 28 occurrences of the terms νίκη or νικάω in the whole NT, 25 occur in John and out of it 17 in the Apocalypse. For this eschatological sense of victory, cf. J. COMBLIN, *Le Christ dans l'Apocalypse*, Paris, 1965, pp. 164-167 ; O. BAUERNFEIND, art. νικάω, *TDNT* IV, pp. 944-5.

in this visible reality. It is a relation between two realities that go together, if they are not identical.

D. *Victory of the divinely born over the world through Faith*

V. 4 that is parallel to v. 1 says that "everyone born of God is victorious over the world", and as the construction of the verse shows, faith becomes the determining element in the divine begetting in acquiring this victory over the world. Though the theme of victory in the NT is essentially eschatological [29], in Jn, in whom the eschatological realities are radically anticipated, this victory also is anticipated in Christ and in those who are united with Him in Faith[30].

A	Because everyone *Born of God*
B	is VICTORIOUS OVER THE WORLD
B'	And this is the victory that is VICTORIOUS OVER THE WORLD
A'	Our *Faith*.

Faith, making it possible for the divinely begotten to overcome the world, also becomes a subjective experience in the life of sonship [31]. This idea of victory is brought as the reason why the observance of commandments is not burdensome [32]. The observance of commandments is identified with the love of God (cf. 5:3). And already in 2:5, the love of the world stands against the love of the Father. So the world represents the enemy that hinders the children of God in their observance of the commandments. The world is therefore the sinful world, which is in the power of the evil one (cf. 5:19) [33]. So it is over this sinful world that the 'God – Begotten' is victorious. Note the neuter and abstract 'πᾶν τὸ γεγεννημένον' instead of the usual concrete 'πᾶς ὁ γ. which seems to emphasize the quality, namely, the divine energy that is active in the divinely begotten in bringing about his victory, rather than attributing victory to the individuals [34].

---

[30] Cf. I. DE LA POTTERIE, art. " La connaissance de Dieu dans le dualisme eschatologique d'après I Jn II, 12-14 ", pp. 96-99.

[31] Note how by a strong metonymy, the victory itself is identified with the means — faith — by which it is won.

[32] Cf. ὅτι in the beginning of v. 4 which marks a distinct fact (objective) — here the victory over the world proper to the divinely begotten — which is itself an adequate cause or explanation of that with which it is connected. Cf. WESTCOTT, *Epistles*, p. 72.

[33] Note I Jn 3:1 where the world is put in antithetical parallelism to the children of God and its parallelism with v. 6 shows the world as the one who sins.

[34] Cf. BLASS-DEBRUNNER, *A Greek Grammar*, 138, 1; cf. also BROOKE, *Epistles*, p. 130; E. GAUGLER, *Die Johannesbriefe*, Zürich, 1964, p. 256: " Es

Now, in v. 4b he specifies that this power of conquering the world consists concretely in faith. The use of the aorist νικήσασα seems to refer to the victory of Christ (cf. Jn 16:33) which becomes ours through faith [35]. Here it seems that we have the use of an effective aorist referring to the victory as both past and present, namely, the past victory of Christ made present to each one through faith [36].

In other terms, Jn resumes here the idea of sonship and righteousness, because the victory over the sinful world resulting in observing the commandments certainly refers to righteousness and sinlessness. As we saw above speaking of righteousness in relation to the divine sonship, it is Christ who is pre-eminently Righteous in his quality of Son of God, and He made this righteousness possible for us (cf. I Jn 2:29; 3:5,8). There we saw too how righteousness is an indispensable expression of our sonship. Here Jn emphasizes the role of faith that mediates this appropriation of the righteousness of Christ, triumph over sin, which thus becomes an everyday experience in the life of the children of God.

III. Faith: The root of love in the Children of God (v. 1)

In the section of I Jn 5:1-13 the theme of love appears only here and it is joined to that of faith in two ways. First, by means of the concept of divine generation: " Everyone who believes ... is born of God, and he who loves the one who begot him, loves also the one

---

wird durch das Neutrum nur grundsätzlich ausgedrückt, dass die Neuzeugung durch Gott diesen Sieg schaffe, als wenn maskulinisch gesagt wäre: die aus Gott gezeugten ". Note the indicative present νικᾷ which shows the permanent and active character of this victory that is inherent in the divinely begotten.

[35] This aorist has been variously explained: as indicating that from the beginning faith overcame the world (cf. Huther as quoted by R. LAW, Tests of Life, p. 276); as referring definitely to the victory over false teachers (BROOKE, Epistles, p. 131); as a constative aorist in which the whole action is comprised in one view (R. LAW, Tests of Life, p. 276, note 1). But the emphatic ἡ πίστις ἡμῶν and the present νικᾷ all point to a victory that is constantly taking place, though in some way it took place in the past. Besides, we cannot speak of a definite victory over the antichrists that took place in the history from the part of the believers, unless considered as happened in the victory of Christ, because the fight against antichrists is not ended once for all as we can see from the frequent warnings in I Jn against the false teachers (cf. I Jn 2:26; 3:7 etc.).

[36] Cf. M. ZERWICK, Analysis Philologica... p. 559; cf. also WESTCOTT, Epistles, p. 180; R. SCHNACKENBURG, Die Johannesbriefe, p. 254.

born of God" (v. 1). Second, by means of the concept of observing God's commandments. The love of God on which the brotherly love is grounded, consists in the observance of His commandments, and as children of God we are able to observe His commandments (and be victorious over the world) through faith (vv. 2-4).

A. Love - Flowing from the Life of the Children of God (v. 1)

First, we speak of v. 1 where the 'love' and 'faith' are joined by means of the concept of divine generation.

1. The 'Begetter' and the 'Begotten'

" He who loves the one who begot, loves also [37] the one born of Him ". V. 1b takes up again what is said in 4:21 [38]. This taking up again of what is said in 4:21 regarding love towards God and love towards our brother, but using the terms ' begetter ' and ' begotten ', just after speaking of birth from God in 5:1ª, undoubtedly points to the same idea, but considered under the new aspect of the divine begetting.

The use of the pres. indicative ' ὁ ἀγαπῶν ' and ἀγαπᾷ shows that Jn brings the argument from the common rule of relation between father and children, without, however, limiting himself to it [39]. If in 4:21 he presented the connection of the love of God with brotherly love as the commandment of God, here he presents it as something spontaneous, arising from the very nature of our existence as ' being born of God '. The ' τὸν γεννήσαντα ' and the τὸν γεγεννημένον ἐξ αὐτοῦ explain what is said in ' ἐκ τοῦ Θεοῦ γεγέννηται ' of v. 1ª. By the fact of being born of God, God becomes the γεννήσας and the Christian becomes the ' γεγεννημένος ' [40], and a relation between the

---

[37] Καί is attested by X A K Vg Clement, Syr, while it is omitted by B Ψ's 048 r Hil and Aug.

[38] The understanding of this verse in a purely general sense, namely, in family relations (the one who loves the father loves also his children) is not fully justified in the context, though the principle is understood here (cf. DODD, Epistles, p. 124 and BROOKE, Epistles, p. 129 where they seem to understand this verse in such a purely general sense), because the context shows that here we are on the level of divine generation (ἐκ τοῦ Θεοῦ γεγέννηται, τὸν γεγεννημένον ἐξ αὐτοῦ). Besides, to express the tenderness of the child in a mere natural sense, one would expect the verb στέργειν. (Cf. C. SPICQ, Agapè ..., III, p. 304).

[39] Cf. R. SCHNACKENBURG, Die Johannesbriefe, p. 251.

[40] St. AUGUSTINE (PL 35, 2054-2055) applies the τὸν γεγεννημένον to Christ (cf. also H. WINDISCH, Die katholischen Briefe, p. 131, where he speaks of the possibility of applying it to both Christ and the Christians), which is,

begetter and begotten is established between God and man. And it is on the basis of this new relation established by the new birth, that Jn connects the love of God with brotherly love.

Love follows directly from life. And this love is directed to one's nature, and not to the person apart from his nature. So this love should be naturally directed to all those, to whom this nature is communicated [41]. Following this principle, love to God is love to the person of God as having the character of the one who begot, or who is the source of the life and nature of the child of God. Hence this love implies that it be naturally directed also to persons of other believers, who have the same life and nature from God as he himself has [42].

2. *Difference between I Jn 4:7 and 5:1*

Here we see both difference and progress, comparing it with the argument in 4:7. In 4:7 brotherly love was an expression of the divine begetting, while here it is a completion of our love to God as Father, which is the natural consequence of our life of sonship through faith. In 4:7 it was the nature and property of the child of God ' to love ', because it was his father's nature to do so. But here the emphasis is on the child of God ' to be loved ', on account of his parentage from God. In 4:7, being the criterion, the movement was ascending, namely, from brotherly love to the source of love in God. Here the movement is descending, namely, from the love of God the Father to the love of the children of God.

One principle that links 1a and 1b is here understood, namely, ' the one who is born of God loves God his begetter ' [43]. The sonship of men is a sharing in the sonship of Christ, in whom it is in its fulness. And sonship in Christ was characterized supremely by love

---

however, not supported by the context. On the other hand, it shows how real this relation of divine birth is.

[41] Cf. WESTCOTT, *Epistles*, p. 177.

[42] Note the singular τὸν γεγεννημένον (in contrast to the plural τὰ τέκνα τοῦ Θεοῦ of v. 2), which certainly emphasizes the relation of love as direct and personal between the Father and child and also brother and brother (cf. WESTCOTT, *Epistles*, p. 177). On the relationship between love of God and love of neighbour, see Ph. DELHAYE – M. HUFTIER, " L'amour de Dieu et l'amour de l'homme ", *EspVie* 82 (1972), pp. 193-204, 225-236, 241-250.

[43] This supposition is usually taken by the authors as a natural supposition in the father-son relationship (cf. R. SCHNACKENBURG, *Die Johannesbriefe*, p. 251; WESTCOTT, *Epistles*, p. 177). But here it seems to be more than a merely natural supposition. Love of God is a natural consequence of the divine birth itself. Cf. above what we said of the relation of love as equivalent to the father-son relationship between God and the believers on pp. 307-309.

between the Father and himself. Christ's whole life was the expression of his sonship in intimate union of love with the Father, manifested in moral harmony with His will [44]. It is this life of sonship that is shared by men through faith. So the very fact of 'being born of God' is characterized by love between the children and God. Jn could, therefore, take it for granted, that the children of God love their Father. So if the relation of love to the Father is something intrinsic to the sonship, the love to the other children of God is simply a natural consequence of it.

B. *Love for God — Proof of genuine love for the children of God (v. 2)*

In vv. 2-4 brotherly love and faith are connected by means of 'love for God' which consists in the observance of His commandments. V. 2 says: " In this we know that we love the children of God, when we love God and obey His commandments ".

1. " Ἐν τούτῳ ... ὅτι ... ὅταν ... " (v. 2)

The usual Johannine order is reversed here. Till now 'brotherly love was the criterion' of 'love for God' (cf. 4:20), while here 'love for God' seems to be the criterion for 'brotherly love' [45]. Because of this change of tone, some have tried to connect the ἐν τούτῳ to the preceding, thus taking v. 2 as a mere conclusion of v. 1b, which they understand in a merely general sense [46]. But as we have seen above, v. 1b is not a mere general principle, but a real affirmation of love of God and brotherly love. Besides, the usual usage of ἐν τούτῳ in the Epistle refers to what follows, though in such cases it is mostly followded by ἐάν, ὅτι or a disconnected sentence. It seems that with ὅταν too it should be interpreted in the usual way [47], beca-

---

[44] Cf. what we said about the father-son relationship proper to the relation of love between the Father and the Son on p. 308.

[45] This difficulty seems to have caused the variations in the Ethiopian version (in this we know that we love God, when we ...) and Arabic translation (In this we know that they are pure children of God, when we love ...).

[46] Cf. for instance, DODD, *Epistles*, p. 125 ; SCHNACKENBURG, *Die Johannesbriefe*, p. 252 ; B. WEISS, *Briefe*, p. 150. In this interpretation they translate : " by this we know that, when we love God, we love the children of God ". But this translation changes the order of words in the verse and is also against the usual Johannine construction with ἐν τούτῳ. This interpretation would make v. 2 a mere repetition of v. 1b thus destroying the progress of the argument.

[47] It is admitted by the Grammarians that ἐάν and ὅταν are interchangeable (cf. F. M. ABEL, *Grammaire du grec biblique*, Paris, 1927, 68d ; BLASS-DEBRUNNER, *A Greek Grammar*, 382, 4, specially 394 where he gives the ὅταν

use the difficulty of taking love of God as a test of brotherly love is not so serious as it appears at first sight, because Jn brings the love of God here not as an external criterion, but as a proof of the genuineness of brotherly love [48].

So we take the ' ἐν τούτῳ ' as usual, referring to the following with ὅταν and primarily with ὅταν τὸν Θεὸν ἀγαπῶμεν. The particle ὅταν with present tense expresses either an action repeated indefinitely (cf. Jn 8:44 ; 9:5 etc.) or an action at an indefinite time, regarded as actually going on (cf. Jn 7:27 ; 16:21 etc.) [49]. So the ' love of God ' and ' keeping the commandments ' are considered here as actions without any time limit. Whenever we love God as Father [50], keeping His commandments, we know that our love to others is a real love to the children of God, namely, a supernatural love communicated to us by God, and with which we love God himself. So it is this love that is divine and has the quality of family love, that Jn wants to show by this reversal of order here.

2. Τὰ τέκνα τοῦ Θεοῦ

Note that Jn uses here ' τὰ τέκνα τοῦ Θεοῦ ' as the object of brotherly love and not ἀδελφόν or ἀλλήλους as is usual, which points to his intention of marking this quality of brotherly love as divine, as originating from the Father - son relationship between God and man, and hence expressed in the love of God. The genuine love of a Christian for God the Father is the proof of authenticity of his love towards the other children of the same Father [51].

Certainly, there is no authentic love for God without obedience to His will, namely, observance of his commandments. So real love

---

in I Jn 5:2 as standing for epexegetical infinitive and generally expressed by John with ἐάν.

[48] Others have tried to avoid the apparent difficulty by disregarding the love of God, and bringing the keeping of the commandments as the real criterion, taking both love of God and keeping the commandments as a Hendiadyon. Bultmann is inclined to this interpretation and sees in v. 3 an argument for such an interpretation; cf. *Die Johannesbriefe*, p. 81 ; cf. also E. GAUGLER, *Die Johannesbriefe*, Zürich, 1964, pp. 252-254.

[49] Cf. F. M. ABEL, *Grammaire* ..., 68c, e ; 79 ; BLASS–DEBRUNNER, *A Greek Grammar* ..., 382, 4.

[50] Note how in the structure this is parallel to ' everyone who loves him who begot ' (CC').

[51] Cf. C. SPICQ, *Agapè* ..., III, p. 307 where he expresses this specific character of ' agape ' that John wants to emphasize in the following words : " L'agapè est tout autre chose que φιλανθρωπία, ἔρως, στοργή, φιλία. Elle n'existe que dans une âme consacrée à Dieu qui étendent à leurs frères l'attachement qui les lie à leur Père commun ".

for God always goes with the observance of His commandments, and this is guaranteed by their life of faith. Hence the authentic love for the children of God is rooted in the love for God, and is expressed in the observance of His commandments. Only a loving, obedient child of God is capable of love with a quality that is divine, because this love is the result of a God-given, God-begotten, life. Hence filial love for God, expressed in the observance of His commandments becomes the touchstone of real brotherly love.

Conclusion

Just as 'love', faith too is an expression of 'birth from God'. It is Christ as the 'Son of God' who is the object of this faith, and since faith in Jn appropriates its object and assimilates the believer to it, it results in a living personal fellowship with the Son and hence it is the basis of the very life of the children of God. So faith belongs to the essence of the divine sonship and is the normal expression of the life of sonship (I Jn 5:1-5).

The formulations of faith and its parallel expressions in the context of I Jn 5:1-5 show that this faith that is the expression of the life of sonship is an experience that had its beginning in Baptism, and remains ever active throughout the Christian life. Faith, making it possible for the divinely begotten to be victorious over the sinful world, becomes also a subjective experience in the life of sonship (I Jn 5:4). This victory identical with the life of faith, is both past and present, namely, the past victory of Christ is made present to each one through faith.

This experience of sonship should be practically expressed in a life of brotherly love in the family of God, because brotherly love follows from the life of sonship. True brotherly love exists only among the children of the same Father. So it is only the children of God (born of God) who can have the life of genuine Christian brotherly love (I Jn 5:1b-2). The proof of a genuine brotherly love is a genuine love for God expressed in observing His commandments, being victorious over the evil one through faith.

CHAPTER XII

The Eschatological Development of the Divine Sonship of Christians (I Jn 3:1-2)

While the NT does not offer a full description of the future life with God, it does give positive and unwavering assurance of the fact of such a life. Furthermore, it teaches that the future life is a continuation and flowering of the spiritual life, which the believer possesses here and now. Jn has provided perhaps the richest and the most lucid conceptions of that life to be found anywhere in the NT. His conception is the natural outgrowth of his vital view of salvation as the experience of divine life imparted to men. What future life shall hold for the child of God, can be only an intensification, a full flowering and a perfect realization of all that Christian sonship involves in the present life: "Now we are children of God ... we shall be as he is" (cf. I Jn 3:2).

I. Present Life of sonship — Foretaste of the Future Life (I Jn 3:1-2a)

A. *Community of Life and similarity of Nature with God*

In I Jn 3:2 the eschatological perfection of the divine sonship is said to consist in a likeness to Christ and God. Hence the divine begetting and sonship in this world should mark the state prior to, but connatural with this likeness to Christ or God [1]. The universal law that like begets like seems to make its way also in the Johannine concept of the divine begetting of the children of God [2].

This seems to be already affirmed by Jn 3:6: "That which is born of the flesh, is flesh; and that which is born of the Spirit is

---

[1] Note how spontaneously the thought of divine begetting and sonship (I Jn 2:29 – 3:1) recalls to John's mind that of an assimilation to the Only Son or to the Father (I Jn 3:2).

[2] This does not in any way mean that men becoming children of God, cease thereby to be what they are by nature, but that remaining human beings as they are, they receive within themselves something (the divine life-giving principle) which inwardly renews their whole being and turns it to the likeness of their divine begetter (Cf. A. M. DONATUS, art. cit., p. 26).

Spirit ". As a man cannot but beget another man, so he who is born of the Spirit, becomes himself Spirit. He is renewed and changed to such an extent by the action of the Spirit, that he becomes like to him [3]. As those who are born of the flesh, being flesh, lead a fleshly life, namely act according to their nature, so those who are born of the Spirit, having been renewed after the likeness of the Spirit, naturally lead a life which corresponds to their new nature. So the substantives σάρξ and πνεῦμα seem to refer to the very similarity of nature between the Begotten and the Begetter [4].

1. *The Use of the Term* 'τέκνα Θεοῦ'

This community of life producing a similarity of nature between the begetter and the begotten seems to be emphasized in the different expressions of v. 1 of I Jn ch. 3, describing the present state of the children of God. The very term 'τέκνα Θεοῦ' characteristic of Jn to signify the divine sonship of men points to this. As we have already observed, the Johannine use of τέκνα Θεοῦ for men in the state of sonship, is not merely to distinguish clearly the unique and natural sonship of Christ (υἱός) from the God-given supernatural sonship of the Christians [5] but also seems to emphasize the community of life and nature with God the Father, as distinct from the Pauline emphasis on the dignity of the divine sonship through adoption [6]. Note the anarthrous τέκνα Θεοῦ different from the 'τὰ τέκνα τοῦ Θεοῦ' in contradistinction to 'τὰ τέκνα τοῦ διαβόλου' in v. 10. This shows that it is not the individuals that are of interest here but the character and quality of the children of God [7].

---

[3] It is in the light of these and similar assertions that the Fathers, specially Greek Fathers, speak of Christians as become deified or gods in virtue of their supernatural generation. Cf. J. GROSS, *La divinisation du chrétien d'après les Pères grecs*, Paris, 1938.

[4] Cf. B. F. WESTCOTT, *Gospel*, p. 51 where he emphasizes the fact that which is born of the flesh and the Spirit is described as 'flesh' and 'Spirit', and not 'fleshy' and 'Spiritual', which shows that the child is of the same nature as the parent and does not only partake of his qualities.

[5] Note that this distinction is shown, as also in Paul, by the absolute use of ὁ υἱός. It seems to be also more than a mere result of linguistic development (Cf. R. SCHNACKENBURG, *Die Johannesbriefe*, p. 169).

[6] Here it is to be remarked that this distinction is not to be taken exclusively, because we see also in Paul the use of τέκνα Θεοῦ (cf. Gal 4:7; Rom 8:17), while in Jn 3:1 the expression 'are called' (κληθῶμεν) though it includes the idea of 'being', lays special stress on the dignity of the Christian title and position (Cf. A. E. BROOKE, *Epistles*, p. 80).

[7] Cf. what we said above on ἀγάπη as the very life and nature of God as Father revealed in Christ His Son on p. 307.

Also the presentation of the idea of τέκνα Θεοῦ by Jn is enlightening in this respect. First, he speaks of the power of becoming children of God that is given (Jn 1:12) through a communication of divine life in a divine begetting (Jn 3:3,5). Then he speaks of the realization of this position at present through the gift of love (I Jn 3:1), which is the very life of the Father Himself (I Jn 4:7-8), and its orientation towards the future (I Jn 3:2). Finally he speaks of the expression and manifestation of this realized position of the children of God (I Jn 3:10). This presentation shows that divine sonship for Jn is the result of the new life, shared with God the Father, which advances from vital germ to full maturity.

2. *The Use of the Term* ' ὁ πατήρ '

The use of the term ' ὁ πατήρ ' here in immediate connection with sonship, certainly refers to God as the one who communicates his life and nature expressed in love [7] (ἀγάπην δέδωκεν), and as a result of which our divine sonship is realized.

a. In the Baptismal Contexts parallel to I Jn 3:1-2

It is interesting to note that the same title ' πατήρ ' occurs in the other baptismal contexts parallel to I Jn 3:1-2, also in connection with the divine begetting and sonship [8]. Rom 8:15 and Gal 4:6 show that the first Christians addressed God, making use of the invocation used by Jesus Christ Himself, when he was on earth — ' Abba ' [9]. This was the result of the gradual consciousness of Christians regarding their union with Christ, the Only Son of God. In virtue of this union with Christ, the Firstborn among many brothers (Rom 8:29), they considered themselves to be in a filial relation to the Father, similar to that of Jesus. Thus the Father of Jesus became their Father too [10]. This concept is manifested in the fact that in their prayers Jesus Christ is almost always connected with the Father [11].

---

[8] Cf. I Pet 1:2,3,17; Rom 8:15; Gal 4:6; Jam 1:17-18. Note that in I Pet this invocation occurs only in this baptismal hymn speaking of the eschatological vocation of Christians under the aspect of divine begetting and that in Paul the absolute use of ὁ πατήρ as an invocation together with ' Abba ' occurs only in these two contexts.

[9] Cf. W. MARCHEL, *Abba Père*, Rome, 1963, p. 211.

[10] Cf. G. SCHRENK, art. πατήρ in *TDNT* V, p. 1006: " The cry ' Abba ' is here regarded as an experience of fundamental significance ... Paul views it as the working of the Spirit of adoption given in the heart ".

[11] Cf. I Thes 3:11,13; II Thes 1:2; 2:16; Gal 1:3; I Cor 1:3; II Cor 1:2; Rom 1:7; Eph 1:2; 6:23; Phil 1:2; I Tim 1:2; II Tim 1:2; Tit 1:4.

Moreover, Paul never calls God 'Our Father', without speaking of Christ in the context [12]. Thus 'ὁ πατήρ' in the Pauline texts above shows the invocation that referred to the father-son relationship between God and the Christians who had a sonship similar to that of Christ.

b. The Johannine Usage

The very use of the title 'ὁ πατήρ' in Jn confirms the above affirmation. We find the absolute form 75 times in Jn, 12 times in I Jn and twice in II Jn, while in the Synoptics we find it only twice [13]. Paul always uses πατήρ with some complements. In Jn we never find the Synoptic phrases 'ὁ πατήρ μου (ὑμῶν) ὁ ἐν οὐρανοῖς' or the Pauline phrase 'ὁ πατήρ ἡμῶν'. In I Jn the absolute form exclusively is used. This exclusive use shows that Jn conceives the divine Fatherhood in its present and eternal realization. And the frequent juxtaposition of 'ὁ πατήρ μου' and 'ὁ πατήρ' in Jn [14] presents to us the sonship of Christ as the foundation of the sonship of men. See how in Jn 20:17 this juxtaposition is explicitly made:

$$\pi\rho\grave{o}\varsigma \ \tau\grave{o}\nu \ \pi\alpha\tau\acute{\epsilon}\rho\alpha \ ... \ \Bigg\{ \begin{array}{l} \pi\rho\grave{o}\varsigma \ \tau\grave{o}\nu \ \pi\alpha\tau\acute{\epsilon}\rho\alpha \ \mu o\upsilon \\ \kappa\alpha\grave{\iota} \ \pi\alpha\tau\acute{\epsilon}\rho\alpha \ \acute{\upsilon}\mu\tilde{\omega}\nu \ ^{15} \end{array}$$

This means that the absolute title 'ὁ πατήρ' has an important signification in this context, being in immediate connection with the sonship — with the sonship of Christ and of Christians, in as much as God is the author of our sonship through the sonship of Christ. Thus the 'ὁ πατήρ' here could be taken in the twofold sense: 'ὁ πατήρ τοῦ υἱοῦ' and 'ὁ πατήρ τῶν τέκνων' [16], and as such it illustrates and to some extent explains the gift of love which God has given men, which makes men children of God as Christ Himself.

Hence I Jn 3:1 emphasizes a community of life and nature with

---

[12] Cf. I Thes 1:3 ; 3:11,13 ; II Thes 1:1 ; 2:16 ; Gal 1:3,4 ; I Cor 1:3 ; 8:6 ; II Cor 1:2 ; Rom 1:7 ; Phil 1:2 ; 4:20 ; Col 1:2 ; Eph 1:2 ; Philm 3.

[13] Cf. Mt 1:27 = Lk 10:21 ; Mt 24:36 = Mk 13:32.

[14] Cf. Jn 5:43,45 ; 6:27,32 ; 10:27,29 ; 14:7,9 ; 20:17.

[15] Hence we find it difficult to approve the statement of G. Schrenk that " none of the statements regarding the children of God, who are said to be begotten or born of Him, is in explanation of ὁ πατήρ " (cf. G. SCHRENK, art. πατήρ, *TDNT* V, p. 997, note 311).

[16] H. ASMUSSEN, *Wahrheit und Liebe, Eine Einführung in die Johannesbriefe*, Hamburg, 1957, p. 86 : " Der ' Vater ' steht hier ganz in dem Doppelsinn welcher diesem Worte im Neuen Testament anhaften muss. Denn Gott ist ' Vater ' Jesu Christi, aber gerade als solcher auch Vater der Christen ".

the Father in the children of God and at the same time a similarity in sonship with Christ. This is quite consistent with the preceding and following verses in the context. If the preceding v. 29 compares Christ the Righteous and Christians ' doing righteousness ' as manifesting their divine birth [17], the following v. 2 says that the children of God will be similar to Christ (God) in the full development of the divine sonship in the future [18].

B. *Community of Life and Knowledge of God (Christ)*

In Jn 17:3 eternal life had already been defined as the ' knowledge of God and Jesus Christ '. So the life of the children of God is inextricably connected with the knowledge of God. Now I Jn 3:1 speaks of the world lacking the knowledge of the children of God and the knowledge of God: " The reason why the world does not know us is that it did not know Him " [19].

1. *Incapability of the world to know the children of God*

The incapability of the world to know the children of God is a typically Johannine concept, as it does not occur anywhere in the parallel texts outside Jn. The term ' κόσμος ' in the Epistle of Jn has two different senses: i) that of humanity in general (cf. I Jn 2:2 ; 4:14 etc.) ; ii) that of men under the influence of the diabolic power that is inimical to Christ and Christians. Out of the 22 occurrences in I Jn, 14 are used in this latter sense [20]. In the structural

---

[17] Cf. what we said about the righteousness of Christ as manifesting His filial relation to God the Father on pp. 250-251.

[18] Note that John underlines the similarity of the Unique Son of God with the children of God more than any other NT Writers. As He is of God (Jn 8:42,47 ; 16:25) they are of God (I Jn 4:4,6 ; 5:19). As He is begotten of the Father (Jn 1:13 ; 18:37 ; I Jn 5:18) they too are begotten of Him (I Jn 2:29 ; 3:9 ; 4:7 ; 5:1,18). As the ' world ' cannot know Him (Jn 1:10 ; 14:19-20), it cannot know the children either (Jn 16:3 ; I Jn 3:1). For a detailed study on this similarity of the Son of God with the children of God in John, cf. E. MERSCH, ' Filii in Filio ', NRT 65 (1938), pp. 558-565.

[19] Note that γινώσκειν in I Jn has usually God as object and not Christ (cf. 2:13-14 ; 4:6,7,8 ; 5:20). Besides, γινώσκειν τὸν Θεόν is a formula that comes all over the Epistle to express the Communion with God. The fact that John easily passes from God to Christ and from Christ to God makes the argument of Bultmann unconvincing. His argument is that the αὐτόν here should be Christ, because in v. 2 the φανερωθῆναι is of Christ (cf. R. BULTMANN, *Die Johannesbriefe*, p. 52).

[20] In this sense κόσμος is a collective person who is represented by the ἄρχων τοῦ κόσμου τούτου (cf. Jn 12:31 ; 16:11). This antithetical opposition appears in different contexts (Cf. I Jn 2:15,16-17 ; 3:13 ; 4:3-5 ; 5:4,5,19).

division of the section I Jn 2:29 – 3:10 we can see how the 'ὁ ἁμαρ-τάνων' and 'τὰ τέκνα τοῦ διαβόλου' come as parallel to 'ὁ κόσμος' being antithetically opposite to the children of God:

I Jn 3: 1 Children of God + The World — did not know Him
    3: 6   + The sinner — did not know Him
    3:10 Children of God + Children of the devil.

Thus the 'κόσμος' is here the children of the devil, namely, those who are under sin and the devil, and hence are not children of God, nor born of God.

So the lack of knowledge of God is due to the lack of community of life with God by means of a birth from God. This is clear from the very nature of the knowledge of God, which is essentially a knowledge which involves a deep personal communion and hence a 'knowledge of communion and love'. So without having as a common possession the love that is the Life of God, it is impossible to have the mutual knowledge of communion. So the world (children of the devil) who lack this life of God in common with the Father and the children of God, naturally are not able to have the knowledge of the Father which the children have; neither do they know the children.

The very construction of the sentence 3:1b makes it clear. Two reasons are given for the lack of knowledge of the children of God in the world: namely, i) because they are children of God; and ii) because the world did not know the Father, the latter explaining the former [21]. So the main reason for the lack of knowledge is that we are children of God, and there is no common possession of the same life (of God) in the world and in the children of God, and hence there is no 'knowledge of communion' between them [22]. This is further illustrated by the lack of the same 'knowledge of communion' between the world and God [23].

---

[21] Note that the διὰ τοῦτο which is frequent in the Gospel (5:16,18; 8:47; 10:17; 12:18,39) refers to the preceding assertion, but with ὅτι gives further explanation to the assertion, and not principally to the following ὅτι sentence (So A. E. BROOKE, *Epistles*, p. 81; R. SCHNACKENBURG, *Die Johannesbriefe*, p. 169 and note 4).

[22] The explanation of this lack of knowledge as a mere lack of recognition (cf. A. E. BROOKE, *Epistles*, p. 81) or understanding (cf. B. F. WESTCOTT, *Epistles*, p. 97) or acknowledgement (cf. R. BULTMANN, *Die Johannesbriefe*, p. 52) does not seem to give the full sense of the Johannine affirmattion.

[23] Note the aorist tense of ἔγνω which being a verb that of its nature indicates a state, must here be understood as indicating the inception of the state of knowledge, hence meaning that 'they did not even arrive at the knowledge of God'.

2. Children of God and the knowledge of God

This contrasting picture of the world lacking the 'knowledge of communion' with the Father and with the children of God, highlights the idea of the children of God possessing a communion of life with God and hence having a 'knowledge of communion' with the Father. This naturally prepares the ground for v. 2, in which the future state of the children of God is described as consisting in a likeness to and a vision of Christ, because, possessing the same life of the Father, the Son and the children of God already stand in a relation of similarity [24], and the 'knowledge of communion' with the Father necessarily implies the same relationship with the Son which develops into vision [25]. Note that the concept of 'τέκνα Θεοῦ' besides expressing a community of life and nature, and hence the 'knowledge of communion' and similarity between the Father and the Son and the children, implies also a prospect of growth and development along the same lines, because the community of life between the Father and the children implies a communication of life, which is certainly destined to growth and development. This is in fact demonstrated by Jn in the following v. 2.

It is evident then according to John, that in Christianity the children of God partake even now in the eternal life common to the Father and the Son which they shall have hereafter, in kind and quality, if not in measure, extent and intensity. As the true children of the Father, His life is in them, as in the Son, which enables them to have the 'knowledge of communion' with the Father and the Son, and this is certainly a pledge of the future life of sonship in perfect likeness with the Son enjoying the vision of communion with the Son and thereby also with the Father.

II. The Future state of sonship — Unfolding of the present state (I Jn 3:2b)

Though in Jn we have a realized or anticipated eschatology, still it remains an eschatology. Jn sees in the present events and experiences something beyond themselves. He views everything under the aspect of eternity, in the light of the consummation of all things.

---

[24] Note how also in the external manifestation of this sonship through righteousness Christ the righteous and Christians doing righteousness stand in the same relation of mutual similarity (I Jn 2:29).

[25] Here it is interesting to note how John in the structure of I Jn 2:29 - 3:10, resuming B (vv. 1-2) in B' (v. 6b) (the one who sins, has not seen Him and has not known Him), gives both elements of knowledge (v. 1) and vision (v. 2).

This is illustrated by his teaching concerning the eschatological significance or the future outcome of the present life of God's children. They enter into eternal life — life of the children of God — here on earth. But there is a consummating sense in which they enter into this life here-after. The final and future entrance will be the inevitable result of the present experience [26]. They are now children of God, and hence like the Son of God. But they will be like Him in a more complete realization than they experience now. They shall indeed be what they are now; no completely new element is to be added to their being. Yet what they shall be is an advanced stage or condition beyond that of the present and hidden at the moment, but is vitally related to it, even as the full fruit is related to the Spring blossom or as the mature man is related to the embryo [27].

A. The Vocabulary

1. Τί ἐσόμεθα

In I Jn 3:2ᵃ he resumes emphatically the statement already made in v. 1 regarding our present condition as children of God [28]. Then he affirms that the future condition of these children of God is hidden for the moment. Now, what does this distinction between the present and future mean? Does it imply that 'what we shall be' will be essentially other or more than 'what we are now'? [29]. The future 'τί ἐσόμεθα' may seem to suggest that it is something essentially different from that which we are now [30]. But the future τί ἐσόμεθα does not inevitably call for such an explanation. It means only that 'what we are' can be fully realized only in 'what we shall be', which is, however, hidden for the moment [31]. We do not await when we

---

[26] Cf. H. ODEBERG, *The Fourth Gospel*, p. 70.

[27] Cf. R. LAW, *Tests of Life*, p. 333 : " As every faculty and every feature of the full grown man are possessed by the new born child, so the image of God's Son is already found in everyone who is begotten of God, is there in embryo, in organic completeness, awaiting its full development ".

[28] The νῦν is to be taken in strictly temporal sense antithetic to οὔπω (Cf. R. LAW, *Tests of Life*, p. 386).

[29] H. J. HOLTZMANN, *Briefe und Offenbarung des Johannes*, 3rd ed. Tübingen, 1908, p. 340 : " So gewiss wir schon Gottes Kinder sind, so gewiss wartet unser noch grösseres " ; cf. also B. WEISS, *Briefe*, p. 81 where he suggests that in future τεκνότης becomes the full υἱότης.

[30] In fact Haupt contends that, to express that what we will be is only a manifestation of what we are now, the Apostle would have written τί ἐσμεν and not τί ἐσόμεθα (Cf. as quoted by R. LAW, *Tests of Life*, p. 386).

[31] Cf. R. LAW, *Tests of Life*, p. 386 ; A. E. BROOKE, *Epistles*, p. 81 : " ... the future which will bring the complete unfolding of that which is even now present ...".

shall become children of God, but when, as children we shall give perfect evidence of his likeness. Note that John uses here the neuter interrogative pronoun τί (what) rather than the masculine form τίς (who).

2. Οὔπω ἐφανερώθη

The verb ' to manifest ' (φανεροῦν) is a word of notable significance in the vocabulary of the Epistle [32]. This word may be said to contain the Johannine conception of history, since history is for Jn a manifestation, namely, each of its successive events is merely the emergence into visibility of what already exists. This does not mean that it is a simple removing of a veil in the sense of an ' ἀποκαλύπτειν ' from that which, though as yet unseen, exists in definite completed form. It is the natural unfolding from within of what already exists, though only in essence, the germination of the seed, the embodiment of potential in actual fact [33]. So the manifestation of what we will be, is an embodiment in actual fact of what we are now potentially, the natural unfolding of the sonship that we possess now in a germinal and hidden state. It is to this state that Jn refers when he says " It has not yet appeared, what we shall be ". Hence the insistence on the definite aoristic sense of ἐφανερώθη and to read into it a reference to the manifestation of Christ after the resurrection, when this revelation might have been expected [34], seems to be out of context. It is the context that should decide whether the aorist refers to a definite or indefinite past. Cf. for example, Mk 11:2 ; I Cor 8:2 ; Heb 12:4 ; Apoc 17:10,12 where we have οὔπω with the aorist, without any reference to a definite time [35].

B. *Comparison with Parallel Texts*

This is clear also from a comparison with other texts that are parallel to I Jn 3:1-2, though in these texts, this hidden condition of the state of sonship to be revealed, is called by different names such

---

[32] Note that the word φανεροῦν occurs in the Johannine Writings 20 times, while in the Synoptics it occurs only in Mk, and that 3 times, and in Paul 22 times in all.

[33] Cf. R. LAW, *Tests of Life*, pp. 315-316, where he illustrates this with numerous examples from John.

[34] Cf. B. F. WESTCOTT, *Epistles*, p. 98.

[35] Cf. F. C. SYNGE, " I Jn 3:2 ", *JTS* 3 (1952), p. 79, where he gives a new explanation to it by a change of punctuation, and refers this to Christ's appearance. But it has no textual evidence, and it disturbs the parallel ἐσμέν — ἐσόμεθα, to which are related the νῦν — οὔπω. Cf. R. SCHNACKENBURG, *Die Johannesbriefe*, p. 170, note 5.

as 'the heritage kept in heaven' (I Pet 1:4), 'salvation ready to be revealed at the last hour' (I Pet 1:5), 'glory ... in the revelation of Jesus Christ' (I Pet 1:7), 'heirs according to the hope' (Tit 3:7), 'according to the promise' (Gal 3:29), 'co-heirs with Christ to be also glorified with Him' (Rom 8:17), 'the future glory to be revealed' (Rom 8:18), 'the revelation of the sons of God' (Rom 8:19), 'freedom of the glory of the sons of God' (Rom 8:21), 'your life hidden with Christ, so that when Christ appears, you also may be revealed in glory with Him' (Col 3:3-4). All these texts come after the texts speaking of the present condition as the 'children of God' or 'born of God'[36]. For this reason, the terminology of these parallel texts will be also enlightening for the understanding of our text.

III. Nature of the Future State of Sonship (I Jn 3:2cd)

After asserting the hidden state of the present life of sonship, Jn goes on to describe the future condition of sonship, as far as he knows from the knowledge of faith, even if no complete revelation has as yet been made : " We know that when He appears we shall be like Him, because we shall see Him as He is ".

The term ' οἴδαμεν ' as we already know, refers to the knowledge of faith, and the parallel (baptismal) texts show that it refers to the knowledge of the faithful drawn from this baptismal tradition of the community[37]. Note the absence of any connective particle in the text[38]. It may be thought to set the confident οἴδαμεν in bolder relief.

A. *A State of perfect Likeness to and Vision of Christ (God)*

1. ' Ἐὰν φανερωθῇ '

There is great discussion regarding the interpretation of ' ἐὰν φανερωθῇ ', whether it is to be understood in an impersonal sense, namely, ' when it (what we will be) appears '[39], or in a personal sense,

---

[36] Only Col 3:3-4 makes an exception to it, making use of another terminology.

[37] Cf. R. SCHNACKENBURG, *Die Johannesbriefe*, p. 170, where he says that the οἴδαμεν refers to the eschatological knowledge drawn from the tradition and the theology of the Community. Cf. also R. BULTMANN, *Die Johannesbriefe*, p. 53 : " Das οἴδαμεν beruft sich auf die Christliche Tradition, aus der die Gemeinde lebt, wie das οἴδατε in v. 5 und v. 15 ".

[38] The δέ after οἴδαμεν attested by certain Mss is not textcritically certain.

[39] So R. SCHNACKENBURG, *Die Johannesbriefe*, p. 170 ; H. BRAUN, art. cit., in *ZThK* 48 (1951), pp. 262-292. Also authors like Huther, Haupt, Holtzmann favour this interpretation.

namely, ' when Christ appears ' [40]. As far as grammar is concerned, the first interpretation is the more natural one because of the repetition of the verb ' οὔπω ἐφανερώθη ... ἐὰν φανερωθῇ '. But the general sense of the passage seems to favour the second interpretation. Throughout the passage, the Writer's thought is turned to the revelation of Christ in his glory at the ' parousia ' [41], and out of the 18 occurrences of the word in Jn, 12 refer to Christ as the subject. The fact that the revelation of Christ in his glory at his parousia forms the tenor of the passage throughout, seems to suggest that in this context, where Jn ponders over the future glory of the children of God, ' ἐὰν φανερωθῇ ' refers better to the manifestation of the Son of God Himself [42]. Besides, the parallel baptismal texts always refer to Christ and his glory at the end of time, and the glorification of the children of God with Christ [43], which seems to be a decisive argument in favour of the second interpretation.

2. Ὅμοιοι αὐτῷ ἐσόμεθα

The idea of being like Him and of seeing Him as He is, is something characteristic of Jn, as it is not found in the parallel texts of other NT Writings. Actually the idea of similarity with Him cannot be said to be entirely new, because the following development regarding purification is based on this likeness with God or Christ also in the Pre-Johannine parallels (cf. I Pet. 1:15-16). If we accept the subject of ' φανερωθῇ ' as Christ, then the ' αὐτῷ ' should also be Christ. Thus here Jn affirms our similitude with Christ coming in glory, which means indirectly also our similitude with God [44]. An explicit reference to our likeness to God is not found in the NT [45].

---

[40] Cf. C. H. Dodd, *Epistles*, pp. 69-71. Also Westcott, Law, Häring, Windisch and Bonsirven favour this interpretation.

[41] Note that in 2:28 the very expression ἐὰν φανερωθῇ has just been used with unmistakable reference to Christ.

[42] Note that the manifestation of Christ is also the means of the revelation of perfect likeness to Him because ἐὰν φανερωθῇ is the prerequisite of ὀψόμεθα αὐτὸν καθώς ἐστιν. Cf. R. Law, *Tests of Life*, p. 387.

[43] Cf. I Pet 1:7,13 ; Rom 8:17 ; Col 3:3-4.

[44] There are authors who apply the αὐτῷ and αὐτόν directly to God (Cf. B. Weiss, *Die drei Briefe des Apostel Johannes*, p. 82 ; R. Schnackenburg, *Die Johannesbriefe*, p. 170 ; W. Twisselmann, op. cit., pp. 90-91). But the whole tenor of the NT teaching demands that the object of vision and assimilation be Christ (Cf. H. J. Holtzmann, *Briefe ... des Johannes*, pp. 340-341).

[45] It is interesting to note here the difference of the Biblical concept in this respect from that of Hellenism, where the idea of a divinisation of man and his similarity with God is very frequent (Cf. C. H. 1:26 ; XIII : 1,7,10 etc.). Cf. R. Schnackenburg, *Die Johannesbriefe*, p. 171, note 2. Note also

On the contrary, a similarity and likeness to Christ is a well known idea in the NT, and specially in contexts giving similar baptismal traditions. Cf. Rom 8:29 which, having spoken of the expectation of the glory of the children of God, says that ' God predestined them to be conformable to the image of His Son, so that he may be the First-born among many brothers '. But for Jn the glorious Christ is the revelation of God Himself. So the similitude with Christ is a similitude with God too.

3. Ὅτι ὀψόμεθα αὐτὸν καθώς ἐστιν

In the phrase ' because we will see Him as He is ', αὐτόν according to the explanation given above must be applied also directly to Christ and not to God.

a. History of Interpretation

The Greek Fathers understood this verse as referring to God and to a vision that is more of an intellectual and speculative nature [46]. The Latin Fathers, though, refer the vision to Christ, but remain also in the intellectual or speculative sphere [47]. It seems that this patristic interpretation was influenced by Greek philosophy and paved the way later to the explanation and reduction of the whole heavenly beatitude by speculative theology as a ' face to face vision of God ' [48]. Some modern authors also understand it directly as a vision of God and similarity with God based on texts like Mt 5:8 ; I Cor 13:12 [49], though they exclude the hellenistic concept of a purely intellectual vision.

---

that ' to be like God ' in the Biblical Tradition is even considered to be as a temptation (cf. Gen 3:5) and in the case of Christ, Phil 2:6 says : " He did not count equality with God a thing to be grasped ".

[46] Cf. CLEMENT OF ALEXANDRIA, PG 9, 737-738 ; DYDIMUS ALEX., PG 39, 1785 ; OECUMENIUS, PG 119, 648 " οἱ γὰρ υἱοὶ πάντως ὅμοιοι τῷ πατρί " ; THEOPHYLACTUS, PG 126, 37.

[47] Cf. AUGUSTINUS, PL 35, 208 : " ... will see ' formam Dei ', the evil will see only ' formam servi ' — (human form) " ; BEDE THE VENERABLE, PL 93, 98-99 : " See Him as He is, quando hunc in ipsa deitatis suae substantia contemplabimur " ; GLOSSA ORDINARIA, PL 114, 698 : " Quomodo Verbum in principio erat apud Patrem videbunt soli justi : tolleretur impius ne videat gloriam Dei ".

[48] Cf. E. BAERT, " Het Thema van de zalige godsaanschouwing in de griekse patriestik tot Origenes ", *TsTNijm* 1 (1961), pp. 289-308, where he shows the change of emphasis on the description of the heavenly beatitude as a beatific vision, which was not so strongly emphasized in the Primitive Christian thought ; cf. also A. ROETS, " De Hemel ", *CollBG* 7 (1961), pp. 486-504.

[49] Cf. the Commentaries of B. Weiss and Schnackenburg ; cf. also W. TWISSELMANN, op. cit., pp. 90-91.

b. Vision of Christ (God) — Fulfilment of the Knowledge of Communion

The purely intellectual concept of a vision of God is certainly excluded here, as it is foreign to the Biblical concept of the vision of God, which always belonged to the context of worship in the OT[50]. In the NT too sanctity is the necessary condition of seeing God [51]. And in Jn the theme of the vision of Christ (God) is connected with the theme of purifying oneself [52]. So the vision here is not a matter of intellectual contemplation, but of a presence — of a familiar communion.

This is in perfect agreement with what we said above on the knowledge of communion with the Father and the Son, that exists in the children of God, in contrast to the world (children of the devil), which lacks this knowledge, because it is this present knowledge and community of life that develops into the future vision and resemblance [53]. This connection of the future vision with the present knowledge of God is perhaps indicated also by the fact that Jn uses the verbs of 'seeing' and 'knowing' interchangeably. So the phrase 'we will see him as he is' of I Jn 3:2 should unmistakably refer to an eschatological fulfilment of this 'knowledge of communion' with the Father and the Son.

c. Christ — The Direct Object of Vision

Now we have to note the fact that in the Johannine teaching, it is through Christ and in Christ the Son that the believers have their relation to God the Father. It is a communion and union with the Son that brings the believers to communion with the Father [54]. In the matter of the 'knowledge of communion' this is all the more explicit. It is through a 'knowledge of communion' with the Son that we come to the 'knowledge of communion' with the Father. This is clear from I Jn 5:20, which puts as parallels 'knowledge of

---

[50] Note that in the OT 'to see God' meant 'to appear in the presence of God in the temple', for which special purity was required (cf. Ps 24:3-6).

[51] Cf. Mt 5:8 and Heb 12:14. Note Apoc 22:4 "They serve Him λατρεύσουσιν and will see His face", where λατρεύειν points to the cultic terminology in connection with seeing God.

[52] Note the cultic term ἁγνίζει in v. 3.

[53] Note what we said on the 'knowledge of God' as a formula of Communion recurring throughout the Epistle of John on p. 309.

[54] Cf. E. F. HARRISON, "A Key to the Understanding of First John", BS 3 (1954), pp. 39-46 where he tries to illustrate this point as central to the whole doctrine of St. John.

God' and 'being in God', which is realized in proportion to our being in His Son Jesus Christ, namely, our 'knowledge of communion' with the Son. The phrase ' ἐν ... Χριστῷ ' cannot be taken as a mere apposition to ' ἐν τῷ ἀληθινῷ ', because then the Son would be identical with ἀληθινός which refers to God (cf. Jn 7:28 ; 17:3), but it must be taken as an explanation of the former assertion [55]. This shows that in I Jn 3:2 we can certainly take αὐτόν as referring to Christ. This is quite coherent with the context and also with the Johannine doctrine elsewhere, and hence the direct object of the vision is Christ, and only indirectly of God in Christ.

Besides, a direct vision of the Father as He is, is never suggested in the NT, nay more, it is assumed to be impossible [56]. In fact, the NT conception of Christ as the revealer of the Father, in the Johannine doctrine on the Logos, and the words of Jn 14:9 " He that hath seen me hath seen the Father " all imply that no other perfect vision of the Father is possible to men than that which is given in Christ [57].

' Καθώς ἐστιν ' — ' Just as He is ' seems to refer to the sonship of Christ, namely, we will see Christ in as much as he is the Son of the Father, because the whole context of I Jn 2:29 - 3:10 speaks of a similarity of the believers with Christ in his sonship, and the 'knowledge' and 'vision' of Communion possessed by the believers is that of God as the Father and Christ as the Son. So ' to see Him as He is ' means ' to have the vision of Christ in the full splendour of glory of his sonship '.

B. *Assimilation through Vision*

I Jn 3:2d says : " ... because we shall see Him as He is ", with the insinuation that the assimilation to Christ is consequent to the vision.

1. *The Meaning of* ὅτι

The causal particle ' ὅτι ' is ambiguous here. The vision of Christ could be the cause of our being like Christ [58], or of our knowing that

---

[55] Cf. R. BULTMANN, *Die Johannesbriefe*, p. 92 where he translates : " dadurch dass wir (oder : sofern wir) in seinem Sohne Jesus Christus sind ". Cf. also R. SCHNACKENBURG, *Die Johannesbriefe*, pp. 291-292 ; J. BONSIRVEN, *Épîtres*, p. 247 ; B. F. WESTCOTT, *Epistles*, p. 196.

[56] Cf. B. F. WESTCOTT, *Epistles*, p. 100.

[57] Note how God becomes the object of faith and knowledge only through His manifestations (Rom 1:20 ; Jn 1:18) and is said to dwell in unapproachable light, whom no man has ever seen or can see (I Tim 6:16).

[58] So R. LAW, *Tests of Life*, p. 388 ; R. BULTMANN, *Die Johannesbriefe*, p. 54.

we shall be like Him [59]. Some find here an allusion to the hellenistic doctrine of divinization through vision, and hence the likeness as a consequence of the divine vision [60]. Grammatically ὅτι could be connected with ' οἴδαμεν ' or ' ὅμοιοι αὐτῷ ἐσόμεθα ' [61], though usually when connected with ' οἴδαμεν ' Jn uses ' ἐν τούτῳ '. But we find also such constructions without ' ἐν τούτῳ ' (cf. I Jn 3:14) [62]. In this situation we have to determine the meaning according to the context, remote and proximate.

2. The Johannine Text in the Light of Parallel NT Texts

All the parallel texts of I Jn 3:2 speak of the eschatological manifestation of ' δόξα ' of Christ and of Christians with Him [63]. In I Pet out of the 10 occurrences of ' δόξα ', 5 are in this eschatological sense [64]. In Jn it does not have the distinctive eschatological sense, but is an essential part of being the Son of God [65]. And a decisive and eschatological manifestation of this glory of Christ as Son of God was certainly part of the early Christian expectation, going back to Christ Himself (cf. Mk 8:38 ; 13:36). And the share of the Christians in this glory of Christ to be revealed also belongs to the primitive eschatological expectation (I Pet 1:7,13 ; 4:13 ; 5:1).

As we saw above, a vision of God or God in Christ is also a fact

---

[59] So R. SCHNACKENBURG, *Die Johannesbriefe*, pp. 172-174, but applying it to God.

[60] Cf. W. BOUSSET, *Kyrios Christos*, (FRLANT 21), Göttingen, 1913, pp. 163ff. ; R. REITZENSTEIN, *Die hellenistischen Mysterienreligionen*, Leipzig, 1927, pp. 357ff ; cf. also B. E. GÄRTNER, " The Pauline and Johannine Idea of ' To know God ' against the Hellenistic Background ", *NTS* 14 (1968), pp. 209-231 where he applies the Greek philosophical principle ' like by like ' to the Johannine knowledge (vision) of God. But as we said above, here it is not a question of a direct intuitive vision of God.

[61] Because of this some authors have tried to combine both ideas. Cf. B. F. WESTCOTT, *Epistles*, p. 99 : " We see that which we have sympathetic power of seeing, and we gain greater power of seeing, by exercise of the power which we have ". Cf. J. HERING, " Y a-t-il des Aramaismes dans la Première Epître Johannique ? ", *RHPR* 36 (1956), pp. 119-120 where he tries to solve the problem by taking ὅτι as equivalent of ὅτε and translating : " semblables, au moment où nous le verrons ...".

[62] Some take the ' seeing Him as He is ' as the effect and the proof of ' being like Him ' (cf. the Commentaries of Calvin and Huther). Though it is true that our power to see depends on what we are (cf. Mt 5:8), here in the context this seems to go against the construction of the sentence. Cf. R. LAW, *Tests of Life*, p. 388.

[63] Cf. I Pet 1:7,21 ; Tit 2:13 ; Rom 8:17,21 ; Col 3:4.

[64] Cf. E. G. SELWYN, *The First Epistle of St. Peter*, London, 1947, p. 254.

[65] Cf. Jn 1:14 ; 2:11 ; 12:41 ; 17:5,22,24.

of eschatological perfection and one connected with divine sonship (cf. Mt 5:8-9 and Heb 12:14)[66]. Hence I Jn 3:2 refers to the eschatological participation in the glory of Christ as Son of God and a vision of Him as such. Thus it refers to our eschatological glorious state of sonship, which consists in seeing Christ in his splendour and glory of sonship, and participating in it.

3. Faith unfolded in Vision

Now, as we already saw, our condition of sonship, here at present is for Jn a participation in the sonship of Christ, and that is attained through, and practically consists in, a life of faith in Christ, as Son of God. This seems to suggest that our glorious state of sonship too should be obtained through something that corresponds to the life of faith in Christ, namely, through a vision of Christ.

Perhaps, I Pet 1:6-9 comes to our aid in illustrating this. There he says that the heritage — the result of the regeneration — to be revealed in the end is to be kept 'through faith unto salvation prepared to be revealed in the end'. And then he asks them to rejoice because of this, looking forward to the revelation of Christ, in whom now they believe 'without seeing' (μὴ ὁρῶντες), because they will attain the end of this faith that is the 'σωτηρία'[67]. Now 'σωτηρία' and 'δόξα' are used in I Pet in parallel eschatological sense (cf. I Pet 1:5,9; 2:2). So the mentioning of 'not seeing Christ' in the present stage of faith seems to look forward to the final stage of salvation 'σωτηρία' and glory 'δόξα' as a stage of 'seeing Christ'. Hence there is no wonder that Jn who already makes use of the verbs 'knowing' and 'seeing' to express communion with the Son and the Father in the Son, speaks of its final stage as a 'seeing as He is'. And since the present stage of sonship is attained through a life of adhesion to (faith in — not seeing) the Son, the final stage of sonship seems to be attained through the perfection of this life of adhesion to (vision — seeing) the Son[68]. So the vision of Christ as

---

[66] Cf. Jn 17:21-24 which speak of the glory of Christ given to those who believe, which comes to its fulfilment in a beholding of this glory of Christ, which shows that a full participation in the glory of Christ as Son of God implies also a vision of Him in His glory.

[67] Cf. the parallelism between this section and I Jn 3:1-2 as delineated in the comparison we made between I Pet 1:3-23 and I Jn 2:29 – 3:10 on p. 235.

[68] Cf. R. LAW, *Tests of Life*, p. 331 where he connects the present faith to the future vision: "The Christian's faith, when he sees Christ as He is, will then appear to himself a far grander thing than it does now. What looks mean and meagure in the semi-darkness of this life will shine forth like the sun at the rising of the sun".

the Son in his glory seems to be the cause of our future state of likeness to Him as Son (cf. II Cor 3:18).

The process involved is the same. In the present life of sonship, 'faith' leads to the 'communication of life' in the divine begetting, and this 'communication of life' (community of life with the Son) makes it possible to lead a 'life of faith' (life of the children of God). Thus in the future state of sonship also, the 'vision of Christ' leads to 'perfect likeness with the Son', while this 'perfect likeness' makes it possible to have a 'life of vision' of the Son, and of the Father in the Son, which is the perfect, eschatological, stage of the life of the children of God [69]. This shows too that the future stage of sonship is a natural unfolding of the sonship that we possess now in a germinal and hidden state.

IV. Filial Hope and Confidence of the Children of God (I Jn 4:17-18; 3:3)

A. *The Eschatological Confidence of the Children of God* (I Jn 4:17-18)

The filial hope and confidence in view of the manifestation of the children of God is well expressed in I Jn 4:17-18: "In this is love perfected in us that we may have confidence for the day of judgement, because as He is so we are ...".

1. *Condition of the children of God: Basis of confidence*

Vv. 17-18 speak of confidence of Christians, because they are in this world as Christ (ἐκεῖνος) is [70]. The phrase 'ἐν τούτῳ' refers to the preceding affirmation of communion with God, the mutual dwelling of God and man [71], in which love is perfected in us, which is the basis of our eschatological confidence, and the following ὅτι sentence gives the reason why it gives this confidence [72].

The absolute use of ἀγάπη shows that it is conceived here as a

---

[69] We may call it the stage of beatific vision in the language of the Speculative Theologians.

[70] Note that ἐκεῖνος occurs in I Jn 2:6; 3:3,5,7,16 and is always referring to Christ. Cf. B. F. WESTCOTT, *Epistles*, p. 51.

[71] Some take the ἐν τούτῳ as referring to the following, considering the ἵνα as having the value of an epexegetical infinitive (cf. R. BULTMANN, *Die Johannesbriefe*, p. 76, note 3). But the construction ἐν τούτῳ ... ἵνα occurs in Jn apart from here only in Jn 15:8 and there it refers to that which precedes. Compare 8:23; 14:13.

[72] The eschatological aspect of these texts are seen in the explicit mentioning of the final judgement, and also in the abundance of the eschatological terms as κρίσις, φόβος, κόλασις, ὁ κόσμος οὗτος and βάλλειν ἔξω.

reality in us, the reality of the divine life, that is perfected in us, which in its turn makes us perfect children of God and is manifested in our brotherly love. It is this condition that gives us confidence now in view of the last judgment [73]. So the present condition of our perfected life of the children of God, the perfected 'agape' in us gives us confidence here and now in view of the future judgment, a judgment already present in the Johannine realized eschatology. So it is a filial confidence [74].

2. Similarity with Christ gives Confidence

In the ὅτι sentence in v. 17cd the author again gives an argument that strengthens what is said in v. 17ab, namely, a similarity of our condition here on earth to that of Christ. The expression 'ἐν τῷ κόσμῳ τούτῳ' in this eschatological context refers to our present state in relation to the state of Christ who is considered here as belonging to the coming (eschatological) world, namely, celestial glory[75]. So Jn affirms a similarity between us here on earth and Christ in his celestial glory. Hence the interpretations that see a similarity to Christ as 'God-man' [76], or as a merely moral exemplar in his terrestrial life [77] are not adequate. The heavenly Christ, who lives in the perfect love of the Father, is the exemplar and origin of our life of perfect love, namely, of our divine sonship. Just as we in this world are compared to Christ who is Righteous, pure and without sin (cf. I Jn 2:29 ; 3:3,5,7) so also, we, in whom the reality of love, that is the life of God, is perfected, are compared to the celestial Christ, whose sonship also consists in the life of a relation of perfect love with the Father [78]. And this similarity between Christ the Son of God and us the children of God possessing the same 'ἀγάπη', the life of God, gives us the filial confidence in view of the judgment.

---

[73] 'On the day of judgment' used with the present tense of ἔχωμεν shows that the reality of the judgment is seen already as present. Cf. I Jn 3:19-21 where also we find the theme of anticipated judgment in speaking of the confidence in the judgment of the conscience.

[74] For the eschatological aspect of agape, cf. L. CERFAUX "La charité fraternelle et le retour du Christ (Jn XIII, 33-38)", *Recueil L. Cerfaux*, II, pp. 27-40 ; on p. 36 he says : "La charité fait donc le lien entre le temps présent et le temps futur".

[75] Note the formula ἐν τῷ κόσμῳ τούτῳ which comes solely here. It belongs to the apocalyptic tradition, where it is opposed to the future or eschatological world.

[76] Cf. C. SPICQ, *Agapè* ..., III, p. 295.

[77] Cf. R. SCHNACKENBURG, *Die Johannesbriefe*, p. 247.

[78] Because of the apparent difficulty to compare our present state with the heavenly state of Christ, some have tried to deny the genuineness of the text

The fear that is excluded here in v. 18 is not to be explained in a purely subjective sense [79]. Such an explanation would require a love towards God, while here the whole context is about brotherly love, as an objective and divine reality in us. Hence the fear that is excluded here is a servile fear [80]. Our similarity with Christ as children of God is the objective (not psychological) basis of our confidence, and hence there is no objective reason for fear [81].

B. *Filial Hope — Incentive for a Dynamic Life of Sonship*

In fact, participation in the glory of Christ as Son of God in the eschatological manifestation as described in I Jn 3:2 presupposes participation in and similarity to His filial life as the Son of God. This similarity to the Son of God creates a filial hope and confidence centered on the Son of God (ἐπ' αὐτῷ).

This eschatological hope and confidence gives also incentive to the children of God to become more and more similar to Christ the Son of God in their daily life: " He who has this hope in Him, purifies himself as He is pure " (I Jn 3:3).

So the ethical duty of righteousness or sinlessness in the Christian, who is a child of God, is not a legal injunction but an internal necessity of life. Righteous living is the criterion and test of having this filial hope, while this hope is an incentive and a challenge to the progressive striving after likeness to the Son of God here and now.

---

and to reconstruct the original text (cf. R. BULTMANN, *Die Johannesbriefe*, p. 77). But when we see that for John the eschatological state is nothing but a natural unfolding of the present state of sonship, and that John has the concept of a realized eschatology (cf. P. RICCA, *Die Eschatologie des Vierten Evangeliums*, Zürich, 1966, pp. 167-178 where he speaks of ' Das eschatologische NYN - Continuum eschatologicum '), the apparent difficulty disappears.

[79] Cf. K. ROMANIUK, " Die vollkommene Liebe treibt die Furcht aus ", Eine Auslegung von I Jn 4:17-18, *BibLeb* 5 (1964), pp. 80-84; Cf. also the Commentaries of Chaine, Westcott, Brooke, all of which speak of an incompatibility of love and fear.

[80] Cf. Rom 8:15 where Paul speaks of the servile fear which is to be totally excluded from the spirit of divine sonship of Christians.

[81] It is this hope which is focussed upon Christ that will lead to present self-purification as described in I Jn 3:3f. Note the prepositional phrase ' ἐπ' αὐτῷ ' in I Jn 3:3 with the locative case, being locational in force, and hence in an objective sense rather than in a subjective sense, thus referring αὐτῷ to Christ rather than to the believer. This is in accord with the general New Testament teaching on hope which is presented as an objective certainty related to the promise of God and the person of Christ, rather than a subjective feeling residing in the believer (cf. Col 1:27; I Tim 1:1) (Cf. W. R. COOK, " Hamartiological Problems in First John ", *BS* 123 (1966), p. 254, note 14).

This shows once again the dynamic working of the divine sonship of men. Though the character of sonship is divinely bestowed upon the Christian, and he must inevitably be what he actually has become by God's grace, yet the child of God must also earnestly strive to make the ethical relation correspond to the spiritual fact. And both elements — divine and human — work together in the harmonious development of the divine sonship to a perfect likeness to and vision of the Son of God, and the Father through the Son.

Conclusion

The Johannine concept of the future life is the natural outgrowth of his view of salvation as the experience of divine life imparted to men. The future life for the child of God will only be an intensification, a full flowering and a perfect realization of all that christian sonship involves in the present life.

Thus Jn describes the present life of sonship as a foretaste of the future life. If the future life of sonship consists in a similarity with the Son (and the Father), the present life of sonship should anticipate this similarity. The very term τέκνα Θεοῦ emphasizes the community of life with the Father. The use of ὁ πατήρ in Jn presenting God as the Father both of Christ and of the Christian, also indicates a similarity with the Son of God in His relation to the Father. This common possession of life with the Father is demonstrated also by denying to the 'world' the 'knowledge' of the children of God (I Jn 3:1).

The very fact that the present life of sonship is a foretaste of the future life shows that there is a future state, which is an unfolding of the present hidden state of sonship, and which is not yet fully revealed. Even if no complete revelation of it has been made, the knowledge of faith gives us the conviction that it would be a state of perfect likeness to Christ and through Christ to God. It is a vision of Christ as Son in his glory that causes this perfect likeness to Christ. At the same time this perfect likeness to the Son makes it possible to have a life of vision of the Son and the Father in the Son. So the future state of sonship is a natural unfolding of the present state, for it will be, a future life of vision corresponding to the present life of faith and a future state of likeness corresponding to the present state of common possession of life.

This eschatological sonship is not yet realized fully. But it presupposes participation in and similarity to the filial life of the Son of God, and it constitutes an assurance of filial hope and confidence in the children of God. It is a hope and confidence in view of the future judgment, which is, however, made present in the realized eschatology of John. Hence it is a hope and confidence that is actually present and is fully existential in the present life of the children of God (I Jn 4:17-18). While righteous living is the criterion and test of having this filial hope and confidence, this hope becomes also an incentive and a challenge to the progressive striving after a likeness to the Son of God here and now, namely, a striving after making the ethical relation correspond to the spiritual fact (I Jn 3:3ff). Thus the filial hope becomes the driving force of a dynamic life of the children of God.

GENERAL CONCLUSION

At the end of this long treatise we should like to offer a brief panoramic view of the Johannine concept of Christian sonship and evaluate it against the traditions that lie behind. First we give a theological synthesis by summing up shortly the main characteristics of the Johannine concept of sonship and then we will try to outline its originality in relation to its background.

I. The Theological Synthesis

Jn expresses his concept of the divine sonship of men, using mainly two phrases: τέκνα Θεοῦ and γεννηθῆναι ἐκ τοῦ Θεοῦ. The use of τέκνα Θεοῦ as antithetically parallel to τέκνα τοῦ διαβόλου and in parallelism with εἶναι ἐκ τοῦ Θεοῦ shows in the children of God a moral connection of derivation from and dependence on God. But the use of γεγέννηται ἐκ τοῦ Θεοῦ in the perfect exclusively for the divine sonship of men shows that, unlike the diabolic sonship, it is based on an initial communication of life from the part of God, which remains active throughout and which determines the nature of the children of God. It is by virtue of this communicated life that one grows into a τέκνον Θεοῦ. Thus the two phrases γεγέννηται ἐκ τοῦ Θεοῦ and τέκνα Θεοῦ εἶναι seem to be identical in sense. Hence for Jn the divine sonship of christians is more than a mere moral relationship and is essentially dynamic, destined to growth and development to full maturity.

The divine sonship of man in Jn implies a change from the state of 'not being children of God' into that of 'being children of God'. This change supposes a process of a continuous becoming children of God, and the dynamic element in this process is faith in the characteristically Johannine form πιστεύειν εἰς τὸ ὄνομα αὐτοῦ, namely, a life of adhesion and commitment to Christ (Jn 1:12) as Son of God (Born of God – Jn 1:13), which enables the believer to share in the divine sonship and birth. Hence this dynamic element of the life of faith is called by Jn 'the power to become children of God' (Jn 1:12). This power is totally a gift from God (ἔδωκεν) and, at the same time, it is a real power — ability (ἐξουσία) — to become children of God.

The divine sonship of man is a sharing from the fulness of the divine sonship by virtue of which Jesus was the fulness of Revelation (Grace and Truth) (Jn 1:16). Hence the starting point of the process of becoming the children of God is the definite step taken in accepting the Revelation in Christ.

A spiritual birth, having the Holy Spirit as the principle, is an indispensable condition for this life of sonship (Jn 3:3,5), because man, left to himself, is in a condition of absolute and radical inability to enter into the life of the children of God, which belongs necessarily to the sphere of the Spirit of God (Jn 3:6).

This begetting is said to be 'from above' (3:3) and 'from the Spirit' (Jn 3:5), which being parallel to 'from God' refers to the divine principle communicating the life of sonship. The Spirit in Jn is the 'Spirit of Truth' (Jn 14:17), who makes present in us the Truth of Christ through faith, and therefore the action of begetting by the Spirit consists in the action of bringing man to the life of faith in Christ. In Jn 3 the result of the supernatural begetting is presented as 'seeing and entering the Kingdom of God'.

In Jn the Kingdom of God is strictly connected with the person of Christ, almost bordering on an identification. And the progressive use of 'seeing' (v. 3) and 'entering' (v. 5) the Kingdom of God shows the faith that results in a life of communion with the person of Christ. So the life of the children of God resulting from the supernatural birth is really a life of faith and communion with the person of Christ.

Speaking, on the one hand, of a begetting to a life of faith (children of God) through the Spirit, and on the other, of a divine sonship conditioned by faith (accepting the Revelation — Word of God), Jn shows the interaction of the Spirit and the Word of God in the life of the children of God. It is through the Word of God that the Holy Spirit works in us, and it is the Holy Spirit, who begets in us faith in the Word of God and gives efficacy to it. This shows also that, though the initiative in this begetting lies with God, the realization of it is always inextricably connected with human conditions and response.

The fact that this new life of sonship has a definite beginning at a specific chronological point of one's conscious experience is indicated by the use of the verb γεννηθῇ in the inceptive aorist form (Jn 3:3,4[bis],5,7). This beginning is the definite step in accepting the Revelation of Christ in the beginning of Christian life, and this is identical with the moment of Baptism (Jn 3:5). Hence Baptism (Water) and Faith (Spirit) become the two basic conditions of this begetting.

The reference to 'Water' and 'Spirit' as two co-ordinated conditions is also significant. The Spirit refers to the life of faith that should accompany Baptism, and it is not something that is fully realized at the moment of Baptism, but something that accompanies and then goes on progressing towards perfection.

This dynamic character of the life of the children of God is also indicated in the Johannine usage of γεννηθῆναι referring to the divine begetting of man. It is used in the aorist only when he speaks of it as a condition to enter the life of the children of God. On all other occasions he makes use of the perfect tense γεγέννηται or γεγεννημένος showing thereby that, in this divine begetting the elements (divine and human) that are at work in the beginning go on working, contributing thus to the sustenance and growth of the life that is begotten.

Though God the Father is the ultimate source of this newly begotten life, it is Christ who possesses the divine life in its fulness, and it is he who becomes the mediator of this life to man. Christ revealing the Father in his earthly life and work becomes a sort of existential definition of the condition of the children of God and hence through faith in him, man participates in this condition of sonship.

Christ imparts this life to men, putting them thus in a filial relationship with God through his death on the cross (exaltation) (3:14-15), which is the supreme revelation of the Life of God who is Love (I Jn 4:8,16). Thus through the death of Christ, the dispersed children of God are gathered together into one (Jn 11:52).

As the natural life has breath or spirit as its principle so also the divine life has as principle the Spirit of God (Jn 3:5-8). Jn explains this aspect of the Spirit mainly in I Jn 3:24 and 4:13. In these texts Jn describes the Holy Spirit as ' given' and becoming the interior principle of the life of the children of God, manifested in faith and love.

The necessity of a birth having the Holy Spirit as principle for receiving the life of the children of God is proved by the fact that for Jn the nature is determined by its origin expressed by ' εἶναι ἐκ ' or ' γεννηθῆναι ἐκ '. One who is born of the flesh is and remains necessarily flesh (human). So a being and life that is divine in character requires necessarily also a principle that is divine, namely, the Holy Spirit (Jn 3:8).

The one who is begotten of the Spirit shares the unfathomable character of the Spirit, and this life in the Spirit remains rather mysterious and cannot be perceived except in the outward manifestations of his life (Jn 3:8).

In his First Epistle, Jn tries to give evidence of this birth to the life of the children of God which could be perceived only in its effects. Jn, in fact, presents the theme of sonship in two stages: one, in the initial stage of ' being begotten of God (Spirit) ', and the other, in the progressive stage of ' having been begotten of God (Spirit) '. The fact that the Epistle exclusively makes use of the perfect γεγέννηται (γεγεννημένος) ἐκ τοῦ Θεοῦ to speak of the divine begetting of man shows that here Jn presents the life of the children of God in the progressive stage, namely, as actually possessed and manifested in its effects. Thus Jn gives righteousness, love and faith as manifestations of the interior reality of sonship (I Jn 2:29; 4:7; 5:1). At the same time he presents them as spontaneous expressions of the very reality of sonship (I Jn 3:9; 5:4,18). So, if the sonship is the foundation and source of its outward manifestations, these outward manifestations prove and testify that one is really a ' child of God '.

The sonship according to Jn is manifested in conduct that shows a moral and spiritual likeness to the one who is claimed as father. ' To commit sin ' is concretely to reject Christ who bears witness to the Truth, and therefore is the criterion of one's diabolic sonship, because it manifests a conduct showing moral likeness to the devil who is a ' murderer from the beginning ' and ' liar ' (Jn 8:31-47).

On the contrary, ' to do righteousness ' is the criterion of one's divine sonship, for it entails a dynamic adherence to Christ who in his triumphant righteousness (sinlessness and triumph over sin) stands in a filial relationship with God, and hence implies a sharing in his sonship (I Jn 2:29 – 3:10). As Christ the righteous is the Revelation of God the Father who is righteous, the ' doing righteousness ' in the children of God shows also a moral likeness to God their Father. This moral likeness to God the Father, unlike the diabolic sonship, is derived from the communication of the divine life which remains active in the children of God throughout their filial life.

The fruit of the life of the children of God is impeccability because the children of God share in the eschatological gift of impeccability which was realized in Christ as Son of God (I Jn 3:5,8), by adhering to him through faith. So in their theological reality, the children of God are impeccable (I Jn 3:9). But as they still live on earth in danger of losing it, this impeccability is guaranteed only as a result of a constant and dynamic life of faith and communion with Christ, through a mutual remaining of the Word of God in us (I Jn 3:9) and our remaining in Him (I Jn 3:6) and in his Word (Jn 8:31). So impeccability is guaranteed only as a fruit of the sonship that is lived.

It is their solidarity with Christ, the Only Begotten of the Father, that keeps them impeccable. He keeps them from sin and enables them to be victorious over the evil one, by giving them understanding and knowledge of the Truthful one by means of his Word interiorized through the Spirit (I Jn 5:18-20).

Though the freedom enjoyed by the children of God is above all a freedom from the bondage of sin, it is a freedom proper to the son having a permanent standing in the household of his Father (Jn 8: 31-36). Therefore it is a freedom proper to the children of God who live in an abiding communion with the Father and the Son and hence a freedom that is the expression of their true nature, allowing a true self-determination.

As brotherly love shows forth the righteousness, it becomes also a manifestation of divine sonship, while the lack of brotherly love is the manifestation of the diabolic sonship (I Jn 3:10-12). As the diabolic sonship is also the source of hatred, the brotherly love is for Jn more than a mere criterion of divine sonship. Since 'God is Love' and since it is the participation of this Love (Life) of God (I Jn 3:1) and its perfection in them (I Jn 4:12), that makes men children of God, love is a need of the very nature of those who are born of God (I Jn 4:7-8). So the divine sonship is not only manifested in love, but in a way defined by love. This means that the life of sonship (life of love) leads men more and more to an experiential knowledge of God the Father, who is 'Love'. The parallelism between 'birth from God' and 'knowledge of God' in relation to ὁ ἀγαπῶν (I Jn 4:7-8) shows that this filial knowledge grows parallel to the sonship.

The brotherly love proper to the children of God has necessarily a family character, because it is a love between the children of the same Father (I Jn 3:10-12). Besides, this love flows directly from their life and is directed to the sonship and not to the person apart from the character. So it should be naturally directed to all those to whom this character is communicated (I Jn 5:1b). Thus love for God the Father becomes for Jn a test of the genuineness of brotherly love towards the other children of the same Father (I Jn 5:2).

Since the object of faith is Christ the Son of God, it results in a living and personal fellowship with the Son and hence it is the basis of the very life of the children of God. So faith in Christ the Son of God belongs to the very essence of the divine sonship of man and is its normal expression (I Jn 5:1-5). Therefore the experience of sonship is a faith-experience that had its beginning in Baptism and that remains ever active throughout the Christian life. Hence this faith-experience is the root or basis of brotherly love too, because true brotherly love exists only among those who experience and live the life of divine sonship, namely, the life proper to the children of the heavenly Father.

Though the divine sonship of men is realized at present in the life of the believers, the full flowering of it is reserved to the future. Hence the eschatological character of the Johannine concept of sonship. But in the realized eschatology of Jn the present life of sonship becomes a foretaste of the future life. If the present life of sonship is a life of faith in the Son, the future state of sonship is a life of vision of the Son in his glory. If the present life of sonship is, in a way, a state of common possession of life with the Father and the Son, the future state of sonship is a state of likeness to the Son (I Jn 3:2). As the present faith in the Son of God leads men to the divine begetting and a resulting community of life and nature with the Son and the Father, so the future vision of Christ in his glory of sonship causes a likeness with him in his glorious condition of sonship. On the other hand, as the divine sonship (birth) makes it possible to have a perfect life of faith (life of the children of God), so the future likeness with the Son makes it possible to have a life of vision of the Son and of the Father in the Son. So the future state of sonship is really an unfolding of the present hidden state of sonship.

It is the filial hope and confidence that is created by this eschatological condition of sonship (I Jn 4:17-18), that becomes a real incentive to acquire more and more a moral likeness to the Son at present (I Jn 3:3), and thus gives dynamism to the present life of sonship.

II. The Originality of the Johannine Concept of Sonship

Having seen the main characteristics of the Johannine doctrine on the divine sonship of Christians, now we can proceed to evaluate it against the background of the pre-Johannine literature in the light of the conclusions reached as a result of our study of this literature in Part One.

A. *Against the OT and Jewish background*

In the OT and Judaism, it is Israel, the people of God, that stands in filial relationship to Yahweh, and that through a formation into a people by means of the saving act of Exodus and by the Covenant. In Jn too it is the new people of God (λαός), who stands in filial relationship to God, and that also through a gathering together into one, by means of a saving act, death on the cross (Jn 11: 47-53). But Jn takes up the distinction between the people of God and others outside, in a manner that is characteristically his own. For him the ' new people of God ' are all ' those who believe in Christ' and those outside are all those who do not believe.

If in the OT it is Yahweh who forms the people by making them a national unity, and by establishing a father-son relationship between himself and them, in Jn it is Christ who gathers the people, bringing them into one entirely spiritual communion, by imparting to them the same divine life and thus making them ' children of God '.

If the Davidic King and Israel share the divine sonship on the same titles of Election and Covenant, in Jn Christ's sonship is singular and unique, as He is Son of God ' by nature ', while the Christians are children of God only ' by participation '. Besides, the sonship of Christians is absolutely dependent on that of Christ, which is not the case with that of the King and Israel.

The dualistic presentation of Qumran putting the ' sons of light ' who believe in the Teacher of righteousness over against the ' sons of darkness ' is perhaps recalled in the Johannine presentation of the ' children of God ' over against the ' children of the devil ', because the children of God, for Jn, are ' sons of Light ' who believe in Christ the Light (Jn 12:36), while the children of the devil are those who reject the Son, who is the Revelation of the Father. But again here Jn remains original by presenting Christ as the revelation of the Father in his sonship, and the ' sons of light ' as those who participate in the very sonship of Christ.

The presentation of the sons of God by the Qumran literature as ' sons of his truth ' or those who give positive reponse to the truth may be viewed as a preparation for the Johannine concept of becoming children of God through faith or a positive response to Christ the Truth. The uniqueness of Jn in this respect comes from the uniqueness of Christ as the Truth or the Revelation, while in Qumran the truth is the plan of God revealed mainly through the Law.

In the OT as well as in Jn, though the initiative lies always with God, the realization of sonship is inextricably connected with human response. In both, the divine sonship results in a loving communion between the Father and the children. Thus the dynamism is kept up in both. But as to the intimate nature of sonship they differ. In the OT it is an adoptive relationship, but in Jn it is based on a communication of a vital principle (Spirit) from the side of God which makes man a ' child of God ' and enables him to carry on the life of sonship. The mutual communion between the Father and the children in Jn is also the result of this vital communication.

Though in a general sense the Spirit of Yahweh appears to be the principle in the realization of Israel's Covenantal and filial relationship with Yahweh, a real communication of the Spirit as the vital principle of the life of sonship is lacking in the OT and Judaism. Though OT presents the concept of a new life in the individuals having the Spirit of Yahweh as its origin and source (Ez 36:26f), it does not present any parallel at all for the explicit Johannine teaching that the believing individuals are actually born of God. When speaking of a begetting by Yahweh, it is the creation of the Community that is meant. Also the Later Jewish literature speaks of a birth from the power of God, but it is again of the Community and not of the individual (I QH 3:1-18).

The dynamism implied in the Johannine doctrine on impeccability of the children of God through the remaining of the ' seed ' of God may have been prepared also by the OT concept of the new life with the Law and the Spirit of Yahweh as its interior principle implying a moral renewal of the individual. Also the interior change from iniquity to justice required by the Qumran literature to enter the filial relationship with God may be the antecedent of this Johannine doctrine, as this change is worked out by the Spirit through the truth and the Law of God.

Also in the eschatological character of sonship, Jn differs from the OT and Judaism. In the later Books of the OT and Judaism sonship becomes something wholly to be attained in the Future. The New Creation itself, having the Holy Spirit as the principle, is presented by the OT as a promise looking forward to the future alone for its fulfilment. But in Jn sonship is actually realized in the present life of the believers, and the eschatological expectation is only for a manifestation and unfolding of the present life of sonship.

B. *Against the Background of Hellenism and Philo*

In Hellenism, the father-son relationship between God and man is a result of the initiative of man, transferring the human relationships to God. But in Jn, as also in the other Books of the Bible, it is God who takes the initiative to establish this father-son relationship. In Hellenism this relation is based on creation and providence, and all men are sons of God by creation. But in Jn men have to become children of God, and the divine sonship is something that is reserved to the believers, elevating them above other men, giving an individual consciousness of a personal relation to God the Father. In Hellenism, the individualization is only in the case of men who are distinguished by wisdom or power, such as kings, priests or teachers.

The kinship of men with God by divine origin, implied in the Hellenistic view of the divine sonship of men, and the consequent communion with God with an equal spiritual and moral stand with God, is quite foreign to Jn, as also to other NT Writers, who stress always the incomparable transcendence of God above men.

C. H. XIII speaking of a rebirth making men children of God

adopts the same way of procedure in the discourse as that in Jn 3, and both use the key words 'Life', 'Light' and 'Truth' in the handling of this mystical experience. Both suggest a close relationship between the moral attitude of man and his attainment of higher knowledge. Both give more stress to the inward experience of the reborn. And there are other analogous expressions and notions specially in the Johannine texts regarding the sonship and regeneration.

However, there are many and essential dissimilarities between the doctrine in Jn and C. H. XIII. In C. H. XIII the state of the reborn is undestroyable, while the Christian state of rebirth could be lost. In C. H. XIII too the reborn is impeccable, but it is because the reborn is divinized (παῖς Θεοῦ Θεός) and hence necessarily in a condition in which it is impossible to sin, while in Jn the impeccability of the reborn is necessarily conditioned by the dynamic working of the life of sonship. The rebirth takes place through definite rites, but it happens almost magically, reducing the part of the individual to a minimum, while in Jn the individual role is of utmost importance in the rebirth taking place in baptism. Above all, the expressions that are typical of Jn regarding the divine sonship of men such as τέκνα Θεοῦ, γεννηθῆναι ἐκ Θεοῦ etc. are not found in C. H. XIII.

Philo in his terminology regarding the father-son relationship does not differ much from Hellenism, except for its colouring derived from his Jewish heritage. Unlike the Hellenistic writers, Philo speaks of a special divine sonship of those who do what is pleasing to God and that according to the Law of Moses, and hence having Israel as type. But he describes it as a kinship with God based on a common belief. All these remain on a purely ethical level, while the sonship in Jn is the result of a supernatural endowment. Philo attributes to the sons of God a knowledge of God, but it is presented as a vision of God or a mystical awareness of the Absolute Being, and not as an experiential knowledge of communion with the Father as presented by Jn. Philo gives also faith together with personal piety, as an element of the sonship, but brings it into closest relation with the philosophical ideal of the apprehension of the Invisible. So it is far away from the Johannine concept of a dynamic faith in the Son of God fundamental to his concept of divine sonship.

In Philo the Logos in his quality of being the 'first-born' son of God (πρωτόγονος υἱός) becomes the mediator of men to become sons of God. This results from the general Philonic doctrine that 'Logos' is the medium of intercourse between God and this world. The metaphor of son here means only that Logos has its source in God and hence the word of God carries the image of God. Since the image of God (λόγος) is also immanent in men, they have a kinship with this universal Logos, the Firstborn of God, and thus through him arrive at the perfect knowledge of God, and become perfect images of God, sons of God. So, in spite of all the personification, Philo is not really thinking of a 'Logos' that is personal and historical as mediator, which is fundamental to the Johannine doctrine of Sonship.

Though Philo does not speak of a birth from God, he speaks of a spiritual generation that makes men sons of God, and he presents Isaac as the symbol of this sonship. But the sonship, resulting from this spiritual generation, has a mystical character, rather than moral and personal, while in Jn the sonship is quite personal and of moral character.

C. *Against the Background of Other NT Writings*

1. *The Synoptic Gospels*

Coming to the NT, we see that Jn is only building upon the foundation laid in the other Books of the NT. Presenting the divine sonship as a becoming children of God through faith, Jn takes up the Synoptic teaching on conversion and becoming like children to enter the Kingdom of heaven (Mt 18:3 ; Mk 10:15 ; Lk 18:17). This is quite evident, because Jn presents the life of the children of God which is a life of faith, as a life in the Kingdom (Jn 3:3,5), while also for the Synoptics the 'sons of God' are members of the Kingdom. But Jn is more radical in demanding a rebirth to become a member of the Kingdom. If the Synoptics demand a 'conversion' and 'becoming like a child' to enter the Kingdom, Jn demands a 'being born as a child', having the Holy Spirit as the principle of this new life. While the Synoptics speak more from the view-point of man (conversion, becoming), Jn speaks more from that of God (begetting from the Spirit).

The difference between the sonship of Christ and that of Christians is made already in the Synoptics. But it is linguistically worked out only in Jn by means of the exclusive use of ' υἱός ' and ' τέκνα '. Also in the Synoptics men are sons of God together with Christ (Mt 17:25-27 ; 12:48-50), who is both the exemplar and mediator of sonship (Mt 11:25-27). But in Jn Christ is not only exemplar and mediator, but he is the very existential definition of sonship, in whom one believes and of whom one participates.

Synoptics bring also love (peace-making) as characteristic of the sons of God, and thus producing certain similarity of life and nature with God the Father, which really contribute to becoming perfect sons of God (Mt 5:9,45). But it is again from the view-point of man, rather than from that of God. Jn, on the other hand, speaks of love as a communicated life of God in His children, and thus producing a community of life and similarity of nature with God (I Jn 3:1 ;

4:7) and, therefore, love as a permanent quality or nature of the children of God always tending towards action.

The Synoptics speak of the sonship mostly in an eschatological perspective as something to be realized in the future at the resurrection (Lk 20:36), though at present there is a participation of this future sonship, while Jn in his realized eschatology sees the divine sonship of men already realized (I Jn 3:1), though the full flowering and manifestation of it is looked forward to in the future.

2. The Pauline Epistles

Though Paul, on the one hand, makes use of the term τέκνα θεοῦ (Rom 8:16,17,21; 9:7f; Phil 2:15) and speaks of a begetting through the Gospel (I Cor 4:15), and on the other, presents the Holy Spirit as the principle of the life of the Children of God (Rom 8:14-16; Gal 4:4-6) he never speaks explicitly of a begetting by God. Paul emphasizes in divine sonship the belonging to God, rather than the origin from God. Hence the typical Pauline term υἱοθεσία to indicate the divine sonship of men, by adoption.

Also in Paul as in John men become children of God through faith. But Paul emphasizes rather the objective faith, namely, the whole happening in Christ (Gal 3:19-29), while in Jn it is the subjective life of faith, that is given greater emphasis, though in both we cannot speak exclusively of subjective or objective faith. The birth through the Gospel in Paul (I Cor 4:15) seems to lie behind the Johannine doctrine of rebirth through the remaining of the seed (Word) of God.

Paul emphasizes also the fact that our sonship is based on the sonship of Christ, and is a participation of it. It is by becoming one with Christ through faith, that men become sons of God. Now, it is the Holy Spirit who is the principle that brings about this union, and thus becomes the principle of the life of sonship (cf. Rom Ch. 8). In Jn too the Holy Spirit remains as the principle of the life of sonship, and that working through faith, which brings about the communion with the Son. The only difference is that Jn presents it as a ' begetting '.

Paul presents the moral life of the children of God as obligations incumbent upon their position as adopted children of God. For Jn, on the contrary, the moral life manifested in righteousness and concretized in brotherly love is a need of the very nature of those who are born of God.

Adoption in Paul is both present (already) and eschatological (not yet) (Rom 8:23), while in Jn the sonship is present. It is only a manifestation of it that is postponed to the future.

From the above comparison, we see the originality of the Johannine doctrine of sonship. In presenting the doctrine of the Christian Sonship, Jn was not fabricating a fanciful, unfamiliar teaching from materials that he uncovered in the nooks and crannies of his own imagination, nor was he depending upon heathen sources. Also regarding the expressions we could say the same thing. Even though we find in Jn many expressions analogous to those found in Hellenism, it is quite significant that nowhere in the Hellenistic Literature we find a direct parallel to the expression ' γεννηθῆναι ἐκ τοῦ Θεοῦ ' which is decisive and fundamental to the Johannine doctrine of sonship. On the other hand, we find close parallels to the Johannine doctrine and expressions regarding the Christian sonship in the Primitive Christian Tradition and in the teachings of Jesus, prepared to a certain extent in the OT and Later Judaism.

Hence we can only conclude by saying that John draws his doctrine of Christian Sonship from the Early Christian Tradition based on the teachings of Jesus, a tradition prepared in the OT and Later Judaism, and presents it in a manner that is characteristically his own. At the same time, expressions analogous to those found in Hellenism show that, in presenting his doctrine of Christian Sonship, John was quite open and sensitive to the movements and currents of the time. Hence the genuineness and the originality of the Johannine Doctrine of the Divine Sonship of Christians.

INDICES

Numbers in bold face indicate pages of special importance

INDEX OF AUTHORS

Abbott, E.A.   143, 168, 186
Abel, F.M.   244, 328, 329
Aland, K.   176
Albert the Great   106, 107, 182
Albrecht, A.   20
Alcuinus, B.   106, 107, 184, 214, 215, 223
Alexander, N.   230
Alfaro, J.   313
Allen, W.C.   65
Ambrose, St.   83, 114, 188
Amiot, F.   78
Ammonius Alexandrinus   181-182, 214 215
Appollinarius of Laodicea   115, 188
Argyle, A.W.   268
Arnaldez, R.   51
Arndt, W.F.   172
Asmussen, H.   334
Athanasius, St.   79
Augustine, St.   83, 102, 110, 114, 172, 184, 199, 223, 232, 266, 269, 214, 215, 223, 270, 298, 326, 342
Augustinović, A.   267
Auzou, G.   12, 13

Baert, E.   342
Bailey, R.F.   179
Baillet, M.   30
Balague, M.   164
Bann, G.   111
Barberis, A.   188
Bardtke, H.   32
Barker, F.E.   16
Barrett, C.K.   84, 113, 147, 172, 199 201, 207, 215, 219

Barth, G.   58
Barth, Karl   248
Barth, M.   180
Basil, St.   182
Bates, H.W.   171, 180
Batiffol, P.   9
Bauer, G.   99, 101
Bauer, W.   54, 90, 95, 98, 139, 146, 147, 148, 149, 150, 151, 172, 194, 214, 243, 278, 284
Bauernfeind, O.   25, 323
Baumann, E.   293
Baur, P.   9, 16
Bede the Venerable   106, 107, 184, 199, 214, 215, 223, 269, 276, 298, 342
Behm, J.   284
Beilner, W.   149
Belser, J.E.   164, 265, 266, 274, 312
Benoit, P.   83, 84
Bernard, J.H.   109, 139, 146, 148, 164, 165, 170, 199, 207, 217
Berrouard, M.F.   248
Bertram, G.   159, 220
Betz, O.   35, 40, 41, 42
Beutler, J.   189
Beyer, H.W.   78, 233
Beyer, K.L.   279
Beyerlin, W.   13
Bieler, L.   46
Bieneck, J.   250
Black, M.   35, 41
Blass, F.   113, 328
Blass-Debrunner   142, 153, 158, 244, 277, 298, 324, 328
Bligh, J.   164

Boismard, M.E. 29, 113, 117, 118, 133, 134, 150, 178, 188, 222, 229, 231, 234, 235, 236, 239, 241, 258, 270, 284, 310
Bonaventure, St. 110, 182
Bonnard, P. 54, 56, 60, 61
Bonsirven, J. 29, 35, 258, 266, 274, 278, 279, 284, 285, 308, 312, 341, 344
Bott, J.C. 157
Botterweck, G. 293
Bornkamm, G. 35, 222, 234
Bousset, W. 29, 301, 345
Bouttier, M. 299
Bouwman G. 4
Bouyer, L. 145, 204
Braun, F.M. 113, 115, 116, 148, 170, 172, 246, 253
Braun, H. 233, 252, 340
Bréhier, A. 52
Bretschneider G. 111
Brinkmann, B. 105
Brooke, A.E. 258, 266, 269, 276, 278, 279, 297, 299, 306, 312, 320, 325, 326, 332, 336, 338
Brown, R.E. 35, 37, 111, 112, 113, 141, 143, 147, 148, 150, 153, 157, 164, 177, 187, 191, 199, 214, 252, 259, 287
Brown, S. 40
Bruno Astensis, St. 110
Büchsel, F. 48, 52, 74, 92, 113, 124, 159, 234, 244, 246, 258, 312, 314
Bultmann, R. 95, 105, 112, 124, 127, 128, 139, 147, 148, 150, 154, 164, 170, 172, 199, 207, 216, 219, 233, 234, 239, 244, 245, 246, 248, 249, 275, 276, 279, 293, 299, 301, 304, 307, 310, 311, 314, 317, 318, 320, 329, 335, 336, 340, 347, 349
Burkitt, W. 115
Burney, F.C. 113
Burton, E. 78
Burton, E.D. 72

Caekel, J. De 293
Calder, W.M. 69
Calle, F. De La 84

Calmes, Th. 109, 146, 160, 164, 172, 214, 248, 258
Calmet, A. 108, 182
Calvin, J. 111, 180, 345
Camelot, Th. 142
Campitelli, A. 293
Carmignac, J. 30, 31, 34, 41
Carpenter, J.W. 171, 180
Castellini, G. 112
Cerfaux, L. 75, 78, 348
Chaine, J. 244, 246, 258, 265, 312, 317, 319
Charlier, C. 113, 311
Charue, A.M. 259, 266, 274
Chmiel, J. 298
Chromatius of Aquileja 276
Chrysostom, John 60, 79, 106, 107, 114, 172, 181, 182, 188, 199, 204, 214, 248
Clarke, W.N. 4
Clement of Alexandria 114, 259, 269, 342
Clement of Rome 184
Clifford, M.F. 273
Comblin, J. 55, 323
Conchas, D.A. 85
Conrad, Martin 108
Cook, W.R. 259, 266, 349
Cooke, G. 18, 20
Cornely, R. 78
Courtney, M.J. 14
Couture, P. 279, 284, 285
Cramer, J.A. 228, 266
Creed, J.M. 62
Croix, M. De La 186
Cullmann, O. 172, 199, 202, 206, 223, 322
Cyril of Alexandria 79, 106, 114, 148, 156, 165, 172, 182, 199, 204, 214

Dahl, N.A. 220
D'Aragon J.L. 215, 217
Daube, D. 11
Decourtray, A. 143
Deissmann, A. 74, 91, 158
Delcor, M. 34
Delhaye, Ph. 327
Delling, G. 147

Depke, A. 91
Descamps, A. 248, 250
Dey, J. 173
Dibelius, M. 276
Dieterich, A. 47
Dillersberger, J. 62
Denechin, O. De 193
Dobschütz, E. Von 233
Dodd, C.H. 51, 95, 143, 148, 211, 216, 252, 254, 266, 269, 273, 276, 278, 279, 284, 286, 287, 288, 293, 299, 307, 312, 323, 326, 328, 341
Donatus Ab Hamrum 2
(Donatus A Marsa) 2, 129, 152, 180, 195, 232, 331
Dorado, Simon 150
Driver, S. 12
Dupont, J. 53, 58, 59, 61, 220, 229, 298
Dupont-Sommer, A. 40, 41
Duprez, A. 78
Dydymus Alexandrinus 106, 269, 276, 277

Eichholz, G. 239
Elmert, W. 71
Ely, M.R. 293
Enslin, M.S. 314
Ephrem, St. 83
Erigena, J. Scotus 106, 107, 184, 185, 204
Eusebius of Caesaria 188, 203
Euthymius 106, 107, 182, 199, 204, 214, 215, 248

Feine, P. 69, 267
Fensham, F.C. 13
Festugière, A.J. 48, 133
Feuillet, A. 4, 125, 133, 134, 170, 211, 233, 241, 307, 313, 317
Foerster, W. 56, 149
Forestell, J.T. 157
Fowler, R. 180

Gaeta, G. 167, 171, 209
Gaffney, J. 142, 144
Galbiati, E. 10
Galtier, P. 258, 265, 266

Galot, J. 113, 115, 116, 118, 119, 131, 132
Garrigues, J.M. 154
Gärtner, B.E. 345
Gärtner, J.B. 38, 41
Gaugler, E. 324, 329
Geldenhuys, N. 62
Gingrich, F.W. 172
Goguel, M. 216
Goodrick, A.T.S. 22
Grässer, E. 260
Gray, G.B. 21
Gross, J. 332
Grossouw, W. 4
Grotius, H. 180
Grundmann, W. 54, 55, 60, 61, 63, 64, 66, 67, 176, 177, 186
Guerrier, L. 114
Guhrt, J. 139
Guilbert, P. 34
Guillerand, A. 109, 110
Gundry, R.H. 290
Gutierrez, P. 160
Gyllenberg, R. 16

Habermann, A.M. 32
Häring, T. 241, 341
Haller, A.H. 183
Hamilton, N.Q. 87
Hanse, H. 321
Harnack, A.V.s.c. 70, 71, 113, 114, 118, 120, 122, 124, 126, 276, 277, 279, 280
Harrison, F. 343
Hauck, F. 196
Hawthorne, G.F. 142, 144
Hehn, J. 174
Heise, J. 273
Hering, J. 345
Herkenrath, J. 267, 278
Hester, J.D. 69, 71
Holtzmann, H.J. 338, 340, 341
Holzmeister, U. 164
Hort, J.A. 129
Hoskyns, E.C. 112, 148, 164, 171, 172, 179, 199, 201
Houssiau, A. 112
Howard, W.D. 308

Howard, W.F.   91, 158, 180
Hubg, J.   327
Huftier, M.   327
Huther, J.E.   97, 325, 340, 345

Iersel, B.M.F. Van   29
Ignatius of Antioch   115, 131, 199
Ireneus, St.   114, 115, 184, 203
Irigoin, J.   133

Jaubert, A.   209
Jeremias, J.   10, 29, 171, 176
Jerome, St.   172, 188, 276
Jervell, J.   125
Johnson, S.E.   65
Jones, G.H.   19
Jonghe, M.De   206
Josephus   33
Justin, St.   115, 172, 184, 203

Kaçur, P.   153
Käsemann, E.   233
Kennedy, H.A.A.   284
Kern, O.   47
Kern, W.   252
Klein, F.N.   298
Klostermann, E.   56
Knabenbauer, J.   148, 214
Knight, G.A.F.   9
Knox, R.A.   274
Kohler, M.   284
Kümmel, W.G.   4, 154
Kuhn, K.G.   302
Kuschke, A.   159
Kuss, O.   78
Kuyper, L.J.   153

Lacan, M.Fr.   133, 134
Lacoque, A.   11, 12
Lagrange, M.J.   9, 16, 18, 46, 60, 72, 74, 78, 111, 118, 129, 130, 139, 148, 150, 164, 172, 199, 201, 203, 204, 248
Lamarche, P.   112, 124, 188
Lammers, B.   273
Lapide, Cornelius, A.   182, 215
Law, R.   97, 195, 210, 249, 257, 259,

268, 296, 298, 322, 325, 338, 339, 341, 344, 345, 346
Lazure, N.   210, 239, 257, 259, 267, 284, 312, 314
Lee, E.K.   183
Leenhardt, F.J.   84
Legasse, S.   61, 67
Leipoldt, J.   75
Lelong, A.   183
Léon-Dufour, X.   170, 198
Lewis, A.S.   115
Lewis, E.   86
Lietzmann, H.   72
Light, J.   33, 41
Lightfoot, R.H.   214, 219, 222
Lindblom, J.   211, 214
Loewe, H.   83
Lofthouse, W.F.   127
Lohmeyer, E.   279
Lohmeyer, H.   241
Lohmeyer, R.   66
Loisy, A.   105, 113, 117, 118, 139, 148, 199, 214, 246, 248, 258
Louw, J.   181
Lührmann, D.   58
Luther, M.   111, 185
Lyonnet, S.   72, 78, 84, 85, 273

Mac Gregor, G.H.C.   113, 148
Malatesta, E.   273
Maldonatus, J.   108, 182, 214, 217, 248
Manson, T.W.   65, 212
Marchel, W.   9, 21, 22, 23, 29, 35, 45, 46, 76, 333
Martin, D.   111
Massaux, E.   184
Maximus the Confessor   228, 266
McCarthy, D.J.   17, 18, 20
McCarthy, D.J.   17, 18, 20
McHugh, J.   113
McKenzie, J.L.   9, 18, 21, 23
McNeile, A.H.   64
McPolin, J.   120
Melanchton, Philip   111
Mendner, S.   164
Mensching, G.   45
Mersch, E.   309, 335

Meyer, H.A.W. 151
Meyer, W. 77
Michaelis, W. 86
Michel, O. 80, 84, 322
Michl, J. 274
Miller, J.W. 285
Milligan, W.M. 288, 292
Miranda, J.P. 125
Moffat, J. 190, 312
Mollat, D. 121, 128, 142, 170, 177, 188
Montefiore, C.G. 29, 89
Moore, G.F. 260, 302
Moraldi, L. 16, 37
Morin, D.G. 114
Moulton, J.H. 91, 147, 158
Mouroux, J. 310
Mowinckel, S. 41
Mülhaupt, E. 111
Mussner, F. 193, 195, 196, 211

Nagl, E. 241
Natalis, A. 108, 182, 183
Nauck, W. 189, 194, 232, 233, 234, 235, 258, 274, 275, 276, 279, 281, 318, 322, 323
Neugebauer, F. 75
Niederwimmer, K. 70
Nilsson, M.P. 45
Nielson, S.H. 33, 38, 41
Nötscher, F. 33, 37, 293
Noth, M. 19
Nygren, A. 305

O'Connell, M. 17
Odeberg, H. 180, 259, 260, 338
Oepke, A. 75, 78, 90, 160
Oke, C.C. 86, 160, 241
Oliveira, C.J.P. De 153
O'Neill, J.C. 278
Origen 83, 114, 172, 184, 214, 219, 222, 279
Otzen, B. 37

Padovani, Anti. 108
Panimolle, S.A. 133, 134, 135, 154
Pascher, J. 198
Pecorara, G. 273

Percy, E. 85
Philips, G.L. 206
Philo, 50, 51, 52, 53, 361
Photius 228, 266, 269
Piper, O. 233
Places, É. Des 45, 46
Plummer, A. 59, 60, 63
Porter, F.C. 260
Potterie, I. De La 34, 76, 120, 130, 143, 144, 147, 154, 163, 164, 170, 171, 176, 178, 183, 184, 186, 187, 189, 191, 234, 239, 244, 245, 257, 258, 265, 266, 267, 269, 272, 274, 275, 293, 324
Powell, J.U. 45
Preisker, H. 233
Preiss. T. 248
Procksch, O. 9
Prunet, O. 265, 291
Pseudo Athanasius 115

Radermacher, L. 91
Ramsay, W.M. 69
Randall, J.F. 196, 217
Ratzinger, J. 299
Reitzenstein, R. 48, 274, 345
Resch, A. 113, 114, 125, 183
Resch, G. 183
Reuss, J. 228
Reville, J. 105
Ribera, Francis 108, 182, 183
Ricca, P. 239, 349
Richardson, A. 205
Richter, G. 187
Richter, W. 20
Ridderbos, H. 133, 134
Riedl, J. 129
Riedmatten, H. de 115
Riesenfeld, H. 285
Rigaux, B. 62
Robert, A. 4
Robinson, D.W.B. 180
Robinson, H.W. 212
Robinson, J.A.T. 105
Robinson, T.E. 98
Roets, A. 342
Rolla, A. 172
Romaniuk, K. 79, 349

Roosen, A. 79
Rossell, W.H. 69, 70
Rost, L. 19
Rothe 97
Roustang, F. 164, 198
Rupertus Abbatus Tuitiensis 106, 107, 185, 191, 214
Ryle, J.C. 190

Saillard, M. 77
Sasse, H. 211
Schaefer, O. 298
Schanz, P. 109, 148, 200, 214, 219
Scharbert, G. 12
Schlafer, F.G. 2
Schlatter, A. 148, 201, 214
Schlier, H. 72, 74, 75, 76, 77, 78, 202, 207
Schmid, J. 54, 60, 112, 117, 118, 120, 121, 122, 126
Schmidt, C. 114, 115, 116
Schmidt, K.L. 205, 221, 222
Schnackenburg, R. 111, 112, 113, 120, 126, 132, 139, 145, 150, 153, 159, 164, 173, 181, 183, 189, 196, 199, 204, 205, 211, 233, 244, 246, 250, 258, 266, 269, 273, 274, 275, 276, 278, 279, 280, 284, 299, 304, 307, 310, 312, 313, 317, 325, 326, 327, 328, 332, 336, 339, 340, 341, 342, 344, 345, 348
Schniewind, J. 60, 297
Schoenberg, M.W. 69, 70
Schrenk, G. 65, 128, 333, 334
Schruners, P. 66
Schürmann, H. 64
Schutz, R. 307, 312
Schweizer, E. 64, 69, 186, 189, 198, 203
Schwertschlager, R. 241
Scott, W. 48
Seebass, H. 250
Seeberg, A. 322
Seesemann, H. 159, 196
Segalla, G. 113, 120
Segond, A. 279, 280
Selwyn, E.G. 345
Severius, Sulpice 115

Severus of Antioch 228, 266
Sidebottom, E.M. 61
Sieffert, Fr. 76
Sisti, P.A. 304
Sjöberg, E. 25, 35, 37
Skrinjar, A. 259, 311
Slipyj, J. 211, 214
Smalley, S. 186
Soden, Von 98, 276
Soiron, Th. 60
Spicq, C. 57, 59, 303, 307, 308, 312, 313, 326, 329, 348
Stählin, G. 239
Stauffer, E. 307
Stevens, G.B. 3, 150, 232
Strathmann, H. 219, 220, 221
Straub, W. 75
Streeter, B.H. 116
Suitbertus, A. 310
Sukenik, E.L. 32
Summers, R. 199, 203
Surjansky, A.J. 129
Sutcliffe, E.F. 37
Swetnam, J. 84
Synge, F.C. 339

Tenney, M.C. 179
Tertullian 113, 114, 116, 172, 188, 203
Thayer, J.H. 276
Theodore of Mopsuestia 114, 156, 181
Theophylactus 106, 107, 165, 182, 199, 204, 214, 215, 228, 248, 266, 269, 276, 297, 342
Theron, D.J. 70
Thomas Aquinas, St. 59, 110, 185, 270
Thompson, W.G. 66
Thüsing, W. 201
Tietze, G. 293
Tillmann, F. 105, 109, 148, 164, 172, 267
Tinegan, J. 216
Tischendorf, C. 115, 276
Toletus, F. 200
Tracts, C. 164, 188, 207, 208
Twisselmann, W. 2, 45, 47, 71, 74, 173, 341, 342

INDICES

Vallisoleto, X.M. 74
Vancells, J.O.T. 286
Van Den Bussche, H. 111, 139, 145, 160, 164, 170, 188, 248
Van Hartingsveld, L. 239
Vanhoye, A. 256
Van Imschoot, P. 9, 174
Vawter, B. 188, 189
Vellanickal, M. 128
Venard, L. 129
Vergote, A. 214
Viard, A. 112
Viau, E. 293
Villette, L. 183
Vincent, M.R. 69, 169, 173, 201
Von Rad, G. 13
Voste, J.M. 150, 183
Vrede, W. 246, 274
Vriezen, Th. C. 14

Walter F. Adeney 163
Walvoord, J.F. 212
Warnach, V. 312
Weisengoff, J.P. 160
Weiss, B. 54, 55, 248, 276, 279, 280, 283, 305, 328, 338, 341, 342

Wellhausen, J. 54, 55, 170
Wendt, H.H. 170
Westcott, B.F. 95, 96, 105, 109, 120, 129, 146, 148, 164, 173, 179, 204, 207, 214, 219, 222, 229, 244, 247, 248, 249, 251, 258, 278, 279, 294, 296, 300, 301, 306, 313, 317, 320, 324, 325, 327, 332, 336, 339, 341, 344, 345, 347
Whaling, T. 69
White, R.E.O. 212
Wikenhauser, A. 113, 196
Williams, A.L. 29
Windisch, H. 54, 55, 56, 233, 258, 266, 279, 312, 318, 326, 341
Wittichen, C. 9
Wohlenberg, G. 279, 280
Wolfson, H.A. 50
Wuest, K.S. 130
Zahn, Th. 59, 72, 76, 98, 109, 113, 114, 118, 151, 179, 203, 212, 214
Zedda, S. 78, 79

Zerwick, M. 78, 138, 158, 168, 291, 306, 312, 325
Zorell, F. 11, 12, 98, 150, 168, 194

INDEX OF SUBJECTS

Abba : 78-80
Abel : prototype of Sonship, 301
Abiding of God : 195-196
Abraham : 51, 255
 blessing of, 70
 children of, 93
 seed of, 255
 son of, 173
 sons of, 70
Adam : 23, 37
Adoption : 19
 eschatological, 80-81, 83-87
 Pauline doctrine of, 69-73
Agape : 57, 308
 eschatological aspect of, 348
 perfected, 348

Ahaz : 15
Anti-Christs : 257
Aratos : 43, 45
Assimilation to Christ (God) : 343-346
Attis : 47

Baptism : 75, 171, 181, 183, 190-191
 and faith, 187-190
 and freedom from sin, 108
 infant, 171
Become : 59-61
Begetting :
 divine,
  effect of, 232
  three stages of, 238-239
  from above, 169-174

from God, 96-97, 98-102
from the Spirit, 174-179, 191-192
  in later Judaism, 175
  in the Old Testament, 174-175
from water and spirit, 179-190
by baptism, 190
by God, 101-103
of Israel, 23
spiritual, absolute necessity, 168-169
supernatural, 121ff
  absolute necessity of, 167ff
  condition of, 168
  nature of, 169-197
Begotten of God : 117, 278
Believe : 141-146
  in Christ, 143-145
  in his name, 145-146
Birth :
  divine,
    in baptismal tradition, 295
    of the believers, 122
    from God, 98ff
    and love of the Father, 236
    into the life of the children of God, 163-202
  Messianic, 38
  of Christ, 122
  of the community, 38-41
  spiritual, 51, 132
  through the gospel, 77, 270
  through the teacher, 175
  through Truth, 42
Blood : 187-189
Born :
  of God, criterion, 262
  of the flesh, 197-198
  of the Spirit, 197-202
Brother : 299

Caiaphas : 218, 219, 223
Cain : 299, 300, 301, 315
  prototype of diabolic sonship, 301
Child of God : 211, 302
Children of God : 91-95, 242, 261, 313-314, 325-326, 328
  become, 138, 139-141
  birth into the life of, 163-225
  confidence of, 347-349

criterion or fruit of, 242
existential definition of, 302-303
freedom of, 286-294
future condition of, 338
gathering of, 223
glory of, 341
impeccability of, 265-294
life of, 210, 211
love for, 319
power to become, 105-161
scattered, 215
similar to Christ, 335
Christ :
  advocate, 249
  birth of, 125
  divine origin of, 118-119
  divinity of, 127
  exemplar, 262
  expiation, 249
  kingship of, 205-206
  light, 140, 157-158, 161
  likeness to, 340-342
  object of faith, 146
  putting on, 75-76
  revelation, 145
  righteous, 244, 246-251, 261
  salvific revealer, 134-135
  son of God, 119, 128
  sonship of,
    expression of, 328
    fulness of, 153-156
  the only begotten, 92, 120-121
  virginal birth of, 132
  vision of, 343-344
Christians : 4
Cleanth : 45
Commandment : 193
Commandments : observance of, 296
Communion : 195-197
  knowledge of, 335, 336, 337, 343
  meal of, 15
  with Christ, 81
  with God, 241, 320
  with the Father and Son, 216
  with the Truth, 293
Community :
  born of the power of God, 41
  covenantal, 35

messianic, 40
Confidence : eschatological, 347-349
Conversion : 76, 176-177
Covenant : 31, 35-36, 70
  Davidic, 19, 30
  Mosaic, 30
  New, 25, 175
  Old, 25
  restoration of, 14
  Sinaitic, 15, 20

Demeter : 47
Devil : children of, 93-94, 96, 243, 267
Disciples : 296
  becoming, 291
  of Moses, 291
Discipleship :
  change into, 140
  manifestation of, 291

Election : 31
Eleusian Mysteries : 47
Emmanuel : 41
Ephraim : 15
Epictetus : 46
Exodus : 10, 13, 14

Faith : 76
  and spirit, 190
  as conversion, 176-177
  confession of, 320
  content of, 143
  dynamic, 139, 144
  elements of, 319
  gift of, 190
  life of, 82-83, 191
  of the Jews, 164-165
Father : the righteous, 249
Fatherhood :
  of devil, 94
  of God, 22-23
Fellowship between God and man : 249
First-born :
  of Egypt, 10
  of Yahweh, 12-13
Flesh : 198, 202
  begotten of, 197-199
  born of, 179

Free : 288, 290
Freedom :
  from sin, 282ff
  of the children of God, 290-292
  of the Son, 290
  through Christ, 286
  through the Truth, 292
  self determination, 290

Generation :
  from God, 92, 102, 180
  of Christ, 121ff
    divine, 123
    eternal, 92
    eternal and temporal, 126, 130-131
    natural, 93
    prototype, 126
    temporal, 95, 123
    virginal, 131
  of Christians, divine, 123
  supernatural, 93, 100
Glory :
  eschatological, 63
  freedom of, 87
  manifestation of, 144
God :
  abiding of, 196
  begotten of, 96-97
  being from, 296
  birth from, 309
  communion with, 193, 304, 304-305
  family of, 300
  father of the disciples, 64-66
  heir of, 86
  indwelling of, 192
  ' is love ' 307-309
  knowledge of, 50, 309, 310, 311-312
  love for, 328-329
  our Father, 334-335
  people of, 223
  providence of, 23
  revelation of, 298
  righteous, 247
  seer of, 50
  the Father, 12
  to be from, 96-97, 230
  to know, 309-310

Gospel: birth through, 77
Grace of Truth: 155-156

Homer: 45
Hope: filial, 347-350

Impeccability:
  and mutual indwelling, 272-274
  and the Holy Spirit, 273
  and the Word, 271-272
  and understanding, 284-286
  eschatological gift, 267, 294
  fruit of the life of sonship, 265-294
  nature of, 286
  of the children of God, 265-294
  participation in, 267
Indwelling: 272
Isaac: 51-52, 71
Isis: 47
Israel: 9, 50
  and love of Yahweh, 16
  election of, 70
  family of God, 15
  first-born of Yahweh, 11
  liberation and adoption of, 70

Jesus:
  Christ, 153-154
  faith in, 321
  righteousness of, 262
  son of God, 143
  the only begotten, 129-130
  the Truth, 292
Jews:
  of the dispersion, 214
  slaves to sin, 288
John the Baptist: 179, 201
Judgment: 348
Just: 21-22, 35-36
Justice:
  covenantal, 21
  personal, 21
  son of, 36

King: 18-20
Kingdom:
  entering in, 60
  of God, 205, 209
  membership in, 211-213
  seeing and entering, 203, 207
  of heaven, 203
Know: 245
Knowledge:
  of communion, 343
  of God, 50, 305, 335-337
  experiential, 310
  of the Father, 283
  of the Truth, 292

Law: interiorization of, 175
Liberation:
  and adoption, 71-72
  from Egypt, 10
  of Israel, 11
Life:
  Christian, beginning of, 323
  community of, 335
  eternal, 208-211
  ethical, 159-160
  of divine sonship, 309, 317 ff
  of faith, 82
  of sonship, 194, 320, 331, 349
  of the children of God, 210, 326
  of the sons of God, 82
Light:
  God is, 298
  in Hellenistic philosophy and Gnosticism, 298
  prince of, 36
  'self revelation of God', 298
  Sons of, 34, 37, 41, 125, 157-160
Likeness:
  moral, 18
  of conduct, 261
  to Christ, 340-341
Logos:
  reception of, 138
  the first-born, 51
  the mediator, 51
Love:
  and the Spirit, 193-194
  brotherly, 295-297, 299, 300
  basis of, 314
  criterion of, 328
  object of, 329
  relation to sonship, 296-300

root of, 318
test of, 329
covenantal, 16, 27
direction of, 327
divine and infused, 307
divine, natural expression of, 315
exemplar and origin of, 348
  expression of divine sonship, 295-316
father-son relationship, 308
gift of God, 314
God is, 51, 303, 307-309
' is of God ', 306-307
life of God, 315
merciful, 59
movement of, 327
observance of commandments, 324
communion with God, 304
of enemies, 56, 61
of God, 326
of Israel, 16
of the Father, 57
origin and communication of, 312
perfection of, 192
to the Father, 328
Trinitarian life, 308, 309

Loving :
  criterion of ' birth from God ', 305
  fruit of ' birth from God ', 305

Message : christian, 297
Messiah : 54
Messianic peace : 54
Mithraic Liturgy : 47
Mithras : 47
Moses : 80
Nathan : 19
Nation :
  in the New Testament, 220-222
  in the LXX, 219-220
  Jewish, 223

Nicodemus : 163-166, 170, 172-175, 179-180

Only begotten of God : 129-130

Peace-makers : 53-55
Peace : messianic, 54
People :
  in the New Testament, 220-222
  in the LXX, 219-220
  of God, 220
  of Israel, 219
Perfection : 57 ff
  of the Father, 57
Pharaoh : 12
Power : 149-152
  diabolic, 259
  divine life, 149
Prayer of intercession : 30

Rebirth in the Mystery Religions : 47-49
Redemption :
  of Israel, 11
  of the bodies, 87
Regeneration :
  baptismal, 212
  gnostic, 49
  in Corpus Hermeticum, 47-49
  pantheistic, 49
Remain in my Word : 293
Repentance : 212
Revelation : response and participation, 134-135
Righteous : Christ as, 246-250
Righteousness : 250
  criterion of divine sonship, 227-263
  doing, 295
  ethical duty of, 349
  of Christ, 248
    source and exemplar, 250
  of the Father, 251
  teacher of, 38
  triumphant, 251, 296

Sacrifice : substitutional, 12
Sadducees : 62
Salvation :
  economy of, 124
  eschatological, 204-205
  final stage of, 346
See : 203
Seed :

of Abraham, 268, 288, 289, 290
of God, 103, 266, 268 ff
Seeing : 207
Sin : 257-260
   diabolic power, 258
   eschatological, 259
   freedom from, 289
   iniquity, 258-260
   Jewish concept, 260
   opposition to the will of God, 259
Sins : works of the devil, 258
Sinlessness : 272-274
Slavery of sin : 287-288
Slaves : son and, 287-288
Son :
   communion with, 292
   obedience of, 250
   of God, 51
      and Christ, 128
      and Christ's mission, 128
      and the Son of man, 251
   of Yahweh, 18
   and Truth, 254
Sons :
   adoption of, 70
   of darkness, 36, 37, 41
   of God, 35, 45, 50, 51, 53-55, 56-58, 60
      adoption of, 70
      freedom of, 288-290
      glory of, 85, 288-290
      in Christ, 74-77
      sons of the Resurrection, 63
      the just, 35
   of his Covenant, 34
   of his Truth, 34, 35
   of light, 36-37
   of the Resurrection, 60-61
   of the kingdom, 66
   of the promise, 70
   of your Father in Heaven, 58
Sonship : 3
   adoptive, 33
   and discipleship, 254
   christian, 136
      and faith and love, 311
      Pauline doctrine of, 69-87
   communication of, 123

covenantal, 13
criterion of, 255
diabolic, 102
   criteria, 243, 252
   manifestation of, 256-260, 289, 300-302
   of man, 95
   of the Jews, 255-257
   source of hatred, 302
divine, 102
   and beatific vision, 346-347
   and brotherly love, 295
   and individual, 20-21
   dynamism of, 107
   expression of, 316
   and faith experience, 319-325
   and fraternal charity, 46
   freedom proper to, 286-294
   germinal, 106
   gift of, 135
   gift of God, 92
   grace of, 156
   grades of, 108
   growth in the life of, 309
   individual, 46
   in two stages, 228
   and joy 52
   life of, 317-330
   love the expression of, 295-316
   manifestation of, 261-262, 289, 298
   means of growing in, 316
   of Christ, 92, 127-128
      eternal and temporal, 145
      manifestation of, 145
   of Christians, 78
      in Synoptic Gospels, 53-68
   of Israel, 10-15
      as begetting by God, 23-24
   of Jesus, 66
      Messiahship, 128
   of Man, 95
      and Christ, 66-67
      in Hellenism, 45-49
      in Later Judaism, 29-43
      in Philo, 50-52
      in the Old Testament, 9-27
   of men, 92

of the believers, 136
of the community, 29, 31
of the king, 18
temporal evolution of, 109
through election and covenant, 29-35
through the death of Christ, 214-224
through the Truth, 175
universality of, 107, 299
dynamic, 105-110
eschatological, 63
eschatological manifestation of, 345
freedom of, 254
future state of, 337 ff
grace of, 154
hidden condition of, 339-340
Israel's, 17
life of, 194, 312, 321
life of and incentive for, 349
manifestation, two fold Johannine scheme, 231-232
of Christ, 261
   temporal, 92
of Christians, 261
   eschatological development, 331-351
of Israel, 31, 69, 70, 71, 80
   adoptive, 15
   eschatological, 25-26
of the disciples, 67
of the Jews, 255
present life of, 331 ff
source of, 312
static, 110-112
Spirit : 181, 183, 186
and eschatological adoption, 86
as wind, 199-203
begetting from, 174-178, 191-193
born of, 41, 197-199, 200
communication of, 191
given to us, 192
Holy, 41, 191-193
   active principle of sonship 80
   cause of adoption, 79-80
   principle of new life, 177
   witness of adoption, 78-79

of Yahweh, 25
of the Son, 81, 82
of Truth, 177
principle of impeccability, 270
principle of life, 193-195
seal of, 187
source of new life, 175
Suffering : 83

Truth : 292
revelation, 154
sons of, 36, 37

Unction : 274-275
by God, 187
Understanding : 84-86

Victory :
baptismal character, 323
baptismal tradition, 323
eschatological, 324
of the divinely born, 324-325
over the evil one, 283
over the world, 272
past and present, 325
the anticipation of 324
Vision :
Consequence of, 344-346
possibility of, 347
the direct object of, 343-344
Voice : 201

Water : 167, 179-181, 182-183, 186, 191
Word :
dwelling of the, 271
remain in the, 293
remaining in the, 253-254
the Truth, 254
World : 96
conquering the, 325
hatred of the, 299
incapability of the, 335
sinful, 282
victory over the, 324
Worship : 51

Zeus : 45

INDEX OF REFERENCES

BIBLICAL REFERENCES

OLD TESTAMENT

Genesis

1:2 ff	174
3:5	342
3:14 ff	23
6:2	9
22:18	23
42:5	90
45:21	90
46:12	90
49:3	13
49:8	13

Exodus

1-15	11
1:1	90
1:1-2:22	10
1:1-7:7	10
1:22	12
2:23-3:12	10
2:23-7:7	10
3:12	13
3:13-6:9	10
4:21-23	10
4:22	9, 12, 16, 19, 31, 40
4:22-23	10, 11, 273
4:23	13
6:4-7	17
6:6	10
6:8	13
6:10-7:7	10
13:2	12
13:11-16	12
19:5	13
24:5-8	15, 19
24:11	15
30:33	36
30:38	36
33:13	220
33:20	18
34:6	153, 154
34:19-20	11
34:24	14

Leviticus

11:44-45	18
11:45	18
17:9	36
17:14	36
18:19	270
18:24	14
19:2	18
19:23	11
20:7	18
20:26	18
25:44	14
26:12	17
26:16	220

Numbers

3:12	11, 12
3:41	11
8:16	12
8:16-17	11
11:12	40
14:15	14
18:15	12
18:15-16	11

Deuteronomy

1:31	16
4:27	14
5:16	16
7:6	220
7:7-8	16
7:8	14, 26
7:8-9	15
8:2-5	80
8:5	16, 31

10:14	13	**I Kings**	
12:31	11		
14:1	**16**, 31, 36, 50, 56	8:58	19
14:1-2	14, 220		
21:17	13	**II Kings**	
21:18-21	16		
26:17-18	17	10:6	24
28:47	285	16:7	15
30:1-3	215	23:3	19
30:11-14	25		
32:4-5	18	**I Chronicles**	
32:5-12	80		
32:6	14, 50	2:3	90
32:10	16	2:10	90
32:11-14	16	16:34	26
32:15	14	16:41	26
32:15-18	**23-24**, 99, 175		
32:17-19	17	**II Chronicles**	
32:18	14, 50		
		5:13	26
		7:3	26
Joshua		7:6	26
2:14	153		
14:8	285	**Job**	
24:1-28	19		
		1:2	9
		2:1	62
I Samuel			
		Psalms	
9:16	20		
10:1	20	2:7	18, 19, 20, 99
13:14	20	10:14	34
25:30	20	23:3-6	343
26:19	25	23:15	343
		23:16	343
		31:7	56
II Samuel		33:6	174
		36:31	270
2:6	153	47	23
5:2	20	50:12	23
6:21	20	71:3	54
7:8	20	71:7	55
7:9-10	18	77:38	55
7:11-14	20	84(85):11	153
7:14	9, 18, 19	85:5	55
7:14-17	20	85:10	26
15:20	153	89:7	62
22:5	40	89:26-27	19
22:47	24		

89:27	12, 18, 22, 24	23:1	22
95:1	24	23:4	22
100:5	26	24:26	270
102:8 f	55	51:10	22
103:7	26		
103:13	16	**Isaiah**	
110:3	18, 19, 99		
118:11	270	1:2	16, 24, 99, 175
120:7 f	55	1:2-3	17, 25
136	26	1:2-4	22
139:1	17	3:12-15	14
139:21	56	5:13	14
144:8 f	55	6:10	14
145:9	23	7:14	315
147:18	174	8:6	14
		8:14	17
Proverbs		9:6	54
		9:7	54
4:4	285	11:4	174
9:6	270	23:4	24
27:19	285	26:3	54
		26:12	54
Canticle of Canticles		30:1	25
		30:1-5	17
8:2	24	30:9	25
		32:15	174
Wisdom		32:17	54, 249
		34:16	174
2:12	22	35:9	11
2:13	9, **21-22**, 26	37:3	40
2:16	**21-22**, 26	40:7	200
2:18	**21-22**, 26	41:10	249
5:5	26	43:5	215
9:4	22	43:5-6	80
9:7	22	43:6	31
9:12	21	43:6-7	14
11:10	21	43:7	31
12:7	22	43:16	23
12:19	22	44:3	174
12:20	22	45:9-11	24, 99, 175
12:21	22	49:7	10
14:3	23	49:13	33
16:26	21	49:21	24
18:13	12	50:3	75
		51:9	24
		51:18	24
Ecclesiasticus		52:1	75
4:10	21	52:7	54

53:3	40	34:11-13	215
54:10	54	34:25	54
55:3	26	36:16	25
56:1-66:24	10	36:25-26	25, 174
59:17	75	36:25-27	270, 284
59:20	10	36:25-28	26
59:21	26, 285	36:26 ff	175, 359
60:11	23	36:26,27	285
60:17	54	37:9	175
61:8	26	37:21 ff	215
63:7-64:11	80	37:26	54
63:8	14, 16, 220		
63:16	11		
64	215	**Daniel**	
64:7	16	9:25	20
64:8	64, 220		
65:16	285	**Hosea**	
66:7-8	40		
66:7-14	25	1:10	12, 220
66:12	54	2:1	220
		2:1-24	175
Jeremiah		2:16	15
		2:25	220
2:26-27	24, 99, 175	8:1	15
3:19-22	25	9:12	24
7:31	11	11:1	15
12:7	15		
12:15	23		
23:1-3	215	**Joel**	
24:7	284	2:28-29	174
31:1-9	14		
31:8-9	80	**Amos**	
31:8-11	215		
31:9	10, 13, 19	3:2	17
31:31	26		
31:31-34	24, 175, 284-285	**Micah**	
31:33-34	270, 272		
33:6	54	4:3	54
33:9	54	5:5	54
48:41	40		
49:22	40	**Haggai**	
		2:10	54
Baruch			
6:61	200	**Zachariah**	
		6:13	54
Ezekiel		9:10	54
20:34	215		

12:10a	188	5:45a	58
12:10-13:1	188	5:45b	57
12:10b-14:7	188	5:46	61, 64
13:1	188	5:46-47	65
		5:47	56
		5:48	53, 57, 58, 59
		6:1	53, 65

Malachi

1:6	16, 17	6:4	53, 65
2:10	14	6:6	53, 65
3:17	14, 220	6:7	149
		6:8	53
		6:9	53, 65
		6:10	64
		6:14	53

NEW TESTAMENT

Matthew

		6:14-15	57, 65
1:3-5	98	6:15	53
1:16	99, 100	6:16	60
1:20	98, 130, 202	6:18	53, 65
1:21-25	98	6:26	53
1:25	12	6:26-32	64-66
1:27	334	6:32	53
2:18	90	7:6	60
3:9	90	7:7-11	65
3:15	250	7:11	53
3:17	250	7:14	212
4:3-11	250	7:21	210, 212
4:17	17, 171	7:25	200
4:23	105	7:27	200
5:1-2	65	7:28-29	65
5:7	57	9:2	90
5:7-9	55	9:22	60
5:8	342, 343, 345	9:35	205
5:8-9	346	9:36	55
5:9	**53-56**, 64, 65, 66, 211, 212, 229, 362	10:7-8	205
		10:16	60, 139
5:12	65	10:20	53, 64
5:16	53, 65	10:22	212
5:19	56, 64	10:29	53
5:20	210	11:1	65
5:39	60	11:25-27	66, 67, 362
5:39-48	58	11:27	251
5:43	59	12:20	249
5:43-48	**56-60**, 61	12:28	64, 205
5:44	56	12:46 ff	212
5:44-45	59, 61, 64, 66	12:48-50	66, 67, 362
5:44-48	57	13:3-8	270
5:45	53, 55, 59, 60, 61, 64, 66, 211, 229, 362	13:19-23	270
		13:22	139

INDICES

13:37-43	66	26:29		64
13:43	53, 64	26:42		67
13:53	65	26:53		65
14:23	251	26:63 ff		251
15:13	65	27:3		60
16:17	65	27:51		172
16:21-23	251	27:54		251
16:23	60	28:19		53, 186
16:28	205, 206			
17:1-8	251	**Mark**		
17:22-23	251			
17:22-18:35	66	1:15	76, 171,	176
17:25-27	**66**, 362	3:31 ff		212
18:1-4	**60-61**, 212	3:31-35		67
18:3	171, 176, 362	3:35		67
18:8	210, 212	4:19		139
18:9	206, 210	8:38		345
18:10	65	9:1	205,	206
18:14	64, 65	9:43		206
18:19	65	9:45		206
18:19-20	65	9:46		206
18:21	57	10:14 ff		212
18:35	65	10:15	171, 176,	362
19:1	65	10:17		206
19:12	100	10:23		206
19:16	206, 212	10:29		205
19:17	210	10:30		210
19:19	59	11:2		339
19:21	59	11:10		205
19:23	206	11:17		56
19:29	205, 210, 212	11:25	53,	57
20:28	55	11:26		53
21:13	64	13:12		90
21:28	90	13:32		334
21:28-32	212	13:36		345
21:31	64	14:36		74
21:43	64	15:39		251
22:39	59	16:15-16	186,	190
23:9	53, 65	16:16		170
23:12	61			
23:31	56	**Luke**		
23:35	302			
23:37	91	1:3		172
24:36	334	1:7		90
24:44	60	1:17		90
25:34	65, 210	1:31		192
25:46	210, 212	1:32	64,	315
26:1	65	1:35	64, 98, 99, 100, 130,	315

1:36	315	20:36	53, **61-63**, 229, 363
1:50	57	21:28	85
1:54	57	23:2	221
1:58	57	23:47	251
1:78	57	24:6	63
2:2-11	205	24:32	63
2:7	12		
2:14	54	**John**	
4:1	80		
6:27	56	1:1-2	126
6:27-28	56	1:1-18	132, 134, 135, 309
6:27-36	58	1:2-18	124
6:32-36	56	1:3-18	133
6:35	53, 64	1:4-5	141
6:35b	61	1:4-16	157
6:36	53, 57, **58**	1:7	177
7:5	221	1:9	298
7:22	63	1:9-14	125, 131
7:36-50	57	1:10	335
7:47	57	1:10-11	257
7:47-48	307	1:10-12	148
7:50	212	1:11	152
8:19	212	1:11-13	147
9:1	149	1:12	1, 4, 90, 92, 96, 97, 144, 160, 163, 170, 178, 224, 227, 228, 261, 288, 310, 333, 353
9:27	205, 206		
10:21	334		
10:25	63, 212		
11:2	53		
11:4	57	1:12-13	2, **105-152**, 163, 207, 213, 215
11:13	53		
11:20	205	1:12-14	124, 126, 140
12:5	149	1:12-15	118
12:15	210	1:12-16	161
12:30	53	1:12-18	129, 155, 156
12:32	53	1:13	1, 92, 100, 172, 177, 178, 154, 198, 255, 262, 280, 335, 353
12:57	216		
14:14	63		
16:25	90, 210	1:14	92, 117, 130, 345
18:14	61	1:14-17	153
18:17	171, 176, 212, 362	1:14-18	124
18:18	63, 206	1:16	**152-156**, 354
18:29	205	1:16-18	154
18:30	210	1:17	292
19:9	212	1:18	92, 121, 308, 344
19:38	205	1:19	118
19:42-45	54	1:23	201
20:34-36	**62-63**	1:25-33	151
20:35-36	63	1:29	114

1:31	245	3:16	127, 130, 160, 210, 310, 313
1:32	201	3:16-18	129, 213
1:33	179, 245	3:18	120, 145, 146, 213
1:42	315	3:18-21	144
1:44	201	3:19	125, 198, 300
1:51	201	3:19-21	157, 298
2:11	143, 345	3:22	181
2:23	120, 213	3:23	181
2:23-3:2	164	3:26	181
2:23-3:21	163, 213	3:29	201
2:24	127	3:31	95, 128, 172, 198, 201, 307
2:29-3:10	227		
3:1	332	3:33	177
3:1-16	123	3:35	201, 309, 313
3:2-3	206	3:36	177, 206, 210
3:2-10	171	3:63	177
3:3	170, 177, 197, 203, 209, 312, 215, 227, 333, 354, 362	4:1-2	181
		4:1-6	198
3:3-5	167	4:10	245
3:3-6	117	4:24	307
3:3-8	1, 121	4:27	203
3:3-9	122	4:32	245
3:3-10	**163-213**	4:34	260
3:4	254	4:47	302
3:5	60, 107, 171, 172, 176-178, 181, 183-185, 190-192, 197, 209, 213, 215, 224, 227, 333, 354, 362	4:50	142, 210
		4:51	210
		4:53	210
		5:4-9	140
		5:6	201
3:5-6	177	5:14-21	281
3:5-8	355	5:15	203
3:6	172, 177, 179, 198, 202, 228, 269, 273, 280, 307, 331, 354	5:16	336
		5:17	309
		5:18	127, 336
3:7	229, 254	5:18-26	357
3:8	172, 198, 200, 225, 228, 267, 280, 355	5:19	168, 198, 309
		5:20	201, 203, 309
3:10	198	5:21	200, 201, 309
3:11-12	177	5:23	309
3:11-14	209	5:24	144, 210
3:11-21	164, **208-213**	5:25	201
3:11-33	147	5:26	157, 200
3:12	198	5:27	149
3:14	200	5:28	201, 203
3:14-15	214, 355	5:30	248
3:14-18	209	5:35	201
3:15	210	5:36	314

5:37	201	8:14-23	119
5:39	210	8:15	198
5:40	201, 210	8:21	257
5:43	147, 334	8:23	95, 177, 198, 307, 347
5:45	334	8:24	257
5:46-47	142	8:26	292
6	201	8:28	245, 309
6:11	201	8:29	309
6:18	200	8:29-55	260
6:21	201	8:30-47	271
6:27	334	8:30-59	259
6:29	144, 259	8:31	253, 273, 274, 284, 288, 291, 294, 356
6:32	334		
6:35	144	8:31-32	261, 274, 275, 293
6:37	314	8:31-36	265, 286, 292, 357
6:38	260	8:31-47	119, 227, **252-260**, 261, 262, 293, 356
6:39	314		
6:40	144, 210	8:32	245, 293
6:45	144	8:33	268, 288
6:46	95, 309	8:34	256, 257, 258, 287, 289
6:47	144, 210, 245	8:35	288
6:51-56	198	8:35-36	287
6:53 ff	210	8:36	261, 288
6:54	144	8:37	256, 268
6:57	157	8:38	256, 260, 287
6:57 ff	210	8:39	56, 93, 256
6:63	180, 198	8:40	256, 260, 287, 300
6:67	201	8:41 ff	56
6:69	245	8:42	128, 255, 256, 260, 335
7:7	300	8:42-47	101, 177
7:8-23	144	8:43	256
7:15	203	8:43-44	287
7:17	94, 201	8:43-47	144
7:18	260	8:44	93, 97, 198, 255, 256, 260, 290, 292, 329
7:21	203		
7:24	248	8:45	256
7:27	128, 329	8:46	257, 260, 261
7:27-29	119	8:47	94, 97, 198, 232, 260, 290, 335, 336
7:28	128, 344		
7:29	95, 293, 309	8:54-55	22
7:33	157	8:55	309
7:37-38	144	8:58	140
7:39	147	8:59	118
7:44	201	9:1	118
8:2	285	9:5	329
8:12	157-160	9:5-37	157
8:12-58	252	9:12	315
8:14	202	9:16	95

9:16-33	168	12:42	140
9:22	140	12:45	144
9:27	140, 201, 291	12:46	125, 160, 298
9:28	291	12:50	200
9:33	95	13:1	309
9:39	140	13:2	97
10:3	201, 310	13:14	314
10:4	201, 310	13:20	147
10:5	201	13:33-38	348
10:7-9	207	13:35	291
10:11	210	13:37	210
10:14	310	14:2	290
10:15	210, 293, 309	14:5	245
10:16	80, 140, 141, 201, 217	14:6	207, 292
10:17	210, 309, 313, 336	14:7	334
10:18	149	14:7-9	310
10:24	210	14:7-10	144
10:25-26	177	14:9	247, 334, 344
10:26	310	14:10	143, 247, 309
10:27	201, 310, 334	14:10-12	127
10:29	334	14:11	309
10:30	127, 217, 309	14:12	201
10:38	142, 168, 245, 309	14:13	347
11:22	245	14:16-17	79
11:24	245	14:17	271, 274, 354
11:27	143	14:19-20	335
11:37	168	14:20	245, 309, 310
11:43	201	14:21 ff	313
11:47-53	**214-224**, 358	14:26	178
11:48-52	220	14:27	54
11:50	222	14:31	200, 309, 314
11:50-52	221	15:1	200
11:51	219	15:1-10	195
11:52	1, 121, 214, 217, 219, 225, 355	15:3	271
		15:4	200
12:18	336	15:7	201, 245
12:21	201	15:8	140, 245, 291
12:25	210	15:9	309, 313
12:27	210	15:12	309, 314
12:28	201	15:13	210
12:30	201	15:18	245, 347
12:31	335	15:19	177, 198
12:33	127	15:21-22	257
12:35-36	125, **157-160**, 298	16:3	335
12:35-46	157	16:8-9	287
12:36	140, 161	16:8-10	248
12:39	336	16:10	251
12:41	345	16:11	248, 257, 335

Reference	Page(s)
16:13-15	178
16:15	127
16:19	201
16:21	329
16:21-22	40
16:25	335
16:27-28	128
16:28	101, 125
16:33	325
17:1	201
17:2	149, 198, 278
17:3	177, 245, 285, 335, 344
17:4	201
17:5	345
17:8	245
17:10	127
17:11	217, 281
17:12	158, 281
17:14	198
17:14-16	177
17:15	281
17:16	198
17:20-23	217
17:21	216, 310
17:21-24	346
17:21-26	216
17:22	217, 345
17:22-23	127
17:23	216, 217, 309, 310
17:23 ff	313
17:24	201, 345
17:25	245, 247, 251, 293
17:26	201, 298, 309, 310
18:8	147
18:14	221, 222
18:35	221
18:36-37	205
18:37	125, 144, 201, 335
18:46 ff	198
19:10-11	149
19:11	172, 257
19:23	172
19:33-37	187, 188
19:34	180, 189
19:35	177, 245
19:38	291
20:9	245
20:14	245
20:17	299, 334
20:22	147, 202
20:31	127, 128, 169, 210
21:4	245
21:12	245
21:18	201
21:22	201
21:23	299
21:24	245

Acts

Reference	Page(s)
1:22	63
2:2	202
2:31	63
2:38	266
2:39	90
3:15	63
3:19-26	266
3:26	63
5:4	149
5:31	266
5:39	94
7:5	90
8:12	186
8:36 ff	322
8:36-37	186, 234
9:31	289
10:22	221
10:43	266
10:45	254
11:2	254
11:17-18	176
11:26	4
13:23	80
13:23-33	81
13:30-34	63
13:33	63, 80, 261
13:38	266
15:5	254
15:14	220
16:14-15	186
16:30-33	186
17:29	3
17:31	248
18:8	186
18:10	220
19:4	176

19:4-5	186	8:17-21	239
20:21	176	8:18	340
21:20	254	8:18-39	76
23:6	63	8:19	69, 340
24:10	221	8:21	69, 71, 340, 345, 363
24:17	221	8:21-23	80
25:8	63	8:22	40
26:5	172	8:23	69, 71, 72, 76, 83, 84, 85, 363
26:18-20	176	8:26	76
26:28	4	8:28	73
28:19	221	8:29	85, 333, 342
		9:4	69, 70
		9:7 ff	363
		9:7-8	70, 71

Romans

		9:8	69, 70
1:3-4	261	9:21	149
1:4	63	9:25-27	220
1:7	333, 334	9:26	69
1:17	107	10:8	77
1:20	344	10:14	70, 234
3:22	74	10:17	234, 270
3:26	74	12:1	85
5:3-5	193, 194	13:4	85
5:5	73	13:14	75, 83
5:10	56	14:19	289
6:3-11	75	15:21	289
6:4	75		
6:10	75		
6:16-20	71		
6:17-20	259	**I Corinthians**	
7:14	85		
8	**80-87**	1:3	333, 334
8:3	73	1:30	85
8:9	289	3:9	289
8:11	81, 83, 289	4:13	85
8:14	69, 76, 79, 80, 83, 238, 239	4:14	91
8:14-16	363	4:15	77, 270, 363
8:14-17	78, 238	4:15-17	99
8:14-18	84	4:17	91
8:15	69, 70, 73, 78, 79, 178, 193, 333, 349	7:14	90
		8:1	289
8:15-16	79	8:2	339
8:15-23	108	8:6	334
8:16	69, 71, 178, 239, 363	10:23	289
8:17	69, 83, 85, 239, 332, 340, 341, 341, 345, 363	13:12	342
		14:3-5	289
		15:1-2	77

II Corinthians

1:2	333, 334
1:21-22	187
1:22	73
3:18	347
4:4-6	298
5:1	85
5:5	73
6:14 ff	220
6:18	69
11:9	277

Galatians

1:3	33, 334
1:4	333, 334
2:16	74
2:20	74, 270
3:5	73
3:10-12	72
3:10-14	70
3:13	72
3:14	72
3:17-18	254
3:19-29	75, 76, 363
3:22	74
3:22-23	72
3:23	83, 239
3:24-27	238
3:25	72
3:26	69, 77, 82, 83, 238,
3:26	69, 77, 82, 83, 238, 239
3:26-27	75, 83, 254
3:26-28	74-77
3:29	70, 239, 340
4:1-3	72
4:1-5	70
4:1-7	84
4:1-10	254
4:3-7	71
4:4	72
4:4-6	238, 363
4:4-7	71, 73, **78-79**
4:5	69, 72
4:6	70, 83, 178, 193, 239, 333
4:7	239, 323, 332
4:8	71
4:8-11	84
4:9	172
4:19	40, 79, 90
4:21-31	71, 254
4:23	100
4:24	99
4:28	69, 91
5:1-14	254
5:18	83

Ephesians

1:2	333, 334
1:5	69, 73
1:7	85
1:13	187
1:14	85
1:15	74
1:18	298
2:3	91
2:14	54
3:6	77
3:12	74
4:24	75
5:30	85
5:8-9	298
5:13-15	298
5:26	180
6:23	333

Philippians

1:2	333, 334
1:27	74
2:6	342
2:15	69, 363
3:9	74
4:9	54
4:20	334

Colossians

1:2	334
1:4	74
1:14	85
1:20	53, 54
1:21	56

1:27 349
2:5 74
2:11-12 75
2:12 . . . . 74, 83
3:1-2 238
3:3 239
3:3-4 . . . . 340, 341
3:4 . . . . 239, 345
3:10 75

I Thessalonians

1:3 334
1:9 285
3:11 . . . . 333, 334
3:13 . . . . 333, 334
5:23 54

II Thessalonians

1:1 334
1:2 333
2:13 74
2:14 77
2:16 . . . . 333, 334

I Timothy

1:1 349
1:2 . . . . 91, 333
1:14 74
3:13 74
5:22 277
6:16 344

II Timothy

1:2 333
1:10-11 77
1:13 74
3:15 . . . . 56, 74

Titus

1:4 333
2:13 345
2:14 220

3:5 . . . . 173, 178, 187, 238
3:7 . . . . 239, 323, 340

Philemon

3 334
10 99

Hebrews

2:4 107
2:10 80
3:1 234
4:14 234
7:26-27 249
10:7 67
10:23 234
11:4 302
11:12 98
12:4 339
12:11 54
12:14 . . . . 343, 346

James

1:17 172
1:17-18 . . . . . . 178, 314, 333
1:18 . . . . 180, 270
1:21 270
1:27 277
2:17 107
3:17 54
3:18 249
4:4 56

I Peter

1:2-3 333
1:3 . . . . 173, 238
1:3-5 236
1:3-22 323
1:3-23 . . . . **235-240**, 346
1:4 . . . . 236, 239, 340
1:4-5 239
1:5 . . . . 236, 340, 346
1:6-9 . . . . 326, 346
1:7 . . . . 333, 340, 341, 345
1:9 346

1:13	341, 345
1:13-16	236
1:13-20	236
1:13-2:10	236
1:14	91
1:15-16	341
1:18-20	236
1:21	345
1:22	178
1:22 ff	236
1:22-23	194, 236, 295
1:23	173, 178, 180, 238
1:23-25	270
2:2	346
2:21	61
3:9	61
3:23	178
4:13	345
4:16	4
5:1	345

II Peter

1:3-4	3

I John

1:1	234
1:3	196, 216, 296
1:4	169, 229, 240
1:5	266, 297, 298, 307
1:5-2:2	257
1:6	196
1:7	196, 214, 247, 259
1:8	265
1:9	247, 249, 251, 259, 289
1:9-2:2	247
1:10	265
2:1	247, 251, 289
2:1-2	**249**
2:2	214, 335
2:3	244, 245, 309, 311
2:3-6	296, 309
2:3-11	295, 303
2:4	309
2:4-5	311
2:5	244, 245
2:6	246, 247, 250, 347
2:7	234
2:7-11	296, 317
2:12-14	**271-272**, 283, 324
2:12-28	317
2:13	234
2:13-14	335
2:14	271, 274
2:15	335
2:16	95, 198
2:16-17	335
2:17	259
2:18	234, 245
2:18-26	321
2:19	95
2:20-21	234, 245, 275
2:22-23	234, 257, 322
2:22-24	275
2:23	278, 320, 321
2:24	234, 271, 273, 274
2:25	210, 297
2:26	325
2:27	274, 275, 278
2:28	233, 244, 246
2:29	1, 90, 102, 106, 121, 122, 172, 177, 227, 229, 231, 236, 238-240, 242-244, 246, 247, 251, 261, 289, 319, 325, 335, 348, 356
2:29-3:1	331
2:29-3:2	216, 228, 238
2:29-3:9	242
2:29-3:10	203, 230, **232-262**, 272, 281, 286, 315, 323, 336, 337, 344, 346, 356
2:29-3:10a	240
2:29-3:10b	295
2:29-4:6	241
3:1	1, 92, 123, 239, 240, 244, 246, 253, 272, 283, 298, 307, 308, 309, **313-315**, 324, 332-335, 350, 357, 362, 363
3:1-2	227, 236, 243, 261, 308, 314, **331-347**

3:1-4	247	3:13 ff	233
3:1-10 ff	121	3:14	211, 214, 234, 299, 345
3:2	1, 112, 170, 233, 234, 239, 245, 323, 331, 333, 343-346, 349, 358	3:14-15	245
		3:15	211, 214, 234
		3:16	210, 244-247, 250, 282, 307, 310, 314, 347
3:2a	236, 338	3:17	299
3:2b	236	3:19	244, 245
3:2d	344	3:19-21	233, 348
3:3	236, 246, 347, 348, **349-350**, 358	3:23	143, 259
		3:23-24	193, 320
3:3 ff	351	3:24	192, 244, 245, 355
3:3-10b	236	4:1	94, 278, 320, 321
3:4	240, 243, 257, 258, 268	4:1-6	320
3:4-10	276, 283	4:2	94, 234, 244, 245, 320, 322
3:5	97, 234, 236, 245, 246, 247, 256, 267, 294, 325, 347, 348	4:3	94, 234, 320, 322
		4:3-5	335
3:6	197, 231, 243, 247, 266, **272-274**, 282, 283, 309, 356	4:4	96, 335
		4:5-6	95, 299
		4:6	244, 245, 335
3:7	236, 240, 246, 247, 289, 309, 325, 348	4:6-8	309
		4:7	1, 94, 121, 172, 177, 192, 194, 203, 227, 228, 229, 231, 244, 262, 300, 302, 310, 319, 327, 335, 356, 363
3:7-8	301		
3:8	96, 97, 177, 232, 234, 236, 240, 243, 247, 257, 260, 265, 282, 294, 301, 309, 325, 356		
		4:7-8	**302-312**, 333, 357
3:9	1, 103, 121, 122, 172, 177, 178, 197, 227, 228, 231, 236, 257, 261, **265-270**, **272-274**, 277, 280, 284, 289, 294, 309, 335, 356	4:7-13	311
		4:7-21	**303-304**, 305, 311, 317
		4:8	214, 296, 297, 335, 355
		4:9	122, 123, 129, 130, 308, 310, 318, 322
		4:9 ff	307, 313, 315
		4:9-10	214, 308
3:10	1, 93, 94, 96, 97, 101, 102, 170, 177, 232, 236, 240, 243, 253, 254, 260, 282, 289, 295, 298, 333	4:10	278, 314
		4:11	244
		4:11	244
		4:12	311, 315, 357
		4:12-13	**312-313**
3:10c ff	236	4:13	244, 245, 355
3:10-12	192, **295-302**, 304, 315, 357	4:13d	192
		4:14	318, 335
3:10-24	303, 317	4:14-15	177
3:11	234	4:15	234, 320, 322
3:12	232, 315	4:16	214, 247, 296, 297, 307, 310, 318, 355
3:13	203, 335		

4:16-18	314
4:17	233, 246, 247, 250
4:17-18	**347-349**, 358
4:18	278
4:19	313, 314
4:20-21	299, 314
4:21	318, 326
5:1	1, 123, 172, 177, 178, 227-229, 231, 262, 272, 280, 310, 335, 356
5:1a	319, 326
5:1-2	216, 299, 314
5:1-4	**317-330**
5:1-5	128, 321, 330, 357
5:1-12	317, 318
5:1-13	127, 325
5:1-18	121
5:2	1, 244, 245, 329, 357
5:4	1, 177, 227, 228, 231, 262, 267, **272**, 280, 335, 356
5:4 ff	249
5:4-5	178, 323
5:5	335
5:5-12	323
5:6	177
5:6-8	180, 189
5:8	191
5:10	145
5:11-12	322
5:12	206, 278
5:12 ff	210
5:13	120, 145, 169, 196, 210, 216, 229, 240, 245
5:13-21	276
5:15	234
5:16	267, 299, 357
5:17	259
5:18	1, 92, 100, 123, 130, 169, 172, 177, 227, 228, 231, 233, 234, 262, 267, 271, 277, 280, 281, 285, 289, 294, 335, 356
5:18b+c	279
5:18-20	96, 265, **276-286**, 294
5:19	96, 177, 234, 254, 324, 335
5:20	234, 245, 283, 284, 285, 310, 335, 343
5:21	285

II John

1	91
1-2	275
2	271, 274
4	91
9	274, 278
13	91

III John

3	299
5	299
10	299
11	97

Jude

21	277

Revelation

3:7	285
3:12	323
3:14	285
7:1	200
12:4	90, 91
12:4-13	98
12:5	90, 91
12:7	41
12:10	205
13:5	149
17:10	339
17:12	339
19:11	248, 249, 285
21:6	323
21:7	5, 56
22:4	343

NON BIBLICAL REFERENCES

APOCRYPHA

The Assumption of Moses
10:3 35

The second Book of Baruch
13:9 35
48:24 270

The Book of Enoch
6:8 270
62:4-5 38
62:11-12 36

The Fourth Book of Esdras
4:42 38
6:58 35
9:31 270

The Book of Jubilees
1:23-25 . . . . 36, 175
1:25 36
1:28 36
2:20 35
19:29 35
22:11 35

The Third Book of Maccabees
5:7 36
6:8 36
6:18 285
7:6 36

The Psalms of Solomon
1:8 35
8:14 35
9:11-15 36
10:5 36
17:17 36
17:21 36
18:4 35

The Testaments of the Twelve Patriarchs:

Testament of Levi
18:9 270

QUMRAN LITERATURE

The Damascus Document (C.D.)
6:19 35
8:14-17 30
19:16 35
20:12 35

The Habakkuk Commentary (I Qp Hab)
2:1-6 37
7:10 34
7:10-12 34
8:1 37
8:2 37
10:14-11:2 37

The Hymn Scroll (IQH)
1:1-7 37
3:1-8 38
3:1-18 . . . . . 38-42, 175, 360
3:5-20 41
3:14 ff 41
4:31-33 34
5:5-6a 42
6:29 34
7:6 ff 41
7:6-25 32
7:20 ff 42
7:29 34
9:30-36 32-34
9:35 32
9:35-36 33
10:20 37
10:27 . . . . 34, 37
10:29 37
11:7 34
11:9-11 34
11:11 34

The Manual of Discipline
(IQS)

1:7-8	36
1:8	35
1:9-10	36
1:12	34
1:12-13	36
1:15	34
2:16	36
2:24	35
2:26	35
3:3	35
3:4-9	35, 175
3:20	36
3:24-25	36
4:20 ff	175
4:20-23	270
4:21-23	35, 41
4:23	37
4:49	41
5:7-10	30
7:29-31	175
8:1-7	30
9:30-36	175
11:4-5	41
11:10-12	175

The War scroll (IQM)

9:15,16	36
13:9,10	36
17:6-7	36
17:8	34, 35

PHILO

Conf. Ling. 142-145	51
145	6
145	50
146	51
Congr. 10,51	50
De Praem. 43-45	50
De Sacr. 36,120	50
De Sobr. 55-56	51
Leg. All. III 219	51
Migr. Ab. 140	52
142	52
Mut. Nom. 131	52
Op. Mund. 84	50
Post. Cain. 26	51
92	51
Quest. in Gen. I 66	51
92	51
Quest. in Gen. III 60	51
Somn. I 173	51
Spec. Leg. I 58	50
317	50
318	50
Spec. Leg. II 30 ff	50
Spec. Leg. III 189	50
Vit. Contem. 68	52

GREEK PHILOSOPHY

Aratos:

Phenomena	45

Cleanth:

Hymn of Zeus 4-5	45

Hellenism:
Epictetus,

Dissert. I 3:1-3	45, 46
9:6 ff	46
9:22	46
9:25	46
13:3	46
17:29	46
19:8 ff	46
19:9	46
Dissert. II 8:11	46
16:44	46
Dissert IV 10:14	46

CORPUS HERMETICUM

C.H. I: 6	49
C.H. XIII	47, 360, 361
C.H. XIII: 1-8a	48
C.H. XIII: 2	47, 49
C.H. XIII: 8b-14	48
14	49
15-20	48
18	49

INDEX OF GREEK WORDS

ἀβαρής 277
ἀββᾶ 70
ἀββᾶ ὁ πατήρ 79
'Αβραάμ 92, 140
ἀγαπάω 56, 57, 123, 192, 298, 299, 300, 302, 303, 304, 305, 307, 311, 313, 314, 316, 318, 326, 329, 357
ἀγάπη 123, 236, 277, 303, 305, 307, 308, 313, 314, 332, 333, 347, 348
ἀγαπητός 250, 251
ἀγγελία 297
ἄγγελος 62
ἄγειν 80
ἁγνίζω 343
ἁγνός 277
ἀδελφός 299, 318, 329
ἀδικία 259, 260
αθανασία 47
αἰών 62
αἰώνιος 210, 211
ἀκούω 234, 275, 297
ἀλήθεια 153, 154, 178, 270, 292
ἀληθής 260, 292
ἀληθινός 177, 281, 285, 344
ἀλλήλους 329
ἁμαρτάνω 277, 279, 336
ἁμαρτία 237, 241, 252, 257, 258, 259, 261, 277, 281
ἀναγεννάω 48, 173, 270
ἀνάστασις 63
ἄνεμος 200
ἀνομία 258, 259
ἄνω 177
ἄνωθεν 100, 128, 166, 170, 171, 172-174, 181, 199, 262
ἀπαρχή 86
ἀπεκδέχομαι 85
ἀποκαλύπτω 67, 339
ἀποκαραδοκία 85
ἀπόλλυμι 223
ἀπολύτρωσις 85
ἀπολύτρωσις τοῦ σώματος 85
ἀποσυνάγωγος 140
ἀρνέομαι 322

ἀρχή 107, 234, 275, 297
ἄρχων 135
ἄσπιλος 277
αὐλή 217
βάλλω 347
βαπτίζω 76
βασιλεία 205
βασιλεία τοῦ Θεοῦ 171, 176, 183, 206
γένεσις 48, 276, 277
γεννᾶσθαι 99-101, 112, 113, 117, 125, 126, 130, 131, 136, 137, 138, 151, 152, 163, 168, 169, 170, 171, 174, 176, 177, 186, 191, 198, 199, 202, 254, 354, 355
γεννᾶσθαι ἐκ Θεοῦ 1-3, 90, 96-103, 105, 121, 172, 353, 361, 364
γεννᾶσθαι ἐκ πνεύματος 174, 202
γεννάω 24, 46, 48, 77, 92, 109, 122, 123, 124, 126, 165, 166, 169, 173, 178, 191, 194, 197, 200, 203, 216, 227, 228, 229, 230, 239, 246, 254, 261, 262, 273, 276, 277, 279, 280, 281, 283, 285, 302, 304, 306, 318, 319, 323, 324, 326, 327, 355, 356
γεννηθείς 123, 169, 276, 277, 278, 285
γεννηθείς ἐκ Θεοῦ 92, 95, 123, 279-281
γένος 45
γίνομαι 56, 59, 60, 61, 64, 72, 101, 105, 106, 110, 124, 125, 139, 140, 141, 150, 152, 158, 161, 176, 229, 254, 291
γινώσκω 168, 234, 244, **245**, 246, 254, 281, 285, 293, 306, 307, 309, 310, 311, 320, 335, 336
δεύτερον 172
δέχομαι 176, 177
διάβολος 92, 177, 252, 260, 290, 301, 302
διάνοια 284, 285, 286
δίδωμι 105, 106, 123, 137, 138, 149, 150, 151, 152, 193, 194, 210, 224, 313, 314, 333, 353
δίκαιος **246**, **247**, 249, 251, 296
δικαιοσύνη 237, 248, 250, 252, 259, 261, 262
δόξα 85, 153, 345, 346
δόσις 314

δουλεύω 287
δοῦλος 287
δύναμαι 168, 169, 171, 176
δυνάμεις Θεοῦ 48
δύναμις 149, 228
δώρημα 314
ἔθνος 218-224
εἶναι 64, 94, 124, 139, 140, 196, 338, 339, 341, 342
εἶναι ἐκ 94-97, 177, 198, 202, 230, 239, 254, 302, 307
εἶναι ἐκ τοῦ διαβόλου 94, 97, 103
εἶναι ἐκ τοῦ Θεοῦ 94-97, 103, **230**, 254, 297, 302, 353
εἶναι παρα θεοῦ 95
εἶπον 216
εἰρήνη 53
εἰρηνοποιέω 53
εἰρηνοποιός 53, 54
εἷς εἶναι 74
εἰσέρχομαι 165, 166, 168, 171, 176, 204, 207, 209
ἐκ τῆς γῆς 95
ἐκ τῆς σαρκός 172
ἐκ τοῦ Θεοῦ 95
ἐκ τοῦ κόσμου 94, 95
ἐκ τοῦ οὐρανοῦ 95
ἐκ τοῦ πατρός 95
ἐκ τοῦ πνεύματος 171, 172, 193, 262
ἐκ τῶν ἄνω 95
ἐκ τῶν κάτω 95
ἐλέγχω 252
ἐλεήμων 55
ἔλεος 153, 236
ἐλεύθερος 292
ἐλευθερόω 254
ἐλπίζω 85
ἐλπίς 85
ἔμφυτος 270
ἔν 217
ἐνδύω 75, 76
ἑνός 98
ἐντολή 192, 280, 303
ἐν χριστῷ 344
ἐν χριστῷ Ἰησοῦ 74, 75, 77
ἐξαγοράζω 70, 72
ἐξαποστέλλω 73, 79
ἐξηγέομαι 154

ἐξουσία 106, 138, 149, 150, 151, 163, 224, 353
ἐξ ὕδατος 170, 172, 262
ἐξ ὕδατος καί πνεύματος 100
ἐπαγγελία 297
ἐπίγεια 200, 201
ἐπουράνια 201
ἔργον 302
ἔρχομαι 95, 124, 125, 128, 144, 152, 166, 189, 201, 202, 255
ἔρχομαι ἐκ θεοῦ 101
ἔρως 329
εὐαγγελίζω 270
εὐαγγέλιον 77, 176, 270
ἔχειν τὸν θεόν 278
ἐχθρός 56
ἔχω 123, 209, 210, 321, 348
ζάω 123, 209, 210, 239, 270
ζωή 123, 157, 169, 195, 206, 209, 210, 211
ζωοποιέω 149, 177, 210
θαυμάζω 203
θεάομαι 308
θεῖος 3
θεῖος ἀνήρ 46
θέλημα 113, 262
θέλω 201, 254
θεός 24, 100, 119, 120, 177, 305, 307
θυγατέρες 69
ἴδια 126
ἴδιος (οἱ) 46, 125, 148
Ἰησοῦς 324
Ἰουδαῖος 254
ἰσάγγελος 62, 63
ἰσχύς 149
καθώς 193, 300, 341, 342, 344
καλεῖσθαι 56
καλέω 53, 64, 106, 229, 315, 332
καρδία 285
καταλαμβάνω 148
καταξιόω 62, 63
κάτω 177
κληρονομέω 323
κληρονόμος 83
κοινωνία 196
κοινωνός 196
κόλασις 347

κόσμος 96, 125, 126, 148, 177, 283, 318, 335, 336, 347, 348
κράζω 79
κράτος 149
κρινώ 149
κρίσις 347
κτίζω 124
κύριος 119
λαλέω 216
λαμβάνω 124, 125, 137, 138, 146, 147, 148, 149, 152, 156, 161, 163, 208, 224
λαός 148, 218-224, 258
λατρεύω 343
λέγω 165, 216
λόγος 48, 215, 252, 270, 271, 280, 361
λόγος ἐνδιάθετος 51
λόγος προφορικός 51
μαθητής 140, 144, 253, 291
μαρτυρέω 118, 124, 128
μαρτυρία 118, 189
μένω 141, 195, 196, 244, 270, 271, 273, 274, 277, 293
μετανοεῖν 76
μετανοέω 176
μετάνοια 76, 176
μήτρα 48
μισέω 299
μισθός 61, 64
μοναί 290
μονογενής 92, 120, 121, 123, 124, 129, 130, 146, 163, 213
νήπιος 67
νικάω 318, 323, 325
νόμος 76
οἶδα 166, 171, 199, 206, 234, 245, 281, 283, 340, 345
οἰκία 289
οἰκτιρμός 58
ὅλος 96
ὅμοιοι αὐτῷ 341-342
ὅμοιος 342, 345
ὁμολογέω 234, 320, 322
ὄνομα 109, 119, 120, 321
ὁράω 176, 206, 239, 323, 341, 342, 346
ὁρῶν θεόν 50
ὅτι 23, 344, 345
οὐρανός 334
παιδίον 176
παῖς 48, 90
παῖς θεοῦ 47, 49, 361
παλιγγενεσία 47
πάντες 218
παραλαμβάνω 125, 147, 152
παρουσία 237
πατήρ 23, 48, 59, 65, 92, 119, 120, 127, 128, 129, 145, 251, 333, 334, 350
πατήρ ὁ 333-335
περιπατέω 158, 160
πιστεύειν 109, 113, 141-146, 272
πιστεύειν εἰς 157, 159, 160
πιστεύειν εἰς τινα 142, 143-145
πιστεύειν εἰς τὸ ὄνομα τινος 120, 141, 142, 145-146, 163, 213, 353
πιστεύειν ὅτι 143
πιστεύειν τινί 141
πιστεύειν τῷ ὀνόματι 143
πιστεύω 76, 113, 117, 122, 137, 138, 139, 141, 142, 143, 147, 148, 151, 152, 158, 159, 165, 176, 206, 208, 209, 216, 218, 287, 289, 318, 319, 320, 321, 323, 324
πίστις 76, 77, 83, 106, 141, 176, 215, 319, 320, 325
πίστις εἰς χριστόν 74
πίστις πρὸς τὸνκύριον Ἰησοῦν 74
πίστις χριστοῦ 74
πιστός 215, 247
πλήρης 153
πλήρωμα 153
πνεῦμα 1, 79, 100, 130, 177, 178, 186, 191, 192, 194, 197, 198, 199, 200, 201, 203, 285, 332
πνέω 200
πόθεν 202
ποιέω 93, 106, 124, 216, 237, 241, 244, 252, 254, 257, 259, 261, 262, 277
ποίμνη 140, 217
πολλοί 143, 287
πολυέλεος 154
πονηρός 281, 282, 300, 301, 302
πορνεία 255
προορίζω 72
προσεύχομαι 56
πρωτόγονος 361
πρωτότοκος 12, 83, 85
ῥῆμα 270
σάββατον 280